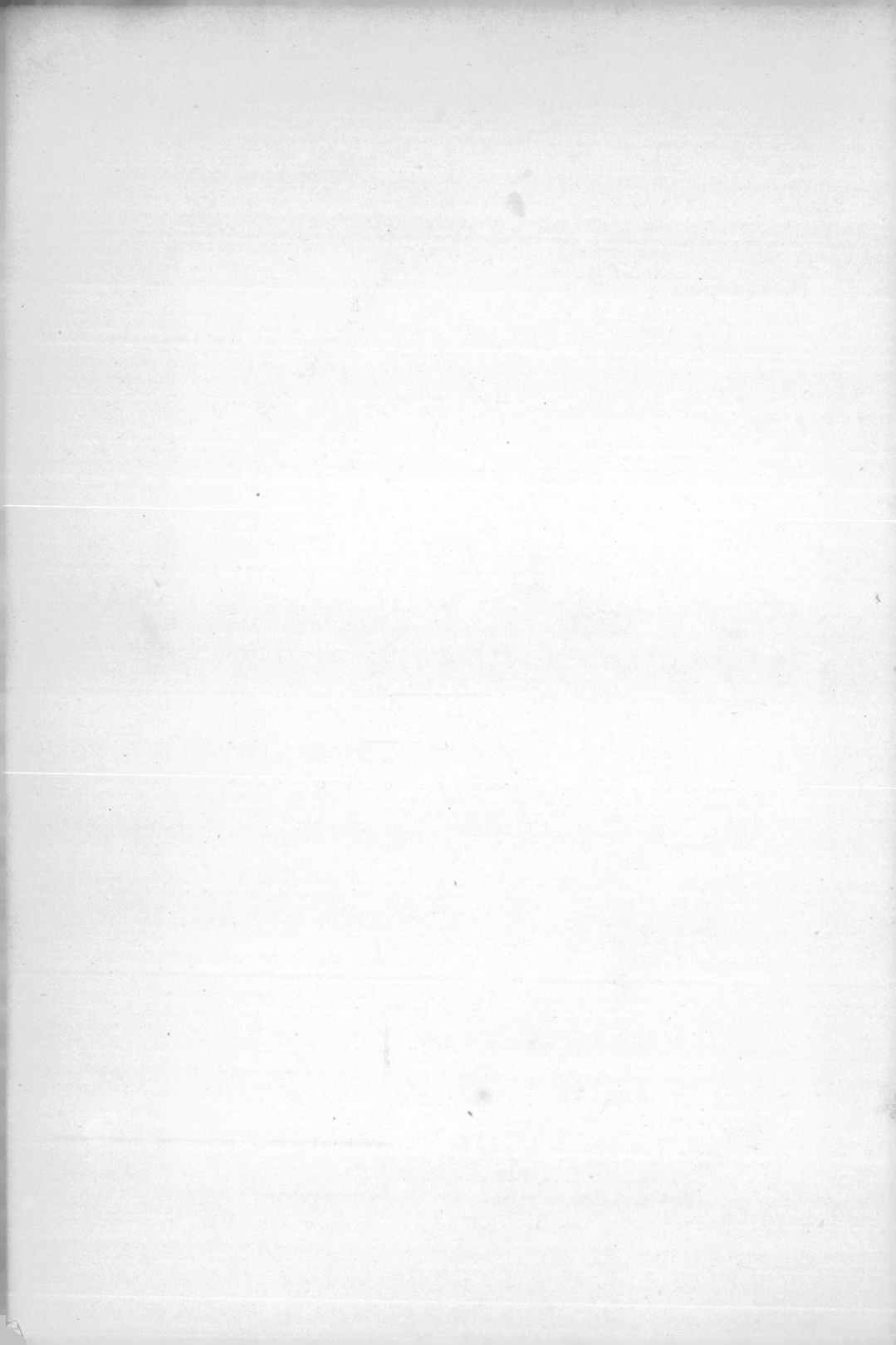

A NEW
SHAKESPEAREAN
DICTIONARY

"When good will is show'd, though't come too short,
The actor may plead pardon."

—*Antony and Cleopatra*, II, 5, 8.

A NEW SHAKESPEAREAN DICTIONARY

BY

RICHARD JOHN CUNLIFFE

M.A. LL.B.

BLACKIE AND SON LIMITED

50 OLD BAILEY LONDON E.C.

GLASGOW AND BOMBAY

1910

PREFACE

This book embodies the results of a fresh and systematic examination of the language of the Shakespeare Canon, and aims at presenting and defining concisely the constituents of that language in so far as they have passed from our modern speech. I have endeavoured to exclude all words and senses of words which are still in good literary use, and, except where there is obscurity, all senses which are merely contextual and do not represent an authenticated usage. It has proved in practice to be very difficult in many cases to determine whether a word or sense is to be considered to have disappeared from the living language; one is naturally inclined to err on the side of inclusion; but I hope that not much that is superfluous will be found. On the other hand, I am not so foolishly confident as to suppose that there are no omissions. Words or senses may have been excluded which to others may seem to require explanation; and no doubt I have been guilty of other omissions through inadvertence. It is, of course, the duty of a compiler to make no omissions; but perhaps some indulgence may be extended to one dealing single-handed with a vocabulary so extensive, and often differing so subtly from that of to-day. I can only hope that not much that is of importance will be sought for in vain. The distinction between Shakespearean and modern usage implied in the inclusion of some words and senses may appear to some to be minute; but such distinctions have their interest and their effect on the meaning; and they are, of course, just those which are most apt to be overlooked. In pursuance of my design to register all words no longer forming part of the language, I have included a certain number, such as *ingrateful, livery* (vb.), *neglection, unsatiate,* the meanings of which are evident, but which have become obsolete.

Quotations as well as references to the text have throughout been appended to the definitions. In the case of a work of this nature mere references are of little service, as, apart from the trouble and loss of time involved in referring to the text, there cannot, if references only are given, be the same facility of comparison, and of seeing how the use of a word in one passage throws light on its use in another, as is afforded by the passages being exhibited to the eye together. It has not been possible to make the references and quotations exhaustive; and in the cases of words and senses of frequent occurrence I have accordingly generally limited myself to three or four. Where not more than two are given it may, as a rule, be assumed that there are no other clear examples of the use.

The references are to the Globe edition, and for the quotations that text has been used. In printing the quotations the only deviation from the Globe text which I have allowed myself, in addition to a few mentioned in the body of the work, is the omission of the apostrophe in genuine aphetic forms such as *gin, gree, long,* and in *a* (= he). In a few cases, where a portion only of a sentence has been quoted, it has been necessary slightly to modify the punctuation. I have found that later issues of the Globe differ somewhat from the first issue, and have recorded one or two such differences which I have noticed.

The Works are cited substantially as in Schmidt's Lexicon. A table of the contractions used, which for the most part explain themselves, is appended. Small numerals attached to leading words indicate that the words so distinguished, although identical in form, differ in origin.

The following words have not, as a rule, been considered to fall within the scope of the undertaking—(1) Latin words and words in foreign languages; (2) the blunders and perversions of the illiterate characters and of such manglers of English as Sir Hugh Evans and Fluellen; and (3) proper names. Information as to the proper names is for the most part easily accessible in the usual Biographical and Mytho-logical Dictionaries; but room has been found for a few—chiefly place-names—in regard to which it was thought that some difficulty might be experienced. In particular, the London place-names, in so far as likely to give trouble, have been briefly treated. Etymologies have seldom been given. It was felt that the place for these was rather in a general dictionary than in one dealing only with a single, and that not a very early, section of the literature, and aiming at presenting materials rather for an accurate exegesis of a particular text than for a historical study of the language.

I have aimed at helping those who wish to read Shakespeare in a scholarly spirit, with a full understanding of the sense, and at providing the means of forming an accurate idea of the extent to which the Shake-spearean vocabulary differs from our own, and of the details of the difference. The Shakespearean language is, to an extent greater than is sometimes supposed, a dead tongue to us, and can be thoroughly mastered only by study with the aid of grammar, dictionary and com-ment. In the matter of grammar the student's needs are amply supplied; there is at his disposal a body of comment, of varying excellence, it is true, but of great extent; but there seems to be room for a dictionary on the lines of the present work, showing the results of a reconsideration of the vocabulary in the light of recent research. In particular the time seems to have come for a fresh treatment of the subject in view of the fact that the New English Dictionary, to which further reference is made below, is so far advanced towards completion. So far as I am aware this is the first work of the kind on a considerable scale in which the materials furnished by the Dictionary have been systematically drawn upon, and in which the scientific guidance to the treatment of the words which it affords has been fully made use of—a feature which may of itself be thought to entitle the book to some consideration.

In using a book of this sort difficulty does not arise chiefly in the case of words which are obsolete, or which, though they are still part of the language, are used in senses which are obviously unfamiliar. In

such cases the reader is on his guard; he seeks enlightenment; and I
hope that I have in all cases succeeded in supplying the information
which he requires.   It is different in the case of words which are in
themselves familiar, and are so used that, taken in a modern sense, they
give a meaning to the passages in which they occur which seems to be
satisfactory, but which yet is not the true meaning; or are used in a sense
which differs from the modern sense in such a way that, while the reader
may feel vaguely that there is a difference, he yet finds a sense for the
passage which he is apt to accept as sufficient, thus attaining only a
blurred and imperfect idea of the meaning.   Take for example the
following passages out of many which might be quoted :—*Travelling*
along *this* coast—LLL V 2 557; *Last scene of all, That ends this strange
eventful* history—As II 7 163; *They are* generally *fools and cowards*—2 H4
IV 3 101; *Which had* return'd *To the* inheritance of *Fortinbras, Had he
been vanquisher*—Hml I 1 91.   Here all the words are quite familiar;
they seem, taken as a modern writer would use them, to give a good
sense; unless he is on his guard, the reader is likely to take this as the
true sense; but, as will be seen on referring in the following pages to the
words printed in Roman type, the sense which the author intended to
convey is very different.   Take again the following :—*If you do love
Rosalind so near the heart as your* gesture *cries it out*—As V 2 68; *An
honest method . . . by very much more* handsome *than fine*—Hml II 2 465;
For want of these required conveniences, *her delicate tenderness will find itself
abused*—Oth II 1 234; *Lest . . . by some mortal stroke She do* defeat *us*—
Ant V 1 64.   Here the words printed in Roman type do not, taken in
a modern sense, give so deceptively a sense which seems to be satisfactory; a difference from modern usage is more or less felt to exist,
and, as will be seen on referring to the words, does in fact exist; but
unless the reader exercises some vigilance, and seeks for guidance, he is
apt to give a wrong turn to the passage, and to fail to grasp its true
meaning.   Of words of this sort many examples will be found in the
Dictionary.   Of course the trouble is that the reader cannot always tell
exactly at what point he ought to look for help.   If I may make the

suggestion the occasional perusal of a page or two of the Dictionary would often show him that he has been taking passages not quite rightly, and would put him on the right lines. To some, such a minute attention to the text may be repugnant, and may seem to be inconsistent with the enjoyment of poetry. It will, however, probably be conceded on reflection that an accurate apprehension of a poet's meaning is a condition precedent to a full appreciation of his poetry. To whatever extent we take a meaning which is not the poet's, to that extent we are making poetry for ourselves, and not reading that which is given to us.

In using the Dictionary it should be borne in mind that, in the case of a good many of the quotations, other words besides those under which the quotations are placed will require explanation. The reader is accordingly recommended to seek for further information under other heads in all cases where he seems to have grounds for thinking that he is not apprehending the meaning fully.

In the case of such a work as this the use of the labours of one's predecessors is, of course, presupposed. As it has not been practicable to make acknowledgments of indebtedness under the words, it is right to indicate here the chief authorities of which use has been made.

Schmidt's Lexicon (supplemented occasionally by Bartlett's Concordance) has been of much service throughout. In matters of grouping and definition Schmidt is hardly a safe guide; but his full references to the occurrences of the words are very useful. The Glossaries of Nares and of Dyce have been consulted.

The annotated editions have, of course, been referred to at many points. Of these probably the most useful have been the Variorum Edition of 1821, and, as far as they go, the New Variorum Edition of Dr. Horace Howard Furness, in which fifteen plays have up to now appeared,* the Clarendon Press series (seventeen plays), and the Warwick Shakespeare (eighteen plays). Of course in many cases the same play is included in each series. On the whole, however, the assistance

* The volume last published, containing King Richard III, is edited by Mr. Horace Howard Furness, Junior.

to be got from the commentators for a work dealing so minutely with the text as this does is less than might perhaps be expected.   The fact is that while some plays have been edited over and over again with varying degrees of philological minuteness, we still await an edition in which the whole body of the works shall be edited with full attention to a thorough exegesis of the text.   Even in the case of plays which have been often edited, help from the commentators has not infrequently been found wanting.

Among books which have been drawn upon to a greater or less extent may be mentioned Douce's *Illustrations*, Hunter's *New Illustrations*, Lord Campbell's *Shakespeare's Legal Acquirements*, and Craik's *English of Shakespeare* (a commentary on *Julius Cæsar*).   For the London place-names use has been made of Loftie's *History of London* and of Wheatley and Cunningham's *London Past and Present*.

In connection with the terms of art in Woodcraft, Falconry, the Manage and Coursing, special acknowledgments are due to *The Diary of Master William Silence*, by the Right Hon. D. H. Madden (Longmans, 1897), a work which is at once delightful as literature and valuable as a mine of information on all subjects connected with Elizabethan sport. It is undoubtedly the most valuable contribution to this aspect of Shakespearean study which has yet appeared.

I put last in order the work to which I owe most.   No one engaged in a task like this can possibly afford to neglect the assistance of the *New English Dictionary*,* to which I have already referred.   Words of commendation on my part would be at once superfluous and impertinent.   I shall content myself with saying that my debt is very heavy and is very gratefully acknowledged.   Only one who has systematically used the Dictionary in connection with some such work as this can fully know its matchless thoroughness and wealth of illustration, and appreciate

---

* A New English Dictionary on Historical Principles; Founded Mainly on the Materials Collected by The Philological Society; Edited by Sir James A. H. Murray.   Oxford, at the Clarendon Press.   To be completed in ten volumes.   Vol. I was published in 1888.   With the exception of a small portion at the end of R, the Dictionary is now complete to Sau.   Dr. Henry Bradley and Dr. W. A. Craigie have for some time been acting as editors along with Sir James Murray.

the enormous advantage which its guidance gives to a compiler of these days. It is not too much to say that in very many cases the difference between then and now is the difference between groping in darkness and walking in daylight. For the portion of the alphabet not yet covered by the New English Dictionary some use has been made of the Century Dictionary.

In using the materials I have endeavoured throughout to bring a fresh mind to bear on the problems arising, and, except of course as regards matters of fact, have in no case been content merely to record the opinions of others without examination. Even the august authority of the New English Dictionary has not always been followed. In consequence some of the explanations of difficult passages will be found to differ somewhat (I hope for the better) from those formerly given, while in other cases explanations are offered which do not appear to have occurred to previous workers.

My friend, Mr. J. B. Douglas, M.A., has very kindly gone over the proofs, and has made many valuable suggestions. I owe much to his scholarly care. For the references and quotations, however, I alone am responsible. All have been checked in proof with the text, and I have some confidence in their accuracy.

If the reader who makes the volume a companion to his study of the text finds that he is thereby helped, even in a small degree, to a clearer comprehension, and consequently to a higher appreciation, of the plays and poems, I shall feel that the not inconsiderable labour which the compilation has entailed has been well bestowed.

R. J. C.

February, 1910.

TABLE OF THE CONTRACTIONS USED
IN CITING THE WORKS

Ado	*Much Ado about Nothing.*	Mcb	*Macbeth.*
All's	*All's Well that Ends Well.*	Meas	*Measure for Measure.*
Ant	*Antony and Cleopatra.*	Merch	*The Merchant of Venice.*
As	*As You Like It.*	Mids	*A Midsummer-Night's Dream.*
Cæs	*Julius Cæsar.*	Oth	*Othello.*
Compl	*A Lover's Complaint.*	Per	*Pericles.*
Cor	*Coriolanus.*	Phœn	*The Phœnix and the Turtle.*
Cymb	*Cymbeline.*	Pilgr	*The Passionate Pilgrim.*
Err	*The Comedy of Errors.*	R2	*King Richard II.*
Gent	*The Two Gentlemen of Verona.*	R3	*King Richard III.*
1 H4	*The First Part of King Henry IV.*	Rom	*Romeo and Juliet.*
2 H4	*The Second Part of King Henry IV.*	Shr	*The Taming of the Shrew.*
H5	*King Henry V.*	Sonn	*Sonnets.*
1 H6	*The First Part of King Henry VI.*	Tim	*Timon of Athens.*
2 H6	*The Second Part of King Henry VI.*	Tit	*Titus Andronicus.*
3 H6	*The Third Part of King Henry VI.*	Tp	*The Tempest.*
H8	*King Henry VIII.*	Troil	*Troilus and Cressida.*
Hml	*Hamlet.*	Tw	*Twelfth Night.*
John	*King John.*	Ven	*Venus and Adonis.*
LLL	*Love's Labour's Lost.*	Wint	*The Winter's Tale.*
Lr	*King Lear.*	Wiv	*The Merry Wives of Windsor.*
Lucr	*The Rape of Lucrece.*		

A NEW
SHAKESPEAREAN DICTIONARY

A

A form of He, used by Mercutio and Claudio as well as by Launcelot and Verges: *Tickling a parson's nose as a lies asleep*—Rom I 4 80. *A brushes his hat o' mornings*—Ado III 2 41. *Let his father be what a will*—Merch II 2 56. *That I think a cannot*—Ado III 3 82.

ABATE

(1) To blunt: *Abate the edge of traitors, gracious Lord*—R3 V 5 35.

(2) To deprive of temper: *His metal . . .; Which once in him abated . . .*—2 H4 I 1 116.

(3) To humble: *Abated captives*—Cor III 3 132.

(4) To estimate at a smaller value: *I would abate her nothing*—Cymb I 4 73.

(5) To curtail: *She hath abated me of half my train*—Lr II 4 161.

(6) To leave out of count, except: *Abate [a] throw at novum*—LLL V 2 547.

ABATEMENT

A state of depreciation: *Falls into abatement and low price*—Tw I 1 13.

ABHOMINABLE

A form of Abominable due to a mistaken derivation from *ab homine*: *This is abhominable*—LLL V 1 26.

ABHOR

(1) To fill with disgust: *It doth abhor me*—Oth IV 2 162. Sim. *abhorring*, a state of causing disgust: *Let the water-flies Blow me into abhorring*—Ant V 2 59.

(2) A term of the canon law, to refuse to accept (as a judge): *I utterly abhor, yea . . . Refuse you for my judge*—H8 II 4 81.

ABHORRED

Detestable, abominable: *Her earthy and abhorr'd commands*—Tp I 2 273. *Such abhorr'd pollution*—Meas II 4 183. *Abhorred villain*—Lr I 2 81.

ABIDE

(1) To face, encounter: *Abide me, if thou darest*—Mids III 2 422. *To abide a field* [of battle]—2 H4 II 3 36.

(2) To submit to, suffer: *What fates impose, that men must needs abide*—3 H6 IV 3 58. To be exposed to, suffer: *I shall here abide the hourly shot Of angry eyes*—Cymb I 1 89.

(3) To suffer for, bear the consequences of (an act of another): *Whiles lions war . . . Poor harmless lambs abide their enmity*—3 H6 II 5 74.

(4) Used erroneously for *Aby* (q.v.): *Let no man abide this deed, But we the doers*—Cæs III 1 94. *Some will dear abide it*—III 2 119.

ABJECT

One brought low: *The queen's abjects*, the lowest of her subjects: *We are the queen's abjects, and must obey*—R3 I 1 106. In Cæs IV 1 37, *abjects* is read by some as an amendment for *objects*, app. to mean things cast off.

ABLE

To warrant, vouch for: *None does offend . . . I'll able 'em*—Lr IV 6 172.

ABODE (sb.)

Delay: *Your patience for my long abode*—Merch II 6 21

1

ABODE (vb.)

To presage: *The night-crow cried, aboding luckless time*—3 H6 V 6 45. *This tempest, Dashing the garment of this peace, aboded The sudden breach on't*—H8 I 1 92.

ABODEMENT

An omen: *Abodements must not now affright us*—3 H6 IV 7 13.

ABORTIVE (adj.)

Unseasonable: *Allay this thy abortive pride*—2 H6 IV 1 60.

ABORTIVE (sb.)

Something issuing untimely or unseasonably: *Meteors, prodigies and signs, Abortives, presages and tongues of heaven*—John III 4 157.

ABRIDGEMENT

A means of shortening time: *What abridgement have you for this evening?*—Mids V 39. In Hml II 2 439 (*Look, where my abridgement comes*), prob., that which will cut me short.

ABROOK

To endure: *Ill can thy noble mind abrook The abject people*—2 H6 II 4 10.

ABRUPTION

A breaking off (of speech): *What makes this pretty abruption?*—Troil III 2 69.

ABSEY (*i.e.* A B C) BOOK

A primer in catechism form: *Then comes answer like an Absey book*—John I 196.

ABSOLUTE

(1) Resolved: *Be absolute for death*—Meas III 1 5. Positive, peremptory: *With an absolute 'Sir, not I', The cloudy messenger turns me his back*—Mcb III 6 40. Positive, certain: *I am absolute 'Twas very Cloten*—Cymb IV 2 106. Uncompromising: *You are too absolute*—Cor III 2 39.

(2) Precise: *How absolute the knave is!*—Hml V 1 148.

(3) Faultless, perfect: *Thou wouldst make an absolute courtier*—Wiv III 3 66. *As just, as absolute As Angelo*—Meas V 54. *A most absolute and excellent horse*—H5 III 7 27.

ABSTRACT

(1) A compendium; *An abstract of success*, successful strokes compressed into a short space of time—All's IV 3 99.

(2) An inventory: *He hath an abstract for the remembrance of such places*—Wiv IV 2 63.

ABSURD

Not in harmony with reason or propriety: *To reason most absurd*—Hml I 2 103. *Absurd pomp*

—III 2 65. In Ant V 2 226 (*Their most absurd intents*) app. used proleptically in the usual modern sense, the intents being already foiled in Cleopatra's thought.

ABUSE (sb.)

(1) Deceit, imposture: *This is a strange abuse*—Meas V 205. *Is it some abuse, and no such thing?*—Hml IV 7 51.

(2) Ill-usage, wrong: *The abuse done to my niece*—3 H6 III 3 188. *They'll take no offence at our abuse*—IV 1 13. *Him I lose through my unkind abuse*—Sonn 134 12.

ABUSE (vb.)

(1) To corrupt, pervert: *Charms By which the property of youth . . . May be abused*—Oth I 1 172. *Thou hast . . . Abused her delicate youth*—I 2 73. *Unless my sins abuse my divination*—Cymb IV 2 351.

(2) To deceive: *Abuses me to damn me*—Hml II 2 632. *The food of thy abused father's wrath*—Lr IV 1 24. *The Moor's abused by some most villanous knave*—Oth IV 2 139.

(3) To calumniate: *O my follies! then Edgar was abused*—Lr III 7 91. [I will] *Abuse him to the Moor in the rank garb*—Oth II 1 315.

ABUSER

One who corrupts or perverts: *An abuser of the world*—Oth I 2 78.

ABY

To pay the penalty for, expiate (an offence): *Lest . . . thou aby it dear*—Mids III 2 175. *Thou shalt aby it*—335.

ABYSM

Abyss—Tp I 2 50; Ant III 13 147; Sonn 112 9.

ACCEPT

Accepted: *Our accept and peremptory answer*—H5 V 2 82. Also taken as sb. = acceptance.

ACCEPTED

Acceptable: *Most accepted pain*—Troil III 3 30.

ACCESSIBLE

Affording access, practicable: *Accessible is none but Milford way*—Cymb III 2 84.

ACCIDENT

An occurrence, event: *These happen'd accidents*—Tp V 250. *An accident of hourly proof*—Ado II 1 188. *Signs of future accidents*—1 H6 V 3 4.

ACCITE

(1) To summon: *We will accite . . . all our state*—2 H4 V 2 141. *He by the senate is accited home*—Tit I 27.

(2) To incite: *What accites your most worshipful thought to think so?*—2 H4 II 2 64.

ACCOMMODATE

(1) To minister convenience to: *Accommodated by the place*, favoured by the nature of the ground —Cymb V 3 32.

(2) To supply, equip: *A soldier is better accommodated than with a wife*—2 H4 III 2 72. *The safer sense will ne'er accommodate His master thus*—Lr IV 6 81.

ACCOMPLICE

In good sense, an associate: *Success unto our valiant general, And happiness to his accomplices!* —1 H6 V 2 8.

ACCOMPLISH

(1) To supply, equip: *They shall think we are accomplished With that we lack*—Merch III 4 61. *So look'd he Accomplish'd with the number of thy hours* (*i.e.* when he was of your age)—R2 II 1 176. *The armourers accomplishing the knights*—H5 IV Chor 12.

(2) To achieve the gaining of: *More unlikely Than to accomplish twenty golden crowns*—3 H6 III 2 151.

ACCOMPT

Account—H5 Prol 17; 2 H6 IV 2 93.

ACCORD

Jove's accord, with the accord or countenance of Jove—Troil I 3 238 (after *nothing* in the next line supply *is*).

ACCORDANT

Willing: *If he found her accordant, he meant . . .* —Ado I 2 14.

ACCORDINGLY

Correspondingly, in the same measure: *Great in knowledge and accordingly valiant*—All's II 5 9.

ACCOST

To approach for any purpose, make up to: *Accost, Sir Andrew, accost*—Tw I 3 52 (cf. '*Accost*' is *front her, board her, woo her, assail her*—59). *Accosting* (vbl. sb.): *That give accosting welcome ere it comes*—Troil IV 5 59.

ACCOUNT

App., store, array: *A beggarly account of empty boxes*—Rom V 1 45.

ACCOUNTANT

Accountable, responsible: *Accountant to the law upon that pain*—Meas II 4 86. *Though peradventure I stand accountant for as great a sin*—Oth II 1 301.

ACCUSE

Accusation: *By false accuse doth level at my life* —2 H6 III 1 160.

ACHE

Pronounced like the name of the letter H: Beat. *. . . I am exceeding ill . . .* Marg. *For a hawk, a horse, or a husband?* Beat. *For the letter that begins them all, H*—Ado III 4 53. Accordingly dissyllabic in pl.: *Fill all thy bones with aches, make thee roar*—Tp I 2 370. *Aches contract and starve your supple joints!*—Tim I 1 257.

ACHIEVE

To gain, win (a material acquisition): *Provided that your fortune Achieved her mistress*—Merch III 2 209. *The treasure in this field achieved and city* —Cor I 9 33. *He hath achieved a maid That paragons description*—Oth II 1 61.

ACHIEVEMENT

A gaining, winning (of a material acquisition): *All the soil of the achievement* (*i.e.* of the crown) *goes With me into the earth*—2 H4 IV 5 190.

ACKNOWN

To be acknown of, to confess knowledge of: *Be not acknown on't*—Oth III 3 319.

ACONITUM

Wolf's-bane or monk's-hood: *Though it do work as strong As aconitum or rash gunpowder*— 2 H4 IV 4 47.

ACQUIT

(1) To atone for: *Till life to death acquit my forced offence*—Lucr 1071.

(2) *To acquit of*, to repay, requite for: Por. (to Bass.) *. . . As I hear, he was much bound for you.* Ant. *No more than I am well acquitted of*—Merch V 137.

(3) To set free from an obligation or burden: *Acquitted Of grievous penalties*—Merch IV 1 409. Oli. *How with mine honour may I . . .* Vio. *I will acquit you*—Tw III 4 234.

(4) *Acquit of*, rid of: *I am glad I am so acquit of this tinder-box*—Wiv I 3 27.

ACQUITTANCE (sb.)

Exoneration from a charge, acquittal: *Now must your conscience my acquittance seal*—Hml IV 7 1.

ACQUITTANCE (vb.)

To clear, free: *Your mere enforcement shall acquittance me*—R3 III 7 233.

ACRE

An acre length, 40 poles: *Ere With spur we heat an acre*—Wint I 2 95

ACT (sb.)

Operation, action: *Distill'd Almost to jelly with the act of fear*—Hml I 2 204. *Dangerous conceits . . . with a little act upon the blood, Burn like the mines of sulphur*—Oth III 3 326. *To . . . apply Allayments to their act*—Cymb I 5 21.

ACT (vb.)

(1) To perform, carry out: *To act her earthy and abhorr'd commands*—Tp I 2 273. *I will consent to act any villany against him*—Wiv II 1 101. [Things] *Which must be acted ere they may be scann'd*—Mcb III 4 140.

(2) To bring into action or operation: *To act controlling laws*—2 H6 V 1 103. *True love acted*—Rom III 2 16. *Let the world see His nobleness well acted*—Ant V 2 44.

ACTION-TAKING

Going to law instead of fighting: *A lily-livered, action-taking knave*—Lr II 2 18.

ACTUAL

Exhibited in deeds: *Her walking and other actual performances*—Mcb V 1 13. Superfluously in a sim. sense: *In discourse of thought or actual deed*—Oth IV 2 153.

ACTURE

The process of acting, action: *With acture they* (*i.e.* his offences) *may be Where neither party is nor true nor kind*—Compl 185.

ADAM

Gen. taken as referring to Adam Bell, an outlaw of the English Border celebrated for archery: *He that hits me, let him be clapped on the shoulder, and called Adam*—Ado I 1 260.

ADAMANT

(1) An alleged mineral, very hard: *Spurn in pieces posts of adamant*—1 H6 I 4 52.

(2) Identified with the loadstone: *You draw me, you hard-hearted adamant*—Mids II 1 195. *As true . . . As iron to adamant*—Troil III 2 184.

ADDICT

Having an inclination or leaning: *If he be addict to vice*—Pilgr 415.

ADDICTION

Inclination, bent, leaning: *His addiction was to courses vain*—H5 I 1 54. *Each man to what sport and revels his addiction leads him*—Oth II 2 5.

ADDITION

(1) A name, title, 'style' of address: *They are devils' additions, the names of fiends*—Wiv II 2 312. *They clepe us drunkards, and with swinish phrase Soil our addition*—Hml I 4 19. *We still retain The name, and all the additions to a king*—Lr I 1 137. Iago. *How do you now, lieutenant?* Cas. *The worser that you give me the addition*—Oth IV 1 104. Something conducing to one's reputation: [I] *think it no addition, nor*

my wish, To have him see me woman'd—Oth III 4 194.

(2) In heraldry, something added to a coat of arms as a mark of honour: *A great addition earned in thy death*—Troil IV 5 141.

ADDRESS

(1) To direct: *All my powers, address your love and might To honour Helen*—Mids II 2 143. *Address thy gait unto her*—Tw I 4 15. *Address, directing one's course: Toward that shade I might behold address The king and his companions*—LLL V 2 92.

(2) To prepare, make ready, equip: *Address'd a mighty power*—As V 4 162. *All imminence that gods and men Address their dangers in*—Troil V 10 13. *Even in your armours, as you are address'd*—Per II 3 94. *Addressed, prepared, ready: Navarre . . . and his competitors in oath Were all address'd to meet you*—LLL II 81. Dec. *Where is Metellus Cimber? . . .* Bru. *He is address'd*—Cæs III 1 27.

(3) To prepare, get oneself ready: *Let us address to tend on Hector's heels*—Troil IV 4 148.

(4) *To address towards*, to address oneself to in speech: *We first address towards you*—Lr I 1 193.

ADHERE

To be coherent: *They do no more adhere and keep place together than . . .*—Wiv II 1 62. *Everything adheres together*—Tw III 4 86. To be consistent with the execution of a design: *Nor time nor place Did then adhere*—Mcb I 7 51.

ADJUDGE

To judge, pass sentence on: *As he adjudged your brother*—Meas V 408.

ADJUNCT

Annexed, consequent: *Though that my death were adjunct to my act*—John III 3 57. *Though death be adjunct*—Lucr 133.

ADMIRABLE

To be wondered at: *Strange and admirable*—Mids V 27.

ADMIRAL

The admiral's ship: *Thou art our admiral, thou bearest the lantern in the poop*—1 H4 III 3 28. *The Antoniad, the Egyptian admiral*—Ant III 10 2.

ADMIRATION

Wonder: *Very notes of admiration*—Wint V 2 12. *Season your admiration for a while With an attent ear*—Hml I 2 192. *What makes your admiration?*—Cymb I 6 38.

ADMIRE

To wonder, marvel: *These lords At this encounter do so much admire*—Tp V 153. *Wonder not, nor admire not*—Tw III 4 165.

ADMIRED

(1) To be admired, admirable: *Admired Miranda!*—Tp III 1 37. *Admired Octavia*—Ant II 2 121.

(2) To be wondered at, strange: *With most admired disorder*—Mcb III 4 110.

ADMÏTTANCE

Of great admittance, admitted to the society of the great—Wiv II 2 235. *Of Venetian admittance*, accepted as fashionable at Venice: *Any tire of Venetian admittance*—Wiv III 3 61.

ADOPTIOUS

Adopted for the nonce: *Pretty, fond, adoptious christendoms*—All's I 1 188.

ADORNED

App., adorned themselves: *Whose men and dames so jetted and adorn'd*—Per I 4 26.

ADULTERATE (adj.)

Adulterous: *I am possess'd with an adulterate blot*—Err II 2 142. *The adulterate Hastings*—R3 IV 4 69. *That incestuous, that adulterate beast*—Hml I 5 42.

ADULTERATE (vb.)

To commit adultery: *Adulterates hourly with thine uncle John*—John III 1 56.

ADVANCE

To raise, uplift: *The fringed curtains of thine eye advance*—Tp I 2 408. *That never war advance His bleeding sword*—H5 V 2 382. *Advance your standards*—R3 V 3 264.

ADVANTAGE (sb.)

(1) A favourable occasion, opportunity: *Bring them after in the best advantage*—Oth I 3 298. *Can stamp and counterfeit advantages*—II 1 247. *Make use of time, let not advantage slip*—Ven 129. *To the advantage*, making use of a favourable opportunity: *To the advantage, I, being here, took't up*—Oth III 3 312. *At more advantage*, at a more suitable time: *We'll read it at more advantage*—1 H4 II 4 593. *In advantage lingering*, protracting his resistance by the advantage of a strong post: *In advantage lingering looks for rescue*—1 H6 IV 4 19.

(2) Pecuniary profit, interest on money lent: *You neither lend nor borrow Upon advantage*—Merch I 3 70. Sim., of stolen money repaid: *The money shall be paid back again with advantage*—1 H4 II 4 599. Fig.: *With advantage means to pay thy love*—John III 3 22. *He'll remember with advantages What feats he did that day*—H5 IV 3 50.

ADVANTAGE (vb.)

To add to the amount or value of: *Advantaging their loan with interest*—R3 IV 4 323.

ADVANTAGEABLE

Tending to advantage, advantageous: *As your wisdoms best Shall see advantageable for our dignity*—H5 V 2 87.

ADVENTURE

(1) Hap, chance: *Searching of thy wound, I have by hard adventure found mine own*—As II 4 44. *To try the fair adventure of to-morrow*—John V 5 22.

(2) A hazarding: *The adventure of her person*—Wint V 1 156.

(3) *At all adventures*, at all hazards, whatever the consequences may be: *And in this mist at all adventures go*—Err II 2 218. *So I would he were, and I by him, at all adventures*—H5 IV 1 121.

ADVERSITY

Perversity; perverse one, quibbler: *Well said, adversity!*—Troil V 1 14.

ADVERTISE

To admonish, instruct: *I do bend my speech To one that can my part in him advertise*—Meas I 1 41.

ADVERTISEMENT

(1) Notification, information: *This advertisement is five days old*—1 H4 III 2 172.

(2) Admonition, warning, precept: *My griefs cry louder than advertisement*—Ado V 1 32. *An advertisement to a proper maid . . . to take heed of . . .*—All's IV 3 240. *Yet doth he give us bold advertisement That . . . we should on*—1 H4 IV 1 36.

ADVERTISING

Attending, attentive: *I was then Advertising and holy to your business*—Meas V 387.

ADVICE

Consideration, deliberation: *How shall I dote on her with more advice, That thus without advice begin to love her!*—Gent II 4 207. *Yet did repent me, after more advice*—Meas V 469. *Make yourself some comfort Out of your best advice*—Cymb I 1 155.

ADVISE

(1) To consider, take thought: *Lay hand on heart, advise*—Rom III 5 192. Refl.: *Advise you what you say*—Tw IV 2 102. *Advise yourself*—Lr II 1 29. So, *to be advised*: [The prince] *bids you be advised there's nought in France That can be with a nimble galliard won*—H5 I 2 251. Hence *advised*, deliberate, careful, taking thought: *With more advised watch*—Merch I 1 142. *More upon humour than advised respect*—John IV 2 214. *The advised head defends itself at home*—H5 I 2 179. The result of deliberation: *Nor never by advised purpose meet*—R2 I 3 188. *Well-advised,*

acting with due consideration, discreet, well-judging: *Be well advised, tell o'er thy tale again—* John III 1 5. *Being well advised. For had I cursed now, I had cursed myself—*R3 I 3 318. *Any well-advised friend—*IV 4 517. In one's sober senses: *Sleeping or waking? mad or well-advised?* —Err II 2 215.

(2) To prevail on by counsel, induce: *Let the friar advise you—*Ado IV 1 246. *Or whether since he is advised by aught To change the course* —Lr V 1 2. *Be advised*, be ruled by me, take heed: *What say you, Hermia? be advised, fair maid—*Mids I 1 46. *Good cousin, be advised; stir not to-night—*1 H4 IV 3 5.

(3) To instruct: *I shall anon advise you Further in the proceeding—*H8 I 2 107. *Advise your fellows so—*Lr I 3 23.

ADVISEDLY

(1) Attentively, carefully: *This ill presage advisedly she marketh—*Ven 457. *This picture she advisedly perused—*Lucr 1527.

(2) Prudently, judiciously: [He] *arm'd his long-hid wits advisedly—*Lucr 1816.

(3) Deliberately: *And to the flame* [he] *thus speaks advisedly—*Lucr 180. After deliberation: *We will not now be troubled with reply: We offer fair; take it advisedly—*1 H4 V 1 113.

ADVOCATION

Advocacy, pleading: *My advocation is not now in tune—*Oth III 4 123.

AERY

The young of a bird of prey: *Our aery buildeth in the cedar's top —* R3 I 3 264. *Your aery buildeth in our aery's nest—*270. Fig.: *An aery of children—*Hml II 2 354.

AFEARD

Afraid: *Be not afeard—*Tp II 2 106. *I am afeard you make a wanton of me—*Hml V 2 310. *He is afeard to come—*Ant II 5 81.

AFFECT (sb.)

(1) Natural tendency, inclination: *For every man with his affects is born—*LLL I 1 152. *The young affects In me defunct—*Oth I 3 264.

(2) Kind feeling, affection: *Wooing poor craftsmen . . . As 'twere to banish their affects with him—*R2 I 4 28.

AFFECT (vb.)

(1) To aim at, seek to attain: *Have I affected wealth or honour?—*2 H6 IV 7 104. *In this point charge him home, that he affects Tyrannical power* —Cor III 3 1. *Affecting one sole throne—*IV 6 32.

(2) To have affection or liking for a person: *There is a lady . . . Whom I affect—*Gent III 1 81. *Maria once told me she* (*i.e.* Olivia) *did*

*affect me—*Tw II 5 27. *I thought the king had more affected the Duke of Albany than Cornwall* —Lr I 1 1. To be drawn to or like a thing: *How doth your grace affect their motion?—*1 H6 V 1 7. *The affected merit—*Troil II 2 60 (in the preceding line *itself* appears to refer to the will, and *affects* to be the other verb of the same form in the still current sense, lays hold of like a disease). *Not to affect many proposed matches—*Oth III 3 229. To incline or like: *Making peace or war As thou affect'st* —Ant I 3 70.

(3) To partake of the character of, be reminiscent of: *The accent of his tongue affecteth him* —John I 86.

AFFECTED

(1) Inclined, disposed: *As I find her, so am I affected—*Wiv III 4 95. *How he doth stand affected to our purpose—*R3 III 1 171.

(2) *Affected to*, in love with: *I stand affected to her—*Gent II 1 90. *Is thine own heart to thine own face affected?—*Ven 157.

AFFECTEDLY

With studied art, fancifully: *Feat and affectedly Enswathed—*Compl 48.

AFFECTING

Affected: *A drawling, affecting rogue—*Wiv II 1 145. *Such antic, lisping, affecting fantasticoes—* Rom II 4 29.

AFFECTION

(1) Emotion, feeling, desire in gen.: *The affection that now guides me most—*Meas II 4 168. *With affection wondrous sensible—*Merch II 8 48. *The appetite and affection common Of the whole body—*Cor I 1 107. In pl.: *Your affections Would become tender—*Tp V 18. *I have not known when his affections sway'd More than his reason—*Cæs II 1 20.

(2) Mental tendency, disposition: *Affection, Mistress of passion—*Merch IV 1 50. *The affection of nobleness which nature shows above her breeding—*Wint V 2 40. *My most ill-composed affection—*Mcb IV 3 77.

(3) Tendency, wish, inclination: *It is the king's most sweet pleasure and affection to . . .—*LLL V 1 92. *Thy affections, which do hold a wing Quite from the flight of all thy ancestors—*1 H4 III 2 30. *Affections of delight*, inclinations to pleasure—2 H4 II 3 29.

(4) Affectation: *Witty without affection—*LLL V 1 4.

AFFECTIONED

Affected: *An affectioned ass—*Tw II 3 160.

AFFEER

To settle, confirm: *The title is affeer'd—*Mcb IV 3 34.

AFFIANCE

Trust, confidence: *The sweetness of affiance*—H5 II 2 127. *This fond affiance*—2 H6 III 1 74. *To know if your affiance Were deeply rooted*—Cymb I 6 163.

AFFINED

(1) Related: *Seem all affined and kin*—Troil I 3 25.

(2) Bound by any tie: *Whether I in any just term am affined To love the Moor*—Oth I 1 39. *If partially affined, or leagued in office, Thou dost . . .*—II 3 218.

AFFRAY

To frighten: *That voice doth us affray*—Rom III 5 33.

AFFRONT (sb.)

An attack, assault: *That gave the affront with them*—Cymb V 3 87.

AFFRONT (vb.)

(1) To meet, address a person: *That he, as 'twere by accident, may here Affront Ophelia*—Hml III 1 30.

(2) To front, face in position: *Unless another . . . Affront his eye*—Wint V 1 73.

(3) To face anticipatively, prepare to meet: *Your preparation can affront no less Than what you hear of*—Cymb IV 3 29.

(4) To confront one thing with another, set face to face: *That my integrity . . . Might be affronted with the match and weight Of . . .*—Troil III 2 172.

AFFY

(1) To confide: *So I do affy In thy uprightness and integrity . . . That . . .*—Tit I 1 47.

(2) To betroth: *Where then do you know best We be affied?*—Shr IV 4 48.

AFORE

Afore God, afore me, by God, by my life: R2 II 1 200; Rom III 4 34.

A-FRONT

In a front, abreast: *These four came all a-front*—1 H4 II 4 222.

AFTER

At the rate of: *I'll rent the fairest house in it after three-pence a bay*—Meas II 1 254. *After fourteen years' purchase*—Tw IV 1 24.

AFTER-SUPPER

A collation after supper, dessert: *Between our after-supper and 'ed-time*—Mids V 34.

AGAINST

Towards, to: *My love and duty Against your sacred person*—H8 II 4 40. *It is hypocrisy against the devil*—Oth IV 1 6.

AGATE

A figure cut in agate as a symbol of smallness: *If low, an agate very vilely cut*—Ado III 1 65. *I was never manned with an agate till now*—2 H4 I 2 18.

AGAZED

Agazed on, astounded, amazed at: *All the whole army stood agazed on him*—1 H6 I 1 126.

AGGRAVATE

To increase, add to: *To aggravate thy store*—Sonn 146 10.

AGLET-BABY

A doll decked with aglets or tags; or perh., a small figure forming the head of the tag of a lace: *Marry him to a puppet or an aglet-baby*—Shr I 2 79.

AGNIZE

To acknowledge: *I do agnize A natural and prompt alacrity I find in hardness*—Oth I 3 232.

AGONE

Ago: *Long agone I have forgot to court*—Gent III 1 85. *An hour agone*—Tw V 204.

AGONY

The death struggle: *Mirth cannot move a soul in agony*—LLL V 2 867. *Sprawl'st thou? take that, to end thy agony*—3 H6 V 5 39.

AGOOD

In good earnest, heartily: *I made her weep agood*—Gent IV 4 170.

A-HOLD

To lay a-hold, to bring to the wind: *Lay her a-hold, a-hold!*—Tp I 1 52.

AIDANT

Aiding, helpful: *Be aidant and remediate In the good man's distress*—Lr IV 4 17.

AIM (sb.)

(1) A guess, conjecture: *A man may prophesy, With a near aim, of the main chance of things*—2 H4 III 1 82. *What you would work me to, I have some aim*—Cæs I 2 163. *Where the aim reports*—Oth I 3 6.

(2) *Give me aim*, explained as, give room and scope to my thoughts—Tit V 3 149. *To cry aim*, to encourage archers by crying out 'aim'; hence to encourage, abet: *Cried I aim? said I well?*—Wiv II 3 92. *To these violent proceedings all my neighbours shall cry aim*—III 2 44. *To cry aim To these ill-tuned repetitions*—John II 196.

(3) A thing aimed at, a mark: *Arrows fled not swifter toward their aim*—2 H4 I 1 123. *To be the aim of every dangerous shot*—R3 IV 4 90.

AIM (vb.)

(1) To guess, conjecture: *Well aim'd of such a young one*—Shr II 237. *Thou aimest all awry* —2 H6 II 4 58. With *at: Aiming, belike, at your interior hatred*—R3 I 3 65. *They aim at it*— Hml IV 5 9.

(2) To devise, plan: *It is exceedingly well aim'd* —1 H4 I 3 282.

AIR

In air of, perh., trusting (merely) to the outward appearance, apparent character of: *Who builds his hopes in air of your good looks*—R3 III 4 100. *To take air,* to get abroad, be exposed: *Lest the device take air and taint*—Tw III 4 144.

AIR-BRAVING

Defying the heavens: *Your stately and air-braving towers*—1 H6 IV 2 13.

ALARUM (sb.)

(1) A call to arms—All's IV 1 69 (Stage Dir.). *Our stern alarums*—R3 I 1 7. *When the alarum were struck*—Cor II 2 80. *Alarum-bell*—Mcb II 3 79; V 5 51.

(2) A loud noise, din: *To endure her loud alarums*—Shr I 1 131.

ALARUM (vb.)

To rouse to action: *Alarum'd by his sentinel, the wolf*—Mcb II 1 53. *My best alarum'd spirits* —Lr II 1 55.

ALDER-LIEFEST

Dearest of all: *Mine alder-liefest sovereign*— 2 H6 I 1 28.

ALE

An ale-house: *To go to the ale with a Christian* —Gent II 5 61.

ALIGHT

To alight from: *Vouchsafe, thou wonder, to alight thy steed*—Ven 13.

ALL

Used in addressing two persons: *Good morrow to you all, my lords* (*i.e.* Warwick and Surrey)— 2 H4 III 1 35. *As all you know* (*i.e.* Salisbury and Warwick)—2 H6 II 2 26.

ALLAY (sb.)

A means of abatement: *To whose feeling sorrows I might be some allay*—Wint IV 2 8.

ALLAY (vb.)

(1) To detract from: *It does allay The good precedence*—Ant II 5 50.

(2) To dilute: *A drop of allaying Tiber*—Cor II 1 53.

(3) To abate, cease: *When the rage allays, the rain begins*—3 H6 I 4 146. *With the mischief of your person it* (*i.e.* Gloucester's displeasure) *would scarcely allay*—Lr I 2 178.

ALLAYMENT

An admixture of a modifying element, mitigation: *The like allayment could I give my grief*— Troil IV 4 8. *To try the vigour of them and apply Allayments to their act*—Cymb I 5 21.

ALL-BUILDING

That on which all is built: *The all-building law*—Meas II 4 94.

ALLEGIANT

Loyal: *Allegiant thanks*—H8 III 2 176.

ALL-HALLOND EVE

The eve of Hallowmas or All Saints Day—Meas II 1 130.

ALL-HALLOWMAS

All Saints Day—Wiv I 1 211.

ALL-HALLOWN SUMMER

Summer falling late, at All-hallowmas. Fig. (of Falstaff): *Farewell, thou latter spring! farewell, All-hallown summer!*—1 H4 I 2 177.

ALL HID

Hide and seek: *All hid, all hid; an old infant play*—LLL IV 3 78.

ALL-OBEYING

Obeyed by all: *His all-obeying breath*—Ant III 13 77.

ALL-OBLIVIOUS

Wrapping everything in oblivion: *Death and all-oblivious enmity*—Sonn 55 9.

ALLOTTERY

A portion allotted: *The poor allottery my father left me*—As I 1 76.

ALLOW

(1) To license: *Go, you are allow'd* (*i.e.* as a fool)—LLL V 2 478. *There is no slander in an allowed fool*—Tw I 5 101.

(2) To acknowledge, recognize: *I do demand, If you . . . Allow their officers*—Cor III 3 43. *Allow'd with absolute power*—Tim V 1 165. To cause to be acknowledged: *That will allow me very worth his service*—Tw I 2 59.

(3) To approve of, sanction: *I like them all, and do allow them well*—2 H4 IV 2 54. *If your sweet sway Allow obedience*—Lr II 4 193. *Who, wondering at him, did his words allow*—Lucr 1845.

(4) Refl., to lend oneself to: *His roguish madness Allows itself to anything*—Lr III 7 104.

(5) To assign as one's due: *The law allows it, and the court awards it*—Merch IV 1 303.

ALLOWANCE

(1) Praise, applause: *A stirring dwarf we do allowance give Before a sleeping giant*—Troil II 3 146.

(2) Approval, sanction: [Words] *Of no allowance to your bosom's truth*—Cor III 2 57. *Under the allowance of your great aspect*—Lr II 2 112. *Your allowance*, a thing sanctioned by you: *If this be known to you and your allowance*—Oth I 1 128.

(3) Acknowledgment: *Give him allowance for the better man*—Troil I 3 377. *The censure of the which one must in your allowance o'erweigh . . .*—Hml III 2 30. *Of very expert and approved allowance*, of tried and acknowledged skill—Oth II 1 49.

ALL-THING

Altogether, in every way: *All-thing unbecoming*—Mcb III 1 13.

ALL-TO

All-to topple (properly *all to-topple*), quite topple in pieces (*to* = asunder): *The very principals did seem to rend, And all-to topple*—Per III 2 16. *All-to*, wholly, completely: *It was not she that call'd him all-to naught*—Ven 993.

ALLUSION

A jest, riddle: *The allusion holds in the exchange*—LLL IV 2 42.

ALLY

A relative, kinsman: *You to your land and love and great allies*—As V 4 195. *This gentleman, the prince's near ally*—Rom III 1 114.

ALMAIN

A German: *He sweats not to overthrow your Almain*—Oth II 3 85.

ALMOST

Used to intensify a rhetorical interrogative: *Or do you almost think, although you see, That you do see?*—John IV 3 43. *Would you imagine, or almost believe?*—R3 III 5 35.

ALMS

At fortune's alms, as something coming by chance: *Your lord, who hath received you At fortune's alms*—Lr I 1 280. *To fortune's alms*, to whatever may chance: *And shut myself up in some other course, To fortune's alms*—Oth III 4 121.

ALMS-DRINK

Drink beyond a man's share contributed to intoxicate him: *They have made him drink alms-drink*—Ant II 7 5.

ALONG (adv.)

(1) At full length: [We] *Did steal behind him as he lay along*—As II 1 30. *Under yond yew-trees lay thee all along*—Rom V 3 3. *To lie along*, to lie low: *When he lies along*—Cor V 6 57. *That now on Pompey's basis lies along*—Cæs III 1 115.

(2) *To go along*, to accompany a person: *Soft! I will go along*—Rom I 1 201. *Gallus, go you along*—Ant V 1 69.

ALONG (prep.)

Of space traversed, throughout the length of, from end to end of: *Travelling along this coast*—LLL V 2 557 (see *Coast*). *The brook that brawls along this wood*—As II 1 32. *Along the field I will the Trojan trail*—Troil V 8 22.

ALTER

To exchange: *She that would alter services with thee*—Tw II 5 171.

AMAZE (sb.)

Astonishment, wonder: *His face's own margent did quote such amazes*—LLL II 246.

AMAZE (vb.)

(1) To bewilder, perplex, confound: *Yet you are amazed; but this shall absolutely resolve you*—Meas IV 2 224. *Lest your retirement do amaze your friends*—1 H4 V 4 6. *Who can be wise, amazed, temperate and furious . . . in a moment?*—Mcb II 3 114. *Like a labyrinth to amaze his foes*—Ven 684.

(2) To fill with consternation, terrify: *The French amazed vouchsafe a parle*—John II 226. *Like amazing thunder*—R2 I 3 81. *It would amaze the proudest of you all*—1 H6 IV 7 84.

AMAZEDLY

(1) In bewilderment: *I shall reply amazedly*—Mids IV 1 150. *I speak amazedly*—Wint V 1 187.

(2) In consternation: *Why Stands Macbeth thus amazedly?*—Mcb IV 1 125.

AMAZEDNESS

(1) Bewilderment: *After a little amazedness we were all commanded out of the chamber*—Wint V 2 5.

(2) Consternation, panic: *We two in great amazedness will fly*—Wiv IV 4 55.

AMAZEMENT

(1) Mental stupefaction: *Distraction, frenzy and amazement*—Troil V 3 85.

(2) Bewilderment, perplexity: *Put not yourself into amazement*—Meas IV 2 219. *Wild amazement hurries up and down The little number of your doubtful friends*—John V 1 35.

(3) Consternation, alarm: *Be collected: no more amazement*—Tp I 2 13. *I flamed amazement*—198. *Look, amazement on thy mother sits*—Hml III 4 112.

AMBIGUITY

An uncertainty, dubiety: *Till we can clear these ambiguities*—Rom V 3 217.

AMBLE

An artificial pace, easy and swift, in which the horse's legs on each side moved together (see also *Trot* vb.): *I will rather trust . . . a thief to walk my ambling gelding*—Wiv II 2 316. *I'll tell you who Time ambles withal*—As III 2 327. [Time ambles] *with a priest that lacks Latin and a rich man that hath not the gout*, 337. Of persons, to walk affectedly: *The skipping king, he ambled up and down*—1 H4 III 2 60. *A wanton ambling nymph*—R3 I 1 17. *You jig, you amble, and you lisp*—Hml III 1 150.

AMENDS

Improvement in health, recovery: *Now Lord be thanked for my good amends!*—Shr Ind 2 99.

AMES-ACE

Both aces, the lowest throw at dice: *I had rather be in this choice than throw ames-ace for my life* (spoken ironically)—All's II 3 84.

AMIABLE

(1) Lovable, inducing love: *Thy amiable cheeks*—Mids IV 1 2. *'Twould make her amiable and subdue my father Entirely to her love*—Oth III 4 59.

(2) Importing love: *To lay an amiable siege to the honesty of this Ford's wife*—Wiv II 2 243. *This amiable encounter*—Ado III 3 161.

AMISS

(1) A calamity, misfortune: *Each toy seems prologue to some great amiss*—Hml IV 5 18.

(2) An offence: *Myself corrupting, salving thy amiss, Excusing thy sins, more than thy sins are*—Sonn 35 7 (so prob. the passage should be pointed, *salving* and *excusing* explaining, and *more . . .* are qualifying *corrupting*). *Urge not my amiss*—151 3.

AMONG

All the while: *Lusty lads roam here and there So merrily, And ever among so merrily*—2 H4 V 3 21.

AMORT

Spiritless, dejected: *What, sweeting, all amort?*—Shr IV 3 36. *What, all amort?*—1 H6 III 2 124.

AN

If: *An he were, I would burn my study*—Ado I 1 80. *Good, an God will!*—2 H4 I 1 13. So *an if*: *These be fine things, an if they be not sprites*—Tp II 2 120. *An if my brother had my shape*—John I 138. *An* = as if: *I will roar you an 'twere any nightingale*—Mids I 2 85. [A] *went*

away an it had been any christom child—H5 II 3 11. *An 'twere a cloud in autumn*—Troil I 2 139.

ANATOMY

(1) A skeleton: *That fell anatomy* (*i.e.* Death)—John III 4 40. A 'walking skeleton': *A hungry lean-faced villain, A mere anatomy*—Err V 237.

(2) The body (depreciatively): *I'll eat the rest of the anatomy*—Tw III 2 67. *In what vile part of this anatomy Doth my name lodge?*—Rom III 3 106.

ANCHOR

An anchorite: *An anchor's cheer in prison be my scope!*—Hml III 2 229.

ANCHORAGE

A ship's set of anchors: *From whence at first she weigh'd her anchorage*—Tit I 73.

ANCIENT (adj.)

Former: *Call home thy ancient thoughts from banishment*—Shr Ind 2 33. *Till you had recovered your ancient freedom*—2 H6 IV 8 27. *Where is your ancient courage?*—Cor IV 1 3.

ANCIENT (sb.)

(1) An ensign, standard: *An old faced ancient*—1 H4 IV 2 34.

(2) He who bears the ancient, an ensign: *Ancients, corporals, lieutenants*—1 H4 IV 2 26. *His Moorship's ancient*—Oth I 1 33.

ANCIENTRY

(1) The old people: *Wronging the ancientry*—Wint III 3 62.

(2) Old-fashioned formality: *A measure, full of state and ancientry*—Ado II 1 80.

AND

Used redundantly: *When that I was and a little tiny boy*—Tw V 398. *He that has and a little tiny wit*—Lr III 2 74.

ANDREW

The name of a ship: *My wealthy Andrew dock'd in sand*—Merch I 1 27.

AN END

On end, standing up: *Each particular hair to stand an end*—Hml I 5 19. *Your bedded hair . . . Starts up, and stands an end*—III 4 121.

ANGEL

(1) A gold coin, in Shakespeare's time = 10*s.*: *I had myself twenty angels given me this morning*—Wiv II 2 73. *When his fair angels would salute my palm*—John II 590. Described in Merch II 7 55.

(2) In Shr IV 2 61 (*An ancient angel coming down the hill*) possibly, a worthy old fellow.

ANGERLY

Angrily: *How angerly I taught my brow to frown!*—Gent I 2 62. *Nor look upon the iron angerly*—John IV 1 82. *Why, how now, Hecate! you look angerly*—Mcb III 5 1.

ANGLE

A fishing-hook: *The angle that plucks our son thither*—Wint IV 2 52. [He that hath] *Thrown out his angle for my proper life*—Hml V 2 66. Extended to tackle and rod: *Give me mine angle*—Ant II 5 10.

A-NIGHT

At night: *For coming a-night to Jane Smile*—As II 4 48.

ANNEXION

An addition, adjunct: *With the annexions of fair gems enrich'd*—Compl 208.

ANNOTHANIZE

Anatomize; app., to explain: *Which to annothanize in the vulgar*—LLL IV 1 68.

ANNOY (sb.)

(1) Pain, grief: *Farewell sour annoy!*—3 H6 V 7 45. *For mirth doth search the bottom of annoy*—Lucr 1109. *That which causes pain: Receivest with pleasure thine annoy*—Sonn 8 4.

(2) Injury, harm: *Good angels guard thee from the boar's annoy!*—R3 V 3 156.

ANNOY (vb.)

To injure, harm: *One spark of evil That might annoy my finger*—H5 II 2 101. *Thorns that would annoy our foot*—2 H6 III 1 67. *Went surly by, Without annoying me*—Cæs I 3 21.

ANNOYANCE

(1) Injury, harm: *Doing annoyance to the treacherous feet*—R2 III 2 16. *Remove from her the means of all annoyance*—Mcb V 1 84.

(2) That which harms: *To souse annoyance that comes near his nest*—John V 2 150.

ANON

Straightway, directly. More or less of this (the older) sense may be seen in many passages, *e.g.*: *Hard by; at street end; he will be here anon*—Wiv IV 2 40. *Anon, anon, sir* (the drawer's regular cry)—1 H4 II 4 41. *I hear some noise within . . . Anon, good nurse!*—Rom II 2 136. *I come, anon*—150. Porter . . . [Knocking within.] *Anon, anon!*—Mcb II 3 22. *Ever and anon*, every now and then—*And ever and anon they made a doubt*—LLL V 2 101. *A pouncet-box, which ever and anon He gave his nose*—1 H4 I 3 38.

ANOTHER

The other: *When they hold one an opinion of another's dotage*—Ado II 3 223. *One side will mock another*—Lr III 7 71. *Such another*, such a: *It is such another Nan*—Wiv I 4 160. *'Tis such another fitchew!*—Oth IV 1 150.

ANSWER (sb.)

(1) Account: *This is not, no, Laid to thy answer*—Wint III 2 199. *He'll call you to so hot an answer of it*—H5 II 4 123. In reference to breaches of the law: *Arrest them to the answer of the law*—H5 II 2 143. *That which we have done, whose answer would be death*—Cymb IV 4 12. *At heaviest answer*, to pay the full penalty—Tim V 4 63.

(2) A return, retaliation: *Great the answer be Britons must take*—Cymb V 3 79.

(3) An acceptance of a challenge: *And wake him to the answer, think you?*—Troil I 3 332. *If your lordship would vouchsafe the answer . . . I mean, my lord, the opposition of your person in trial*—Hml V 2 175. Cf. H5 IV 7 142 (*Quite from the answer of his degree*).

(4) In fencing, a stroke after parrying or being hit: *On the answer, he pays you as surely as . . .*—Tw III 4 305.

ANSWER (vb.)

(1) To face, encounter: *That dare as well answer a man indeed As . . .*—Ado V 1 89. *He will answer the letter's master*—Rom II 4 11. *To answer with thy uncovered body this extremity of the skies*—Lr III 4 106. To respond to an attack: *To answer royally in our defences*—H5 II 4 3. *Arming to answer in a night alarm*—Troil I 3 171. To accept a challenge: Mer. *A challenge, on my life.* Ben. *Romeo will answer it*—Rom II 4 8.

(2) Not to let slip: *Answer the time of request*—All's I 1 168. *Observe and answer The vantage of his anger*—Cor II 3 267.

(3) To perform, carry out: *To answer other business*—Tp I 2 367. *To answer matters of this consequence*—H5 II 4 146.

(4) To fulfil the desires of, satisfy (a person): *Answer me to-morrow, Or . . . I'll prove a tyrant to him*—Meas IV 1 167. To pay (a debt, &c.): *As dear As all the metal in your shop will answer*—Err IV 1 81. *To answer all the debt he owes to you*—1 H4 I 3 185. To pay (a person): *Say whether you'll answer me or no*—Err IV 1 60. *Answering us With our own charge*—Cor V 6 67.

(5) To meet charges in regard to, accept responsibility for: *The offences we have made you do we'll answer*—Wint I 2 83. *I'll answer the coinage*—1 H4 IV 2 8. *And will answer well The death I gave him*—Hml III 4 176. To atone for, pay for: *This shall be answered*—Wiv I 1 117. *If she convey Letters to Richmond, you shall answer it*—R3 IV 2 95. Of an accounting, to make it: *Her audit, though delay'd, answer'd must be*—Sonn

126 13. To make good (an assertion): *What I speak . . . my divine soul* [shall] *answer it in heaven*—R2 I 1 36. To make good (a loss caused to one): *A shall answer it* (*i.e.* the loss of the sack)—2 H4 V 1 27. To repay, make a return for: *A surplus of your grace, which never My life may last to answer*—Wint V 3 7. To give back in kind, return: *Who mutually hath answer'd my affection*—Wiv IV 6 10. *To answer for*, to make up for: *Could all but answer for that peevish brat?* —R3 I 3 194.

ANSWERABLE

Corresponding, commensurate: *All things answerable to this portion*—Shr II 361. *Thou shalt see an answerable sequestration*—Oth I 3 350.

ANTHROPOPHAGI

Eaters of men, cannibals: *The Cannibals that each other eat, The Anthropophagi*—Oth I 3 143. In Wiv IV 5 10 the Host uses the form *Anthropophaginian.*

ANTIC, ANTIQUE (adj.)

Fantastic, grotesque: *The pox of such antic, lisping, affecting fantasticoes*—Rom II 4 29. *To put an antic disposition on*—Hml I 5 172. *Draw no lines there with thine antique pen*—Sonn 19 10.

ANTIC, ANTIQUE (sb.)

(1) A grotesque theatrical representation: *Or pageant, or antique, or firework*—LLL V 1 118. *We will have, if this fadge not, an antique*—154.

(2) A grotesque figure: *Nature, drawing of an antique, Made a foul blot*—Ado III 1 63. *Were he the veriest antic in the world*—Shr Ind 1 101. *Winking, there appears Quick-shifting antics, ugly in her eyes*—Lucr 458.

ANTIC (vb.)

To make buffoons of: *The wild disguise hath almost Antick'd us all*—Ant II 7 131.

ANTIQUARY

Of antiquity, ancient: *Instructed by the antiquary times*—Troil II 3 262.

ANTIQUE

See *Antic.*

ANTIQUITY

Old age: *An oak, whose . . . high top* [was] *bald with dry antiquity*—As IV 3 105. *Hadst thou not the privilege of antiquity upon thee*—All's II 3 220. *Every part about you blasted with antiquity*—2 H4 I 2 207.

ANTRE

A cavern: *Antres vast and deserts idle*—Oth I 3 140.

APART

To put apart, to make away with: *Humphrey being dead . . . And Henry put apart, the next for me*—2 H6 III 1 382.

APE-BEARER

One who carries an ape about for exhibition: *He hath been since an ape-bearer*—Wint IV 3 101.

APES

To lead apes into (or *in*) *hell*, the punishment of old maids—Ado II 1 43; Shr II 34.

APOLOGY

An explanation or justification (of an incident): *He shall present Hercules in minority . . and I will have an apology for that purpose*—LLL V 1 140. *Make this haste as your own good proceeding, Strengthen'd with what apology you think May make it probable need*—All's II 4 50. App., a setting out or displaying (of a thing): *What needeth then apologies be made, To set forth that which is so singular?*—Lucr 31.

APOSTRAPHA

Apostrophe, the sign indicating the omission of a letter: *You find not the apostraphas, and so miss the accent*, app., *you neglect such signs, and so spoil the scansion*—LLL IV 2 123.

APPAID

Contented, pleased: *Thou art well appaid As well to hear as grant what he hath said*—Lucr 914.

APPAL

(1) To make pale: *Your looks are sad, your cheer appall'd*—1 H6 I 2 48.

(2) To impair: *Property was thus appalled*—Phœn 37.

APPARENT

(1) Visible, plainly seen: *By some apparent sign Let us have knowledge*—1 H6 II 1 3.

(2) Evident, manifest: *Apparent hazard of his life*—Gent III 1 116. Prov. . . . *His fact . . . came not to an undoubtful proof.* Duke. *It is now apparent?* Prov. *Most manifest*—Meas IV 2 141. *Some apparent danger seen in him*—R2 I 1 13.

(3) In the position of heir apparent: *He's Apparent to my heart*—Wint I 2 176. *I'll draw it* (*i.e.* his sword) *as apparent to the crown*—3 H6 II 2 64.

APPARENTLY

Openly, manifestly: *If he should scorn me so apparently*—Err IV 1 78.

APPEACH

To impeach, accuse: *Your passions Have to the full appeach'd*—All's I 3 196. *I will appeach the villain*—R2 V 2 79.

APPEAL (sb.)

A criminal charge made by one who undertook to prove it by combat: *The boisterous late appeal . . . Against the Duke of Norfolk*—R2 I 1 4. *His honour is as true In this appeal as thou art all unjust*—IV 44. An accusation in gen.: *Upon his own appeal, seizes him*—Ant III 5 11.

APPEAL (vb.)

To impeach, accuse by way of 'appeal': *To appeal each other of high treason*—R2 I 1 27. *Against the Duke of Hereford that appeals me*—I 3 21. With the charge as obj.: *As for the rest appeal'd*—I 1 142.

APPEARER

Reverend appearer, one who appears to' be reverend—Per V 3 18.

APPELLANT

One one 'appeals' another: *Come I appellant to this princely presence*—R2 I 1 34. *The summons of the appellant's trumpet*—I 3 4. *Ready are the appellant and defendant*—2 H6 II 3 49.

APPENDIX

An appendage: *To bid the priest be ready to come against you come with your appendix (i.e. the bride)*—Shr IV 4 103.

APPERIL

Peril, risk: *Let me stay at thine apperil*—Tim I 2 32.

APPERTAINING

An appurtenance, belonging: *Gave life and grace To appertainings and to ornament*—Compl 114.

APPERTAINMENT

An appurtenance, prerogative: *We lay by Our appertainments, visiting of him*—Troil II 3 86.

APPLE-JOHN

A kind of apple said to keep two years and to be in perfection when shrivelled: *I am withered like an old apple-john*—1 H4 III 3 4; *What the devil hast thou brought there? apple-johns?*—2 H4 II 4 1.

APPLIANCE

Compliance: *To conserve a life In base appliances*—Meas III 1 88. In All's II 1 116 (*I come to tender it (i.e. the receipt) and my appliance*), perh., willing service. ,

APPLY

(1) To devote or attach oneself to: *Virtue and that part of philosophy Will I apply that . . .*—Shr I 1 18. So *to apply to*: *Let your remembrance apply to Banquo*—Mcb III 2 30.

(2) *To apply to*, to suit or adapt oneself to: *Would it apply well to the vehemency of your affection, that . . .*—Wiv II 2 247. So refl.: *If you apply yourself to our intents*—Ant V 2 126.

APPOINT

(1) To assign: *I do appoint him store of provender*—Cæs IV 1 30.

(2) To order, direct: *I'll appoint my men to carry the basket again*—Wiv IV 2 96. *I can . . . appoint her to look out*—Ado II 2 16.

(3) To equip, array: *To appoint myself in this vexation*—Wint I 2 326 (cf. *I am so attired in wonder*—Ado IV 1 146. *Attired in discontent*—Lucr 1601). *To have you royally appointed*—IV 4 602. *That . . . You may be armed and appointed well*—Tit IV 2 15.

APPOINTMENT

(1) Direction, orders: *That good fellow . . . follows my appointment*—H8 II 2 133.

(2) A resolution, purpose: *My appointments have in them a need*—All's II 5 72. *Where their appointment we may best discover*—Ant IV 10 8.

(3) Preparation, equipment: *Your best appointment make with speed*—Meas III 1 60. *We'll set forth In best appointment all our regiments*—John II 295. *A pirate of very warlike appointment*—Hml IV 6 15. An article of equipment: *Our habits and . . . every other appointment*—1 H4 I 2 196.

APPREHENSION

App., wit: *How long have you professed apprehension?*—Ado III 4 67.

APPREHENSIVE

(1) Intelligent: *Apprehensive, quick, forgetive*—2 H4 IV 3 107. *Men are flesh and blood, and apprehensive*—Cæs III 1 67.

(2) App., ruled by caprices: *Younger spirits, whose apprehensive senses All but new things disdain*—All's I 2 60.

APPROBATION

(1) Attestation, making good: *Gives manhood more approbation than . . .*—Tw III 4 198. *Shall drop their blood in approbation Of what your reverence shall incite us to*—H5 I 2 19. Proof: *That lack'd sight only, nought for approbation But only seeing*—Wint II 1 177. Confirmation (in office): *The people . . . are summon'd To meet anon, upon your approbation*—Cor II 3 151. Trial: *Would I had put my estate . . . on the approbation of what I have spoke!*—Cymb I 4 133.

(2) Probation, novitiate: *This day my sister should the cloister enter And there receive her approbation*—Meas I 2 182.

APPROOF

(1) Proof, trial: *So in approof lives not his epitaph As in your royal speech*—All's I 2 50. *My*

farthest band *Shall pass on thy approof*—Ant III 2 26. *Valiant approof*, tried valour—All's II 5 3.

(2) Approval: *Either of condemnation or ap-proof*—Meas II 4 174.

APPROPRIATION

A special attribute: *A great appropriation to his own good parts*—Merch I 2 45.

APPROVE

(1) To test, try: *On whose eyes I might approve This flower's force in stirring love*—Mids II 2 68. *Task me to my word; approve me, lord*—1 H4 IV 1 9. *Approved*, tried: *Of approved valour*—Ado II 1 394. *That ever-valiant and approved Scot*—1 H4 I 1 54. Convicted: *An approved wanton*—Ado IV 1 45. *He that is approved in this offence*—Oth II 3 211.

(2) To prove: *To approve Henry of Hereford . . . disloyal*—R2 I 3 112. *Which approves him an intelligent party*—Lr III 5 12. *Thou dost approve thyself the very same*—Cymb IV 2 380. To make good, confirm: *Will bless it and approve it with a text*—Merch III 2 79. *This approves her letter*—Lr II 4 186. *He approves the common liar*—Ant I 1 60.

(3) To show to advantage: *It would not much approve me*—Hml V 2 141. *All that may men approve or men detect*—Per II 1 55.

APPROVER

One who makes trial: *Will make known To their approvers*—Cymb II 4 24.

APRICOCK

Apricot—Mids III 1 169; R2 III 4 29.

APT

(1) Ready, inclined: *I find an apt remission in myself*—Meas V 503. *They (i.e. his hands) are apt enough to dislocate and tear Thy flesh and bones*—Lr IV 2 65. Ready, about to: *But so I am apt to do myself wrong*—Ado II 1 213.

(2) Fitted, prepared: *I shall not find myself so apt to die*—Cæs III 1 160.

(3) Likely: *It were a mock Apt to be render'd*—Cæs II 2 96. Easily accounted for, natural: *Vain though apt affection*—Meas I 4 48.

(4) Credible: *That she loves him, 'tis apt and of great credit*—Oth II 1 296. *No more Than what he found himself was apt and true*—V 2 176.

(5) Fitting, suitable: *The fit and apt construc-tion of thy name*—Cymb V 5 444.

(6) Easily impressed, susceptible, amenable, pliable: *I have a heart as little apt as yours*—Cor III 2 29. *She is young and apt*—Tim I 1 132. *The apt thoughts of men*—Cæs V 3 68. As adv.: *As apt as new-fall'n snow takes any dint*—Ven 354.

APTLY

Readily: *His youth will aptly receive it*—Tw III

4 211. *A frock or livery, That aptly is put on*—Hml III 4 164. *What's sweet to do, to do will aptly find*—Compl 88.

AQUILON

The north wind: *Blow . . . till thy . . . cheek Out-swell the colic of puff'd Aquilon*—Troil IV 5 8.

ARABIAN BIRD

The phœnix: *O Antony! O thou Arabian bird!*—Ant III 2 12. *She is alone the Arabian bird*—Cymb I 6 17.

ARAISE

To raise (from the dead): *Powerful to araise King Pepin*—All's II 1 79.

ARBITRATE

To give an authoritative decision with regard to, decide: *Which now the manage of two kingdoms must . . . arbitrate*—John I 37. *Certain issue strokes must arbitrate*—Mcb V 4 20.

ARCH

A chief one, a master, chief: *My worthy arch and patron*—Lr II 1 61.

ARGIER

Algiers—Tp I 2 261 265.

ARGOSY

A large merchant ship: *Your argosies with portly sail*—Merch I 1 9. *An argosy That now is lying in Marseilles' road*—Shr II 376. *As doth a sail . . . Command an argosy to stem the waves*—3 H6 II 6 35.

ARGUMENT

(1) Proof, evidence, token: *No great argument of her folly*—Ado II 3 242. *This (i.e. the dream) was nothing but an argument That . . .*—2 H6 I 2 32. *An argument that he is pluck'd*—Ant III 12 3.

(2) Skill in argument: *For bearing, argument and valour, Goes foremost in report*—Ado III 1 96.

(3) Subject of contention: *Sheathed their swords for lack of argument*—H5 III 1 21. *I cannot fight upon this argument*—Troil I 1 95. *All the argu-ment is a cuckold and a whore*—II 3 78.

(4) Subject-matter, theme: *Thou wilt prove a notable argument*—Ado I 1 258. *The argument of his own scorn*—II 3 11. *It would be argument for a week*—1 H4 II 2 100. *The argument of your praise*—Lr I 1 218. An occasion, moving cause: *Displeasure . . . Grounded upon no other argument But that . . .*—As I 2 290. *Not to stir without great argument*—Hml IV 4 54. The subject or plot of a play: *The argument (i.e. of the extem-pore play) shall be thy running away*—1 H4 II 4 310. *There was . . . no money bid for argument, unless the poet and the player went to cuffs*—Hml

II 2 371. *Have you heard the argument? Is there no offence in't?*—III 2 242. *In argument of praise,* in the matter of merit—All's III 5 62.

(5) A summary of a book; fig., of the heart, the contents: [If I would] *try the argument of hearts by borrowing*—Tim II 2 187.

ARM

To take into the arms: *Come, arm him*—Cymb IV 2 400.

ARMADO

A fleet: *Whole armadoes of caracks*—Err III 2 140. *A whole armado of convicted sail*—John III 4 2.

ARM-GAUNT

An unexplained word, no doubt a corruption: *And soberly did mount an arm-gaunt steed*—Ant I 5 48.

ARMIGERO

Ablative (misused) of *armiger,* one entitled to bear arms: *Who writes himself 'Armigero'*—Wiv I 1 9.

ARMIPOTENT

Mighty in arms: *The armipotent Mars*—LLL V 2 650. *The armipotent soldier*—All's IV 3 265.

ARMOUR

A suit of mail: *Would have walked ten mile a-foot to see a good armour*—Ado II 3 16. *Like a rich armour worn in heat of day*—2 H4 IV 5 30. *'Tis turned to a rusty armour*—Per II 1 125.

AROINT THEE

Begone: *Aroint thee, witch!*—Mcb I 3 6. *Aroint thee, witch, aroint thee!*—Lr III 4 129.

A-ROW

In a row, in turn: *My master and his man . . .* [have] *Beaten the maids a-row*—Err V 169.

ARRAS

Tapestry: *I will ensconce me behind the arras*—Wiv III 3 96. *Be you and I behind an arras then*—Hml II 2 163. Attrib.: *My arras counterpoints*—Shr II 353.

ARRAY

To afflict, distress: *These rebel powers that thee array*—Sonn 146 2.

ARREARAGES

Arrears: *He'll grant the tribute, send the arrearages*—Cymb II 4 13.

ARREST (sb.)

A formal restraining order: *Sends out arrests On Fortinbras*—Hml II 2 67.

ARREST (vb.)

To arrest one's word or words, to take one at his word: *We arrest your word*—LLL II 160. *I do arrest your words*—Meas II 4 134.

ARRIVANCE

Arrivals, persons arriving: *Every minute is expectancy Of more arrivance*—Oth II 1 41.

ARRIVE

To arrive at, reach: *Arriving A place of potency*—Cor II 3 189. *Ere we could arrive the point proposed*—Cæs I 2 110. *Ere he arrive his weary noon-tide prick*—Lucr 781.

ART

(1) Scholarship, learning: *Where all those pleasures live that art would comprehend*—LLL IV 2 114. *The commission of thy years and art*—Rom IV 1 64.

(2) Technical or professional skill: *That labouring art can never ransom nature From her inaidible estate*—All's II 1 121. *Tell me, if your art Can tell so much*—Mcb IV 1 101. *Their malady convinces The great assay of art*—IV 3 142.

ARTHUR'S SHOW

An exhibition by archers who took the names of the Knights of the Round Table: *I was then Sir Dagonet in Arthur's show*—2 H4 III 2 299.

ARTICLE

(1) A stipulation: *Which easily endures not article Tying him to aught*—Cor II 3 204.

(2) *Articles,* heads of interrogatories: *To draw my answer from thy articles*—John II 111.

(3) *Of great article,* of great weight or moment: *A soul of great article*—Hml V 2 122.

(4) *The article of,* the matter of: *Thou shouldst not alter the article of thy gentry*—Wiv II 1 52.

ARTICULATE

(1) To come to terms, negotiate: *Send us to Rome The best, with whom we may articulate*—Cor I 9 76.

(2) To set out in articles: *These things indeed you have articulate*—1 H4 V 1 72.

ARTIFICIAL

Produced by art: *Artificial sprites*—Mcb III 5 27. Of persons, skilled in constructive art: *Like two artificial gods*—Mids III 2 203. Of actions, displaying technical skill: *Thy prosperous and artificial feat*—Per V 1 72. *Artificial strife,* strife of art to equal nature—Tim I 1 37. (Cf. *The red blood reek'd, to show the painter's strife*—Lucr 1377).

ARTIST

A man of learning or technical skill: *The wise and fool, the artist and unread*—Troil I 3 24. *In*

framing an artist, art hath thus decreed—Per II
3 15. Specifically, a physician or surgeon: *To be
relinquished of the artists*—All's II 3 10.

ARTLESS

Unskilful: *So full of artless jealousy is guilt*—
Hml IV 5 19.

ARTS-MAN

A man of learning: *Arts-man, preambulate, we
will be singuled from the barbarous*—LLL V 1 85.

AS

(1) So that: *We will play our part, As he shall
think . . .*—Shr Ind I 69. *For myself mine own
worth* [I] *do define, As I all other in all worths
surmount*—Sonn 62 7.

(2) As for instance: *The seasons' difference, as
the icy fang And churlish chiding of the winter's
wind*—As II 1 6. *Our recountments . . . As how
I came into that desert place*—IV 3 141. Namely:
Two Cliffords, as the father and the son—3 H6 V
7 7.

(3) As far as: *As I remember, this should be the
house*—Rom V 1 55. *Now, as I can remember . . .
I never did her hurt*—Per IV 1 74.

(4) As if: *As it were doomsday*—Cæs III 1 98.
As he would draw it—Hml II 1 91.

(5) With expressions of time with restrictive
force: *That he should hither come as this dire
night*—Rom V 3 247. *This is my birth-day; as
this very day Was Cassius born*—Cæs V 1 72.

ASK

(1) To ask about: *The dead man's knell Is there
scarce ask'd for who*—Mcb IV 3 170.

(2) To call for, require: *That will ask some
tears*—Mids I 2 27. *My business asketh haste*—
Shr II 115. *These great affairs do ask some charge*
—R2 II 1 159.

ASKANCE

To turn aside: *That from their own misdeeds
askance their eyes*—Lucr 637.

ASPECT

(1) Beholding, gaze: *Render'd such aspect As
cloudy men use to their adversaries*—1 H4 III 2
82. *There would he anchor his aspect*—Ant I 5 33.

(2) A look, glance: *Some other mistress hath
thy sweet aspects*—Err II 2 113.

(3) In astrology, the relative positions of the
heavenly bodies at a given time: *Till the heavens
look With an aspect more favourable*—Wint I 1 106.
The ill aspects of planets evil—Troil I 3 92. Fig.:
Under the allowance of your great aspect—Lr II 2
112.

ASPIC

Asp: *Aspics' tongues*—Oth III 3 450. *Have I
the aspic in my lips?*—Ant V 2 296.

ASPIRE

To mount to: *That gallant spirit hath aspired
the clouds*—Rom III 1 122. So with *to*, to attain:
*Safer triumph is this funeral pomp, That hath
aspired to Solon's happiness*—Tit I 176.

ASSAY (sb.)

(1) A trial, testing: *An assay of her virtue*
—Meas III 1 164. *By no assay of reason*—Oth
I 3 18.

(2) An attempt: *Help, angels! Make assay!*—
Hml III 3 69. *After many . . . sick and short
assays*—Lucr 1719. The putting forth of one's
best effort: *Their malady convinces The great
assay of art*—Mcb IV 3 142. *Assays of bias*,
roundabout attempts like the path of a bowl which
moves in a curve under the influence of the bias—
Hml II 1 65.

(3) An attack, assault: *Galling the gleaned
land with hot assays*—H5 I 2 151. *To give the
assay of arms against your majesty*—Hml II 2 71.

ASSAY (vb.)

(1) To make trial of: *Assay the power you have*
—Meas I 4 76. To have proof of, know by ex-
perience: *The destined ill she must herself assay*
—Compl 156.

(2) To attack, assault: *I will assay thee: so,
defend thyself*—1 H4 V 4 34. To challenge to a
trial of strength, skill, &c.: *Did you assay him To
any pastime?*—Hml III 1 14. To assail with
words or arguments: *Bid herself assay him*—
Meas I 2 186. With love-proposals: *That he
dares in this manner assay me*—Wiv II 1 25.

ASSEMBLANCE

Semblance, appearance: *The stature, bulk, and
big assemblance of a man*—2 H4 III 2 277.

ASSIGN

An appurtenance, belonging: *Six French rapiers
and poniards, with their assigns*—Hml V 2 156
(see also 169).

ASSINEGO

A little ass, an ass: *An assinego may tutor thee*
—Troil II 1 49.

ASSIST

To join, attend, accompany: *The king and prince
at prayers! let's assist them*—Tp I 1 57. *Yourself,
assisted with your honour'd friends, Bring them*—
Wint V 1 113. Absol.—Cor V 6 156.

ASSISTANCE

Assessors, associates: *Affecting one sole throne,
Without assistance*—Cor IV 6 32.

ASSOCIATE

To accompany: *Going to find a bare-foot brother
out . . . to associate me*—Rom V 2 5.

ASSUBJUGATE

To subjugate, bring into subjection: *Nor . . .* [must he] *assubjugate his merit . . . By going to Achilles*—Troil II 3 202.

ASSURANCE

(1) Legal guarantee or security: *Let your father make her the assurance*—Shr II 389. *To pass assurance of a dower in marriage*—IV 2 117. *Better assurance than Bardolph*—2 H4 I 2 36.

(2) Security, safety: *His head's assurance is but frail*—R3 IV 4 498. *The way which promises assurance*—Ant III 7 47.

ASSURE

(1) To give legal guarantee or security for: *He of both That can assure my daughter greatest dower*—Shr II 344. So *to assure of*: *I'll assure her of Her widowhood*—II 124.

(2) To betroth: *Swore I was assured to her*—Err III 2 145. *I did so when I was first assured*—John II 535.

ASTONISH

(1) To stun mentally: *Stone-still, astonish'd with this deadly deed*—Lucr 1730. Sim.: *Neither he, nor his compeers by night . . . my verse astonished*—Sonn 86 7.

(2) To dismay, terrify: *Enough, captain: you have astonished him*—H5 V 1 40. *That with the very shaking of their chains They may astonish these fell-lurking curs*—2 H6 V 1 145. *Such dreadful heralds to astonish us*—Cæs I 3 56.

ASTRINGER

A hawker who used the goshawk or estridge; distinguished from the falconer, who used the long-winged hawk or falcon: *Enter a gentle Astringer*—All's V 1 6 (Stage Dir.). (So the First Folio).

ATOMY[1]

(1) An atom, mote: *As easy to count atomies*—As III 2 245. *Eyes . . . Who shut their coward gates on atomies*—III 5 12.

(2) A tiny being, a mite: *Drawn with a team of little atomies*—Rom I 4 57.

ATOMY[2]

= *Anatomy*, a 'walking skeleton': *You starved blood-hound . . . Thou atomy, thou!*—2 H4 V 4 31.

ATONE

(1) To reconcile: *Since we can not atone you*—R2 I 1 202. *I would do much To atone them*—Oth IV 1 243. To bring into concord: *To atone your fears With my more noble meaning*—Tim V 4 58.

(2) To come into unity or concord: *When earthly things made even Atone together*—As V 4 115. *He and Aufidius can no more atone Than violentest contrariety*—Cor IV 6 72.

ATONEMENT

Reconciliation: *If we do now make our atonement well*—2 H4 IV 1 221. *To make atonement Betwixt the Duke of Gloucester and your brothers*—R3 I 3 36.

ATTACH

To seize, lay hold of; fig., of feelings, &c.: *Who am myself attach'd with weariness*—Tp III 3 5. *I had thought weariness durst not have attached one of so high blood*—2 H4 II 2 2. To seize with the hand: *Every man attach the hand Of his fair mistress*—LLL IV 3 375.

ATTACHMENT

Arrest, confinement; fig.: [Sleep] *give as soft attachment to thy senses As infants' empty of all thought!*—Troil IV 2 5.

ATTAINDER

(1) Fig., condemnation: *Stands in attainder of eternal shame*—LLL I 1 158. A dishonouring accusation: *Have mine honour soil'd With the attainder of his slanderous lips*—R2 IV 23.

(2) Stain of dishonour: *He lived from all attainder of suspect*—R3 III 5 32.

ATTAINT (sb.)

(1) App., impeachment, accusation: *I arrest thee . . . and, in thine attaint, This gilded serpent*—Lr V 3 82.

(2) A taint, stain: *What simple thief brags of his own attaint?*—Err III 2 16. *Nor* [hath] *any man an attaint but he carries some stain of it*—Troil I 2 26.

(3) App., exhaustion, weariness: *Freshly looks and over-bears attaint*—H5 IV Chor 39.

ATTAINT (vb.)

(1) To condemn to the penalties and forfeitures attaching to treason: *And, by his treason, stand'st not thou attainted?*—1 H6 II 4 92. *I must offend before I be attainted*—2 H6 II 4 59.

(2) To taint, stain: *You are attaint with faults and perjury*—LLL V 2 829. *Faults conceal'd, wherein I am attainted*—Sonn 88 7.

ATTAINTURE

Attainder, conviction: *Her attainture will be Humphrey's fall*—2 H6 I 2 106.

ATTASK

To take to task, blame: *Attask'd for want of wisdom*—Lr I 4 366.

ATTEMPT

(1) To try to seduce: *He will never . . . in the way of waste, attempt us again*—Wiv IV 2 225.

(2) To try to obtain or attract: *How can that be true love which is falsely attempted?*—LLL

2

I 2 176. *This man of thine Attempts her love—*
Tim I 1 125.

(3) To try to move, seek to influence: *That
neither my coat, integrity, nor persuasion can with
ease attempt you*—Meas IV 2 204. *Of force I must
attempt you further*—Merch IV 1 421.

(4) To try to master, assail: *Him attempting
who was self-subdued*—Lr II 2 129.

ATTEMPTABLE

Open to attempts: *Less attemptable than any the
rarest of our ladies in France*—Cymb I 4 65.

ATTEND

(1) To listen to, attend to: *She will attend it
better in thy youth*—Tw I 4 27. *When my betossed
soul Did not attend him as we rode*—Rom V 3 76.
*I do condemn mine ears that have So long attended
thee*—Cymb I 6 141. To regard, consider, mark:
Could not with graceful eyes attend those wars—
Ant II 2 60. *Which speechless woe of his poor
she attendeth*—Lucr 1674.

(2) To apply oneself to, look after: *Each hath
his place and function to attend*—1 H6 I 1 173.
*No place, That guard . . . Does not attend my
taking*—Lr II 3 3.

(3) To tend, guard: *To attend the emperor's
person carefully*—Tit II 2 8. *They are in a trunk,
Attended by my men*—Cymb I 6 196.

(4) To wait: *At the deanery, where a priest
attends*—Wiv IV 6 31. *He attendeth here hard
by*—Merch IV 1 145. *In the base court he doth
attend*—R2 III 3 176. To dance attendance: *This
life Is nobler than attending for a check*—Cymb
III 3 21.

(5) To await (a person): *We here attend you*—
Ado V 4 36. *Who attended him In secret ambush*
—3 H6 IV 6 82. *On the market-place, I know,
they do attend us*—Cor II 2 163. To look for, expect: *If, after two days' shine, Athens contain thee,
Attend our weightier judgement*—Tim III 5 101.

ATTENT

Attentive: *With an attent ear*—Hml I 2 193.
Be attent—Per III Prol 11.

ATTEST (sb.)

Evidence, testimony: *That doth invert the attest
of eyes and ears*—Troil V 2 122.

ATTEST (vb.)

To call to witness: *I attest the gods*—Troil II
2 132.

ATTORNEYED

In employment as attorney: *I am still Attorney'd at your service*—Meas V 389. Performed
by attorney: *Their encounters . . . have been
royally attorneyed*—Wint I 1 29.

ATTORNEY-GENERAL

One with general authority to act in all the
principal's affairs: *By his attorneys-general to sue
His livery*—R2 II 1 203.

ATTRIBUTE

Reputation: *Much attribute he hath*—Troil II
3 125. *The pith and marrow of our attribute*—
Hml I 4 22. [Unless you] *for an honest attribute
cry out 'She died by foul play'*—Per IV 3 18.

ATTRIBUTION

Character ascribed to one: *Such attribution
should the Douglas have, As . . .*—1 H4 IV 1 3.

ATTRIBUTIVE

Characterized by attributing (honour): *The will
dotes that is attributive To what infectiously itself
affects, Without . . .*—Troil II 2 58.

AUBURN

This word seems to have denoted in Shakespeare's time a yellowish or brownish-white colour:
Her hair is auburn, mine is perfect yellow—Gent
IV 4 194. *Not that our heads are some brown,
some black, some auburn*—Cor II 3 20.

AUDACIOUS

Bold, in good sense: *Audacious without impu-
dency*—LLL V 1 5.

AUDACIOUSLY

Boldly, in good sense: *Yet fear not thou, but
speak audaciously*—LLL V 2 104. *Durst not ask
of her audaciously*—Lucr 1223.

AUDACITY

Boldness, in good sense: *Who would e'er suppose They had such courage and audacity?*—1 H6
I 2 35. *It was defect Of spirit, life, and bold
audacity*—Lucr 1345.

AUDIBLE

Able to hear; and hence app., quick of hearing:
*Let me have war . . . it's spritely, waking, audible,
and full of vent*—Cor IV 5 236.

AUDIT

An account: *A brief span To keep your earthly
audit*—H8 III 2 140. *How his audit stands who
knows save heaven?*—Hml III 3 82. An accounting, rendering of accounts: *To make their audit
at your highness' pleasure*—Mcb I 6 27. *If you
will take this audit, take this life*—Cymb V 4 27.
Her audit, though delay'd, answer'd must be—Sonn
126 13.

AUGUR

Augury: *Augurs and understood relations have
. . . brought forth The secret'st man of blood*—
Mcb III 4 124.

AUNT

(1) An old dame: *The wisest aunt, telling the saddest tale*—Mids II 1 51.

(2) A loose woman: *Summer songs for me and my aunts, While we lie tumbling in the hay*—Wint IV 3 11.

(3) In Troil II 2 77 (*An old aunt whom the Greeks held captive*) the reference is to Hesione, sister of Priam.

AUSTERELY

By outward signs of seriousness: *Mightst thou perceive austerely in his eye That he did plead in earnest?*—Err IV 2 2.

AUTHENTIC

Recognized, authoritative: *Authentic in your place and person*—Wiv II 2 235. *How could communities, Degrees in schools . . . But by degree, stand in authentic place?*—Troil I 3 103. *Truth's authentic author to be cited*—III 2 188. Legally qualified: *To be relinquished . . . of all the learned and authentic fellows*—All's II 3 10.

AUTHORIZE

To vouch for the truth of, confirm: *A woman's story at a winter's fire, Authorized by her grandam*—Mcb III 4 65.

AVAIL

Profit, benefit: *I charge thee, As heaven shall work in me for thine avail*—All's I 3 189. *When better fall, for your avails they fell*—III 1 22.

AVISED

A form of Advised; informed, aware: *Are you avised o' that? do you see that?*—Wiv I 4 106. Sim., *Art avised o' that? more on't*—Meas II 2 132. Be advised, yield to reason: *Be avised, sir, and pass good humours*—Wiv I 1 169.

AVOID

(1) To make of no effect, get rid of the consequences of: *As the matter now stands, he will avoid your accusation*—Meas III 1 200. *All these you may avoid but the Lie Direct; and you may avoid that too, with an If*—As V 4 101.

(2) To get rid of: *I will no longer endure it, though yet I know no wise remedy how to avoid it*—As I 1 25. *How may I avoid . . . The wife I chose?*—Troil II 2 65.

(3) To depart, withdraw: *Come, Camillo . . . let*

us avoid—Wint I 2 460. *Here's no place for you; pray you, avoid*—Cor IV 5 33.

(4) To depart from, quit: *Avoid the gallery*—H8 V 1 85. *Pray you, avoid the house*—Cor IV 5 25.

AVOUCH (sb.)

Testimony, assurance: *The sensible and true avouch Of mine own eyes*—Hml I 1 57.

AVOUCH (vb.)

(1) To answer for, make good: *If the duke avouch the justice of your dealing*—Meas IV 2 200. *Dare not avouch in your deeds any of your words*—H5 V 1 76. *What I have said I will avouch in presence of the king*—R3 I 3 114. *I could . . . sweep him from my sight And bid my will avouch it*—Mcb III 1 118.

(2) To own, acknowledge: *Avouch the thoughts of your heart*—H5 V 2 253. *If you'll avouch 'twas wisdom Paris went . . . If you'll confess . . .*—Troil II 2 84.

AWAY

She never could away with me, she never could endure me—2 H4 III 2 213.

AWELESS

Inspiring no awe: *The innocent and aweless throne*—R3 II 4 52.

AWFUL

(1) Worthy of or commanding profound respect: *Awful rule and right supremacy*—Shr V 109. *To pluck down justice from your awful bench*—2 H4 V 2 86.

(2) Respectful, duly regardful: *How dare thy joints forget To pay their awful duty to our presence?*—R2 III 3 75. *We come within our awful banks again*—2 H4 IV 1 176. Regardful of obligations, conscientious: *Such as the fury of ungovern'd youth Thrust from the company of awful men*—Gent IV 1 45. *A better prince . . . That will prove awful both in deed and word*—Per II Prol 3.

AWKWARD

(1) Oblique, not straightforward: *No sinister nor no awkward claim*—H5 II 4 85.

(2) Adverse, thwarting: *Was I for this . . . by awkward wind from England's bank Drove back?*—2 H6 III 2 82. *Awkward casualties*—Per V 1 94.

B

BABE

Doing nothing for a babe, perh., administering, and neglecting, the estate of an infant ward—Cymb III 3 23. (The reading of the Folios.)

BABY

Perh., a doll: *Protest me The baby of a girl*—Mcb III 4 106. Cf. John III 4 58 (*A babe of clouts*).

BACCARE

Go back, give way; a cant expression of doubtful origin: *Baccare! you are marvellous forward*—Shr II 73.

BACK

A support, backing: *This project Should have a back or second*—Hml IV 7 153.

BACK-FRIEND

Of a bailiff, who comes from behind to arrest one: *A fellow all in buff; A back-friend, a shoulder-clapper*—Err IV 2 36.

BACKSWORD MAN

A fencer with backsword, *i.e.* single-stick: *I knew him a good backsword man*—2 H4 III 2 69.

BACK-TRICK

A caper backwards in dancing: *I have the back-trick simply as strong as any man in Illyria*—Tw I 3 131.

BACKWARDLY

Perversely: *Does he think so backwardly of me now, That I'll requite it last?*—Tim III 3 18.

BADGE

To mark (as with a badge): *Their hands and faces were all badged with blood*—Mcb II 3 107.

BAFFLE

To subject to public disgrace; esp., so to treat a perjured knight: *An I do not, call me villain and baffle me*—1 H4 I 2 113 (Sir John's speech). Gen., to use with indignity: *I will baffle Sir Toby*—Tw II 5 176. *Alas, poor fool, how have they baffled thee!*—V 377. *I am disgraced, impeach'd and baffled here*—R2 I 1 170.

BAITE

See *Bate* (vb.)².

BAKE

(1) To form into a thick mass: [She] *bakes the elf-locks in foul sluttish hairs*—Rom I 4 90.

(2) *Baked meat*, pastry, a pie: *Look to the baked meats, good Angelica*—Rom IV 4 5. *The funeral baked meats Did coldly furnish forth the marriage tables*—Hml I 2 180.

BALD

Bare-headed: [The senators] *stand bald before him*—Cor IV 5 206.

BALDRICK

A shoulder-belt: *Or hang my bugle in an invisible baldrick*—Ado I 1 243.

BALK

(1) To miss, fail to seize: *Make slow pursuit, or altogether balk The prey*—Lucr 696. To let slip an opportunity of doing (something): *This was looked for at your hand, and this was balked*—Tw III 2 25.

(2) *To balk logic*, to quibble: *Balk logic with acquaintance that you have*—Shr I 1 34.

(3) *Balked*, prob., piled in a heap: *Two and twenty knights Balk'd in their own blood*—1 H4 I 1 68.

BALLAST

To freight, load: *Who sent whole armadoes of caracks to be ballast at her nose*—Err III 2 140. Prob. confused with Balance: *Then had my prize Been less, and so more equal ballasting To thee*—Cymb III 6 77. Instances of this confusion are not wanting. For *Prize* see *Price* (3).

BALLOW

App., a cudgel: *Ise try whether your costard or my ballow be the harder*—Lr IV 6 246.

BALM

The oil of consecration of kings: *Can wash the balm off from an anointed king*—R2 III 2 55. *The balm, the sceptre and the ball*—H5 IV 1 277.

BALSAMUM

Balm, fragrant oil or ointment: *I have bought The oil, the balsamum and aqua-vitæ*—Err IV 1 88.

BANBURY CHEESE

A thin cheese, nothing but paring: *You Banbury cheese!*—Wiv I 1 130 (to Slender).

BAND

(1) A shackle, manacle: *Release me from my bands*—Tp Epil 9. *Die in bands for this unmanly deed!*—3 H6 I 1 186.

(2) A bond or obligation; (*a*) Moral: *Now will I charge you in the band of truth*—All's IV 2 56. *The end of life cancels all bands*—1 H4 III 2 157. (*b*) Legal: *Was he arrested on a band?*—Err IV 2 49. *He would not take his band and yours*—2 H4 I 2 36.

BAN-DOG

A dog tied up: *The time when screech-owls cry and ban-dogs howl*—2 H6 I 4 21.

BANDY

To contend, strive: *I will bandy with thee in faction*—As V 1 61. *One fit to bandy with thy lawless sons*—Tit I 312. *The prince expressly hath Forbidden bandying in Verona streets*—Rom III 1 91.

BANE (sb.)

Death, destruction: *I will not be afraid of death and bane*—Mcb V 3 59. *Though nothing but my body's bane would cure thee*—Ven 372.

BANE (vb.)

To kill, esp. by poison: *What if my house be troubled with a rat And I be pleased to give ten thousand ducats To have it baned?*—Merch IV 1 44.

BANK

To coast, skirt: *As I have bank'd their towns*—John V 2 104.

BANQUET

(1) A course of sweetmeats, &c., served after a principal meal, often in another room: *Come, let us to the banquet*—Ado II 1 178 (this being after supper; see 1). *My banquet is to close our stomachs up, After our great good cheer*—Shr V 2 9. *We have a trifling foolish banquet towards*—Rom I 5 124 (this also being after supper; see the beginning of the scene).

(2) *A running banquet*, a repast between meals. Fig.: *Some of these Should find a running banquet ere they rested, I think would better please 'em*—H8 I 4 11. *The running banquet of two beadles that is to come*—V 4 69.

BAR

A barrier separating the parties at an interview; hence, a place of congress: *To bring your most imperial majesties Unto this bar and royal interview*—H5 V 2 26.

BARBED

Of horses, provided with barbs (properly bards), protective coverings for the breast and flanks: *His glittering arms he will commend to rust, His barbed steeds to stables*—R2 III 3 116. *Instead of mounting barbed steeds*—R3 I 1 10.

BARBER-MONGER

A frequenter of barbers' shops, a fop: *You whoreson cullionly barber-monger*—Lr II 2 35.

BARE (adj.)

(1) Lean: *Methinks they are exceeding poor and bare, too beggarly*—1 H4 IV 2 74.

(2) Indigent, needy: *Art thou so bare and full of wretchedness, And fear'st to die?*—Rom V 1 68.

(3) Poor in quality, paltry, worthless: *Such poor, such bare, such lewd, such mean attempts*—1 H4 III 2 13. *What bare excuses makest thou to be gone!*—Ven 188.

BARE (sb.)

Bareness: *That termless skin Whose bare outbragg'd the web it seem'd to wear*—Compl 94.

BARELY

(1) Merely, only: *Shall I not have barely my principal?*—Merch IV 1 342. Ross. . . . *For now his son is duke.* Willo. *Barely in title, not in revenues*—R2 II 1 225.

(2) Nakedly; *barely leave*, leave bare: *When you have our roses, You barely leave our thorns to prick ourselves*—All's IV 2 18.

BARENESS

Leanness: *For their bareness, I am sure they never learned that of me*—1 H4 IV 2 77.

BARFUL

Full of bars or hindrances: *A barful strife!*—Tw I 4 41.

BARGAIN

To sell one a bargain, to make a fool of him: *The boy hath sold him a bargain*—LLL III 102.

BARK

To cover as with bark, encrust: *A most instant tetter bark'd about . . . All my smooth body*—Hml I 5 71.

BARLEY-BROTH

Beer, in contempt: *Sodden water, A drench for sur-rein'd jades, their barley-broth*—H5 III 5 18.

BARM

Yeast, leaven: *And sometime make the drink to bear no barm*—Mids II 1 38.

BARN

To store in a barn: *And useless barns the harvest of his wits*—Lucr 859.

BARNACLE

A species of wild goose supposed to be produced from shell-fish growing on trees; or perh. the shell-fish are meant: *[We shall] all be turn'd to barnacles*—Tp IV 249.

BARNE

A child: *They say barnes are blessings*—All's I 3 28. *A barne; a very pretty barne!*—Wint III 3 70. With a play on the word: *If your husband have stables enough, you'll see he shall lack no barns*—Ado III 4 48.

BARTHOLOMEW BOAR-PIG

A roasted pig from Bartholomew Fair (held at the time of the festival of St. Bartholomew): *Thou whoreson little tidy Bartholomew boar-pig* 2 H4 II 4 250.

BARTHOLOMEW-TIDE

The festival of St. Bartholomew (24th August): *Like flies at Bartholomew-tide*—H5 V 2 335.

BASAN

Bashan (see Ps. xxii 12): *O, that I were Upon the hill of Basan, to outroar The horned herd!*— Ant III 13 126.

BASE (adj.)

(1) Of small height: *The cedar stoops not to the base shrub's foot*—Lucr 664.

(2) Occupying a low position, low-lying: *I see thy glory like a shooting star Fall to the base earth from the firmament*—R2 II 4 19.

(3) Illegitimate: *Why bastard? wherefore base?* —Lr I 2 6. *Why brand they us With base? with baseness?*—9.

BASE (sb.)

A country game consisting chiefly in running: *Lads more like to run The country base than to commit such slaughter*—Cymb V 3 19. *To bid the* or *a base*, to challenge in the game. Fig.: *I bid the base for Proteus*—Gent I 2 97. *To bid the wind a base he now prepares*—Ven 303.

BASE COURT

The lower or outer court of a castle: *In the base court he doth attend*—R2 III 3 176. *In the base ourt? Base court, where kings grow base*—180.

BASENESS

Illegitimacy of birth: *That forced baseness Which he has put upon't*—Wint II 3 78. *Why brand they us With base? with baseness?*—Lr I 2 9.

BASES

A plaited skirt appended to the doublet and reaching to the knee: *I yet am unprovided Of a pair of bases*—Per II 1 166.

BASILISCO-LIKE

Like Basilisco, a foolish knight in the old play *Soliman and Perseda* (reprinted in Hazlitt's Dodsley, vol. v): *Knight, knight, good mother, Basilisco-like*—John I 244.

BASILISK

(1) A fabulous serpent, supposed to kill by its look: *Make me not sighted like the basilisk: I have look'd on thousands, who have sped the better By my regard, but kill'd none so*—Wint I 2 388. *Come, basilisk, And kill the innocent gazer with thy sight*—2 H6 III 2 52. *I'll slay more gazers than the basilisk*—3 H6 III 2 187.

(2) A heavy piece of ordnance: *And thou hast talk'd . . . Of basilisks, of cannon, culverin*—1 H4 II 3 53.

(3) The two senses blended: *Your eyes, which hitherto have borne in them . . . The fatal balls of murdering basilisks: The venom of such looks, we fairly hope, Have lost their quality*—H5 V 2 15.

BASIS

A pedestal: *Cæsar . . . That now on Pompey's basis lies along*—Cæs III 1 114.

BASS

To utter or proclaim with bass voice: *The thunder . . . did bass my trespass*—Tp III 3 97.

BASTA

Enough (Italian): *Basta; content thee*—Shr I 1 203.

BASTARD

A sweet Spanish wine: *We shall have all the world drink brown and white bastard*—Meas III 2 3. *Score a pint of bastard in the Half-moon*— 1 H4 II 4 29.

BASTINADO

A cudgelling (not referring, as in the mod. usage, to the Eastern punishment): *He of Wales, that gave Amamon the bastinado*—1 H4 II 4 370. Fig.: *He gives the bastinado with his tongue*— John II 463. Cudgelling, stick-play: *I will deal in poison with thee, or in bastinado*—As V 1 59.

BAT

A staff, a cudgel: *Where go you With bats and clubs?*—Cor I 1 56. *Make you ready your stiff bats and clubs*—165. *So slides he down upon his grained bat*—Compl 64.

BATCH

The produce of baking, a loaf: *Thou crusty batch of nature, what's the news?*—Troil V 1 5.

BATE (sb.)

Contention, strife: *[He] breeds no bate with telling of discreet stories*—2 H4 II 4 271.

BATE (vb.)[1]

(1) To blunt: *That honour which shall bate his scythe's keen edge*—LLL I 1 6.

(2) To reduce, diminish, lower: *These griefs and losses have so bated me*—Merch III 3 32. *Bate thy rage*—H5 III 2 26. *Who bates mine honour shall not know my coin*—Tim III 3 26. To fall off, decrease: *Do I not bate? do I not dwindle?*—1 H4 III 3 2.

(3) To remit: *Thou didst promise To bate me a full year*—Tp I 2 249. *I will not bate thee a scruple*—All's II 3 233. To lay aside: *Rather than she will bate one breath of her accustomed crossness*—Ado II 3 183. To except: *Demetrius*

being bated—Mids I 1 190. *No leisure bated*, without exception (from the strictness of the injunction) of any time of inaction: *That, on the supervise, no leisure bated . . . My head should be struck off*—Hml V 2 23. To leave undone: *Of my instruction hast thou nothing bated*—Tp III 3 85. To depart from one's custom in respect of: *Bid the main flood bate his usual height*—Merch IV 1 72. To modify what one has said: *Who long'st, like me, to see thy lord; who long'st,—O, let me bate,—but not like me*—Cymb III 2 55. *To bate of*, to depreciate, belittle: *You bate too much of your own merits*—Tim I 2 212. *To be bated of*, to get a price asked made lower than: *I cannot be bated one doit of a thousand pieces*—Per IV 2 55.

BATE (vb.)², BAITE

In falconry, of a hawk, to beat the wings, flutter: *As we watch these kites That bate and beat and will not be obedient* — Shr IV 1 198. *Like estridges that with the wind Baited*—1 H4 IV 1 98. *'Tis a hooded valour; and when it appears, it will bate*—H5 III 7 121. *Hood my unmann'd blood, bating in my cheeks*—Rom III 2 14.

BATE-BREEDING

Stirring up strife: *This sour informer, this bate-breeding spy*—Ven 655.

BATELESS

That cannot be blunted: *Unhappily set This bateless edge on his keen appetite*—Lucr 8.

BAT-FOWLING

Catching birds at night when at roost: *We would so, and then go a bat-fowling*—Tp II 1 185.

BATLET

Prob., a staff for beating clothes: *And I remember the kissing of her batlet*—As II 4 49.

BATTALION

An army: *Why, our battalion trebles that account*—R3 V 3 11.

BATTEN

To feed gluttonously: *Go, and batten on cold bits*—Cor IV 5 35. *Could you on this fair mountain leave to feed, And batten on this moor?*—Hml III 4 66.

BATTERY

(1) A mark of beating, a wound or bruise: *For where a heart is hard they make no battery*—Ven 426.

(2) Bombardment: *This union shall do more than battery can To our fast-closed gates*—John II 446. *If I begin the battery once again*—H5 III 3 7. Fig.: *Her sighs will make a battery in his breast*—3 H6 III 1 37. *The seven-fold shield of Ajax cannot keep The battery from my heart*—Ant IV 14 38.

BATTLE

(1) An army or a division of an army: *What may the king's whole battle reach unto?*—1 H4 IV 1 129. *Our main battle's front*—3 H6 I 1 8. *How lies their battle?*—Cor I 6 51. *You, worthy uncle, Shall . . . Lead our first battle*—Mcb V 6 2.

(2) The disposition of troops for battle: *I'll draw the form and model of our battle*—R3 V 3 24.

(3) Fig., a martial array, a line: *On his bow-back he hath a battle set Of bristly pikes*—Ven 619.

BAUBLE

A baton with a fantastically carved head carried by a fool or jester: *And I would give his wife my bauble, sir, to do her service*—All's IV 5 32. *For that I know An idiot holds his bauble for a god*—Tit V 1 78.

BAVIN

Brushwood, firewood; attrib. and fig.: *Rash bavin wits, Soon kindled and soon burnt*—1 H4 III 2 61.

BAWBLING

Insignificant, paltry: *A bawbling vessel was he captain of*—Tw V 57.

BAWCOCK

Fr. *Beau coq*; fine fellow: *Why, how now, my bawcock!*—Tw III 4 125. *Good bawcock, bate thy rage!*—H5 III 2 26. *The king's a bawcock, and a heart of gold*—IV 1 44.

BAY (sb.)¹

A section of a building: *I'll rent the fairest house in it after three-pence a bay*—Meas II 1 254.

BAY (sb.)²

At bay, the state of the chase when a hunted animal, unable to flee farther, turns on the hounds; hence *at this bay, at such a bay, in such a bay*, in such extremity or straits: *Ah, that I had my lady at this bay*—Pilgr 155. *I would we had a thousand Roman dames At such a bay*—Tit IV 2 41. *In such a desperate bay of death*—R3 IV 4 232.

BAYNARD'S CASTLE

Built by Humphrey, Duke of Gloucester, in 1428, and destroyed in the Great Fire. It stood on the river bank not far east of the mouth of the Fleet. (The Fleet is now covered over by Farringdon Street and New Bridge Street.) *If you thrive well, bring them to Baynard's Castle*—R3 III 5 98. See also III 7 (Stage Dir.).

BEACHED

Covered with beach, *i.e.* shingle, pebbly: *In the beached margent of the sea*—Mids II 1 85. *Upon the beached verge of the salt flood*—Tim V 1 219.

BEACHY

The same as *Beached*: *The beachy girdle of the ocean*—2 H4 III 1 50.

BEADSMAN

(1) One who prays for another: *For I will be thy beadsman, Valentine*—Gent I 1 18.

(2) A pensioner or almsman bound to pray for the soul of his benefactor: *Thy very beadsmen learn to bend their bows . . . against thy state*—R2 III 2 116.

BEAR (sb.)

Along with a ragged staff the cognizance of the Nevils, Earls of Warwick; referred to—2 H6 V 1 144.

BEAR (vb.)

(1) To conduct, bring: *Bear me forthwith unto his creditor*—Err IV 4 123. *Let Diomedes bear him*—Troil III 3 30.

(2) To manage, carry on: *The manner how this action hath been borne*—2 H4 IV 4 88. *O, if he Had borne the business!*—Cor I 1 273.

(3) To win, gain: *His honesty rewards him in itself; It must not bear my daughter*—Tim I 1 130. *So may he with more facile question bear it* (*i.e.* Cyprus)—Oth I 3 23.

(4) To bear down, load: *Tempest of commotion, like the south Borne with black vapour*—2 H4 II 4 392.

(5) *To bear hard* or *hardly*, to resent: *Who bears hard His brother's death at Bristol*—1 H4 I 3 270. *If I . . . Have aught committed that is hardly borne*—R3 II 1 56. *To bear* (one) *hard*, to have a grudge against (him): *Cæsar doth bear me hard*—Cæs I 2 317. *Caius Ligarius doth bear Cæsar hard*—II 1 215.

(6) *To bear in hand*, to deceive with pretences: *What, bear her in hand until they come to take hands!*—Ado IV 1 305. *To bear a gentleman in hand, and then stand upon security!*—2 H4 I 2 41. *That so his sickness, age and impotence Was falsely borne in hand*—Hml II 2 66. To pretend: *Your daughter, whom she bore in hand to love*—Cymb V 5 43.

(7) *To bear off*, to bear and so keep off: *Here's neither bush nor shrub, to bear off any weather at all*—Tp II 2 18.

BEARING-CLOTH

A child's christening-robe: *A bearing-cloth for a squire's child!*—Wint III 3 118. *Thy scarlet robes as a child's bearing-cloth I'll use to carry thee out of this place*—1 H6 I 3 42.

BEAR-WARD

A keeper of bears: *I will even take sixpence in earnest of the bear-ward*—Ado II 1 42. *We'll bait thy bears to death, And manacle the bear-ward in their chains*—2 H6 V 1 148.

BEASTLY

In the manner of a beast: *How beastly she doth court him!*—Shr IV 2 34. [We] *will give you that Like beasts which you shun beastly*—Cymb V 3 26.

BEAUTY

To beautify: *The harlot's cheek, beautied with plastering art*—Hml III 1 51.

BEAVER

The visor of a helmet: *Their armed staves in charge, their beavers down*—2 H4 IV 1 120. Ham. *Then saw you not his face?* Hor. *O, yes, my lord; he wore his beaver up*—Hml I 2 229. App. of the helmet itself: *I saw young Harry, with his beaver on*—1 H4 IV 1 104.

BECAUSE

To the end that, in order that: *The splitting rocks . . . would not dash me with their ragged sides, Because thy flinty heart . . . Might in thy palace perish Margaret*—2 H6 III 2 97.

BECK

An obeisance, bow: *What a coil's here! Serving of becks and jutting-out of bums!*—Tim I 2 236.

BECOME

To get to, betake oneself to: *Until I be resolved Where our right valiant father is become*—3 H6 II 1 9. *Where is Warwick then become?*—IV 4 25.

BECOMED

Becoming, befitting: *And gave him what becomed love I might*—Rom IV 2 26.

BECOMING

That which becomes or graces: *My becomings kill me, when they do not Eye well to you*—Ant I 3 96.

BEDDED

Laid in a smooth layer: *Your bedded hair . . . Starts up, and stands an end*—Hml III 4 121.

BEDLAM

A lunatic: *Bedlam, have done*—John II 183. Esp. one discharged from an asylum and licensed to beg: *Let's follow the old earl, and get the Bedlam To lead him where he would*—Lr III 7 103 (it is doubtful whether this refers to Edgar). As adj.: *The bedlam brain-sick duchess*—2 H6 III 1 51. *A bedlam and ambitious humour*—V 1 132.

BED-SWERVER

One false to the marriage-bed: *A bed-swerver, even as bad as those That vulgars give bold'st titles*—Wint II 1 93.

BEEF

An ox: *Flesh of muttons, beefs, or goats*—Merch I 3 168. *Now has he land and beefs*—2 H4 III 2 352. So, *bull-beeves: They want their porridge and their fat bull-beeves*—1 H6 I 2 9.

BEEF-WITTED

With no more brains than an ox: *Thou mongrel beef-witted lord!*—Troil II 1 13.

BEEN

3rd pers. pl. pres. of To be = are: *To seas, Where when men been, there's seldom ease*—Per II Prol 27.

BEETLE-HEADED

From beetle, a mallet or rammer, block-headed, stupid: *A whoreson beetle-headed, flap-ear'd knave!*—Shr IV 1 160.

BEFORTUNE

To befall, bechance: *I wish all good befortune you*—Gent IV 3 41.

BEG

To beg a person, to petition the Court of Wards for custody of him as an idiot; fig., to make a fool of: *You cannot beg us, sir, I can assure you, sir*—LLL V 2 490. Sim., to petition for custody of a minor: *I think he means to beg a child of her*—3 H6 III 2 27 (with a play).

BEGET

(1) To get, acquire: *You must acquire and beget a temperance that may give it smoothness*—Hml III 2 8.

(2) To get (with child): *There's one Whom he begot with child*—Meas V 516.

BEGGARY

Beggarliness, contemptible meanness: *Not I, Inclined to this intelligence, pronounce The beggary of his change*—Cymb I 6 113.

BEGUILE

To cheat, disappoint (hopes): *Thou hast beguiled my hopes*—Gent V 4 64.

BEGUILED

Guilefully dressed up: *So beguiled With outward honesty*—Lucr 1544.

BEHALF OF

In behalf of, with regard to, in the matter of: *Will you give me a copy of the sonnet you writ to Diana in behalf of* (i.e. warning her against) *the Count Rousillon?*—All's IV 3 354.

BEHAVE

To govern, manage: *With such sober and unnoted passion He did behave his anger . . . As if . . .* —Tim III 5 21.

BEHAVIOUR

The bearing of the character of another, 'person': *Thus . . . speaks the King of France In my behaviour to the majesty . . . of England here* —John I 2.

BEHOLDING

Obliged, indebted: *A justice of peace sometime may be beholding to his friend for a man*—Wiv I 1 283. *Little are we beholding to your love*—R2 IV 1 160. *For Brutus' sake, I am beholding to you*—Cæs III 2 70.

BEHOVE

Behoof, advantage: *It was very sweet, To contract, O, the time, for, ah, my behove*—Hml V 1 70.

BEHOVEFUL

Needful, necessary: *Such necessaries As are behoveful for our state to-morrow*—Rom IV 3 7.

BEING

Mode or conditions of life: *My health and happy being at your court*—Gent III 1 57. *To shift his being Is to exchange one misery with another*—Cymb I 5 54.

BEING, BEING THAT

Inasmuch as, seeing that: *Being that I flow in grief, The smallest twine may lead me*—Ado IV 1 251. *You loiter here too long, being you are to take soldiers up in counties as you go*—2 H4 II 1 198.

BELDAM

(1) A grandmother: *To show the beldam daughters of her daughter*—Lucr 953.

(2) An aged woman (without depreciation being necessarily implied): *Old men and beldams in the streets*—John IV 2 185. *And shapes her sorrow to the beldam's woes*—Lucr 1458.

BE-LEE

To get (a ship) into such a position that the wind is intercepted from her; fig.: *And I . . . must be be-lee'd and calm'd By debitor and creditor* —Oth I 1 28.

BELIE

(1) To speak falsely of a person (to his credit): *Thou dost belie him, Percy . . . He never did encounter with Glendower*—1 H4 I 3 113.

(2) To fill with lies: *Slander . . . whose breath . . . doth belie All corners of the world*—Cymb III 4 35. So app., *belied*, contrived so as to convey a false impression: *She concludes the picture was belied*—Lucr 1533.

BELIKE

As it seems, no doubt, perhaps: *Belike, boy, then, you are in love*—Gent II 1 85. *A scar*

*nobly got . . . is a good livery of honour; so belike
is that*—All's IV 5 105. *Belike this show imports
the argument of the play*—Hml III 2 149.

BELL

Used with the book of offices and a candle in
the ceremony of excommunication: *Bell, book, and
candle shall not drive me back, When gold and
silver becks me to come on*—John III 3 12. In
hawking bells were attached to the hawk's legs,
to enable an erring hawk to be traced, and to
terrify the prey: *As the ox hath his bow . . . and
the falcon her bells*—As III 3 80. *Nor . . . The
proudest he that holds up Lancaster Dares stir a
wing, if Warwick shake his bells*—3 H6 I 1 45.
*Lies Harmless Lucretia . . . With trembling fear,
as fowl hear falcon's bells*—Lucr 509.

BEMAD

To madden: *Unnatural and bemadding sorrow*
—Lr III 1 38.

BEMOIL

To bemire, dirty: *Thou shouldst have heard how
her horse fell . . . how she was bemoiled*—Shr IV
1 75.

BE-MONSTER

Be-monster not thy feature, do not show thy
(hitherto concealed) hideous fiendishness in thy
outward form—Lr IV 2 63.

BENCH

(1) To sit on the seat of justice: *And thou, his
yoke-fellow of equity, Bench by his side*—Lr III 6
39.

(2) To raise to the bench: *Whom I from meaner
form Have bench'd and rear'd to worship*—Wint I
2 313.

BENCH-HOLE

A privy: *We'll beat 'em into bench-holes*—Ant
IV 7 9.

BEND (sb.)

An inclination of the eye, glance: *That same
eye whose bend doth awe the world*—Cæs I 2 123.

BEND (vb.)

(1) Of weapons, to direct, bring to bear: *Our
cannon shall be bent Against the brows of this re-
sisting town*—John II 37. *Thy murderous fal-
chion . . . The which thou once didst bend against
her breast*—R3 I 2 94. *Bending his sword To his
great master*—Lr IV 2 74.

(2) To direct one's course: *For thence we came,
And, after some dispatch in hand at court, Thither
we bend again*—All's III 2 55. *Or bends with the
remover to remove*—Sonn 116 4. So refl.: *You . . .
Towards York shall bend you with your dearest
speed*—1 H4 V 5 35.

(3) Refl., to incline, dispose oneself: *We beseech
you, bend you to remain Here*—Hml I 2 115.

(4) *Bent*, resolved, determined; with infin.: *I see
you all are bent To set against me for your merriment*—Mids III 2 145. *For now I am bent to
know, By the worst means, the worst*—Mcb III 4
134. Inclined, disposed, ready: *Speak on with
favour; we are bent to hear*—John II 422. *All
his mind is bent to holiness*—2 H6 I 3 58. *A sort
of naughty persons, lewdly bent*—II 1 167. Ready,
prepared: *Everything is bent For England*—Hml
IV 3 47. Intent; with infin.: *Whose busy care is
bent To follow that which flies before her face*—
Sonn 143 6. *Bent to* or *with,* intent on: *With a
power Of high-resolved men, bent to the spoil*—Tit
IV 4 63. *How Thaliard came full bent with sin*
—Per II Prol 23. *Bent on* or *against,* hostilely
disposed against: *Met us again and madly bent on
us Chased us away*—Err V 152. *There is but one
mind in all these men, and it is bent against Cæsar*
—Cæs II 3 5.

BENEFIT

(1) A benefaction (in a legal sense): *Accept the
title thou usurp'st, Of benefit proceeding from our
king*—1 H6 V 4 151. *Take to your royal self
This proffer'd benefit of dignity*—R3 III 7 195.

(2) A natural advantage or gift: *Disable all the
benefits of your own country*—As IV 1 34. *When
these so noble benefits shall prove Not well disposed*
—H8 I 2 115.

BENEVOLENCE

To do one's benevolence, to lend one's friendly
offices: *I . . . will be glad to do my benevolence to
make atonements . . . between you*—Wiv I 1 32.

BENNET

Saint Bennet, identified by some with the church
of St. Benet (Benedict) Hude or Hythe, Paul's
Wharf, nearly opposite the Globe Theatre, de-
stroyed in the Great Fire. *The bells of Saint
Bennet, sir, may put you in mind; one, two, three*
—Tw V 41.

BENT

Degree of tension: *It seems her affections have
their full bent*—Ado II 3 231. *And here give up
ourselves, in the full bent To lay our service freely
at your feet*—Hml II 2 30. *To hold the bent,* to
endure: *Thy affection cannot hold the bent*—Tw
II 4 38. Extent to which a bow may be bent or
a spring wound up; hence, limit of capacity: *They
fool me to the top of my bent*—Hml III 2 401.

BERATTLE

To rattle away at, assail with din: *[These] so
berattle the common stages*—Hml II 2 357.

BEREAVE

To snatch or take away: *If thou live to see like
right bereft*—Err I 1 40. *Whose dismal tune bereft my vital powers*—2 H6 III 2 41. *What can
man's wisdom In the restoring his bereaved sense?*
—Lr IV 4 8.

BERGOMASK

Bergomask dance, a rustic dance in imitation of the clownish people of Bergamo in Italy: *Will it please you . . . to hear a Bergomask dance*—Mids V 359. So *Bergomask* alone: *But, come, your Bergomask*—368.

BERMOOTHES

The Bermudas: *The still-vex'd Bermoothes*—Tp I 2 229.

BESEECH

Beseeching, entreaty: *Achievement is command; ungain'd, beseech*—Troil I 2 319.

BESEEMING

Appearance: *The soldier that did company these three In poor beseeming*—Cymb V 5 408.

BESHREW

To objurgate, blame greatly: *She will beshrew me much that Romeo Hath had no notice of these accidents*—Rom V 2 25. As a minor imprecation: *Beshrew my hand, If it should give your age such cause of fear*—Ado V 1 55. Tenderly or playfully: *Beshrew your heart, Fair daughter, you do draw my spirits from me*—2 H4 II 3 45. *If thou wantest any thing, and wilt not call, beshrew thy heart*—V 3 58. In asseveration: *Beshrew me but I love her heartily*—Merch II 6 52.

BESIDE

By the side so as to miss, by: *Yet sometimes falls an orient drop beside, Which her cheek melts, as scorning it should pass*—Ven 981. Perh. as prep. in the same sense: *We have met with foes That strike beside us* (*i.e.* they deliberately miss)—Mcb V 7 28; or the meaning may be the more obvious one, on our side.

BESIDES

Beside: *How fell you besides your five wits?*—Tw IV 2 92. *Quite besides The government of patience!*—Cymb II 4 149.

BESONIAN

See *Bezonian*.

BESORT (sb.)

Suitable company: *Such accommodation and besort As levels with her breeding*—Oth I 3 239.

BESORT (vb.)

To befit: *Such men as may besort your age*—Lr I 4 272.

BESPEAK

To request (a person to do something): *Then fairly I bespoke the officer To go in person with me to my house*—Err V 233.

BEST

In the best, at best: *Murder most foul, as in the best it is*—Hml I 5 27.

BESTOW

(1) To place, dispose of (in a place): *Bestow your luggage where you found it*—Tp V 298. *How should I bestow him?*—Wiv IV 2 47. *I will bestow you where you shall have time To speak your bosom freely*—Oth III 1 57. To deposit for safe-keeping: *Answer me In what safe place you have bestow'd my money*—Err I 2 77. To lodge (a person): *Will you see the players well bestowed?*—Hml II 2 546. *This house is little: the old man and his people Cannot be well bestow'd*—Lr II 4 291. Refl., to dwell: *Can you tell Where he bestows himself?*—Mcb III 6 23. So in pass.: *We hear, our bloody cousins are bestow'd In England and in Ireland*—Mcb III 1 30. *To bestow oneself*, to take up one's position: *Bestow yourself with speed: The French are bravely in their battles set*—H5 IV 3 68.

(2) To settle in marriage: *Not to bestow my youngest daughter Before I have a husband for the elder*—Shr I 1 50. *Willing . . . to have her so bestow'd*—IV 4 34.

(3) Of money, to lay out, spend: *How little is the cost I have bestow'd*—Merch III 4 19. *I would have bestowed the thousand pound I borrowed of you*—2 H4 V 5 12.

(4) To confer as a gift, give, grant, with dative of pronoun, *of* or *to*: *You must needs bestow her funeral*—Tit IV 2 163. *How shall I feast him? what bestow of him?*—Tw III 4 2. *And bestow Your needful counsel to our business*—Lr II 1 128.

(5) *To bestow oneself*, to conduct or deport oneself: *How . . . I may bestow myself To be regarded in her sun-bright eye*—Gent III 1 87. *Bestows himself Like a ripe sister*—As IV 3 87. *How might we see Falstaff bestow himself to-night in his true colours?*—2 H4 II 2 186.

BESTOWING

App., endowments: *All my powers do their bestowing lose*—Troil III 2 39.

BESTRAUGHT

Distracted: *What! I am not bestraught*—Shr Ind II 26.

BETEEM

(1) To grant, accord: *For want of rain, which I could well Beteem them from the tempest of my eyes*—Mids I 1 130.

(2) To allow, permit: *That he might not beteem the winds of heaven Visit her face too roughly*—Hml I 2 141.

BETHINK

To devise, contrive: *While we bethink a means to break it off*—3 H6 III 3 39.

BETIDE

To betide of, to become of: *If he were dead, what would betide of me?*—R3 I 3 6.

BETIME (vb.)

To betide, happen: *No time shall be omitted That will betime, and may by us be fitted*—LLL IV 3 381.

BETIME (adv.)

(1) In good time, seasonably: *Put up thy sword betime*—John IV 3 98. *Send succours, lords, and stop the rage betime*—2 H6 III 1 285.

(2) Early in the day: *All in the morning betime* —Hml IV 5 49. *To business that we love we rise betime*—Ant IV 4 20.

BETRAY

(1) Loosely, to cheat, disappoint: *Do not betray me, sir. I fear you love Mistress Page*—Wiv III 3 82. *Win us with honest trifles, to betray's In deepest consequence*—Mcb I 3 125.

(2) To give up or expose (*to* punishment): *To betray him to another punishment*—Wiv III 3 208. *She did betray me to my own reproof*—Err V 90.

BEVIS

Bevis of Southampton, a knight of romance: [So] *that former fabulous story . . . got credit, That Bevis was believed*—H8 I 1 36.

BEWARE

To take care of, guard: *Priest, beware your beard*—1 H6 I 3 47.

BEWRAY

To disclose, make known, show: *Our raiment . . . would bewray what life We have led since thy exile*—Cor V 3 94. *Write down thy mind, bewray thy meaning so*—Tit II 4 3. *Thyself bewray, When false opinion . . . repeals and reconciles thee*—Lr III 6 118.

BEZONIAN, BESONIAN

A needy beggar, base fellow: *Under which king, Besonian? speak, or die*—2 H4 V 3 119. *Great men oft die by vile bezonians*—2 H6 IV 1 134.

BIAS (adj.)

Thy sphered bias cheek, swelled like a bowl on the biased side—Troil IV 5 8.

BIAS (adv.)

Awry, wrong: *Every action . . . trial did draw Bias and thwart, not answering the aim*—Troil I 3 13.

BID

To bid battle, to offer battle: *The king will bid you battle presently*—1 H4 V 2 31. *Let's . . . issue forth and bid them battle straight*—3 H6 I 2 70. For *Bid the base* see *Base* (sb.).

BID

Past tense of *To bide*. See quotation from R3 under *Bide* (2).

BIDDY

A chicken, fowl; as a term of endearment: *Ay, Biddy, come with me*—Tw III 4 128.

BIDE

(1) To face, encounter: *Wilt thou . . . bide the mortal fortune of the field?*—3 H6 II 2 81. *She will not . . . bide the encounter of assailing eyes* —Rom I 1 218.

(2) To undergo, suffer: *A night of groans Endured of her, for whom you bid like sorrow*—R3 IV 4 303. *Poor naked wretches . . . That bide the pelting of this pitiless storm*—Lr III 4 28. To endure, stand: *There is no woman's sides Can bide the beating of so strong a passion As love doth give my heart*—Tw II 4 96. *My love can give no place, bide no denay*—127.

(3) *To bide upon it*, my abiding or fixed opinion is: *To bide upon 't, thou art not honest*—Wint I 2 242.

BIDING

An abiding place, habitation: *I'll lead you to some biding*—Lr IV 6 228. *Some gentle gust . . . Which blows these pitchy vapours from their biding* —Lucr 549.

BIGAMY

In ecclesiastical law, marriage of or with a widow or widower—R3 III 7 189.

BIGGEN

A night-cap: *He whose brow with homely biggen bound Snores out the watch of night*—2 H4 IV 5 27.

BILBO

A sword, properly one of Bilbao: *Compassed, like a good bilbo, in the circumference of a peck*— Wiv III 5 112. App., one who bears a bilbo: *I combat challenge of this latten bilbo*—Wiv I 1 165. In pl. an iron bar with shackles to confine the ankles: *Worse than the mutines in the bilboes*— Hml V 2 6.

BILL¹

A weapon like a Halberd (*q.v.*): *Only, have a care that your bills be not stolen*—Ado III 3 43. *Manage rusty bills*—R2 III 2 118. *Clubs, bills, and partisans! strike! beat them down!*—Rom I 1 80. Distinct forms of bills seem to have been painted or varnished in different colours; hence *brown bills*: *Many a time, but for a sallet, my brain-pan had been cleft with a brown bill*—2 H6 IV 10 12. *Bring up the brown bills*—Lr IV 6 91.

BILL²

(1) A deed: *Writes himself 'Armigero', in any bill . . . or obligation*—Wiv I 1 9. Any written paper, a billet: *Ride, and give these bills Unto the legions on the other side*—Cæs V 2 1. A note or

memorandum: *Error i' the bill, sir*—Shr IV 3 146 (cf. 130).

(2) A list or inventory: *I will draw a bill of properties, such as our play wants*—Mids I 2 107. *He does receive Particular addition, from the bill That writes them all alike*—Mcb III 1 99.

BIRD

The young of a bird: *That ungentle gull, the cuckoo's bird*—1 H4 V I 60. *If thou be that princely eagle's bird*—3 H6 II 1 91.

BIRD-BOLT

A blunt-headed arrow for shooting birds: *Challenged him at the bird-bolt*—Ado I 1 42. *Thou hast thumped him with thy bird-bolt*—LLL IV 3 24.

BIRDING

Fowling: *We'll a-birding together*—Wiv III 3 246. *Her husband goes this morning a-birding*—III 5 45.

BIRDING-PIECE

A fowling-piece: *There they always use to discharge their birding-pieces*—Wiv IV 2 58.

BIRTH-CHILD

Thetis' birth-child (as having been born at sea)—Per IV 4 41.

BIRTHDOM

Inheritance, birthright: *Let us . . . Bestride our down-fall'n birthdom*—Mcb IV 3 2.

BISSON

Blind, or perh., purblind: *Your bisson conspectuities*—Cor II 1 70. *This bisson multitude*—III 1 131. Prob., blinding: *Threatening the flames With bisson rheum*—Hml II 2 528.

BITE

To bite the thumb, to defy or insult by jerking the thumb-nail from behind the upper teeth with a crack: *I will bite my thumb at them; which is a disgrace to them, if they bear it*—Rom I 1 48. *To bite by the ear*, an endearment: *I will bite thee by the ear for that jest*—Rom II 4 81. *To bite by the nose*, to set at defiance: *Affections . . . That thus can make him bite the law by the nose*—Meas III 1 108.

BITTER SWEETING

The bitter-sweet apple: *Thy wit is a very bitter sweeting*—Rom II 4 83.

BITUMED

Smeared with bitumen, *i.e.* mineral pitch: *We have a chest beneath the hatches, caulked and bitumed ready*—Per III 1 71. *How close 'tis caulk'd and bitumed!*—III 2 57.

BLACK

Having black hair, dark-complexioned: *If black, why, Nature, drawing of an antique, Made a foul blot*—Ado III 1 63. *How if she be black and witty?*—Oth II 1 132.

BLACK-CORNERED

Explained as, as obscure as a dark corner: *Black-corner'd night*—Tim V 1 47.

BLACK-FRIARS

A church, precinct and sanctuary lying between Baynard's Castle (*q.v.*) and the Fleet: *The most convenient place that I can think of For such receipt of learning is Black-Friars*—H8 II 2 138. See also II 4 (Stage Dir.).

BLACK-MONDAY

Easter Monday: *It was not for nothing that my nose fell a-bleeding on Black-Monday last*—Merch II 5 24.

BLACKS

Black stuffs or clothes: *False As o'er-dyed blacks*—Wint I 2 131.

BLADED

(1) Abounding in blades: *Decking with liquid pearl the bladed grass*—Mids I 1 211.

(2) Prob., enclosed in the blade, not yet in full ear: *Though bladed corn be lodged and trees blown down*—Mcb IV 1 55.

BLAME

A fault: *My high-repented blames . . . pardon to me*—All 's V 3 36. *'Tis his own blame*—Lr II 4 293. Blameworthiness: *Authority for sin, warrant for blame*—Lucr 620. *Perjured, murderous, bloody, full of blame*—Sonn 129 3.

BLANK (sb.)

(1) The white spot in the centre of a target, anything aimed at: *As level as the cannon to his blank*—Hml IV 1 42. *Let me still remain The true blank of thine eye*—Lr I 1 160.

(2) The range of the aim: *Quite beyond mine arm, out of the blank And level of my brain*—Wint II 3 5. *Stood within the blank of his displeasure*—Oth III 4 128.

(3) A document with spaces left blank to be filled up at pleasure: *New exactions . . . As blanks, benevolences, and I wot not what*—R2 II 1 249. *Seals a commission to a blank of danger*—Troil III 3 231. So *blank charters*: *Our substitutes at home shall have blank charters*—R2 I 4 48.

BLANK (vb.)

To blanch, make pale: *Each opposite that blanks the face of joy*—Hml III 2 230.

BLASPHEME

To speak evil of, calumniate: *The truest issue of thy throne . . . does blaspheme his breed*—Mcb IV 3 106.

BLAST

To din by trumpeting: *With brazen din blast you the city's ear*—Ant IV 8 36. *To blast in proof*: *This project Should have a back or second, that might hold, If this should blast in proof*—Hml IV 7 153, explained as a figure taken from the testing of fire-arms, to burst, fail.

BLASTMENT

A blasting, blighting: *Contagious blastments are most imminent*—Hml I 3 42.

BLAZE

To divulge, make known: *Till we can find a time To blaze your marriage*—Rom III 3 150.

BLAZON (sb.)

(1) Armorial bearings: *Each fair instalment, coat, and several crest, With loyal blazon*—Wiv V 5 67.

(2) A description: *I' faith, lady, I think your blazon to be true*—Ado II 1 307. *The blazon of sweet beauty's best*—Sonn 106 5.

(3) Disclosure, divulgation, proclamation: *'I am a gentleman'. I'll be sworn thou art; Thy tongue, thy face, thy limbs, actions and spirit, Do give thee five-fold blazon* (i.e. proclaim it with five-fold voice)—Tw I 5 310. *Eternal blazon*, a disclosure of the things of eternity: *This eternal blazon must not be To ears of flesh and blood*—Hml I 5 21.

BLAZON (vb.)

To describe: *If . . . thy skill be more To blazon it*—Rom II 6 24. *One that excels the quirks of blazoning pens*—Oth II 1 63.

BLEAR

To blear the eyes, to deceive, hoodwink: *While counterfeit supposes blear'd thine eyne*—Shr V 1 120.

BLENCH (sb.)

A turning of the eyes askance: *These blenches gave my heart another youth*—Sonn 110 7.

BLENCH (vb.)

To flinch; hence, to swerve, be unsettled, inconsistent: *Hold you ever to our special drift; Though sometimes you do blench from this to that*—Meas IV 5 4. *Could man so blench?*—Wint I 2 333.

BLEND

Blended: *The opal blend With objects manifold*—Compl 215.

BLIND-WORM

Newts and blind-worms, do no wrong—Mids II 2 11. *Adder's fork and blind-worm's sting*—Mcb IV 1 16. The blind-worm is harmless; but it appears to have been thought poisonous in Shakespeare's time.

BLISTERED

Ornamented with puffs: *Short blister'd breeches*—H8 I 3 31.

BLOAT

Puffy, puffed, swollen: *The bloat king*—Hml III 4 182.

BLOCK

A mould for a hat: *He wears his faith but as the fashion of his hat; it ever changes with the next block*—Ado I 1 75. In Lr IV 6 187 (*This' a good block*) perh., the shape or style of a hat.

BLOOD

(1) Disposition, temper: *It better fits my blood*—Ado I 3 29. *Undone by goodness! Strange, unusual blood, When man's worst sin is, he does too much good!*—Tim IV 2 38. *Though the conflict be sore between that and my blood*—Lr III 5 23. Mood: *When you perceive his blood inclined to mirth*—2 H4 IV 4 38. *Humours of blood*, caprices of temperament: *In . . . humours of blood He was the mark and glass . . . That fashion'd others*—2 H4 II 3 30.

(2) Spirit, courage: *Thy Fates open their hands; let thy blood and spirit embrace them*—Tw II 5 159. *Though sometimes it show greatness, courage, blood*—1 H4 III 1 181. Passion: *Blest are those Whose blood and judgement are so well commingled, That . . .*—Hml III 2 73. *Were't my fitness To let these hands obey my blood*—Lr IV 2 63. *The blood and baseness of our natures*—Oth I 3 332. *Of the blood*, app., heartfelt: *Thy due from me Is tears and heavy sorrows of the blood*—2 H4 IV 5 37.

(3) *In blood*, in full vigour: *If we be English deer, be then in blood*—1 H6 IV 2 48. *When they shall see, sir, his crest up again, and the man in blood*—Cor IV 5 224. *Worst in blood*, in the worst condition: *Thou rascal, that art worst in blood to run*—Cor I 1 163.

BLOOD-BOLTERED

Having the hair matted with blood: *The blood-bolter'd Banquo smiles upon me*—Mcb IV 1 123.

BLOODY

(1) In the blood: *Lust is but a bloody fire*—Wiv V 5 99.

(2) *The bloody flag*, the red flag, the signal of battle: *Stand for your own; unwind your bloody flag*—H5 I 2 101. [You] *set up the bloody flag against all patience*—Cor II 1 84. So *bloody sign* of battle: *Their bloody sign of battle is hung out*—Cæs V 1 14.

BLOW

(1) To blow upon: *Air, quoth he, thy cheeks may blow*—LLL IV 3 109. *And the very ports they* (*i.e.* the winds) *blow*—Mcb I 3 15.

(2) To inflate; hence, to make full to bursting: *This blows my heart*—Ant IV 6 34.

(3) Of insects, to deposit eggs, to fill with eggs: *And would no more endure This wooden slavery than to suffer The flesh-fly blow my mouth*—Tp III 1 61. [Honest] *as summer flies are in the shambles, That quicken even with blowing*—Oth IV 2 66. *Let the water-flies Blow me into abhorring!*—Ant V 2 59.

BLOWSE

A ruddy fat-faced wench: *Sweet blowse, you are a beauteous blossom, sure*—Tit IV 2 72.

BLUE

Of the eyes, having livid circles round them: *A lean cheek . . . a blue eye and sunken*—As III 2 392.

BLUE-BOTTLE

You blue-bottle rogue, you filthy famished correctioner—2 H4 V 4 22, alluding to the beadle's blue coat.

BLUE-CAPS

Scots, from their blue bonnets: *He* (*i.e.* Douglas) *is there too . . . and a thousand blue-caps more*—1 H4 II 4 390.

BLUE COAT

The common dress of serving men: [Let] *their* (*i.e.* the servants') *blue coats* [be] *brushed*—Shr IV 1 93. *Draw, men . . . Blue coats to tawny coats*—1 H6 I 3 46.

BLUNT

(1) Dull, obtuse: *Blunt Thurio's dull proceeding*—Gent II 6 41. *The blunt monster with uncounted heads, The still-discordant wavering multitude*—2 H4 Ind 18. *What a blunt fellow is this grown to be! He was quick mettle when he went to school*—Cæs I 2 299.

(2) Unfeeling, harsh, unsparing: *Vicious, ungentle, foolish, blunt, unkind*—Err IV 2 21. *So harsh, so blunt, unnatural*—3 H6 V 1 86. *No gentle chase, But the blunt boar, rough bear, or lion proud*—Ven 883.

BLURT

To blurt at, to puff at in scorn with the lips: *Ours was blurted at and held a malkin*—Per IV 3 34.

BOARD

The same as *Accost* (*q.v.*): *Unless he know . . . he would never have boarded me in this fury*—Wiv II 1 90. *'Accost' is front her, board her, woo her, assail her*—Tw I 3 59. *I'll board him presently*—Hml II 2 170.

BOAST

A noise, clamour: *Every thing doth make a gleeful boast*—Tit II 3 11.

BOB (sb.)

A firm rap; fig., a rap with the tongue: *He that a fool doth very wisely hit Doth very foolishly . . . Not to seem senseless of the bob*—As II 7 53.

BOB (vb.)[1]

To get by craft: *Gold and jewels that I bobb'd from him*—Oth V 1 16. *To bob out of*, to cheat of: *You shall not bob us out of our melody*—Troil III 1 75.

BOB (vb.)[2]

To pommel: *Whom our fathers Have in their own land beaten, bobb'd, and thump'd*—R3 V 3 333. *I have bobbed his brain more than he has beat my bones*—Troil II 1 75.

BODGE

Botch; to do a thing unskilfully: *With this, we charged again: but, out, alas! We bodged again*—3 H6 I 4 18.

BODKIN

A short pointed weapon, a poniard: *Biron. Because thou hast no face. Hol. What is this? . . . Dum. The head of a bodkin*—LLL V 2 612. *When he himself might his quietus make With a bare bodkin*—Hml III 1 75.

BODYKINS

God's bodykins, God's dear body—Hml II 2 554. *So bodykins alone*—Wiv II 3 46.

BOGGLER

One who plays fast and loose: *You have been a boggler ever*—Ant III 13 110.

BOILED

Such boil'd stuff—Cymb I 6 125. An allusion to the treatment mentioned under *Tub*.

BOISTEROUS

(1) Rough to the feelings, painfully rough: *Feeling what small things are boisterous there* (*i.e.* in the eye)—John IV 1 95. *Is love a tender thing? it is too rough, Too rude, too boisterous*—Rom I 4 25.

(2) Fierce, savage: *O Clifford, boisterous Clifford! thou hast slain The flower of Europe for his chivalry*—3 H6 II 1 70.

BOLD (adj.)

(1) *To make* or *be bold with* or *upon*, to take liberties with, make free with: *I will first make bold with your money*—Wiv II 2 262. *If I cut my finger, I shall make bold with you*—Mids III 1 186. *I will only be bold with Benedick for his company*—Ado III 2 8. *We are too bold upon your rest*—Cæs II 1 86.

(2) Confident, certain: *Bold of your worthiness, we single you*—LLL II 28. *Be bold you do so grow in my requital As* . . .—All's V 1 5. *Be bold in us*—Tit V 1 13. *I am bold her honour Will remain hers*—Cymb II 4 2.

BOLD (vb.)

To encourage (practically = *Comfort* (vb.) (2)): *For this business, It toucheth us, as France invades our land, Not bolds the king*—Lr V 1 24.

BOLD-BEATING

App. a confusion of bold-faced and brow-beating: *Your bold-beating oaths*—Wiv II 2 28.

BOLDEN

To embolden: *Art thou thus bolden'd, man, by thy distress?*—As II 7 91. *Am bolden'd Under your promised pardon*—H8 I 2 55.

BOLIN

Bowline; a rope for steadying the edge of a sail: *Slack the bolins there!*—Per III 1 43.

BOLLEN

Swollen: *Here one being throng'd bears back, all boll'n and red*—Lucr 1417.

BOLT (sb.)

A short arrow with a blunt head as opposed to a shaft, the regular sharp-pointed war arrow: *I'll make a shaft or a bolt on't*—Wiv III 4 24.

BOLT (vb.)

To sift: *The fann'd snow that's bolted By the northern blasts twice o'er*—Wint IV 4 374. Tro. *Have I not tarried?* Pan. *Ay, the bolting, but you must tarry the leavening*—Troil I 1 18. Fig.: *Such and so finely bolted didst thou seem*—H5 II 2 137. [He] *is ill school'd In bolted language*—Cor III 1 321.

BOLTER

A sieve, strainer: *I have given them* (i.e. the shirts) *away to bakers' wives, and they have made bolters of them*—1 H4 III 3 79.

BOLTING-HUTCH

A receptacle into which meal is sifted: *Why dost thou converse with* . . . *that bolting-hutch of beastliness?*—1 H4 II 4 494.

BOMBARD

A leather jug or bottle for liquor: *Yond* . . . *cloud* . . . *looks like a foul bombard that would shed his liquor*—Tp II 2 20. *Why dost thou converse with* . . . *that huge bombard of sack?*—1 H4 II 4 494.

BOMBAST

Pa. pple. of *To bombase*, to stuff; fig., puffed, inflated: *A bombast circumstance Horribly stuff'd with epithets of war*—Oth I 1 13.

BOMBAST

Cotton-wool used as padding: *My sweet creature of bombast*—1 H4 II 4 359 (of Falstaff). Fig.: [We] *rated them* (i.e. the letters) . . . *As bombast and as lining to the time*—LLL V 2 789.

BONA-ROBA

A showy wanton: *We knew where the bona-robas were*—2 H4 III 2 26. *She was then a bona-roba*—217.

BOND

Obligation, duty: *I knew it for my bond*—Ant I 4 84.

BONDAGE

Binding force, obligation: *The vows of women Of no more bondage be* . . . *Than they are to their virtues*—Cymb II 4 110.

BONES

Bobbins made of bone for weaving bonelace: *The free maids that weave their thread with bones*—Tw II 4 46.

BONNET

To take off the bonnet in token of respect: *Those who, having been supple and courteous to the people, bonneted*—Cor II 2 29.

BONNY

(1) Comely: *Bonny Kate*—Shr II 187. *The bonny beast he loved so well*—2 H6 V 2 12.

(2) Of fine size, lusty: *The bonny priser of the humorous duke*—As II 3 8.

(3) Gladsome: *Be you blithe and bonny*—Ado II 3 69.

BOOK

(1) A writing, document: *By that time will our book, I think, be drawn*—1 H4 III 1 224.

(2) Learning: *The tenour of my book*—Ado IV 1 169. *Because my book preferr'd me to the king*—2 H6 IV 7 77.

BOOT (sb.)[1]

Booty, spoil: *This prisoner freely give I thee; And thou* . . . *make boot of this*—2 H6 IV 1 12. To make boot upon, to despoil: *Others* . . . *Make boot upon the summer's velvet buds*—H5 I 2 193.

BOOT (sb.)[2]

(1) Profit, use: *Vail your stomachs, for it is no boot*—Shr V 2 176. *Make boot of his distraction*—Ant IV 1 9.

(2) Something thrown in or given in addition: *Though the pennyworth on his side be the worst, yet hold thee, there's some boot*—Wint IV 4 649. *I'll give you boot, I'll give you three for one*—Troil IV 5 40. With boot, giving something into the bargain: *My gravity* . . . *Could I with boot change for an idle plume*—Meas II 4 9.

(3) *Grace to boot!* an apprecatory phrase, grace to my help—Wint I 2 80. Sim. *Saint George to boot!*—R3 V 3 301.

(4) A resource, alternative: *Norfolk, throw down, we bid; there is no boot*—R2 I 1 164.

BOOT (vb.)

To benefit, enrich: *I will boot thee with what gift beside Thy modesty can beg*—Ant II 5 71.

BOOT-HOSE

An over-stocking covering the leg like a jack-boot: *A kersey boot-hose on the other* [leg]—Shr III 2 68.

BOOTLESS

Having gained nothing: *Thrice . . . have I sent him Bootless home and weather-beaten back*—1 H4 III 1 65.

BOOTS

To give one the boots, to make him a laughing-stock: *Over the boots? nay, give me not the boots*—Gent I 1 27.   Or the torture of the boots may be alluded to.

BORDER

To keep within bounds, limit: *That nature, which contemns it origin, Cannot be border'd certain in itself*—Lr IV 2 32.

BORE (sb.)

A hole, aperture: *Your franchises . . . confined Into an auger's bore*—Cor IV 6 86.   *The bores of hearing*—Cymb III 2 59.

BORE (vb.)

To cheat, overreach: *At this instant He bores me with some trick*—H8 I 1 127.

BORROW

A borrowing: *Yet of your royal presence I'll adventure The borrow of a week*—Wint I 2 38.

BOSKY, BUSKY

Covered with bushes or underwood: *My bosky acres and my unshrubb'd down*—Tp IV 81.   *Yon busky hill*—1 H4 V 1 2.

BOSOM

One's inward thoughts or wishes: *Where you shall have time To speak your bosom freely*—Oth III 1 57.   One's heart's desire: *You shall have your bosom on this wretch*—Meas IV 3 139.   *Of one's bosom,* in his confidence: *I know you are of her bosom*—Lr IV 5 26.   Attrib., *bosom interest,* confidential affection: *No more that thane of Cawdor shall deceive Our bosom interest*—Mcb I 2 63.

BOTCH

A botched place, a flaw or blemish: *To leave no rubs nor botches in the work*—Mcb III 1 134.

BOTCHY

Covered with botches, *i.e.* excrescences: *Were not that a botchy core?*—Troil II 1 6.

BOTH

Of more than two objects: *She was both pantler, butler, cook*—Wint IV 4 56.   *Both he and they and you*—1 H4 V 1 107.

BOTS

Worms or maggots in horses—*Begnawn with the bots*—Shr III 2 55.   *The next way to give poor jades the bots*—1 H4 II 1 10.   *Bots on't,* as an imprecation—Per II 1 124.

BOTTLE[1]

Hang me in a bottle like a cat and shoot at me—Ado I 1 259.   App. some vessel made of wicker-work is meant.

BOTTLE[2]

A bundle or truss (of hay or straw): *I have a great desire to a bottle of hay*—Mids IV 1 34.

BOTTLED

Like a bottle, swollen, bloated: *That bottled spider*—R3 I 3 242; IV 4 81.

BOTTOM (sb.)

A nucleus on which to wind thread; and hence, a skein or ball of thread: *Beat me to death with a bottom of brown thread*—Shr IV 3 137.

BOTTOM (vb.)

To wind on a bottom: *As you unwind her love from him . . . You must provide to bottom it on me*—Gent III 2 51.

BOUNCE

The loud burst of noise produced by an explosion: *He speaks plain cannon fire, and smoke and bounce*—John II 462.

BOUND

Ready, prepared: *Speak; I am bound to hear*—Hml I 5 6.   *Like a man to double business bound*—III 3 41.   *We are bound to the like*—Lr III 7 11.

BOUNTY

Kindness, hospitality: *This entertainment May . . . derive a liberty From heartiness, from bounty, fertile bosom*—Wint I 2 111.   *As Hector's leisure and your bounties shall Concur together, severally entreat him*—Troil IV 5 273.   A kind act: *To you This honourable bounty shall belong*—1 H4 V 5 25.

BOURN[1]

A boundary (between fields, &c.): *Bourn, bound of land, tilth, vineyard, none*—Tp II 1 152.   *One that fixes No bourn 'twixt his and mine*—Wint I 2 133.   A limit, frontier: *Thy wisdom, Which,*

3

like a bourn . . . confines Thy . . . parts—Troil
II 3 259. *The undiscover'd country from whose
bourn No traveller returns*—Hml III 1 79. *I'll
set a bourn how far to be beloved*—Ant I 1 16.

BOURN²

A brook: *Come o'er the bourn, Bessy, to me*—
Lr III 6 27.

BOW (sb.)

A yoke for oxen: *As the ox hath his bow . . .
so man hath his desires*—As III 3 80.

BOW (vb.)

(1) To assume a bent or crooked shape or atti-
tude, bend: *An ass whose back with ingots bows*—
Meas III 1 26. *Which in weight to re-answer,
his pettiness would bow under*—H5 III 6 136.
That bows unto the grave with mickle age—2 H6
V 1 174.

(2) To cause to bend, curve, crook: *I . . .
bow'd her hand to teach her fingering*—Shr II 150.
A three-pence bow'd would hire me—H8 II 3 36.
You're a young foolish sapling, and must be bowed
—Per IV 2 93. Fig.: *God forbid . . . That you
should fashion, wrest, or bow your reading*—H5
I 2 13. *He bow'd his nature*—Cor V 6 25.

BOY

To personate as a boy actor: *I shall see Some
squeaking Cleopatra boy my greatness*—Ant V
2 219.

BOY-QUELLER

A slayer of boys: *Come, come, thou boy-queller,
show thy face*—Troil V 5 45.

BRABBLE

A brawl, quarrel: *In private brabble did we
apprehend him*—Tw V 68. *This petty brabble will
undo us all*—Tit II 1 62.

BRABBLER

(1) A brawler, quarrelsome person: *We hold our
time too precious to be spent With such a brabbler*
—John V 2 161.

(2) A hound that gives tongue too freely; as
the name of a hound: *He will spend his mouth,
and promise, like Brabbler the hound*—Troil V 1
98.

BRACE

A piece of armour covering the arm: *' It hath
been a shield' Twixt me and death ;'—and pointed
to this brace*—Per II 1 132. Fig., state of defence:
It stands not in such warlike brace—Oth I 3 24.

BRACH

A female running hound: *I had rather hear
Lady, my brach, howl in Irish*—1 H4 III 1 240.
*When Lady the brach may stand by the fire and
stink*—Lr I 4 125.

BRAID (adj.)

App., deceitful: *Since Frenchmen are so braid,
Marry that will, I live and die a maid*—All's IV
2 73.

BRAID (vb.)

To upbraid, reproach: *'Twould braid yourself
too near for me to tell it*—Per I 1 93.

BRAIN

To conceive in the brain: *Such stuff as madmen
Tongue and brain not*—Cymb V 4 146.

BRAINISH

Headstrong, impetuous: *In this brainish apprehension*—Hml IV 1 11.

BRAVE (adj.)

(1) Of things, excellent, splendid, making a fine
show: *O brave new world!*—Tp V 183. *I'll
devise thee brave punishments for him*—Ado V 4
129. *Their brave pavilions*—Troil Prol 15. *This
brave o'erhanging firmament*—Hml II 2 312.
*When I do . . . see the brave day sunk in hideous
night*—Sonn 12 1.

(2) Of persons, goodly, gallant: *My brave spirit!*
—Tp I 2 206. *O, that's a brave man!*—As III
4 43. *My brave Egyptians all*—Ant III 13 164.
In fine array: *Enter Tranio brave*—Shr I 2 218
(Stage Dir.). App., defiant, warlike: *Is Lewis so
brave? belike he thinks me Henry*—3 H6 IV 1 96.
Are you so brave? I'll have you talked with anon
—Cor IV 5 18.

BRAVE (sb.)

A bravado: *There end thy brave*—John V 2 159.
This brave shall oft make thee to hide thy head—
Troil IV 4 139. *To bear me down with braves*—
Tit II 1 30.

BRAVE (vb.)

(1) To deck out, adorn: *Thou hast braved many
men*—Shr IV 3 125. *He (i.e. the sun) should have
braved the east an hour ago*—R3 V 3 279.

(2) To make a gay show: *Lucius and I'll go
brave it at the court*—Tit IV 1 121.

(3) To defy; *braving*, defying each other: *Enter Demetrius and Chiron, braving*—Tit II 1 25
(Stage Dir.).

BRAVELY

Excellently, capitally, in fine style: *Bravely the
figure of this harpy hast thou Perform'd*—Tp III
3 83. *The French are bravely in their battles set*
—H5 IV 3 69. *Here we may see most bravely*—
Troil I 2 198. *How bravely thou becomest thy bed*
—Cymb II 2 15.

BRAVERY

(1) Finery, splendour: *With scarfs and fans and
double change of bravery*—Shr IV 3 57. *Hiding
thy bravery in their rotten smoke*—Sonn 34 4.

(2) Ostentatious display: *They . . . come down With fearful bravery, thinking by this face To . . .* —Cæs V 1 8. *The bravery of his grief*—Hml V 2 79.

(3) Bravado: *Upon malicious bravery dost thou come To start my quiet*—Oth I 1 100.

(4) Defiance, power to defy: *The natural bravery of your isle*—Cymb III 1 18.

BRAVING

Defiant: *A braving war*—All's I 2 3. *In braving arms*—R2 II 3 112.

BRAWL (sb.)

A French dance resembling a cotillon: *Will you win your love with a French brawl?*—LLL III 8.

BRAWL (vb.)

As the times do brawl, in consequence of the brawls on foot—2 H4 I 3 70.

BRAWN

(1) The arm: *And in my vantbrace* [I'll] *put this wither'd brawn*—Troil I 3 297. *To hew thy target from thy brawn*—Cor IV 5 126. *The brawns of Hercules*—Cymb IV 2 311.

(2) A boar or swine fattened for the table; of persons: *That damned brawn shall play Dame Mortimer his wife*—1 H4 II 4 123. *Harry Monmouth's brawn, the hulk Sir John*—2 H4 I 1 19.

(3) *A brawn buttock*, a fleshy one: *A barber's chair that fits all buttocks . . . the brawn buttock, or any buttock*—All's II 2 17.

BREAK

(1) To disclose, communicate: *Break thy mind to me in broken English*—H5 V 2 265. *That made you break this enterprise to me*—Mcb I 7 48. *To break with* or *to* (a person), to make a disclosure or communication to (him): *I'll . . . Break with your wives of your departure hence*—1 H4 III 1 143. *Then after to her father will I break*—Ado I 1 328. But in Wiv III 2 57 *to break with* = to break one's word to.

(2) *To break up*, to carve: *Boyet, you can carve; Break up this capon*—LLL IV 1 55.

(3) *To break cross*, in tilting, to break the spear across the adversary's body and not by the push of the point: *Give him another staff; this last was broke cross*—Ado V 1 138. So *to break traverse*: *Swears brave oaths and breaks them bravely, quite traverse . . . as a puisny tilter . . . breaks his staff*—As III 4 44.

(4) To break off: *Break the parle*—Tit V 3 19. *Broken*, interrupted: *A broken banquet*—H8 I 4 61. *A single famish'd kiss, Distasted with the salt of broken tears*—Troil IV 4 49.

(5) *A broken mouth*, one that has lost some teeth: *I'ld give . . . My mouth no more were broken than these boys'*—All's II 3 65.

(6) To break up, be disbanded: *The army*

breaking, My husband hies him home—All's IV 4 11.

BREAST

Breath, voice in singing: *The fool has an excellent breast*—Tw II 3 19.

BREATH

Exercise (properly of the respiratory organs): *An after-dinner's breath*—Troil II 3 121. *The order of their fight . . . either to the uttermost, Or else a breath*—IV 5 90.

BREATHE

(1) To make a stay (in a place): *Here* (*i.e.* in Padua) *let us breathe and haply institute A course of learning*—Shr I 1 8. To delay: *We breathe too long*—1 H4 V 4 15. *Breathing*, delay: *You shake the head at so long a breathing*—Ado II 1 377. *After many accents and delays, Untimely breathings, sick and short assays*—Lucr 1719.

(2) To exercise oneself, take exercise: *Our gentry, who are sick For breathing and exploit*—All's I 2 16. *'Tis the breathing time of day with me*—Hml V 2 181. Refl.: *I think thou wast created for men to breathe themselves upon thee*—All's II 3 271.

(3) To endow with breath: *What . . . had my father lost, That need to be revived and breathed in me?*—2 H4 IV 1 113.

BREATHED

(1) Having long wind: *A man so breathed, that certain he would fight; yea From morn till night*—LLL V 2 659. *Breathed, as it were, To an untirable . . . goodness*—Tim I 1 10.

(2) In good wind, in full display of strength: *I am not yet well breathed*—As I 2 229. *As swift As breathed stags*—Shr Ind 2 49.

BREATHER

A living being, creature: *I will chide no breather in the world but myself*—As III 2 297. *A statue* [rather] *than a breather*—Ant III 3 24. *When all the breathers of this world are dead*—Sonn 81 12.

BRED OUT

Degenerated: *Our madams . . . plainly say Our mettle is bred out*—H5 III 5 28. *The strain of man's bred out Into baboon and monkey*—Tim I 1 259.

BREECH (sb.)

Breeches: *And ne'er have stol'n the breech from Lancaster*—3 H6 V 5 24.

BREECH (vb.)

To cover (as with breeches). Fig.: *Their daggers Unmannerly breech'd with gore*—Mcb II 3 121.

BREECHING

A breeching scholar, one still subject to the rod: *I am no breeching scholar in the schools*—Shr III 1 18.

BREED

Offspring, children: *And nothing 'gainst Time's scythe can make defence Save breed*—Sonn 12 13. Fig., of interest: *When did friendship take A breed for barren metal of his friend?*—Merch I 3 134.

BREED-BATE

A stirrer of strife: *No tell-tale nor no breed-bate* —Wiv I 4 12.

BREEDING

Parentage, extraction: *Your names, your ages, of what having, breeding . . . discover*—Wint IV 4 739. *Honest gentleman, I know not your breeding*—2 H4 V 3 111.

BREESE

The gadfly: *The herd hath more annoyance by the breese Than by the tiger*—Troil I 3 48. *The breese upon her, like a cow in June, Hoists sails and flies*—Ant III 10 14.

BRIBE BUCK

Venison given as a present to bespeak goodwill: *Divide me like a bribe buck, each a haunch*—Wiv V 5 27.

BRIDGE

They account his head upon the bridge—R3 III 2 72, the heads of traitors being exposed on old London Bridge.

BRIEF (adj.)

(1) Hasty, speedy, expeditious: *If you will live, lament; if die, be brief*—R3 II 2 43. Hect. *Nay, I have done already.* Achil. *Thou art too brief*— Troil IV 5 236. *Quickly send, Be brief in it, to the castle*—Lr V 3 243.

(2) Limited, restricted. *Postures beyond brief nature*—Cymb V 5 165.

(3) Calling for despatch: *A thousand businesses are brief in hand*—John IV 3 158.

(4) As quasi-adv., in few words, quickly: *It were a grief, so brief to part with thee*—Rom III 3 174. Briefly, in brief: *Brief, I recover'd him, bound up his wound*—As IV 3 151.

BRIEF (sb.)

(1) A letter: *Bear this sealed brief . . . to the lord marshal*—1 H4 IV 4 1.

(2) A short statement, an abstract: *A sweet verbal brief*—All's V 3 137. *The hand of time Shall draw this brief into as huge a volume*—John II 102.

(3) A list, inventory: *There is a brief how many sports are ripe*—Mids V 42. *This is the brief of money, plate, and jewels, I am possess'd of*—Ant V 2 138.

(4) *Expedient on the now-born brief*, perh., fitting in view of the occasion for despatch which now presents itself (cf. *Brief* (adj.) (3)): *This contract, whose ceremony Shall seem expedient on the now-born brief, And be perform'd to-night*—All's II 3 185.

BRIEFLY

(1) Lately: *Briefly we heard their drums*—Cor I 6 16.

(2) Quickly, soon: *Briefly die their joys That place them on the truth of girls and boys*—Cymb V 5 106. *Time that is so briefly spent*—Per III Prol 12. Forthwith: Ant. . . . *Go put on thy defences.* Eros. *Briefly, sir*—Ant IV 4 10.

BRIEFNESS

Quickness, celerity: *Briefness and fortune, work!* —Lr II 1 20. *In feather'd briefness sails are fill'd* —Per V 2 15. Shortness, summariness: *I hope the briefness of your answer made The speediness of your return*—Cymb II 4 30.

BRING

(1) To conduct, accompany: *Yet give leave, my lord, That we may bring you something on the way* —Meas I 1 61. *Let me bring thee to Staines*—H5 II 3 1. *Good even, Casca: brought you Cæsar home?*—Cæs I 3 1.

(2) To deduce, derive: *He From John of Gaunt doth bring his pedigree*—1 H6 II 5 76.

(3) To cause to come into a certain state: *A nurse's song Of lullaby to bring her babe asleep*— Tit II 3 28.

(4) *To bring out*, to put out, disconcert: *They do not mark me, and that brings me out*—LLL V 2 172. So *to bring out of tune*—As III 2 262.

(5) *To be with one to bring*, a cant expression, formerly common, the meaning of which is lost: Pan. *I'll be with you, niece, by and by.* Cres. *To bring, uncle?*—Troil I 2 304.

BRISK

Smartly dressed, spruce: *To see him shine so brisk and smell so sweet*—1 H4 I 3 54.

BROACH

To spit, transfix: *Bringing rebellion broached on his sword*—H5 V Chor 32. *I'll broach the tadpole on my rapier's point*—Tit IV 2 85.

BROAD

Widely diffused, spread all abroad: *As broad and general as the casing air*—Mcb III 4 23.

BROCK

A badger (of a person in disparagement): *Marry, hang thee, brock!*—Tw II 5 114.

BROKE

(1) To act as a go-between (in love affairs): *He . . . brokes with all that can in such a suit Corrupt the tender honour of a maid*—All's III 5 73.

(2) *Broking pawn*, the security held by a broker: *Redeem from broking pawn the blemish'd crown*—R2 II 1 293.

BROKEN MUSIC

Music arranged for different instruments, concerted music; referred to (with a play): *Is there any else longs to see this broken music in his sides?* —As I 2 149. *Come, your answer in broken music; for thy voice is music and thy English broken*—H5 V 2 262.

BROKER

(1) A go-between (in love affairs): *Now, by my modesty, a goodly broker!*—Gent I 2 41. *Do not believe his vows, for they are brokers*—Hml I 3 127. So *broker-between*: [Let] *all brokers-between* [be called] *Pandars!*—Troil III 2 211. *Broker-lackey*: Hence, *broker-lackey!*—V 10 33.

(2) An intermediary generally (with implied censure): *That broker (i.e. Commodity) that still breaks the pate of faith*—John II 568.

BROOCH (sb.)

Worn in a man's hat: *Saint George's half-cheek in a brooch . . . worn in the cap of a tooth-drawer* —LLL V 2 620.

BROOCH (vb.)

To adorn (as with a brooch): *Not the imperious show Of the full-fortuned Cæsar ever shall Be brooch'd with me*—Ant IV 15 23.

BROODED

Perh., having a brood (to watch over), or, brooding: *Then, in despite of brooded watchful day, I would into thy bosom pour my thoughts*—John III 3 52.

BROOK (sb.)

Flying at the brook, hawking for water-fowl: *For flying at the brook, I saw not better sport these seven years' day*—2 H6 II 1 1.

BROOK (vb.)

To be affected by a thing in a particular way: *This shadowy desert . . . I better brook than flourishing peopled towns*—Gent V 4 2. *How brooks your grace the air?*—R2 III 2 2.

BROWNIST

An adherent of the principles of Robert Brown, an English puritan and nonconformist: *I had as lief be a Brownist as a politician*—Tw III 2 33.

BRUIT

To announce by or with noise: *By this great clatter, one of greatest note Seems bruited*—Mcb V

7 21. *The king's rouse the heavens shall bruit again*—Hml I 2 127.

BRUSH

A hostile encounter; hence of hurtful effects in gen.: *Who in rage forgets Aged contusions and all brush of time*—2 H6 V 3 2.

BUBUKLE

A confusion of bubo, *i.e.* an inflamed abscess, and carbuncle: *His face is all bubukles, and whelks, and knobs*—H5 III 6 108.

BUCK

A quantity of clothes bucked at once (see *Bucking*): *She washes bucks here at home*—2 H6 IV 2 51.

BUCK-BASKET

A basket for clothes to be bucked (see *Bucking*): *They conveyed me into a buck-basket*—Wiv III 5 87. *This 'tis to have linen and buck-baskets!*—144.

BUCKING

The operation of steeping clothes in lye: *Throw foul linen upon him, as if it were going to bucking* —Wiv III 3 139.

BUCKLE

To buckle with, to close or grapple with (an adversary), engage (him): *In single combat thou shalt buckle with me*—1 H6 I 2 95. *All our general force Might with a sally of the very town Be buckled with*—IV 4 3. With cognate accus.: *I will not bandy with thee word for word, But buckle with thee blows, twice two for one*—3 H6 I 4 49.

BUCKLER

To give the bucklers, to yield the victory: *I give thee the bucklers*—Ado V 2 17.

BUCKLERSBURY

Many druggists dwelt here: *That . . . smell like Bucklersbury in simple time*—Wiv III 3 78.

BUCK OF THE FIRST HEAD

A male fallow deer in his fifth year: *I assure ye, it was a buck of the first head*—LLL IV 2 10.

BUCK-WASHING

The process of washing clothes by steeping them in lye and afterwards beating and rinsing them in clear water: *You were best meddle with buck-washing*—Wiv III 3 165.

BUDGET

A wallet, usually of leather: *If tinkers may have leave to live, And bear the sow-skin budget*—Wint IV 3 19.

BUFF

Buff-leather, a very stout kind of leather made of ox-hide; commonly worn by bailiffs and catch-poles: *A fellow all in buff* [hath him]—Err IV 2 36. *He's in a suit of buff which 'rested him*—45. App. of a prison dress: *Is not a buff jerkin a most sweet robe of durance?*—1 H4 I 2 48.

BUG

An object of terror, bogy: *Fear boys with bugs*—Shr I 2 211. *The bug which you would fright me with I seek*—Wint III 2 93. *With, ho! such bugs and goblins in my life*—Hml V 2 22.

BUGLE

A glass bead, usually black; attrib.: *Your bugle eyeballs*—As III 5 47. *Bugle bracelet*—Wint IV 4 224.

BUILDING

Style of construction, build: *I am a worthless boat, He of tall building and of goodly pride*—Sonn 80 11.

BULK¹

The bodily frame, body: *The envious flood . . . smother'd it* (*i.e.* his soul) *within my panting bulk*—R3 I 4 37. *Nature, crescent, does not grow alone In thews and bulk*—Hml I 3 11. *As it did seem to shatter all his bulk*—II 1 95. *May feel her heart . . . Beating her bulk*—Lucr 465.

BULK²

A framework projecting from the front of a shop: *Stalls, bulks, windows, Are smother'd up*—Cor II 1 226. *Here, stand behind this bulk*—Oth V 1 1.

BULLY

A fine fellow, jolly comrade: *My hand, bully*—Wiv II 1 225. *What sayest thou, bully Bottom?*—Mids III 1 8. *I love the lovely bully*—H5 IV 1 48.

BULLY-ROOK

The same as the foregoing: *What says my bully-rook?*—Wiv I 3 2. Cf. *Bully-monster*—Tp V 258.

BUM-BAILY

A contemptuous synonym of bailiff: *Scout me for him . . . like a bum-baily*—Tw III 4 193.

BUNCH-BACKED

Hump-backed: *That poisonous bunch-back'd toad*—R3 I 3 246. *That bottled spider, that foul bunch-back'd toad*—IV 4 81.

BUNG

A purse; hence app., a stealer of purses, a pick-pocket: *Away, you cut-purse rascal! you filthy bung, away!*—2 H4 II 4 137.

BUOY

To rise, swell: *The sea . . . would have buoy'd up, And quench'd the stelled fires*—Lr III 7 59.

BURDEN, BURTHEN

(1) An undersong, accompaniment: *Clap's into 'Light o' Love'; that goes without a burden*—Ado III 4 44. *I would sing my song without a burden: thou bringest me out of tune*—As III 2 261. So *burden-wise*: *Burden-wise I'll hum on Tarquin still*—Lucr 1133.
(2) A refrain, chorus: *Foot it featly here and there; And, sweet sprites, the burthen bear.* Burthen [dispersedly]. *Hark, Hark! . . .*—Tp I 2 380.

BURGONET

A kind of helmet: *And that I'll write upon thy burgonet*—2 H6 V 1 200. Fig.: *The demi-Atlas of this earth, the arm And burgonet of men*—Ant I 5 23.

BURST

To break: *You will not pay for the glasses you have burst?*—Shr Ind 1 7. *And then he burst his head for crowding among the marshal's men*—2 H4 III 2 347.

BURTHEN

See *Burden*.

BURTHENED

Imposed as a burden: *Now thy proud neck bears half my burthen'd yoke*—R3 IV 4 111.

BUSH

A branch of ivy as a vintner's sign: *Good wine needs no bush*—As Epil 3.

BUSKY

See *Bosky*.

BUSS (sb.)

A kiss, smack: *Thou dost give me flattering busses*—2 H4 II 4 291.

BUSS (vb.)

To kiss: *I will . . . buss thee as thy wife*—John III 4 34. Fig.: *Yond towers, whose wanton tops do buss the clouds*—Troil IV 5 220.

BUTCHERY

A slaughter-house: *This house is but a butchery*—As II 3 27.

BUTTERY

A place for storing liquor or provisions: *Go, sirrah, take them to the buttery*—Shr Ind 1 102.

BUTTERY-BAR

A ledge on the top of the buttery-hatch: *Bring your hand to the buttery-bar and let it drink*—Tw I 3 74.

BUTTON

A bud: *The canker galls the infants of the spring, Too oft before their buttons be disclosed*—Hml I 3 39.

BUTT-SHAFT

An unbarbed arrow for shooting at butts: *The blind bow-boy's butt-shaft*—Rom II 4 16.

BUXOM

(1) Lively, alert: *Bardolph, a soldier, firm and sound of heart, And of buxom valour*—H5 III 6 26.

(2) Either in this sense or in the usual modern sense, well-favoured, plump, comely: *A female heir, So buxom, blithe, and full of face, As . . .*—Per. Prol. 22.

BUY

The same as *Aby* (*q.v.*), of which it is prob. an aphetic form: *Thou shalt buy this dear*—Mids III 2 426.

BUZ

An interjection said to mean 'stale news': Pol. *The actors are come hither, my lord.* Ham. *Buz, buz!*—Hml II 2 411.

BUZZ

A groundless fancy, whim: *That, on every dream, Each buzz, each fancy . . . He may en-guard his dotage with their powers*—Lr I 4 347.

BUZZARD¹

A large moth or cockchafer: *Well ta'en, and like a buzzard*—Shr II 207.

BUZZARD²

An inferior kind of hawk, useless for falconry: *O slow-wing'd turtle! shall a buzzard take thee?*—Shr II 208 (in the next line, *Ay, for a turtle, as he takes a buzzard*, the sense is uncertain). *More pity that the eagle should be mew'd, While kites and buzzards prey at liberty*—R3 I 1 132.

BY

Of, with reference to, in the matter of: [She] *always hath been just and virtuous In any thing that I do know by her*—Ado V 1 312. *That 'many' may be meant By the fool multitude*—Merch II 9 25. *Opinion's but a fool, that makes us scan The outward habit by the inward man*—Per II 2 56.

BY AND BY

Straightway, directly. More or less of this (the older) sense may be seen in many passages, *e.g.*: *I'll be with her by and by; I'll but bring my young man here to school*—Wiv IV 1 7. May. *Sirrah, go fetch the beadle hither straight.* Glou. *Now fetch me a stool hither by and by*—2 H6 II 1 140. *Ay, by and by; But we will drink together*—Cor V 3 202. Nurse. *Madam!* Jul. *By and by, I come*—Rom II 2 151.

BY-DEPENDENCIES

Subsidiary details: *All the other by-dependencies, From chance to chance*—Cymb V 5 390.

BY-PEEP

To cast sidelong glances: *By-peeping in an eye Base and unlustrous as . . .*—Cymb I 6 108.

BY'R LAKIN

By our ladykin: *By'r lakin, I can go no further, sir*—Tp III 3 1. *By'r lakin, a parlous fear*—Mids III 1 14.

C

CABIN

To shut up as in a cabin, to confine within narrow and hampering bounds: *Cabin'd, cribb'd, confined, bound in*—Mcb III 4 24.

CACODEMON

An evil spirit: *Hie thee to hell . . . Thou caco-demon!*—R3 I 3 143.

CADDIS

A worsted tape used for garters, &c.: [He hath] *inkles, caddisses, cambrics, lawns*—Wint IV 4 208. Attrib.: *caddis-garter*—1 H4 II 4 79.

CADE

A cask, barrel: *Stealing a cade of herrings*—2 H6 IV 2 35.

CADENT

Falling: *With cadent tears fret channels in her cheeks*—Lr I 4 307.

CAGE

(1) A prison for petty malefactors: *His father had never a house but the cage*—2 H6 IV 2 56.

(2) Applied to a basket: *I must up-fill this osier cage of ours With . . .*—Rom II 3 7.

CAIN-COLOURED

Reddish-yellow, the traditional colour of Cain's beard: *A little yellow beard, a Cain-coloured beard*—Wiv I 4 23.

CAITIFF (adj.)

Wretched, miserable: *Here lives a caitiff wretch would sell it him*—Rom V 1 52.

CAITIFF (sb.)

A poor wretch, one in a piteous case: *A very caitiff crown'd with care*—R3 IV 4 100. Of an animal: *She finds a hound, And asks the weary caitiff for his master*—Ven 913. By way of endearment: *Alas, poor caitiff!*—Oth IV I 109 (said by Cassio of Bianca).

CALIPOLIS

A character in Peele's *Battle of Alcazar*: *Then feed, and be fat, my fair Calipolis*—2 H4 II 4 193. The line is a parody of lines in speeches of Muly Mahamet in Act II (vol. 2, pp. 109 and 110 of Dyce's 2d ed., 1829).

CALIVER

A light musket: *Such as fear the report of a caliver worse than a struck fowl*—1 H4 IV 2 20. *Put me a caliver into Wart's hand*—2 H4 III 2 289.

CALL (sb.)

A decoy-bird: *If but a dozen French Were there in arms, they would be as a call To train ten thousand English to their side*—John III 4 173.

CALL (vb.)

(1) To call upon, visit: *I'll call you at your house*—Meas IV 4 18. *We'll call thee at the cubiculo*—Tw III 2 56. *To call to*, in the same sense: Tim. . . . *I'll call to you.* All Lords. *O, none so welcome*—Tim I 2 223.

(2) *Call on him for it*, call him to account for it: *If he fill'd His vacancy with his voluptuousness, Full surfeits . . . Call on him for't*—Ant I 4 25.

CALLET

A lewd woman, trull: *A beggar in his drink Could not have laid such terms upon his callet*—Oth IV 2 120. As a (somewhat vague) term of abuse: *Contemptuous base-born callet as she is*—2 H6 I 3 86. Perh. = scold: *A callet Of boundless tongue*—Wint II 3 90. *A wisp of straw were worth a thousand crowns, To make this shameless callet know herself* (cf. *Wisp*)—3 H6 II 2 144.

CALLING

An appellation, name: *[I] would not change that calling, To be adopted heir to Frederick*—As I 2 246.

CALM

To becalm: *Like to a ship that . . . Is straightway calm'd*—2 H6 IV 9 32. Fig.: *And I . . . must be be-lee'd and calm'd By debitor and creditor*—Oth I 1 28.

CAMBYSES' VEIN

I must speak in passion, and I will do it in

King Cambyses' vein—1 H4 II 4 424. An allusion to the ranting hero of Thomas Preston's *Cambises King of Percia* (reprinted in Hazlitt's Dodsley, vol. 4).

CAMELOT

Often mentioned in the Arthurian romances: *Goose, if I had you upon Sarum plain, I'ld drive ye cackling home to Camelot*—Lr II 2 89. It has by some been identified with Cadbury in Somersetshire. The allusion has not been explained.

CAMLET

A garment of camlet, a light kind of cloth: *You i' the camlet, get up o' the rail*—H8 V 4 93.

CAMP

To serve as camp for, lodge: *Had our great palace the capacity To camp this host, we all would sup together*—Ant IV 8 32.

CAN¹

(1) To know: *[When] I ha' strew'd his grave, And on it said a century of prayers, Such as I can*—Cymb IV 2 390.

(2) To have skill: *They can well on horseback*—Hml IV 7 85. To have skill in (a thing): *The priest in surplice white, That defunctive music can*—Phœn 13.

CAN²

Gan, began; as a mere auxiliary = did: *Through the velvet leaves the wind, All unseen, can passage find*—LLL IV 3 105. *And every one with claps can sound, 'Our heir-apparent is a king!'*—Per III Prol 36. Cf. *Gin* (2).

CANARY (sb.)

(1) A lively Spanish dance: *A medicine That's able to breathe life into a stone . . . and make you dance canary*—All's II I 75.

(2) A light sweet wine from the Canary Islands: *I will to my honest knight Falstaff, and drink canary with him*—Wiv III 2 88. *O knight, thou lackest a cup of canary*—Tw I 3 85. In pl.: *You have drunk too much canaries*—2 H4 II 4 29.

CANARY (vb.)

To dance the canary: *To jig off a tune at the tongue's end, canary to it with your feet*—LLL III 11.

CANDLE-MINE

A mine of fat: *You whoreson candle-mine*—2 H4 II 4 326.

CANDLE-WASTER

One who consumes candles in late study: *Make misfortune drunk With candle-wasters*—Ado V 1 17.

CANDY

(1) To congeal: *Twenty consciences, That stand 'twixt me and Milan, candied be they And melt ere they molest!*—Tp II 1 278.

(2) *Candied*, incrusted with sugar; fig., sugared, honied: *Let the candied tongue lick absurd pomp*—Hml III 2 65. Covered (with ice): *The cold brook, Candied with ice*—Tim IV 3 225.

CANKER (sb.)

(1) A canker-worm: *Some to kill cankers in the musk-rose buds*—Mids II 2 3. *And loathsome canker lives in sweetest bud*—Sonn 35 4. Attrib.: *Now will canker sorrow eat my bud*—John III 4 82. *Full soon the canker death eats up that plant*—Rom II 3 30.

(2) A dog-rose: *I had rather be a canker in a hedge than a rose in his grace*—Ado I 3 28. *To put down Richard, that sweet lovely rose, And plant this thorn, this canker, Bolingbroke*—1 H4 I 3 175. So *canker-bloom: The canker-blooms have full as deep a dye As the perfumed tincture of the roses*—Sonn 54 5.

CANKER (vb.)

(1) To rust, tarnish: *Canker'd heaps of strange-achieved gold*—2 H4 IV 5 72. *Old partisans . . . Canker'd with peace*—Rom I 1 101.

(2) To become evil: *As with age his body uglier grows, So his mind cankers*—Tp IV 191. *Cankered*, corrupt, depraved: *I will fight Against my canker'd country*—Cor IV 5 96. Malignant, spiteful: *A canker'd grandam's will*—John II 194. *This ingrate and canker'd Bolingbroke*—1 H4 I 3 137. *To part your canker'd hate*—Rom I 1 102.

CANKER-BLOSSOM

A worm that eats away and destroys a blossom, a canker-worm: *You canker-blossom! You thief of love!*—Mids III 2 282.

CANONIZED

Prob., buried with canonical rites: *Thy canonized bones*—Hml I 4 47.

CANOPY

To bear the canopy, to render homage: *Were't aught to me I bore the canopy, With my extern the outward honouring*—Sonn 125 1.

CANSTICK

A candlestick: *I had rather hear a brazen canstick turn'd*—1 H4 III 1 131.

CANTLE

A segment cut out: *And cuts me from the best of all my land . . . a monstrous cantle out*—1 H4 III 1 99. A segment of a sphere: *The greater cantle of the world is lost With very ignorance*—Ant III 10 6.

CANTON

A song: [I would] *Write loyal cantons of contemned love*—Tw I 5 289.

CANVASS

To toss in a sheet in punishment or sport: *I'll canvass thee in thy broad cardinal's hat*—1 H6 I 3 36. Cf. Fal. *. . . I will toss the rogue in a blanket.* Dol. *. . . An thou dost, I'll canvass thee between a pair of sheets*—2 H4 II 4 240.

CANZONET

A short song: *Let me supervise the canzonet*—LLL IV 2 124.

CAPABLE

(1) Comprehensive: *A capable and wide revenge*—Oth III 3 459.

(2) *Capable of*, liable to be affected by, open to: *Heart too capable Of every line and trick of his sweet favour*—All's I 1 106. *You were advised his flesh was capable Of wounds*—2 H4 I 1 172. *Capable of our flesh*, subject to the temptations of the flesh—H8 V 3 11.

(3) Sentient: *His form and cause conjoin'd, preaching to stones, Would make them capable*—Hml III 4 126.

(4) Having legal capacity of inheritance: *Of my land . . . I'll work the means To make thee capable*—Lr II 1 85.

(5) Sensible, perceptible: *The cicatrice and capable impressure Thy palm some moment keeps*—As III 5 23.

CAP AND KNEE

With cap and knee, bareheaded and bowing or kneeling: *The more and less came in with cap and knee*—1 H4 IV 3 68. Cf. *Cap and knee slaves*—Tim III 6 107. *Give them title, knee and approbation*—IV 3 36.

CAP-A-PE

From head to foot: *I am courtier cap-a-pe*—Wint IV 4 760. *Armed at point exactly, cap-a-pe*—Hml I 2 200.

CAPE

A neck-band or collar: *A small compassed cape*—Shr IV 3 140. *Will you buy any . . . lace for your cape?*—Wint IV 4 322.

CAPITAL

Deadly, fatal: *To poor we Thine enmity's most capital*—Cor V 3 103.

CAPITE

To hold in capite, to hold (lands) immediately of the crown: *Men shall hold of me in capite*—2 H6 IV 7 131.

CAPITULATE

To draw up articles of agreement, arrange terms, treat: *Percy, Northumberland . . . Capitulate against us and are up*—1 H4 III 2 118. *Do not bid me . . . capitulate Again with Rome's mechanics*—Cor V 3 81.

CAPOCCHIA

Italian; fem. of *capocchio*, silly, simple: *Alas, poor wretch! ah, poor capocchia!*—Troil IV 2 32.

CAPON

A billet-doux: *Boyet, you can carve; Break up this capon*—LLL IV 1 55.

CAPRICCIO

A caprice: *Will this capriccio hold in thee?*—All's II 3 310.

CAPRICIOUS

Displaying wit or fancy: *I am here with thee and thy goats, as the most capricious poet, honest Ovid, was among the Goths*—As III 3 7 (with a play on Lat. *caper*, a goat).

CAPTAIN

As adj., chief, predominant: *Captain jewels in the carcanet*—Sonn 52 8. *Captive good attending captain ill*—66 12.

CAPTIOUS

Capacious: *This captious and intenible sieve*—All's I 3 208.

CAPTIVATE

To make captive, take prisoner: *Thou hast Wasted our country . . . And sent our sons and husbands captivate*—1 H6 II 3 40. *Their woes whom fortune captivates*—5 H6 I 4 115. To hold captive: *Thou wert immured, restrained, captivated, bound*—LLL III 1 125.

CAPTIVE

To make captive: *And all our princes captived*—H5 II 4 55.

CARACK

A large ship, a galleon: *Whole armadoes of caracks*—Err III 2 140. *He to-night hath boarded a land carack*—Oth I 2 50.

CARAT

Worth, estimate (by confusion with Caract, Character): *Other [gold], less fine in carat, is more precious*—2 H4 IV 5 162.

CARAWAY

A sweetmeat containing caraway-seeds: *A dish of caraways*—2 H4 V 3 3.

CARBONADO (sb.)

A piece of flesh scored across and grilled on the coals: *If I come in his [way] willingly, let him make a carbonado of me*—1 H4 V 3 60. *He scotched him and notched him like a carbonado*—Cor IV 5 198.

CARBONADO (vb.)

To make a carbonado of: *It is your carbonadoed face*—All's IV 5 107. *How she longed to eat adders' heads and toads carbonadoed*—Wint IV 4 267. *Draw, you rogue, or I'll so carbonado your shanks*—Lr II 2 40.

CARCANET

A necklace; *To see the making of her carcanet*—Err III 1 4. *Captain jewels in the carcanet*—Sonn 52 8.

CARD (sb.)

(1) A map or plan: *The card or calendar of gentry*—Hml V 2 114.

(2) The face of a compass: *All the quarters that they* (*i.e.* the winds) *know I' the shipman's card*—Mcb I 3 16. Fig., *to speak by the card*, to speak with precision: *We must speak by the card, or equivocation will undo us*—Hml V 1 148.

(3) *A card of ten*, one with ten pips; fig., from its function in some game, *to face it with a card of ten*, to bluff, put on a bold front: *Yet I have faced it with a card of ten*—Shr II 407. See *Face* (2).

(4) *A cooling card*, a term of some game, applied to anything that cools or dashes one's hopes: *There all is marr'd; there lies a cooling card*—1 H6 V 3 83.

CARD (vb.)

To stir together, mix; fig.: *Carded his state, Mingled his royalty with capering fools*—1 H4 III 2 62.

CARD-MAKER

A maker of cards for combing wool: *By birth a pedlar, by education a card-maker*—Shr Ind 2 20.

CARDUUS BENEDICTUS

Blessed or holy thistle: *Get you some of this distilled Carduus Benedictus, and lay it to your heart*—Ado III 4 73.

CARE

(1) With inf., to be solicitous or anxious: *Those that care to keep your royal person*—2 H6 III 1 173.

(2) To be careful, take measures: *What was first but fear what might be done, Grows elder now and cares it be not done*—Per I 2 14.

CAREER, CAREIRE

(1) A short gallop at full speed: *Full merrily Hath this brave manage, this career, been run*—LLL V 2 481. *To pass a career*, to run one's course: *And so conclusions passed the careires*—Wiv I 1 184 (a phrase intentionally obscure).

(2) A charge or encounter (at a tournament): *I shall meet your wit in the career, an you charge it against me*—Ado V 1 135. *If misfortune miss the first career*—R2 I 2 49.

(3) The short turning of a nimble horse to and fro; hence, a frisk, gambol: *He passes some humours and careers*—H5 II 1 132.

CAREFUL

Full of care, anxious, concerned: *Careful wives* —H5 IV 1 248. *Is not careful what they mean thereby*—Tit IV 4 84. Of things, fraught or attended with care: *Careful hours*—Err V 298. *Careful business* — R2 II 2 75. *This careful height*—R2 I 3 83.

CAREIRE

See *Career.*

CARELESS

(1) Free from care: *Sleep she as sound as careless infancy*—Wiv V 5 56. *The light and careless livery that it (i.e. youth) wears*—Hml IV 7 80.

(2) Uncared for: *A careless trifle*—Mcb I 4 11.

CARL

A peasant: *Could this carl . . . have subdued me In my profession?*—Cymb V 2 4.

CARLOT

The same as the foregoing; prob. specifically, a churlish fellow, a niggard: *The cottage and the bounds That the old carlot once was master of*— As III 5 107 (cf. the description of him, II 4 80).

CARNAL

Carnivorous; hence, bloody, cruel: *This carnal cur*—R3 IV 4 56. *Carnal, bloody, and unnatural acts*—Hml V 2 392.

CAROUSE

A full bumper: *And quaff carouses to our mistress' health*—Shr I 2 277. *And drink carouses to the next day's fate*—Ant IV 8 34.

CARPET

A table-cloth: *Be the jacks fair within, the jills fair without, the carpets laid, and every thing in order?*—Shr IV 1 51.

CARPET CONSIDERATION

Dubbed on carpet consideration, of a knight distinguished in the lady's chamber rather than in the field: *Dubbed with unhatched rapier and on carpet consideration*—Tw III 4 257.

CARPET-MONGER

A frequenter of ladies' chambers: *A whole bookful of these quondam carpet-mongers*—Ado V 2 32.

CARRIAGE

(1) Capacity for carrying: *Samson, master: he was a man of good carriage, great carriage*— LLL I 2 73.

(2) A burden, load: *Time Goes upright with his carriage*—Tp V 2. Perh. also: *Many carriages he hath dispatch'd To the sea-side*—John V 7 90.

(3) Import, purport: *[The] carriage of the article design'd*—Hml I 1 94.

(4) Deportment, behaviour: *Teach sin the carriage of a holy saint*—Err III 2 14. *Let them be men of good repute and carriage*—LLL I 2 71.

(5) Management, conduct: *The violent carriage of it Will clear or end the business*—Wint III 1 17. *The passage and whole carriage of this action*— Troil II 3 140.

CARRY

(1) To manage, conduct: *This well carried shall on her behalf Change slander to remorse*— Ado IV 1 212. *This sport, well carried, shall be chronicled*—Mids III 2 240. *To carry it,* to conduct matters, act: *We may carry it thus, for our pleasure and his penance, till . . .*—Tw III 4 150. *What a full fortune does the thick-lips owe, If he can carry 't thus!*—Oth I 1 66.

(2) *To carry coals,* to do degrading work, to submit to insult: *I knew by that piece of service the men would carry coals*—H5 III 2 49. *Gregory, o' my word, we'll not carry coals*—Rom I 1 1. *To carry crochets,* in a similar sense: *I will carry no crotchets*—Rom IV 5 120.

(3) *To carry out one's side,* to win one's game as at cards: *Hardly shall I carry out my side, Her husband being alive*—Lr V 1 61.

CART (sb.)

A chariot, car: *Full thirty times hath Phœbus' cart gone round Neptune's salt wash . . .*—Hml III 2 165.

CART (vb.)

To expose in a cart by way of punishment: *To cart her rather: she's too rough for me*—Shr I 1 55.

CARVE

(1) To show courtesy and affability: *I spy entertainment in her; she discourses, she carves, she . . .* —Wiv I 3 48. *A can carve too, and lisp*—LLL V 2 323.

(2) *To carve for,* to indulge, gratify: *He may not . . . Carve for himself*—Hml I 3 19. *He that stirs next to carve for his own rage Holds his soul light*—Oth II 3 173.

CASE (sb.)[1]

(1) The skin: *When time hath sow'd a grizzle on thy case*—Tw V 168. With a play: *Though*

my case be a pitiful one, I hope I shall not be flayed out of it—Wint IV 4 843.

(2) Applied to dress: *O place, O form, How often dost thou with thy case, thy habit, Wrench awe from fools*—Meas II 4 12. And, app., to something adventitious: *Accomplish'd in himself, not in his case*—Compl 116.

(3) An outer protective or covering part; hence the covering of the eye, the eyelid: *They seemed almost, with staring on one another, to tear the cases of their eyes*—Wint V 2 12. *Lear. Read. Glou. What, with the case of eyes?*—Lr IV 6 146. Cf. *Behold, Her eyelids, cases to those heavenly jewels . . . Begin to part their fringes of bright gold*—Per III 2 98.

(4) A set of things: *I have not a case of lives*—H5 III 2 4.

CASE (sb.)²

(1) *In case to*, in a condition to (do something): *I am in case to justle a constable*—Tp III 2 28.

(2) *If case* [be that], if it should happen that, if perchance: *If case some one of you would fly from us*—3 H6 V 4 34.

CASE (vb.)

To skin: *We'll make you some sport with the fox ere we case him*—All's III 6 110.

CASHIERED

In Wiv I 1 183 (*And being fap, sir, was, as they say, cashiered*) Bardolph seems to mean, relieved of his cash.

CASK

A casket: *A jewel, lock'd into the wofull'st cask That ever did contain a thing of worth*—2 H6 III 2 409.

CASQUE

A helmet: *Let thy blows . . . Fall like amazing thunder on the casque Of . . .*—R2 I 3 80. *The very casques That did affright the air at Agincourt*—H5 Prol 13. *Were it a casque composed by Vulcan's skill*—Troil V 2 170.

CASSOCK

A soldier's cloak: *Half of the which dare not shake the snow from off their cassocks, lest . . .*—All's IV 3 190.

CAST (sb.)

A tinge, hue: *Sicklied o'er with the pale cast of thought*—Hml III 1 85.

CAST (vb.)

(1) To throw off, discard: *A pair of cast lips of Diana*—As III 4 16.

(2) To shed in process of growth: *Your colt's tooth is not cast yet*—H8 1 3 48.

(3) To dismiss: *Our general cast us thus early for the love of his Desdemona*—Oth II 3 14. To dismiss from service: *The state . . . Cannot with safety cast him*—Oth I 1 148. *You are but now cast in his mood*—II 3 273.

(4) To reckon, calculate, estimate: *You cast the event of war . . . before you said . . .*—2 H4 I 1 166. *It is as proper to our age To cast beyond ourselves in our opinions As . . .*—Hml II 1 114.

(5) *To cast water*, to diagnose disease by inspection of the water: *If thou couldst, doctor, cast The water of my land, find her disease*—Mcb V 3 50.

(6) *To cast filth*, of a hawk when dosed with 'castings' (*i.e.* fur or feathers given with her food) after confinement to purge her of grease; fig.: *His filth within being cast, he would appear A pond as deep as hell*—Meas III 1 93.

(7) *To cast oneself in wonder*, to throw oneself into wonder as into a garment: *You look pale and gaze And put on fear and cast yourself in wonder*—Cæs I 3 59. Cf. Wint I 2 326 quoted under *Appoint* (3).

CASTLE

Explained as meaning a helmet: *Rear'd aloft the bloody battle-axe, Writing destruction on the enemy's castle*—Tit III 1 169.

CASUAL

Subject to chance or accident: *The one is but frail and the other casual*—Cymb I 4 99.

CASUALLY

Too casually, through blameworthy exposure to the risks of accident: *A jewel that too casually Hath left mine arm*—Cymb II 3 146.

CAT

(1) App., the wild cat: *Be it ounce, or cat, or bear, Pard, or boar with bristled hair*—Mids II 2 30 (but the word was in Shakespeare's time, as it still is, extended to the members of the genus *Felis* generally).

(2) The civet-cat: *Civet is . . . the very uncleanly flux of a cat*—As III 2 69. *Thou owest . . . the cat no perfume*—Lr III 4 108.

CATAIAN

A Chinese, disparagingly: *I will not believe such a Cataian*—Wiv II 1 148. *My lady's a Cataian*—Tw II 3 80.

CATARACT

A waterspout (hardly to be distinguished from *Hurricano*): *You cataracts and hurricanoes, spout*—Lr III 2 2.

CATASTROPHE

Humorously, the posteriors: *I'll tickle your catastrophe*—2 H4 II 1 66.

CATER-COUSINS

Persons on terms of intimate friendship; perh. so called from being catered for together: *His master and he . . . are scarce cater-cousins*—Merch II 2 138.

CATLING

A piece of catgut: *Unless the fiddler Apollo get his sinews to make catlings on*—Troil III 3 305. As proper name—Rom IV 5 132.

CAT O' MOUNTAIN, CAT-A-MOUN-TAIN

Applied vaguely to various feline beasts: *More pinch-spotted make them Than pard or cat o' moun-tain*—Tp IV 261. Attrib.: *Your cat-a-mountain looks*—Wiv II 2 27.

CAUSE

(1) A matter, affair: *The extreme parts of time extremely forms All causes to the purpose of his speed*—LLL V 2 750. *All your just proceedings in this cause*—R3 III 5 66. *Sith I am enter'd in this cause so far . . . I will go on*—Oth III 3 411. An affair to be decided: *What counsel give you in this weighty cause?*—2 H6 III 1 289. A charge, accusation: *I pardon that man's life. What was thy cause?*—Lr IV 6 111. App., dispute, argument: *O madness of discourse, That cause sets up with and against itself!*—Troil V 2 142.

(2) Disease, sickness: *Hearing your high majesty is touch'd With that malignant cause*—All's II 1 113. *Leave us to cure this cause*—Cor III 1 235.

(3) *The first and second cause*: *The first and second cause will not serve my turn*—LLL I 2 183. *A gentleman . . . of the first and second cause*—Rom II 4 25. For this see As V 4 51 and foll.

CAUTEL

A crafty device, artifice: *Now no soil nor cautel doth besmirch The virtue of his will*—Hml I 3 15. *A plenitude of subtle matter, Applied to cautels*—Compl 302.

CAUTELOUS

(1) Deceitful, crafty: *Cautelous baits and prac-tice*—Cor IV 1 33.

(2) Cautious, circumspect: *Swear priests and cowards and men cautelous*—Cæs II 1 129.

CAVALERO, CAVALEIRO

A roistering fellow, a jolly companion: *I'll drink to . . . all the cavaleros about London*—2 H4 V 3 61. Sim. *Cavaleiro-justice*—Wiv II 1 201.

CEASE (sb.)

Ceasing, extinction: *The cease of majesty Dies not alone*—Hml III 3 15.

CEASE (vb.)

(1) To put a stop to, stop: *Heaven cease this idle humour in your honour!*—Shr Ind 2 14. *Let the general trumpet blow his blast, Particu-larities and petty sounds To cease!*—2 H6 V 2 43. To stop an agent's action, silence him: *Be not ceased With slight denial*—Tim II 1 16.

(2) To cease to exist, fail, pass away: *Both (i.e. her age and honour) shall cease, without your remedy*—All's V 3 164. *Things at the worst will cease*—Mcb IV 2 24. *Fall, and cease!*—Lr V 3 264. *If all were minded so, the times should cease*—Sonn 11 7.

CENSER

A vessel for burning perfumes. In Shr IV 3 90 (*Snip and nip . . . Like to a censer in a barber's shop*) and 2 H4 V 4 20 (*You thin man in a censer*) allusions have been seen to its perforated lid and to thin embossed figures thereon.

CENSURE (sb.)

(1) Judicial sentence: *Content To suffer lawful censure for such faults As shall be proved upon you*—Cor III 3 45. *The censure of this hellish villain*—Oth V 2 368.

(2) Opinion, judgement: *Betray themselves to every modern censure worse than drunkards*—As IV 1 6. *Will you go To give your censures in this weighty business?*—R3 II 2 143. *Take each man's censure, but reserve thy judgement*—Hml I 3 69. *Your name is great In mouths of wisest censure*—Oth II 3 192.

CENSURE (vb.)

(1) To pronounce judicial sentence on: *Has censured him Already*—Meas I 4 72. *Until their greater pleasures first be known That are to cen-sure them*—Lr V 3 2.

(2) To judge, estimate: *Whose equality By our best eyes cannot be censured*—John II 327. *Cen-sure me in your wisdom*—Cæs III 2 16. *How . . . I may be censured . . . something fears me to think of*—Lr III 5 3. *To censure on*, to express one's opinion of: *'Tis a passing shame That I . . . Should censure thus on lovely gentlemen*—Gent I 2 17.

CENTRE

The centre of the earth: *I will find Where truth is hid, though it were hid indeed Within the centre*—Hml II 2 157. The earth itself (as the supposed centre of the universe): *The centre is not big enough to bear A school-boy's top*—Wint II 1 102. *The heavens themselves, the planets and this centre*—Troil I 3 85.

CENTURY

A body of a hundred men: *Dispatch Those cen-turies to our aid*—Cor I 7 2. *A century send forth*—Lr IV 4 6. Loosely of an indefinite number of things: *A century of prayers*—Cymb IV 2 391.

CERECLOTH

A waxed winding-sheet, a winding-sheet in gen.: *It were too gross To rib her cerecloth in the obscure grave*—Merch II 7 50.

CEREMENTS

Waxed grave-clothes, grave-clothes in gen.: *Why thy canonized bones . . . Have burst their cerements*—Hml I 4 47.

CEREMONY

(1) Ceremonial display, pomp: *What have kings, that privates have not too, Save ceremony*—H5 IV 1 255, and *passim* in the speech.

(2) An accessory or symbol of worship or pomp: *No ceremony that to great ones longs, Not the king's crown, nor . . .*—Meas II 2 59. *Disrobe the images, If you do find them deck'd with ceremonies*—Cæs I 1 69. A sacred emblem: *The thing held as a ceremony*—Merch V 206.

(3) A portent, omen (prob. originally drawn from the performance of a rite): *Of fantasy, of dreams and ceremonies*—Cæs II 1 197. *I never stood on ceremonies, Yet now they fright me*—II 2 13.

CERTES

Certainly; dissyll.: *For, certes, these are people of the island*—Tp III 3 30. Monosyll.: *One, certes, that promises no element In such a business*—H8 I 1 48.

CESS

Assessment, estimation; *out of all cess*, excessively: *Poor jade, is wrung in the withers out of all cess*—1 H4 II 1 7.

CESSE

Cease: *Ere they meet, in me, O nature, cesse!*—All's V 3 72.

CHACE

In tennis applied to the second impact of a ball not returned by the opponent: *All the courts of France will be disturb'd With chaces*—H5 I 2 265.

CHAFE

Heat of temper, anger: *How this Herculean Roman does become The carriage of his chafe*—Ant I 3 84.

CHAIN

To embrace, enclasp: *O thou day o' the world, Chain mine arm'd neck*—Ant IV 8 13.

CHAIR

A pulpit: *Hath not a tomb so evident as a chair To extol what it hath done*—Cor IV 7 52. Applied to the Roman *rostra*: *Let him go up into the public chair*—Cæs III 2 68.

CHALICE

A drinking-cup, goblet: *Take away these chalices*—Wiv III 5 29. *Commends the ingredients of our poison'd chalice To our own lips*—Mcb I 7 11.

CHALICED

Having a cup-shaped blossom: *Those springs On chaliced flowers that lies*—Cymb II 3 24.

CHALLENGE (sb.)

A claim: *Accept the title thou usurp'st . . . not of any challenge of desert*—1 H6 V 4 151.

CHALLENGE (vb.)

(1) To accuse: *Dishonour'd thus, and challenged of wrongs*—Tit I 340. To find fault with, reprehend: *Who may I rather challenge for unkindness Than pity for mischance*—Mcb III 4 42.

(2) To claim: *I am a subject, And I challenge law*—R2 II 3 133. *Where nature doth with merit challenge*—Lr I 1 54. *These white flakes Had challenged pity of them*—IV 7 30. *So much I challenge that I may profess Due to the Moor my lord*—Oth I 3 188.

CHALLENGER

A claimant: *The native and true challenger*—H5 II 4 95.

CHAM

The Khan of Tartary, or perh., the Emperor of China: [I will] *fetch you a hair off the great Cham's beard*—Ado II 1 276.

CHAMBER

(1) A small cannon (properly a small piece without a carriage used to fire salutes): *To venture upon the charged chambers bravely*—2 H4 II 4 56. *Alarum, and chambers go off*—H5 III Chor 33 (Stage Dir.)

(2) A capital, royal residence: *Welcome, sweet prince, to London, to your chamber*—R3 III 1 1.

CHAMBERER

A frequenter of ladies' chambers: *Those soft parts of conversation That chamberers have*—Oth III 3 264.

CHAMBER-LIE

Urine: *Your chamber-lie breeds fleas like a loach*—1 H4 II 1 23.

CHAMPAIN

Champaign; open country, a plain: *Daylight and champain discovers not more*—Tw II 5 174. *With shadowy forests and with champains rich'd*—Lr I 1 65.

CHAMPION

To challenge to a contest: *Come fate into the list, And champion me to the utterance!*—Mcb III 1 71.

CHANCE

(1) An event: *All the other by-dependencies, From chance to chance*—Cymb V 5 390. A mishap, mischance: *What chance is this that suddenly hath cross'd us?*—1 H6 I 4 72. *Had I but died an hour before this chance, I had lived a blessed time*—Mcb II 3 96.

(2) One's hap, fortune: *If it be thy chance to kill me*—Tw III 4 177. *I'll yet follow The wounded chance of Antony*—Ant III 10 35.

(3) *On what a chance*, with what (fair) prospects: *Think what a chance thou changest on*—Cymb I 5 68.

CHANGE (sb.)

(1) Prob., a round in dancing: *In our measure do but vouchsafe one change*—LLL V 2 209.

(2) Exchange: *Maintain'd the change of words with any creature*—Ado IV 1 185. *He that I gave it to in change promised to wear it in his cap*—H5 IV 8 30.

(3) Changefulness, fickleness, a caprice: *You see how full of changes his age is*—Lr I 1 291. *A woman's gentle heart, but not acquainted With shifting change*—Sonn 20 3.

(4) In music, variation, modulation: *Hark, what fine change is in the music!*—Gent IV 2 68.

(5) *Change of honours*, fresh honours: *From whom I have received not only greetings, But with them change of honours*—Cor II 1 213.

(6) *In one's own change*, app., by a change in one's conduct or in his disposition towards another: *Your master, Pindarus, In his own change, or by ill officers, Hath given me some worthy cause . . .*—Cæs IV 2 6.

CHANGE (vb.)

To exchange: *What we changed Was innocence for innocence*—Wint I 2 68. *I'll change that name with you*—Hml I 2 163. *Then I scorn to change my state with kings*—Sonn 29 14.

CHANGEABLE

Changing-coloured, shot: *The tailor make thy doublet of changeable taffeta*—Tw II 4 76.

CHANGELING

(1) An inconstant person, swerver: *Fickle changelings and poor discontents*—1 H4 V 1 76. *His nature In that's no changeling*—Cor IV 7 10.

(2) A child taken by fairies in exchange for one surreptitiously substituted (elsewhere applied to the child substituted): *She (i.e.* Titania) *never had so sweet a changeling*—Mids II 1 23. Attrib.: *I do but beg a little changeling boy*—120. *I then did ask of her her changeling child*—IV 1 62.

CHANNEL

A kennel, gutter: *Throw the quean in the channel*—2 H4 II 1 51. *As if a channel should be call'd the sea*—3 H6 II 2 141.

CHANSON

A song: *The first row of the pious chanson will show you more*—Hml II 2 438.

CHAPE

The metal plate covering the point of a scabbard, or perh., the scabbard itself: *That had . . . the practice* [of war] *in the chape of his dagger*—All's IV 3 162.

CHAPELESS

Without a chape: *An old rusty sword . . . with a broken hilt, and chapeless*—Shr III 2 46 (the scabbard itself seems here to be referred to).

CHAPLESS

Without the lower jaw: *Yellow chapless skulls*—Rom IV 1 83. *Chapless, and knocked about the mazzard with a sexton's spade*—Hml V 1 97.

CHAPMAN

(1) A merchant, trader: *Not utter'd by base sale of chapmen's tongues*—LLL II 16.

(2) A customer, purchaser: *You do as chapmen do, Dispraise the thing that you desire to buy*—Troil IV 1 75.

CHARACT

A distinctive mark: *All his dressings, characts, titles, forms*—Meas V 56.

CHARACTER (sb.)

(1) A figure, numeral: *Whose grossness little characters sum up*—Troil I 3 325.

(2) Writing: *There is a kind of character in thy life*—Meas I 1 28. *With character too gross*—I 2 159. Something written: *Blossom, speed thee well! There lie, and there thy character*—Wint III 3 46. *The character I'll take with wax*—Tim V 3 6. One's handwriting: *'Tis Hamlet's character*—Hml IV 7 52. *You know the character to be your brother's?*—Lr I 2 66. So in pl.: *Learn'd indeed were that astronomer That knew the stars as I his characters*—Cymb III 2 27.

(3) The face or features, personal appearance: *Thy fair and outward character*—Tw I 2 51.

(4) *In the character*, as he really is: *I paint him in the character*—Cor V 4 28.

CHARACTER (vb.)

To write: *In their barks my thoughts I'll character*—As III 2 6. *These few precepts in thy memory See thou character*—Hml I 3 58. *Charac'd in my brow, The story . . .*—Lucr 807.

CHARACTERLESS

Unrecorded; or perh., featureless: [When] *mighty states characterless are grated To dusty nothing*—Troil III 2 195.

CHARACTERY

Symbols used in writing collectively: *Fairies use flowers for their charactery*—Wiv V 5 77. That which is written: *All the charactery of my sad brows*—Cæs II 1 308.

CHARGE (sb.)

(1) Importance, moment: *Many parcels of charge*—Wint IV 4 261. *The letter was not nice but full of charge*—Rom V 2 18. *Many such-like 'As'es of great charge* — Hml V 2 43 (with a play on the sense load).

(2) Expense, cost: *This expedition's charge*—John I 49. *These great affairs do ask some charge*—R2 II 1 159. *Answering us With our own charge*—Cor V 6 67. *A charge we bear i' the war*—Ant III 7 17. So in pl.: *The charges of the action*—Cor V 6 79. *To be at charges for*, to lay out the cost of: *I'll be at charges for a looking-glass*—R3 I 2 256.

(3) A military command: *I'll procure this fat rogue a charge of foot*—1 H4 II 4 596. So the troops under one's command: *My whole charge consists of ancients, corporals . . .*—1 H4 IV 2 25. *Bid our commanders lead their charges off*—Cæs IV 2 48.

(4) *In charge*, of a weapon, in position for action: *Their armed staves in charge*—2 H4 IV 1 120.

CHARGE (vb.)

(1) To oppress, burden, weigh down: *Nicely charge your understanding soul*—H5 I 2 15. *The heart is sorely charged*—Mcb V 1 59. *If sleep charge nature*—Cymb III 4 44. *It charges me*, it is incumbent on me: *It charges me in manners the rather to express myself*—Tw II 1 15.

(2) To put to expense: *I sue for* [your acquaintance]; *not to charge you*—Wiv II 2 170.

(3) *To charge to an answer*, to call upon to answer: *Thou canst not, cardinal, devise a name So slight . . . To charge me to an answer, as the pope*—John III 1 149. *To charge upon interrogatories*, in the language of Queen's Bench practice, to cause a person to swear that he will answer certain questions truly: *Let us go in; And charge us there upon inter'gatories, And we will answer all things faithfully*—Merch V 297.

(4) To put (a weapon) in position for action: *I shall meet your wit in the career, an you charge it against me*—Ado V 1 135. *What are they That charge their breath against us?*—LLL V 2 87.

CHARGEFUL

Expensive, costly: *The fineness of the gold and chargeful fashion*—Err IV 1 29.

CHARGE-HOUSE

A school, app. as being a house for the charge of youth: *Do you not educate youth at the charge-house on the top of the mountain?*—LLL V 1 86.

CHARINESS

Carefully preserved state, scrupulous integrity: *Any villany against him, that may not sully the chariness of our honesty*—Wiv II 1 101.

CHARM

(1) To entreat, conjure: *I charm you, by my once-commended beauty*—Cæs II 1 271.

(2) To produce as by a charm: *Music, such as charmeth sleep*—Mids IV 1 86.

(3) To appease, silence; esp. of the tongue: *Therefore shall it charm thy riotous tongue*—2 H6 IV 1 64. *Go to, charm your tongue*—Oth V 2 183.

CHARNECO

A kind of wine, prob. Portuguese: *Here's a cup of charneco*—2 H6 II 3 62.

CHARTREUX

A monk of the Chartreux, a Carthusian monk: Bran. *A monk o' the Chartreux.* Buck. *O, Nicholas Hopkins?* Bran. *He*—H8 I 1 221. So *a Chartreux friar*: *A Chartreux friar, His confessor*—H8 I 2 148.

CHAT

To talk about: *While she chats him*—Cor II 1 224.

CHAUDRON

The entrails of a beast: *Add thereto a tiger's chaudron*—Mcb IV 1 33.

CHEAP

Bargain, purchase; *good cheap*, cheaply: *Would have bought me lights as good cheap at the dearest chandler's in Europe*—1 H4 III 3 51.

CHEAPEN

To bargain for, make an offer for: *Virtuous, or I'll never cheapen her*—Ado II 3 33. *If he should cheapen a kiss of her*—Per IV 6 10.

CHEAT

In thieves' cant used in general sense 'thing', 'article', usually preceded by a descriptive word. Thus *a smelling cheat* was the nose, *a grunting cheat* a pig; and in Wint IV 3 28 (*My revenue is the silly cheat*) a *silly cheat* is a dupe.

CHEATER

(1) Escheator; an officer who looked after the king's escheats: *I will be cheater to them both, and they shall be exchequers to me*—Wiv I 3 77. *I play'd the cheater for thy father's hand*—Tit V 1 111. *Gentle cheater, urge not my amiss*—Sonn 151 3. (In all the cases with a play.)

(2) A dishonest gamester, a sharper: *Disguised cheaters, prating mountebanks*—Err I 2 101. *Thou abominable damned cheater*—2 H4 II 4 151. *A*

tame cheater, perh., in thieves' cant, a decoy: *He's no swaggerer, hostess; a tame cheater, i' faith—* 2 H4 II 4 105.

CHECK (sb.)

A reproof, reprimand: *You might keep that check for it till . . .*—As IV 1 169. *Worthy shameful check*—Ant IV 4 31.

CHECK (vb.)

(1) To reprove, reprimand: *Be check'd for silence, But never tax'd for speech*—All's I 1 76. *The good king his master Will check him for't*—Lr II 2 148.

(2) In hawking, of the hawk, when she forsakes the quarry and flies *at* a chance bird: *With what wing the staniel checks at it!*—Tw II 5 124. *Like the haggard, check at every feather That comes before his eye*—III 1 71.

(3) Intr. for refl., to shy *at*, stick *at*: *If he be now return'd, As checking at his voyage*—Hml IV 7 62.

CHEER (sb.)

(1) The face: *All fancy-sick she is and pale of cheer*—Mids III 2 96. *Show a merry cheer*—Merch III 2 315. *Your looks are sad, your cheer appall'd*—1 H6 I 2 48.

(2) Disposition, mood: *If they sing, 'tis with so dull a cheer That leaves look pale*—Sonn 97 13.

(3) Cheerfulness: *I have not that alacrity of spirit, Nor cheer of mind, that I was wont to have*—R3 V 3 73. *You are so sick of late, So far from cheer*—Hml III 2 173.

(4) Kindly welcome; *to give the cheer: You do not give the cheer*—Mcb III 4 33. *To give good cheer: She securely gives good cheer And reverend welcome to her princely guest*—Lucr 89.

CHEER (vb.)

To give oneself or assume such and such a state of mind; *how cheer you?* how fare you? how do you? *How cheer'st thou, Jessica?*—Merch III 5 75.

CHEERLY

Cheerily, cheerfully: *Cheerly, cheerly, my hearts!*—Tp I 1 6. *Thou lookest cheerly*—As II 6 14. *Cheerly on, courageous friends*—R3 V 2 14.

CHEQUIN

An Italian and Turkish gold coin: *Three or four thousand chequins were as pretty a proportion to live quietly, and so give over*—Per IV 2 28.

CHERRY-PIT

A child's game played with cherry-stones: *'Tis not for gravity to play at cherry-pit with Satan*—Tw III 4 129.

CHERUBIN

Cherub: *O, a cherubin Thou wast that did preserve me*—Tp I 2 152. *Still quiring to the young-eyed cherubins*—Merch V 62.

CHEVERIL

Kid-leather: *Here's a wit of cheveril, that stretches . . .*—Rom II 4 87. Attrib.: *A cheveril glove*—Tw III 1 13. *Your soft cheveril conscience*—H8 II 3 32.

CHEWET

Equivalent to *Chough* (q.v.): *Peace, chewet, peace!*—1 H4 V 1 29.

CHIDE

(1) To wrangle, brawl: *We shall chide downright, if I longer stay*—Mids II 1 145.

(2) To express dissatisfaction or displeasure loudly or angrily, rail: *I will board her, though she chide as loud As thunder*—Shr I 2 95. *He calls me boy; and chides, as he had power To beat me out of Egypt*—Ant IV 1 1.

(3) *To chide with*, to complain aloud against, to dispute or quarrel with: *The business of the state does him offence, And he does chide with you*—Oth IV 2 166. [No more] *With Mars fall out, with Juno chide*—Cymb V 4 32. *For my sake do you with Fortune chide*—Sonn 111 1.

(4) *To chide at*, to scold: *You chid at Sir Proteus for going ungartered*—Gent II 1 78. *Chid I for that at frugal nature's frame?*—Ado IV 1 130.

CHILD

(1) A female infant: *A very pretty barne! A boy or a child, I wonder?*—Wint III 3 71.

(2) A youth of gentle birth; used as a kind of title: *Child Rowland to the dark tower came*—Lr III 4 187.

CHILD-CHANGED

Perh., changed into a child; or, changed by his children's conduct: *This child-changed father*—Lr IV 7 17.

CHILDHOOD

Childship, filial relation: *The offices of nature, bond of childhood*—Lr II 4 181.

CHILDING

Fruitful: *The childing autumn*—Mids II 1 112.

CHILDNESS

Childish humour, childishness: *With his varying childness cures in me Thoughts . . .*—Wint I 2 170.

CHINKS

Coins, money: *He that can lay hold of her Shall have the chinks*—Rom I 5 118.

4

CHIRURGEONLY

Like a skilful surgeon: Gon. . . . *You rub the sore, When you should bring the plaster.* Seb. *Very well.* Ant. *And most chirurgeonly*—Tp II 1 138.

CHOICE

Special value, estimation: *This ring he holds In most rich choice*—All's III 7 25.

CHOOSE

Cannot choose, have no alternative, must of necessity: *'Tis a good dulness, And give it way: I know thou canst not choose*—Tp I 2 185. Rom. . . . *Tullus Aufidius will appear well in these wars* . . . Vols. *He cannot choose*—Cor IV 3 35. Sim. *Shall not choose: You shall not choose, sir! come, come*—Wiv I 1 316.

CHOP

To thrust with sudden force: *We will chop him in the malmsey-butt*—R3 I 4 160.

CHOPINE

A shoe with a high sole: *Your ladyship is nearer to heaven . . . by the altitude of a chopine*—Hml II 2 445.

CHOP-LOGIC

A sophistical arguer: *How now, chop-logic! What is this?*—Rom III 5 150.

CHOPPED

Chapped; fissured, cracked: *Her pretty chopt hands*—As II 4 50. *Chopp'd with tann'd antiquity*—Sonn 62 10.

CHOPPING

Jerky, coming in fits and starts: *The chopping French we do not understand*—R2 V 3 124.

CHOPPY

Chappy; fissured, cracked: *Her choppy finger*—Mcb I 3 44.

CHOPS

An appellation for a person with fat or bloated cheeks: *You will, chops?*—1 H4 I 2 151. *Come on, you whoreson chops*—2 H4 II 4 235.

CHOUGH

A bird of the crow family, applied esp. to the jackdaw: *I myself could make A chough of as deep chat*—Tp II 1 265. *Choughs' language*—All's IV 1 22. *Magot-pies and choughs and rooks*—Mcb III 4 125. In Lr IV 6 13 (*The crows and choughs that wing the midway air*) perh., the red-legged crow, which was probably common on the Kentish coast.

CHRISOM

A chrisom (corrupted to *christom*) *child,* a child in the first month, during which it wore its chrisom-cloth or christening-robe: *Went away an it had been any christom child*—H5 II 3 11.

CHRISTEN

Christian: *Ne'er a king christen could be better bit*—1 H4 II 1 19. [I] *can call them all by their christen names*—II 4 8.

CHRISTENDOM

(1) Christianity: *Their clothes are after such a pagan cut too, That, sure, they've worn out Christendom*—H8 I 3 14. *By my christendom, as I am a Christian*—John IV 1 16.

(2) App., an appellation, name: *Pretty, fond, adoptious christendoms*—All's I 1 188.

CHRISTOM

See *Chrisom.*

CHRYSOLITE

A name given to several gems of a green colour: *Such another world Of one entire and perfect chrysolite*—Oth V 2 144.

CHUFF

An old hunks: *Are ye undone? No, ye fat chuffs; I would your store were here!*—1 H4 II 2 93.

CHURL

A niggard, miser: *O churl! drunk all, and left no friendly drop To help me after?*—Rom V 3 163. *And, tender churl, makest waste in niggarding*—Sonn 1 12.

CHURLISH

Niggardly, miserly: *My master is of churlish disposition And little recks to find the way to heaven By doing deeds of hospitality*—As II 4 80. Grudging of praise: *Though churlish thoughts themselves should be your judge*—John II 519.

CICATRICE

Loosely, a scar-like mark: *Lean but upon a rush, The cicatrice . . . Thy palm some moment keeps*—As III 5 22.

CINQUE PACE, SINK-A-PACE

A lively dance, the steps of which appear to have been regulated by the number five: *Wooing, wedding, and repenting, is as a Scotch jig, a measure, and a cinque pace*—Ado II 1 76. *I would not so much as make water but in a sink-a-pace*—Tw I 3 138.

CINQUE-SPOTTED

Having five spots: *A mole cinque-spotted*—Cymb II 2 38.

CIPHER

(1) To express, portray: *Some loathsome dash the herald will contrive, To cipher me how fondly I did dote*—Lucr 206. *The face of either cipher'd either's heart*—1396.

(2) To decipher: *The illiterate, that know not how To cipher what is writ in learned books*—Lucr 810.

CIRCUIT

A crown: *The golden circuit on my head*—2 H6 III 1 352.

CIRCUMSTANCE

(1) A condition or state of affairs: *So, by your circumstance, I fear you'll prove*—Gent I 1 37. *Unsifted in such perilous circumstance* — Hml I 3 102.

(2) The conditioning surroundings of an action: *The circumstance consider'd*—1 H4 I 3 70. *What is the quality of mine offence, Being constrain'd with dreadful circumstance?*—Lucr 1702. Events happening: *But, lady, That policy may . . . breed itself so out of circumstance*—Oth III 3 13.

(3) The particulars or details of an action or case: *I know the knight is incensed . . . but nothing of the circumstance more*—Tw III 4 285. *One scene of it comes near the circumstance . . . of my father's death*—Hml III 2 81. *You do remember all the circumstance?*—V 2 2. Detail in narration or assertion: *It must with circumstance be spoken* —Gent III 2 36. *With circumstance and oaths so to deny This chain*—Err V 16. *Is thy news good, or bad? . . . Say either, and I'll stay the circumstance*—Rom II 5 36. By circumstance, by adducing particulars: *Give me leave, By circumstance, but to acquit myself*—R3 I 2 76; sim. in 80. By particulars adduced: *Most true, if ever truth were pregnant by circumstance* — Wint V 2 33. *Without circumstance*, without further particulars: *The true ground . . . We cannot without circumstance descry*—Rom V 3 180. *Circumstance of thought*, details from which the mind draws conclusions: *In our circumstance and course of thought, 'Tis heavy with him*—Hml III 3 83. *The Lie with Circumstance = the Lie Circumstantial* (see *Circumstantial*)—As V 4 100.

(4) Long-winded speech, phrases: [You] *spend but time To wind about my love with circumstance* —Merch I 1 153. *This peroration with such circumstance*—2 H6 I 1 105. *Evades them, with a bombast circumstance Horribly stuff'd with epithets of war*—Oth I 1 13. So in pl.: *To leave frivolous circumstances, I pray you, tell . . .*—Shr V 1 27.

(5) Circumlocution, indirectness: *And can you, by no drift of circumstance, Get from him why he . . .?*—Hml III 1 1.

(6) An argument, proof: *So, by your circumstance, you call me fool*—Gent I 1 36. *Nay, that I can deny by a circumstance*—84. *Who, in his circumstance, expressly proves That . . .*—Troil III 3 114.

(7) Ceremony, formality: *And so, without more circumstance at all, I hold it fit that we shake hands and part*—Hml I 5 127. Ceremony, pomp: *All quality, Pride, pomp and circumstance of glorious war*—Oth III 3 353. *Out of circumstance*, unceremonious: *His approach, So out of circumstance and sudden*—Wint V 1 89.

(8) Something adventitious or casual: *Nor he that loves himself Hath not essentially but by circumstance The name of valour*—2 H6 V 2 38.

CIRCUMSTANCED

Governed by circumstances: *'Tis very good; I must be circumstanced*—Oth III 4 201.

CIRCUMSTANTIAL

The Lie Circumstantial—As V 4 85, a contradiction given indirectly by circumstances or details.

CITAL

A recital, mention; or perh., a reproof, impeachment: *He made a blushing cital of himself*—1 H4 V 2 62.

CITE

(1) To incite, urge: *For Valentine, I need not cite him to it*—Gent II 4 85. *Had I not been cited so by them, Yet did I purpose as they do entreat*—2 H6 III 2 281. *I think it cites us, brother, to the field*—3 H6 II 1 34.

(2) To bespeak, evidence: *Yourself, Whose aged honour cites a virtuous youth*—All's I 3 215.

CITIZEN

Citizenish, city-bred: *So citizen a wanton*—Cymb IV 2 8.

CITTERN

An instrument of the guitar kind, strung with wire and played with a quill, usually having a grotesquely carved head: *A cittern-head*—LLL V 2 614.

CIVIL

(1) Well-ordered, orderly: *They are reformed, civil, full of good*—Gent V 4 156. *The civil citizens*—H5 I 2 199. *Bringing them to civil discipline*—2 H6 I 1 195. Civilized: *Who's here? If anything that's civil, speak; if savage, Take or lend*—Cymb IV 6 22. *Civil sayings*, bearing the mark of civilization: *Tongues I'll hang on every tree, That shall civil sayings show*—As III 2 135.

(2) Well-bred, well-mannered: *Where is Malvolio? he is sad and civil*—Tw III 4 5. *The mere form of civil and humane seeming*—Oth II 1 243. Sober, grave: *Come, civil night*—Rom III 2 10. Gentle, calm: *The rude sea grew civil at her song*—Mids II 1 152.

(3) *A civil doctor*, a doctor of the Civil Law—Merch V 210.

(4) *Civil arms, swords*, used in civil war: *The king of heaven forbid our lord the king Should so with civil and uncivil arms Be rush'd upon!*—R2 III 3 101. *Our Italy Shines o'er with civil swords*—Ant I 3 44. But in 2 H4 V 5 112 (*We bear our civil swords and native fire As far as France*) app., borne by us as citizens of this state.

(5) With a pun on Seville (formerly spelt Civil): *The count is neither sad, nor sick, nor merry, nor well; but civil count, civil as an orange*—Ado II 1 303. A Civil orange is defined as one between sweet and sour.

CIVILITY

Good breeding, good manners: *Use all the observance of civility*—Merch II 2 204. *Honour untaught, Civility not seen from other*—Cymb IV 2 178.

CIVILLY

Decorously: *I have savage cause; And to proclaim it civilly, were like . . .*—Ant III 13 128.

CLACK-DISH

A beggar's wooden dish with a lid which was clacked to attract notice: *His use was to put a ducat in her clack-dish*—Meas III 2 134.

CLAMOUR

Said to be a term in bell-ringing signifying to increase the rapidity of the strokes before silencing the bells; hence gen., to silence, stop from noise: *Clamour your tongues*—Wint IV 4 250.

CLAP

(1) *To clap hands*, to shake hands in token of a bargain: *And so clap hands and a bargain*—H5 V 2 133. Cf. *And clap thyself my love*—Wint I 2 104.

(2) *To clap* [an arrow] *in the clout*, to hit the mark: *A would have clapped i' the clout at twelve score*—2 H4 III 2 51.

CLAPPER-CLAW

To thrash, drub: *He will clapper-claw thee tightly, bully*—Wiv II 3 67. *Now they are clapper-clawing one another*—Troil V 4 1.

CLASP

To cling or fix oneself: *Clasping to the mast*—Per IV 1 56.

CLAW

To flatter, wheedle: [I must] *laugh when I am merry and claw no man in his humour*—Ado I 3 18.

CLEANLY

Cleverly, neatly: *Hast not thou full often struck a doe, And borne her cleanly by the keeper's nose?*—Tit II 1 93. *Till they have singled With much ado the cold fault cleanly out*—Ven 693.

CLEAR

(1) Brightly shining, brilliant: *Those clear rays which she infused on me*—1 H6 I 2 85. *O thou clear god* (*i.e.* the sun)—Ven 860. Fully light, opposed to dusk or twilight: *It is almost clear dawn*—Meas IV 2 226.

(2) Illustrious, glorious: *Roots, you clear heavens!*—Tim IV 3 27. *The clearest gods*—Lr IV 6 73.

(3) Serene, cheerful: *You, the murderer, look as bright, as clear, As yonder Venus*—Mids III 2 60. *Say that she frown; I'll say she looks as clear As morning roses*—Shr II 173. *A countenance as clear As friendship wears at feasts*—Wint I 2 343.

CLEARLY

Completely, entirely: *A most extracting frenzy of mine own From my remembrance clearly banish'd his*—Tw V 288. Perh. also: *Wound our tattering colours clearly up*—John V 5 7 (or perh. the meaning may be, clear of opposition).

CLEARNESS

Freedom (from suspicion): *Always thought That I require a clearness*—Mcb III 1 132.

CLEARSTORE

Clerestory; the upper part of a cathedral or other building containing a series of windows: *The clearstores toward the south north are as lustrous as ebony*—Tw IV 2 41.

CLEFT

Divided, twofold: *O cleft effect!*—Compl 293.

CLEPE

To call, name: *He clepeth a calf, cauf*—LLL V 1 24. *As hounds and greyhounds . . . are clept All by the name of dogs*—Mcb III 1 93. *They clepe us drunkards*—Hml I 4 19.

CLERK

A man of book learning, a scholar: *Great clerks*—Mids V 93. *All the clerks, I mean the learned ones, in Christian kingdoms*—H8 II 2 92. *Deep clerks she dumbs*—Per V Prol 5.

CLERK-LIKE

Like a scholar, in a scholarly way: *As you are certainly a gentleman, thereto Clerk-like experienced*—Wint I 2 391.

CLERKLY

Scholarly: *Thou art clerkly, Sir John*—Wiv IV 5 58. As adv., in a scholarly way: *'Tis very clerkly done*—Gent II 1 114. *Ignominious words, though clerkly couch'd*—2 H6 III 1 179.

CLEW

A ball of thread; fig.: *You have wound a goodly clew*—All's I 3 188.

CLIFF

Clef: *Any man may sing her, if he can take her cliff*—Troil V 2 10.

CLIMATE (sb.)

A region, clime: *A Christian climate*—R2 IV 130. *They are portentous things Unto the climate that they point upon*—Cæs I 3 31. App. of a region of the sky: *By this hand I swear, That sways the earth this climate overlooks*—John II 343.

CLIMATE (vb.)

To sojourn in a region: *Whilst you Do climate here*—Wint V 1 169.

CLIMATURE

Prob., a region, clime: *Have heaven and earth together demonstrated Unto our climatures and countrymen*—Hml I 1 124. Or perh. *Climatures* = persons living in the same clime.

CLING

To parch, shrivel: *Till famine cling thee*—Mcb V 5 40.

CLINQUANT

Glittering with gold: *All clinquant, all in gold*—H8 I 1 19.

CLIP

To embrace, hug, enfold: *Neptune's arms, who clippeth thee about*—John V 2 34. *O, let me clip ye In arms as sound as when I woo'd*—Cor I 6 29. *No grave upon the earth shall clip in it A pair so famous*—Ant V 2 362.

CLOAK-BAG

A portmanteau, valise: *That stuffed cloak-bag of guts*—1 H4 II 4 497. *'Tis in my cloak-bag*—Cymb III 4 172.

CLOCK

The hour as struck by the clock: *To weep 'twixt clock and clock*—Cymb III 4 44.

CLOISTERED

Confined, restricted (as within the limits of a cloister): *Ere the bat hath flown His cloister'd flight*—Mcb III 2 40.

CLOISTRESS

A nun: *Like a cloistress she will veiled walk*—Tw I 1 28.

CLOSE (adj.)

Of acts, &c., secret, covert: *Another secret close intent*—R3 I 1 158. *A close exploit of death*—IV 2 35. *The close enacts and counsels of the heart*—Tit IV 2 118.

CLOSE (sb.)

(1) A closing or uniting together, union: *Let me be blest to make this happy close*—Gent V 4 117. *Attested by the holy close of lips*—Tw V 161.

(2) A closing in fight: *Furious close of civil butchery*—1 H4 I 1 13.

CLOSE (vb.)

(1) To enclose, shut up: *Poor living corse, closed in a dead man's tomb!*—Rom V 2 29. *Some purer chest to close so pure a mind*—Lucr 761.

(2) To conjoin, unite: *Young princes, close your hands*—John II 533. *Do thou but close our hands with holy words*—Rom II 6 6.

(3) *He closes with you in this consequence*, he takes your lead and goes on thus—Hml II 1 45.

CLOSE (adv.)

Secretly, covertly: *In a napkin being close convey'd*—Shr Ind I 127.

CLOSELY

Secretly, covertly: *Go closely in with me*—John IV 1 133. *Meaning to keep her closely at my cell*—Rom V 3 255. *We have closely sent for Hamlet hither*—Hml III 1 29.

CLOSENESS

Retirement, seclusion: *All dedicated To closeness*—Tp I 2 89.

CLOSET

(1) A room for privacy or retirement: *She desires to speak with you in her closet*—Hml III 2 343. *I found it thrown in at the casement of my closet*—Lr I 2 64.

(2) A private repository for valuables: *I found it in his closet, 'tis his will*—Cæs III 2 134. *I have locked the letter in my closet*—Lr III 3 11. Attrib.: *A closet lock and key of villanous secrets*—Oth IV 2 22.

CLOSURE

(1) Bound, circuit: *Within the guilty closure of thy walls*—R3 III 3 11. *Within the gentle closure of my breast*—Sonn 48 11. An enclosure: *Into the quiet closure of my breast*—Ven 782.

(2) An end, close: *And make a mutual closure of our house*—Tit V 3 134.

CLOTH

A livery: *A hilding for a livery, a squire's cloth*—Cymb II 3 128.

CLOTHIER'S YARD

A cloth-yard shaft, the arrow of the long bow: *Draw me a clothier's yard*—Lr IV 6 88.

CLOTPOLL

A thick or 'wooden' head: *I have sent Cloten's clotpoll down the stream*—Cymb IV 2 184.

CLOUD

A patch on a surface of another colour; esp. a dark spot on the face of a horse: *Eno. Will Cæsar weep? Agr. He has a cloud in's face. Eno. He were the worse for that, were he a horse*—Ant III 2 51.

CLOUDY

Of persons, full of gloom, sullen, frowning: *It is foul weather in us all, good sir, When you are cloudy*—Tp II 1 141. *Such aspect As cloudy men use to their adversaries*—1 H4 III 2 82. *The cloudy messenger*—Mcb III 6 41.

CLOUT

In archery, the mark: *A must shoot nearer, or he'll ne'er hit the clout*—LLL IV 1 136. *A would have clapped i' the clout at twelve score*—2 H4 III 2 51.

CLOUTED

Studded with clout-nails; or perh., patched: *Such as go in clouted shoon*—2 H6 IV 2 195. *I thought he slept, and put My clouted brogues from off my feet*—Cymb IV 2 213 (here prob. in the first sense).

CLOY¹

To fill up, stop up: *[When they] have both their eyes And ears so cloy'd importantly as now*—Cymb IV 4 18.

CLOY²

To scratch with the claw; or perh., to strike (the beak) together: *His royal bird Prunes the immortal wing and cloys his beak*—Cymb V 4 117.

CLOYMENT

Satiety: *That suffer surfeit, cloyment and revolt*—Tw II 4 102.

'CLUBS'

The rallying cry of the London apprentices, nominally to keep the peace, but often to engage in a brawl: *I . . . hit that woman; who cried out 'Clubs!'*—H8 V 4 52. *Clubs, clubs! these lovers will not keep the peace*—Tit II 1 37. Cf. *Clubs cannot part them*—As V 2 44. Mayor. *I'll call for clubs, if you will not away*—1 H6 I 3 84. *Clubs, bills, and partisans! strike! beat them down!*—Rom I 1 80.

CLUTCH

To clench (the hand): *Putting the hand in the pocket and extracting it clutched*—Meas III 2 48. *The power to clutch my hand*—John II 589. *Within thine eyes sat twenty thousand deaths, In thy hands clutch'd [sat] as many millions . . . I would say . . .*—Cor III 3 70.

COACH-FELLOW

A horse yoked with another; hence, a companion: *You and your coach-fellow Nym*—Wiv II 2 7.

COAST (sb.)

A region of the earth, country: *Travelling along this coast*—LLL V 2 557 (see *Along* (prep.)). *Spare England, for it is your native coast*—2 H6 IV 8 52. *The thunderer, whose bolt . . . batters all rebelling coasts*—Cymb V 4 95.

COAST (vb.), COST

(1) To go to work in a roundabout way: *How he coasts And hedges his own way*—H8 III 2 38.

(2) To make one's way to a place: *And all in haste she coasteth to the cry*—Ven 870.

(3) To attack, assail: *Whose haughty spirit . . . Will cost my crown*—3 H6 I 1 267.

COAT

A petticoat: *I could shake them off my coat*—As I 3 16.

COBLOAF

A little loaf with a round head; applied to Thersites: Troil II 1 41.

COCK¹

A weather-cock: *Spout Till you have drench'd our steeples, drown'd the cocks!*—Lr III 2 2.

COCK²

A cock-boat: *Yond tall anchoring bark, Diminish'd to her cock*—Lr IV 6 18.

COCK³

A perversion of God: *By cock, they are to blame*—Hml IV 5 62. *By cock and pie*, supposed to be by God and the pie, the ordinal of the Roman Catholic church: *By cock and pie, you shall not choose*—Wiv I 1 316. *By cock and pie, sir, you shall not away to-night*—2 H4 V 1 1. See also *Passion* (sb.) (1).

COCK-A-HOOP

To set cock-a-hoop, to give a loose to disorder, set all by the ears: *You will set cock-a-hoop! you'll be the man!*—Rom I 5 83.

COCKATRICE

Identified with the basilisk (see *Basilisk* (1)): *They will kill one another by the look, like cockatrices*—Tw III 4 214. *A cockatrice hast thou hatch'd to the world, Whose unavoided eye is murderous*—R3 IV 1 55.

COCKLED

Furnished with a shell: *The tender horns of cockled snails*—LLL IV 3 338.

COCKLE HAT

A hat with a scallop-shell, worn by pilgrims to the shrine of St. James of Compostella: *By his cockle hat and staff*—Hml IV 5 25.

COCKNEY

An effeminate person, a milksop: *I am afraid this great lubber, the world, will prove a cockney*—Tw IV 1 14. A town-bred person (derisively): *Cry to it, nuncle, as the cockney did to the eels when she put 'em i' the paste alive*—Lr II 4 123.

COCK-SHUT TIME

Prob., the time when poultry go to roost and are shut up: *Much about cock-shut time*—R3 V 3 70.

COD

See *Peascod.*

CODDING

Lustful, lecherous: *That codding spirit had they from their mother*—Tit V 1 99.

CODLING

An immature apple: [As] *a codling* [is] *when 'tis almost an apple*—Tw I 5 167.

CODPIECE

A bagged appendage in front of the hose or breeches: *You must needs have them* (*i.e.* the breeches) *with a codpiece*—Gent II 7 53. *Like . . . Hercules in the . . . tapestry, where his codpiece seems as massy as his club*—Ado III 3 145. *'Twas nothing to geld a codpiece of a purse*—Wint IV 4 622.

COFFIN

A mould of paste for a pie: *Of the paste a coffin I will rear And make two pasties of your shameful heads*—Tit V 2 189. *Custard-coffin*, such a mould for a custard, which was a kind of open pie: *It is a paltry cap, A custard-coffin, a bauble, a silken pie*—Shr IV 3 81.

COG

(1) To use fraud or deceit, cheat: *Fashion-monging boys, That lie and cog and flout*—Ado V 1 94. *Some cogging, cozening slave*—Oth IV 2 132.

(2) To flatter, fawn, wheedle: *I cannot cog and say thou art this and that*—Wiv III 3 76. *Because I cannot flatter and speak fair . . . smooth, deceive and cog*—R3 I 3 47.

(3) To gain by wheedling: *I'll . . . Cog their hearts from them*—Cor III 2 132.

COGNIZANCE

An emblem, token: *This pale and angry rose, As cognizance of my blood-drinking hate*—1 H6 II 4 107. *The cognizance of her incontinency Is this*—Cymb II 4 127. In heraldry, a device borne by retainers; so in Cæs II 2 88 (*Great men shall press For tinctures, stains, relics and cognizance*) a badge to show whose followers the wearers were. *Cognizance* here is pl.

COHERE

To combine congruously, agree: *Had time cohered with place*—Meas II 1 11. *Till each circumstance . . . do cohere and jump That I am Viola*—Tw V 258.

COHERENCE

Agreement; *semblable coherence*, agreement in likeness: *The semblable coherence of his men's spirits and his*—2 H4 V 1 72.

COHERENT

Harmoniously accordant: *That time and place with this deceit so lawful May prove coherent*—All's III 7 38.

COIGN

(1) A corner: *The four opposing coigns Which the world together joins*—Per III Prol 17.

(2) A corner-stone: *See you yon coign o' the Capitol, yon corner-stone?*—Cor V 4 1. A projecting corner: *Coign of vantage* (*i.e.* one lending itself to the use of the birds)—Mcb I 6 7.

COIL

(1) Turmoil, bustle, stir: *Who was so firm, so constant, that this coil Would not infect his reason?* Tp I 2 207. *The wedding being there to-morrow, there is a great coil to-night*—Ado III 3 99. *What a coil's here!*—Tim I 2 236.

(2) Fuss, ado: *I am not worth this coil that's made for me*—John II 165. *To keep a coil*, to make a fuss; so, app., in a passive construction: *I am commanded here, and kept a coil with ' Too young' . . .*—All's II 1 27.

(3) *This mortal coil*, the turmoil of this life: *When we have shuffled off this mortal coil*—Hml III 1 67.

COISTREL

See *Coystrill.*

COLBRAND

A Danish giant, overthrown by Sir Guy of Warwick: *Colbrand the giant, that same mighty man*—John I 225. *I am not Samson, nor Sir Guy, nor Colbrand*—H8 V 4 22.

COLD

(1) Deliberate, cool: *He's like to be a cold soldier*—2 H4 III 2 134. *After this cold considerance, sentence me*—V 2 98. *The most patient man in loss, the most coldest that ever turned up ace*—Cymb II 3 1.

(2) Void of sensual passion: *To make cold nymphs chaste crowns*—Tp IV 66. *Our cold maids*—Hml IV 7 172. *As Dian had hot dreams, And she alone were cold*—Cymb V 5 180.

(3) In hunting, of the scent, not strong, faint: *How Silver made it good . . . in the coldest fault*— Shr Ind I 19. *He is now at a cold scent*—Tw II 5 133. *Till they have singled With much ado the cold fault cleanly out*—Ven 693. Of deficiency in the sense of smell: *You smell this business with a sense as cold As is a dead man's nose*—Wint II 1 151.

COLDLY

Without heat, patiently, calmly: *If he were mad, he would not plead so coldly*—Err V 272. *Bear it coldly but till midnight*—Ado III 2 132. *Reason coldly of your grievances*—Rom III 1 55.

COLLAR

(1) Perh., a hangman's halter: Sam. . . . *An we be in choler, we'll draw.* Gre. *Ay, while you live, draw your neck out o' the collar*—Rom I 1 4. Cf. for a similar play 2 H4 V 5 90.

(2) *Collar of SS,* a chain with a series of S's, originally worn by adherents of the House of Lancaster, still part of the official dress of various officers—H8 IV 1 36 (Stage Dir).

COLLEAGUE

To unite in alliance, ally: *Colleagued with the dream of his advantage*—Hml I 2 21.

COLLECT

To deduce, infer: *The reverent care I bear unto my lord Made me collect these dangers in the duke*—2 H6 III 1 34.

COLLECTION

Deduction, inference: *Her speech is nothing, Yet the unshaped use of it doth move The hearers to collection*—Hml IV 5 7. *To make collection of,* app., to deduce or find out the meaning of: *This label . . . whose containing Is so from sense in hardness, that I can Make no collection of it*—Cymb V 5 430.

COLLIED

Dark, murky: *Brief as the lightning in the collied night*—Mids I 1 145.

COLLIER

One who carries coal for sale: Sam. . . . *We'll not carry coals.* Gre. *No, for then we should be colliers*—Rom I 1 1. See *Carry* (2).

COLLOP

A piece of flesh; used of offspring: *Sweet villain! Most dear'st! my collop!*—Wint I 2 136. *God knows thou art a collop of my flesh*—1 H6 V 4 18.

COLLY

To darken, obscure: *Passion, having my best judgement collied, Assays to lead the way*—Oth II 3 206.

COLOQUINTIDA

Colocynth; the bitter-apple: *As bitter as coloquintida*—Oth I 3 355.

COLOUR

(1) *Colourable colours,* perh., plausible shows of reason or sophistries: Nath. . . . *As a certain father saith,—* Hol. *Sir, tell not me of the father; I do fear colourable colours (i.e. in what might be cited from the writings of the father)*—LLL IV 2 153.

(2) *To fear no colours,* to fear no foe; and gen., to have no fear: *He that is well hanged in this world needs to fear no colours*—Tw I 5 5. *Fear no colours*—2 H4 V 5 94.

COLT

To befool: *What a plague mean ye to colt me thus?*—1 H4 II 2 39.

COMBINATE

App., bound by agreement, affianced: *Her combinate husband*—Meas III 1 231. Cf. *Combine.*

COMBINATION

An alliance: *A solemn combination shall be made Of our dear souls*—Tw V 392. A treaty: *This cunning cardinal The articles o' the combination drew As himself pleased*—H8 I 1 168.

COMBINE

App., to bind: *I am combined by a sacred vow*—Meas IV 3 149. Cf. *Thy faith my fancy to thee doth combine*—As V 4 156, and *Combinate.*

COMBUSTIOUS

Combustible: *As dry combustious matter is to fire*—Ven 1162.

COME

(1) *To come near,* to touch, 'get': *Indeed, you come near me now, Hal*—1 H4 I 2 14. *She that makes dainty, She, I'll swear, hath corns; am I come near ye now?*—Rom I 5 21.

(2) *To come off,* to acquit oneself: *Bravely came we off*—John V 5 4. To turn out, come to an issue: *This comes off well and excellent*—Tim I 1 29. *This overdone, or come tardy off*—Hml III 2 27. To pay: *I'll make them pay . . . they must come off*—Wiv IV 3 10.

(3) *To come over,* to surpass: *In so high a style, Margaret, that no man living shall come over it*—Ado V 2 6. To twit, taunt: *How he comes o'er us with our wilder days*—H5 I 2 267.

(4) *To come up,* to come into fashion: *It was never merry world in England since gentlemen came up*—2 H6 IV 2 9.

COMFECT

Comfit: *A goodly count, Count Comfect; a sweet gallant, surely!*—Ado IV 1 318.

COMFORT (sb.)

(1) Relief, aid, succour: *I spy comfort; I cry bail*—Meas III 2 43. *Thy comforts can do me no good at all*—Lr IV 1 17. *A comfort of retirement*, a resource consisting in something to fall back upon: *A comfort of retirement lives in this*—1 H4 IV 1 56. Encouragement: *Give him a show of comfort in his suit*—Wiv II 1 98. *Expectations and comforts of sudden respect and acquaintance*—Oth IV 2 191.

(2) Delight, joy, happiness: *Which should Make our eyes flow with joy, hearts dance with comforts*—Cor V 3 98. *Such comfort as do lusty young men feel . . . even such delight . . . shall you this night Inherit*—Rom I 2 26. *My soul hath her content so absolute That not another comfort like to this Succeeds*—Oth II 1 193.

(3) *Comfort, be of comfort, have comfort*, be of good cheer: *Comfort, my liege: why looks your grace so pale?*—R2 III 2 75. *Be of comfort*—Tp I 2 495. *Have comfort, lady*—Ado IV 1 119. *What comfort? what cheer? What comfort, man? how is't with aged Gaunt?*—R2 II 1 72.

COMFORT (vb.)

(1) To strengthen, invigorate (faculties): *God comfort thy capacity!*—LLL IV 2 44.

(2) To support, assist, abet (more or less in a legal sense): *Comforting your evils*—Wint II 3 56. *If I find him comforting the king, it will stuff his suspicion more fully*—Lr III 5 21.

(3) To help, aid, in gen.: *Why dost not comfort me, and help me out (i.e. from the pit)?*—Tit II 3 209.

(4) To cheer, gladden: *To keep with you at meals, comfort your bed*—Cæs II 1 284. *Her eyes are fierce; but thine Do comfort and not burn*—Lr II 4 175.

(5) To take comfort: *Live a little; comfort a little; cheer thyself a little*—As II 6 5.

COMFORTABLE

(1) Characterized by willingness or desire to promote the wellbeing of others, helpful, serviceable: *Be comfortable to my mother . . . and make much of her*—All's I 1 85. *Had I a steward So true, so just, and now so comfortable?*—Tim IV 3 497. *Yet have I left a daughter, Who, I am sure, is kind and comfortable*—Lr I 4 327. *Thy comfortable beams*—II 2 171.

(2) Pleasant, enjoyable: *What comfortable hour canst thou name, That ever graced me in thy company?*—R3 IV 4 173.

(3) Of good comfort, cheerful: *For my sake be comfortable*—As II 6 9. *Express yourself in a more comfortable sort*—Cor I 3 1. *His comfortable temper has forsook him*—Tim III 4 71.

COMFORTLESS

Giving no comfort: *That kiss is comfortless As frozen water to a starved snake*—Tit III 1 251.

COMMA

(1) A short member of a sentence: *No levell'd malice Infects one comma in the course I hold*—Tim I 1 47.

(2) The punctuation mark, viewed as standing between clauses which are to be joined in thought (as opposed to the full stop, which divides): *As peace should still . . . stand a comma 'tween their amities*—Hml V 2 41.

COMMANDMENT

(1) Bidding, command: *The countenance Of stern commandment*—As II 7 108. So *At commandment, at one's commandment*: *[We] had the best of them all at commandment*—2 H4 III 2 26. *The laws of England are at my commandment*—V 3 143.

(2) Authority, control: *Have I commandment on the pulse of life?*—John IV 2 92.

COMMENCE

To admit to a degree; fig.: *Learning [is] a mere hoard of gold kept by a devil, till sack commences it*—2 H4 IV 3 124.

COMMEND (sb.)

(1) Commendation: *Can any way speak in his just commend*—Per II 2 49.

(2) In pl., greetings, compliments: *Besides commends . . . Gifts of rich value*—Merch II 9 90. *I send to her my kind commends*—R2 III 1 38. *Speak to his gentle hearing kind commends*—III 3 126.

COMMEND (vb.)

(1) To commit, deliver, present: *To her white hand see thou do commend This seal'd-up counsel*—LLL III 169. *His glittering arms he will commend to rust*—R2 III 3 116. *I did commend your highness' letters to them*—Lr II 4 28. To communicate: *[I] durst commend a secret to your ear*—H8 V 1 17. *[I] dare . . . Commend a dear thing to you*—Lr III 1 18.

(2) To recommend to kindly remembrance or thought: *Your friends are well and have them much commended*—Gent II 4 123. *If thou seest her before me, commend me*—Wiv I 4 168. *Signor Antonio Commends him to you*—Merch III 2 234. *With all my love I do commend me to you*—Hml I 5 184.

COMMENDATIONS

Greetings, compliments: *No princely commendations to my king?*—1 H6 V 3 176. *Sends you his princely commendations*—H8 IV 2 118.

COMMENT

To meditate, ponder: *Fearful commenting Is leaden servitor to dull delay*—R3 IV 3 51

COMMIT

To commit an offence: *I do as truly suffer As e'er I did commit*—Gent V 4 76. To commit adultery: *Commit not with man's sworn spouse*—Lr III 4 83 (cf. Oth IV 2 7c and foll.).

COMMIXTION

Commixture, blending of ingredients: *Were thy commixtion Greek and Trojan*—Troil IV 5 124.

COMMODITY

(1) Facilities for trading: *The commodity that strangers have With us in Venice*—Merch III 3 27.

(2) Advantage, benefit, profit: *To me can life be no commodity*—Wint III 2 94. *I will turn diseases to commodity*—2 H4 I 2 277. *The commodity wages not with the danger*—Per IV 2 34.

(3) Expediency: *Tickling Commodity, Commodity, the bias of the world*—John II 573, and *passim* in the speech.

(4) A quantity of wares, lot: *A commodity of brown paper and old ginger*—Meas IV 3 5. *Now Jove, in his next commodity of hair, send thee a beard!*—Tw III 1 50. *I would . . . I knew where a commodity of good names were to be bought*—1 H4 I 2 92. Sim. of persons: *A commodity of warm slaves*—1 H4 IV 2 18.

COMMON

The commons, the common people: *The weal o' the common*—Cor I 1 155. *Hath he not pass'd the noble and the common?*—III 1 29.

COMMONER

A common harlot: *A commoner o' the camp*—All's V 3 194. *O thou public commoner!*—Oth IV 2 73.

COMMOTION

Insurrection, sedition: *Idly to profane the precious time, When tempest of commotion . . . doth begin to melt*—2 H4 II 4 391. *Damn'd commotion*—IV I 36. *Commotions, uproars, with a general taint Of the whole state*—H8 V 3 28.

COMMUNICATE

To communicate with, to participate in: *Makes me with thy strength to communicate*—Err II 2 178.

COMMUNITY

Commonness, familiarity: *Sick and blunted with community*—1 H4 III 2 77.

COMPACT (ppl. adj.)[1]

Joined in compact, leagued: *Thou pernicious woman, Compact with her that's gone*—Meas V 241.

COMPACT (ppl. adj.)[2]

Framed, composed: *Of imagination all compact*—Mids V 8. *If he, compact of jars, grow musical*—As II 7 5. *Well compact*, well framed: *My dimensions are as well compact*—Lr I 2 7.

COMPACT (vb.)

To confirm, give consistency to: *Such reasons . . . As may compact it more*—Lr I 4 361.

COMPANION

Fellow (slightingly): *This companion with the saffron face*—Err IV 4 64. *I abhor such . . . point-devise companions*—LLL V I 19. *What an equivocal companion is this!*—All's V 3 250. *Now, you companion, I'll say an errand for you*—Cor V 2 65.

COMPANY

A companion: *To seek new friends and stranger companies*—Mids I 1 219. *I would gladly have him see his company anatomized*—All's IV 3 36. *His addiction was to courses vain, His companies unletter'd*—H5 I 1 54.

COMPARATIVE (adj.)

(1) Quick at or dealing in scoffing similitudes: *The most comparative, rascalliest, sweet young prince*—1 H4 I 2 90.

(2) Perh., serving as a means of comparison: *Thou wert dignified enough . . . if 'twere made Comparative for your virtues, to be styled . . .* —Cymb II 3 132.

COMPARATIVE (sb.)

One who is quick at or deals in scoffing similitudes: *[To] stand the push Of every beardless vain comparative*—1 H4 III 2 66.

COMPARISON

(1) A scoffing similitude: *He'll but break a comparison or two on me*—Ado II 1 152. *Full of comparisons and wounding flouts*—LLL V 2 854.

(2) *His gay comparisons*, his gay and triumphant condition as compared with the speaker in his declined or fallen state: *I dare him therefore To lay his gay comparisons apart, And answer me declined, sword against sword*—Ant III 13 25.

COMPASS

(1) To bend into a circle: *To be compassed . . . in the circumference of a peck*—Wiv III 5 112.

(2) *Compassed*, circular: *A small compassed cape*—Shr IV 3 140. Arched: *His (i.e.* the horse's) *compass'd crest*—Ven 272. *A compassed window*, a semicircular bay-window—Troil I 2 120.

COMPASSION

To pity: *Can you hear a good man groan, And not . . . compassion him?*—Tit IV I 123.

COMPASSIONATE

Lamenting; or perh., moving pity: *It boots thee not to be compassionate*—R2 I 3 174.

COMPEER

To be the equal of: *In my rights, By me invested, he compeers the best*—Lr V 3 68.

COMPEL

To take by force, extort: *An I were not a very coward, I'ld compel it* (*i.e.* the copy of the sonnet) *of you*—All's IV 3 356. *Express charge, that . . . there be nothing compelled from the villages*—H5 III 6 114. *Commissions, which compel from each The sixth part of his substance*—H8 I 2 57.

COMPETENCE

An adequate supply, sufficiency: *For competence of life I will allow you*—2 H4 V 5 70.

COMPETITOR

An associate: *He and his competitors in oath*—LLL II 82. *Every hour more competitors Flock to their aid*—R3 IV 4 506. *Thou, my brother, my competitor In top of all design*—Ant V I 42.

COMPILE

To compose (as original work): *Longaville Did never sonnet for her sake compile*—LLL IV 3 133. *Be most proud of that which I compile, Whose influence is thine and born of thee*—Sonn 78 9.

COMPLAIN

(1) To make moan, lament: *A wretched soul . . . We bid be quiet when we hear it cry ; But were we burden'd with like weight of pain, As much or more we should ourselves complain*—Err II 1 34. *Humbly complaining to her deity Got my lord chamberlain his liberty*—R3 I 1 76. *Thou movest no less with thy complaining than Thy master in bleeding*—Cymb IV 2 375.

(2) To beweep, bewail: *What I want it boots not to complain*—R2 III 4 18. *That late complain'd Her wrongs to us*—Lucr 1839.

COMPLAINT

A lament: *Give me no help in lamentation; I am not barren to bring forth complaints*—R3 II 2 66. Cf. ' A Lover's Complaint '.

COMPLEMENT, COMPLIMENT

(1) Ceremoniousness, outward show: *Not only . . . in the simple office of love, but in all the accoutrement, complement and ceremony of it*—Wiv IV 2 4. *Farewell compliment!*—Rom II 2 89. *In compliment extern*—Oth I 1 63. Formal civility, courtesy: *That they call compliment is like the encounter of two dog-apes*—As II 5 26. *'Twas never merry world Since lowly feigning was call'd compliment*—Tw III 1 109. *Dialogue of compliment*—John I 201. In pl., etiquette: *A man of complements*—LLL I 1 169. *The courageous captain of complements*—Rom II 4 20.

(2) That which goes to complete the gentleman: *Garnish'd and deck'd in modest complement*—H5 II 2 134.

COMPLETE

(1) Accomplished, finished (of persons): *The varnish of a complete man*—LLL I 2 46. *A pestilent complete knave*—Oth II 1 252.

(2) Fully armoured: *A complete bosom*—Meas I 3 3.

COMPLEXION

(1) One of the four ' humours ' (see *Humour* (3)): Arm. *Of what complexion?* Moth. *Of all the four*—LLL I 2 82 and foll.

(2) Bodily habit: *It is very sultry and hot for my complexion*—Hml V 2 101.

(3) Natural disposition, nature: *Then it is the complexion of them all to leave the dam*—Merch III 1 32. A mental tendency: *The o'ergrowth of some complexion*—Hml I 4 27.

(4) External appearance: *How near the god drew to the complexion of a goose!*—Wiv V 5 8. *Thing like a man, but of no woman bred! Thou art no man, though of a man's complexion*—Ven 214.

(5) The countenance: *Turn thy complexion there*—Oth IV 2 62.

COMPLICE

(1) An associate: *All your loving complices*—2 H4 I 1 163.

(2) An accomplice, confederate in wrong-doing: *Bushy, Bagot and their complices*—R2 II 3 165. *The rebels and their complices*—2 H6 V 1 212.

COMPLIMENT

See *Complement*.

COMPLOT (sb.)

Prob. the original from which Plot is abbreviated: *Their complot is to have my life*—2 H6 III 1 147. *A complot to betray thy foes*—Tit V 2 147.

COMPLOT (vb.)

To plot (see *Complot* (sb.)): *All the treasons . . . Complotted and contrived in this land*—R2 I 1 95. *To plot, contrive, or complot any ill*—I 3 189.

COMPLY

To use compliments or ceremonies: *Let me comply with you in this garb*—Hml II 2 389. *He did comply with his dug, before he sucked it*—V 2 195.

COMPOSE

(1) Of a manufactured article, to put together, construct: *A casque composed by Vulcan's skill*—Troil V 2 170.

(2) Of the body, to fashion, frame: *Nature . . . Hath well composed thee*—All's I 2 20.

(3) To come to an agreement: *If we compose well here*—Ant II 2 15.

COMPOSED

Elaborately contrived: *Wailful sonnets, whose composed rhymes . . .*—Gent III 2 69.

COMPOSITION

(1) Constitution of body: *The large composition of this man*—John I 88.

(2) An agreement, terms: *If the duke . . . come not to composition with the King . . .*—Meas I 2 1. *Came short of composition*—V 220. *Thus we are agreed: I crave our composition may be written*—Ant II 6 58. A coming to terms: *Which caused Our swifter composition*—Cor III 1 2.

(3) Consistency: *There is no composition in these news*—Oth I 3 1.

COMPOSTURE

Compost, manure: *A composture stolen From general excrement*—Tim IV 3 444.

COMPOSURE

(1) Personal constitution, temperament: *Thou art of sweet composure*—Troil II 3 251. *His composure must be rare indeed Whom these things cannot blemish*—Ant I 4 22.

(2) A combination, union: *It was a strong composure a fool could disunite*—Troil II 3 108.

COMPOUND

(1) To settle or compose (strife, &c.): *We will compound this quarrel*—Shr I 2 27. *I would to God all strifes were well compounded*—R3 II 1 74.

(2) To agree, come to terms, contract: *Compound with him by the year*—Meas IV 2 25. *Till you compound whose right is worthiest*—John II 281. *What We have compounded on*—Cor V 6 83.

COMPROMISE

To be compromised, to be agreed, to have come to terms: *When Laban and himself were compromised That . . .*—Merch I 3 79.

COMPT

An account, reckoning: *Strikes some scores away From the great compt*—All's V 3 56. *In compt,* subject to an accounting: *Have theirs, themselves and what is theirs, in compt*—Mcb I 6 26. App., jotted down for reference: *Take the bonds along with you, And have the dates in compt*—Tim II 1 34. *At compt,* at the Judgement: *When we shall meet at compt*—Oth V 2 273.

COMPTIBLE

Sensitive: *I am very comptible, even to the least sinister usage*—Tw I 5 187.

COMPTROLLER

See *Controller.*

COMPULSATORY

Compulsory: *By strong hand And terms compulsatory*—Hml I 1 102.

COMPULSIVE

In a physical sense, driving or forcing onward: *Icy current and compulsive course*—Oth III 3 454.

CON

To con thanks, to avow one's gratitude: *I con him no thanks for't*—All's IV 3 174. *Thanks I must you con That . . .*—Tim IV 3 428.

CONCEALMENT

A secret art: *Profited In strange concealments*—1 H4 III 1 166.

CONCEIT (sb.)

(1) The faculty of conceiving, apprehension: *Wisdom, gravity, profound conceit*—Merch I 1 92. *I know you are a gentleman of good conceit*—As V 2 58. *Thy conceit is soaking*—Wint I 2 224.

(2) The faculty in exercise, thought, imagination: *Conceit, more rich in matter than in words, Brags of his substance, not of ornament*—Rom II 6 30. *Conceit in weakest bodies strongest works*—Hml III 4 114. *I know not how conceit may rob The treasury of life*—Lr IV 6 42. Morbid brooding: *The prince your son, with mere conceit and fear Of the queen's speed, is gone*—Wint III 2 145. *Conceit upon her father*—Hml IV 5 45.

(3) A conception, notion: *His conceit is false*—Ado II 1 308. *You have a noble and a true conceit Of god-like amity*—Merch III 4 2. *As if thou then hadst shut up in thy brain Some horrible conceit*—Oth III 3 114.

(4) Design, device: *Of very liberal conceit*—Hml V 2 160. Ingenuity embodied in something devised: *With forged quaint conceit*—1 H6 IV 1 102. *Much imaginary work was there (i.e.* in the picture); *Conceit deceitful, so compact, so kind, That . . .*—Lucr 1422. An invention, device: *She would applaud Andronicus' conceit*—Tit IV 2 30. A thing fancifully devised: *Rings, gawds, conceits*—Mids I 1 33.

(5) A whim, caprice: *Let it be as humours and conceits shall govern*—Merch III 5 68.

(6) Gaiety of imagination, wit: *He a good wit? . . . there's no more conceit in him than is in a mallet*—2 H4 II 4 261.

CONCEIT (vb.)

(1) To form a conception, think: *That your wisdom yet, From one that so imperfectly conceits, Would take no notice*—Oth III 3 148. To form an ingenious or fanciful conception: *Well conceited, Davy*—2 H4 V 1 39.

(2) To form a conception or notion of: *Him and his worth . . . You have right well conceited*—Cæs I 3 161. *One of two bad ways you must conceit me*—III 1 192.

CONCEITED

(1) Possessed with an idea (of such and such a kind): *He is as horribly conceited of him*—Tw III 4 322.

(2) Having an intelligence (of such and such a kind): *An admirable conceited fellow*—Wint IV 4 203.

(3) Ingenious, clever: *The conceited painter*—Lucr 1371. Of things, showing ingenuity: *Is not the humour conceited?*—Wiv I 3 25. *Conceited characters*—Compl 16.

CONCEITLESS

Without intelligence: *Think'st thou I am so shallow, so conceitless*—Gent IV 2 96.

CONCEPTIOUS

Able to conceive, fruitful: *Thy* (*i.e.* the earth's) *fertile and conceptious womb*—Tim IV 3 187.

CONCERN

Absol. or intr., to be of importance, matter: *It will not lie where it concerns, Unless it have a false interpreter*—Gent I 2 77. *It may concern much*—LLL IV 2 146. *What concerns his freedom unto me?*—1 H6 V 3 116. *Concerns more than avails*, is your business, is (naturally) the course which you take, but it avails you nothing: *Which to deny concerns more than avails*—Wint III 2 87.

CONCERNANCY

A matter in hand: *The concernancy, sir?*—Hml V 2 128.

CONCERNING

A matter that concerns one, an affair: *As time and our concernings shall importune*—Meas I 1 57. [Who would] *Such dear concernings hide?*—Hml III 4 191.

CONCERT

See *Consort* (sb.).

CONCLUDE

(1) To demonstrate, prove: *You conclude that my master is a shepherd?*—Gent I 1 76. *Thou dost conclude hairy men plain dealers*—Err II 2 87. *The text most infallibly concludes it*—LLL IV 2 169.

(2) To come to an agreement or decision: *Conclude and be agreed*—R2 I 1 156. *Where gentry . . . Cannot conclude but by the yea and no Of general ignorance,—it must omit Real necessities*—Cor III 1 144. *Concluded*, app., resolved upon formally: Riv. *Is it concluded he shall be protector?* Q. Eliz. *It is determined, not concluded yet*—R3 I 3 14. To conclude of or on, to agree upon, arrange: *To have a godly peace concluded of*—1 H6 V 1 5. *Suffolk concluded on the articles*—2 H6 I 1 217. To acknowledge, admit: *Reprove my allegation, if you can; Or else conclude my words effectual*—

2 H6 III 1 40. *Then, grandam, you conclude that he is dead*—R3 II 2 12.

CONCLUSION

(1) An experiment: *She hath pursued conclusions infinite Of easy ways to die*—Ant V 2 358. *Is't not meet That I did amplify my judgement in Other conclusions?*—Cymb I 5 16. *A foregone conclusion*, a previous experience, *i.e.* a basis of fact: Iago. *Nay, this was but his dream.* Oth. *But this denoted a foregone conclusion*—Oth III 3 427.

(2) A riddle: *Read the conclusion, then: Which read and not expounded, 'tis decreed . . .*—Per I 1 56.

(3) The act of inferring; *still conclusion*, quiet drawing of inferences: *Her modest eyes And still conclusion*—Ant IV 15 27.

CONCOLINEL

App., a snatch, or the burden, of a song: LLL III 3.

CONCUPISCIBLE

Vehemently desiring: *His concupiscible intemperate lust*—Meas V 98.

CONCUPY

App. an abbreviation or perversion of Concubine: *He'll tickle it for his concupy*—Troil V 2 177.

CONDIGN

Well deserved: *In thy condign praise*—LLL I 2 27.

CONDITION

(1) A covenant, contract, agreement: *Such sum or sums as are Express'd in the condition*—Merch I 3 148. *Your oaths Are words and poor conditions, but unseal'd*—All's IV 2 29. *Shall our condition stand?*—1 H6 V 4 165. Terms: *'Twill be deliver'd back on good condition*—Cor I 10 2. *In the gentle condition of blood*—As I 1 47, prob. (by transference of epithet) = in the condition of gentle blood, *i.e.*, because of the (implied) covenant to which those of good blood must be held to be parties.

(2) Disposition, character, temper: *The condition of a saint*—Merch I 2 142. *I have a touch of your condition*—R3 IV 4 157. *Is't possible that so short a time can alter the condition of a man?*—Cor V 4 9. Mood, temper: *Such is now the duke's condition That . . .*—As I 2 276. In pl., manners, morals, ways: *Yes, and* [knows] *his ill conditions*—Ado III 2 68. *They know his conditions and lay him in straw*—All's IV 3 288.

(3) Nature, quality: *Our haste from hence is of so quick condition That . . .*—Meas I 1 54. *The condition of that fardel*—Wint IV 4 738. *A rage whose heat hath this condition, That . . .*—John III 1 341.

(4) App., official capacity: *I, in my condition,*

Shall better speak of you than you deserve—2 H4 IV 3 90.

(5) App., medium: *This throne, this Fortune . . . would be well express'd In our condition*—Tim I 1 73 (said by the Painter).

CONDOLE

(1) To make lament: *That will ask some tears . . . I will condole in some measure*—Mids I 2 27. *A lover is more condoling*—42.

(2) To express sympathy with: *Let us condole the knight*—H5 II 1 133.

CONDOLEMENT

(1) Lamentation, sorrowing: *To persever In obstinate condolement*—Hml I 2 92.

(2) A solatium: *There are certain condolements, certain vails*—Per II 1 156.

CONDUCE

Perh. intr. for refl., to conduct itself, carry itself on: *Within my soul there doth conduce a fight*—Troil V 2 147.

CONDUCT

(1) Provision for safety on a journey, an escort, convoy: *I will . . . desire some conduct of the lady*—Tw III 4 264. *An honourable conduct let him have*—John I 29. *I desire of you A conduct over-land to Milford-Haven*—Cymb III 5 7.

(2) A person who escorts, a guide, conductor: *There is in this business more than nature Was ever conduct of*—Tp V 243. *I will be his conduct*—R2 IV 157. *Come, bitter conduct, come, unsavoury guide!*—Rom V 3 116.

(3) Leadership, command: *A mighty power; which were on foot, In his own conduct*—As V 4 162. *Under whose conduct came those powers of France?*—John IV 2 129. *A speedy power . . . Under the conduct of young Lancaster*—2 H4 I 1 133.

CONFECTION

A medicinal preparation: *My confections*—Cymb I 5 15. *If Pisanio Have . . . given his mistress that confection Which I gave him for cordial . . .*—V 5 245.

CONFER

To converse, talk: *I'll leave you to confer of home affairs*—Gent II 4 119. *They sit conferring by the parlour fire*—Shr V 2 102. Der. . . . [We] *Are come from visiting his majesty . . . Q. Eliz. . . . Did you confer with him?*—R3 I 3 32.

CONFERENCE

Conversation: *The conference was sadly borne*—Ado II 3 229. *So sensible Seemeth their conference*—LLL V 2 259. *Let's not confound the time with conference harsh*—Ant I 1 45.

CONFESSION

(1) Avowal of another's merits: *He made confession of you, And gave you such a masterly report*—Hml IV 7 96.

(2) App., profession: *If there be one . . . That loves his mistress more than in confession*—Troil I 3 265.

CONFIDENT

(1) Trustful, confiding: *Be as just and gracious unto me As I am confident and kind to thee*—Tit I 1 60. *I am confident,* I trust you: First Gent. *Let me have it (i.e.* the secret); *I do not talk much.* Sec. Gent. *I am confident; You shall, sir*—H8 II 1 145.

(2) Over-bold, impudent: *A confident brow*—2 H4 II 1 121.

CONFINE (sb.)

(1) A region, territory: *It irks me the poor dappled fools . . . Should in their own confines . . . Have their round haunches gored*—As II 1 22. *This kingdom, this confine of blood and breath*—John IV 2 246. *Here in these confines slily have I lurk'd*—R3 IV 4 3.

(2) A boundary, limit: *Nature in you stands on the very verge Of her confine*—Lr II 4 149. *Vow, bond, nor space, In thee hath neither sting, knot, nor confine*—Compl 264.

(3) Confinement, limitation: *Put into circumscription and confine*—Oth I 2 27. *Till death enlarge his confine*—Ant III 5 13.

(4) A place of confinement, an enclosure: *The extravagant and erring spirit hies To his confine*—Hml I 1 154. *Many confines, wards and dungeons*—II 2 251. *In whose confine immured is the store*—Sonn 84 3.

CONFINE (vb.)

To relegate to certain limits, banish: *So have we thought it good From our free person she should be confined*—Wint II 1 193. *To England send him, or confine him where Your wisdom best shall think*—Hml III 1 194. Refl., *To confine yourself To Asher House*—H8 III 2 230.

CONFINELESS

Boundless, unlimited: *Compared With my confineless harms*—Mcb IV 3 54.

CONFINER

An inhabitant of a region: *The confiners And gentlemen of Italy*—Cymb IV 2 337.

CONFOUND

(1) To destroy, undo: *What willingly he did confound he wail'd*—Ant III 2 58. *By such toys that would . . . have confounded one the other, or have fallen both*—Cymb I 4 53. *When he himself himself confounds*—Lucr 160.

(2) To waste, consume: *As fearfully as doth a galled rock O'erhang and jutty his confounded base* —H5 III 1 12. *Who confounds In singleness the parts that thou shouldst bear*—Sonn 8 7. Of time, to spend, consume: *He did confound the best part of an hour*—1 H4 I 3 100. *How couldst thou in a mile confound an hour?*—Cor I 6 17. *Let's not confound the time with conference harsh*—Ant I 1 45.

CONFUSION

Destruction: *So quick bright things come to confusion*—Mids I 1 149. *How soon confusion May . . . take The one by the other*—Cor III 1 110. *Confusion now hath made his masterpiece!*—Mcb II 3 71.

CONGEE, CONGY

(1) To take formal leave: *I have congied with the duke*—All's IV 3 100.
(2) To bow: *They first congee unto her*—H8 IV 2 82 (Stage Dir).

CONGEST

To gather together, heap up: [You] *Must for your victory us all congest*—Compl 258.

CONGRATULATE

To salute: *It is the king's . . . pleasure . . . to congratulate the princess at her pavilion*—LLL V 1 92.

CONGREE

To agree together, accord: *Congreeing in a full and natural close, Like music*—H5 I 2 182.

CONGREET

To greet mutually: *Face to face and royal eye to eye, You have congreeted*—H5 V 2 30.

CONGRUE

To agree: *Letters congruing to that effect*—Hml IV 3 66.

CONGY

See *Congee*.

CONJECTURE

(1) Supposition: *Now entertain conjecture of a time*—H5 IV Chor 1.
(2) Suspicion: *On my eyelids shall conjecture hang*—Ado IV 1 107. An evil surmise: *She may strew Dangerous conjectures in ill-breeding minds*—Hml IV 5 14.

CONJUNCTION

Persons conjoined, an assembled force: *That with our small conjunction we should on*—1 H4 IV 1 37.

CONJUNCTIVE

Closely united: *Conjunctive to my life and soul*—Hml IV 7 14. Acting in unison: *Let us be conjunctive in our revenge*—Oth I 3 374.

CONJURATION

A solemn appeal, adjuration: *Mock not my senseless conjuration*—R2 III 2 23. *Under this conjuration speak*—H5 I 2 29. *An earnest conjuration from the king*—Hml V 2 38.

CONJURE

To charm, bewitch: *Some dram conjured to this effect*—Oth I 3 105.

CONQUEST

In legal phrase, an acquisition by 'purchase' (see *Purchase* (vb.) (4)): *How to divide the conquest of thy sight*—Sonn 46 2.

CONSCIENCE

(1) Consciousness: *Thus conscience does make cowards of us all*—Hml III 1 83 (*i.e.* the fact that the mind is conscious of the considerations mentioned).
(2) Internal or mental recognition or acknowledgment: *I appeal To your own conscience . . . how . . .*—Wint III 2 46. *Now must your conscience my acquittance seal*—Hml IV 7 1. *This will witness outwardly, As strongly as the conscience does within*—Cymb II 2 35. Inmost thought: *'Tis your graces That from my mutest conscience to my tongue Charms this report out*—Cymb I 6 115. To speak one's conscience, to speak one's mind: *I will speak my conscience of the king*—H5 IV 1 123. *Shall I speak my conscience?*—2 H6 III 1 68.
(3) Reasonableness, understanding, 'sense': *Canst thou the conscience lack, To think I shall lack friends?*—Tim II 2 184.
(4) Regard to the dictates of conscience, conscientiousness: *I cannot with conscience take it*—Wint IV 4 658. *Is't not perfect conscience, To quit him with this arm?*—Hml V 2 67. *Their best conscience Is not to leave 't undone, but keep 't unknown*—Oth III 3 203.

CONSCIONABLE

Conscientious: *No further conscionable than in putting on the mere form of . . .*—Oth II 1 242.

CONSENT (sb.)

(1) Agreement as to a course of action, concert: *They fell together all, as by consent*—Tp II 1 203. *Here was a consent . . . To . . .*—LLL V 2 460. *Government . . . doth keep in one consent*—H5 I 2 180. *To be of consent*, to be accessary: *Some villains of my court Are of consent and sufferance in this*—As II 2 2.
(2) Feeling, opinion: *By my consent, we'll even let them alone*—1 H6 I 2 44.

CONSENT (vb.)

(1) To agree in opinion: *All your writers do consent that ipse is he*—As V 1 47.

(2) To come to agreement as to a course of action, &c.: [We should] *Consent upon a sure foundation*—2 H4 I 3 52. *As you and . . . Consent upon the order of their fight, So be it*—Troil IV 5 89. *Did you and he consent in Cassio's death?*—Oth V 2 297.

CONSEQUENCE

(1) Sequel: *A dire induction am I witness to, And will to France, hoping the consequence Will prove . . .*—R3 IV 4 5. *He closes with you in this consequence*—Hml II 1 45. *If consequence do but approve my dream*—Oth II 3 64.

(2) *Consequence of*, app., succession to: *You are curb'd from that enlargement by The consequence o' the crown*—Cymb II 3 125.

CONSIDER

To take account of the services of (a person), requite, remunerate: *You that have worn your eyes almost out in the service, you will be considered*—Meas I 2 113. *Being something gently considered, I'll . . .*—Wint IV 4 824. To requite, reward (services, &c.): *Which (i.e. the services) if I have not enough considered . . .*—Wint IV 2 19. *I will consider your music*—Cymb II 3 31.

CONSIDERANCE

Consideration, reflection: *After this cold considerance, sentence me*—2 H4 V 2 98.

CONSIDERATE

Marked by consideration or thought: *None are for me That look into me with considerate eyes*—R3 IV 2 29. *Your considerate stone*, (here I stand like) a thoughtful (and of course silent) stone: *Ant. . . . Therefore speak no more.* Eno. *Go to, then; your considerate stone*—Ant II 2 111.

CONSIDERED

Characterized by, or giving opportunity for, consideration: *At our more consider'd time we'll read*—Hml II 2 81.

CONSIGN

(1) To subscribe, agree: *God consigning to my good intents*—2 H4 V 2 143. *We'll consign thereto*—H5 V 2 90. *A hard condition for a maid to consign to*—326.

(2) To submit to the same terms with another: *All lovers must Consign to thee*—Cymb IV 2 274.

(3) *Consign'd kisses*, prob., committed, delivered: *As many farewells as be stars in heaven, With distinct breath and consign'd kisses to them*—Troil IV 4 46.

CONSIST

(1) *To consist upon*, to insist or stand upon: *Such large terms . . . As our conditions shall consist upon*—2 H4 IV 1 186.

(2) App., to be bent on: *Welcome is peace, if he on peace consist*—Per I 4 83.

CONSISTORY

A council-chamber; fig.: *My other self, my counsel's consistory*—R3 II 2 151.

CONSOLATE

To console: *To consolate thine ear*—All's III 2 131.

CONSORT (sb.), CONCERT

(1) A fellowship, company: *Wilt thou be of our consort?*—Gent IV 1 64. *He was of that consort*—Lr II 1 99.

(2) Music in harmony: *And boding screech-owls make the concert full!*—2 H6 III 2 327. A company of musicians: *Visit by night your lady's chamber-window With some sweet concert; to their instruments Tune a deploring dump*—Gent III 2 83. This last sense alluded to (with a play)—Rom III 1 48 and foll.

CONSORT (vb.)

To accompany, attend: *Afterward [I'll] consort you till bed-time*—Err I 2 28. *Sweet health and fair desires consort your grace!*—LLL II 178. *Thou . . . that didst consort him here*—Rom III 1 135. *Who to Philippi here consorted us*—Cæs V 1 83.

CONSPECTUITY

Faculty of sight, vision: *Your bisson conspectuities*—Cor II 1 70.

CONSPIRANT

Engaged in a conspiracy or plot: *Conspirant 'gainst this high-illustrious prince*—Lr V 3 135.

CONSTANCY

(1) Persistence, perseverance: *If you will now unite in your complaints, And force them with a constancy*—H8 III 2 1.

(2) Certainty, or perh., consistency, coherency: [The story] *grows to something of great constancy*—Mids V 26.

CONSTANT

(1) Consecutive, regularly conducted: *Make the trial of it in any constant question*—Tw IV 2 52.

(2) Settled, steady (physically): *My stomach is not constant*—Tp II 2 118.

CONSTANTLY

(1) With assurance or certitude, confidently, firmly: *I do constantly believe you*—Meas IV 1 21. *I constantly do think*—Troil IV 1 40.

(2) Continuously, permanently: *The devil a puritan that he is, or any thing constantly*—Tw II 3 159.

CONSTANT-QUALIFIED

Constant in the possession of (good) qualities: *More fair, virtuous . . . constant-qualified and less attemptable*—Cymb I 4 64.

CONSTELLATION

Disposition or character as determined by one's 'stars': *I know thy constellation is right apt For this affair*—Tw I 4 35.

CONSTRUE

To inform by way of explanation, explain: *I will construe to them whence you come*—Tw III 1 63.

CONTAGIOUS

Noxious, pernicious: *Contagious fogs*—Mids II 1 90. *This night, whose black contagious breath . . .*—John V 4 33. *Contagious blastments*—Hml I 3 42.

CONTAIN

To retain (in various shades of meaning): *Cannot contain their urine*—Merch IV 1 50. *If you had known . . . your own honour to contain the ring, You would not then have parted with the ring*—V 199. *What thy memory can not contain*—Sonn 77 9.

CONTAINING

Contents: *This label . . . whose containing Is so from sense in hardness, that . . .*—Cymb V 5 430.

CONTEMPTIBLE

Contemptuous: *The man . . . hath a contemptible spirit*—Ado II 3 187.

CONTEMPTUOUS

Contemptible: *Contemptuous base-born callet as she is*—2 H6 I 3 86.

CONTENT (adj.)

(1) Consenting, willing: *Are you content to be our general?*—Gent IV 1 61. *I have been content, sir, you should lay my countenance to pawn*—Wiv II 2 4. *Be you content to lend your patience to us*—Hml IV 5 210. *Content*, agreed! all right! *Content, i' faith: I'll seal to such a bond*—Merch I 3 153. First Sold. . . . *Let's see how it* (i.e. the noise) *will give off.* All. *Content*—Ant IV 3 23.

(2) Satisfied in mind, calm, not uneasy: *Cassius, be content; Speak your griefs softly*—Cæs IV 2 41. *I pray you, be content; 'tis but his humour*—Oth IV 2 165. *Be content; Your low-laid son our godhead will uplift*—Cymb V 4 102. *Hold you content*—Ado V 1 92.

CONTENT (sb.)¹

That which is contained: *Though my heart's content firm love doth bear*—Troil I 2 320.

CONTENT (sb.)²

(1) Pleasure, delight: *Your gallery Have we pass'd through, not without much content*—Wint V 3 10. *This night he dedicates To fair content and you*—H8 I 4 2. *It gives me wonder great as my content To see you*—Oth II 1 185. *My soul hath her content so absolute That . . .*—193.

(2) App., faculty of pleasing, pleasing quality: *Examine every married lineament And see how one another lends content*—Rom I 3 83.

CONTENT (vb.)

(1) To please, gratify: *A woman sometimes scorns what best contents her*—Gent III 1 93. *Is the adder better than the eel, Because his painted skin contents the eye?*—Shr IV 3 179. *It doth much content me To hear him so inclined*—Hml III 1 24.

(2) To remunerate: *Come the next Sabbath, and I will content you*—R3 III 2 113. To reward (services): *I will content your pains*—Oth III 1 1.

(3) To be content, acquiesce: *'Tis Clifford; Who not contented that he lopp'd the branch . . . But set his murdering knife unto the root*—3 H6 II 6 46. *Forced to content, but never to obey, Panting he lies*—Ven 61.

CONTINENT (adj.)

Restraining, restrictive: *Thy . . . edict and continent canon*—LLL I 1 262. *My desire All continent impediments would o'erbear*—Mcb IV 3 63. (In both cases no doubt with a reference also to the meaning *chaste*).

CONTINENT (sb.)

(1) That which contains or holds: *They* (i.e. the rivers) *have overborne their continents*—Mids II 1 92. *Which is not tomb enough and continent To hide the slain*—Hml IV 4 64. *Heart, once be stronger than thy continent*—Ant IV 14 40.

(2) A summary, abstract: *Ay, my continent of beauty*—LLL IV 1 111. *The continent and summary of my fortune*—Merch III 2 131. *You shall find in him the continent of what part a gentleman would see*—Hml V 2 114.

(3) The land as opposed to the water: [*That one might see*] *the continent . . . melt itself Into the sea*—2 H4 III 1 47. Of a river bank: *Mark how he* (i.e. the Trent) *bears his course . . . Gelding the opposed continent*—1 H4 III 1 108.

(4) The orb of the sun: *As true . . . As doth that orbed continent the fire That severs day from night*—Tw V 277.

CONTINUANCE

Permanence, persistency: *The continuance of his love*—Tw I 4 6. *The continuance of their parents' rage*—Rom Prol 10.

CONTINUATE

(1) Lasting: *An untirable and continuate goodness*—Tim I 1 11.

5

(2) Uninterrupted: *A more continuate time*—Oth III 4 178.

CONTRACTION

The making of marriage vows: *Such a deed As from the body of contraction plucks The very soul*—Hml III 4 45.

CONTRADICT

To oppose, forbid: *To contradict his claim*—John II 280. *A greater power than we can contradict*—Rom V 3 153. *I, her husband, contradict your bans*—Lr V 3 87.

CONTRARIOUS

Self-contradictory (in result): *False and most contrarious quests*—Meas IV 1 62.

CONTRARIOUSLY

In (apparent) opposition, in different directions: *Many things, having full reference To one consent, may work contrariously*—H5 I 2 205.

CONTRARY (adj.)

(1) Of things, wrong, the wrong: *Set a deep glass of rhenish wine on the contrary casket*—Merch I 2 104. *Slippers . . . falsely thrust upon contrary feet*—John IV 2 197.

(2) Of persons, antagonistic, hostile: *'Tis your counsel My lord should to the heavens be contrary, Oppose against their wills*—Wint V 1 44. *To their lives bad friends were contrary*—R3 IV 4 216.

CONTRARY (vb.)

To oppose, cross: *You must contrary me!*—Rom I 5 87.

CONTRIVE ¹

To spend, pass (time): *Please ye we may contrive this afternoon*—Shr I 2 276.

CONTRIVE ²

To plan evil devices, plot, conspire: *Thou hast contrived against the very life Of the defendant*—Merch IV 1 360. *Was't you that did so oft contrive to kill him?*—As IV 3 135. *We charge you, that you have contrived to take From Rome all season'd office*—Cor III 3 63. *The Fates with traitors do contrive*—Cæs II 3 16. *Most generous and free from all contriving*—Hml IV 7 136.

CONTRIVER

A plotter, conspirator: *A secret and villanous contriver against me*—As I 1 150.

CONTROL (sb.)

(1) Constraint, compulsion: *The proud control of fierce and bloody war*—John I 17.

(2) *At control*, subject to orders: *Are their males' subjects and at their controls*—Err II 1 19. *I am too high-born . . . To be a secondary at control*—John V 2 79.

CONTROL (vb.)

(1) To rebuke, reprove (a person): *When soon I heard The crying babe controll'd with this discourse*—Tit V 1 25. *If then they chanced to slack you, We could control them*—Lr II 4 248. To confute: *The Duke of Milan . . . could control thee*—Tp I 2 438.

(2) To find fault with, censure (a thing): *No more will I control thy griefs*—Tit III 1 260. *And justly thus controls his thoughts unjust*—Lucr 189.

(3) To overmaster, overpower: *His art is of such power, It would control my dam's god, Setebos*—Tp I 2 372. *The ill which doth control't*—Cor III 1 161. *With her own white fleece her voice controll'd Entombs her outcry in her lips' sweet fold*—Lucr 678.

CONTROLLER, COMPTROLLER

(1) A steward; *comptrollers*, app., masters of the ceremonies: *I was spoke to, with . . . This night to be comptrollers*—H8 I 3 66.

(2) A censurer, detractor: *He dares not calm his contumelious spirit Nor cease to be an arrogant controller*—2 H6 III 2 204.

CONTROLMENT

Constraint, compulsion: *War for war . . . Controlment for controlment*—John I 19.

CONVENIENCE

(1) An agreement, correspondence: *For want of these required conveniences, her delicate tenderness will find itself abused*—Oth II 1 234.

(2) Fitness, propriety: *And [that] the place answer to convenience*—Meas III 1 257. *All the honour That good convenience claims*—All's III 2 74.

CONVENIENT

(1) Appropriate, suitable (*for* a thing): *A marvellous convenient place for our rehearsal*—Mids III 1 2. *The most convenient place . . . For such receipt of learning*—H8 II 2 138. Suitable to the circumstances, appropriate, proper: *I go with all convenient speed*—Merch III 4 56. *It shall be convenient . . . that you be by her*—2 H6 I 4 9. *Take Convenient numbers to make good the city*—Cor I 5 12. *I'll frame convenient peace*—V 3 191.

(2) Ethically suitable, becoming, fitting: *'Tis not convenient you should be cozened*—Wiv IV 5 83. *Caitiff . . . That under covert and convenient seeming Hast practised on man's life*—Lr III 2 55. Reg. *Sister, you'll go with us?* Gon. *No.* Reg. *'Tis most convenient; pray you, go with us*—V 1 34.

CONVENIENTLY

Becomingly, fittingly: *Such fair ostents of love As shall conveniently become you there*—Merch II 8 44.

CONVENT

(1) To summon: *What he . . . will make up full clear, Whensoever he's convented*—Meas V 156.

(2) To cause to come together, assemble: *We are convented Upon a pleasing treaty*—Cor II 2 58.

(3) To suit: *When . . . golden time convents*—Tw V 391. (But sense (1) is possible.)

CONVENTICLE

A secret gathering for a sinister purpose: *Myself had notice of your conventicles*—2 H6 III 1 166.

CONVERSATION

(1) Intercourse, commerce: *The king Had from the conversation of my thoughts Haply been absent*—All's I 3 239. *Thou art e'en as just a man As e'er my conversation coped withal*—Hml III 2 59. Implying sexual intercourse: *His conversation with Shore's wife*—R3 III 5 31.

(2) Behaviour, mode or course of life: *What an unweighed behaviour hath* [he] *picked . . . out of my conversation?*—Wiv II 1 23. *Banish'd till their conversations Appear more wise and modest to the world*—2 H4 V 5 106. *Those soft parts of conversation That chamberers have*—Oth III 3 264.

CONVERSE

(1) To hold intercourse: *I have, since I was three year old, conversed with a magician*—As V 2 66. *Why dost thou converse with that trunk of humours?*—1 H4 II 4 494. *One that converses more with the buttock of the night than with the forehead of the morning*—Cor II 1 56.

(2) To interchange ideas (*with* a person): *Did you converse, sir, with this gentlewoman?* (*i.e.* have you been laying plans together?)—Err II 2 162.

CONVERT

(1) To change the direction of: *The eyes, 'fore duteous, now converted are From his low tract*—Sonn 7 11.

(2) To turn oneself away: *When thou from youth convertest*—Sonn 11 4.

(3) To turn, change (*to* something else): *The love of wicked men converts to fear*—R2 V 1 66. *This intrusion shall Now seeming sweet convert to bitter gall*—Rom I 5 93. *Let grief Convert to anger*—Mcb IV 3 228.

CONVEY

(1) To escort, lead away: *Convey my tristful queen*—1 H4 II 4 434. *Convey them with safe conduct*—H5 I 2 297.

(2) To carry away or cause to go clandestinely: *Thence she cannot be convey'd away*—Gent III 1 37. *If you have a friend here, convey, convey him out*—Wiv III 3 124. *War. . . . How made he escape?* *Post. He was convey'd by Richard Duke*

of Gloucester—3 H6 IV 6 80. Refl.: *Behind the arras I'll convey myself*—Hml III 3 28. To put into a thing clandestinely: *They conveyed me into a buck-basket*—Wiv III 5 87. *An onion . . . Which in a napkin being close convey'd Shall . . .*—Shr Ind 1 126.

(3) As a euphemism, to steal: *'Convey', the wise it call. 'Steal!' foh!*—Wiv I 3 32.

(4) To bring down by succession, derive: *Convey'd himself as heir to the Lady Lingare*—H5 I 2 74.

(5) To carry on or manage clandestinely: *You may Convey your pleasures in a spacious plenty*—Mcb IV 3 70. *I will . . . convey the business as I shall find means*—Lr I 2 109.

CONVEYANCE

(1) Convoying, escorting: *To his conveyance I assign my wife*—Oth I 3 286.

(2) Removal, riddance: *Madest quick conveyance with her good aunt Anne*—R3 IV 4 283.

(3) Underhand dealing, trickery: *I fear there is conveyance*—1 H6 I 3 2. *Thy sly conveyance and thy lord's false love*—3 H6 III 3 160. Dexterity, jugglery: *Huddling jest upon jest with such impossible conveyance upon me that . . .*—Ado II 1 252.

CONVEYER

As a euphemism, a thief: *Convey? conveyers are you all, That rise thus nimbly by a true king's fall*—R2 IV 317.

CONVICT

To discomfit, put to flight: *A whole armado of convicted sail*—John III 4 2.

CONVINCE

(1) To overcome: *His two chamberlains Will I with wine and wassail so convince That . . .*—Mcb I 7 63. *Their malady convinces The great assay of art*—IV 3 142. *Who having . . . Convinced or supplied them* (*i.e.* their mistresses), *cannot choose But they must blab*—Oth IV 1 26. *To convince the honour of my mistress*—Cymb I 4 104. App., to overcome opposition in, prevail in: *The holy suit which fain it would convince*—LLL V 2 756.

(2) To convict: *Else might the world convince of levity As well my undertakings as your counsels*—Troil II 2 130.

CONVIVE

To feast together, banquet: *There in the full convive we*—Troil IV 5 272.

CONVOY

Means of conveyance: *To which place We have convenient convoy*—All's IV 4 9. *As the winds give benefit And convoy is assistant*—Hml I 3 2. Road money: *His passport shall be made And crowns for convoy put into his purse*—H5 IV 3 36.

A thing that conducts, a way or path: *A tackled stair; Which to the high top-gallant of my joy Must be my convoy*—Rom II 4 201.

CONY-CATCH

(1) To cheat, trick: *Your cony-catching rascals*—Wiv I 1 128. *There is no remedy; I must cony-catch; I must shift*—I 3 36. *Take heed . . . lest you be cony-catched in this business*—Shr V 1 101.

(2) App., to mock, gibe: *Come, you are so full of cony-catching!*—Shr IV 1 45.

COPATAIN HAT

A high-crowned hat in the form of a sugar-loaf: *A scarlet cloak! and a copatain hat!*—Shr V 1 69.

COPE

(1) To come into relation or contact with, have to do with, meet; intr.: *Who of force must know The royal fool thou copest with*—Wint IV 4 433. *Thou art e'en as just a man As e'er my conversation coped withal*—Hml III 2 59. *She, that never coped with stranger eyes*—Lucr 99. Trans.: *I love to cope him in these sullen fits*—As II 1 67. *He yesterday coped Hector in the battle*—Troil I 2 34. *Where . . . and when He hath, and is again to cope your wife*—Oth IV 1 86.

(2) To match with an equivalent: *Three thousand ducats . . . We freely cope your courteous pains withal*—Merch IV 1 411.

COPESMATE

A companion, associate: *Mis-shapen Time, copesmate of ugly Night*—Lucr 925.

COPPED

Rising to a top or head: *The blind mole casts Copp'd hills towards heaven*—Per I 1 100.

COPULATIVES

Persons desiring to be coupled in marriage: *I press in here, sir, amongst the rest of the country copulatives*—As V 4 57.

COPY

(1) A holding by copy, copyhold; fig.: *In them nature's copy's not eterne*—Mcb III 2 38.

(2) *Copy of a conference*, memorandum or minutes of it; hence app., subject matter, theme: *It was the copy of our conference*—Err V 62.

CORAM

By confusion for Quorum: *Justice of peace and 'Coram'*—Wiv I 1 5.

CORANTO

A dance characterized by a running or gliding step: *He's able to lead her a coranto*—All's II 3 49. *Why dost thou not . . . come home in a coranto?*—Tw I 3 136. *Lavoltas high and swift corantos*—H5 III 5 33.

CORE

A boil (properly the mass of dead tissue in the centre of a boil): *Were not that a botchy core?*—Troil II 1 6. *How now, thou core of envy!*—V I 4.

CORINTH

The luxurious Greek city; allusively, a house of ill fame: *Would we could see you at Corinth!*—Tim II 2 72.

CORINTHIAN

A gay, spirited fellow: *[They] tell me flatly I am no proud Jack . . . but a Corinthian, a lad of mettle*—1 H4 II 4 12.

CORKY

Withered, sapless: *Bind fast his corky arms*—Lr III 7 29.

CORNER-CAP

A three-cornered cap worn by divines: *Thou makest the triumviry, the corner-cap of society*—LLL IV 3 53.

CORNET

A company of horse: *Somerset, who in proud heart Doth stop my cornets*—1 H6 IV 3 24.

CORNUTO

A cuckold: *The peaking Cornuto her husband*—Wiv III 5 71.

COROLLARY

A supernumerary: *Bring a corollary, Rather than want a spirit*—Tp IV 57.

CORPORAL

Corporeal, material: *What seem'd corporal melted As breath into the wind*—Mcb I 3 81.

CORPORAL OF THE FIELD

An officer of superior rank: *I to be a corporal of his (i.e. Cupid's) field!*—LLL III 189.

CORPSE

Unchanged in plural: *Upon whose dead corpse there was such misuse*—1 H4 I 1 43. *My lord your son had only but the corpse, But shadows and the shows of men, to fight*—2 H4 I 1 192.

CORRECTIONER

One who administers punishment: *You filthy famished correctioner*—2 H4 V 4 22 (to the beadle).

CORRESPONDENT

Compliant, submissive: *I will be correspondent to command*—Tp I 2 297.

CORRIGIBLE

Corrective: *The power and corrigible authority of this lies in our wills*—Oth I 3 329.

CORRIVAL

A compeer, associate: *Many moe corrivals and dear men*—1 H4 IV 4 31.

CORRUPTIBLY

So as to be corrupted: *The life of all his blood Is touch'd corruptibly*—John V 7 1.

CORRUPTION

Putrid matter, pus; fig.: *When it breaks, I fear will issue thence The foul corruption of a sweet child's death*—John IV 2 80. *The time will come, that foul sin, gathering head, Shall break into corruption*—2 H4 III 1 76. *Stew'd in corruption*—Hml III 4 93.

COST (sb.)

(1) Outlay, expenditure: *The fashion of the world is to avoid cost*—Ado I 1 97. *How little is the cost I have bestow'd*—Merch III 4 19. *Command what cost Your heart has mind to*—Ant III 4 37. *Costs*, expenses: *Costs and charges in transporting her*—2 H6 I 1 134.

(2) That on which money is expended; ornament, show, pomp: *Where youth, and cost, and witless bravery keeps*—Meas I 3 10. *The citywoman bears The cost of princes on unworthy shoulders*—As II 7 75. *This queen, worth all our mundane cost*—Per III 2 71. A costly or gorgeous thing: *His part-created cost* (i.e. his half-built house)—2 H4 I 3 60. *By Time's fell hand defaced The rich proud cost of outworn buried age*—Sonn 64 1.

COST (vb.)

See *Coast* (vb.).

COSTARD

A large apple; applied to the head: *I will knog his urinals about his knave's costard*—Wiv III 1 14. *Take him over the costard with the hilts of thy sword*—R3 I 4 159. *Ise try whether your costard or my ballow be the harder*—Lr IV 6 246.

COSTLY

Gorgeous, rich: *Costly summer*—Merch II 9 94. *The canopies of costly state*—2 H4 III 1 13. *Costly thy habit as thy purse can buy*—Hml I 3 70.

COTE (sb.)

A cottage: *His cote, his flocks and bounds of feed Are now on sale*—As II 4 83. *Come every day to my cote*—III 2 447.

COTE (vb.)

In coursing, of a hound, to outstrip his competitor; fig., to outstrip, pass (on the way): *We coted them on the way*—Hml II 2 330.

COT-QUEAN

A man who acts the house-wife: *Go, you cotquean, go*—Rom IV 4 6 (addressed to Capulet).

COTSALL

Cotswold in Gloucestershire, the recognized home and centre of coursing: *How does your fallow greyhound, sir? I heard say he wa: outrun on Cotsall*—Wiv I 1 91.

COUCH

(1) To lay to rest: *Where unbruised youth . . . Doth couch his limbs*—Rom II 3 37.

(2) Of a falcon, to cause to crouch close: *Which, like a falcon towering in the skies, Coucheth the fowl below with his wings' shade*—Lucr 506. Fig.: *One cloud of winter showers, These flies are couch'd*—Tim II 2 180.

COUCHINGS

Obeisances: *These couchings and these lowly courtesies*—Cæs III 1 36.

COUNSEL (sb.)

(1) A secret design or thought: *Their several counsels they unbosom shall To loves mistook*—LLL V 2 141. *They of Rome are enter'd in our counsels*—Cor I 2 2. *The close enacts and counsels of the heart*—Tit IV 2 118. Of a letter: *To her white hand see thou do commend This seal'd-up counsel*—LLL III 1 169. Collectively, secret designs or thoughts: *Buckingham No more shall be the neighbour to my counsel*—R3 IV 2 42. *What man art thou that . . . So stumblest on my counsel?*—Rom II 2 52. *These locks of counsel* (i.e. the seals of the letter)—Cymb III 2 36.

(2) *In counsel*, admitted to confidence; *of one's counsel*, in his confidence: *This night he meaneth . . . To climb celestial Silvia's chamber-window, Myself in counsel*—Gent II 6 33. *When I told thee he was of my counsel*—Oth III 3 111.

(3) *In counsel*, in confidence, in private: *'Twere better for you if it were known in counsel: you'll be laughed at*—Wiv I 1 121.

(4) *To speak to* (a person's) *counsel*, app., to speak to him in confidence: *What to your sworn counsel I have spoken*—All's III 7 9.

COUNSEL (vb.)

In pass., to yield to counsel: *Pray, be counsell'd*—Cor III 2 28. *So I lose none . . . I shall be counsell'd*—Mcb II 1 26.

COUNT (sb.)

Account, calling to account: *The other motive, Why to a public count I might not go* (i.e. against Hamlet for the murder)—Hml IV 7 16.

COUNT (vb.)

To count of, to make account of, mark: *So painted . . . that no man counts of her beauty*—Gent II 1 64. *Count of this, the count's a fool*—All's IV 3 258.

COUNTENANCE (sb.)

(1) Bearing, demeanour: *The something that nature gave me his countenance seems to take from me*—As I 1 18. *Unkind usage, dangerous countenance*—1 H4 V 1 69. *The strangeness of his alter'd countenance*—2 H6 III 1 5. *Found you no displeasure in him by word or countenance?*—Lr I 2 171.

(2) Appearance, aspect: *Puts my apparel and my countenance on*—Shr I 1 234. *To cozen somebody in this city under my countenance*—V 1 40. *He did bear my countenance in the town*—129. Feigned appearance, seeming: *Unfold the evil which is here wrapt up In countenance!*—Meas V 117.

COUNTENANCE (vb.)

To be in keeping with, match: *As from your graves rise up, and walk like sprites, To countenance this horror!*—Mcb II 3 84.

COUNTER

In hunting, backwards in the line of the hunted hart: *You hunt counter: hence! avaunt!*—2 H4 I 2 102. *How cheerfully on the false trail they cry! O, this is counter, you false Danish dogs!*—Hml IV 5 109. In Err IV 2 39 (*A hound that runs counter*, said of the catchpole) with a play on Counter or Compter; see *Counter-gate*.

COUNTER-CASTER

One who reckons with counters; applied contemptuously to a 'great arithmetician': *This counter-caster . . . must his lieutenant be*—Oth I 1 31.

COUNTERCHANGE

Reciprocation: *She . . . throws her eye . . . hitting Each object with a joy: the counterchange Is severally in all*—Cymb V 5 394.

COUNTERCHECK

A 'check' or rebuke in return for another: *This is called the Countercheck Quarrelsome*—As V 4 84.

COUNTERFEIT (sb.)

A portrait: *Fair Portia's counterfeit!*—Merch III 2 116. *Thou draw'st a counterfeit Best in all Athens*—Tim I 1 83. *Much liker than your painted counterfeit*—Sonn 16 8. As adj., portrayed: *The counterfeit presentment of two brothers*—Hml III 4 54.

COUNTERFEIT (vb.)

To make a portrait: *Thou counterfeit'st most lively*—Tim V 1 85. Cf. 83 quoted under the preceding word.

COUNTER-GATE

Thou mightst as well say I love to walk by the Counter-gate—Wiv III 3 84. There were two prisons in London with the name Counter or Compter, one in Wood Street and the other in the Poultry. There was also a Compter in Southwark.

COUNTERMAND

(1) To go counter to, oppose: *My heart shall never countermand mine eye*—Lucr 276.

(2) To keep under command, control: *That countermands The passages of alleys*—Err IV 2 37.

COUNTERPART

A duplicate, exact copy: *Let him but copy what in you is writ . . . And such a counterpart shall fame his wit*—Sonn 84 9.

COUNTERPOINT

A counterpane: *My arras counterpoints*—Shr II 353.

COUNTER-SEAL

To seal with an additional seal by way of sanction: *Which* (*i.e.* the treaty) *we . . . will have counter-seal'd*—Cor V 3 204.

COUNTRY

Attrib., of one's country: *I know our country disposition well*—Oth III 3 201. *Each of us fell in praise of our country mistresses*—Cymb I 4 61. *Our country rights*—Lucr 1838.

COUNTY

Count: *The County Palatine*—Merch I 2 49. *A ring the county wears*—All's III 7 22. *The county stays*—Rom I 3 105.

COUPLEMENT

(1) A coupling together: *Making a couplement of proud compare, With sun and moon, with . . .*—Sonn 21 5.

(2) A pair: *I wish you the peace of mind, most royal couplement!*—LLL V 2 534.

COURAGE

(1) Mind, temper: *This soft courage makes your followers faint*—3 H6 II 2 57.

(2) Spirit, vigour: *So did this horse excel a common one In shape, in courage, colour, pace and bone*—Ven 293. In 276 (*His hot courage and his high desire*) with the notion of sexual vigour.

(3) Spirit, haughtiness: [I would not] *check my courage for what they can give*—Cor III 3 92.

(4) Inclination, leaning: *I'd such a courage to do him good*—Tim III 3 24.

COURSE

(1) In pl., points of the compass: *Set her two courses off to sea again*—Tp I 1 52.

(2) In bear-baiting, an attack of the dogs: *Bear-like, I must fight the course*—Mcb V 7 2. *I am tied to the stake, and I must stand the course*—Lr III 7 54.

COURSER'S HAIR

Much is breeding, Which, like the courser's hair, hath yet but life, And not a serpent's poison—Ant I 2 199. It was believed that a horse's hair placed in water would become a living creature.

COURT-CUPBOARD

A sideboard or cabinet: *Remove the court-cupboard, look to the plate*—Rom I 5 7.

COURTESY (sb.)

(1) A bow (by a man): *If a man will make courtesy and say nothing, he is virtuous*—2 H4 II 1 135. *These couchings and these lowly courtesies*—Cæs III 1 36. *An excellent courtesy!*—Oth II 1 176. Bowing: *The elephant hath joints, but none for courtesy*—Troil II 3 113. *Leave your courtesy*, app., leave off bowing, never mind about your bow—Mids IV 1 21.

(2) App., deferential treatment; and so, the amenities of life: *The certainty of this hard life; aye hopeless To have the courtesy your cradle promised*—Cymb IV 4 27.

(3) *Remember thy courtesy*, be covered: *I do beseech thee, remember thy courtesy; I beseech thee, apparel thy head*—LLL V 1 102. Cf. Hml V 2 108: Ham. *I beseech you, remember* — [Hamlet moves him to put on his hat.

(4) *The courtesy of it*, the ceremony with which it is introduced: *Sure, you have some hideous matter to deliver, when the courtesy of it is so fearful*—Tw I 5 221. *The courtesy of nations*, the ceremonial laws governing society: *The courtesy of nations allows you my better*—As I 1 49.

COURTESY (vb.), CURTSY

To make a bow (of men): *Let them curtsy with their left legs*—Shr IV 1 95. *Toby approaches; courtesies there to me*—Tw II 5 67. *To dog his heels and curtsy at his frowns*—1 H4 III 2 127.

COURT HOLY-WATER

Fair empty words: *Court holy-water in a dry house is better than this rain-water out o' door*—Lr III 2 10.

COURTIER

One who courts, a wooer: *Courtiers of beauteous freedom*—Ant II 6 17.

COURT OF GUARD

The post occupied by a military guard: *The lieutenant to-night watches on the court of guard*—Oth II 1 219. *We must return to the court of guard*—Ant IV 9 2. Sim. *the court and guard of safety*: *To manage private and domestic quarrel, In night, and on the court and guard of safety!*—Oth II 3 215.

COURTSHIP

(1) Behaviour befitting a court, courtliness of manners: *Trim gallants, full of courtship and of state*—LLL V 2 363. *One that knew courtship too well, for there he fell in love*—As III 2 363 (there seems to mean, at court). *I thought King Henry had resembled thee In courage, courtship and proportion*—2 H6 I 3 56.

(2) The condition befitting a courtier: *More validity, More honourable state, more courtship lives In carrion-flies than Romeo*—Rom III 3 33.

(3) The paying of courteous attentions: *His courtship to the common people*—R2 I 4 24.

COUSIN

A kinsman, a relative; applied to a nephew: *Peace, cousin, say no more*—1 H4 I 3 187 (Worcester to Hotspur). A niece: *Your cousin, my lady, takes great exceptions to your ill hours*—Tw I 3 5 (to Sir Toby, referring to Olivia). An uncle: *Cousin, cousin, how have you come so early by this lethargy?*—Tw I 5 131 (Olivia to Sir Toby). A brother-in-law: *Peace, cousin Percy*—1 H4 III 1 52 (Mortimer to Hotspur; applied also by Hotspur to Glendower, Mortimer's father-in-law: 3; and by Glendower to Hotspur: 35). A grandchild: *Farewell, gentle cousin*—John III 3 17 (Queen Elinor to the Bastard). *You'll have your daughter covered with a Barbary horse . . . you'll have coursers for cousins*—Oth I 1 111.

COVENT

Convent: *One of our covent*—Meas IV 3 133. *Where the reverend abbot, With all his covent, honourably received him*—H8 IV 2 18.

COVETOUSNESS

Inordinate desire, over-eagerness: *When workmen strive to do better than well, They do confound their skill in covetousness*—John IV 2 28.

COWARD

To daunt: *That hath so cowarded and chased your blood Out of appearance*—H5 II 2 75.

COWARDSHIP

Cowardice: *For his cowardship, ask Fabian*—Tw III 4 423.

COWISH

Of the nature of a cow; hence, cowardly: *The cowish terror of his spirit*—Lr IV 2 12.

COWL-STAFF

A pole used for carrying a burden (*e.g.* a basket) borne by two persons: *Go take up these clothes here quickly. Where's the cowl-staff?*—Wiv III 3 155.

COX

Cock's, God's; see *Passion* (sb.) (1).

COXCOMB

(1) A fool's cap: *Shall I have a coxcomb of frize?*—Wiv V 5 146. *Here's my coxcomb* [Offering Kent his cap—Lr I 4 105.

(2) The head: *A bloody coxcomb*—Tw V 193. *It is good for your green wound and your ploody coxcomb*—H5 V 1 44. *She knapped 'em o' the coxcombs with a stick*—Lr II 4 124.

(3) A fool, simpleton: *Off, coxcomb!*—Ado IV 2 71. *An ass and a fool and a prating coxcomb*—H5 IV 1 78. *O murderous coxcomb! what should such a fool Do with so good a woman?*—Oth V 2 233.

COY (adj.)

Disdainful: *Where scorn is bought with groans; Coy looks with heart-sore sighs*—Gent I 1 29. *Her spirits are as coy and wild As haggerds of the rock*—Ado III 1 35. *'Twas told me you were rough and coy and sullen*—Shr II 245.

COY (vb.)

(1) To caress: *While I thy amiable cheeks do coy*—Mids IV 1 2.

(2) To disdain: *If he coy'd To hear Cominius speak, I'll keep at home*—Cor V 1 6.

COYSTRILL, COISTREL

A knight's groom; or perh. a form of Kestrel, a worthless kind of hawk; hence, a base fellow: *A coward and a coystrill*—Tw I 3 42. *Every Coistrel that comes inquiring for his Tib*—Per IV 6 175.

COZIER

A cobbler: *Ye squeak out your coziers' catches*—Tw II 3 97.

CRACK (sb.)

A lively lad, 'young rogue': *When a was a crack not thus high*—2 H4 III 2 34. *Val. Indeed, la, 'tis a noble child. Vir. A crack, madam*—Cor I 3 73.

CRACK (vb.)

(1) To boast: *Ethiopes of their sweet complexion crack*—LLL IV 3 268. So, to utter boastfully: *Our brags Were crack'd of kitchen-trulls*—Cymb V 5 176.

(2) To drink, 'discuss': *You'll crack a quart together*—2 H4 V 3 66.

CRACKER

A blusterer: *What cracker is this same that deafs our ears?*—John II 147.

CRACK-HEMP

A gallows-bird: *Come hither, crack-hemp*—Shr V 1 46.

CRAFT

To make a job of it: *You have made fair hands, You and your crafts! you have crafted fair!*—Cor IV 6 117.

CRANK (sb.)

A winding passage: *Through the cranks and offices of man*—Cor I 1 141.

CRANK (vb.)

To zigzag, wind: *See how this river comes me cranking in*—1 H4 III 1 98. *He (i.e. the hare) cranks and crosses with a thousand doubles*—Ven 682.

CRANTS

A garland, chaplet: *She is allow'd her virgin crants*—Hml V 1 255.

CRARE

A small trading vessel: *To show what coast thy sluggish crare Might easiliest harbour in*—Cymb IV 2 205.

CRAVEN

A cock that is not game: *You crow too like a craven*—Shr II 228.

CRAZE

To impair: *So many miseries have crazed my voice*—R3 IV 4 17. *Crazed*, having a flaw; fig.: *Yield Thy crazed title to my certain right*—Mids I 1 91.

CRAZY

Frail, infirm: *Some better place, Fitter for sickness and for crazy age*—1 H6 III 2 88.

CREDENCE

Trust in, reliance on (a person): *[We] lay our best love and credence Upon thy promising fortune*—All's III 3 2.

CREDENT

(1) Having credit or repute: *My authority bears of a credent bulk*—Meas IV 4 29.

(2) Credible: *Then 'tis very credent Thou mayst co-join with something*—Wint I 2 142.

CREDIT (sb.)

(1) A belief, report: *There I found this credit, That he did range the town to seek me out*—Tw IV 3 6.

(2) Trustworthiness, credibility: *What does else want credit . . . I'll be sworn 'tis true*—Tp III 3 25. *An oath of credit*—Merch V 246. *There is no composition in these news That gives them credit*—Oth I 3 1.

CREDIT (vb.)

To do credit to: *I call them forth to credit her*—Shr IV 1 106.

CREEK

A narrow or winding passage: *The passages of alleys, creeks and narrow lands*—Err IV 2 38.

CRESCIVE

Capable of growth: *Unseen, yet crescive in his faculty*—H5 I 1 66.

CRESSET

A vessel containing fire, gen. mounted on a pole or suspended from a roof; fig.: *The front of heaven was full of fiery shapes, Of burning cressets* —1 H4 III 1 14.

CRESSIDA, CRESSID

Cressida was a beggar—Tw III 1 62. *The lazar kite of Cressid's kind*—H5 II 1 80. In Henryson's Testament of Cresseid (l. 342 in Skeat's Chaucerian and other Pieces, 1897) Cressida is condemned to go "begging . . . lyk ane lazarous". See *Lazar* (adj.) and (sb.).

CRIB

To shut up as in a crib, to confine within narrow and hampering bounds: *Cabin'd, cribb'd, confined, bound in*—Mcb III 4 24.

CRINGE

To draw together or distort through pain: *Whip him, fellows, Till, like a boy, you see him cringe his face*—Ant III 13 99.

CRISP

App., bright, shining: *Crisp heaven*—Tim IV 3 183.

CRISPIN and CRISPIAN

The patron saints of shoemakers: H5 IV 3 40 and foll. *Crispin Crispian*, their feast (October 25th): 57.

CROSBY PLACE

R3 I 2 213; I 3 345; III 1 190.   Built by Sir John Crosby about 1470 on the east side of Bishopsgate Street.   It was taken down in 1908.   Much of the old work had been replaced.

CROSS (adj.)

Quarrelsome, contrarious: *Nor hast thou pleasure to be cross in talk*—Shr II 251. *My Lord of York will still be cross in talk*—R3 III 1 126. *Bassianus comes: Be cross with him*—Tit II 3 52. Malignant, thwarting: *What cross devil Made me put this main secret in the packet?*—H8 III 2 214. Perverse, froward: *To move the heavens to smile upon my state, Which . . . is cross and full of sin* —Rom IV 3 4.

CROSS (sb.)

A coin bearing the figure of a cross; and gen., a coin: Arm. *I love not to be crossed*. Moth. [Aside] *He speaks the mere contrary; crosses love not him*—LLL I 2 34. *I should bear no cross if I did bear you, for I think you have no money in your purse*—As II 4 12. *Not a penny; you are too impatient to bear crosses*—2 H4 I 2 252. (In all the cases with a play.)

CROSS (vb.)

(1) To debar, hinder *from*: *To cross me from the golden time I look for*—3 H6 III 2 127.

(2) To contradict, traverse (a statement): *I'll say so.   Who can cross it?*—Per IV 3 16.

(3) App., to provide with money (with a play): *There is no crossing him in 's humour; Else I should tell him . . . When all's spent, he'ld be cross'd then, an he could*—Tim I 2 166.

CROSS (adv.)

To break cross, see *Break* (3).

CROSS (prep.)

Across: *I charge thee waft me safely cross the Channel*—2 H6 IV 1 114.

CROSS-GARTERED

Wearing the garters both above and below the knee and crossed behind: *Remember who . . . wished to see thee ever cross-gartered*—Tw II 5 166.

CROSS-GARTERING

The wearing of the garters as explained under the foregoing word: *This does make some obstruction in the blood, this cross-gartering*—Tw III 421.

CROSSNESS

Perversity, spirit of contradiction: *Rather than she will bate one breath of her accustomed crossness* —Ado II 3 183.

CROSS-ROW

The alphabet: *From the cross-row plucks the letter G*—R3 I 1 55.

CROW-FLOWER

The buttercup: *Fantastic garlands . . . Of crow-flowers, nettles . . .*—Hml IV 7 169.

CROW-KEEPER

(1) A scare-crow: *Scaring the ladies like a crow-keeper*—Rom I 4 6.

(2) One who guards fields from crows: *That fellow handles his bow like a crow-keeper*—Lr IV 6 87.

CROWNER

Coroner: *Seek the crowner, and let him sit o' my coz*—Tw I 5 142.   *The crowner hath sat on her*—Hml V 1 4.   *Crowner's quest law*—24.

CROWNET

Coronet: *Sixty and nine, that wore Their crownets regal*—Troil Prol 5.   *Whose bosom was my crownet, my chief end*—Ant IV 12 27.   *In his livery Walk'd crowns and crownets*—V 2 90.

CROWN IMPERIAL

A species of Fritillary: *Bold oxlips and The crown imperial*—Wint IV 4 125.

CRUDY

Curdy; curd-like in appearance: *Foolish and dull and crudy vapours*—2 H4 IV 3 106.

CRUELTY

To brother born an household cruelty—2 H4 IV 1 95, perh., an act of cruelty touching the speaker in his domestic relations, viz. the death of his born brother (the Lord Scroop, see 1 H4 I 3 270), as distinguished from the cause of his *brother general* mentioned in the preceding line.

CRUSADO

A Portuguese coin: *I had rather have lost my purse Full of crusadoes*—Oth III 4 25.

CRUSH

(1) *To crush a cup*, to drink, 'discuss' it: *Come and crush a cup of wine*—Rom I 2 85.

(2) *Crushed*, strained, forced: *Yet that is but a crush'd necessity*—H5 I 2 175.

CRY (sb.)

(1) A rumour, report: *The cry goes that you shall marry her*—Oth IV 1 126. The public voice (in admiration or applause): *The cry went once on thee, And still it might*—Troil III 3 184.

(2) A pack of hounds: *A cry more tuneable Was never holla'd to*—Mids IV 1 128. *You common cry of curs!*—Cor III 3 120. A company of persons: *A fellowship in a cry of players*—Hml III 2 288.

CRY (vb.)

(1) To beg for: *Monarch's hands that let not bounty fall Where want cries some, but where excess begs all*—Compl 41.

(2) To call for, require: *The affair cries haste*—Oth I 3 277.

(3) To cry up, extol: *Now this masque Was cried incomparable*—H8 I 1 26.

(4) *To cry out on the top of question*, to dominate discussion—Hml II 2 355. *To cry in the top of one's judgement*, to dominate it—Hml II 2 459.

(5) *To cry on*, to exclaim against: *His mangled Myrmidons . . . Crying on Hector*—Troil V 5 33. So *to cry out of: They say he cried out of sack*—H5 II 3 29.

(6) *To cry on*, to utter the cry of: *Their souls . . . Came to my tent, and cried on victory*—R3 V 3 230. *Whose noise is this that cries on murder?*—Oth V 1 48.

(7) *To cry* (fame, &c.) *on* or *upon*, to invoke (fame, &c.) by outcry on or upon: *That very envy . . . Cried fame and honour on him*—Tw V 61. *All the country . . . Cried hate upon him*—2 H4 IV 1 136.

(8) *I cry you mercy*, I beg your pardon: *O, I cry you mercy, friend*—Ado I 2 26. *I cry you mercy, then*—Oth IV 2 88. So *I cry your wor-*

ships mercy—Mids III 1 182. Sim. *to cry pardon*: *I cry you gentle pardon*—Oth V 1 93. Also *to cry grace: Cry These dreadful summoners grace*—Lr III 2 58.

CUBICULO

A bedroom: *We'll call thee at the cubiculo*—Tw III 2 56.

CUCKOO-BUD

A wild flower which cannot be identified: *Cuckoo-buds of yellow hue*—LLL V 2 906.

CUDGELLED

Made by cudgelling: *Patches will I get unto these cudgell'd scars*—H5 V 1 93.

CUISSES

Armour for the thighs: *His cuisses on his thighs*—1 H4 IV 1 105.

CULLION

A despicable fellow, rascal: *Such a one as leaves a gentleman, And makes a god of such a cullion*—Shr IV 2 19. *Avaunt, you cullions!*—H5 III 2 21. *Away, base cullions!*—2 H6 I 3 43.

CULLIONLY

Despicable: *You whoreson cullionly barbermonger*—Lr II 2 35.

CULVERIN

A large cannon, very long in proportion to its bore: *Of basilisks, of cannon, culverin*—1 H4 II 3 56.

CUNNING (adj.)

(1) Learned: *This learned constable is too cunning to be understood*—Ado V 1 233. *To cunning men I will be very kind*—Shr I 1 97. *Cunning in Greek, Latin, and other languages*—II 81.

(2) Skilful: *Be cunning in the working this*—Ado II 2 53. *Cunning in fence*—Tw III 4 312. *This bodiless creation ecstasy Is very cunning in*—Hml III 4 138.

(3) Having magical or occult knowledge or skill: *Margery Jourdain, the cunning witch*—2 H6 I 2 75. *A cunning man did calculate my birth*—IV 1 34.

CUNNING (sb.)

(1) Knowledge: *That errs in ignorance and not in cunning*—Oth III 3 49. Learning, erudition: *I hold it ever, Virtue and cunning were endowments greater Than nobleness and riches*—Per III 2 26.

(2) Wisdom, intelligence: *We have been guided by thee hitherto And of thy cunning had no diffidence*—1 H6 III 3 9. *Shame that they wanted cunning, in excess Hath broke their hearts*—Tim V 4 28.

(3) Skill, ability, cleverness: *I have no cunning in protestation*—H5 V 2 150. *An excellent play . . . set down with as much modesty as cunning*—Hml II 2 459. *We'll make a solemn wager on your cunnings*—IV 7 156. *In our sports my better cunning faints Under his chance*—Ant II 3 34.

(4) Magical skill: *A sorcerer that by his cunning hath cheated me of the island*—Tp III 2 49.

(5) A profession: *Shame not these woods, By putting on the cunning of a carper*—Tim IV 3 208.

(6) *In the boldness of my cunning*, in confidence of my insight: *In the boldness of my cunning, I will lay myself in hazard*—Meas IV 2 165.

CUP

To supply with cups, *i.e.* with liquor: *Cup us, till the world go round*—Ant II 7 124.

CURATE

The parson of a parish: LLL V 1 120 (of Sir Nathaniel). *Make him believe thou art Sir Topas the curate*—Tw IV 2 2.

CURB

To bow, cringe: *Virtue itself of vice must pardon beg, Yea, curb and woo for leave to do him good*—Hml III 4 154.

CURDY

To congeal: *The icicle That's curdied by the frost from purest snow*—Cor V 3 65.

CURE

Perh., responsibility, charge: *For my little cure, Let me alone*—H8 I 4 33.

CURFEW

Applied to a bell rung at a fixed hour in the morning: *The second cock hath crow'd, The curfew-bell hath rung*—Rom IV 4 3.

CURIOSITY

Nicety, fastidiousness: *When thou wast in thy gilt and thy perfume, they mocked thee for too much curiosity*—Tim IV 3 301. Critical scrutiny, punctiliousness: *Curiosity in neither can make choice of either's moiety*—Lr I 1 6. *Wherefore should I . . . permit The curiosity of nations to deprive me?*—I 2 2. *Which I have rather blamed as mine own jealous curiosity than as a very pretence and purpose of unkindness*—I 4 74.

CURIOUS

(1) Bestowing care or pains: *Frank nature, rather curious than in haste, Hath well composed thee*—All's I 2 20.

(2) Anxious, solicitous: *I am something curious . . . To have them in safe stowage*—Cymb I 6 191. Sim. perh. in Troil III 2 70 (*What too curious dreg espies my sweet lady in the fountain of our love?*) suggesting trouble to come.

(3) Difficult to satisfy, nice: *You shall not find, Though you be therein curious, the least cause For what you seem to fear*—Ant III 2 34. *These curious days*—Sonn 38 13.

(4) Particular, cautious: *Curious I cannot be with you . . . of whom I hear so well*—Shr IV 4 36.

(5) Careful in observation: *What care I What curious eye doth quote deformities?*—Rom I 4 30.

(6) Exquisitely wrought or prepared: *His body couched in a curious bed*—3 H6 II 5 53. *Lapp'd In a most curious mantle*—Cymb V 5 360. *Those mothers who, to nousle up their babes, Thought nought too curious*—Per I 4 42. Of workmanship, careful: *The curious workmanship of nature*—Ven 734.

(7) Elaborate: *Mar a curious tale in telling it*—Lr I 4 35. *With sleided silk . . . Enswathed, and seal'd to curious secrecy*—Compl 48. Exquisite: *Curious pleasures*—Per I 1 16. So perh., intricate, various: *Fraught with curious business*—Wint IV 4 524.

CURIOUS-GOOD

Elaborately worked up: *This (i.e. in the letter) is too curious-good, this blunt and ill*—Lucr 1300.

CURIOUS-KNOTTED

Elaborately laid out in plots: *Thy curious-knotted garden*—LLL I 1 249.

CURIOUSLY

(1) With careful art, elaborately: *The which if I do not carve most curiously, say my knife's naught*—Ado V 1 156. *The sleeves curiously cut*—Shr IV 3 144. *That he might take a measure of his own judgements, wherein so curiously he had set this counterfeit*—All's IV 3 38.

(2) Minutely: *'Twere to consider too curiously, to consider so*—Hml V 1 227.

CURRANCE

Current, flow: *With such a heady currance, scouring faults*—H5 I 1 34.

CURRY

To employ blandishment so as to win favour: *If [I had a suit] to his men, I would curry with Master Shallow that . . .*—2 H4 V 1 81.

CURSORARY

Cursory, hasty: *I have but with a cursorary eye O'erglanced the articles*—H5 V 2 77.

CURST

(1) Ill-tempered, virulent, harsh: *Curst wives*—LLL IV 1 36. *Her elder sister is so curst and shrewd That . . .*—Shr I 1 185. *Write it in a martial hand; be curst and brief*—Tw III 2 45. *Sweet saint, for charity, be not so curst*—R3 I 2 49. Of speech, sharp, biting: *As bitter-searching*

*terms, As curst, as harsh and horrible to hear . . .
As . . .*—2 H6 III 2 311. *With curst speech I
threaten'd to discover him*—Lr II 1 67.

(2) Of animals, savage, fierce: *They (i.e. the
bears) are never curst but when they are hungry*—
Wint III 3 134. *Finding their enemy (i.e. the
boar) to be so curst*—Ven 887.

CURSTNESS

Bad humour, ill temper: *Touch you the sourest
points with sweetest terms, Nor curstness grow to
the matter*—Ant II 2 24.

CURTAIL

See *Curtal.*

CURTAIN

Applied to an ensign: *Their ragged curtains
poorly are let loose*—H5 IV 2 41.

CURTAL, CURTAIL

Having the tail cut short or off:

(1) Of a dog: *My curtail dog . . . Plays not at
all*—Pilgr 273. Applied to a dog that misses his
game: *Hope is a curtal dog in some affairs*—Wiv
II 1 114. And to a common dog not meant for
sport: *She had transform'd me to a curtal dog and
made me turn i' the wheel*—Err III 2 151.

(2) The name of a horse: *Bay Curtal and his
furniture*—All's II 3 65.

CURTLE-AXE

A cutlass: *A gallant curtle-axe upon my thigh*
—As I 3 119. *Scarce blood enough . . . To give
each naked curtle-axe a stain*—H5 IV 2 20.

CURTSY

See *Courtesy* (vb.).

CUSTALORUM

By confusion for *Custos Rotulorum*, Keeper of
the Rolls: Wiv I 1 7.

CUSTARD

Like him that leaped into the custard—All's II
5 40. *Custard-coffin*—Shr IV 3 82. For these
see *Coffin.*

CUSTOM

App. adverbially, by custom: *But custom what*

they did begin Was with long use account no sin—
Per Prol 29.

CUSTOMED

Usual, customary: *No common wind, no customed
event*—John III 4 155. *To wring the widow from
her custom'd right*—2 H6 V 1 188.

CUSTOMER

(1) A familiar associate: *You minion, you, are
these your customers?*—Err IV 4 63.

(2) A common woman: *I think thee now some
common customer*—All's V 3 287. *I marry her!
what? a customer!*—Oth IV 1 122.

CUT

(1) A slash in a garment for ornament: *Cloth
o' gold, and cuts, and laced with silver*—Ado III
4 19.

(2) A common or labouring horse, either as
being a cut-tail horse or as being a gelding; as a
term of abuse: *If thou hast her not i' the end, call
me cut*—Tw II 3 202. The name of a horse:
Beat Cut's saddle—1 H4 II 1 6.

CUT AND LONG-TAIL

Curtal curs and all; all kinds, everybody: *Ay,
that I will, come cut and long-tail, under the degree
of a squire*—Wiv III 4 47.

CUTTLE

A knife; hence perh. one over-ready to use his
knife, a bully, bravo: *An you play the saucy cuttle
with me*—2 H4 II 4 139.

CYME

Perh. an error for Cynne, Senna: *What rhubarb,
cyme, or what purgative drug, Would scour these
English hence?*—Mcb V 3 55.

CYPRESS, CYPRUS

(1) A light transparent material like crape:
Cyprus black as e'er was crow—Wint IV 4 221.
So perh. in Tw II 4 52 (*Come away, come away,
death, And in sad cypress let me be laid*); but there
a coffin of cypress wood or sprigs of cypress as
symbols of mourning may be meant.

(2) Of a piece of cypress used as a kerchief: *A
cypress, not a bosom, Hideth my heart*—Tw III 1
132.

D

DAFF

(1) To divest oneself of: *To daff't for our repose*
—Ant IV 4 13. *There my white stole of chastity
I daff'd*—Compl 297.

(2) To thrust aside, put aside: *I would have
daffed all other respects*—Ado II 3 176. *That
daff'd the world aside, And bid it pass*—1 H4 IV

1 96. To put off: *Every day thou daffest me with
some device*—Oth IV 2 176.

DAGONET

*Sir Dagonet: I was then Sir Dagonet in Arthur's
show*—2 H4 III 2 299. See *Arthur's Show.* Sir
Dagonet was King Arthur's attendant fool.

DAINTRY

Daventry: *By this* [he is] *at Daintry, with a puissant troop*—3 H6 V 1 6.

DAINTY

To make dainty, to hold back affectedly: *She that makes dainty, She, I'll swear, hath corns*—Rom I 5 21. *Dainty of*, particular or scrupulous about: *Grows dainty of his worth*—Troil I 3 145. *Let us not be dainty of leave-taking*—Mcb III 3 150.

DALLIANCE

Putting off time by trifling, wilful delay: *You use this dalliance to excuse Your breach of promise*—Err IV 1 48. *My business cannot brook this dalliance*—59.

DAMASCUS

This be Damascus, thou be cursed Cain—1 H6 I 3 39. Cain was said to have slain Abel here.

DAMASK

(1) *Damask rose*, a species or variety of rose supposed to have been originally brought from Damascus: *Gloves as sweet as damask roses*—Wint IV 4 222.

(2) The colour of the damask rose, especially as seen in the face of a woman, blush-colour: *The war of white and damask in Their nicely-gawded cheeks*—Cor II 1 232.

(3) Applied to mingled red and white: *Just the difference Betwixt the constant red and mingled damask*—As III 5 122. This cannot refer to the damask rose, which is not known to be variegated. Probably the reference is to damask silk fabrics.

(4) Attrib., of the colour of the damask rose, blush-coloured: *Her damask cheek*—Tw II 4 115. *A lily pale, with damask dye to grace her*—Pilgr 89. Red and white mingled (see (3)): *Their damask sweet commixture shown*—LLL V 2 296. So *damasked*: *Roses damask'd, red and white*—Sonn 130 5.

DAMN

To condemn: *Look, with a spot I damn him*—Cæs IV 1 6. *Perform't, or else we damn thee*—Ant I 1 24.

DAN

Dominus; Master, Sir: *Dan Cupid*—LLL III 182.

DANCING HORSE

The dancing horse, a horse named 'Morocco' taught by one Bankes, a Staffordshire man, to perform many remarkable tricks: *How easy it is to . . . the dancing horse will tell you*—LLL I 2 55.

DANCING-RAPIER

A sword worn only for ornament in dancing: *Although our mother, unadvised, Gave you a dancing-rapier by your side*—Tit II 1 38. Cf. *No sword worn But one to dance with*—All's II 1 32. *He at Philippi kept His sword e'en like a dancer*—Ant III 11 35.

DANGER (sb.)

(1) The power, reach, range (of a person or weapon): *Out of the shot and danger of desire*—Hml I 3 35. *Within one's danger*, in his reach or power: *You stand within his danger, do you not?*—Merch IV 1 180. *Come not within his danger*—Ven 639.

(2) Mischief, harm: *The neglecting it May do much danger*—Rom V 2 19. *We put a sting in him, That at his will he may do danger with*—Cæs II 1 16.

DANGER (vb.)

To endanger: *Whose quality, going on, The sides o' the world may danger*—Ant I 2 198.

DANGEROUS

(1) Haughty, rigorous: *Unkind usage, dangerous countenance*—1 H4 V 1 69.

(2) In danger (as from disease): *You may salve so, Not what is dangerous present, but the loss Of what is past*—Cor III 2 70 (*not* = not only; see *Not*).

DANKISH

Dank, wet: *A dark and dankish vault*—Err V 247.

DANSKER

A Dane: *Inquire me first what Danskers are in Paris*—Hml II 1 7.

DARE (sb.)

(1) A defiance, challenge: *Sextus Pompeius Hath given the dare to Cæsar*—Ant I 2 190.

(2) Daring, boldness: *It lends . . . A larger dare to our great enterprise*—1 H4 IV 1 77.

DARE (vb.)

To fascinate and daze a lark by the approach of a hawk, or by a mirror or a piece of scarlet cloth, so that it lay close and was caught: *Our approach shall so much dare the field That England shall couch down in fear and yield*—H5 IV 2 36. *Let his grace go forward, And dare us with his cap* (*i.e.* his scarlet cardinal's hat) *like larks*—H8 III 2 281.

DAREFUL

Full of defiance: *We might have met them dareful, beard to beard*—Mcb V 5 6.

DARK

To obscure: *This so darks In Philoten all graceful marks*—Per IV Prol 35.

DARRAIGN

To set in array: *Darraign your battle, for they are at hand*—3 H6 II 2 72.

DASH (sb.)

At first dash, from the first: *She takes upon her bravely at first dash*—1 H6 I 2 71.

DASH (vb.)

To cancel, bring to nothing, frustrate: *Here was a consent, Knowing aforehand of our merriment, To dash it*—LLL V 2 460. *With a full intent To dash our late decree in parliament*—3 H6 II 1 117.

DATE

(1) Limit, term: *Thy end is truth's and beauty's doom and date*—Sonn 14 14.

(2) *Teeming date*, period of child-bearing: *Is not my teeming date drunk up with time?*—R2 V 2 91.

DATE-BROKE

Not met when due: *Clamorous demands of date-broke bonds*—Tim II 2 38.

DAUB

(1) To cloak, gloss: *So smooth he daub'd his vice with show of virtue*—R3 III 5 29.

(2) To dissemble: *I cannot daub it further*—Lr IV 1 54.

DAUBERY

Specious pretences: *She works by charms . . . and such daubery as this is*—Wiv IV 2 184.

DAY

A space (of time), the extent being defined by accompanying words; thus *seven years' day*: *I saw not better sport these seven years' day*—2 H6 II 1 2.

DAY-BED

A sofa, couch: *Having come from a day-bed, where I have left Olivia sleeping*—Tw II 5 54. *Lolling on a lewd day-bed*—R3 III 7 72.

DAY-WOMAN

Dey = dairy-woman; comb. in same sense, *dey-woman, day-woman*: *She is allowed for the day-woman*—LLL I 2 136.

DAZZLE

Of the eyes, to lose the power of distinct or steady vision: *Dazzle mine eyes, or do I see three suns?*—3 H6 II 1 25. *Thy sight is young, And thou shalt read when mine begin to dazzle*—Tit III 2 84. *Her sight dazzling makes the wound seem three*—Ven 1064.

DEAD

(1) Deadly: *Though full of our displeasure, yet we free thee From the dead blow of it*—Wint IV 4 443. *You breathe these dead news in as dead an ear*—John V 7 65.

(2) Deadly pale: *So should a murderer look, so dead, so grim*—Mids III 2 57. *Honest Iago, that look'st dead with grieving*—Oth II 3 177.

DEADLY (adj.)

Deadly use, such use as is made of dead things: *She that herself will sliver . . . From her material sap, perforce must wither And come to deadly use*—Lr IV 2 34.

DEADLY (adv.)

Mortally, fatally: *The venom clamours of a jealous woman Poisons more deadly than a mad dog's tooth*—Err V 69. *Deadly hurt*—Troil V 5 12.

DEADLY-STANDING

With a dull, fixed stare: *My deadly-standing eye*—Tit II 3 32.

DEAF

To deafen: *Sickly ears, Deaf'd with the clamours of their own dear groans*—LLL V 2 873. *What cracker is this same that deafs our ears?*—John II 147.

DEAL (sb.)

A part, portion; hence, *some deal*, somewhat: *To weep with them that weep doth ease some deal*—Tit III 1 245. *No deal*, not at all: *My shepherd's pipe can sound no deal*—Pilgr 271.

DEAL (vb.)

(1) To take action, act, proceed (*in* an affair): *Do not you meddle; let me deal in this*—Ado V 1 101. *To deal upon*, to set to work upon: *They that I would have thee deal upon*—R3 IV 2 75.

(2) *To deal on lieutenantry*, to act by substitutes: *He alone Dealt on lieutenantry*—Ant III 11 38. *A witch . . . that could . . . deal in her command without her power*—Tp V 269, that could act by her power of commanding (that is, by calling for the aid of others more powerful in a particular case than herself) in matters beyond her (personal) power. For an instance see I 2 274 (*She did confine thee, By help of her more potent ministers . . . Into a cloven pine*), and cf. I 2 289 (*It was a torment . . . which Sycorax (i.e. Sycorax unaided) Could not again undo*). See also *Without* (prep.).

DEAR (adj.)[1]

(1) Noble, honourable: *Dear men Of estimation*—1 H4 IV 4 31. *Death hath not struck so fat a deer to-day, Though many dearer*—V 4 107.

(2) Affectionate, loving: *What dear good will I bear unto the banish'd Valentine*—Gent IV 3 14. *This is dear mercy, and thou seest it not*—Rom III

3 23 (or perh. here, rare, unusual). *No less no-bility of love Than that which dearest father bears his son*—Hml I 2 110.

(3) Precious, valuable, prized: *A dear happiness to women*—Ado I 1 129. *Your worth is very dear in my regard*—Merch I 1 62. *With old woes new wail my dear time's waste*—Sonn 30 4. *A dearer birth than this his love had brought*—32 11. In-volving a large sum: *Claudio shall render me a dear account*—Ado IV 1 337. *Upon remainder of a dear account*—R2 I 1 130. *I have bred her at my dearest cost*—Tim I 1 124.

(4) Important, of moment: *The letter was not nice but full of charge Of dear import*—Rom V 2 18. *A ring that I must use In dear employment*—V 3 31. [I dare] *Commend a dear thing to you*—Lr III 1 19. *Some dear cause Will in conceal-ment wrap me up awhile*—IV 3 53.

(5) Touching one nearly: *Their dear causes*—Mcb V 2 3. Heartfelt: *So dear a show of zeal*—1 H4 V 4 95. *Out of dear respect*—H8 V 3 119. So, earnest, zealous: *Towards York shall bend you with your dearest speed*—1 H4 V 5 36. *Loud and dear petition*—Troil V 3 9.

(6) *Dearer*, greater in degree: *A dearer merit . . . Have I deserved at your highness' hands*—R2 I 3 156.

(7) *Dearest enemy*: *Which art my near'st and dearest enemy*—1 H4 III 2 123; and *dearest foe*: *Would I had met my dearest foe in heaven*—Hml I 2 182 (cf. Tw V 74: *Whom thou, in terms so bloody and so dear, Hast made thine enemies*) may have been suggested by 'dearest friend'; or perh. these quotations should come under the next word.

DEAR (adj.)²

Grievous, heavy, dire: *The dearest groans of a mother*—All's IV 5 11. *The dateless limit of thy dear exile*—R2 I 3 151. *Our dear peril*—Tim V 1 231. *I, made lame by fortune's dearest spite*—Sonn 37 3.

DEAR (adv.)¹

Heartily: *I will love you dear*—Merch III 2 316. *So dear I loved the man*— R3 III 5 24.

DEAR (adv.)²

Deeply, keenly: *Shall it not grieve thee dearer than thy death?*—Cæs III 1 196.

DEARED

Endeared: *The ebb'd man . . . Comes dear'd by being lack'd*—Ant I 4 43.

DEARLY¹

(1) Exquisitely, excellently: *Man, how dearly ever parted . . . Cannot*—Troil III 3 96. *One kiss! Rubies unparagon'd, How dearly they do't!*—Cymb II 2 17.

(2) Heartily: *Most dearly welcome to the Greeks*—Troil IV 5 18. *Greets your highness dearly*—Cymb I 6 13.

DEARLY²

Deeply, keenly: *How dearly would it touch thee to the quick*—Err II 2 132. *My father hated his father dearly*—As I 3 34. *We dearly grieve For that which thou hast done*—Hml IV 3 43.

DEARTH

Dearness, costliness; fig.: [I take] *his infusion* [to be] *of such dearth and rareness, as . . .*—Hml V 2 122.

DEATH-PRACTISED

Whose death is plotted: *The death-practised duke*—Lr IV 6 284.

DEATH-TOKENS

See *Tokens.*

DEBASE

To lower (in a physical sense): *Will she yet debase her eyes on me?*—R3 I 2 247.

DEBATE (sb.)

Strife, contention: *From our debate, from our dissension*—Mids II 1 116. *This debate that bleedeth at our doors*—2 H4 IV 4 2. *For thee against myself I'll vow debate*—Sonn 89 13.

DEBATE (vb.)

To combat, fight: *It seem'd they would debate with angry swords*—Lucr 1421. To fight out: *Two thousand souls . . . Will not debate the ques-tion of this straw*—Hml IV 4 25.

DEBATEMENT

Deliberation, consideration: *After much aebate-ment*—Meas V 99. *Without debatement further*—Hml V 2 45.

DEBILE

Weak, feeble: *A most weak and debile minister*—All's II 3 39. *Foil'd some debile wretch*—Cor I 9 48.

DEBITOR

Debtor: *You have no true debitor and creditor but it*—Cymb V 4 171. *Debitor and creditor*, applied contemptuously to a 'great arithmetician': [I] *must be be-lee'd and calm'd By debitor and creditor*—Oth I 1 30.

DEBOSHED

Debauched: *Thou deboshed fish*—Tp III 2 29. *Men so disorder'd, so debosh'd and bold*—Lr I 4 263. Debased: *The mere word's a slave Debosh'd on every tomb*—All's II 3 144. Defiled, dis-credited: *With all the spots o' the world tax'd and debosh'd*—All's V 3 206.

DEBTED

Indebted: *Three odd ducats more Than I stand debted to this gentleman*—Err IV 1 30.

DECAY (sb.)

(1) Ruin, destruction: *Be thou the trumpet of our wrath And sullen presage of your own decay*—John I 1 27. *Death, desolation, ruin and decay*—R3 IV 4 409. *To kill thine honour with thy life's decay*—Lucr 516.

(2) That which causes ruin: *My love was my decay*—Sonn 80 14. That which has been ruined: *What comfort to this great decay may come Shall be applied*—Lr V 3 297.

DECAY (vb.)

(1) To cause to deteriorate, impair: *Infirmity, that decays the wise*—Tw I 5 82

(2) To destroy, bring to nothing: *Every day that comes comes to decay A day's work in him*—Cymb I 5 56.

DECEIVEABLE

Deceptive, deceitful: *There's something in't That is deceiveable*—Tw IV 3 20. *Show me thy humble heart, and not thy knee, Whose duty is deceiveable and false*—R2 II 3 83.

DECENT

Seemly, becoming: *Honesty and decent carriage*—H8 IV 2 145.

DECEPTIOUS

Deceiving: *As if those organs had deceptious functions*—Troil V 2 123.

DECIPHER

(1) To detect, find out: *That you are both decipher'd, that's the news*—Tit IV 2 8.

(2) To reveal, indicate, make known: *The white will decipher her well enough*—Wiv V 2 10. *We should have seen decipher'd there More rancorous spite*—1 H6 IV 1 184. To indicate the distinction between: *Which is the natural man, And which the spirit? who deciphers them?*—Err V 333.

DECK (sb.)

A pack of cards: *The king was slily finger'd from the deck*—3 H6 V 1 44.

DECK (vb.)

To cover, clothe: *Coats To deck our soldiers for these Irish wars*—R2 I 4 61. So possibly in Tp I 2 155 (*When I have deck'd the sea with drops full salt*); but some explain sprinkled, a meaning borne by the word in some dialects.

DECLARE

(1) To explain, expound: *Read, and declare the meaning*—Cymb V 5 434.

(2) To unfold, make known, describe: *This suit of mine, that thou declare What incidency thou dost guess of harm Is creeping toward me*—Wint I 2 402. *His embassy; Which I could with a ready guess declare*—H5 I 1 95. *And now declare . . . Why didst thou say, of late thou wert despised?*—1 H6 II 5 41.

DECLINE

(1) To incline, lean: *Far more to you do I decline*—Err III 2 44.

(2) To come down, sink: *When thou hast hung thy advanced sword i' the air, Not letting it decline*—Troil IV 5 188. *In's nervy arm . . . Which, being advanced, declines, and then men die*—Cor II 1 177. *His sword, Which was declining on the milky head Of reverend Priam*—Hml II 2 499.

(3) Trans., to lower, bend down: *Declining their rich aspect*—Err III 2 138. *Decline your head*—Lr IV 2 22.

(4) To go through in order: *Decline all this, and see what now thou art*—R3 IV 4 97. *I'll decline the whole question*—Troil II 3 55.

DECOCT

To warm (as in cooking): *Can sodden water . . . Decoct their cold blood to such valiant heat?*—H5 III 5 18.

DECREE (sb.)

A resolve: *On our quick'st decrees The inaudible and noiseless foot of Time Steals ere we can effect them*—All's V 3 40. *That so my sad decrees may fly away*—Tit V 2 11. *How now, wife! Have you deliver'd to her our decree?*—Rom III 5 138. *Poor hand, why quiver'st thou at this decree?*—Lucr 1030.

DECREE (vb.)

To resolve, decide: *Therefore I have decreed not to sing in my cage*—Ado I 3 35. To resolve upon (a course): *What yesternight our council did decree*—1 H4 I 1 32.

DEED-ACHIEVING

Won by the achieving of deeds: *By deed-achieving honour newly named . . . Coriolanus*—Cor II 1 190.

DEED OF SAYING

The deed of saying, the performance of what has been promised: *The deed of saying is quite out of use*—Tim V 1 28.

DEEM (sb.)

A thought, surmise: *I true! how now! what wicked deem is this?*—Troil IV 4 61.

DEEM (vb.)

To judge of, estimate: *In eye of Imogen, that best Could deem his dignity*—Cymb V 4 56. With of: *How the world may deem of me*—2 H6 III 2 65.

DEEP

Grave, weighty: *Matter deep and dangerous*—1 H4 I 3 190. *To betray's In deepest consequence*

—Mcb I 3 125. *If you but said so, 'twere as deep with me*—Cymb II 3 96.

DEEP-FET

Deep-fetched: *To see my tears and hear my deep-fet groans*—2 H6 II 4 33.

DEEPLY

With deep seriousness, solemnly: *Sworn as deeply*—R3 III 1 158. *'Tis deeply sworn*—Hml III 2 235.

DEER

A beast in general: *Mice and rats, and such small deer*—Lr III 4 144.

DEFAME (sb.)

Infamy, disgrace: *Dark harbour for defame!*—Lucr 768. *Feast-finding minstrels, tuning my defame*—817. *If I live, thou livest in my defame*—1033.

DEFAME (vb.)

To bring dishonour upon, disgrace: *England was defamed by tyranny*—2 H6 III 1 123.

DEFAULT

(1) Fault: *Are penitent for your default*—Err I 2 52. *This was your default*—1 H6 II 1 60.

(2) *In the default*, at a pinch: *That I may say in the default, he is a man I know*—All's II 3 241.

DEFEAT (sb.)

Ruin, destruction: *Made defeat of her virginity*—Ado IV 1 48. *A king, Upon whose property and most dear life A damn'd defeat was made*—Hml II 2 596. *Their defeat Does by their own insinuation grow*—V 2 58.

DEFEAT (vb.)

(1) To destroy: *His unkindness may defeat my life*—Oth IV 2 160. [It is] *Mine own true love that doth my rest defeat*—Sonn 61 11.

(2) To deface, disfigure: *Defeat thy favour with an usurped beard*—Oth I 3 346.

(3) To disappoint, defraud, evade: *If these men have defeated the law*—H5 IV 1 175. *Alleged Many sharp reasons to defeat the law*—H8 II 1 13. *Thou strikest not me, 'tis Cæsar thou defeat'st*—Ant IV 14 68. *Lest . . . by some mortal stroke She do defeat us*—V 1 64. *By addition me of thee defeated*—Sonn 20 11.

DEFEATURE

Disfigurement, defacement: *Then is he the ground Of my defeatures*—Err II 1 97. *Careful hours . . . Have written strange defeatures in my face*—V 298. *To mingle beauty with infirmities, And pure perfection with impure defeature*—Ven 735.

DEFECT

Defectiveness: *Being unprepared, Our will became the servant to defect*—Mcb II 1 17. *All my best doth worship thy defect*—Sonn 149 11.

DEFENCE

(1) Capacity of defence: *The city being but of small defence*—3 H6 V 1 64.

(2) The art of defending oneself; fencing, sword-play: *That defence thou hast, betake thee to't*—Tw III 4 240. *A masterly report For art and exercise in your defence*—Hml IV 7 97.

(3) *Defences*, armour: *Go put on thy defences*—Ant IV 4 10.

DEFEND

To prohibit, forbid; with obj. and obj. clause: *Heaven defend your good souls, that you think I will . . .*—Oth I 3 267. With this sense and the sense avert app. united; *God, &c., defend*, God, &c., forbid: *God defend the lute should be like the case!*—Ado II 1 97. *God defend but still I should stand so*—1 H4 IV 3 38. *Which God defend that I should **wring** from him!*—R3 III 7 173. *Hath he seen majesty? Isis else defend, And serving you so long!*—Ant III 3 46.

DEFENDANT

Affording defence, defensive: *To line . . . our towns of war With men of courage and with means defendant*—H5 II 4 7.

DEFENSIBLE

Capable of affording defence: *A field Where nothing but the sound of Hotspur's name Did seem defensible*—2 H4 II 3 36. Capable of defending oneself: *Enter our gates . . . For we no longer are defensible*—H5 III 3 49.

DEFER

To put off, waste (time): *Defer no time, delays have dangerous ends*—1 H6 III 2 33.

DEFIANCE

A declaration of aversion, rejection: *Take my defiance! Die, perish!*—Meas III 1 143.

DEFICIENT

Failing, fainting: *Lest my brain turn, and the deficient sight Topple down headlong*—Lr IV 6 23.

DEFINEMENT

Definition, description: *His definement suffers no perdition in you*—Hml V 2 117.

DEFINITIVE

Of a person, resolved: *Never crave him; we are definitive*—Meas V 432.

DEFLOUR

Deflower: *Let my spleenful sons this trull deflour*—Tit II 3 191.

6

DEFORMED

Deforming: *Time's deformed hand*—Err V 298.

DEFUNCTION

Death: *After defunction of King Pharamond*—H5 I 2 58.

DEFUNCTIVE

Funereal: *The priest in surplice white, That defunctive music can*—Phœn 13.

DEFUSE

See *Diffuse.*

DEFY

To revolt at, set at nought, renounce: *Breaths that I defied not*—As Epil 20. *I defy lechery*—Tw I 5 133. *All studies here I solemnly defy, Save . . .*—1 H4 I 3 228. *We defy augury*—Hml V 2 230.

DEGREE

(1) A step or rung: *His ascent is not by such easy degrees as . . .*—Cor II 2 28. *Scorning the base degrees By which he did ascend*—Cæs II 1 26. Fig.: *That's a degree to love*—Tw III 1 134. *The next degree is England's royal throne*—3 H6 II 1 193.

(2) Way, respect: *Hector is not Troilus in some degrees*—Troil I 2 73.

DEIGN

To accept, not to disdain: *I fear my Julia would not deign my lines*—Gent I 1 160. *Thy palate then did deign The roughest berry*—Ant I 4 63.

DEJECT

Dejected, downcast, dispirited: *Reason and respect Make livers pale and lustihood deject*—Troil II 2 49. *I, of ladies most deject and wretched*—Hml III 1 163.

DEJECTED

Abased, lowly: *The lowest and most dejected thing of fortune*—Lr IV 1 3. *The dejected state wherein he is*—Per II 2 46.

DELATE

See *Dilate.*

DELICATE (adj.)

(1) Delightful, charming: *Love-songs . . . with such delicate burthens*—Wint IV 4 193. *Till that the conquering wine hath steep'd our sense In soft and delicate Lethe*—Ant II 7 113. *That most delicate lodging*—Cymb II 4 136. *A delicate odour*—Per III 2 61. Said of climate or the air: *[The island] must needs be of subtle, tender and delicate temperance*—Tp II 1 41. *The climate's delicate*—Wint III 1 1. *The air is delicate*—Mcb I 6 10.

(2) Voluptuous: *Soft and delicate desires*—Ado I 1 305.

(3) Of persons and their parts, dainty to behold, lovely, graceful: *Delicate Ariel*—Tp I 2 441. *Thou ever young, fresh, loved and delicate wooer*—Tim IV 3 385. *Her delicate cheek*—Lr IV 3 15. *A most fresh and delicate creature*—Oth II 3 20.

(4) Tenderly reared, dainty: *A delicate and tender prince*—Hml IV 4 48. *Her delicate youth*—Oth I 2 74.

(5) Characterized by skilful action, finely ingenious: *A delicate stratagem*—Lr IV 6 188.

DELICATE (sb.)

A luxury: *Far beyond a prince's delicates*—3 H6 II 5 51.

DELIGHTED

Endowed with delight; and hence

(1) Affording delight: *If virtue no delighted beauty lack*—Oth I 3 290. *To make my gift, The more delay'd, delighted*—Cymb V 4 101.

(2) Perh., having capacity for delight, and so turning naturally to happiness (rather than to pain): *To die . . . and the delighted spirit To bathe in fiery floods, or . . .*—Meas III 1 118.

DELIVER

(1) To state, report, make known: *More depends on it than we must yet deliver*—Meas IV 2 128. *Were . . . not with such strength denied As is deliver'd to your majesty*—1 H4 I 3 25. *More, More fearful, is deliver'd*—Cor IV 6 62. To speak, make a statement: *And thus deliver*—R2 III 3 34. *But, an't please you, deliver*—Cor I 1 98.

(2) To hand over, present (in a weakened sense): *O that I served that lady And might not be delivered to the world Till I had made mine own occasion mellow*—Tw I 2 41. *The sorrow that delivers us thus changed*—Cor V 3 39. *I'll deliver Myself your loyal servant*—V 6 141.

(3) In passive, of offspring, to be brought forth: *There are many events in the womb of time which will be delivered*—Oth I 3 377. *Those children nursed, deliver'd from thy brain*—Sonn 77 11.

DELIVERANCE

Manner of speaking: *If seriously I may convey my thoughts In this my light deliverance*—All's II 1 84. Utterance, enunciation: *If we should . . . at each word's deliverance Stab poniards in our flesh*—3 H6 II 1 96. A making of statements: *You have it from his own deliverance*—All's II 5 4.

DELIVERY

A statement, narration: *I make a broken delivery of the business*—Wint V 2 10.

DEMAND (sb.)

A question: *Come you more nearer Than your particular demands will touch it*—Hml II 1 11. *Your answers To my demands*—Cymb I 6 88. Questioning: *Acquaint my daughter no further with any thing you know than comes from her demand out of the letter*—Lr I 5 2.

DEMAND (vb.)

To put a question, ask: *Well demanded, wench* —Tp I 2 139. *You will demand of me why I do this*—Meas I 3 17. Trans., to question: *To be demanded of a sponge!*—Hml IV 2 12. *Demand that demi-devil Why . . .*—Oth V 2 301.

DEMERIT

(1) Merit, desert (in good sense): *Opinion . . . shall Of his demerits rob Cominius*—Cor I 1 275. *My demerits May speak unbonneted to as proud a fortune As this that I have reach'd*—Oth I 2 22.

(2) A blameworthy act, offence: *Not for their own demerits, but for mine, Fell slaughter on their souls*—Mcb IV 3 226.

DEMI-CANNON

A kind of large gun: *What's this? a sleeve? 'tis like a demi-cannon*—Shr IV 3 88.

DEMISE

To transmit: *What honour Canst thou demise to any child of mine?*—R3 IV 4 246.

DEMI-WOLF

A cross between a dog and a wolf—Mcb III 1 94.

DEMON

Equivalent to *Genius* (1): *Thy demon, that's thy spirit which keeps thee*—Ant II 3 19.

DEMONSTRABLE

Evident, apparent: *Some unhatch'd practice Made demonstrable here in Cyprus to him*—Oth III 4 141.

DEMURE

App., to look demurely: *Octavia . . . shall acquire no honour Demuring upon me*—Ant IV 15 27.

DEMURELY

In a subdued manner: *The drums Demurely wake the sleepers*—Ant IV 9 30.

DENAY (sb.)

Denial, refusal: *My love can give no place, bide no denay*—Tw II 4 127.

DENAY (vb.)

To deny, refuse: *Then let him be denay'd the regentship*—2 H6 I 3 107.

DENIER

A small French copper coin; as a type of a small sum: [I will] *not* [pay] *a denier*—Shr Ind 1 9. *I'll not pay a denier*—1 H4 III 3 91. *My dukedom to a beggarly denier*—R3 I 2 252.

DENOTEMENT

An emendation for *devotement*, app. to mean noting, marking: *The contemplation, mark, and denotement of her parts and graces*—Oth II 3 322.

DENOUNCE

Of war, to proclaim, declare: Cleo. *Thou hast forspoke my being in these wars, And say'st it is not fit.* Eno. *Well, is it, is it?* Cleo. *If not, denounced against us, why should not we Be there in person?*—Ant III 7 3. After the second *not* app. must be supplied *in general, yet since the wars have been.* The comma inserted after the *not* seems to help out the sense.

DENUNCIATION

Formal announcement: *She is fast my wife, Save that we do the denunciation lack Of outward order*—Meas I 2 151.

DENY

(1) To refuse (to do a thing): *If you deny to dance*—LLL V 2 228. *Deny to speak with me?* —Lr II 4 89.

(2) To refuse permission to, to forbid: *I am denied to sue my livery here*—R2 II 3 129. *One thing more That womanhood denies my tongue to tell*—Tit II 3 173.

(3) To refuse to accept: *I do desire you Not to deny this imposition*—Merch III 4 32. [If you] *deny his offer'd homage*—R2 II 1 204.

(4) To refuse admittance to (a visitor): *If you will deny the sheriff, so*—1 H4 II 4 544. Cf. Err IV 4 66: *Whilst upon me the guilty doors were shut And I denied to enter in my house.*

DEPART (sb.)

Departure: *At my depart I gave this unto Julia* —Gent V 4 96. *At my depart for France*—2 H6 I 1 2. Of death: *Tidings . . . Were brought me of your loss and his depart*—3 H6 II 1 109.

DEPART (vb.)

(1) To go away from, leave: *Depart the chamber* —2 H4 IV 5 91. *Ere I depart his house*—Lr III 5 1.

(2) To go asunder, to part from each other: *Ere we depart, we'll share a bounteous time In different pleasures*—Tim I 1 263. *Should we be taking leave As long a term as yet we have to live, The loathness to depart would grow*—Cymb I 1 106. *As easy might I from myself depart*—Sonn 109 3.

(3) *To depart with*, to give up, surrender: *Hath willingly departed with a part*—John II 563. *So to depart withal: Which we much rather had depart withal*—LLL II 147.

DEPARTING

Parting, separation: *A deadly groan, like life and death's departing*—3 H6 II 6 43.

DEPEND

(1) To hang down: *Her andirons . . . were two winking Cupids . . . nicely Depending on their brands*—Cymb II 4 88.

(2) To be dependent: *Canst thou believe thy living is a life, So stinkingly depending?*—Meas III 2 27. To be a dependant: *The remainder, that shall still depend*—Lr I 4 271.

(3) To impend: *This day's black fate on more days doth depend*—Rom III 1 124. *Our jealousy Does yet depend*—Cymb IV 3 22. *In me moe woes than words are now depending*—Lucr 1615.

DEPENDANT

Impending: *The curse dependant on those that war for a placket*—Troil II 3 21.

DEPENDENCY

Things depending: *On whom there is no more dependency But brats and beggary*—Cymb II 3 123.

DEPLORE

To tell of with grief: *Never more Will I my master's tears to you deplore*—Tw III 1 173.

DEPOSE

(1) To take away: *You may my glories and my state depose*—R2 IV 1 192.

(2) To divest, deprive: *That Lepidus of the triumvirate Should be deposed*—Ant III 6 28.

(3) To promise formally on oath to do something: *Seeing 'twas he that made you to depose*—3 H6 I 2 26. Cf. 15: *I took an oath that he should quietly reign.*

(4) To examine on oath: *Depose him in the justice of his cause*—R2 I 3 30.

DEPRAVATION

Vilification, detraction: *Stubborn critics, apt, without a theme, For depravation*—Troil V 2 131.

DEPRAVE

To vilify, defame: *That lie and cog and flout, deprave and slander*—Ado V 1 95. *Who lives that's not depraved or depraves?*—Tim I 2 145.

DEPRIVE

To take away: *Some other horrible form, Which might deprive your sovereignty of reason*—Hml I 4 72. *'Tis honour to deprive dishonour'd life*—Lucr 1186. In a passive construction: *Is wretchedness deprived that benefit?*—Lr IV 6 61. Absol., to debar from what one would otherwise have: *Wherefore should I . . . permit The curiosity of nations to deprive me?*—Lr I 2 2.

DEPUTATION

The office of a deputy or substitute: *[We have] given his deputation all the organs Of our own power*—Meas I 1 21. *Sometime, great Agamemnon, Thy topless deputation* (*i.e.* as substitute of Jove) *he puts on*—Troil I 3 151.

DEPUTY

The deputy of the alderman of the ward: *Maid Marian may be the deputy's wife of the ward to thee*—1 H4 III 3 129. *I was before Master Tisick, the debuty, t'other day*—2 H4 II 4 92.

DERIVE

(1) To cause to come upon one, bring down: *Things which would derive me ill will to speak of*—All's V 3 265. *Friend of mine That had to him derived your anger*—H8 II 4 31.

(2) Refl., to pass by descent: *This imperial crown, Which, as immediate from thy place and blood, Derives itself to me*—2 H4 IV 5 41.

DERN

Dark, wild, drear: *By many a dern and painful perch Of Pericles the careful search*—Per III Prol 15.

DEROGATE

Debased: *Her derogate body*—Lr I 4 302.

DEROGATELY

With disparagement: *That I should Once name you derogately*—Ant II 2 33.

DESCANT (sb.)

A melodious accompaniment to a simple musical theme: *[You] mar the concord with too harsh a descant*—Gent I 2 94. Hence, a comment: *On that ground I'll build a holy descant*—R3 III 7 49. Cf. *Ground* (3).

DESCANT (vb.)

To sing: *While thou on Tereus descant'st better skill*—Lucr 1134.

DESCEND

To come down from: *Descend my throne*—3 H6 I 1 74. To hang down from: *Some [hair], untuck'd, descended her sheaved hat*—Compl 31.

DESCENDING

Lineage, parentage: *Didst thou not say . . . that thou camest From good descending?*—Per V 1 127.

DESCRY (sb.)

A descrying, perception: *The main descry Stands on the hourly thought*, we hourly expect to descry the main body—Lr IV 6 217.

DESCRY (vb.)

To spy out, find out, reconnoitre: *Who hath descried the number of the foe?*—R3 V 3 9. [Is gone] *to descry The strength o' the enemy*—Lr IV 5 13.

DESERT

A meritorious action: *Many good and great deserts to Rome*—Tit I 24. *That set thee on to this desert*—Cymb I 5 73.

DESERVED

Deserving, meritorious: *Gratitude Towards her deserved children*—Cor III 1 291.

DESIGN

To point out, indicate: *We shall see Justice design the victor's chivalry*—R2 I 1 202.

DESIGNMENT

A design, undertaking: *Served his designments In mine own person*—Cor V 6 35. *Their designment halts*—Oth II 1 22.

DESIRE

To request the presence of, invite: *Desire them all to my pavilion*—H5 IV 1 27. *I would desire My famous cousin to our Grecian tents*—Troil IV 5 150. To invite (*to the doing of something*): *Shall we dance, if they desire us to't?*—LLL V 2 145.

DESPAIR

To cease to expect aid from: *Despair thy charm*—Mcb V 8 13.

DESPERATE

(1) *Desperate of*, having lost hope, despairing, in regard to (something): *I am desperate of obtaining her*—Gent III 2 5. *Yon island carrions, desperate of their bones*—H5 IV 2 39. *I am desperate of my fortunes*—Oth II 3 337. *Desperate assurance*, one leaving no room for hope: *Put your lord into a desperate assurance she will none of him*—Tw II 2 8.

(2) Expressing or indicating despair: *Did he live now, This sight would make him do a desperate turn*—Oth V 2 206. *To find some desperate instrument of death*—Lucr 1038.

(3) Utterly disregardful: *Desperate of shame and state*, of disgrace and the danger of his position—Tw V 67.

(4) Involving risk, dangerous: *Desperate studies*—As V 4 32.

DESPERATELY

In despair: *Your eldest daughters have fordone themselves, And desperately are dead*—Lr V 3 291. *Insensible of mortality, and desperately mortal*—Meas IV 2 152, prob., taking no thought for death, and (yet) bound to die, and to die without hope.

DESPISED

Despicable: *Despised substance of divinest show!*—Rom III 2 77. *Yond despised and ruinous man*—Tim IV 3 465. Hateful: *Expire the term Of a despised life*—Rom I 4 109. *What's to come of my despised time Is nought but bitterness*—Oth I 1 162. In R2 II 3 95 (*Ostentation of despised arms*) the word may app. be taken in one or the other of these senses.

DESPITE

(1) *In despite of*, in contempt or scorn of, so as to mortify: *A verse to this note that I made yesterday in despite of my invention*—As II 5 48. So *in one's despite*: *Whiles he is vaulting variable ramps In your despite*—Cymb I 6 134. *She framed thee in high heaven's despite*—Ven 731. Sim. *in the despite of*: *An obstinate heretic in the despite of beauty*—Ado I 1 236.

(2) *In despite*, notwithstanding opposition: [An onion] *Shall in despite enforce a watery eye*—Shr Ind 1 128. *I enforce thy rotten jaws to open, And, in despite, I'll cram thee with more food!*—Rom V 3 47.

DETECT

To expose, betray: *To let thy tongue detect thy base-born heart*—3 H6 II 2 143. *Some Tereus hath deflowered thee, And, lest thou shouldst detect him, cut thy tongue*—Tit II 4 26. To accuse: *I never heard the absent duke much detected for women*—Meas III 2 129. *He cannot lie with his neighbour's wife, but it (i.e. his conscience) detects him*—R3 I 4 140.

DETECTION

An accusation, charge: *Could I come to her with any detection in my hand*—Wiv II 2 254.

DETERMINATE

To put a limit or end to, cancel: *The sly slow hours shall not determinate The dateless limit of thy dear exile*—R2 I 3 150. *My bonds in thee are all determinate*—Sonn 87 4.

DETEST

To express abhorrence of, denounce, execrate. Something of this sense may be traced in: *From these that my poor company detest*—Mids II 2 434. *The gods Detest my baseness*—Ant IV 14 56. *I'll write against them, Detest them, curse them*—Cymb II 5 32. And of the sense to renounce in: *'Tis a hard bondage to become the wife Of a detesting lord*—All's III 5 67. *Ay me, detested! how am I beguiled!*—Tw V 142.

DETESTED

Detestable, abominable: *The detested blot Of murderous subornation*—1 H4 I 3 162. *Detested parasites*—Tim III 6 104. *Unnatural, detested, brutish villain!*—Lr I 2 81.

DEUCE-ACE

At dice, two and one: *How much the gross sum of deuce-ace amounts to*—LLL I 2 48.

DEVEST

To undress: *Like bride and groom Devesting them for bed*—Oth II 3 180.

DEVICE

(1) Inventive faculty, ingenuity: *Full of noble device*—As I 1 173.

(2) Applied to the cut and ornaments of one's dress: *Habit and device, Exterior form, outward accoutrement*—John I 210.

(3) A fanciful dramatic representation; a mask played by private persons: *I will forward with my device*—LLL V 2 668. *That is an old device; and it was play'd When I from Thebes came last a conqueror*—Mids V 50.

DEVISE

(1) To conjecture, conceive: *[I] love thee better than thou canst devise*—Rom III 1 72.

(2) To think, meditate: *My lord, where are you? what devise you on?*—1 H6 I 2 124.

DEXTERIOUSLY

A variant of dexterously: *Oli. Can you do it? Clo. Dexteriously, good madonna*—Tw I 5 65.

DIAL

A watch or clock: *He drew a dial from his poke*—As II 7 20. *Then my dial goes not true*—All's II 5 6.

DIAPASON

A bass in octaves: *With deep groans the diapason bear*—Lucr 1132.

DICH

App. = do it, may it do: *Much good dich thy good heart*—Tim I 2 73.

DICK

Like *Jack*, as a term of disparagement: *Some mumble-news, some trencher-knight, some Dick*—LLL V 2 464.

DICKON

Dick: *Dickon thy master is bought and sold*—R3 V 3 305.

DIET (sb.)

Course of life, way of living: *O, he hath kept an evil diet long*—R3 I 1 139.

DIET (vb.)

(1) To regulate, limit: *He is dieted to his hour*—All's IV 3 34.

(2) App. (from putting on a diet) to treat severely: *You, that have turn'd off a first so noble wife, May justly diet me*—All's V 3 220.

DIETER

One who feeds another according to the rules of medicine: *As Juno had been sick And he her dieter*—Cymb IV 2 50.

DIFFERENCE

(1) A characteristic quality: *An absolute gentleman, full of most excellent differences*—Hml V 2 111.

(2) In heraldry, a distinctive alteration on or addition to a coat of arms: *Let him bear it for a difference between himself and his horse*—Ado I 1 69. *You must wear your rue with a difference*—Hml IV 5 182.

(3) Distinction, discrimination: *As long as I have an eye to make difference of men's liking*—Wiv II 1 56.

(4) *At difference*, at variance: *Thou hast set thy mercy and thy honour At difference in thee*—Cor V 3 200. *Of some difference*, conflicting: *Vexed I am Of late with passions of some difference*—Cæs I 2 39.

DIFFERENCY

Difference: *There is differency between a grub and a butterfly*—Cor V 4 11.

DIFFERING

Inconstant in opinion, unstable: *That nothing-gift of differing multitudes*—Cymb III 6 86.

DIFFIDENCE

Distrust, suspicion: *Thou dost shame thy mother And wound her honour with this diffidence*—John I 64. *Needless diffidences*—Lr I 2 161. Want of confidence, misgiving: [We have] *of thy cunning had no diffidence*—1 H6 III 3 10.

DIFFUSE, DEFUSE

To disorder, render confused, indistinct or shapeless: *Some diffused song*—Wiv IV 4 54. *Defused attire*—H5 V 2 61. *Defused infection of a man*—R3 I 2 78. *Other accents . . . That can my speech defuse*—Lr I 4 1.

DIGEST

To divide and dispose of: *Cornwall and Albany, With my two daughters' dowers digest this third*—Lr I 1 129.

DIGRESS

(1) To deviate, fall off (from the due course, &c.): *I am come to keep my word, Though in some part enforced to digress*—Shr III 2 108. *Digressing from the valour of a man*—Rom III 3 127.

(2) To transgress: *This deadly blot in thy digressing son*—R2 V 3 66.

DIGRESSION

Transgression: *That I may example my digression by some mighty precedent*—LLL I 2 121. *My digression is so vile*—Lucr 202.

DILATE, DELATE

To relate or describe at length: *Do me the favour to dilate at full What hath befall'n*—Err I 1 123. *That I would all my pilgrimage dilate*—Oth I 3 153. *Delated*, set out at large: *These delated articles*—Hml I 2 38.

DILDO

A word of obscure origin and meaning; used as a refrain: *With such delicate burthens of dildos and fadings*—Wint IV 4 194.

DILEMMAS

App., pros and cons: *I will presently pen down my dilemmas*—All's III 6 79.

DILIGENT

Observant, attentive: *My too diligent ear*—Tp III 1 42.

DIMENSION

Bodily frame: *In dimension . . . A gracious person*—Tw I 5 280. *[I] am in that dimension grossly clad Which from the womb I did participate*—V 244. In pl., the parts of the body: *Hath not a Jew hands, organs, dimensions?*—Merch III 1 61. *My dimensions are as well compact*—Lr I 2 7.

DIMINISH

To take away, remove: *As [they may] diminish One dowle that's in my plume*—Tp III 3 64.

DIMINUTIVE

Something very small: *Such waterflies, diminutives of nature*—Troil V 1 38. App., a small piece of money: *Shown For poor'st diminutives, for doits*—Ant IV 12 36.

DINT

The dealing of blows; violence, force; *by dint of sword*, by force of arms: *That . . . by dint of sword Have since miscarried*—2 H4 IV 1 128.

DIRECTION

Capacity for directing: *Call for some men of sound direction*—R3 V 3 16.

DIRECTIVE

Subject to direction: *In no less working than are swords and bows Directive by the limbs*—Troil I 3 355.

DISABLE

To depreciate, belittle: *A weak disabling of myself*—Merch II 7 30. *Look you . . . disable all the benefits of your own country*—As IV 1 33. *He disabled my judgement*—V 80.

DISALLOW

To *disallow of*, to refuse approval to, reject: *What follows if we disallow of this?*—John I 16.

DISANIMATE

To discourage, dishearten: *It disanimates his enemies*—1 H6 III 1 183.

DISAPPOINTED

Unprepared: *Unhousel'd, disappointed, unaneled*—Hml I 5 77.

DISASTER (sb.)

In astrology, an unfavourable aspect: *Disasters in the sun*—Hml I 1 118.

DISASTER (vb.)

To damage, injure: *Which pitifully disaster the cheeks*—Ant II 7 18.

DISBENCH

To drive from one's seat: *I hope My words disbench'd you not*—Cor II 2 74.

DISBRANCH

To break off like a branch: *She that herself will sliver and disbranch From her material sap*—Lr IV 2 34.

DISCANDY

To melt away: *The discandying of this pelleted storm*—Ant III 13 165. *The hearts That spaniel'd me at heels . . . do discandy, melt their sweets On blossoming Cæsar*—IV 12 20.

DISCASE

To undress: *I will discase me*—Tp V 85. *Discase thee instantly*—Wint IV 4 647.

DISCERNINGS

Perceptive faculties: *His discernings Are lethargied*—Lr I 4 248.

DISCHARGE (sb.)

Perh., an (official) sending away: *My Lord of Somerset will keep me here, Without discharge, money, or furniture*—2 H6 I 3 171.

DISCHARGE (vb.)

(1) To settle with (a creditor), pay (him): *See him presently discharged*—Err IV 1 32. *The present money to discharge the Jew*—Merch III 2 276.

(2) Technically, to perform (a play or a part): *I will discharge it in either . . .*—Mids I 2 95. *A fine tragedy . . . and very notably discharged*—V 367. *A part which never I shall discharge to the life*—Cor III 2 105.

DISCIPLE

To train: *Discipled of the bravest*—All's I 2 28.

DISCIPLINE

Training or skill in military affairs: *Call for our chiefest men of discipline*—John II 39. *Your discipline in war, wisdom in peace*—R3 III 7 16. *To anger Cassio, either by speaking too loud, or tainting his discipline*—Oth II 1 274.

DISCLAIM

To disclaim in, to renounce or disavow all part in: *Nature disclaims in thee*—Lr II 2 59. Sim. *to disclaim from*: *My disclaiming from a purposed evil*—Hml V 2 252.

DISCLOSE (sb.)

A hatching, coming to light: *I do doubt the hatch and the disclose Will be some danger*—Hml III 1 174.

DISCLOSE (vb.)

To open, unfold: *Before their buttons be disclosed*—Hml I 3 40. *When summer's breath their masked buds discloses*—Sonn 54 8. To hatch out: *As patient as the female dove, When that her golden couplets are disclosed*—Hml V 1 309.

DISCOMFIT

Discomfiture: *Uncurable discomfit Reigns in the hearts of all our present parts*—2 H6 V 2 86.

DISCOMFORT (sb.)

(1) Discouragement: *Discomfort guides my tongue And bids me speak of nothing but despair*—R2 III 2 65.

(2) Distress, grief: *What mean you, sir, To give them this discomfort? Look, they weep*—Ant IV 2 33.

DISCOMFORT (vb.)

(1) To discourage: *You do discomfort all the host*—Troil V 10 10. *His funerals shall not be in our camp, Lest it discomfort us*—Cæs V 3 105.

(2) To distress, grieve: *Yet, though I distrust, Discomfort you, my lord, it nothing must*—Hml III 2 175.

DISCOMFORTABLE

Causing discouragement: *Discomfortable cousin!* —R2 III 2 36.

DISCONTENT

(1) Grief, sorrow: *A man of comfort, whose advice Hath often still'd my brawling discontent*—Meas IV 1 8. *My lord leans wondrously to discontent*—Tim III 4 70. *Not prizing her poor infant's discontent*—Sonn 143 8.

(2) A malcontent: *Fickle changelings and poor discontents*—1 H4 V 1 76. *To the ports The discontents repair*—Ant I 4 38.

DISCONTENTING

Discontented, displeased: *Your discontenting father strive to qualify*—Wint IV 4 542.

DISCOURSE (sb.)

(1) Process; *discourse of reason*, process of reasoning: *Is your blood So madly hot that no discourse of reason . . . Can qualify the same?*—Troil II 2 115. So, faculty of reasoning: *A beast, that wants discourse of reason*—Hml I 2 150. *Discourse of thought*, process of thought: *Either in discourse of thought or actual deed*—Oth IV 2 153.

(2) Reasoning: *She hath prosperous art When she will play with reason and discourse*—Meas I 2 189. *O madness of discourse, That cause sets up with and against itself!*—Troil V 2 142. Faculty of reasoning: *He that made us with such large discourse*—Hml IV 4 36.

(3) Conversational power: *A gentleman of excellent breeding, admirable discourse*—Wiv II 2 234. *A wench of excellent discourse*—Err III 1 109.

(4) Narration: *Yet doth this accident . . . So far exceed all instance, all discourse, That . . .*—Tw IV 3 11.

(5) Familiar intercourse: *Your honesty should admit no discourse to your beauty*—Hml III 1 107.

DISCOURSE (vb.)

To tell, narrate: *[To] hear at large discoursed all our fortunes*—Err V 395. *I am to discourse wonders*—Mids IV 2 29. *The manner of their taking may appear At large discoursed in this paper here*—R2 V 6 9.

DISCOVER

(1) To uncover, lay open: *Draw aside the curtains and discover The several caskets*—Merch II 7 1. *Daylight and champain discovers not more*—Tw II 5 174.

(2) To reveal, make known: *I will open my lips in vain, or discover his government*—Meas III 1 198. *I can discover all The unlucky manage of this fatal brawl*—Rom III 1 147. To expose, denounce (a person): *I threaten'd to discover him* —Lr II 1 68.

(3) To spy out, find out, reconnoitre: *Sent me over . . . to discover What power the Duke of York had levied there*—R2 II 3 33. *Thou hast painfully discover'd: are his files As full as thy report?*—Tim V 2 1. To catch sight of, descry: *We discovered Two ships*—Err I 1 92.

(4) To manifest, display: *Frame some feeling line That may discover such integrity*—Gent III 2 76. *Never counterfeit of passion came so near the life of passion as she discovers it*—Ado II 3 109.

(5) To distinguish, discern: *Angelo hath seen them both, and will discover the favour*—Meas IV 2 184. *By no means I may discover them By any mark of favour*—Cæs II 1 75.

DISCOVERER

A scout: *Send discoverers forth To know the numbers of our enemies*—2 H4 IV 1 3.

DISCOVERY

(1) Revelation, disclosure: *'Tis an office of discovery, love; And I should be obscured*—Merch II 6 43. *My fortunes . . . which are here By this discovery (i.e.* by his imparting the information just given) *lost*—Wint I 2 440. *So shall my anticipa-*

tion prevent your discovery—Hml II 2 304. *Having lost the fair discovery of her way* (*i.e.* having nothing to show her her way)—Ven 828. *Preposterous discoveries*, perh., abuses which reveal themselves to the speaker: *The rotten diseases of the south . . . take and take again such preposterous discoveries!*—Troil V 1 20.

(2) Reconnoitring: *Thereby shall we . . . make discovery Err in report of us*—Mcb V 4 5. *Here is the guess of their true strength and forces By diligent discovery*—Lr V 1 52.

DISCREET

Discreet stories, stories calling for discretion in the telling, *i.e.* that ought not to be told: *Breeds no bate with telling of discreet stories*—2 H4 II 4 271.

DISCRETION

The faculty of discrimination: *Have you any discretion? . . . do you know what a man is?*—Troil I 2 273.

DISCUSS

To make known, tell: *I will discuss the humour of this love to Page*—Wiv I 3 104. *You may discuss unto the duke*—H5 III 2 65. *Discuss unto me; art thou officer?*—IV 1 37.

DISDAINED

Disdainful: *The jeering and disdain'd contempt Of this proud king*—1 H4 I 3 183.

DISEASE (sb.)

A trouble: *I'll tell thee my disease*—1 H6 II 5 44. *Provision To shield thee from diseases of the world*—Lr I 1 176.

DISEASE (vb.)

To trouble: *She will but disease our better mirth*—Cor I 3 116.

DISGRACE (sb.)

(1) A dishonour, affront: *And you . . . Causeless have laid disgraces on my head*—2 H6 III 1 161. *I cannot promise But that you shall sustain moe new disgraces, With these you bear already*—H8 III 2 4.

(2) The expression of dishonour, disparagement: *In disgrace Bespoke him thus*—1 H6 IV 6 20.

(3) A marring of grace, disfigurement: *Stealing unseen to west with this disgrace*—Sonn 33 8. *No man well of such a salve can speak That heals the wound and cures not the disgrace*—Sonn 34 7.

DISGRACE (vb.)

To disparage: *You that were so hot at sea, Disgracing of these colours that I wear*—1 H6 III 4 28.

DISGRACEFUL

Unbecoming: *Away with these disgraceful wailing robes!*—1 H6 I 1 86.

DISGRACIOUS

Not finding favour, disliked: *I have done some offence That seems disgracious in the city's eyes*—R3 III 7 111. *If I be so disgracious in your sight, Let me march on*—IV 4 177.

DISGUISE

Disorder by drink: *The wild disguise hath almost Antick'd us all*—Ant II 7 131.

DISHABIT

To dislodge: *Those sleeping stones . . . By this time from their fixed beds of lime Had been dishabited*—John II 216.

DISHONEST

(1) Dishonourable: *O faithless coward! O dishonest wretch!*—Meas III 1 137. *Did not you say you knew that Friar Lodowick to be a dishonest person?*—V 261. *A very dishonest paltry boy*—Tw III 4 420. Loose in one's habits: *You grow dishonest*—Tw I 5 46.

(2) Unchaste, lewd: *Hang him, dishonest rascal!*—Wiv III 3 196. *Holding in disdain the German women For some dishonest manners of their life*—H5 I 2 48.

DISHONESTY

(1) Dishonourable character or conduct: *His dishonesty appears in leaving his friend here in necessity*—Tw III 4 421. *Leon. What, canst not rule her? Paul. From all dishonesty he can*—Wint II 3 46.

(2) Unchastity, lewdness: *Heaven be my witness you do* [suspect without cause], *if you suspect me in any dishonesty*—Wiv IV 2 139.

DISHONOURED

Dishonouring, dishonourable: *This so dishonour'd rub*—Cor III 1 60. *No unchaste action, or dishonour'd step*—Lr I 1 231.

DISJOINT

Disjointed: *Thinking . . . Our state to be disjoint and out of frame*—Hml I 2 19.

DISLIKE (sb.)

(1) Disapproval: *Wisdom, loyalty and mere dislike Of our proceedings*—1 H4 IV 1 64.

(2) Dissension, discord: *I have not sought the day of this dislike*—1 H4 V 1 26. *You feed too much on this dislike*—Troil II 3 235.

DISLIKE (vb.)

(1) To displease: *Neither, fair saint, if either thee dislike*—Rom II 2 61. *I'll do't; but it dislikes me*—Oth II 3 49.

(2) To express disapproval of: *I never heard any soldier dislike it*—Meas I 2 18. *I did dislike the cut of a certain courtier's beard*—As V 4 73.

DISLIKEN

To disguise: *Disliken The truth of your own seeming*—Wint IV 4 665.

DISLODGE

Pass., to shift one's quarters: *The Volscians are dislodged, and Marcius gone*—Cor V 4 44.

DISMANTLE

To strip off (that which covers): [Should] *Commit a thing so monstrous, to dismantle So many folds of favour*—Lr I 1 220.

DISMAY

To be dismayed: *Dismay not, princes, at this accident*—1 H6 III 3 1.

DISME

A tenth part; hence, a tenth man: *Every tithe soul, 'mongst many thousand dismes*—Troil II 2 19.

DISMISS

To remit, forgive: *A dismiss'd offence*—Meas II 2 102.

DISMOUNT

To draw from the sheath: *Dismount thy tuck*—Tw III 4 244.

DISORBED

Dislodged from its orb (see *Orb* (2)): *Like a star disorb'd*—Troil II 2 46.

DISORDERED

Disorderly, riotous: *Men so disorder'd, so debosh'd and bold*—Lr I 4 263. *Your disorder'd rabble*—277.

DISPARK

To throw open (a park): *Dispark'd my parks and fell'd my forest woods*—R2 III 1 23.

DISPATCH (sb.)

(1) Official dismissal on completion of an errand: *To-day we shall have our dispatch*—LLL IV 1 5. *Yet give us our dispatch*—Cor V 3 180. *The several messengers From hence attend dispatch*—Lr II 1 126.

(2) Conduct, management: *You shall put This night's great business into my dispatch*—Mcb I 5 68.

(3) Business to be dispatched or business dispatched: *After some dispatch in hand at court*—All's III 2 56. *These main parcels of dispatch*—IV 3 104.

DISPATCH (vb.)

(1) To dismiss on completion of an errand: Fr. King. *To-morrow shall you know our mind at full.* Exe. *Dispatch us with all speed*—H5 II 4 140. *You shall be soon dispatch'd*—144.

(2) To deprive, bereave: *Of life, of crown, of queen, at once dispatch'd*—Hml I 5 75.

(3) To make haste to go: *Now dispatch we toward the court*—2 H4 IV 3 82. To make haste to do something; in imper.: *Let them go; Dispatch, I say*—Mids IV 1 111. *Come, sir, dispatch*—Mcb V 3 50.

(4) To get through one's business: *How now, son! have you dispatched?*—Wiv V 5 188. *Dispatch with Angelo, that it may be quickly*—Meas III 1 278.

DISPENSE WITH

(1) To compound with: *Canst thou dispense with heaven for such an oath?*—2 H6 V 1 181.

(2) To condone, pardon: *Nature dispenses with the deed so far That it becomes a virtue*—Meas III 1 135. *Unfeeling fools can with such wrongs dispense*—Err II 1 103. *With my trespass [I] never will dispense*—Lucr 1070.

(3) To set aside, disregard: *Dispense with trifles*—Wiv II 1 47. *We must of force dispense with this decree*—LLL I 1 148. *How shall we then dispense with that contract?*—1 H6 V 5 28.

DISPITEOUS

Cruel, pitiless: *Turning dispiteous torture out of door*—John IV 1 34.

DISPLACE

To drive away, banish: *You have displaced the mirth, broke the good meeting*—Mcb III 4 109.

DISPLEASURE

Injury, offence: *To see a wretched man Do outrage and displeasure to himself*—Err IV 4 118. *Doing displeasure to the citizens*—V 142. *Run To meet displeasure farther from the doors*—John V 1 59.

DISPOSE (sb.)

(1) Disposal: *All that is mine I leave at thy dispose*—Gent II 7 86. *Needs must you lay your heart at his dispose*—John I 263.

(2) Disposition, temper: *Carries on the stream of his dispose Without observance or respect of any*—Troil II 3 174. Manner, air: *A person and a smooth dispose To be suspected*—Oth I 3 403.

DISPOSE (vb.)

(1) To order, arrange: *So hot a speed with such advice disposed*—John III 4 11. *How thou pleasest, God, dispose the day!*—H5 IV 3 132. Refl., to order one's doings or course: *To your own bents dispose you*—Wint I 2 179. *By whose letters I'll dispose myself*—Per I 2 117.

(2) To bestow, deal out: *His blows are well disposed (i.e. placed with judgement)*—Troil IV 5 116.

(3) To dispose of: *Of the king's ship The mariners say how thou hast disposed*—Tp I 2 224.

We intend so to dispose you as Yourself shall give us counsel—Ant V 2 186. To deal with: *Put his cause and quarrel To the disposing of the cardinal*—John V 7 91. To use: *When these so noble benefits shall prove Not well disposed*—H8 I 2 115.

(4) To make terms: *You did suspect She had disposed with Cæsar*—Ant IV 14 122.

DISPOSED

Merrily inclined: *Boyet is disposed*—LLL II 249. *To make my lady laugh when she's disposed* —V 2 466. *He does well enough if he be disposed* —Tw II 3 87.

DISPOSER

One who can dispose at pleasure of another: *My disposer Cressida*—Troil III 1 95.

DISPOSITION

(1) A frame of mind, mood: *Entertain a cheerful disposition*—R2 II 2 4. *To put an antic disposition on*—Hml I 5 172. *If our father carry authority with such dispositions as he bears*—Lr I 1 308. *Put away These dispositions*—I 4 241.

(2) An arrangement (for residence and maintenance): *I crave fit disposition for my wife*—Oth I 3 237.

DISPROPERTY

To take away, annul: *Dispropertied their freedoms*—Cor II 1 264.

DISPROPORTIONED

Inconsistent: *They (i.e. the news) are disproportion'd*—Oth I 3 2.

DISPURSE

Disburse: *Many a pound . . . Have I dispursed to the garrisons*—2 H6 III 1 115.

DISPUTABLE

Disputatious; *He is too disputable for my company*—As II 5 36.

DISPUTATION

App., a discourse, conversation: *I understand thy kisses and thou mine, And that's a feeling disputation*—1 H4 III 1 205. *Will you voutsafe me . . . a few disputations with you*—H5 III 2 101.

DISPUTE

To discuss, reason upon: *Can he speak? hear? . . . dispute his own estate?*—Wint IV 4 409.

DISQUANTITY

To diminish: *A little to disquantity your train* —Lr I 4 270.

DISSEMBLE

(1) To disguise: *I will dissemble myself in't*— Tw IV 2 5.

(2) *Dissembling*, prob., fraudful, cheating: *Cheated of feature by dissembling nature*—R3 I 1 19.

(3) *The dissembling colour.* See *Judas.*

DISSIPATION

Scattering, dispersing: *Banishment of friends, dissipation of cohorts*—Lr I 2 161.

DISSOLUTION

Melting by the application of heat: *A man of continual dissolution and thaw*—Wiv III 5 118. *Against love's fire fear's frost hath dissolution*— Lucr 355.

DISSOLVE

(1) To part, sunder: *She and I . . . Are now so sure that nothing can dissolve us*—Wiv V 5 236. [I wish] *I quickly were dissolved from my hive*— All's I 2 66.

(2) To become liquefied with heat: *A figure Trenched in ice, which with an hour's heat Dissolves to water*—Gent III 2 6. *When this hail some heat from Hermia felt, So he dissolved*—Mids I 1 244. *What wax so frozen but dissolves with tempering?*—Ven 565.

DISTANCE

(1) Discord, dissension: *So is he mine (i.e. his enemy); and in such bloody distance, That . . .* —Mcb III 1 116.

(2) In fencing, an interval to be observed between the combatants: *In these times you stand on distance, your passes . . .*—Wiv II 1 233. *He fights as you sing prick-song, keeps time, distance, and proportion*—Rom II 4 21.

DISTASTE

(1) To be unsavoury: *Poisons, Which at the first are scarce found to distaste*—Oth III 3 326.

(2) To spoil the savour of: *Her brain-sick raptures Cannot distaste the goodness of a quarrel Which . . .*—Troil II 2 122. *Distasted with the salt of broken tears*—IV 4 50.

DISTASTEFUL

Full of dislike, malevolent: *Distasteful looks*— Tim II 2 220.

DISTEMPER (sb.)

Intoxication: *Little faults, proceeding on distemper*—H5 II 2 54.

DISTEMPER (vb.)

(1) To intoxicate: *Full of supper and distempering draughts*—Oth I 1 99.

(2) *Distempered*, of weather, inclement: *No distemper'd day, No common wind, no customed event* —John III 4 154 (cf. All's I 3 157 (*This distemper'd messenger of wet, The many-colour'd Iris*)).

Disturbed in temper or feelings: *Once more to-day well met, distemper'd lords!*—John IV 3 21. With a play on sense (1): Guil. [The king] *is in his retirement marvellous distempered.* Ham. *With drink, sir?*—Hml III 2 312.

DISTEMPERATURE

(1) Of atmospheric states, inclemency: *Thorough this distemperature we see The seasons alter*—Mids II 1 106. Of an unusual appearance of a heavenly body: *The day looks pale At his (i.e.* the sun's) *distemperature*—1 H4 V 1 2.

(2) An ailment, disorder: *Pale distemperatures and foes to life*—Err V 82. *At your birth Our grandam earth, having this distemperature, In passion shook*—1 H4 III 1 33.

(3) Uneasiness, trouble: *Thou art up-roused by some distemperature*—Rom II 3 40. *Upon what ground is his distemperature?*—Per V 1 27.

DISTIL

To melt: *Distill'd Almost to jelly with the act of fear*—Hml I 2 204.

DISTINCT

A separate or individual person: *Two distincts, division none*—Phœn 27.

DISTINCTION

App., a variety or abundance of detail: *This fierce abridgement Hath to it circumstantial branches, which Distinction should be rich in*—Cymb V 5 382.

DISTINCTLY

Separately, severally: *On the topmast, The yards and bowsprit, would I flame distinctly*—Tp I 2 199. *The centurions and their charges, distinctly billeted*—Cor IV 3 47. Without confusion: *The office did Distinctly his full function*—H8 I 1 44.

DISTINGUISHMENT

Distinction: *Mannerly distinguishment leave out Betwixt the prince and beggar*—Wint II 1 86.

DISTRACT (ppl. adj.)

(1) Divided: *To your audit comes Their distract parcels in combined sums*—Compl 230.

(2) Deranged in mind: *Mine hair be fix'd on end, as one distract*—2 H6 III 2 318. *With this she fell distract*—Cæs IV 3 155. *She is importunate, indeed distract*—Hml IV 5 2.

DISTRACT (vb.)

To tear asunder, scatter: *To the brightest beams Distracted clouds give way*—All's V 3 34. To parcel out, divide: *Supply it with one gender of herbs, or distract it with many*—Oth I 3 326. *Distracted,* disjointed: *In most uneven and distracted manner*—Meas IV 4 3.

DISTRACTEDLY

Disjointedly: *She did speak in starts distractedly*—Tw II 2 22.

DISTRACTION

A severed or divided form, drawn apart from others: *His power went out in such distractions as Beguiled all spies*—Ant III 7 77.

DISTRAIN

To seize (chattels, &c.) by legal process: *My father's goods are all distrain'd and sold*—R2 II 3 131. Gen., to seize, confiscate: *Beaufort . . . Hath here distrain'd the Tower to his use*—1 H6 I 3 60.

DISTRESSFUL

Gained by toil: *Cramm'd with distressful bread*—H5 IV 1 287.

DISTRUST (sb.)

Want of self-confidence: *Fear and sad distrust*—John V 1 46.

DISTRUST (vb.)

To be anxious about: *You are so sick of late . . . That I distrust you*—Hml III 2 173.

DISTRUSTFUL

Wanting in self-confidence: *Why, no, I say, distrustful recreants!*—1 H6 I 2 126.

DISVALUE

To depreciate, disparage: *Her reputation was disvalued In levity*—Meas V 221.

DISVOUCH

To contradict: *Every letter he hath writ hath disvouched other*—Meas IV 4 1.

DIVE-DAPPER

A dabchick: *Like a dive-dapper peering through a wave*—Ven 86.

DIVERS

Differing from what is good; evil, harmful: *New opinions, Divers and dangerous*—H8 V 3 17.

DIVERSITY

Divers sorts, variety: *Moe diversity of sounds*—Tp V 234.

DIVERT

To turn awry: *Frights, changes, horrors, Divert and crack . . . The unity . . . of states Quite from their fixure!*—Troil I 3 98. *Diverted,* turned from the course of nature: *A diverted blood and bloody brother*—As II 3 37.

DIVIDABLE

Divided: *Peaceful commerce from dividable shores*—Troil I 3 105.

DIVIDANT

Divided, separate: *Twinn'd brothers . . . Whose procreation, residence, and birth, Scarce is dividant* —Tim IV 3 3.

DIVINE

(1) Of the soul, beatified: *Or my divine soul answer it in heaven*—R2 I 1 38.

(2) Holy, pious: *A man divine and holy*—Meas V 144. *With most divine integrity*—Troil IV 5 170.

DIVINELY

Holily, piously: *This right hand, whose protection Is most divinely vow'd upon the right Of him it holds*—John II 236. *He is within . . . Divinely bent to meditation*—R3 III 7 61.

DIVISION

(1) Arrangement, disposition: *Nor the division of a battle knows*—Oth I 1 23. As a term in logic: *Rightly reasoned, and in his own division*—Ado V 1 229.

(2) In music, the execution of a rapid melodic passage: *Some say the lark makes sweet division*—Rom III 5 29. A variation on a theme or plainsong: *Sung by a fair queen . . . With ravishing division, to her lute*—1 H4 III 1 210. Fig., variation: *But abound In the division of each several crime*—Mcb IV 3 95.

DIVORCE

That which separates: *Dear divorce 'Twixt natural son and sire!*—Tim IV 3 382. ' *Hateful divorce of love*',—*thus chides she Death*—Ven 932.

DIVULGE

(1) To publish abroad, make known: *A divulged shame*—All's II 1 174. *That shall be divulged well*—Troil V 2 163.

(2) To proclaim (a person) publicly: *Divulge Page himself for a secure and wilful Actæon*—Wiv III 2 43.

(3) To become known: *To keep it from divulging*—Hml IV 1 22.

(4) *Well divulged*, of good reputation: *In voices well divulged*—Tw I 5 279.

DOCTRINE

(1) A lesson: *From women's eyes this doctrine I derive*—LLL IV 3 350. *I hourly learn A doctrine of obedience*—Ant V 2 30. *I'll pay that doctrine*, I'll give that lesson—Rom I 1 244.

(2) Learning, erudition: *The schools Embowell'd of their doctrine*—All's I 3 246.

DOCUMENT

A lesson: *A document in madness*—Hml IV 5 178.

DOG-APE

A dog-faced baboon; or perh., a male ape: *That they call compliment is like the encounter of two dog-apes*—As II 5 26.

DOGGED

Ill-conditioned, malignant, unfeeling: *These dogged spies*—John IV 1 129. *Dogged war*—IV 3 149. *Dogged York . . . doth level at my life*—2 H6 III 1 158.

DOIT

A small Dutch coin; as a type of a small sum: *And take no doit Of usance*—Merch I 3 141. *A dissension of a doit*—Cor IV 4 17.

DOLE¹

(1) A portion, share: *What great creation and what dole of honour Flies where you bid it*—All's II 3 176. So proverbially: *Happy man be his dole!* —Shr I 1 144; Wint I 2 163.

(2) Dealing, distribution: *It was your presurmise, That, in the dole of blows, your son might drop*—2 H4 I 1 168.

DOLE²

(1) Grief: *In equal scale weighing delight and dole*—Hml I 2 13. *Omit we all their dole and woe*—Per III Prol 42. Something which causes grief: *What dreadful dole is here!*—Mids V 283.

(2) Lamentation: *Making such pitiful dole over them*—As I 2 138.

DOLLAR

The English name for the German Thaler, a large silver coin of varying value: *Till he disbursed . . . Ten thousand dollars to our general use*—Mcb I 2 61. With a play: *Three thousand dolours a year*—Meas I 2 50. See also Tp II 1 16 and foll.

DOLPHIN

Dauphin: *Dolphin my boy, my boy, sessa! let him trot by*—Lr III 4 104. Cf. *Dolphin or dogfish, Your hearts I'll stamp out with my horse's heels*—1 H6 I 4 107.

DOMINEER

To roister, feast riotously: *Go to the feast, revel and domineer*—Shr III 2 226.

DOMINICAL

Short for dominical letter, the letter used in a particular year to denote the Sundays: *My red dominical, my golden letter*—LLL V 2 44.

DOOM (sb.)

(1) A decision come to: *It skills not greatly who impugns our doom*—2 H6 III 1 281. *When they had sworn to this advised doom*—Lucr 1849.

(2) *Day of doom*, the last day of one's life, the

fatal day: [I'll] *triumph, Henry, in thy day of doom*—3 H6 V 6 93. *This is the day of doom for Bassianus*—Tit II 3 42.

DOOM (vb.)

(1) To judge, decide: *Nobly doom'd!*—Cymb V 5 420.

(2) To pronounce as a sentence: *To doom my brother's death*—R3 II 1 102. *The prince will doom thee death*—Rom III 1 139.

DOTANT

A dotard: *Such a decayed dotant as you seem to be*—Cor V 2 47.

DOUBLE

(1) To increase ranks to twice their length by marching other ranks up to them: *To instruct for the doubling of files*—All's IV 3 302.

(2) To speak with repetition of sounds: *This knave's tongue begins to double*—2 H6 II 3 94.

DOUBLE-FATAL

Of yew, the wood being used for bows and the berries being poisonous: *Their bows Of double-fatal yew*—R2 III 2 116.

DOUBLET AND HOSE

(1) The typical masculine attire (cf. *Hose*): *As doublet and hose ought to show itself courageous to petticoat*—As II 4 6. *Dost thou think . . . I have a doublet and hose in my disposition?*—III 2 204.

(2) A sort of undress or dress for active pursuits, implying the absence of cloak, &c.: *Youthful still! in your doublet and hose this raw rheumatic day!*—Wiv III 1 46. *When he goes in his doublet and hose and leaves off his wit*—Ado V 1 202. Cf. *Thou oughtest not to let thy horse wear a cloak, when honester men than thou go in their hose and doublets*—2 H6 IV 7 54.

DOUBLE-VANTAGE

To profit doubly: *The injuries that to myself I do, Doing thee vantage, double-vantage me*—Sonn 88 11.

DOUBLE VOUCHER

His fines, his double vouchers, his recoveries—Hml V 1 114. A recovery with double voucher was so called from two persons being vouched or called upon to warrant the tenant's title. See *Fine* (sb.) (3).

DOUBT (sb.)

(1) A doubtful question, difficulty: *I should be arguing still upon that doubt*—Shr III 1 55.

(2) Apprehension, fear: *Urge doubts to them that fear*—R2 II 1 299. *Deposed 'Tis doubt he will be*—III 4 68. *The smallest fear or doubt of her revolt*—Oth III 3 188. *This is, sir, a doubt In such a time nothing becoming you*—Cymb IV 4 14.

DOUBT (vb.)

To fear, feel fear on account of: *That love the fundamental part of state More than you doubt the change on't*—Cor III 1 151. *But doubt discovery there*, app., but (must) be apprehensive as to what it may find there: *Ambition cannot pierce a wink beyond, But doubt discovery there*—Tp II 1 242.

DOUBTFUL

Apprehensive, full of fear: *My most jealous and too doubtful soul*—Tw IV 3 27. *Doubtful joy*—Mcb III 2 7. *I am doubtful that you have been conjunct And bosom'd with her*—Lr V 1 12. Giving cause for fear: *A doubtful warrant of immediate death*—Err I 1 69.

DOUBTLESS

Free from apprehension or fear: *Sleep doubtless and secure*—John IV 1 130.

DOUT

To put out, extinguish: *That their hot blood may spin in English eyes, And dout them with superfluous courage*—H5 IV 2 10. *A speech of fire, that fain would blaze, But that this folly douts it*—Hml IV 7 191.

DOWLAS

A coarse kind of linen: Host. . . . *I bought you a dozen of shirts to your back.* Fal. *Dowlas, filthy dowlas*—1 H4 III 3 77.

DOWLE

A filament of a feather: [Your swords] *may as well Wound the loud winds . . . as diminish One dowle that's in my plume*—Tp III 3 62.

DOWN-GYVED

Hanging down like fetters: *His stockings . . . down-gyved to his ancle*—Hml II 1 79.

DOWN-ROPING

Flowing down in a glutinous thread: *The gum down-roping from their pale-dead eyes*—H5 IV 2 48.

DOXY

A tramp's trull: *With heigh! the doxy over the dale*—Wint IV 3 2.

DRACHMA

The principal silver coin of the ancient Greeks; spoken of as in use in Rome: *A crack'd drachma*—Cor I 5 6. *To every several man, seventy five drachmas*—Cæs III 2 247.

DRAUGHT

A cesspool, sewer: *Sweet draught: 'sweet' quoth a! sweet sink, sweet sewer*—Troil V 1 82. *Drown them in a draught*—Tim V 1 105.

DRAW

(1) To draw the sword; *to be drawn*, to have the sword drawn: *Why are you drawn?*—Tp II 1 308. *What, drawn, and talk of peace!*—Rom I 1 77.

(2) To muster: *That such an army could be drawn in France*—John IV 2 118. *Shall we go draw our numbers and set on?*—2 H4 I 3 109. To assemble, bring together: *A good quarrel to draw emulous factions*—Troil II 3 79. *There were drawn Upon a heap a hundred ghastly women*—Cæs I 3 22.

(3) To undraw, draw aside: *We will draw the curtain and show you the picture*—Tw I 5 251. *This absence of your father's draws a curtain, That shows the ignorant a kind of fear*—1 H4 IV 1 73.

(4) To withdraw (an action): *Go, wash thy face, and draw the action*—2 H4 II 1 162.

(5) Of a hound, to track: [*There's*] *no more truth in thee than in a drawn fox*—1 H4 III 3 128. *To draw dry-foot*, to track by the mere scent of the foot: *A hound that runs counter and yet draws dry-foot well*—Err IV 2 39.

DRAWER

A tapster: *Give us leave, drawer*—Wiv II 2 165. *I am sworn brother to a leash of drawers*—1 H4 II 4 7. *Wait upon him at his table as drawers*—2 H4 II 2 190.

DREAD

To be anxious about: *Dreading my love, the loss thereof still fearing*—Pilgr 94.

DREADFUL

Full of awe: *This to me In dreadful secrecy impart they did*—Hml I 2 206.

DREADFULLY

With fear: *That apprehends death no more dreadfully but as a drunken sleep*—Meas IV 2 149.

DRESS

To prepare, make ready: *Admonishing That we should dress us fairly for our end*—H5 IV 1 9. *Being drest to some oration*—Troil I 3 166.

DRIBBLING

Of an arrow, shot so that it falls short or wide: *The dribbling dart of love*—Meas I 3 2.

DRIFT

A scheme, design: *Thou hast lent me wit to plot this drift*—Gent II 6 43. *To cross my friend in his intended drift*—III 1 18. *You shall say my cunning drift excels*—IV 2 83. *In the mean time . . . Shall Romeo by my letters know our drift*—Rom IV 1 113.

DROLLERY

(1) A puppet-show: *A living drollery*—Tp III 3 21.

(2) A comic picture: *For thy walls, a pretty slight drollery*—2 H4 II 1 156.

DROVIER

Drover; a dealer in cattle: *That's spoken like an honest drovier; so they sell bullocks*—Ado II 1 201.

DRUG

Drudge: *Such as may the passive drugs . . . Freely command*—Tim IV 3 254.

DRUG-DAMNED

Detestable for its poisons: *Drug-damn'd Italy*—Cymb III 4 15.

DRUMBLE

To move sluggishly: *How you drumble!*—Wiv III 3 156.

DRY

Of a beating, hard, severe: *Lest it make you choleric and purchase me another dry basting*—Err II 2 63. Perh. similarly used in Tp IV 259 (*Charge my goblins that they grind their joints With dry convulsions*).

DRY-BEAT

To beat soundly: *All dry-beaten with pure scoff!*—LLL V 2 263. *One of your nine lives; that I mean to make bold withal, and . . . dry-beat the rest of the eight*—Rom III 1 80.

DRY-FOOT

See *Draw* (5).

DUCAT

A gold coin of varying value formerly in use in most European countries: *His use was to put a ducat in her clack-dish*—Meas III 2 134. *Three thousand ducats; well*—Merch I 3 1. *He has three thousand ducats a year*—Tw I 3 22. *Give twenty . . . an hundred ducats a-piece for his picture in little*—Hml II 2 382. There was an Italian silver ducat; and the ducat was also a money of account at Venice. It is not easy in all cases to say what meaning should be assigned to the word.

DUCDAME

Prob. intentional nonsense: As II 5 56.

DUDGEON

A kind of wood, by some identified with box-wood, used for handles of knives, &c.; hence, the hilt of a dagger: *On thy blade and dudgeon gouts of blood*—Mcb II 1 46.

DUE (sb.)

A debt: *Here is a note of certain dues*—Tim II 2 16. *What remains will hardly stop the mouth Of present dues*—156.

DUE (vb.)

To endue, invest: *This is the latest glory of thy praise That I, thy enemy, due thee withal*—1 H6 IV 2 33.

DUELLO

The duellists' code: *The duello he regards not* —LLL I 2 185. *He cannot by the duello avoid it* —Tw III 4 337.

DUKE

A leader; a chief, ruler, captain. Referring to the King of Navarre: *Which is the duke's own person?*—LLL I 1 182. *I have promised to study three years with the duke*—I 2 37. *Vow-fellows with this virtuous duke*—II 38. Referring to the Player King: *Gonzago is the duke's name*—Hml III 2 249. Applied by Pistol to Fluellen: *Be merciful, great duke*—H5 III 2 23. Used to render the Venetian Doge: *The villain Jew . . . raised the duke*—Merch II 8 4. *Your ships are stay'd at Venice, and the duke . . . Hath publish'd . . .*—Shr IV 2 83. *A voice potential As double as the duke's*—Oth I 2 13, and elsewhere in that play.

DULL

Producing drowsiness, soothing: *Unless some dull and favourable hand Will whisper music to my weary spirit*—2 H4 IV 5 2.

DUMB

To reduce to silence: *Deep clerks she dumbs*— Per V Prol 5. To make unheard: *What I would have spoke Was beastly dumb'd by him*—Ant I 5 49.

DUMP

A mournful melody or song: *To their instruments Tune a deploring dump*—Gent III 2 84. *Distress likes dumps when time is kept with tears* —Lucr 1127.

DUN

A dun horse: *If thou art dun, we'll draw thee from the mire*—Rom I 4 41. An allusion to a game, " Dun is in the mire ", in which a horse represented by a log was supposed to be stuck in the mire and was extricated. The proverb *Dun's the mouse* in the preceding line has not been explained.

DUP

To open: *Dupp'd the chamber-door*—Hml IV 5 53.

DURANCE

Lasting quality: *Gives them suits of durance*— Err IV 3 26. *Is not a buff jerkin a most sweet robe of durance?*—1 H4 I 2 48. In both cases with a play on Durance = Imprisonment.

DUST

A particle of dust: *[She] was in mine eye The dust that did offend it*—All's V 3 54. *Shall blow each dust, each straw . . . Out of the path*—John III 4 128. *Why have those . . . legs Dared once to touch a dust of England's ground?*—R2 II 3 90.

DUTY

One's due: *Do thy duty, and have thy duty*— Shr IV 1 38.

E

EACH

At each, set end to end: *Ten masts at each*— Lr IV 6 53.

EAGER

(1) Pungent, sharp in operation: *Like as, to make our appetites more keen, With eager compounds we our palate urge*—Sonn 118 1. Of words, cold, &c., biting, keen: *The bitter clamour of two eager tongues*—R2 I 1 49. *Vex him with eager words*—3 H6 II 6 68. *A nipping and an eager air*—Hml I 4 2.

(2) Sour, tart: *Eager droppings into milk*— Hml I 5 69.

(3) Ardent, vehement: *What shrill-voiced suppliant makes this eager cry?*—R2 V 3 75. *Hunger will enforce them to be more eager*—1 H6 I 2 38.

EAGERLY

Fiercely, bitterly, malignantly: *How eagerly ye follow my disgraces*—H8 III 2 240. *Eagerly his sickness Pursued him still*—IV 2 24.

EAN

To bring forth lambs: *In eaning time*—Merch I 3 88. *So many weeks ere the poor fools will ean* —3 H6 II 5 36. Of a woman: *That I was shipp'd at sea, I well remember, Even on my eaning time*—Per III 4 5.

EANLING

A young lamb: *All the eanlings which were streak'd and pied*—Merch I 3 80.

EAR

To plough, till: *He that ears my land spares my team*—All's I 3 47. *Let them go To ear the land that hath some hope to grow*—R2 III 2 211. *[I shall] never after ear so barren a land*—Ven Dedic 5.

EARING

Ploughing, tilling: *Our ills told us Is as our earing*—Ant I 2 114.

EARLY

Early days, early in the day: *'Tis but early days* —Troil IV 5 12.

EARTH

To bury: *Who shall be of as little memory When he is earth'd*—Tp II 1 233.

EARTHLY

In the earth: *A sceptre, or an earthly sepulchre!* —3 H6 I 4 17.

EARTHY

Earthly: *What earthy name to interrogatories Can task the free breath of a sacred king?*—John III 1 147.

EASY

Slight, insignificant: *Was this easy? May this be wash'd in Lethe, and forgotten?*—2 H4 V 2 71. *These faults are easy*—2 H6 III 1 133. *A little water clears us of this deed: How easy is it, then!* —Mcb II 2 67.

EASY-HELD

Involving little restraint: *Her easy-held imprisonment*—1 H6 V 3 139.

ECHE

To eke out: *Time . . . With your fine fancies quaintly eche*—Per III Prol 12.

ECSTASY

(1) Mental disturbance, frenzy: *Hinder them from what this ecstasy May now provoke them to*— Tp III 3 108. *The very ecstasy of love*—Hml II 1 102. *That unmatch'd form and feature of blown youth Blasted with ecstasy*—III 1 167.

(2) A trance, swoon: *I shifted him away, And laid good 'scuse upon your ecstasy*—Oth IV 1 79.

EDGE

Ardour, keenness: *Doth rebate and blunt his natural edge*—Meas I 4 60. To give an edge to, to stimulate, incite: *Give him a further edge, And drive his purpose on to these delights*—Hml III 1 26. On edge, all agog: *Doth set my pugging tooth on edge*—Wint IV 3 7.

EFFECT (sb.)

(1) An outward manifestation, sign, symptom: *What effects of passion shows she?*—Ado II 3 112. *Answer in the effect of your reputation* (i.e. so as to display the character borne by him)—2 H4 II 1 142. *To receive at once the benefit of sleep, and do the effects of watching*—Mcb V 1 10. *Lest with this piteous action you convert My stern effects* (i.e. manifestations of sternness, the unbending demeanour befitting his task)—Hml III 4 128. *The warm effects which she in him finds missing*— Ven 605.

(2) Something acquired: *I am still possess'd Of those effects for which I did the murder*—Hml III 3 53.

(3) Accomplishment, fulfilment: *All the fair effects of future hopes*—Gent I 1 50. *The effect of your own purpose*—Meas II 1 13.

(4) Reality, fact: *Words, words . . . The effect doth operate another way*—Troil V 3 108.

(5) A purpose, end: *Base men, that use them to so base effect!*—Gent II 7 73. *With some dram conjured to this effect*—Oth I 3 105.

(6) In pl., app., attributes: *All the large effects That troop with majesty*—Lr I 1 133. *Effects of courtesy, dues of gratitude*—II 4 182.

EFFECT (vb.)

(1) To produce (a state of things): *Sorry am I that our good will effects Bianca's grief*—Shr I 1 86.

(2) To give effect to (a feeling): *Effect your rage with speed!*—Troil V 10 6.

EFFECTUAL

To the point, pertinent, conclusive: *Conclude my words effectual*—2 H6 III 1 41.

EFFECTUALLY

In fact, in reality: [Mine eye] *Seems seeing, but effectually is out*—Sonn 113 4.

EFFEMINATE

Gentle, tender: *Gentle, kind, effeminate remorse* —R3 III 7 211.

EFFIGIES

A likeness, image: *Mine eye doth his effigies witness . . . living in your face*—As II 7 193.

EFFUSE

A pouring out, effusion: *Much effuse of blood doth make me faint*—3 H6 II 6 28.

EFT

Perh., ready, convenient: *That's the eftest way* —Ado IV 2 38.   App. a blunder.

EFTSOONS

Afterwards, by and by: *Eftsoons I'll tell thee why* —Per V 1 256.

EGAL

Equal; impartial: *Egal justice*—Tit IV 4 4.

EGALLY

Equally: *Egally indeed to all estates*—R3 III 7 213.

EGGS

To take eggs for money, to be put off with something worthless: *Will you take eggs for money?* —Wint I 2 161.

7

EGYPTIAN

Either a native of Egypt or a gipsy: *That hand-kerchief Did an Egyptian to my mother give—* Oth III 4 55.

EISEL

Vinegar: *Woo't drink up eisel?*—Hml V 1 299. *I will drink Potions of eisel 'gainst my strong infection*—Sonn 111 9.

ELBOW

To rub the elbow, to show oneself pleased: *One rubb'd his elbow thus*—LLL V 2 109. *Rub the elbow at the news Of hurlyburly innovation*—1 H4 V 1 77.

ELD

(1) Old men: *Thy blessed youth . . . doth beg the alms Of palsied eld*—Meas III 1 34. *Virgins and boys, mid-age and wrinkled eld*—Troil II 2 104.

(2) The men of old: *Idle-headed eld Received and did deliver to our age This tale*—Wiv IV 4 36.

ELDER

Older: *How much more elder art thou than thy looks!*—Merch IV 1 251. *Behold divineness No elder than a boy!*—Cymb III 6 44.

ELDEST

Oldest: *Your eld'st acquaintance cannot be three hours*—Tp V 186. *The primal eldest curse*—Hml III 3 37.

ELECT

To pick out, choose (for a particular purpose or function): *We have with special soul Elected him our absence to supply*—Meas I 1 18. *The elected deer before thee*—Cymb III 4 112.

ELEMENT

The sky: *The cinders of the element*—2 H4 IV 3 57. *The element shows to him as it doth to me* —H5 IV 1 107. *The complexion of the element In favour's like the work we have in hand*—Cæs I 3 128.

ELEVEN AND TWENTY

Tricks eleven and twenty long, said to be a reference (certainly obscure) to the game of bone-ace (see *Two and Thirty*): *That teacheth tricks eleven and twenty long, To tame a shrew and charm her chattering tongue*—Shr IV 2 57.

ELF

To tangle (as an elf might do): *[I'll] elf all my hair in knots*—Lr II 3 10.

ELF-LOCK

A tangled mass of hair: *Bakes the elf-locks in foul sluttish hairs*—Rom I 4 90.

ELSE

Elsewhither: *Since the substance of your perfect self Is else devoted*—Gent IV 2 124.

ELVISH-MARKED

Branded with the stigma of deformity by malicious fairies: *Thou elvish-mark'd, abortive, rooting hog!*—R3 I 3 228. Cf. 3 H6 II 2 136 (*A foul mis-shapen stigmatic, Mark'd by the destinies*).

ELY HOUSE

The town house of the Bishops of Ely—R2 I 4 58; II 1 216. Referred to: R3 III 4 32 and foll. The site is occupied by Ely Place, Holborn.

EMBALLING

An investing with the ball as the symbol of royalty: *For little England You'ld venture an emballing*—H8 II 3 46.

EMBARQUEMENT

A placing under embargo, restraint: *Embarquements all of fury*—Cor I 10 22.

EMBASSADE

Embassy: *When you disgraced me in my embassade*—3 H6 IV 3 32.

EMBASSAGE

The message committed to an ambassador, a message in general: *That well by heart hath conn'd his embassage*—LLL V 2 98. *Doth not thy embassage belong to me, And am I last that knows it?*—R2 III 4 93. *To thee I send this written embassage*—Sonn 26 3.

EMBASSY

The message committed to an ambassador: *Silence, good mother; hear the embassy*—John I 6. *Go we in, to know his embassy*—H5 I 1 95.

EMBATTLE

Intr. for refl., to take up a position for battle: *They say we shall embattle By the second hour i' the morn*—Ant IV 9 3.

EMBLAZE

To set forth by heraldic devices: *Thou shalt wear it as a herald's coat, To emblaze the honour that thy master got*—2 H6 IV 10 75.

EMBOSS

In woodcraft, to drive to extremity: *We have almost embossed him*—All's III 6 107.

EMBOSSED[1]

In woodcraft, exhausted, foaming at the mouth: *The poor cur is emboss'd*—Shr Ind 1 17. *The boar of Thessaly Was never so emboss'd*—Ant IV 13 2. It is uncertain whether in Tim V 1 220 (*His (i.e.* the sea's) *embossed froth*) there is a figurative application of this word, or whether the quotation should be put under the next word.

EMBOSSED²

Swollen, tumid: *All the embossed sores and headed evils*—As II 7 67. *An embossed carbuncle*—Lr II 4 227. Also *Thou whoreson, impudent, embossed rascal*—1 H4 III 3 177 (perh. here with a play on *Embossed¹*. See *Rascal* (sb.)).

EMBRACE

To accept as a friend or servant: *He bears himself more proudlier . . . than I thought he would When first I did embrace him*—Cor IV 7 8. *Desire his service . . . doubtless With joy he will embrace you*—Cymb III 4 176.

EMBRASURE

Embrace: *Forcibly prevents Our lock'd embrasures*—Troil IV 4 38.

EMBREW

See *Imbrue.*

EMINENCE

(1) Superiority, the upper hand: *You should not have the eminence of him*—Troil II 3 266.

(2) Honour paid to one: *Present him eminence, both with eye and tongue*—Mcb III 2 31.

EMMANUEL

Formerly prefixed to letters and deeds: Cade. *. . . What is thy name?* Clerk. *Emmanuel.* Dick. *They use to write it on the top of letters*—2 H6 IV 2 105.

EMMEW

Immew; in hawking, of the falcon, to cow the prey so that it lies close: [This deputy who] *Nips youth i' the head and follies doth emmew As falcon doth the fowl*—Meas III 1 91.

EMPALE

See *Impale.*

EMPERY

(1) The status or dignity of an emperor: *Election for the Roman empery*—Tit I 22. *Thou shalt obtain and ask the empery*—201.

(2) A kingdom: *Your right of birth, your empery, your own*—R3 III 7 136. *Fasten'd to an empery, Would make the great'st king double*—Cymb I 6 120.

(3) Dominion: *Ruling in large and ample empery*—H5 I 2 226. *Princes, that strive . . . for rule and empery*—Tit I 18.

EMPHASIS

An emphatic expression: *Be choked with such another emphasis!*—Ant I 5 68.

EMPIRICUTIC

Empirical: *The most sovereign prescription in Galen is but empiricutic*—Cor II 1 127.

EMPOISON

To kill by poison: *A man by his own alms empoison'd, And with his charity slain*—Cor V 6 11.

EMULATE

Ambitious, emulous: *Thereto prick'd on by a most emulate pride*—Hml I 1 83.

EMULATION

(1) Ambitious rivalry, contention between rivals: *When for so slight and frivolous a cause Such factious emulations shall arise*—1 H6 IV 1 112. *Emulation . . . who shall be nearest*—R3 II 3 25. *The obligation of our blood forbids A gory emulation 'twixt us twain*—Troil IV 5 122.

(2) Grudge against the superiority of others, tendency to disparagement of those who are superior: [You] *Keep off aloof with worthless emulation*—1 H6 IV 4 21. *An envious fever of pale and bloodless emulation*—Troil I 3 133. *Shouting their emulation*—Cor I 1 218. *Virtue cannot live Out of the teeth of emulation*—Cæs II 3 13.

EMULATOR

A disparager: *An envious emulator of every man's good parts*—As I 1 149.

EMULOUS

Greedy of praise or power: *He is not emulous, as Achilles is*—Troil II 3 242.

ENACT (sb.)

A purpose, resolution: *The close enacts and counsels of the heart*—Tit IV 2 118.

ENACT (vb.)

(1) To record: *A little harm done to a great good end For lawful policy remains enacted*—Lucr 528.

(2) To carry into act, accomplish, perform: *Valiant Talbot . . . Enacted wonders*—1 H6 I 1 121. *You see . . . what murder . . . Hath been enacted through your enmity*—III 1 115. *The king enacts more wonders than a man*—R3 V 4 2.

ENACTURE

A carrying into act; or perh., a purpose, resolution: *The violence of either grief or joy Their own enactures with themselves destroy*—Hml III 2 206.

ENCAVE

To hide: *Do but encave yourself*—Oth IV 1 82.

ENCHANTINGLY

As if by the operation of a spell: *Of all sorts enchantingly beloved*—As I 1 174.

ENCOMPASS

To bring under one's influence, 'get round': *Ah, ha! Mistress Ford and Mistress Page, have I encompassed you?*—Wiv II 2 158.

ENCOMPASSMENT

Talking round a subject, circumlocution: *This encompassment and drift of question*—Hml II 1 10.

ENCOUNTER (sb.)

(1) An accosting: *The loose encounters of lascivious men*—Gent II 7 41.

(2) Behaviour: *With what encounter so uncurrent I Have strain'd to appear thus*—Wint III 2 50. *The tune of the time and outward habit of encounter*—Hml V 2 198. Mode of address: *My merry mistress, That with your strange encounter much amazed me*—Shr IV 5 53.

ENCOUNTER (vb.)

To go to meet: *I will encounter darkness as a bride*—Meas III 1 84. *The fashion of the world is to avoid cost, and you encounter it*—Ado I 1 97. *At noon, at midnight, To encounter me with orisons*—Cymb I 3 31. Bombastically, to go to, approach: *Will you encounter the house?*—Tw III 1 82.

ENCOUNTERER

A forward person, coquette: *These encounterers, so glib of tongue*—Troil IV 5 58.

ENCUMBER

Of the arms, to fold: *With arms encumber'd thus*—Hml I 5 174.

END¹

To carry through to the end, finish, accomplish: *This ended action*—Ado I 1 299. *This same day Must end that work the ides of March begun*—Cæs V 1 113. *To end his vow*—Lucr 1843.

END²

Of corn, &c., to get in: *Holp to reap the fame Which he did end all his*—Cor V 6 36.

ENDEAR

To bind by obligations of gratitude: *You broke your word, When you were more endear'd to it than now*—2 H4 II 3 10. First Lord. *We are so virtuously bound*— . . . Sec. Lord. *So infinitely endear'd*—Tim I 2 232. *I am so much endeared to that lord; he's ever sending*—III 2 35.

ENDOWMENTS

Property, possessions: *Base men by his endowments are made great*—R2 II 3 139.

ENDS

Fig., quoted scraps, tags: *Old odd ends stolen out of holy writ*—R3 I 3 337. *To flout old ends*, to quote them with sarcastic purpose: *Ere you flout old ends any further, examine your conscience*—Ado I 1 290.

ENDUE, INDUE

(1) To bring to a certain state: *Let our finger ache, and it indues Our other healthful members even to that sense Of pain*—Oth III 4 146.

(2) To supply (*with* a thing): [More reasons] *I shall indue you with*—John IV 2 43. *The tribunes Endue you with the people's voice*—Cor II 3 146.

(3) *Indued unto that element*, endowed with properties suited to it—Hml IV 7 180.

ENFEOFF

To hand over as a fief, surrender; fig.: [The skipping king] *Enfeoff'd himself to popularity*—1 H4 III 2 69.

ENFORCE

(1) To lay stress upon, emphasize: *Enforce his pride, And his old hate unto you*—Cor II 3 227. *His glory not extenuated . . . nor his offences enforced*—Cæs III 2 42.

(2) To strike with force: *As the flint bears fire; Who, much enforced, shows a hasty spark*—Cæs IV 3 111. To drive by force: *We are enforced from our most quiet there By the rough torrent of occasion*—2 H4 IV 1 71. *As swift as stones Enforced from the old Assyrian slings*—H5 IV 7 64. To force (a lock): *Each [lock] by him enforced retires his ward*—Lucr 303.

(3) To violate, ravish: *Some enforced chastity*—Mids III 1 205. *She was enforced, stain'd, and deflower'd*—Tit V 3 38. *Thy mistress enforced*—Cymb IV 1 18.

(4) To extort, compel: *With a base and boisterous sword enforce A thievish living*—As II 3 32. *His countenance enforces homage*—H5 III 7 30. *We'll enforce it from thee By a sharp torture*—Cymb IV 3 11. *Drops . . . enforced by sympathy*—Lucr 1228.

(5) To press hard upon, urge: *Enforce him with his envy to the people*—Cor III 3 3.

(6) To obtrude: *I will no more enforce mine office on you*—All's II 1 129.

ENFORCEMENT

(I) A bringing of force to bear upon a thing: *The thing that's heavy in itself, Upon enforcement flies with greatest speed*—2 H4 I 1 119.

(2) Violation: *His enforcement of the city wives*—R3 III 7 8. *What wrong . . . By foul enforcement might be done to me*—Lucr 1622.

ENFRANCH

To free (a slave): *My enfranched bondman*—Ant III 13 149.

ENFRANCHISE

To set free from political subjection: *Take in that kingdom, and enfranchise that*—Ant I 1 23.

ENFRANCHISEMENT

Restoration to one's rights: *His coming hither hath no further scope Than . . to beg Enfranchisement immediate*—R2 III 3 112.

ENGAGE

(1) To pledge, mortgage: *This to be true, I do engage my life*—As V 4 171. *'Tis all* (*i.e.* the land) *engaged, some forfeited and gone*—Tim II 2 155. To take up (a pledge): *There is my honour's pawn; Engage it to the trial, if thou darest*—R2 IV 55. To give as a hostage: *Westmoreland, that was engaged, did bear it*—1 H4 V 2 44. [Suffered] *his king to be engaged* (*i.e.* kept as a hostage) *in Wales*—1 H4 IV 3 95.

(2) To render liable for a debt: *I have engaged myself to a dear friend, Engaged my friend to his mere enemy*—Merch III 2 264.

(3) To entangle: *O limed soul, that, struggling to be free, Art more engaged!*—Hml III 3 68. To involve, commit: *Retire, we have engaged ourselves too far*—Ant IV 7 1. *Engaged to,* involved in: *We all that are engaged to this loss*—2 H4 I 1 180.

ENGINE

(1) An artifice, device: *Oaths, tokens, and all these engines of lust*—All's III 5 20. *She shall file our engines with advice*—Tit II 1 123. *Devise engines for my life*—Oth IV 2 221.

(2) An implement, instrument: *An engine fit for my proceeding*—Gent III 1 138. *Once more the engine of her thoughts* (*i.e.* the tongue) *began*—Ven 367. Esp. one for war: *When he walks, he moves like an engine*—Cor V 4 18. *You mortal engines, whose rude throats The immortal Jove's dread clamours counterfeit*—Oth III 3 355.

(3) An instrument of torture: *Like an engine wrench'd my frame of nature From the fix'd place*—Lr I 4 290.

ENGINER

Engineer: *Then there's Achilles, a rare enginer!*—Troil II 3 8. *'Tis the sport to have the enginer Hoist with his own petar*—Hml III 4 206.

ENGIRT

To surround, clasp: *My body round engirt with misery*—2 H6 III 1 200. *That gold must round engirt these brows of mine*—V 1 99. *So white a friend engirts so white a foe*—Ven 364.

ENGRAFFED

Engrafted; closely attached: *You have been so lewd and so much engraffed to Falstaff*—2 H4 II 2 66.

ENGROSS, INGROSS

(1) To get together, to collect from all quarters: *Percy is but my factor . . . To engross up glorious deeds on my behalf*—1 H4 III 2 147. *For this they have engross'd . . . The canker'd heaps of . . .*

gold—2 H4 IV 5 71. *Your mariners are muleters, reapers, people Ingross'd by swift impress*—Ant III 7 36. To lose no chance of securing: *Engrossed opportunities to meet her*—Wiv II 2 203.

(2) To fatten: *Not sleeping, to engross his idle body*—R3 III 7 76.

ENLARD

To fatten: *That were to enlard his fat already pride*—Troil II 3 205.

ENLARGE

To give free expression to: *In my tent, Cassius, enlarge your griefs*—Cæs IV 2 46.

ENLARGEMENT

Freedom of action: *You are curb'd from that enlargement*—Cymb II 3 125.

ENORMOUS

Disordered, monstrous: *This enormous state*—Lr II 2 176.

ENOW

Pl. of enough: *We were Christians enow before*—Merch III 5 23. *Spare for no faggots, let there be enow*—1 H6 V 4 56. *Have napkins enow about you*—Mcb II 3 6. *Evils enow to darken all his goodness*—Ant I 4 11.

ENPATRON

To be the patron saint of: *You enpatron me*—Compl 224.

ENRIDGED

Thrown into ridges: *The enridged sea*—Lr IV 6 71.

ENROUND

To surround, encircle: *How dread an army hath enrounded him*—H5 IV Chor 36.

ENSCHEDULE

To state in writing: *Whose tenours . . . You have enscheduled briefly in your hands*—H5 V 2 72. Cf. Schedule.

ENSCONCE, INSCONCE

To shelter within or behind a fortification: *I must get a sconce for my head and insconce it too*—Err II 2 37. Fig.: [You] *will ensconce your rags . . . under the shelter of your honour!*—Wiv II 2 26. [He] *therein so ensconced his secret evil*—Lucr 1515. Refl. and fig.: *Against that time do I ensconce me here Within the knowledge of mine own desert*—Sonn 49 9.

ENSEAM

To load with grease; fig.: *The rank sweat of an enseamed bed*—Hml III 4 92.

ENSHIELD

Shielded, concealed: *An enshield beauty*—Meas II 4 80.

ENSTEEP

To immerse, station under water: *Rocks and . . . sands,—Traitors ensteep'd to clog the guiltless keel*—Oth II 1 69.

ENSUE

To follow upon, come next to: *Let not to-morrow then ensue to-day*—R2 II 1 197. To follow upon as a result: *Repentant tears ensue the deed*—Lucr 502. To follow as a logical conclusion: *Doth it therefore ensue that you should love his son?*—As I 3 32.

ENTAIL¹

To cut the entail from all remainders, to leave no rights of succession after the holder: *He will sell the fee-simple of his salvation . . . and cut the entail from all remainders*—All's IV 3 311.

ENTAIL²

To make heir *to*: *To entail him and his heirs unto the crown*—3 H6 I 1 235.

ENTER

(1) To instruct; *entered in,* acquainted with: *They of Rome are enter'd in our counsels*—Cor I 2 2. To initiate: *'Tis our hope, sir, After well enter'd soldiers, to return*—All's II 1 5. *Man-entered,* initiated in manhood: *His pupil age Man-enter'd thus*—Cor II 2 102.

(2) *To enter with,* to bring into the service of: *This sword but shown to Cæsar . . . Shall enter me with him*—Ant IV 14 112.

ENTERTAIN (sb.)

Entertainment: *Your entertain shall be As doth befit our honour*—Per I 1 119.

ENTERTAIN (vb.)

(1) To keep up, maintain (a course of action, state of feeling, &c.): *Do a wilful stillness entertain*—Merch I 1 90. *Entertain a cheerful disposition*—R2 II 2 4. *He entertain'd a show so seeming just*—Lucr 1514.

(2) To take into service, engage: *Being entertained for a perfumer*—Ado I 3 60. [I have] *entertained my convoy*—All's IV 3 103. *You, sir, I entertain for one of my hundred*—Lr III 6 83.

(3) To retain in service: [I beg of you] *whilst this poor wealth lasts To entertain me as your steward still*—Tim IV 3 495.

(4) To treat in general: *I'll entertain myself like one that I am not acquainted withal*—Wiv II 1 89. *Yet tell'st thou not how thou wert entertain'd*—1 H6 I 4 38. *Your highness is not enter-*

tained with that ceremonious affection as you were wont—Lr I 4 62.

(5) To receive, admit, accept in general: *I quake, Lest thou a feverous life shouldst entertain*—Meas III 1 74. *Mine own doors refuse to entertain me*—Err III 1 120. *Ring, bells . . . To entertain great England's lawful king*—2 H6 V 1 3. *Let the presents Be worthily entertain'd*—Tim I 2 190.

(6) To engage (an enemy): *O noble English, that could entertain With half their forces the full pride of France*—H5 I 2 111.

(7) Of time, to pass, wile away: *It cannot be That . . . The misplaced John should entertain an hour . . . of rest*—John III 4 131. *I could be well content To entertain the lag-end of my life With quiet hours*—1 H4 V 1 23. *To entertain these fair well-spoken days*—R3 I 1 29.

(8) To come under obligations in regard to, enter into: *Here we entertain a solemn peace*—1 H6 V 4 175.

ENTERTAINMENT

(1) Employment, service: *Some band of strangers i' the adversary's entertainment*—All's IV 1 16. *Canidius and the rest That fell away have entertainment, but No honourable trust*—Ant IV 6 16. *In the entertainment,* app., mobilized: *Rom . . . Have you an army ready, say you?* Vols. *A most royal one; the centurions and their charges, distinctly billeted, already in the entertainment, and to be on foot at an hour's warning*—Cor IV 3 45. A taking again into service: *If your lady strain his entertainment*—Oth III 3 250.

(2) Treatment or reception in general: *I will resist such entertainment*—Tp I 2 465. *I have deserved no better entertainment*—Cor IV 5 10. *Get thee back to Cæsar, Tell him thy entertainment*—Ant III 13 139. Kind treatment, ready reception: *I spy entertainment in her*—Wiv I 3 48. *This entertainment May a free face put on*—Wint I 2 111. *Do not dull thy palm with entertainment Of each new-hatch'd, unfledged comrade*—Hml I 3 64. Of intercourse between lovers: *The stealth of our most mutual entertainment*—Meas I 2 158.

(3) A means of passing (time): *Some entertainment of time, some show*—LLL V 1 125.

(4) The entertaining of an idea, expectation: *This friar hath . . . advised him for the entertainment of death*—Meas III 2 224.

ENTIRE

Of feelings, unfeigned, pure, unmixed: *Your entire affection to Bianca*—Shr IV 2 23. *Pure fear and entire cowardice*—2 H4 II 4 352.

ENTITLED

In heraldry, blazoned, displayed: *Whether beauty, birth, or wealth, or wit . . . Entitled in thy parts do crowned sit*—Sonn 37 5. Cf. *Intituled.*

ENTRANCE

The thirsty entrance of this soil, app., the parched surface figured as a mouth: *No more the thirsty entrance of this soil Shall daub her lips with her own children's blood*—1 H4 I 1 5.

ENTREASURE, INTREASURE

(1) To lay up, store: *Which in their seeds And weak beginnings lie intreasured*—2 H4 III 1 84.

(2) To enrich: *Balm'd and entreasured With full bags of spices*—Per III 2 65.

ENTREAT (sb.)

Entreaty: *Penetrable to your kind entreats*—R3 III 7 225. *Yield at entreats*—Tit I 449. *At my lovely Tamora's entreats*—483.

ENTREAT (vb.)

(1) To treat, use: *Fairly let her be entreated*—R2 III 1 37. *Be patient, and entreat me fair*—R3 IV 4 151. *Entreat her fair*—Troil IV 4 115.

(2) To negotiate: *I'll send some holy bishop to entreat*—2 H6 IV 4 9.

(3) To prevail on by entreaty, persuade: *Thou canst compel no more than she entreat*—Mids III 2 249. *Since the youth will not be entreated*—As I 2 158. *I could hardly entreat him back*—Tw III 4 63. *When we can entreat an hour to serve*—Mcb II 1 22.

ENTREATMENT

A conversation, interview: *Set your entreatments at a higher rate Than a command to parley*—Hml I 3 122.

ENTRENCH

To make (a wound) by cutting: *It was this very sword entrenched it*—All's II 1 44.

ENVENOM

To kill by poison; fig.: *What a world is this, when what is comely Envenoms him that bears it!*—As II 3 14. *Envenom him with words*—John III 1 63.

ENVIOUS

Malignant, spiteful: *My father's rough and envious disposition*—As I 2 253. *Can heaven be so envious?*—Rom III 2 40. *This shall make Our purpose necessary and not envious*—Cæs II 1 177. *An envious sliver broke*—Hml IV 7 174.

ENVIOUSLY

Spitefully: *Spurns enviously at straws*—Hml IV 5 6.

ENVY (sb.)

Malice, spite, ill-will: *Sycorax, who with age and envy Was grown into a hoop*—Tp I 2 258. *She bore a mind that envy could not but call fair*—Tw II 1 30. *His envy to the people*—Cor III 3 3. *Wrath in death and envy afterwards*—Cæs II 1 164.

ENVY (vb.)

To have malevolence or a grudge against: *Do not take His rougher accents for malicious sounds, But . . . such as become a soldier, Rather than envy you*—Cor III 3 54. To have malevolent or grudging feelings: *Now I envy at their liberty, And will again commit them to their bonds*—John III 4 73. *Whose honesty the devil And his disciples only envy at*—H8 V 3 111. *For that he has . . . Envied against the people*—Cor III 3 93.

ENWHEEL

To encircle, surround: *The grace of heaven . . . Enwheel thee round!*—Oth II 1 85.

EPHESIAN

A boon companion: *It is thine host, thine Ephesian, calls*—Wiv IV 5 18. *Prince. What company? Page. Ephesians, my lord, of the old church*—2 H4 II 2 163.

EPICURISM

Sensuality: *Epicurism and lust*—Lr I 4 265.

EPITHET

A phrase, expression: *Suffer love! a good epithet!*—Ado V 2 67. *A bombast circumstance Horribly stuff'd with epithets of war*—Oth I 1 13.

EPITHETON

An epithet: *A congruent epitheton*—LLL I 2 14.

EQUAL (adj.)

(1) Just, impartial: *Justice always whirls in equal measure*—LLL IV 3 384. *Equal friendship and proceeding*—H8 II 4 18.

(2) *An equal pound*, prob., a pound to be accepted as an equivalent for the debt: *Let the forfeit Be nominated for an equal pound Of your fair flesh*—Merch I 3 149.

EQUAL (vb.)

To equal with, to be a match for: *A body strong enough . . . to equal with the king*—2 H4 I 3 66.

EQUALLY

Justly, equitably: *As . . . their merits and our safety May equally determine*—Lr V 3 44.

EQUIPAGE

(1) Equipment: *To march in ranks of better equipage*—Sonn 32 12.

(2) Furnishings in gen.; hence app., (stolen) goods: *I will retort the sum in equipage*—Wiv II 2 3. (So the first two Quartos.)

ERINGO

The candied root of the sea holly, supposed to have aphrodisiac qualities: *[Let the sky] hail kissing-comfits and snow eringoes*—Wiv V 5 22.

ERR

To wander, rove: *How brief the life of man Runs his erring pilgrimage*—As III 2 137. *The extravagant and erring spirit*—Hml I 1 154. In Oth I 3 362 (*A frail vow betwixt an erring barbarian and a supersubtle Venetian*) prob. the meanings roving and blundering (as contrasted with *supersubtle*) are intermingled.

ERRONEOUS

(1) Criminal: *What stratagems, how fell, how butcherly, Erroneous, mutinous and unnatural*—3 H6 II 5 89.

(2) Misguided: *Erroneous vassal!*—R3 I 4 200.

ERROR

(1) An aberration, deviation from the right course: *Many an error by the same example Will rush into the state*—Merch IV 1 221. *It is the very error of the moon*—Oth V 2 109.

(2) A delusion, trick: *My love with words and errors still she feeds*—Troil V 3 111.

ESCAPE

(1) A sally (of wit): *Thousand escapes of wit Make thee the father of their idle dreams*—Meas IV 1 63.

(2) A transgression, escapade (connoting a breach of chastity): *Rome will despise her for this foul escape*—Tit IV 2 113. *Thy escape would teach me tyranny*—Oth I 3 197.

ESCHEW

To avoid, keep clear of: *What cannot be eschew'd must be embraced*—Wiv V 5 251.

ESCOT

To pay a reckoning for, maintain: *Who maintains 'em? how are they escoted?*—Hml II 2 361.

ESPECIAL

(1) Special: *Upon especial cause*—1 H6 IV 1 55. *There is especial commission come from Venice*—Oth IV 2 225.

(2) Individual: *For thine especial safety*—Hml IV 3 42.

(3) Quasi-adv.: *[He] gave you such a masterly report . . . for your rapier most especial*—Hml IV 7 97.

ESPERANCE

Hope: *An esperance so obstinately strong*—Troil V 2 121. *Stands still in esperance, lives not in fear*—Lr IV 1 4. The motto of the Percy family: *O esperance!*—1 H4 II 3 74. *Now, Esperance! Percy! and set on.*—V 2 97.

ESPIAL

A scout, spy: *The prince's espials*—1 H6 I 4 8. *By your espials were discovered Two mightier troops*—IV 3 6. *Her father and myself, lawful espials*—Hml III 1 32.

ESPY

To spy upon, watch: *Question me no more; we are espied*—Tit II 3 48.

ESSAY

A trial, testing: *An essay or taste of my virtue*—Lr I 2 47. *Worse essays proved thee my best of love*—Sonn 110 8.

ESSENCE

(1) Being, existence: *So they loved, as love in twain Had the essence but in one*—Phœn 25.

(2) An entity: *Her honour is an essence that's not seen*—Oth IV 1 16.

(3) Nature, character: *Most ignorant of what he's most assured, His glassy essence*—Meas II 2 119.

(4) Foundation of being: *She is my essence, and I leave to be, If I be not by her fair influence Foster'd*—Gent III 1 182.

ESSENTIAL

Having existence, real; and hence prob., material: *And in the essential vesture of creation Does tire the ingener*—Oth II 1 64.

ESSENTIALLY

(1) On the ground of one's actual nature: *He that loves himself Hath not essentially but by circumstance The name of valour*—2 H6 V 2 38.

(2) In fact, really: *Thou art essentially mad, without seeming so*—1 H4 II 4 540. *I essentially am not in madness, But mad in craft*—Hml III 4 187.

ESTABLISH

Of dignities, &c., to settle (*upon* a person): *We will establish our estate upon Our eldest*—Mcb I 4 37.

ESTATE (sb.)

(1) State or condition in general: *Her inaidible estate*—All's II 1 122. *Having seen me in my worst estate*—Lr V 3 209. *So think of your estate*—Cymb V 5 74. Condition with respect to worldly prosperity: *Is grown into an unspeakable estate*—Wint IV 2 45. [*We should*] *know our own estate, How able such a work to undergo*—2 H4 I 3 53.

(2) A condition or form of existence: *It gives me an estate of seven years' health*—Cor II 1 125. [*I*] *wish the estate o' the world were now undone*—Mcb V 5 50.

(3) Rank, status: *O, that estates, degrees and offices Were not derived corruptly!*—Merch II 9 41. *Fortune, she said, was no goddess, that had put such difference betwixt their two estates*—All's I 3 115. [*The corse*] *was of some estate*—Hml V 1 244. Regal dignity: *We will establish our estate upon Our eldest*—Mcb I 4 37. *He poisons him i' the garden for's estate*—Hml III 2 272. *Robe of*

estate, robe of state: *Duke of Suffolk, in his robe of estate*—H8 IV 1 36 (Stage Dir).

(4) A class in a community: *Flouts, Which you on all estates will execute*—LLL V 2 854. *Your tenderness of heart . . . Which we have noted in you to your kin, And egally indeed to all estates*—R3 III 7 210.

(5) Interest, affairs: [Can he] *dispute his own estate?*—Wint IV 4 410. Political or state affairs: *How wildly then walks my estate in France!*—John IV 2 128. *The terms of our estate may not endure Hazard so near us*—Hml III 3 5. The state: *The estate is green and yet ungovern'd*—R3 II 2 127.

ESTATE (vb.)

To bestow, make over, settle: *Some donation freely to estate On the blest lovers*—Tp IV 85. *All my right of her I do estate unto Demetrius*—Mids I 1 97. *All the revenue . . . will I estate upon you*—As V 2 12.

ESTEEM (sb.)

(1) Estimated value, valuation: *We lost a jewel of her; and our esteem Was made much poorer by it*—All's V 3 1.

(2) Account, worth, reputation: *Gentlemen of good esteem*—Gent I 3 40. *She is of good esteem*—Shr IV 5 64. *Five hundred prisoners of esteem*—1 H6 III 4 8. *Your highness is betroth'd Unto another lady of esteem*—V 5 26.

ESTEEM (vb.)

(1) To estimate, value: *Life itself, my wife . . . Are not with me esteem'd above thy life*—Merch IV 1 284. *What do you esteem it at?*—Cymb I 4 85.

(2) To have such and such an opinion *of*: *We have always truly served you, and beseech you So to esteem of us*—Wint II 3 148.

ESTEEMING

Value, worth: *That love is merchandized whose rich esteeming The owner's tongue doth publish every where*—Sonn 102 3.

ESTIMABLE

(1) Valuable, of worth: *A pound of man's flesh . . . Is not so estimable . . . As flesh of muttons*—Merch I 3 166.

(2) Esteeming; *with such estimable wonder*, with such (highly) esteeming admiration: *I could not with such estimable wonder overfar believe that*—Tw II 1 28.

ESTIMATE

(1) Appraising, valuation; *in thee hath estimate*, app., has a claim to be considered in the valuation of thee: *All that life can rate Worth name of life in thee hath estimate*—All's II 1 182. Measure (of value) attributed: *Value dwells not in particular will; It holds his estimate and dignity . . . in . . .*—

Troil II 2 53. Price: *If he will touch the estimate*—Tim I 1 14. *Thou art too dear for my possessing, And like enough thou know'st thy estimate*—Sonn 87 1.

(2) Repute, reputation: *None else of name and noble estimate*—R2 II 3 56. *My dear wife's estimate*—Cor III 3 114.

ESTIMATION

(1) Appraising, valuation: *Who, in a cheap estimation, is worth all your predecessors*—Cor II 1 100. *In the estimation of*, so as to indicate the weight of: *If the scale do turn But in the estimation of a hair*—Merch IV 1 330.

(2) Worth, value: *Claudio—whose estimation do you mightily hold up*—Ado II 2 24. *If thou be'st rated by thy estimation, Thou dost deserve enough*—Merch II 7 26. *Your son . . . lack'd the sense to know Her estimation home*—All's V 3 2. A thing of worth: [Why do you now] *Beggar the estimation which you prized Richer than sea and land?*—Troil II 2 91. *Your brace of unprizable estimations*—Cymb I 4 98.

(3) Repute, reputation: *He cannot plead his estimation with you*—Meas IV 2 27. *Your yet ungalled estimation*—Err III 1 102. *Dear men Of estimation*—1 H4 IV 4 31. *Do they hold the same estimation they did when I was in the city?*—Hml II 2 348.

(4) Conjecture: *I speak not this in estimation*—1 H4 I 3 272.

ESTRIDGE

The goshawk: *All plumed like estridges that with the wind Baited like eagles having lately bathed*—1 H4 IV 1 98. *In that mood The dove will peck the estridge*—Ant III 13 196.

ETERNAL

(1) Having an eternal resolve: *Never did young man fancy With so eternal and so fix'd a soul*—Troil V 2 165.

(2) Relating to the things of eternity: *This eternal blazon must not be To ears of flesh and blood*—Hml I 5 21.

(3) Used to express abhorrence: *The eternal devil*—Cæs I 2 160. *Some eternal villain*—Oth IV 2 130.

ETERNE

Eternal: *In them nature's copy's not eterne*—Mcb III 2 38. *Mars's armour forged for proof eterne*—Hml II 2 512.

EVEN (adj.)

(1) Of movements or speech, direct, straightforward: *In plain shock and even play of battle*—H5 IV 8 114. *Be even and direct with me*—Hml II 2 297. Steady in the due course: *I know my life so even*—H8 III 1 37. *The even virtue of our enterprise*—Cæs II 1 133.

(2) Exact, precise: *To make the even truth in pleasure flow*—All's V 3 326.

(3) *To make him even o'er*, to give him a clear perception of: *It is danger To make him even o'er the time he has lost*—Lr IV 7 79.

(4) As sb., *the even of it*, the long and short of it: *That's the even of it*—H5 II 1 128.

EVEN (vb.)

(1) To make a person quits (*with* another): *Nothing can or shall content my soul Till I am even'd with him*—Oth II 1 307.

(2) To act up to, keep pace with: *The care I have had to even your content*—All's I 3 3. *We'll even All that good time will give us*—Cymb III 4 184.

EVEN (adv.)

(1) In a right line, straight: *Made to run even upon even ground*—John II 576. *Then he runs straight and even*—1 H4 III 1 114.

(2) *To go even*, to accord, agree: *The rest goes even*—Tw V 246. To conform *with*: *Rather shunned to go even with what I heard than in my every action to be guided by others' experiences*—Cymb I 4 47.

(3) *Even before*, just before: *Even before this truce, but new before*—John III 1 233. *My hunger's gone; but even before, I was At point to sink for food*—Cymb III 6 16. *Even at hand*, just at hand: *Even at hand a drum is ready braced*—John V 2 169.

EVEN CHRISTIAN

Fellow Christian: *The more pity that great folk should have countenance . . . to drown or hang themselves, more than their even Christian*—Hml V 1 29.

EVENLY

In a right line, directly: [The] *Trent shall run In a new channel, fair and evenly*—1 H4 III 1 102. *Evenly derived From his most famed of famous ancestors*—H5 II 4 91.

EVEN-PLEACHED

Smoothly intertwined: *Her hedges even-pleach'd . . . Put forth disorder'd twigs*—H5 V 2 42.

EVIDENCE

A witness: *Comes not that blood as modest evidence To witness simple virtue?*—Ado IV 1 38. *His scarlet lust came evidence to swear That . . .*—Lucr 1650. Collectively, witnesses: *True evidence of good esteem*—2 H6 III 2 21. *Where are the evidence that do accuse me?*—R3 I 4 188. *Bring in the evidence*—Lr III 6 37.

EVIDENT

Indubitable, conclusive: *Render to me some corporal sign about her, More evident than this*—Cymb II 4 119.

EVIL

(1) A wrong-doing, sin, crime: *Those many had not dared to do that evil*—Meas II 2 91. *Of these supposed evils . . . to acquit myself*—R3 I 2 76. *My disclaiming from a purposed evil*—Hml V 2 252. [She] *repented The evils she hatch'd were not effected*—Cymb V 5 59.

(2) A calamity, misfortune: *That I may bear my evils alone*—Tw II 1 6. [I] *broke out To acquaint you with this evil*—John V 6 24. *It is too true an evil: gone she is*—Oth I 1 161.

(3) A disease, malady: *Embossed sores and headed evils*—As II 7 67. *Evils that take leave, On their departure most of all show evil*—John III 4 114. *A sick man's appetite, who desires most that Which would increase his evil*—Cor I 1 182. Specifically, the king's evil, scrofula: Macd. *What's the disease he means?* Mal. *'Tis call'd the evil*—Mcb IV 3 146.

EVITATE

To shun, avoid: *She doth evitate and shun A thousand irreligious cursed hours*—Wiv V 5 241.

EXACT

(1) Consummate, perfect: *Severals and generals of grace exact*—Troil I 3 180.

(2) App., brought fully into a computation, without exception: *Were it good To set the exact wealth of all our states All at one cast?*—1 H4 IV 1 45.

EXACTLY

(1) Completely: *Armed at point exactly*—Hml I 2 200.

(2) In express terms: *I did confess it, and exactly begg'd Your grace's pardon*—R2 I 1 140.

EXAMINE

To call in question, throw doubt upon: *All her deserving Is a reserved honesty, and that I have not heard examined*—All's III 5 64.

EXAMPLE

To furnish a precedent for, justify by a precedent: *That I may example my digression by some mighty precedent*—LLL I 2 121. *Ill, to example ill*—IV 3 124. *Prove a deadly bloodshed but a jest, Exampled by this heinous spectacle*—John IV 3 55.

EXCEEDING

To exceeding, eminently: *Very brief, and to exceeding good sense*—Tw III 4 174.

EXCEPT

(1) To object to; and so, to oppose, take measures against: *Desire is death, which physic did except*—Sonn 147 8.

(2) *Except before excepted*, except as before excepted, a formal law phrase used ludicrously: Mar. *. . . Your cousin, my lady, takes great exceptions to*

your ill hours. Sir To. *Why, let her except before excepted*—Tw I 3 5.

EXCEPTION

(1) Objection, demur: *Knew the true minute when Exception bid him speak* — All's I 2 39. *Modest in exception*—H5 II 4 34. *'Tis positive 'gainst all exceptions*—IV 2 25.

(2) Dislike, dissatisfaction: *What I have done, That might your nature, honour and exception Roughly awake, I here proclaim was madness*—Hml V 2 241.

EXCEPTLESS

Making no exception: *Forgive my general and exceptless rashness*—Tim IV 3 502.

EXCHANGE (sb.)

Change, transmutation: *The allusion holds in the exchange*—LLL IV 2 42. *I am much ashamed of my exchange*—Merch II 6 35.

EXCHANGE (vb.)

(1) To get in exchange: *What shalt thou exchange for rags? robes*—LLL IV 1 84.

(2) To change, alter: *Not with the time exchanged*—Sonn 109 7.

EXCITE

To incite, impel: *Every reason excites to this, that my lady loves me*—Tw II 5 179. *Beaten for loyalty Excited me to treason*—Cymb V 5 344.

EXCITEMENT

An exhortation: *Excitements to the field, or speech for truce*—Troil I 3 182. An incentive: *Excitements of my reason and my blood*—Hml IV 4 58.

EXCLAIM

An exclamation, outcry: *The part I had in Woodstock's blood Doth more solicit me than your exclaims*—R2 I 2 1. *Cursing cries and deep exclaims*—R3 I 2 52. *You are amazed, my liege, at her exclaim*—Troil V 3 91.

EXCREMENT

That which grows out of the body; of hair: [To] *dally with my excrement, with my mustachio*—LLL V 1 109. *How many cowards . . . wear . . . The beards of Hercules and frowning Mars . . . And these assume but valour's excrement*—Merch III 2 83. *Let me pocket up my pedlar's excrement.* [Takes off his false beard]—Wint IV 4 732. *Your bedded hair, like life in excrements, Starts up*—Hml III 4 121.

EXCURSIONS

Rushes, fighting (only in Stage Directions): John II 299; 1 H4 V 4; Troil V 4.

EXCUSE

To beg off from doing (a thing): *To-morrow be in readiness to go: Excuse it not, for I am peremptory*—Gent I 3 70.

EXECUTE

(1) To give effect to (a passion): *Execute thy wrath in me alone*—R3 I 4 71.

(2) To do execution, wreak one's wrath: *Cassio following him with determined sword, To execute upon him*—Oth II 3 227.

(3) To bring (a weapon) into operation: *In fellest manner execute your arms*—Troil V 7 6. (So the Quartos and the Folios, except the First, which has *arme.*)

(4) To put to death, kill: *Thou . . . didst send two of thy men To execute the noble duke at Calais*—R2 IV 81. *Whom with my bare fists I would execute*—1 H6 I 4 36.

EXECUTION

(1) The giving effect to (a passion), the exercise (of powers): *Scarce I can refrain The execution of my big-swoln heart Upon that Clifford*—3 H6 II 2 110. *Those that . . . By reason guide his (i.e.* the ram's) *execution*—Troil I 3 209. *Iago doth give up The execution of his wit, hands, heart, To wrong'd Othello's service*—Oth III 3 465.

(2) Infliction of damage or slaughter: *Retreat is made and execution stay'd*—2 H4 IV 3 78. *His brandish'd steel, Which smoked with bloody execution*—Mcb I 2 17.

EXECUTOR

(1) One who carries out (a work): *Such baseness Had never like executor*—Tp III 1 12.

(2) An executioner: *The sad-eyed justice . . . Delivering o'er to executors pale The lazy yawning drone*—H5 I 2 202.

EXEMPT (ppl. adj.)

Cut off, removed: *Be it my wrong you are from me exempt*—Err II 2 173. *This our life exempt from public haunt*—As II 1 15. *Stand'st not thou attainted, Corrupted, and exempt from ancient gentry?*—1 H6 II 4 92. *Who would not wish to be from wealth exempt, Since riches point to misery and contempt?*—Tim IV 2 31.

EXEMPT (vb.)

To take away, remove: *Exempted be from me the arrogance To choose from forth the royal blood of France*—All's II 1 198.

EXERCISE (sb.)

(1) Exertion, action: *Thy exercise hath been too violent For a second course of fight*—Cor I 5 16. *When these mutualities so marshal the way, hard at hand comes the master and main exercise*—Oth II 1 267.

(2) A habitual occupation: *Hunting was his daily exercise*—3 H6 IV 6 85.

(3) Religious observance, an act of devotion: *Once a day I'll visit The chapel . . . so long as nature Will bear up with this exercise, so long I daily vow to use it*—Wint III 2 239. *In no worldly suit would he be moved, To draw him from his holy exercise*—R3 III 7 63. *Much castigation, exercise devout*—Oth III 4 41. A sermon: *I am in debt for your last exercise*—R3 III 2 112.

(4) Acquired skill: *They have been thoughtful to invest Their sons with arts and martial exercises*—2 H4 IV 5 73. *Swelling o'er with arts and exercise*—Troil IV 4 80. [He] *gave you such a masterly report For art and exercise in your defence*—Hml IV 7 97.

EXERCISE (vb.)

To do one's office: *Urchins Shall . . . All exercise on thee*—Tp I 2 326.

EXHALATION

A meteor (see *Exhale*[1] (2)): *No natural exhalation in the sky*—John III 4 153. *Do you see these meteors? do you behold these exhalations?*—1 H4 II 4 351. *The exhalations whizzing in the air*—Cæs II 1 44.

EXHALE[1]

(1) To draw up (a vapour): *Then thou, fair sun . . . Exhalest this vapour-vow*—LLL IV 3 69. *With rotten damps ravish the morning air; Let their exhaled unwholesome breaths make sick The life of purity*—Lucr 778.

(2) Of meteors (supposed to proceed from vapours drawn up by the sun): *Be no more an exhaled meteor*—1 H4 V 1 19. *It is some meteor that the sun exhales*—Rom III 5 13.

EXHALE[2]

(1) To draw (a sword): *The grave doth gape, and doting death is near: Therefore exhale*—H5 II 1 65.

(2) To cause (blood or tears) to flow: *'Tis thy presence that exhales this blood*—R3 I 2 58. *In that sad time My manly eyes did scorn an humble tear; And what these sorrows could not thence exhale, Thy beauty hath*—164.

EXHAUST

To draw out: *The babe, Whose dimpled smiles from fools exhaust their mercy*—Tim IV 3 118.

EXHIBIT

To present formally, introduce, submit: *I'll exhibit a bill in the parliament for the putting down of men*—Wiv II 1 29. *They should exhibit their petitions in the street*—Meas IV 4 11. *Accept this scroll . . . Which in the right of Richard Plantagenet We do exhibit*—1 H6 III 1 149.

EXHIBITER

One who introduces a bill in parliament: *Rather swaying more upon our part Than cherishing the exhibiters against us*—H5 I 1 73.

EXHIBITION

(1) An allowance, a pension: *Like exhibition thou shalt have from me*—Gent I 3 69. *The king gone to-night! subscribed his power! Confined to exhibition!*—Lr I 2 24. *I crave fit disposition for my wife, Due reference of place and exhibition*—Oth I 3 237.

(2) A present: *I would not do such a thing for a joint-ring . . . nor any petty exhibition*—Oth IV 3 72.

EXIGENT

(1) An emergency, crisis: *Why do you cross me in this exigent?*—Cæs V 1 19. *When the exigent should come, which now Is come indeed*—Ant IV 14 63.

(2) The last pinch, end: *These eyes . . . Wax dim, as drawing to their exigent*—1 H6 II 5 8.

EXORCISER

One who calls up spirits: *No exorciser harm thee!*—Cymb IV 2 276.

EXORCISM

A ceremony for calling up spirits: *Will her ladyship behold and hear our exorcisms?*—2 H6 I 4 4.

EXORCIST

One who calls up spirits: *Is there no exorcist Beguiles the truer office of mine eyes?*—All's V 3 305. *Thou, like an exorcist, hast conjured up My mortified spirit*—Cæs II 1 323.

EXPECT (sb.)

Expectation: *Be't of less expect That . . .*—Troil I 3 70.

EXPECT (vb.)

To await: *My father at the road Expects my coming*—Gent I 1 53. *Let's in, and there expect their coming*—Merch V 49. *A thousand, sir . . . at the port expect you*—Ant IV 4 21.

EXPECTANCE

With indirect question, the state of waiting to know: *There is expectance here from both the sides, What further you will do*—Troil IV 5 146.

EXPECTANCY

That from which one expects: *The expectancy and rose of the fair state*—Hml III 1 160.

EXPEDIENCE

(1) Haste, speed: *Making hither with all due expedience*—R2 II 1 287. *The French . . . will with all expedience charge on us*—H5 IV 3 69.

(2) An enterprise, expedition: *What yesternight our council did decree In forwarding this dear expedience*—1 H4 I 1 32. *I shall break The cause of our expedience to the queen*—Ant I 2 184 (or perh. this should be taken in sense (1)).

EXPEDIENT

Speedy: *His marches are expedient to this town*—John II 60. *Expedient manage must be made*—R2 I 4 39. *A breach that craves a quick expedient stop!*—2 H6 III 1 288.

EXPEDIENTLY

Speedily: *Do this expediently*—As III 1 18.

EXPEDITION

The condition of being set in motion: *Let us deliver Our puissance into the hand of God, Putting it straight in expedition*—H5 II 2 189.

EXPEL

To keep off, keep out: *Should patch a wall to expel the winter's flaw*—Hml V 1 239.

EXPEND

To make away with, consume in outlay: *Careless heirs May the two latter (i.e. nobleness and riches) darken and expend*—Per III 2 28.

EXPENSE

(1) Disbursement, spending (of money): *Wilt thou, after the expense of so much money, be now a gainer?*—Wiv II 2 146. *To have the expense and waste of his revenues*—Lr II 1 102. Wasteful expenditure: *My state being gall'd with my expense*—Wiv III 4 5. *It is a dear expense*, it will be a bitter bargain, will cost me dear: Mids I 1 249.

(2) Expenditure or using up in general: *I implore so much expense of thy . . . breath as . . .*—LLL V 2 523. [They] *husband nature's riches from expense*—Sonn 94 6. *The expense of spirit in a waste of shame*—129 1.

(3) Loss: [Then can I] *moan the expense of many a vanish'd sight*—Sonn 30 8.

EXPIATE (ppl. adj.)

Of an appointed time, fully come: *Make haste; the hour of death is expiate*—R3 III 3 23.

EXPIATE (vb.)

To bring to an end: *Then look I death my days should expiate*—Sonn 22 4.

EXPIRE

To bring to an end: [Some consequence shall] *expire the term Of a despised life*—Rom I 4 109.

EXPLOIT

(1) An act or deed: *A close exploit of death*—R3 IV 2 35. *Time, thou anticipatest my dread exploits*—Mcb IV 1 144.

(2) Military service, action: *Our gentry, who are sick For breathing and exploit*—All's I 2 16. *I must give myself some hurts, and say I got them in exploit*—IV I 40.

EXPOSTULATE

To discourse, discuss: *The time now serves not to expostulate*—Gent III 1 251. *Stay not to expostulate, make speed*—3 H6 II 5 135. *To expostulate What majesty should be, what duty is*—Hml II 2 86.

EXPOSTULATION

Prob., discourse, discussion: *Nay, we must use expostulation kindly, For it is parting from us*—Troil IV 4 62.

EXPOSTURE

Exposure: *A wild exposture to each chance That starts i' the way before thee*—Cor IV I 36.

EXPOSURE

I.e. to danger, perilous situation (meaning power of resistance in that situation): *To weaken and discredit our exposure, How rank soever rounded in with danger*—Troil I 3 195.

EXPRESS

Well framed or modelled: *In form and moving how express and admirable!*—Hml II 2 317.

EXPRESSIVE

Open in speech: *Be more expressive to them*—All's II 1 53.

EXPRESSURE

(1) Expression: *An operation more divine Than breath or pen can give expressure to*—Troil III 3 203.

(2) A description: *The expressure of his eye, forehead, and complexion*—Tw II 3 171.

(3) An image, picture: *Look you sing . . . in a ring: The expressure that it bears, green let it be*—Wiv V 5 69.

EXPULSE

To drive out, expel: *For ever should they be expulsed from France*—1 H6 III 3 25.

EXSUFFLICATE

Perh., puffed up, windy: *Such exsufflicate and blown surmises*—Oth III 3 182.

EXTANT

Of time, present: *In this extant moment*—Troil IV 5 168.

EXTEMPORAL

Able to speak or write extempore: *Assist me, some extemporal god of rhyme*—LLL I 2 189.

EXTEND

(1) To recite or state a person's (good) qualities: Sec. Gent. *You speak him far.* First Gent. *I do*

extend him, sir, within himself (*i.e.* within the limits which his merits permit)—Cymb I 1 24. To magnify in representation: *The approbation of those that weep this lamentable divorce under her colours are wonderfully to extend him*—I 4 19.

(2) To seize upon: *Labienus . . . hath . . . Extended Asia from Euphrates*—Ant I 2 103.

(3) To display: *Nor doth he of himself know them* (*i.e.* his parts) *for aught Till he behold them form'd in the applause Where they're extended*—Troil III 3 118. *Let it not gall your patience . . . That I extend my manners*—Oth II 1 98.

EXTENT

(1) A seizure of lands, &c., by writ of extent: *Make an extent upon his house and lands*—As III 1 17.

(2) An attack, assault: *This uncivil and unjust extent Against thy peace*—Tw IV 1 57.

(3) The exercising or showing (of justice or kindness): *Was ever seen An emperor in Rome . . . for the extent Of egal justice used in such contempt?*—Tit IV 4 1. *My extent to the players, which . . . must show fairly outward*—Hml II 2 390.

EXTENUATE

(1) To mitigate: *The law of Athens . . . Which by no means we may extenuate*—Mids I 1 119.

(2) To depreciate, disparage: *His glory not extenuated . . . nor his offences enforced*—Cæs III 2 42.

EXTENUATION

Mitigation of blame: *Such extenuation let me beg, As . . . I may . . . Find pardon on my true submission*—I H4 III 2 22.

EXTERMINE

Exterminate: *By giving love your sorrow and my grief Were both extermined*—As III 5 88.

EXTERN

External: *In compliment extern*—Oth I 1 63. As sb., outward appearance, exterior: *With my extern the outward honouring*—Sonn 125 2.

EXTINCTED

Extinguished, quenched: [That he may] *Give renew'd fire to our extincted spirits*—Oth II 1 81.

EXTINCTURE

Extinction, quenching: *Cold modesty, hot wrath, Both fire from hence and chill extincture hath*—Compl 293.

EXTIRP

Extirpate: *It is impossible to extirp it quite*—Meas III 2 109. [They should] *be extirped from our provinces*—I H6 III 3 24.

EXTORT

To wring or wrest away: *None of noble sort Would so offend a virgin and extort A poor soul's patience*—Mids III 2 159.

EXTRACTING

App., distracting: *A most extracting frenzy*—Tw V 288.

EXTRAUGHT

Extract = Extracted; derived, descended: *Knowing whence thou art extraught*—3 H6 II 2 142.

EXTRAVAGANCY

Wandering, vagrancy: *My determinate voyage is mere extravagancy*—Tw II 1 11.

EXTRAVAGANT

Wandering, vagrant: *The extravagant and erring spirit*—Hml I 1 154. *An extravagant and wheeling stranger Of here and every where*—Oth I 1 137.

EXTREME (adj.)

Last: *The extreme parts of time extremely forms All causes to the purpose of his speed*—LLL V 2 750. (*Extremely* is app. a nonce-use = at the last, merely repeating and emphasizing the notion conveyed by *extreme*.)

EXTREME (sb.)

(1) An extravagancy: *To chide at your extremes it not becomes me*—Wint IV 4 6. *Do not break into these deep extremes*—Tit III 1 216.

(2) In pl., extremities, straits: *Always resolute in most extremes*—I H6 IV 1 38. *'Twixt my extremes and me this bloody knife Shall play the umpire*—Rom IV 1 62.

EXTREMITY

(1) An extravagancy: *If I find not what I seek, show no colour for my extremity*—Wiv IV 2 168.

(2) Extreme severity or rigour: *O time's extremity, Hast thou so crack'd and splitted my poor tongue . . . that . . .*—Err V 307.

EYAS

A young hawk taken from the nest to be trained, or one incompletely trained; fig.: *An aery of children, little eyases*—Hml II 2 354.

EYAS-MUSKET

A young male sparrow-hawk (the smallest hawk employed in falconry) in the condition of an eyas (see *Eyas*); fig.: *How now, my eyas-musket!*—Wiv III 3 22 (addressed to Robin the little page).

EYE (sb.)

(1) Range of vision, view, sight: *I wonder . . . what it was that next came in her eye*—Mids III

2 1. *There it lies in your eye*—Tw II 2 16. *We shall express our duty in his eye*—Hml IV 4 6.

(2) A slight shade, tinge: *With an eye of green in't*—Tp II 1 55.

EYE (vb.)

(1) To perceive with the eyes, catch sight of, see: *As wild geese that the creeping fowler eye*—Mids III 2 20. *That, when he waked, of force she must be eyed*—40.

(2) To look, appear: *My becomings kill me, when they do not Eye well to you*—Ant I 3 96.

EYE-GLASS

The lens of the eye: *Or your eye-glass Is thicker than a cuckold's horn*— Wint I 2 268.

EYNE

Pl. of eye: *Our watery eyne*—LLL V 2 206. *Hermia's eyne*—Mids I 1 242. *Your bright eyne*—As IV 3 50.

F

FABLE (sb.)

Sans fable, in truth: *Sans fable, she herself reviled you there*—Err IV 4 76.

FABLE (vb.)

To speak falsely: *He fables not; I hear the enemy*—1 H6 IV 2 42.

FACE

(1) To show a false face: *Fair Margaret knows That Suffolk doth not flatter, face, or feign*—1 H6 V 3 141.

(2) To confront with assurance or impudence, bully: *Face not me*—Shr IV 3 125. *Where is that damned villain Tranio, That faced and braved me in this matter so?*—V I 123. With cognate accus., to commit with assurance: *Was this the face that faced so many follies?*—R2 IV 285 (perh. with a tinge of sense (3)). *To face out of*, to bully out of: *Do all they can to face me out of my wits*—Tw IV 2 101. *I will not say so, for fear I should be faced out of my way*—H5 III 7 89. To exclude shamelessly from: *His false cunning . . . Taught him to face me out of his acquaintance*—Tw V 89. *To face it with a card of ten*, see *Card* (sb.) (3).

(3) Fig., to trim, adorn: *To face the garment of rebellion With some fine colour*—1 H4 V 1 74.

FACED

Patched, mended: *An old faced ancient*—1 H4 IV 2 34.

FACE-ROYAL

A kingly face, and the king's face on the coin called a royal: *He will not stick to say his face is a face-royal . . . he may keep it still at a face-royal, for a barber shall never earn sixpence out of it*—2 H4 I 2 25.

FACINERIOUS

Facinorous; wicked: *Of a most facinerious spirit*—All's II 3 34.

FACT

(1) A deed, action: *A sinful fact*—All's III 7 47. *This fact was infamous*—1 H6 IV 1 30.

Those of your fact, those who do as you have done—Wint III 2 86. *In the fact*, in the act: *Whom we have apprehended in the fact*—2 H6 II 1 173.

(2) An evil deed, a crime: *His fact till now . . . came not to an undoubtful proof*—Meas IV 2 141. *There was more than one Confederate in the fact*—Tit IV 1 38.

FACTION

(1) A number of persons secretly banded together for common ends (not conveying an imputation of selfish or mischievous ends): *They are the faction*—Cæs II 1 77 (said by Brutus of his fellows in the projected attempt).

(2) A class or set of persons: *This fellow were a king for our wild faction*—Gent IV 1 37. *I will keep where there is wit stirring and leave the faction of fools*—Troil II 1 129.

FACTIONARY

Taking part in a dissension, actively partisan: *My name is Menenius, always factionary on the party of your general*—Cor V 2 29.

FACTIOUS

(1) The same as the preceding: *You and your husband Grey Were factious for the house of Lancaster*—R3 I 3 127.

(2) Taking an active part with others towards a common end (cf. *Faction* (1)): *Be factious for redress of all these griefs*—Cæs I 3 118.

FACTOR

An agent, deputy: *Not as protector, steward, substitute, Or lowly factor for another's gain*—R3 III 7 133. *You all three . . . Chief factors for the gods*—Ant II 6 8. *Which I, the factor for the rest, have done*—Cymb I 6 188.

FACULTY

(1) A personal quality: *Traduced by ignorant tongues, which neither know My faculties nor person*—H8 I 2 72.

(2) Efficient property or virtue: *Unseen, yet crescive in his faculty*—H5 I 1 66. *Why all these*

things change from their ordinance Their natures and preformed faculties—Cæs I 3 66.

(3) In pl., powers, prerogatives: *This Duncan Hath borne his faculties so meek*—Mcb I 7 16.

FADGE

(1) To turn out: *How will this fadge?*—Tw II 2 34.

(2) To succeed, come off: *We will have, if this fadge not, an antique*—LLL V 1 154.

FADING

The name of a dance, said to have been Irish; used as a refrain: *With such delicate burthens of dildos and fadings*—Wint IV 4 194.

FAIL (sb.)

(1) Failure, neglect: *The fail Of any point in't shall . . . be Death*—Wint II 3 170. Failure, lack: *His highness' fail of issue*—Wint V 1 27. *This my issue's fail*—H8 II 4 198. Moral failure, fault: [The public body] *hath sense withal Of it own fail, restraining aid to Timon*—Tim V 1 150. *Goodly and gallant shall be false and perjured From thy great fail*—Cymb III 4 65.

(2) Death, or perh., failure of issue: *How grounded he his title to the crown, Upon our fail?*—H8 I 2 144.

FAIL (vb.)

(1) To die: *Had the king in his last sickness fail'd*—H8 I 2 184.

(2) *To fail of,* (a) to miss: *If I fail Of the right casket*—Merch II 9 11. (b) To be unsuccessful in, fail to attain: *If he fail of that, He will have other means to cut you off*—As II 3 24. *Failing of her end*—Cymb V 5 57. (c) To come short in: *If I fail not of my cunning*—Shr II 413. (d) To fail to obtain: *The queen Of audience nor desire shall fail*—Ant III 12 20.

(3) To omit, neglect, leave unperformed: *I cannot think my sister in the least Would fail her obligation*—Lr II 4 143. *'Cause he fail'd His presence at (i.e.* absented himself from) *the tyrant's feast*—Mcb III 6 21.

FAIN

Glad, well pleased: *Glad and fain by flight to save themselves*—1 H6 III 2 114. With *of*, fond of: *Man and birds are fain of climbing high*—2 H6 II 1 8.

FAINT (adj.)

Wanting in courage, spiritless: *Women and children of so high a courage, And warriors faint!*—3 H6 V 4 50. *Who is so faint, that dares not be so bold To touch the fire, the weather being cold?*—Ven 401.

FAINT (vb.)

(1) To lose heart, flag, be afraid: *If you faint,*

as fearing to do so, Stay—R2 II 1 297. *How I faint when I of you do write!*—Sonn. 80 1.

(2) To become faint, grow weak: *Fair love, you faint with wandering in the wood*—Mids II 2 35. *I faint almost to death*—As II 4 66.

(3) To make faint, depress: *It faints me, To think what follows*—H8 II 3 103.

FAINTLY

With hesitation, half-heartedly, coldly: *I faintly broke with thee of Arthur's death*—John IV 2 227. *He prays but faintly and would be denied*—R2 3 103. *'Twas very faintly he said 'Rise'*—Cor V 1 66. *He denies it faintly*—Oth IV 1 113.

FAIR (adj.)

(1) Of animals, of good form or appearance: *He's a good dog, and a fair dog*—Wiv I 1 98.

(2) Kind: *Vouchsafe me, for my meed, but one fair look*—Gent V 4 23. *Sometimes from her eyes I did receive fair speechless messages*—Merch I 1 163. *So fair an offer'd chain,* one so kindly offered—Err III 2 186.

(3) Favourable, auspicious: *This most fair occasion*—John V 4 51. *Till whatsoever star that guides my moving Points on me graciously with fair aspect*—Sonn 26 9.

(4) As a general epithet of commendation: *His fair tongue, conceit's expositor*—LLL II 72. *Fair thoughts and happy hours attend on you!*—Merch III 4 41. *Many fair promotions Are daily given*—R3 I 3 80. Used in courteous or respectful address or mention: *What think'st thou of the fair Sir Eglamour?*—Gent I 2 9. *Fair sir, God save you!*—LLL V 2 310. *Fair sir, you spit on me on Wednesday last*—Merch I 3 127. Cf. *Rest you fair, good signior*—Merch I 3 60.

(5) *Fair daylight,* broad day: *Where am I? Fair daylight?*—Lr IV 7 52.

FAIR (sb.)

(1) Beauty: *My decayed fair*—Err II 1 98. *Demetrius loves your fair*—Mids I 1 182. *Having no fair to lose*—Ven 1083.

(2) A beautiful person; generally of a woman: *Or I'll be thine, my fair, Or not my father's*—Wint IV 4 42. *Speak, my fair*—H5 V 2 177. *Farewell, revolted fair!*—Troil V 2 186. Of a youth: *Speak, fair*—Ven 208 (addressed to Adonis).

FAIR (vb.)

To make fair: *Fairing the foul with art's false borrow'd face*—Sonn 127 6.

FAIR (adv.)

(1) Respectfully, courteously: *Be patient, and entreat me fair*—R3 IV 4 151. *Entreat her fair*—Troil IV 4 115.

(2) Auspiciously: *You that choose not by the view, Chance as fair and choose as true!*—Merch

III 2 132. *Since this business so fair is done—* —1 H4 V 5 43. *Fair be to you!* prosperity attend you—Troil III 1 46. Sim. *Fair fall the bones that took the pains for me!*—John I 78.

(3) Gently, quietly: *Soft and fair, friar*—Ado V 4 72. *The... Trent shall run In a new channel, fair and evenly*—1 H4 III 1 102. *Stand fair, I pray thee; let me look on thee*—Troil IV 5 235.

FAIRLY

(1) So as to make a fine appearance, beautifully: *The unworthiest shows as fairly in the mask*—Troil I 3 84. *Was ever book containing such vile matter So fairly bound?*—Rom III 2 83.

(2) Respectfully, courteously: *Fairly I bespoke the officer*—Err V 233. *I pray ye, greet them fairly*—Per V 1 10. Kindly: *They are fairly welcome*—Tim I 2 182. *I shall accept them fairly* —190.

(3) Auspiciously: *Fairly met!*—Meas V 1. *Heavens so shine, That they may fairly note this act of mine!*—Tw IV 3 34. App., successfully: *Let them say 'tis grossly done; so it be fairly done, no matter*—Wiv II 2 148.

(4) Gently, peaceably: *After they closed in earnest, they parted very fairly in jest*—Gent II 5 13.

FAIRNESS

To the fairness of my power, app., in so far as I fairly can—Cor I 9 73.

FAIRY

One possessing more than human power, an enchantress: *To this great fairy* (*i.e.* Cleopatra) *I'll commend thy acts*—Ant IV 8 12.

FAITH

To give credit to, believe: *Would the reposal Of any trust . . . in thee Make thy words faith'd?*—Lr II 1 70.

FAITHFUL

Believing, having Christian faith: *As I am a Christian faithful man*—R3 I 4 4.

FAITHFULLY

Confidently: *If his occasion were not virtuous, I should not urge it half so faithfully*—Tim III 2 45.

FAITOR

A cheat, impostor: *Down, down, dogs! down, faitors!*—2 H4 II 4 172.

FALL (sb.)

(1) The ebb; *to be at fall*, to be in a low condition: *Now they are at fall, want treasure, cannot Do what they would*—Tim II 2 214.

(2) Shedding, effusion (of blood): *Without much fall of blood*—H5 I 2 25.

FALL (vb.)

(1) To shrink, become lean: *A good leg will fall* —H5 V 2 167.

(2) To befall, happen, come to pass: *If any thing fall to you upon this, more than thanks . . .* —Meas IV 2 190. *Whate'er falls more*—All's V I 37. *For fear of what might fall*—Cæs V I 105.

(3) *To fall away, from, off, over*, to revolt, desert: *Canidius and the rest That fell away*—Ant IV 6 16. *The falling-from of his friends*—Tim IV 3 401. *Revolted Mortimer! He never did fall off*—1 H4 I 3 93. *Dost thou now fall over to my foes?*—John III 1 127.

(4) To cause to fall, let fall: *When I rear my hand, do you the like, To fall it on Gonzalo*—Tp II I 295. *Mine eyes . . . Fall fellowly drops*—V 63. *Let us . . . rather cut a little, Than fall, and bruise to death*—Meas II 1 5. *For every tear he falls a Trojan bleeds*—Lucr 1551. So, to bring forth: *Did in eaning time Fall parti-colour'd lambs*—Merch I 3 88.

FALSE (adj.)

(1) *False gallop*, one of the paces which horses were taught, an artificial canter, somewhat jolting: Beat. *What pace is this that thy tongue keeps?* Marg. *Not a false gallop*—Ado III 4 93. *This is the very false gallop of verses*—As III 2 119.

(2) *False fire*, a blank discharge of firearms; fig.: *What, frighted with false fire!*—Hml III 2 277.

FALSE (vb.)

(1) Refl., to betray one's trust: *'Tis gold Which . . . makes Diana's rangers false themselves*—Cymb II 3 72 (or the word may be an adj.).

(2) *Falsing*: Err II 2 95 (*In a thing falsing*), app., deceptive; but the exact sense is not clear.

FALSEHOOD

Faithlessness, dishonesty: *Mine integrity Being counted falsehood*—Wint III 2 27. *Though indirect, Yet indirection thereby grows direct, And falsehood falsehood cures*—John III 1 275. *If you suspect my husbandry or falsehood, Call me before the exactest auditors*—Tim II 2 164.

FALSELY

Improperly: *England's chair, where he is falsely set*—R3 V 3 251.

FAME (sb.)

(1) Rumour, report: *Having heard by fame Of this . . . assembly*—H8 I 4 66. *Unregister'd in vulgar fame*—Ant III 13 119. A rumour, report: *So is the fame*—Ant II 2 166. App., relation, knowledge at second hand: *Too much to know is to know nought but fame*—LLL I 1 92.

(2) One's reputation: *How much he wrongs his fame*—1 H6 II 1 16. *That's their fame in peace* —Troil I 3 236.

FAME (vb.)

To render famous: *When went there by an age . . . But it was famed with more than with one man?*—Cæs I 2 152. *Such a counterpart shall fame his wit*—Sonn 84 11.

FAMOUS

Notorious: *Famous for a scolding tongue*—Shr I 2 254. *This place is famous for the creatures Of prey that keep upon't*—Wint III 3 12. *Menecrates and Menas, famous pirates*—Ant I 4 48.

FAMOUSED

Renowned: *The painful warrior famoused for fight*—Sonn 25 9.

FAN

To winnow; fig., to try: *The love I bear him Made me to fan you thus*—Cymb I 6 176.

FANATICAL

Extravagant: *I abhor such fanatical phantasimes*—LLL V 1 19.

FANCY (sb.)

(1) Fantasticalness: *This child of fancy that Armado hight*—LLL I 1 171. *Costly thy habit as thy purse can buy, But not express'd in fancy*—Hml I 3 70.

(2) Love: *Wishes and tears, poor fancy's followers*—Mids I 1 155. Cam. *Be advised.* Flo. *I am, and by my fancy*—Wint IV 4 491. *I love thee in so strain'd a purity, That the bless'd gods, as angry with my fancy . . .*—Troil IV 4 26. *A martial man to be soft fancy's slave!*—Lucr 200. A person in love: *A reverend man . . . Towards this afflicted fancy fastly drew*—Compl 57. *Look here, what tributes wounded fancies sent me*—197.

(3) In music, an impromptu: *Sware they were his fancies or his good-nights*—2 H4 III 2 342.

(4) 'The humour of forty fancies', prob. the title of some ballad or collection of ballads: *An old hat and 'the humour of forty fancies' prick'd in't for a feather*—Shr III 2 69.

FANCY (vb.)

To love: *Cannot your Grace win her to fancy him?*—Gent III 1 67. *Should she fancy, it should be one of my complexion*—Tw II 5 29. *Never did young man fancy With so eternal and so fix'd a soul*—Troil V 2 165.

FANCY-FREE

Untouched by love: *In maiden meditation, fancy-free*—Mids II 1 164.

FANCY-MONGER

One who makes love his business: *If I could meet that fancy-monger, I would give him some good counsel*—As III 2 381.

FANCY-SICK

Love-sick: *All fancy-sick she is and pale of cheer*—Mids III 2 96.

FANG

To seize upon, catch: *Destruction fang mankind!*—Tim IV 3 23.

FANGLED

Fond of finery and fopperies: *Our fangled world*—Cymb V 4 134.

FANTASIED

Filled with fancies or imaginations: *I find the people strangely fantasied*—John IV 2 144.

FANTASTIC

Imaginary, unreal: [Who can] *wallow naked in December snow By thinking on fantastic summer's heat?*—R2 I 3 298. Fabulous, incredible: *Who hath done to-day Mad and fantastic execution*—Troil V 5 37.

FANTASTICAL

(1) Imaginary, unreal: *Are ye fantastical, or that indeed Which outwardly ye show?*—Mcb I 3 53. *My thought, whose murder yet is but fantastical*—139.

(2) Imaginative: *So full of shapes is fancy That it alone is high fantastical*—Tw I 1 14.

FANTASTICO

A fantastic absurd person: *The pox of such antic, lisping, affecting fantasticoes*—Rom II 4 29.

FANTASY

(1) Delusive imagination, hallucination: *Art thou alive? Or is it fantasy that plays upon our eye-sight?*—1 H4 V 4 137. The habit of deluding oneself by imaginary perceptions: *The main opinion he held once Of fantasy, of dreams and ceremonies*—Cæs II 1 196.

(2) Love: *Fie on sinful fantasy!*—Wiv V 5 97. *How many actions most ridiculous Hast thou been drawn to by thy fantasy?*—As II 4 30. *Stolen the impression of her fantasy,* made surreptitious impression on her love-thoughts, stolen her heart—Mids I 1 32 (cf. *With cunning hast thou filch'd my daughter's heart*—36).

FAP

Drunk: *And being fap, sir, was, as they say, cashiered*—Wiv I 1 183.

FAR

(1) *To speak far,* to praise highly: *You speak him far*—Cymb I 1 24.

(2) As comparative = farther: *Travel you far on, or are you at the farthest?*—Shr IV 2 73. *Far than Deucalion off*—Wint IV 4 441.

FARCED

Stuffed out, tumid: *The farced title running 'fore the king*—H5 IV 1 280.

FARDEL

A bundle, pack: *The condition of that fardel*—Wint IV 4 738. A burden, load: *Who would fardels bear?*—Hml III 1 76.

FARDINGALE

See *Farthingale*.

FARE

State of matters, hap: *Poison'd,—ill fare—dead, forsook, cast off*—John V 7 35. *How now, fair lords! What fare?*—3 H6 II 1 95.

FAR-FET

Subtle, deep: *York, with all his far-fet policy*—2 H6 III 1 293.

FARROW

Her nine farrow, her litter of nine: *Pour in sow's blood, that hath eaten Her nine farrow*—Mcb IV 1 64.

FARTHINGALE, FARDINGALE

A hooped petticoat: *What compass will you wear your farthingale?*—Gent II 7 51. *Ruffs and cuffs and fardingales and things*—Shr IV 3 56.

FASHION (sb.)

(1) Making, workmanship: *The fineness of the gold and chargeful fashion*—Err IV 1 29.

(2) Behaviour, demeanour: [I] *observed your fashion*—LLL IV 3 139. *Puts him thus From fashion of himself*, makes him unlike himself—Hml III 1 182.

(3) Kind, sort: *Thou friend of an ill fashion*—Gent V 4 61. *Gentlemen of all fashions*—Per IV 2 83. *Of all fashion*, app. in the same sense, of all degrees: *The child-bed privilege denied, which 'longs To women of all fashion*—Wint III 2 104. *In the fashion to*, of a kind to: *This reasoning is not in the fashion to choose me a husband*—Merch I 2 22.

(4) A mere form: *Thou but lead'st this fashion of thy malice To the last hour of act*—Merch IV 1 18. A mere temporary feeling: *Hold it a fashion and a toy in blood*—Hml I 3 6.

(5) *Out of fashion*, out of method: *I prattle out of fashion*—Oth II 1 208. *For fashion*, in imitation: *The pretty babes, That mourn'd for fashion, ignorant what to fear*—Err I 1 73.

FASHION (vb.)

(1) To contrive, manage: *I will so fashion the matter that Hero shall be absent*—Ado II 2 47. *Where you and Douglas and our powers at once, As I will fashion it, shall happily meet*—1 H4 I 3 296. *His going thence, which I will fashion to*

fall out between twelve and one—Oth IV 2 241. *To fashion in*, to make an opening for: *To fashion in My sequent protestation*—Troil IV 4 67.

(2) To bring into a desired state: *Send him but hither, and I'll fashion him*—Cæs II 1 220.

(3) To counterfeit: *It better fits my blood to be disdained of all than to fashion a carriage to rob love from any*—Ado I 3 29. To pervert: *God forbid . . . That you should fashion, wrest, or bow your reading*—H5 I 2 13.

FASHIONS

Farcy; a disease of horses: *Infected with the fashions*—Shr III 2 52.

FAST (adj.)

(1) Fixed, constant: *'Tis our fast intent To . . .*—Lr I 1 39. [I] *will continue fast to your affection*—Cymb I 6 138.

(2) Of sleep, deep, sound: *All this while in a most fast sleep*—Mcb V 1 8. Of a person, fast asleep: *Mistress! what, mistress! Juliet! fast, I warrant her, she*—Rom IV 5 1.

FAST (adv.)

Steadily, earnestly: *Thou art so fast mine enemy*—2 H6 V 2 21.

FASTENED

Confirmed, hardened: *Strong and fasten'd villain!*—Lr II 1 79.

FASTLY

Quickly, rapidly: *A reverend man . . . Towards this afflicted fancy fastly drew*—Compl 57.

FAT (adj.)

Full of dense air: *Come out of that fat room*—1 H4 II 4 1.

FAT (sb.)

Vat: *In thy fats our cares be drown'd*—Ant II 7 122.

FATAL

Ominous, boding: *I fear that fatal prophecy*—1 H6 III 1 195. *A canopy most fatal, under which Our army lies*—Cæs V 1 88. *Art thou not, fatal vision, sensible To feeling as to sight?*—Mcb II 1 36. *It was the owl that shriek'd, the fatal bellman*—II 2 3.

FATED

Invested with the power of fate: *The fated sky*—All's I 1 232.

FATHERLY

Vested in one as a father, paternal: *That fatherly and kindly power That you have in her*—Ado IV 1 75.

FATIGATE

Fatigued: *What in flesh was fatigate*—Cor II 2 121.

FAULT

(1) In woodcraft, *cold fault*, cold or lost scent: *Till they have singled With much ado the cold fault cleanly out*—Ven 693.

(2) *For fault of*, in default of: *For fault of a better*—Wiv I 4 17. *For fault of a worse*—Rom II 4 129.

(3) A damaged place, a tear: *Patches set upon a little breach Discredit more in hiding of the fault Than did the fault before it was so patch'd*—John IV 2 32.

FAVOUR

(1) Leave, permission: *By thy favour, sweet welkin, I must sigh in thy face*—LLL III 68. *I am commanded, with your leave and favour, Humbly to kiss your hand*—3 H6 III 3 60. *Pray, give me favour, sir*—H8 I 1 168. *Your leave and favour to return to France*—Hml I 2 51. Pardon: *Give me your favour*—Mcb I 3 149.

(2) Lenity, mildness, mitigation of punishment: *Justice with favour have I always done*—2 H6 IV 7 72. Ant. *Cried he? and begg'd a pardon?* First Att. *He did ask favour*—Ant III 13 132. An act of leniency: *Provided . . . that, for this favour, He presently become a Christian*—Merch IV 1 386.

(3) Something, such as a scarf, worn as a badge of knighthood: *Let my favours hide thy mangled face*—1 H4 V 4 96.

(4) Attractiveness, charm: *Passion, hell itself, She turns to favour and to prettiness*—Hml IV 5 188. *His checks, his frowns . . . have grace and favour in them*—Oth IV 3 20. *Idiots in this case of favour would Be wisely definite*—Cymb I 6 42.

(5) Appearance, aspect: *I do love the favour and the form Of this most fair occasion*—John V 4 50. *As well as I do know your outward favour*—Cæs I 2 91. *The complexion of the element In favour's like the work we have in hand*—I 3 128. The countenance, face: *Angelo hath seen them both, and will discover the favour*—Meas IV 2 184. *My imagination Carries no favour in't but Bertram's*—All's I 1 93. *They were to be known by garment, not by favour*—Wint V 2 52. *Half their faces [are] buried in their cloaks, That by no means I may discover them By any mark of favour*—Cæs II 1 74. A feature: *[I will] stain my favours in a bloody mask*—1 H4 III 2 136. *With robbers' hands my hospitable favours You should not ruffle thus*—Lr III 7 40.

FAVOURABLE

Kindly: *Unless some dull and favourable hand Will whisper music*—2 H4 IV 5 2.

FAY

Faith: *By my fay, a goodly nap*—Shr Ind 2 83. *By my fay, it waxes late*—Rom I 5 128. *By my fay, I cannot reason*—Hml II 2 271.

FEAR (sb.)

(1) Formidableness: *The fear of your adventure would counsel you to a more equal enterprise*—As I 2 187. *My love and fear glued many friends to thee*—3 H6 II 6 5. *There is no fear in him*—Cæs II 1 190.

(2) An object of fear: *In the night, imagining some fear, How easy is a bush supposed a bear!*—Mids V 21. *Environed with all these hideous fears*—Rom IV 3 50. *We will fetters put upon this fear*—Hml III 3 25.

FEAR (vb.)

(1) To alarm, frighten: *The people fear me*—2 H4 IV 4 121. *She hath been then more fear'd than harm'd*—H5 I 2 155. *Thou canst not fear us, Pompey, with thy sails*—Ant II 6 24. To frighten away: *We must not make a scarecrow of the law, Setting it up to fear the birds of prey*—Meas II 1 1.

(2) To be apprehensive or solicitous about: *Fear you not my part of the dialogue*—Ado III 1 31. *You shall not need to fear me*—All's III 5 31. *He was much fear'd by his physicians*—1 H4 IV 1 24. *Fear not your advancements*—2 H4 V 5 84. *Let him go, Gertrude; do not fear our person*—Hml IV 5 122.

FEARFUL

(1) Leaving room for apprehension or uneasiness: *My house, left in the fearful guard Of an unthrifty knave*—Merch I 3 176.

(2) *Fearful of*, anxious or concerned about: *Edward shall be fearful of his life*—3 H6 V 6 87.

FEAT (adj.)

(1) Deft, adroit: *Never master had A page so kind . . . So feat, so nurse-like*—Cymb V 5 85. As adv.: *Feat and affectedly Enswathed*—Compl 48.

(2) Of dress, becoming, graceful: *How well my garments sit upon me; Much feater than before*—Tp II 1 272.

FEAT (sb.)

(1) A deed, action: *All fell feats Enlink'd to waste and desolation*—H5 III 3 17. *[I] bend up Each corporal agent to this terrible feat*—Mcb I 7 79.

(2) An evil deed, a crime: *Tell me Why you proceeded not against these feats*—Hml IV 7 5.

(3) A department of action; action in a matter in which one is skilled: *If that thy prosperous and artificial feat Can . . .*—Per V 1 72.

FEAT (vb.)

App., to constrain to propriety: *A sample to the youngest, to the more mature A glass that feated them*—Cymb I 1 48.

FEATLY

With graceful agility, nimbly: *Foot it featly here and there*—Tp I 2 380. *She dances featly*—Wint IV 4 176.

FEATURE

(1) Bodily shape or make: *He is complete in feature and in mind*—Gent II 4 73. *Her peerless feature*—1 H6 V 5 68. *That unmatch'd form and feature of blown youth*—Hml III 1 167. *Bid him Report the feature of Octavia*—Ant II 5 111.

(2) Good shape, comeliness: *Cheated of feature by dissembling nature*—R3 I 1 19.

FEATURED

Formed, shaped: *I never yet saw man, How wise . . . how rarely featured, But she would spell him backward*—Ado III 1 59. *Wishing me . . . Featured like him*—Sonn 29 5.

FEATURELESS

Shapeless, ugly: *Those whom Nature hath not made for store, Harsh featureless and rude*—Sonn 11 9.

FECKS

A distortion of Fay, Faith, perh. with suffix -kins; *I' fecks*, as an unmeaning asseveration: *I' fecks! Why, that's my bawcock*—Wint I 2 120.

FEDERARY

See *Feodary*.

FEE¹

Property, a possession. Prob. the word should come under this head in Tim III 6 89 (*The rest of your fees, O gods—the senators of Athens, together with the common lag of people*), unless there is corruption. App., a thing available to a person for bringing something about: *Your trespass now becomes a fee; Mine ransoms yours, and yours must ransom me*—Sonn 120 13.

FEE²

(1) A fief, feudal benefice; *in fee*, with absolute and perpetual possession: *Nor will it yield . . . A ranker rate, should it be sold in fee*—Hml IV 4 21. *Three thousand crowns in annual fee*, an estate in land of that yearly value—Hml II 2 73. *At a pin's fee*, at the value of a pin: *I do not set my life at a pin's fee*—Hml I 4 65.

(2) A prize, reward: *Pleading for a lover's fee*—Mids III 2 113. *When he saw his love, his youth's fair fee*—Ven 393. *Her pleading hath deserved a greater fee*—609. A bribe: *Those heaven-moving pearls from his poor eyes, Which heaven shall take in nature of a fee*—John II 169.

FEEBLE

To enfeeble, weaken: *Shall that victorious hand be feebled here?*—John V 2 146. *Making parties strong And feebling such as stand not in their liking*—Cor I 1 198.

FEED

(1) A right of grazing: *His cote, his flocks and bounds of feed*—As II 4 83.

(2) Food (for sheep, &c.), fodder: *Rotted with delicious feed*—Tit IV 4 93.

FEEDER

A servant: *I will your very faithful feeder be*—As II 4 99. *When all our offices have been oppress'd With riotous feeders*—Tim II 2 167. *To be abused By one that looks on feeders*—Ant III 13 108.

FEEDING

A grazing ground: *Boasts himself To have a worthy feeding*—Wint IV 4 168.

FEE-FARM

An absolute and perpetual tenure; fig.: *A kiss in fee-farm!*—Troil III 2 53.

FEE-GRIEF

One that has a particular owner: *Is it a fee-grief Due to some single breast?*—Mcb IV 3 196.

FEELING

Deeply felt, heartfelt: *To whose feeling sorrows I might be some allay*—Wint IV 2 8. *Known and feeling sorrows*—Lr IV 6 226. Sim. *feeling-painful*: *My woe too sensible thy passion maketh More feeling-painful*—Lucr 1678.

FEELINGLY

With exact observation, so as to hit a thing exactly: *Do I speak feelingly now?*—Meas I 2 36. *He shall find himself most feelingly personated*—Tw II 3 172. *To speak feelingly of him*—Hml V 2 113.

FEE-SIMPLE

An estate in land, &c., held for ever without limitation to any particular class of heirs; hence

(1) The tenure by which something is so held: *If the devil have him not in fee-simple*—Wiv IV 2 224.

(2) A piece of land held by such a tenure: *To seize me for a stray, for entering his fee-simple without leave*—2 H6 IV 10 26.

(3) An interest in a thing held by such a tenure: *He will sell the fee-simple of his salvation*—All's IV 3 311. *The fee-simple of my life*—Rom III 1 35.

FEIGN

(1) To represent in fiction, fable: *Therefore the poet Did feign that Orpheus drew trees*—Merch V

79. *All that poets feign of bliss and joy*—3 H6 I 2 31. *I have upon a high and pleasant hill Feign'd Fortune to be throned*—Tim I 1 63.

(2) To sing softly, hum an air: *Thou hast by moonlight at her window sung With feigning voice verses of feigning love*—Mids I 1 30.

FEIGNING

Imaginative: *The truest poetry is the most feigning*—As III 3 19.

FELICITATE

Made happy: *I am alone felicitate In your dear highness' love*—Lr I 1 77.

FELL

Angry, enraged: *Oberon is passing fell and wrath*—Mids II 1 20.

FELLOW (sb.)

A partaker, sharer *of*: *A fellow of the royal bed*—Wint III 2 39.

FELLOW (vb.)

To be associated with, accompany: *With what's unreal thou coactive art, And fellow'st nothing*—Wint I 2 141.

FELLOWLY

Companionable, sympathetic: *Mine eyes . . . Fall fellowly drops*—Tp V 63.

FELLOWSHIP

(1) A partnership: *Would not this . . . get me a fellowship in a cry of players?*—Hml III 2 286.

(2) Intercourse, dealing: *All the fellowship I hold now with him Is only my obedience*—H8 III 1 121.

FEODARY, FEDERARY

A confederate, accomplice: *Camillo is A federary with her*—Wint II 1 89. *Art thou a feodary for this act?*—Cymb III 2 21. *If not a feodary, but only he Owe and succeed thy weakness*, if there is no fellow-sinner, but he alone has it in him and takes up man's weakness—Meas II 4 122. (See *Owe* (1), *Succeed* (2). The reference of *thy* seems to be general—that of which thou hast spoken.)

FERE

A spouse: *The woful fere And father of that chaste dishonour'd dame*—Tit IV 1 89. *This king unto him took a fere*—Per Prol 21.

FERN-SEED

We have the receipt of fern-seed, we walk invisible—1 H4 II 1 95. Ferns were popularly supposed to produce an invisible seed which was capable of making the bearer invisible.

FERTILE

(1) Promoting fertility: [His cold blood] *he hath, like lean . . . land, manured, husbanded and tilled with . . . drinking good and good store of fertile sherris*—2 H4 IV 3 129.

(2) Copious, abundant: Oli. *How does he love me?* Vio. *With adorations, fertile tears*—Tw I 5 273.

FESTINATE

Speedy: *Advise the duke . . . to a most festinate preparation*—Lr III 7 9.

FESTINATELY

Speedily: *Bring him festinately hither*—LLL III 5.

FET

Pa. pple. of To fet = To fetch; derived: *Whose blood is fet from fathers of war-proof*—H5 III 1 18.

FETCH (sb.)

A device, invention: *A fetch of wit*—Hml II 1 38 (the Folios read *A fetch of warrant*, a warranted or approved device). *Mere fetches*—Lr II 4 90.

FETCH (vb.)

(1) To reach, strike: *Come away, or I'll fetch thee with a wanion*—Per II 1 16.

(2) *To fetch in*, to capture: [There are] *Enough to fetch him in*—Ant IV 1 14. [He] *might break out, and swear He'ld fetch us in*—Cymb IV 2 140. To take in, dupe: *You speak this to fetch me in*—Ado I 1 225.

(3) *To fetch off*, to 'do', fleece: *I will fetch off these justices*—2 H4 III 2 324. To do for, make away with: [I] *will fetch off Bohemia*—Wint I 2 334.

FETTLE

To make ready, put in trim: *Fettle your fine joints 'gainst Thursday next*—Rom III 5 154.

FEWNESS AND TRUTH

In few words and truly: *Fewness and truth, 'tis thus*—Meas I 4 39.

FICO

A fig: *A fico for the phrase!*—Wiv I 3 33.

FIDELITY

Word of honour: *By my fidelity, this is not well*—Wiv IV 2 160.

FIELD

In heraldry, the surface of a shield: *Beauty, in that white intituled, From Venus' doves doth challenge that fair field*—Lucr 57. Cf. *Their silent war of lilies and of roses, Which Tarquin view'd in her fair face's field*—71.

FIELDED

Engaged on a field of battle: *To help our fielded friends*—Cor I 4 12.

FIERCE

(1) Proud, haughty: *He is fierce and cannot brook hard language*—2 H6 IV 9 45.

(2) Of a narrative, rapid, covering the ground hastily: *This fierce abridgement*—Cymb V 5 382.

FIFTEEN

See *Fifteenth*.

FIFTEENTH

A tax of one-fifteenth on personal property: *A whole fifteenth For costs and charges in transporting her*—2 H6 I 1 133. So *fifteen: He that made us pay one and twenty fifteens*—IV 7 23.

FIG (sb.)

The fig of Spain!—H5 III 6 62. *The fig*, or *the fig of Spain*, was an insulting gesture consisting in thrusting the thumb between two of the closed fingers or into the mouth. *The fig of Spain* was used also to denote a poisoned fig. This may be referred to.

FIG (vb.)

To insult by making the fig (see above): *Fig me, like The bragging Spaniard*—2 H4 V 3 124.

FIGHTS

Screens used in a naval engagement for protection and concealment: *Clap on more sails; pursue; up with your fights!*—Wiv II 2 142.

FIGO

(1) Equivalent to *Fico* (q.v.): *Figo for thy friendship!*—H5 III 6 60.

(2) Equivalent to *Fig* (sb.) (q.v.): *The figo for thee, then!*—H5 IV 1 60.

FIGURE

(1) The proper or distinctive appearance (of a thing): *Doing, in the figure of a lamb, the feats of a lion*—Ado I 1 14.

(2) An imaginary form, a phantasm: *To scrape the figures out of your husband's brains*—Wiv IV 2 230. *He apprehends a world of figures here*—1 H4 I 3 209. *Thou hast no figures nor no fantasies*—Cæs II 1 231.

(3) A part enacted: *Bravely the figure of this harpy hast thou Perform'd*—Tp III 3 83.

(4) A written character, letter: [Shall] *write in thee the figures of their love, Ever to read them thine*—Tim V 1 157. *Our captain hath in every figure skill*—V 3 7.

(5) In astrology, a horoscope: *She works by charms, by spells, by the figure*—Wiv IV 2 184.

FILE (sb.)

A catalogue, list, roll: *Our present musters grow upon the file To five and twenty thousand*—2 H4 I 3 10. *He makes up the file Of all the gentry*—H8 I 1 75. *If you have a station in the file, Not i' the worst rank of manhood, say't*—Mcb III 1 102. *The valued file*, one in which values are stated: *The valued file Distinguishes the swift, the slow, the . . .*—Mcb III 1 95.

FILE (vb.) [1]

To defile, taint: *For Banquo's issue have I filed my mind*—Mcb III 1 65.

FILE (vb.) [2]

To march in line, keep pace *with: My endeavours Have ever come too short of my desires, Yet filed with my abilities*—H8 III 2 169.

FILL (sb.)

In pl., the thills or shafts of a cart: *An you draw backward, we'll put you i' the fills*—Troil III 2 47.

FILL (vb.)

(1) To put (a liquid) into a vessel with the view of filling it; hence, to pour out: *Fill me some wine*—Tim III 1 8. Absol.: *Fill till the cup be hid*—Ant II 7 93.

(2) To become satisfied or satiated: *Glutton-like she feeds, yet never filleth*—Ven 548.

(3) *To fill up*, to fulfil, satisfy: *To fill up your grace's request in my stead*—Merch IV 1 160. To come up to the measure of, equal: *How many inches doth fill up one mile*—LLL V 2 193.

FILL-HORSE

A shaft-horse (see *Fill* (sb.)): *Dobbin my fill-horse*—Merch II 2 100.

FILM

A filament (of gossamer): *Her whip of cricket's bone, the lash of film*—Rom I 4 63.

FIND

(1) To find out, detect: *Thereby to find That which thyself hast now disclosed to me*—Gent III 1 31. *Inspire me, that I may this treason find!*—Tit IV 1 67. *The old man hath found their guilt*—IV 2 26. To find out (a person's character, his secret, &c.): *You were the first that found me*—All's V 2 45. *My blood hath been too cold . . . And you have found me*—1 H4 I 3 1. *If she find him not, To England send him*—Hml III 1 193.

(2) In H5 I 2 72 (*To find his title with some shows of truth*) perh., to provide, or, to trace out.

FINE (adj.)

Intellectually subtle, clever, ingenious: *Thou art too fine in thy evidence*—All's V 3 269. *Not noted, is't, But of the finer natures?*—Wint I 2 225. *His fine pate*—Hml V 1 116. Cunning, artful: *O for a fine thief!*—1 H4 III 3 211.

FINE (sb.)

(1) End, finish: *Still the fine's the crown*—All's IV 4 35. With a play on this sense and sense (2): *Paying the fine of rated treachery Even with a treacherous fine of all your lives*—John V 4 37. With a play on this sense and sense (3): *Is this the fine of his fines*—Hml V 1 114. Result, conclusion: *The fine is . . . I will live a bachelor*—Ado I 1 247. *In fine*, in the end, at last: *Let her in fine consent*—All's III 7 19. [We'll] *bring you in fine together*—Hml IV 7 134.

(2) A penalty of any kind: *To fine the faults whose fine stands in record*—Meas II 2 40. *What faults he made before the last, I think Might have found easy fines*—Cor V 6 64.

(3) *Fine and recovery*, fictions of law used to convert a limited estate into a fee-simple: *In fee-simple, with fine and recovery*—Wiv IV 2 225. *His fines, his double vouchers, his recoveries*—Hml V 1 114.

FINE (vb.)

(1) To bring to an end: *Time's office is to fine the hate of foes*—Lucr 936.

(2) To punish: *To fine the faults whose fine stands in record*—Meas II 2 40. *Why would he for the momentary trick Be perdurably fined?*—III 1 114.

(3) To agree to pay as a fine or composition: *I have fined these bones of mine for ransom*—H5 IV 7 72.

FINELESS

Boundless, infinite: *Riches fineless*—Oth III 3 173.

FINGER

To filch, pilfer: *Whiles he thought to steal the single ten, The king was slily finger'd from the deck!*—3 H6 V 1 43. *Finger'd their packet*—Hml V 2 15.

FINSBURY

Originally Fensbury, from the fenny nature of the ground, a lordship lying north of the old London Wall; in early documents called the Moor, whence *Moorfields* (q.v.): *As if thou never walk'st further than Finsbury*—1 H4 III 1 257. Finsbury was a favourite walk with the citizens.

FIRAGO

App. a word coined by Sir Toby; or virago may be meant: *He's a very devil; I have not seen such a firago*—Tw III 4 301.

FIRE-DRAKE

A fiery meteor; fig.: *Twenty of the dog-days now reign in's nose . . . that fire-drake did I hit three times on the head*—H8 V 4 43.

FIRK

To beat, trounce: *Master Fer! I'll fer him, and firk him*—H5 IV 4 29.

FIRST

(1) *At first*, at once, immediately: *He whose wife is most obedient To come at first when he doth send for her*—Shr V 2 67. *We are familiar at first*—Cymb I 4 112. Before others: *True is it . . . That I receive the general food at first*—Cor I 1 134. Firstly: *One man in his time plays many parts . . . At first the infant*—As II 7 142. In the beginning, originally: *Let it rest where it began at first*—1 H6 IV 1 121. *Conscience is but a word . . . Devised at first to keep the strong in awe*—R3 V 3 309.

(2) *Two of the first*, in heraldry, a mode of dividing the shield employed in the case of married persons: *With two seeming bodies, but one heart; Two of the first, like coats in heraldry*—Mids III 2 212.

FIRST-CONCEIVED

First perceived, first heard: *The first-conceived sound*—2 H6 III 2 44.

FISH STREET

I.e. New Fish Street, now Fish Street Hill, the approach from the north to old London Bridge: *Up Fish Street! down Saint Magnus' Corner!*—2 H6 IV 8 1.

FISNOMY

Physiognomy: *His fisnomy is more hotter in France than there*—All's IV 5 42.

FIT (adj.)

(1) In a suitable condition for doing or undergoing something, prepared, ready: *I will forestal their repair hither, and say you are not fit*—Hml V 2 228. *If I do find him fit, I'll move your suit*—Oth III 4 166. *I have already fit . . . doublet, hat, hose*—Cymb III 4 171.

(2) Of clothes, accurate in fit, sitting gracefully: *One o' these maids' girdles for your waist should be fit*—LLL IV 1 50. Fig.: *These fix'd evils sit so fit in him*—All's I 1 113. [They] *botch the words up fit to their own thoughts* (*i.e.* to suit their preconceived ideas)—Hml IV 5 10. Quasi-adv.: *Madam Julia's gown, Which served me as fit . . . As if the garment had been made for me*—Gent IV 4 166. *How fit his garments serve me!*—Cymb IV 1 2.

FIT (sb.)[1]

(1) A paroxysm of lunacy (viewed as a periodic disease): *Belike his wife, acquainted with his fits, On purpose shut the doors*—Err IV 3 91. *Unless some fit or frenzy do possess her*—Tit IV 1 17. *In his lawless fit . . . Whips out his rapier*—Hml IV 1 8.

(2) *A fit of the face*, a grimace: *All the good our*

English Have got by the late voyage is but merely A fit or two o' the face—H8 I 3 5.

(3) *The fits of the season*, the critical conjunctures of the time: *He is . . . judicious, and best knows The fits o' the season*—Mcb IV 2 16.

FIT (sb.)²

A division of a poem or song: *You say so in fits*—Troil III 1 61.

FIT (vb.)¹

(1) Intr., to be fit, seemly, suitable: *Where . . . despair most fits*—All's II 1 147. *This staff of honour raught, there let it stand Where it best fits to be*—2 H6 II 3 43. *It fits, when such a villain is a guest*—Rom I 5 77.

(2) To agree or harmonize *with*: *Why dost thou laugh? It fits not with this hour*—Tit III 1 266. *Must make content with his fortunes fit*—Lr III 2 76.

(3) To be well adapted or suitable for: *I thought on her; she'll fit it*—Wiv II 1 165. *That time best fits the work we have in hand*—2 H6 I 4 23. *This valley fits the purpose passing well*—Tit II 3 84.

(4) To supply or provide (a person *with* something): *Fit me with such weeds As may beseem some well-reputed page*—Gent II 7 42. *I will fit thee with the remedy*—Ado I 1 321. [I] *will fit you With dignities becoming your estates*—Cymb V 5 21.

FIT (vb.)²

To displace by paroxysms: *How have mine eyes out of their spheres been fitted In the distraction of this madding fever!*—Sonn 119 7. In Per II 1 57, perh., to give a paroxysm (of madness): *Honest! good fellow, what's that? If it be a day fits you, search out of the calendar*, you must be mad to speak of such a thing as honesty; if it be a (particular) day that gives you the fit (alluding to periodicity in the madness) search (for it and take it) out of the calendar.

FITCHEW

The polecat: *To be a dog . . . a fitchew . . . I would not care; but to be Menelaus!*—Troil V 1 66. *The fitchew, nor the soiled horse, goes to't With a more riotous appetite*—Lr IV 6 124. Of a loose woman: *'Tis such another fitchew!*—Oth IV 1 150.

FITFUL

Vexed by paroxysms: *After life's fitful fever he sleeps well*—Mcb III 2 23.

FITLY

At the fitting time: Tim. . . . *My steward!* Flav. *Here, my lord.* Tim. *So fitly?*—Tim III 4 109. *I will fitly bring you to hear my lord speak*—Lr I 2 184.

FITMENT

(1) A making fit, preparation: *'Twas a fitment for The purpose I then follow'd*—Cymb V 5 409.

(2) That which is fitting, duty: *When she should do for clients her fitment*—Per IV 6 6.

FITNESS

Readiness, inclination: *If his fitness speaks, mine is ready*—Hml V 2 209. *'Tis said a woman's fitness comes by fits*—Cymb IV 1 6.

FIVE-FINGER-TIED

Tied by giving the hand: *With another knot, five-finger-tied, The fractions of her faith . . . are bound to Diomed*—Troil V 2 157.

FIVES

Avives; a swelling of the parotid glands in horses: *Past cure of the fives*—Shr III 2 54.

FIXTURE

The action of planting (the foot): *The firm fixture of thy foot*—Wiv III 3 67.

FIXURE

Fixed condition or position: *The fixure of her eye has motion in't*—Wint V 3 67. *Rend . . . The unity . . . of states Quite from their fixure*—Troil I 3 99.

FLAMEN

At Rome, a priest devoted to the service of a particular god: *Seld-shown flamens*—Cor II 1 229. Applied to a priest at Athens: *Hoar the flamen, That scolds against the quality of flesh*—Tim IV 3 155.

FLAP-DRAGON (sb.)

Equivalent to Snap-dragon; a raisin or other thing caught up out of burning brandy and eaten: *Thou art easier swallowed than a flap-dragon*—LLL V 1 44. *Drinks off candles' ends for flap-dragons*—2 H4 II 4 267.

FLAP-DRAGON (vb.)

To swallow as one would a flap-dragon (see above): *To make an end of the ship, to see how the sea flap-dragoned it*—Wint III 3 99.

FLAP-JACK

A pancake: *We'll have flesh for holidays . . . and moreo'er puddings and flap-jacks*—Per II 1 85.

FLARING

Of hair and the like, spreading out or waving conspicuously: *With ribands pendent, flaring 'bout her head*—Wiv IV 6 42.

FLASK

A powder flask: *The carved-bone face on a flask*—LLL V 2 619. *Like powder in a skilless soldier's flask*—Rom III 3 132.

FLAT

That's flat, that's clear: *The boy hath sold him a bargain, a goose, that's flat*—LLL III 102.

FLAT-LONG

With the flat (of the sword) down: Ant. *What a blow was there given!* Seb. *An it had not fallen flat-long*—Tp II 1 180.

FLATNESS

Absoluteness, completeness: *The flatness of my misery*—Wint III 2 123.

FLATTER

(1) To beguile, charm away (sorrows): *Flatter my sorrows with report of it*—R3 IV 4 245.

(2) *To flatter up,* to pamper: *To flatter up these powers of mine with rest*—LLL V 2 824.

FLAUNTS

Showy dress, finery: *In these my borrow'd flaunts*—Wint IV 4 23.

FLAW¹

(1) A flake of snow: *Flaws congealed in the spring of day*—2 H4 IV 4 35.

(2) A fragment: *This heart Shall break into a hundred thousand flaws, Or ere I'll weep*—Lr II 4 287.

(3) A crack, rift: *Observe how Antony becomes his flaw* (*i.e.* this breach of his fortune)—Ant III 12 34.

FLAW²

A sudden gust of wind: *A great sea-mark, standing every flaw*—Cor V 3 74. *Should patch a wall to expel the winter's flaw*—Hml V 1 239. Fig.: *Falling in the flaws of her own youth*—Meas II 3 11. A burst of feeling or passion: *These flaws and starts*—Mcb III 4 63. A tumult or uproar: *The fury of this mad-bred flaw*—2 H6 III 1 354.

FLEER (sb.)

A mocking look, sneer: *The fleers, the gibes, and notable scorns, That dwell in every region of his face*—Oth IV 1 83.

FLEER (vb.)

To grin, grimace: *One rubb'd his elbow thus, and fleer'd and swore A better speech was never spoke before*—LLL V 2 109.

FLEET

(1) To be afloat, sail: *Our sever'd navy too Have knit again, and fleet, threatening most sea-like*—Ant III 13 170.

(2) To fade, vanish: *How all the other passions fleet to air!*—Merch III 2 108.

(3) To flit, migrate: *Even from the gallows did his fell soul fleet*—Merch IV 1 135. *I, hence fleeting, here remain with thee*—Ant I 3 104. *To darkness fleet souls that fly backwards*—Cymb V 3 25.

(4) Trans., of time, to pass, beguile: *Many young gentlemen flock to him every day, and fleet the time carelessly*—As I 1 123.

FLEETING

Inconstant, unstable: *False, fleeting, perjured Clarence*—R3 I 4 55. *The fleeting moon No planet is of mine*—Ant V 2 240.

FLESH

(1) To reward a hawk or hound with flesh of the game; hence, to initiate in bloodshed: *The kindred of him hath been flesh'd upon us*—H5 II 4 50. *Come, I'll flesh ye; come on, young master*—Lr II 2 49. *Come, my young soldier, put up your iron; you are well fleshed* (*i.e.* the fleshing process has gone far enough)—Tw IV 1 42. *To flesh one's sword,* to use it for the first time: *Full bravely hast thou flesh'd Thy maiden sword*—1 H4 V 4 133. *The young whelp of Talbot's . . . Did flesh his puny sword in Frenchmen's blood*—1 H6 IV 7 35. To make eager for combat: *Princes flesh'd with conquest*—2 H4 I 1 149. *Fleshed,* hardened: *The flesh'd soldier*—H5 III 3 11. *Flesh'd villains, bloody dogs*—R3 IV 3 6.

(2) To plunge into flesh: *The wild dog Shall flesh his tooth on every innocent*—2 H4 IV 5 132.

(3) To gratify (lust or rage): *This night he fleshes his will in the spoil of her honour*—All's IV 3 19. *Shall a beardless boy . . . flesh his spirit in a warlike soil?*—John V 1 69.

FLESHMENT

The excitement of a first success: *In the fleshment of this dread exploit*—Lr II 2 130.

FLESHMONGER

A fornicator: *Was the duke a fleshmonger, a fool, and a coward?*—Meas V 336.

FLEWED

Having flews or large chaps: *My hounds are bred out of the Spartan kind, So flew'd, so sanded*—Mids IV 1 123.

FLIGHT

(1) Flight-shooting, shooting with the flight-arrow, a light well-feathered arrow for long distances: *He set up his bills . . . and challenged Cupid at the flight*—Ado I 1 39.

(2) *Of the same flight,* of arrows, of the same size and weight: *I shot his fellow of the self-same flight The self-same way*—Merch I 1 141.

FLIGHTY

Swift: *The flighty purpose never is o'ertook Unless the deed go with it*—Mcb IV 1 145.

FLIRT-GILL

A loose woman: *I am none of his flirt-gills*—Rom II 4 161.

FLOTE

A wave or billow; the sea: *For the rest o' the fleet . . . they all have met again And are upon the Mediterranean flote*—Tp I 2 232.

FLOURISH (sb.)

Embellishment, gloss, varnish: *My beauty . . . Needs not the painted flourish of your praise*—LLL II 13. *Lend me the flourish of all gentle tongues* — IV 3 238. *Time doth transfix the flourish set on youth*—Sonn 60 9. Something (merely) decorative: *Since brevity is the soul of wit, And tediousness the limbs and outward flourishes*—Hml II 2 90. *Vain flourish of my fortune*, mere empty embellishment of the rank that is properly mine—R3 I 3 241.

FLOURISH (vb.)

(1) To embellish, varnish over: *The justice of your title to him Doth flourish the deceit*—Meas IV 1 74.

(2) To make a flourish, exult, triumph: *Whilst bloody treason flourish'd over us*—Cæs III 2 196.

FLOWER-DE-LUCE

(1) The fleur-de-lis, the flower of a plant of the genus Iris: *Lilies of all kinds, The flower-de-luce being one*—Wint IV 4 126.

(2) The heraldic lily, the armorial device of France: *Cropp'd are the flower-de-luces in your arms*—1 H6 I 1 80. *The flower-de-luce of France* —2 H6 V 1 11. Cf. *What sayest thou, my fair flower-de-luce?*—H5 V 2 223 (King Henry to Katharine).

FLUSH

(1) Of time, fully come: *Now the time is flush, When . . .*—Tim V 4 8.

(2) In full vigour, full-blooded: *With all his crimes broad blown, as flush as May*—Hml III 3 81. *Flush youth revolt*—Ant I 4 52.

FLUXIVE

Running with tears: *These often bathed she in her fluxive eyes*—Compl 50.

FLY

To fly off = *To fall off* (see *Fall* (vb.) (3)): *Mere fetches; The images of revolt and flying off*—Lr II 4 90. *Never Fly off our loves again!*—Ant II 2 154.

FOB, FUB

(1) To impose upon, 'put upon': *Resolution thus fobbed as it is with the rusty curb of old father antic the law*—1 H4 I 2 67.

(2) *To fob, fub off*, to put off: *I have borne, and borne . . . and have been fubbed off, and fubbed off* —2 H4 II 1 36. To set aside (by a trick): *You must not think to fob off our disgrace with a tale*— Cor I 1 96.

FOIL (sb.)¹

The setting (of a jewel): *Esteem [thy exile] as foil wherein thou art to set The precious jewel of thy home return*—R2 I 3 266.

FOIL (sb.)²

A repulse, check: *One sudden foil shall never breed distrust*—1 H6 III 3 11. *To give the foil*, to defeat: *Before that England give the French the foil*—1 H6 V 3 23. *To put to the foil*, to put to shame: *Some defect in her Did quarrel with the noblest grace she owed And put it to the foil*—Tp III 1 44.

FOIL (vb.)

To pollute, mar: *She framed the love, and yet she foil'd the framing*—Pilgr 99.

FOIN (sb.)

A thrust in fencing: *Come; no matter vor your foins*—Lr IV 6 250.

FOIN (vb.)

To thrust in fencing: *To see thee fight, to see thee foin*—Wiv II 3 24. *I'll whip you from your foining fence*—Ado V 1 84. *He will foin like any devil*—2 H4 II 1 17.

FOISON

(1) Plentiful crop or harvest: *Earth's increase, foison plenty*—Tp IV 110. *Blossoming time That from the seedness the bare fallow brings To teeming foison*—Meas I 4 41.

(2) In pl., resources: *Scotland hath foisons to fill up your will*—Mcb IV 3 88.

FOLLOW

To follow up, to pursue (an affair, &c.) to its conclusion: *How with a sportful malice it (i.e. the device) was follow'd*—Tw V 373. *Such a day, So fought, so follow'd and so fairly won*—2 H4 I 1 20. *'The time shall come', thus did he follow it*— III 1 75. *This chase is hotly follow'd*—H5 II 4 68.

FOLLY

(1) Lewdness, wantonness: *He gives her folly motion and advantage*—Wiv III 2 35. *She turn'd to folly, and she was a whore*—Oth V 2 132. *Her sad behaviour feeds his vulture folly*—Lucr 556.

(2) A lewd action or desire: *[This deputy who] Nips youth i' the head and follies doth emmew*— Meas III 1 91.

FOND (adj.)

(1) Foolish: *Fond wretch, thou know'st not what thou speak'st* — Meas V 105. *His fond jealousies*—Wint IV 1 18. *Grant I may never prove so fond, To trust man on his oath or bond*— Tim I 2 65. *I begin to find an idle and fond bondage in the oppression of aged tyranny*—Lr I 2 51.

(2) Foolishly affectionate, doting: *When men were fond, I smiled and wonder'd how*—Meas II 2 187. *In truth, fair Montague, I am too fond*—Rom II 2 98. *If you are so fond over her iniquity, give her patent to offend*—Oth IV 1 208.

(3) Trifling, trivial: *Not with fond shekels of the tested gold*—Meas II 2 149. *All trivial fond records*—Hml I 5 99.

(4) *Fond of*, eager for, anxious to have: *She, poor hen, fond of no second brood*—Cor V 3 162. *Old and fond of issue*—Cymb I 1 37. So *fond with*: *Those that much covet are with gain so fond*—Lucr 134. *Fond to*, eager to: *Why would you be so fond to overcome The bonny priser of the humorous duke?*—As II 3 7.

FOND (vb.)

To dote *on*: *I, poor monster, fond as much on him*—Tw II 2 35.

FONDLY

Foolishly: *How fondly dost thou reason!*—Err IV 2 57. *If you fondly pass our proffer'd offer*—John II 258. *Most shallowly did you these arms commence, Fondly brought here and foolishly sent hence*—2 H4 IV 2 118. *What my great-grandfather and grandsire got My careless father fondly gave away*—3 H6 II 2 37.

FOOL (sb.)

(1) *The shrieve's fool*, a female idiot kept for diversion, as appears sometimes to have been done, though males of the class were more common: *He was whipped for getting the shrieve's fool with child*—All's IV 3 212.

(2) Used as a term of pity or endearment: *Alas, poor fool, how have they baffled thee!*—Tw V 377. *Pretty fool*—Rom I 3 31.

FOOL (vb.)

To make foolish, infatuate: *Fool me not so much To bear it tamely*—Lr II 4 278.

FOOL-BEGGED

Foolish enough to be 'begged' (see *Beg*): *This fool-begg'd patience in thee will be left*—Err II 1 41.

FOOT (sb.)

(1) *To follow at foot*, to follow at the heels, closely: *Follow him at foot*—Hml IV 3 56.

(2) *To come in foot and hand*, stepping forward and dealing a blow at the same time: *I followed me close, came in foot and hand*—1 H4 II 4 240.

FOOT (vb.)

(1) To kick, spurn: *[You that did] foot me as you spurn a stranger cur*—Merch I 3 119. *To the court I'll knock her back, foot her home again*—Cymb III 5 148.

(2) Of a bird of prey, to clutch with the talons: *The holy eagle Stoop'd, as to foot us*—Cymb V 4 115.

FOOT-CLOTH

An ornamented saddle-cloth hanging to the ground: *Thou dost ride in a foot-cloth, dost thou not?*—2 H6 IV 7 51. Attrib.: *Hast thou not ... plodded by my foot-cloth mule?*—2 H6 IV 1 53. *Three times to-day my foot-cloth horse did stumble*—R3 III 4 86.

FOOTED

Having got a foothold, *i.e.* landed: *He is footed in this land already*—H5 II 4 143. *There's part of a power already footed*—Lr III 3 13. *The traitors Late footed in the kingdom*—III 7 44.

FOOTING

(1) Walking, stepping: *I hear the footing of a man*—Merch V 24. *The earth, in love with thee, thy footing trips*—Ven 722.

(2) *To set footing*, to set foot *in*, *on* a place: *Who strongly hath set footing in this land*—R2 II 2 48. *Set no footing on this unkind shore*—2 H6 III 2 87. Sim., *When she set footing here*—H8 III 1 183. Fig.: *Can it be That so degenerate a strain as this Should once set footing in your generous bosoms?*—Troil II 2 153.

(3) Landing: *Whose footing here anticipates our thoughts A se'nnight's speed*—Oth II 1 76.

(4) A footprint: *Like a nymph ... Dance on the sands, and yet no footing seen*—Ven 147.

FOOT LAND-RAKER

A footpad: *I am joined with no foot land-rakers*—1 H4 II 1 81.

FOP (sb.)

A fool, dunce: *A whole tribe of fops, Got 'tween asleep and wake*—Lr I 2 14.

FOP (vb.)

To make a fool of, dupe: *[I] begin to find myself fopped in it*—Oth IV 2 197.

FOPPERY

(1) Folly: *I had as lief have the foppery of freedom as the morality of imprisonment*—Meas I 2 137. *Let not the sound of shallow foppery enter My sober house*—Merch II 5 35. *This is the excellent foppery of the world*—Lr I 2 128.

(2) An imposture, trick: *The guiltiness of my mind ... drove the grossness of the foppery into a received belief*—Wiv V 5 130.

FOPPISH

Foolish: *Wise men are grown foppish*—Lr I 4 182.

FOR (prep.)

With verbs of hindering and the like, from: *Now will I dam up this thy yawning mouth For swallowing the treasure of the realm*—2 H6 IV 1 73. *[They] advise thee to desist For going on death's net*—Per I 1 39.

FOR (conj.)

(1) Because: *For thou wast a spirit too delicate . . . she did confine thee*—Tp I 2 272. *My foolish rival, that her father likes Only for his possessions are so huge*—Gent II 4 174. *You may not so extenuate his offence For I have had such faults*—Meas II 1 27. *For their virtue only is their show, They live unwoo'd*—Sonn 54 9. So for that: *Which was broke off, Partly for that her promised proportions Came short of composition*—Meas V 218. *I return'd the rather For that I heard the clink and fall of swords*—Oth II 3 233. For because: *Not for because Your brows are blacker*—Wint II 1 7. *For because the world is populous . . . I cannot do it*—R2 V 5 3.

(2) In order that: *For the time shall not seem tedious, I'll tell thee what befel me*—3 H6 III 1 9. *For I should not deal in her soft laws, She did corrupt frail nature with some bribe*—III 2 154. So for that: *For that our kingdom's earth should not be soil'd With that dear blood . . . Therefore, we . . .*—R2 I 3 125.

(3) *For and*, and moreover: *A pick-axe, and a spade, a spade, For and a shrouding sheet*—Hml V 1 102.

FORAGE (sb.)

Raging or ravening: *And he from forage will incline to play*—LLL IV 1 93.

FORAGE (vb.)

To raven, to glut oneself as a wild beast: *Shall they seek the lion in his den? . . . O, let it not be said: forage, and run*—John V 1 57. *Having felt the sweetness of the spoil, With blindfold fury she begins to forage*—Ven 553. To revel *in*: *Smiling to behold his lion's whelp Forage in blood of French nobility*—H5 I 2 109.

FORBEAR

(1) To put up with, endure: *A twelvemonth longer, let me entreat you to Forbear the absence of your king*—Per II 4 45.

(2) To keep away from, leave alone: *Forbear his presence*—Lr I 2 175. *Forbear me*—Ant I 2 125. *Forbear me till anon*—II 7 44.

(3) To spare, let alone: *For love of God, forbear him*—Hml V 1 296. *With the little godliness I have I did full hard forbear him*—Oth I 2 9. *Ghost unlaid forbear thee!*—Cymb IV 2 278.

FORBID

To lay under a ban, curse: *He shall live a man forbid*—Mcb I 3 21.

FORBOD

Pa. pple. of To forbid: *To be forbod the sweets that seem so good*—Compl 164.

FORCE (sb.)

(1) Physical strength: *Had [I] force and knowledge More than was ever man's*—Wint IV 4 384.

Force of Greekish sinews—Troil III 1 166. *Some [glory] in their bodies' force*—Sonn 91 2.

(2) Of force, of necessity: *That, when he waked, of force she must be eyed*—Mids III 2 40. *Good reasons must, of force, give place to better*—Cæs IV 3 203.

(3) *In the force of*, exposed to the brunt of: *In the force and road of casualty*—Merch II 9 30.

FORCE (vb.)[1]

(1) To press home, urge: *If you will now unite in your complaints, And force them with a constancy*—H8 III 2 1. *Why force you this?*—Cor III 2 51. *[Who ever] forced examples, 'gainst her own content?*—Compl 157. To enforce (a law): *Has he affections in him, That thus can make him bite the law by the nose, When he would force it?*—Meas III 1 108.

(2) To reinforce, strengthen: *Were they not forced with those that should be ours*—Mcb V 5 5.

(3) To care for, regard: *I force not argument a straw*—Lucr 1021.

(4) To hesitate, scruple: *Your oath once broke, you force not to forswear*—LLL V 2 440.

FORCE (vb.)[2]

Farce; to stuff: *Force him with praises*—Troil II 3 232. *Wit larded with malice and malice forced with wit*—V 1 63.

FORDO

(1) To kill, destroy: *The corse they follow did . . . Fordo it own life*—Hml V 1 243. *That she fordid herself*—Lr V 3 255.

(2) To ruin, undo: *This is the night That either makes me or fordoes me quite*—Oth V 1 128.

FORE-END

The beginning, early part: *Than in all The fore-end of my time*—Cymb III 3 72.

FOREHAND (adj.)

(1) Done before the due time; *a forehand sin*, a sin consisting in anticipation: *You will say she did embrace me as a husband, And so extenuate the forehand sin*—Ado IV 1 50.

(2) *A forehand shaft*, an arrow for shooting straight before one, *i.e.* point blank: [A would have] *carried you a forehand shaft a fourteen and fourteen and a half*—2 H4 III 2 52.

FOREHAND (sb.)

(1) The position in front or above; *to have the forehand of*, to have the upper hand or advantage of: *But for ceremony such a wretch . . . Had the fore-hand and vantage of a king*—H5 IV 1 295.

(2) The mainstay: *The sinew and the forehand of our host*—Troil I 3 143.

FOREHORSE

The forehorse to a smock (*i.e.* a woman), a squire of dames: *I shall stay here the forehorse to a smock*—All's II 1 30.

FOREIGN

(1) Not of one's household: *Say that . . . [the husbands] pour our treasures into foreign laps*—Oth IV 3 88. *I love the king your father, and yourself, With more than foreign heart*—Per IV 1 33.

(2) *A foreign man*, living abroad; or perh., excluded from court or from affairs: *And fearing he would rise . . . [you] Kept him a foreign man still*—H8 II 2 128.

FORE-PAST

Antecedent: *My fore-past proofs*—All's V 3 121.

FORESAY

To say beforehand, to decree: *Let ordinance Come as the gods foresay it*—Cymb IV 2 145.

FORESEE

To provide against or for: *Of his great grace And princely care foreseeing those fell mischiefs*—H8 V 1 48. *Him that, his particular to foresee, Smells from the general weal*—Tim IV 3 159.

FORESPENT

(1) Formerly bestowed: *His goodness forespent on us*—Cymb II 3 64.

(2) Formerly enacted: *His vanities forespent*—H5 II 4 36.

FORESTALL

(1) To bar, deprive: *May This night forestall him of the coming day!*—Cymb III 5 68.

(2) To deal with before the due time, 'go to meet'; so perh. *a forestalled remission*, a pardon asked, not awaited: *Never shall you see that I will beg A ragged and forestall'd remission*—2 H4 V 2 37.

(3) App., to regard with prejudice: *Forestall prescience and esteem no act But that of hand*—Troil I 3 199.

FORETHINK

To plan beforehand, to decree: *The doom Forethought by heaven*—John III 1 311.

FOREWARD

The vanguard: *My foreward shall be drawn out all in length*—R3 V 3 293.

FORFEIT (sb.)

(1) *The forfeits in a barber's shop*, the penalties attached to infractions of regulations detailed in papers put up in such shops, which were great resorts of idlers: *The strong statutes Stand like the forfeits in a barber's shop, As much in mock as mark*—Meas V 322.

(2) *The forfeit of my servant's life*, his forfeited life—R3 II 1 99.

(3) *Forfeits*, lives forfeited (to one's sword): *Despising many forfeits and subduements*—Troil IV 5 187.

FORFEIT (vb.)

To transgress, sin: *Double and treble admonition, and still forfeit in the same kind!*—Meas III 2 205.

FORFEND

To forbid, prohibit: *The forfended place*—Lr V 1 11.

FORGE

(1) Of immaterial things, to contrive, devise, produce: *The best wishes that can be forged in your thoughts*—All's I 1 84. *To me the difference forges dread*—Wint IV 4 17. *Such means As you yourself have forged against yourself*—1 H4 V 1 67.

(2) To 'get up' (a quarrel, &c.): *Forged rebellion*—2 H4 IV 1 92. *I should forge Quarrels unjust*—Mcb IV 3 82.

FORGERY

(1) Devising, inventing: *That I, in forgery of shapes and tricks, Come short of what he did*—Hml IV 7 90.

(2) A fiction, a figment: *These are the forgeries of jealousy*—Mids II 1 81. *Such shadows are the weak brain's forgeries*—Lucr 460. A misleading fiction: *There put on him What forgeries you please*—Hml II 1 19.

(3) False dealing; a deceit: *To soothe your forgery and his Sends me a paper*—3 H6 III 3 175. *Guilty of treason, forgery, and shift*—Lucr 920. *Unskilful in the world's false forgeries*—Pilgr 4.

FORGET

(1) To give up a practice, to drop the discharge of a duty: *Whilst I live [I will] forget to drink after thee*—Meas I 2 40. *May it be that you have quite forgot A husband's office?*—Err III 2 1.

(2) *To forget to do*, to forget how to do: *Long agone I have forgot to court*—Gent III 1 85. *Like men that had forgot to speak*—2 H4 V 2 22.

(3) *Forgotten*, app., forgetting, forgetful: *My oblivion is a very Antony, And I am all forgotten*—Ant I 3 90.

FORGETIVE

Prob., apt at forging (in the sense of *Forge* (1)), inventive, creative: *Makes it (i.e. the brain) apprehensive, quick, forgetive*—2 H4 IV 3 107.

FORK

The forked tongue of a snake: *Thou dost fear the soft and tender fork Of a poor worm*—Meas III 1 16. *Adder's fork and blind-worm's sting*—Mcb IV 1 16. The barbed head of an arrow: *Let it (i.e. the shaft) fall rather, though the fork invade The region of my heart*—Lr I 1 146.

FORKED

(1) Of an arrow-head, barbed: *It irks me the poor dappled fools . . . Should . . . with forked heads Have their round haunches gored*—As II 1 22.

(2) *A forked one*, a horned one, a cuckold: *O'er head and ears a fork'd one!*—Wint I 2 186. Cf. *'Which of these hairs is Paris my husband?' 'The forked one,' quoth he*—Troil I 2 177. *This forked plague*—Oth III 3 276.

FORLORN

Pa. pple. of To forlese, to lose, to destroy:

(1) With the second meaning: *Love hath forlorn me*—Pilgr 265.

(2) Lost, not to be found: *The forlorn soldier, that so nobly fought, He would have well becomed this place*—Cymb V 5 405.

FORLORN (sb.)

A forlorn person: *Forced to live in Scotland a forlorn*—3 H6 III 3 26.

FORM

(1) An image, likeness: *O thou senseless form, Thou shalt be worshipp'd, kiss'd, loved and adored!*—Gent IV 4 203 (of Silvia's portrait). *If my form lie there (i.e. in the casket), Then I am yours*—Merch II 7 61. *The world will . . . weep That thou no form of thee hast left behind*—Sonn 9 5.

(2) Manner, method: *In manner and form following*—LLL I 1 207.

(3) A way of behaving oneself: *If the gentle spirit of moving words Can no way change you to a milder form*—Gent V 4 55. *Then camest in smiling, And in such forms which here were presupposed Upon thee in the letter*—Tw V 357. *However he puts on this tardy form*—Cæs I 2 303. In pl., action: *His whole function suiting With forms to his conceit*—Hml II 2 582.

(4) Beauty, comeliness: *Things base and vile . . . Love can transpose to form and dignity*—Mids I 1 232. *To set a form upon desired change*—Sonn 89 6. Credit: *To bring manslaughter into form*—Tim III 5 27.

FORMAL

(1) Regular, normal: *This is evident to any formal capacity*—Tw II 5 128. *Thou shouldst come like a Fury crown'd with snakes, Not like a formal man*—Ant II 5 40. Conventional: *Thus, like the formal vice, Iniquity, I moralize two meanings in one word*—R3 III 1 82. So, sane: *Till I have used the approved means I have . . . To make of him a formal man again*—Err V 103.

(2) Dignified: *In formal majesty*—2 H4 V 2 133. *With untired spirits and formal constancy*—Cæs II 1 227.

FORMER

Set in front: *Our former ensign*—Cæs V 1 80.

FORMERLY

A little time before, just now: *Thou hast incurr'd The danger formerly by me rehearsed*—Merch IV 1 361.

FORSAKE

To refuse, reject: *Thou hast power to choose, and they none to forsake*—All's II 3 62. *If you forsake the offer of their love*—1 H6 IV 2 14. *Forsook so many noble matches*—Oth IV 2 125.

FORSLOW

To be slow or dilatory: *Forslow no longer, make we hence amain*—3 H6 II 3 56.

FORSOOTH

In truth, truly (without irony or derision): Quick. *And Master Slender's your master?* Sim. *Ay, forsooth*—Wiv I 4 18. *That my master was? no, forsooth*—2 H6 I 3 33. Cap. . . . *Is my daughter gone to Friar Laurence?* Nurse. *Ay, forsooth*—Rom IV 2 11.

FORSPEAK

To speak against: *Thou hast forspoke my being in these wars*—Ant III 7 3.

FORSWEAR

To deny on oath or with strong asseveration; with infin. or sentence as obj.: *That self chain about his neck Which he forswore most monstrously to have*—Err V 10. *By now forswearing that he is forsworn*—1 H4 V 2 39.

FORTED

Fortified: *A forted residence 'gainst the tooth of time*—Meas V 12.

FORTH (prep.)

Out of: *Steal forth thy father's house*—Mids I 1 164. *They fear us not, but issue forth their city*—Cor I 4 23.

FORTH (adv.)

(1) Abroad, not at home, in the field: *At that time . . . her husband will be forth*—Wiv II 2 275. *I have no mind of feasting forth to-night*—Merch II 5 37. *The Volsces have an army forth*—Cor I 3 107.

(2) *To make forth*, to protract: *The boy Fidele's sickness Did make my way long forth*—Cymb IV 2 148.

(3) Used where modern usage would require out: *Wherefore didst thou lock me forth to-day?*—Err IV 4 98. *To find the other forth*—Merch I 1 143. *How he singled Clifford forth*—3 H6 II 1 12.

FORTHCOMING

In custody: *Your lady is forthcoming yet at London*—2 H6 II 1 179.

FORTH ON

Straight on: *Flies an eagle flight, bold and forth on*—Tim I 1 49.

FORTHRIGHT

A straight path: *Through forth-rights and meanders*—Tp III 3 3. *Aside from the direct forthright*—Troil III 3 158.

FORTITUDE

(1) Physical strength: *Despairing of his own arm's fortitude*—1 H6 II 1 17.

(2) Of a place, strength for defence: *The fortitude of the place is best known to you*—Oth I 3 222.

FORTUNE (sb.)

A chance, hap: *Whatever fortune stays him from his word*—Shr III 2 23.

FORTUNE (vb.)

(1) To regulate the fortunes of: *Therefore, dear Isis, keep decorum, and fortune him accordingly!*—Ant I 2 76.

(2) To happen, chance: *You will wonder what hath fortuned*—Gent V 4 169.

FOR WHY

Because: *Then must my earth . . . Become a deluge . . . For why my bowels cannot hide her woes*—Tit III 1 229. *Sorts a sad look to her lady's sorrow, For why her face wore sorrow's livery*—Lucr 1221. *I weep for thee, and yet no cause I have; For why thou left'st me nothing in thy will*—Pilgr 137.

FOSSET-SELLER

A seller of faucets or taps: *A cause between an orange-wife and a fosset-seller*—Cor II 1 78.

FOUL

Ugly: *I thank the gods I am foul*—As III 3 38. *What miserable praise hast thou for her that's foul and foolish?*—Oth II 1 140. *It is a deadly sorrow to behold a foul knave uncuckolded*—Ant I 2 75. Of things, unattractive: *Let us, like merchants, show our foulest wares, And think, perchance, they'll sell*—Troil I 3 359.

FOULNESS

Ugliness: *Well, praised be the gods for thy foulness!*—As III 3 40. *He's fallen in love with your foulness*—III 5 66.

FOURTEEN

I.e. fourteen yards: *A would have . . . carried you a forehand shaft a fourteen and fourteen and a half*—2 H4 III 2 51.

FOUTRE

A foutre for, an expression of contempt (through French from Lat. *futuo*): *A foutre for the world and worldlings base!*—2 H4 V 3 103. *A foutre for thine office!*—121.

FOX

A kind of sword (perh. from the figure of a wolf on certain sword-blades being mistaken for that of a fox): *Thou diest on point of fox*—H5 IV 4 9.

FRACTED

Broken: *His heart is fracted and corroborate*—H5 II 1 130 (*corroborate* is meaningless). Of an engagement and the like, not kept: *His fracted dates*—Tim II 1 22.

FRACTION

(1) Discord, dissension: *Their fraction is more our wish than their faction*—Troil II 3 107.

(2) A fragment: *The fractions of her faith*—Troil V 2 158. So in pl., broken sentences: *After distasteful looks and these hard fractions*—Tim II 2 220.

FRAME (sb.)

(1) Contrivance: *Whose spirits toil in frame of villanies*—Ado IV 1 191.

(2) Definite form, order: *Her madness hath the oddest frame of sense*—Meas V 61. *Put your discourse into some frame*—Hml III 2 320. *Out of frame*, out of order, in disorder: *Like a German clock, Still a-repairing, ever out of frame*—LLL III 192. *Thinking . . . Our state to be disjoint and out of frame*—Hml I 2 19.

FRAME (vb.)

(1) To cause, produce, bring to pass: *And either end in peace, which God so frame! Or . . .*—2 H4 IV 1 180. *All is on the rout; Fear frames disorder*—2 H6 V 2 31.

(2) To discharge (a function): *Those flower-soft hands, That yarely frame the office*—Ant II 2 215.

(3) To betake oneself, resort: *The beauty of this sinful dame Made many princes thither frame*—Per Prol 31.

FRAMPOLD

Quarrelsome: *She leads a very frampold life with him*—Wiv II 2 93.

FRANCHISE

App., freeing from (foreign) control: *Our laws . . . whose repair and franchise Shall . . . be our good deed*—Cymb III 1 56.

FRANCHISED

Kept free (from guilt), guiltless: *So I . . . still keep My bosom franchised and allegiance clear, I shall be counsell'd*—Mcb II 1 26.

FRANK (adj.)

(1) Unrestricted: *Thy frank election make*—All's II 3 61.

(2) Liberal, bounteous: *Frank nature . . . Hath well composed thee*—All's I 2 20. *Your old kind father, whose frank heart gave all*—Lr III 4 20. *'Tis a good hand, A frank one*—Oth III 4 43.

FRANK (sb.)

A sty: *Doth the old boar feed in the old frank?*
—2 H4 II 2 159.

FRANK (vb.)

To frank up, to pen in, or as in a sty: *He is frank'd up to fatting for his pains*—R3 I 3 314. *My son George Stanley is frank'd up in hold*—IV 5 3.

FRANKLIN

A freeholder; one of a class of landowners, of free but not noble birth, and ranking next below the gentry: *A franklin in the wild of Kent*—1 H4 II 1 60. *A riding-suit, no costlier than would fit A franklin's housewife*—Cymb III 2 78.

FRANKLY

Freely, without restraint or hindrance: *Speak frankly as the wind*—Troil I 3 253. *My half-supp'd sword, that frankly would have fed*—V 8 19. *Men and men's fortunes could I frankly use*—Tim II 2 188. *That, seeing, unseen, We may of their encounter frankly judge*—Hml III I 33.

FRAUGHT (sb.)

Freight, cargo: *This is that Antonio That took the Phœnix and her fraught from Candy*—Tw V 63. *The bark that hath discharged her fraught*—Tit I 71. A burden, load: *Swell, bosom, with thy fraught, For 'tis of aspics' tongues!*—Oth III 3 449.

FRAUGHT (vb.)

(1) To burden: *If after this command thou fraught the court With thine unworthiness, thou diest*—Cymb I 1 126.

(2) *Fraughting,* forming the freight: *The good ship . . . and The fraughting souls within her*—Tp I 2 12.

FRAUGHTAGE

Freight, cargo: *Our fraughtage, sir, I have convey'd aboard*—Err IV 1 87. *The deep-drawing barks do there disgorge Their warlike fraughtage*—Troil Prol 12.

FRAY

To frighten: *As if she were frayed with a sprite*—Troil III 2 33.

FREE (adj.)

(1) Noble, honourable; of birth: *I lay my claim To my inheritance of free descent*—R2 II 3 135. Of character: *In voices well divulged, free, learn'd and valiant*—Tw I 5 279. *Your free and noble nature*—Oth III 3 199.

(2) Eager, willing, ready: *Never did captive with a freer heart Cast off his chains*—R2 I 3 88. *Courageously and with a free desire Attending but the signal to begin*—115. *Signior Montano . . .*

With his free duty recommends you thus—Oth I 3 39. *Provided I have your commendation for my more free entertainment*—Cymb I 4 166. Freely offered: *Your free undertaking cannot miss A thriving issue*—Wint II 2 44.

(3) Guiltless, innocent, acquitted: *Would all other women Could speak this with as free a soul as I do!*—H8 III I 31. [He would] *Make mad the guilty and appal the free*—Hml II 2 590. *Hold her free, I do beseech your honour*—Oth III 3 255.

(4) Sound, not infected: *Whether thou art tainted or free*—Meas I 2 43. *They have the plague . . . you are not free*—LLL V 2 421. Of thoughts: *Bear free and patient thoughts*—Lr IV 6 80.

(5) Careless, happy: *The free maids that weave their thread with bones*—Tw II 4 46. *I slept the next night well, was free and merry*—Oth III 3 340.

(6) *Free awe,* still felt, though no longer visibly enforced: *Thy free awe Pays homage to us*—Hml IV 3 63.

FREE (vb.)

(1) To clear from blame or stain, absolve, acquit: *I free you from't*—H8 II 4 157. *I dare so far free him*—Cor IV 7 47. *Let my disclaiming from a purposed evil Free me so far . . . That . . .*—Hml V 2 252. To atone for, expiate: *My life's foul deed, my life's fair end shall free it*—Lucr 1208. To procure the acquittal of: *Mine honour, Which I would free*—Wint III 2 111. To procure absolution for: *Prayer, Which pierces so that it . . . frees all faults*—Tp Epil 16. To grant immunity from the operation of a thing: *Though full of our displeasure, yet we free thee From the dead blow of it*—Wint IV 4 443.

(2) To remove, get rid of, banish: *We may again Give to our tables meat . . . Free from our feasts . . . bloody knives*—Mcb III 6 33. Bel. *He wrings at some distress.* Gui. *Would I could free't!*—Cymb III 6 79.

FREEDOM

In the freedom of my knowledge, freely, sincerely, as warranted by my knowledge: *I speak it in the freedom of my knowledge*—Wint I 1 12.

FREELY

With full possession (of property, &c.): *All their petitions are as freely theirs As they themselves would owe them*—Meas I 4 82. *I must freely have the half of anything That this same paper brings you*—Merch III 2 252. *Thou shalt live as freely as thy lord, To call his fortunes thine*—Tw I 4 39.

FREENESS

Generosity: *Nobly doom'd! We'll learn our freeness of a son-in-law*—Cymb V 5 420.

9

FRENCH CROWN

With a reference to baldness caused by the 'French disease': Bot. *I will discharge it in either . . . or your French-crown-colour beard . . .* Quin. *Some of your French crowns have no hair at all, and then you will play barefaced*—Mids I 2 95. [As fit as] *your French crown for your taffeta punk*—All's II 2 23. See also Meas I 2 52.

FREQUENT (adj.)

(1) Addicted : [He] *is less frequent to his princely exercises than formerly he hath appeared*—Wint IV 2 36.

(2) Familiar : *I have frequent been with unknown minds*—Sonn 117 5.

FREQUENT (vb.)

Absol., to be in a place as a matter of habit : *Inquire at London, 'mongst the taverns there, For there, they say, he daily doth frequent*—R2 V 3 5.

FRESH (adj.)

Ready, eager : *A fresh admirer Of what I saw there*—H8 I 1 3.

FRESH (sb.)

A spring of fresh water : *I'll not show him Where the quick freshes are*—Tp III 2 74.

FRET (vb.)¹

App., to finger the frets of : *Call me what instrument you will, though you can fret me, yet you cannot play upon me*—Hml III 2 387 (with a play).

FRET (vb.)²

To wear, spoil, become corrupt : *Stinking clothes that fretted in their own grease*—Wiv III 5 115. *'Twas a commodity lay fretting by you*—Shr II 330. *He frets like a gummed velvet*—1 H4 II 2 2 (with a play).

FRETFUL

Gnawing, irritating : *Though parting be a fretful corrosive*—2 H6 III 2 403.

FRETTED

Chequered ; fig. : *His fretted fortunes*—Ant IV 12 8.

FRETTEN

Pa. pple. of To fret : *When they (i.e.* the pines) *are fretten with the gusts of heaven*—Merch IV 1 77.

FRIEND (sb.)

(1) A lover or paramour ; masc. : *Naked with her friend in bed*—Oth IV 1 3. Fem. : *He hath got his friend with child*—Meas I 4 29.

(2) *Though I profess myself her adorer, not her friend,* though (I admit that) in so praising her I speak as one that worships her, not (merely) as a lover (and you may make allowance accordingly) —Cymb I 4 73.

(3) To have . . . to friend, to have . . . as a friend or on one's side : *We shall have him well to friend*—Cæs III 1 143. *As I shall find the time to friend*—Mcb IV 3 10. *At friend,* on terms of friendship : *All greetings that a king, at friend, Can send his brother*—Wint V 1 140.

FRIEND (vb.)

To befriend, help : *Disorder, that hath spoil'd us, friend us now!*—H5 IV 5 17. *Be friended With aptness of the season*—Cymb II 3 52.

FRIENDING

Friendliness : *His love and friending to you*—Hml I 5 186.

FRIENDSHIP

A friendly act, a favour, friendly aid : *To buy his favour, I extend this friendship*—Merch I 3 169. *The heaping friendships*—Wint IV 2 22. *Some friendship will it lend you 'gainst the tempest*—Lr III 2 62.

FRIPPERY

An old-clothes shop : *We know what belongs to a frippery*—Tp IV 225.

FRITTERS

Fragments, shreds : *One that makes fritters of English*—Wiv V 5 151. Or perh. the term of cookery is meant.

FRIZE

Frieze : *Shall I have a coxcomb of frize?*—Wiv V 5 146. *My invention Comes from my pate as birdlime does from frize*—Oth II 1 126.

FROM

(1) Differently from, contrary to : *You must not now deny it is your hand : Write from it, if you can*—Tw V 339. *Him that, his particular to foresee, Smells from the general weal*—Tim IV 3 159. *Any thing so overdone is from the purpose of playing*—Hml III 2 22. *At random from the truth vainly express'd*—Sonn 147 12.

(2) Away from : *From thy sight, I should be raging mad*—2 H6 III 2 394. *Thou shalt build from men*—Tim IV 3 533. *Being both from me*—Sonn 144 11. Free from : *He lived from all attainder of suspect*—R3 III 5 32.

FRONT

(1) To serve as a front to : *Yonder walls, that pertly front your town*—Troil IV 5 219.

(2) To march in the front rank : [I] *front but in that file Where others tell steps with me*—H8 I 2 42.

FRONTIER

(1) The forehead; *moody frontier* = frown: *Majesty might never yet endure The moody frontier of a servant brow*—1 H4 I 3 18 (in *servant brow* the emphasis is on *servant*, *brow* merely repeating the idea conveyed by *frontier*).

(2) A frontier fortress or town: *Goes it against the main of Poland, sir, Or for some frontier?*—Hml IV 4 15. An outlying fort: *Thou hast talk'd . . . Of palisadoes, frontiers, parapets*—1 H4 II 3 53.

FRONTLET

A forehead band; fig. of a frown: *How now, daughter! what makes that frontlet on?*—Lr I 4 207.

FRUITFUL

(1) Abundant, copious: *One fruitful meal*—Meas IV 3 161. *A recompense more fruitful*—Tim V 1 153. *The fruitful river in the eye*—Hml I 2 80.

(2) Bounteous: *A hand as fruitful as the land that feeds us*—H8 I 3 56. *She's framed as fruitful As the free elements*—Oth II 3 347.

FRUITFULLY

Copiously, fully: Count. . . . *You understand me?* Clo. *Most fruitfully*—All's II 2 71. *Time and place will be fruitfully offered*—Lr IV 6 269.

FRUITFULNESS

Bounteousness: *This argues fruitfulness and liberal heart*—Oth III 4 38.

FRUSH

To batter, smash: *I like thy armour well; I'll frush it . . . But I'll be master of it*—Troil V 6 28.

FRUSTRATE (ppl. adj.)

Unavailing, useless: *The sea mocks Our frustrate search on land*—Tp III 3 9.

FRUSTRATE (vb.)

To make null and void: *To London all the crew are gone, To frustrate . . . his oath*—3 H6 II 1 174.

FUB

See *Fob*.

FUGITIVE

A deserter: *Who then but English Henry will be lord And thou be thrust out like a fugitive* (whose services are no longer needed)?—1 H6 III 3 66. *A master-leaver and a fugitive*—Ant IV 9 22.

FULFIL

(1) To fill up, make full: *Let it not be hild Poor women's faults, that they are so fulfill'd With men's abuses*—Lucr 1257. *' Will' will fulfil the treasure of thy love*—Sonn 136 5. *Fulfils the law, is its consummation: Charity itself fulfils the law*—LLL IV 3 364.

(2) *Fulfilling*, exactly fitting: *Correspondve and fulfilling bolts*—Troil Prol 18.

FULL

Entitled to a designation in the full sense of the term, perfect: *The man commands Like a full soldier*—Oth II 1 35. *The bidding of the fullest man, and worthiest To have command obey'd*—Ant III 13 87.

FULLAM

Some kind of false dice: *Gourd and fullam holds, And high and low beguiles the rich and poor*—Wiv I 3 94.

FULSOME

(1) Cloying, satiating: *Wash'd to death with fulsome wine*—R3 V 3 132. Fig., wearisome, distasteful: *It is as fat and fulsome to mine ear As howling after music*—Tw V 112.

(2) Physically disgusting, loathsome: [I will] *stop this gap of breath with fulsome dust*—John III 4 32.

(3) Morally foul: *Lie with her! that's fulsome*—Oth IV 1 36.

(4) App., lustful, rank: *The fulsome ewes*—Merch I 3 87.

FUMITER

Fumitory: *Crown'd with rank fumiter*—Lr IV 4 3.

FUNCTION

(1) Mental or moral activity: *My thought . . . Shakes so my single state of man that function Is smother'd in surmise*—Mcb I 3 139.

(2) The outward manifestation of such activity, bearing: *His whole function suiting With forms to his conceit*—Hml II 2 582.

FUNERAL

(1) App., burial, sepulture: *You must needs bestow her funeral*—Tit IV 2 163. See *Bestow* (4).

(2) In pl. with sing. sense: *Wise Laertes' son Did graciously plead for his funerals*—Tit I 380. *His funerals shall not be in our camp*—Cæs V 3 105.

FURNACE

To exhale like a furnace: *He furnaces The thick sighs from him*—Cymb I 6 66.

FURNISH

(1) To supply with what is necessary: *What I stand in need of, To furnish me upon my longing journey*—Gent II 7 84. *We have two hours To furnish us*—Merch II 4 8. *The revenue whereof shall furnish us For our affairs in hand*—R2 I 4 46.

(2) To equip, to prepare for action or a career: *His training such, That he may furnish and instruct great teachers*—H8 I 2 112. *Furnished,* (a) equipped, armed: *All furnish'd, all in arms*—1 H4 IV 1 97. (b) Equipped, dressed: *He was furnished like a hunter*—As III 2 258. *We are not furnish'd like Bohemia's son*—Wint IV 4 598. *Semblably furnish'd like the king himself*—1 H4 V 3 21. (c) Of horses, caparisoned, harnessed: *The horses your lordship sent for . . . I saw well chosen, ridden, and furnished*—H8 II 2 1. (d) Endowed with moral qualities: *He then that is not furnish'd in this sort Doth but usurp the sacred name of knight*—1 H6 IV 1 39. (e) In a position (to do a thing): *To-morrow, Cæsar, I shall be furnish'd to inform you rightly*—Ant I 4 76.

(3) To embellish: *I'll show thee some attires, and have thy counsel Which is the best to furnish me to-morrow*—Ado III 1 102. *Such needful ornaments As you think fit to furnish me to-morrow*—Rom IV 2 34.

FURNISHINGS

Unimportant adjuncts: *Something deeper, Whereof perchance these are but furnishings*—Lr III 1 28.

FURNITURE

(1) Equipment, outfit: *There shalt thou know thy charge; and there receive Money and order for their furniture*—1 H4 III 3 225.

(2) Munitions of war: *My Lord of Somerset will keep me here, Without discharge, money, or furniture*—2 H6 I 3 171.

(3) Apparel, dress: *This poor furniture and mean array*—Shr IV 3 182.

FURY

Inspired frenzy, poetic rage: *What zeal, what fury hath inspired thee now?*—LLL IV 3 229. *A sibyl . . . In her prophetic fury sew'd the work*—Oth III 4 70. *Spend'st thou thy fury on some worthless song?*—Sonn 100 3.

FUST

To become mouldy: *Gave us not That capability and god-like reason To fust in us unused*—Hml IV 4 37.

FUSTILARIAN

Perh., a fat frowsy woman: *Away, you scullion! . . . you fustilarian!*—2 H4 II 1 65.

G

GABERDINE

A loose upper garment: *My best way is to creep under his gaberdine*—Tp II 2 39. *[You] spit upon my Jewish gaberdine*—Merch I 3 113.

GAD

A sharp metal spike: *With a gad of steel [I] will write these words*—Tit IV 1 103. *Upon the gad*, upon the spur of the moment: *All this done Upon the gad!*—Lr I 2 25.

GAGE

(1) To stake, wager, risk: *[Shall it be said] That men of your nobility and power Did gage them both in an unjust behalf*—1 H4 I 3 172. *Against the which, a moiety competent Was gaged by our king*—Hml I 1 90. *One for all, or all for one we gage*—Lucr 144.

(2) To bind, entangle: *The great debts Wherein my time something too prodigal Hath left me gaged*—Merch I 1 128.

(3) App. = Engage; to urge, exhort: *Here is a letter from Queen Hecuba . . . Both taxing me and gaging me to keep An oath that I have sworn*—Troil V 1 44.

GAIN-GIVING

Misgiving: *It is such a kind of gain-giving, as would perhaps trouble a woman*—Hml V 2 225.

GAINSAY

(1) To hinder: *The just gods gainsay That . . . !*—Troil IV 5 132.

(2) To refuse: *In that I'll no gainsaying*—Wint I 2 18.

GAIT

(1) A going, course: *Every fairy take his gait*—Mids V 423. *Address thy gait unto her*—Tw I 4 15. *Pass and stay not here thy gait*—Tim V 4 73.

(2) Proceeding (*in* an affair): *To suppress His further gait herein*—Hml I 2 30.

GALL (sb.)

As a seat of spirit or courage: *When they would seem soldiers, they have galls, Good arms . . .*—Troil I 3 237. *We have galls, and though we have some grace, Yet have we some revenge*—Oth IV 3 93. So, spirit: *I am pigeon-liver'd and lack gall To make oppression bitter*—Hml II 2 605.

GALL (vb.)

(1) To fret or wash away: *A galled rock*—H5 III 1 12. *The galled shore*—Lucr 1440.

(2) *To gall at*, to scoff at, insult: *I have seen you gleeking and galling at this gentleman*—H5 V 1 77.

GALLANTRY

Gallants collectively: *Hector, Deiphobus . . . and all the gallantry of Troy*—Troil III 1 148.

GALLANT-SPRINGING

Waxing in goodly wise: *Gallant-springing brave Plantagenet*—R3 I 4 227.

GALLIAN

Gallic, French: *More than half the Gallian territories*—1 H6 V 4 139. *A Gallian girl*—Cymb I 6 66.

GALLIARD

A lively dance in triple time: *What is thy excellence in a galliard?*—Tw I 3 127. *A nimble galliard*—H5 I 2 252.

GALLIAS

A heavy low-built vessel, larger than a galley: *Two galliases, And twelve tight galleys*—Shr II 380.

GALLIMAUFRY

A medley of persons or things: *He loves the gallimaufry*—Wiv II 1 119. *A dance which the wenches say is a gallimaufry of gambols*—Wint IV 4 334.

GALLOW

To frighten, scare: *The wrathful skies Gallow the very wanderers of the dark*—Lr III 2 43.

GALLOWGLASS

A foot soldier of Ireland or the Western Islands of Scotland: *A mighty power Of gallowglasses and stout kerns*—2 H6 IV 9 25. [Macdonwald] *from the western isles Of kerns and gallowglasses is supplied*—Mcb I 2 12.

GALLOWS

A gallows-bird: *A shrewd unhappy gallows*—LLL V 2 12.

GAMESTER

(1) A player at a game (not necessarily implying addiction to gambling): *When lenity and cruelty play for a kingdom, the gentler gamester is the soonest winner*—H5 III 6 118.

(2) A gamesome or frolicsome person: *You are a merry gamester, My Lord Sands*—H8 I 4 45.

(3) Used somewhat contemptuously, but with no very clearly defined meaning: *Now will I stir this gamester*—As I 1 170. *Sirrah young gamester*—Shr II 402.

(4) A loose woman: [She] *was a common gamester to the camp*—All's V 3 188. *Were you a gamester at five or at seven?*—Per IV 6 80.

GAP

[He] *Stands in the gap and trade of moe preferments*—H8 V 1 36, the opening through which preferments may be expected to come.

GAPE

To bawl, shout: *Ye rude slaves, leave your gaping*—H8 V 4 2. There appears to be a reference to this sense in Hml I 2 245 (*I'll speak to it, though hell itself should gape And bid me hold my peace*). *A gaping pig*: Merch IV 1 47 (*Some men there are love not a gaping pig*), a squealing pig; or perh., one dressed for the table with the mouth open.

GARB

Manner, mode: *Because he could not speak English in the native garb*—H5 V 1 79. *Commanding peace Even with the same austerity and garb As he controll'd the war*—Cor IV 7 43. *Let me comply with you in this garb*—Hml II 2 389. [I'll] *Abuse him to the Moor in the rank garb*—Oth II 1 315.

GARBOIL

A commotion, disturbance: *The garboils she awaked*—Ant I 3 61. *Her garboils . . . Did you too much disquiet*—II 2 67.

GARNISH

Outfit, dress: *In the lovely garnish of a boy*—Merch II 6 45.

GARNISHED

App., endowed (with mental qualities): *I do know A many fools . . . Garnish'd like him*—Merch III 5 72.

GASKINS

A kind of hose or breeches: *If both* [points] *break, your gaskins fall*—Tw I 5 27.

GAST

To terrify, scare: *Gasted by the noise I made*—Lr II 1 57.

GASTNESS

Terrified appearance: *Do you perceive the gastness of her eye?*—Oth V 1 106.

GAUDY

Festive: *Let's have one other gaudy night*—Ant III 13 183.

GAWD

A child's plaything, a toy: *An idle gawd Which in my childhood I did dote upon*—Mids IV 1 171.

GAZE

That which is gazed at: *The show and gaze o' the time*—Mcb V 8 24. *The lovely gaze where every eye doth dwell*—Sonn 5 2.

GEAR

(1) A substance, stuff: *A dram of poison, such soon-speeding gear As . . .*—Rom V 1 60.

(2) Discourse, talk: *I'll grow a talker for this gear*—Merch I 1 110.

(3) A matter, affair: *If Fortune be a woman, she's a good wench for this gear*—Merch II 2 175. *I will remedy this gear ere long*—2 H6 III 1 91. *Come, shall we to this gear?*—R3 I 4 157. Doings, 'goings on': *Here's goodly gear!*—Rom II 4 107.

GECK

One befooled or derided: *The most notorious geck and gull That e'er invention play'd on*—Tw V 351. *To become the geck and scorn O' th' other's villany*—Cymb V 4 67.

GEMINY

A couple, pair: *A geminy of baboons*—Wiv II 2 8.

GENDER (sb.)

(1) Kind, sort: [If we will] *supply it with one gender of herbs, or distract it with many*—Oth I 3 326. *The general gender*, the common sort (of people): *The great love the general gender bear him*—Hml IV 7 18.

(2) Offspring: *That thy sable gender makest With the breath thou givest and takest*—Phœn 18.

GENDER (vb.)

To procreate, breed: *A cistern for foul toads To knot and gender in*—Oth IV 2 61.

GENERAL (adj.)

(1) Common, public: *The other half comes to the general state*—Merch IV 1 371. *Whose ransoms did the general coffers fill*—Cæs III 2 94. *The general ear*—Hml II 2 589.

(2) With collective or pl. sb., all, all collectively: *To square the general sex By Cressid's rule*—Troil V 2 132. *A general abatement of kindness appears . . . in the general dependants*—Lr I 4 64. *If the general camp . . . had tasted her sweet body*—Oth III 3 345.

(3) *In general*, in a body, without exception: *The horses of the enemy In general*—1 H4 IV 3 25. *The greater part, the horse in general, Are come with Cassius*—Cæs IV 2 29. In all respects: *Thou art a grave and noble counsellor, Most wise in general*—Per V 1 184.

GENERAL (sb.)

(1) The whole: *The success, Although particular, shall give a scantling Of good or bad unto the general*—Troil I 3 340.

(2) That which is common to all: *All our abilities . . . Severals and generals of grace exact*—Troil I 3 179.

(3) The people in general, the multitude: *The general, subject to a well-wish'd king*—Meas II 4 27. *I know no personal cause to spurn at him, But for the general*—Cæs II 1 11. *'Twas caviare to the general*—Hml II 2 457.

GENERALLY

(1) In a body, all: *This gentleman, To whom we all rest generally beholding*—Shr I 2 273. *As to be . . . generally thankful*—All's II 3 42.

(2) Universally; with few or no exceptions: *Generally allowed for your many war-like, courtlike, and learned preparations*—Wiv II 2 236. *So many giddy offences as he hath generally taxed their whole sex withal*—As III 2 367. *He that so generally is at all times good*—All's I 1 8. *They are generally fools and cowards*—2 H4 IV 3 101.

GENERATION

(1) Offspring, progeny: *These two beget A generation of still-breeding thoughts*—R2 V 5 7. *Is love a generation of vipers?*—Troil III 1 146. *He that makes his generation messes To gorge his appetite*—Lr I 1 119. In pl.: *Fourteen they shall not see, To bring false generations*—Wint II 1 147.

(2) Race, breed: *Our human generation*—Tp III 3 33. *Ere twice the sun hath made his journal greeting To the under generation*—Meas IV 3 92. *Thy mother's of my generation; what's she, if I be a dog?*—Tim I 1 204.

GENEROSITY

Good birth; those of good birth: *A petition granted them, a strange one—To break the heart of generosity*—Cor I 1 214.

GENEROUS

High-born, noble: *The generous and gravest citizens*—Meas IV 6 13. *Most generous sir*—LLL V 1 96. *The generous islanders By you invited*—Oth III 3 280.

GENIUS

(1) The tutelary spirit supposed to accompany each man through life: *The Genius and the mortal instruments Are then in council*—Cæs II 1 66. *Under him My Genius is rebuked*—Mcb III 1 55. Sometimes two, a good and a bad, were figured: *The strong'st suggestion Our worser genius can*—Tp IV 26.

(2) Disposition, nature: *His very genius hath taken the infection of the device*—Tw III 4 142.

(3) An embodied type of an idea: *A was the very genius of famine*—2 H4 III 2 337.

GENNET

See *Jennet.*

GENTILITY

Good manners, politeness: *A dangerous law against gentility!*—LLL I 1 129.

GENTLE (adj.)

Well-born: *A slave no gentler than my dog*—H5 IV 5 15. *There's many a gentle person made a Jack*—R3 I 3 73. *He said he was gentle, but unfortunate*—Cymb IV 2 39.

GENTLE (sb.)

(1) In pl., gentlefolks: *The gentles are at their game*—LLL IV 2 172.

(2) Used in polite address: *Will you go, gentles?*—Wiv III 2 91. *Gentles, perchance you wonder at this show*—Mids V 128. *Gentles, methinks you frown*—Shr III 2 95.

GENTLE (vb.)

To ennoble: *Be he ne'er so vile, This day shall gentle his condition*—H5 IV 3 62.

GENTLENESS

Courtesy, serviceableness: *Of his gentleness . . . he furnish'd me From mine own library with volumes*—Tp I 2 165. *In humane gentleness, Welcome to Troy!*—Troil IV 1 20. [I] *will with deeds requite thy gentleness*—Tit I 1 237.

GENTLY

In a manner (*i.e.* to an amount) befitting a gentleman: *Being something gently considered, I'll bring you where he is aboard*—Wint IV 4 824.

GENTRY

(1) Rank by birth (high or low): *Thou shouldst not alter the article of thy gentry*—Wiv II 1 52.

(2) The rank or quality of gentleman: *Which no less adorns Our gentry than our parents' noble names*—Wint I 2 392. *Exempt from ancient gentry*—1 H6 II 4 93. *She conjures him . . . By knighthood, gentry, and sweet friendship's oath*—Lucr 568.

(3) Courtesy, kindness: *If it will please you To show us so much gentry and good will As . . .*—Hml II 2 21. Good breeding: *He is the card or calendar of gentry*—Hml V 2 114.

GEORGE

The jewel forming part of the insignia of the Order of the Garter: *Look on my George; I am a gentleman*—2 H6 IV 1 29. *By my George, my garter, and my crown*—R3 IV 4 366.

GEORGE'S FIELD, SAINT

An open space, now built over, on the Surrey side, between Southwark and Lambeth: *Do you remember since we lay all night in the windmill in Saint George's field?*—2 H4 III 2 206. *Meet me to-morrow in Saint George's field*—2 H6 V 1 46. The Elephant and Castle and the Obelisk serve to give an indication of the site.

GERMAN (adj.), GERMANE

Akin: *Those that are germane to him, though removed fifty times*—Wint IV 4 800. *Wert thou a leopard, thou wert german to the lion*—Tim IV 3 343.

GERMAN (sb.)

One sprung from the same stock, a kinsman: *You'll have coursers for cousins and gennets for germans*—Oth I 1 113.

GERMEN

A germ: *Though the treasure Of nature's germens tumble all together*—Mcb IV 1 58. *All germens spill at once, That make ingrateful man!*—Lr III 2 8.

GEST[1]

The time allotted for a stay: *A month behind the gest Prefix'd for's parting*—Wint I 2 41.

GEST[2]

In pl., high deeds: *Let the queen know of our gests*—Ant IV 8 2.

GESTURE

Bearing, carriage, demeanour: *Re-enter . . . Alonso, with a frantic gesture*—Tp V 57 (Stage Dir). *If you do love Rosalind so near the heart as your gesture cries it out*—As V 2 68. *Their gesture sad . . . Presenteth them unto the gazing moon So many horrid ghosts*—H5 IV Chor 25.

GET

To beget: *She is with child; And he that got it, sentenced*—Meas II 3 12. *A whole tribe of fops, Got 'tween asleep and wake*—Lr I 2 14.

GETTER

A begetter: [Peace is] *a getter of more bastard children than war's a destroyer of men*—Cor IV 5 240.

GHASTLY

Full of fear, inspired by fear: *Wherefore this ghastly looking?*—Tp II 1 309. *Ghastly looks*—R3 III 5 8. *A hundred ghastly women, Transformed with their fear*—Cæs I 3 23.

GHOST (sb.)

(1) An incorporeal being, a spirit: *That affable familiar ghost Which nightly gulls him with intelligence*—Sonn 86 9.

(2) A corpse: *A timely-parted ghost, Of ashy semblance*—2 H6 III 2 161.

GHOST (vb.)

To haunt: *Julius Cæsar, Who at Philippi the good Brutus ghosted*—Ant II 6 12.

GIB, GIB CAT

A male cat: [Who] *Would from a paddock, from a bat, a gib, Such dear concernings hide?*—Hml III 4 190. *I am as melancholy as a gib cat*—1 H4 I 2 82.

GIBBET

To gibbet on, to hang on (a sling for carrying): *Come off and on swifter than he that gibbets on the brewer's bucket*—2 H4 III 2 281.

GIDDILY

Carelessly: *The parts that fortune hath bestow'd upon her, Tell her, I hold as giddily as fortune*—Tw II 4 86.

GIG

A whipping-top: *Great Hercules whipping a gig*—LLL IV 3 167. *Go, whip thy gig*—V 1 69.

GIGLOT

A loose woman: *Away with those giglots!*—Meas V 351. As adj.: *Young Talbot was not born To be the pillage of a giglot wench*—1 H6 IV 7 40. *O giglot fortune!*—Cymb III 1 31.

GILD

(1) To smear (with blood): *Their armours . . . Hither return all gilt with Frenchmen's blood*—John II 315. *If he do bleed, I'll gild the faces of the grooms withal*—Mcb II 2 55.
(2) To impart a flush to the face: *This grand liquor that hath gilded 'em*—Tp V 280.

GILLYVOR

Gillyflower; formerly applied especially to the clove-scented pink: *Carnations and streak'd gillyvors*—Wint IV 4 82.

GILT

Gold, money: *For the gilt of France*—H5 II Chor 26.

GIMMAL

Consisting of two similar parts: *In their pale dull mouths the gimmal bit*—H5 IV 2 49.

GIMMORS

Connecting parts in clockwork: *I think, by some odd gimmors or device Their arms are set like clocks, still to strike on*—1 H6 I 2 41.

GIN

(1) Begin: *The bloody Douglas . . . Gan vail his stomach*—2 H4 I 1 127. *The glow-worm . . . gins to pale his uneffectual fire*—Hml I 5 89. *A flower that dies when first it gins to bud*—Pilgr 171.
(2) As a mere auxiliary = did: *Through the velvet leaves the wind, All unseen, gan passage find*—Pilgr 231. Cf. *Can*², which is an altered form of this.

GING

A gang, crew: *There's a knot, a ging, a pack, a conspiracy against me*—Wiv IV 2 123.

GIRD

To gird at, scoff at: *He will not spare to gird the gods*—Cor I 1 260.

GIRDLE

If he be [angry], *he knows how to turn his girdle,*

i.e. let him do so (and so occupy himself) if he is not pleased; implying indifference to Benedick's anger—Ado V 1 142.

GIS

A corruption of Jesus: *By Gis and by Saint Charity*—Hml IV 5 59.

GIVE

(1) To display as an armorial bearing: *They may give the dozen white luces in their coat*—Wiv I 1 16. *Tear the lions out of England's coat . . . give sheep in lions' stead*—1 H6 I 5 28.
(2) To represent, describe: *Us that give you truly*—Cor I 9 55. *Men's reports Give him much wrong'd*—Ant I 4 39.
(3) To account, consider: *Your favour I do give lost*—Wint III 2 95.
(4) Of one's mind, to suggest (something to one), to have a misgiving: *My mind gave me . . . Ye blew the fire that burns ye*—H8 V 3 109. *My mind gave me his clothes made a false report of him*—Cor IV 5 156.
(5) *To give away*, to sacrifice (another's interests): *Thy solicitor shall rather die Than give thy cause away*—Oth III 3 27. To announce: *I thank your grace for this high courtesy, Which I shall give away immediately*—1 H4 V 5 32.
(6) *To give off*, to cease: *Let's see how it* (*i.e.* the noise) *will give off*—Ant IV 3 23.
(7) *To give off, out*, to surrender, resign: *Did not the prophet Say that before Ascension-day at noon My crown I should give off?*—John V 1 25. *I thought ye would never have given out these arms till . . .*—2 H6 IV 8 26.
(8) *To give over*, to abandon, desert: *Pray to the devils; the gods have given us over*—Tit IV 2 48. *Given over*, abandoned by God to one's own evil passions: *Thou art altogether given over*—1 H4 III 3 40.

GLAD

Gladness, joy: *Fortune . . . Threw him ashore, to give him glad*—Per II Prol 37.

GLANCE (sb.)

A satirical hit: *The wise man's folly is anatomized Even by the squandering glances of the fool*—As II 7 56.

GLANCE (vb.)

To glance at, allude to: *In company I often glanced it*—Err V 66.

GLASS

As a measure of time; usually said of the half-hour glass, but in Tp app. of the hour glass (cf. V 186 (*Your eld'st acquaintance cannot be three hours*) with the second quotation): Pros. . . . *What is the time o' the day?* Ari. *Past the mid season.* Pros. *At least two glasses*—Tp I 2 239. *Our ship*

*—Which, but three glasses since, we gave out split
—V 222.*

GLASS-FACED

Reflecting another's looks like a mirror: *The glass-faced flatterer*—Tim I 1 58.

GLEEK (sb.)

A gibe, jest: *Where's the Bastard's braves, and Charles his gleeks?*—1 H6 III 2 123.   First Mus. *What will you give us?* Pet. *No money . . . but the gleek*—Rom IV 5 114.

GLEEK (vb.)

To gibe, jest: *Nay, I can gleek upon occasion*—Mids III 1 149.   *Gleeking and galling at this gentleman*—H5 V 1 78.

GLIB

To geld: *I had rather glib myself*—Wint II 1 149.

GLIMPSE

(1) A tinge, trace: *There is no man hath a virtue that he hath not a glimpse of*—Troil I 2 24.

(2) *The fault and glimpse of newness*, the faulty and imperfect (mental) vision caused by novelty—Meas I 2 162.

GLISTER

Glitter: *All that glisters is not gold*—Merch II 7 65.   *Glistering semblances of piety*—H5 II 2 117.   *His* (i.e. the sun's) *glistering coach*—Tit II 1 7.

GLORIOUS

Eager for distinction: *Most miserable Is the desire that's glorious*—Cymb I 6 6.   *The purchase is to make men glorious*—Per Prol 9.

GLORY

Vaunting: *Ha, majesty! how high thy glory towers!*—John II 350.

GLOSE

See *Gloze*.

GLOW

To make hot: *Fans, whose wind did seem To glow the delicate cheeks*—Ant II 2 208.

GLOZE, GLOSE

(1) To explain, interpret: *Which Salique land the French unjustly glose To be the realm of France*—H5 I 2 40.   To discourse: *On the . . . question now in hand* [you] *Have glozed, but superficially*—Troil II 2 164.

(2) To talk smoothly and speciously: *They whom youth and ease have taught to glose*—R2 II 1 10. *Thus it shall become High-witted Tamora to gloze with all*—Tit IV 4 34.

GLOZES

Specious talk: *Now to plain-dealing; lay these glozes by*—LLL IV 3 370.

GLUT

To swallow up: *Though every drop of water . . . gape at widest to glut him*—Tp I 1 62.

GLUTTON

To feed voraciously: *Thus do I pine and surfeit day by day, Or gluttoning on all, or all away*—Sonn 75 13.

GNARL

To snarl: *Gnarling sorrow hath less power to bite The man that mocks at it*—R2 I 3 292.   *Wolves are gnarling who shall gnaw thee first*—2 H6 III 1 192.

GO

To move step by step, walk: Ste. *We'll not run . . .* Trin. *Nor go neither*—Tp III 2 21.   *Thou must run to him, for thou hast stayed so long that going will scarce serve the turn*—Gent III 1 387.

GOD-A-MERCY

God have mercy:

(1) Used as an exclamation with no very clearly defined meaning: *God-a-mercy, Grumio! then he shall have no odds*—Shr IV 3 154.   *God-a-mercy! so should I be sure to be heart-burned*—1 H4 III 3 58.

(2) As an exclamation of thanks: ' *Good den, sir Richard!* '—' *God-a-mercy, fellow!* '—John I 185.   *God-a-mercy, that thou wilt believe me*—Troil V 4 33.   Pol. . . . *How does my good Lord Hamlet?* Ham. *Well, God-a-mercy*—Hml II 2 171.

GOD-DEN, GOOD DEN

Good even: *God-den to your worships*—Cor II 1 103.   *Good den, sir Richard!*—John I 185.

GOD DIG-YOU-DEN

God give you good even: *God dig-you-den all!*—LLL IV 1 42.

GOD 'ILD

God reward.   See *Yield*.

GOD'S LID

God's eyelid: *By God's lid, it does one's heart good*—Troil I 2 228.

GOD YE

God [give] you: *God ye good even, William*—As V 1 16.   *God ye good morrow, gentlemen*—Rom II 4 115.

GOGS-WOUNS

God's wounds: ' *Ay, by gogs-wouns,' quoth he*—Shr III 2 162.

GOOD-CONCEITED

Ingeniously devised: *A very excellent good-conceited thing*—Cymb II 3 18. Cf. *Conceited* (3).

GOOD DEED

In very deed: *Yet, good deed, Leontes, I love thee*—Wint I 2 42.

GOOD DEN

See *God-den*.

GOOD-JER

See *Good-year*.

GOODNESS

Good fortune, success: *Bliss and goodness on you!*—Meas III 2 228. *The chance of goodness Be like our warranted quarrel!*—Mcb IV 3 136.

GOOD-NIGHT

Per., a composition improvised when going to sleep: *Sware they were his fancies or his good-nights*—2 H4 III 2 342.

GOOD-YEAR, GOOD-JER

What the good-year, good-jer, a meaningless expletive: *We must give folks leave to prate; what, the good-jer!*—Wiv I 4 128. *What the good-year, my lord! why are you thus out of measure sad?*—Ado I 3 1. *What the good-year! one must bear*—2 H4 II 4 64. *The good-years*, used to denote some undefined malefic power: *The good-years shall devour them, flesh and fell*—Lr V 3 24.

GORBELLIED

Big-bellied: *Hang ye, gorbellied knaves*—1 H4 II 2 93.

GORGE

(1) The crop of a bird of prey: *Even as an empty eagle . . . Tires . . . on feathers, flesh and bone . . . Till . . . gorge be stuff'd*—Ven 55.

(2) What has been swallowed; so *to cast, heave the gorge, one's gorge rises*, expressing extreme disgust: *She whom the spital-house . . . Would cast the gorge at*—Tim IV 3 39. *Her delicate tenderness will . . . begin to heave the gorge*—Oth II 1 235. *My gorge rises at it*—Hml V 1 206.

GORGET

A piece of armour for the throat: *With a palsy-fumbling on his gorget*—Troil I 3 174.

GOSPELLED

Imbued with gospel principles: *Are you so gospell'd To pray for this good man . . . Whose heavy hand hath bow'd you to the grave?*—Mcb III 1 88.

GOSS

Gorse: *Sharp furzes, pricking goss and thorns*—Tp IV 180.

GOSSIP (sb.)

(1) A godfather or godmother to one's child: *'Tis not a maid, for she hath had gossips*—Gent III 1 268. *Needful conference About some gossips for your highness*—Wint II 3 40. *My noble gossips, ye have been too prodigal*—H8 V 5 13.

(2) Applied to a woman's female friends invited to be present at a birth: *A gossips' feast*—Err V 405. *Gossip's bowl*, app., that in which the gossip's cup or caudle was made: *Sometime lurk I in a gossip's bowl, In very likeness of a roasted crab*—Mids II 1 47. *Utter your gravity o'er a gossip's bowl*—Rom III 5 175.

GOSSIP (vb.)

(1) To make merry: *I'll gossip at this feast*—Err V 407. *Feasts Full of warm blood, of mirth, of gossiping*—John V 2 58.

(2) App., to be a sponsor at the giving of (a name): *Pretty, fond, adoptious christendoms, That blinking Cupid gossips*—All's I 1 188.

GOURD

Some kind of false dice; see the quotation under *Fullam*.

GOUT

A drop: *On thy blade and dudgeon gouts of blood*—Mcb II 1 46.

GOVERN

(1) To master, prevail over: *[She] govern'd him in strength, though not in lust*—Ven 42.

(2) To guide, direct: *That which governs me to go about*—Sonn 113 2.

(3) To manage, carry out: *Whiles I go tell . . . How I have govern'd our determined jest*—Tit V 2 138.

(4) To manage, manipulate: *Govern these ventages with your fingers and thumb*—Hml III 2 372.

GOVERNESS

A mistress, ruler: *The moon, the governess of floods*—Mids II 1 103. *Their dear governess and lady*—Lucr 443.

GOVERNMENT

(1) Conduct, behaviour: *I will open my lips in vain, or discover his government*—Meas III 1 198. *We be men of good government*—1 H4 I 2 30. Becoming conduct, discretion: *Defect of manners, want of government*—1 H4 III 1 184. *Thy meekness saint-like, wife-like government*—H8 II 4 138. *Fear not my government*—Oth III 3 256.

(2) Period of rule, tenure of office: *His fact, till now in the government of Lord Angelo, came not to an undoubtful proof*—Meas IV 2 141.

GRACE (sb.)

(1) Honour, distinction: *Of worth To undergo such ample grace and honour*—Meas I 1 23. *That*

loose grace Which shallow laughing hearers give to fools—LLL V 2 869. *Ancestry, whose grace Chalks successors their way*—H8 I 1 59. *In grace of*, in honour of: [They] *Came here in grace of our solemnity*—Mids IV 1 138. *In grace whereof, No jocund health that Denmark drinks to-day, But the great cannon to the clouds shall tell*—Hml I 2 124. *To do grace to, to do* (a person or thing) *grace*, to do honour to, distinguish by attentions: *Thyself do grace to them, and bring them in*—Hml II 2 53. To reflect credit on, embellish, set in a good light: *The which for sport sake are content to do the profession some grace*—1 H4 II 1 77. *If there be any good thing to be done, That may to thee do ease and grace to me*—Hml I 1 130. [Thou] *dost him* (*i.e.* the day) *grace when clouds do blot the heaven*—Sonn 28 10. *Since mourning doth thee grace*—132 11.

(2) Something that imparts beauty, an ornament: *This grace of kings*—H5 II Chor 28.

(3) Favour, benignant regard: *You shall have . . . Grace of the duke*—Meas IV 3 139. *I* [am] *in such a poverty of grace*—As III 5 100. Sim.: *Give me grace to lay My duty on your hand*—Ant III 13 81. A favour, kindness: *Your royal graces, Shower'd on me daily*—H8 III 2 166. [We] *shall continue our graces towards him*—Mcb I 6 30.

(4) Good fortune: [I] *Do curse the grace that with such grace hath bless'd them*—Gent III 1 146. *Unless you have the grace by your fair prayer To soften Angelo*—Meas I 4 69. A piece of good fortune: *Every wink of an eye some new grace will be born*—Wint V 2 119.

(5) Beneficent efficacy: *Mickle is the powerful grace that lies In herbs, plants . . .*—Rom II 3 15.

(6) Mercy, pardon: *All the grace I beg*—Meas V 379. *Now, perjured Henry! wilt thou kneel for grace?*—3 H6 II 2 81.

GRACE (vb.)

(1) To honour, distinguish: *Whom they doted on And bless'd and graced indeed, more than the king*—2 H4 IV 1 138. *We grace the yeoman by conversing with him*—1 H6 II 4 81. Refl., to get oneself honour or credit: *If he do not mightily grace himself on thee*—As I 1 155. [That] *goes to the wars, to grace himself . . . under the form of a soldier*—H5 III 6 71.

(2) To show favour to: *Daily graced by the emperor*—Gent I 3 58. *Thy wit wants . . . manners, to intrude where I am graced*—Tit II 1 26.

(3) To give pleasure to: *What comfortable hour canst thou name, That ever graced me in thy company?*—R3 IV 4 173.

GRACED

Full of graces: *The graced person of our Banquo*—Mcb III 4 41. Stately: *A graced palace*—Lr I 4 267.

GRACEFUL

(1) Full of divine grace: *You have a holy father, A graceful gentleman*—Wint V 1 170.

(2) Favourable, friendly: [I] *Could not with graceful eyes attend those wars Which fronted mine own peace*—Ant II 2 60.

GRACIOUS

(1) Enjoying favour, in good odour, acceptable: *If I be foiled, there is but one shamed that was never gracious*—As I 2 199. *Is he gracious in the people's eye?*—3 H6 III 3 117. *If ever Bassianus . . . Were gracious in the eyes of royal Rome*—Tit I 10. *If ever Tamora Were gracious in those princely eyes of thine*—428.

(2) Lovely, attractive: [In] *the shape of nature A gracious person*—Tw I 5 280. *There was not such a gracious creature born*—John III 4 81. *My gracious silence, hail!*—Cor II 1 192. *Methinks no face so gracious is as mine*—Sonn 62 5.

(3) Characterized by or endowed with divine grace, holy, virtuous: [She] *hath made him that gracious denial which he is most glad to receive*—Meas III 1 166. *Kings are . . . unhappy, their issue not being gracious*—Wint IV 2 29. *So hallow'd and so gracious is the time*—Hml I 1 164.

(4) Prosperous, fortunate: *To try her gracious fortune with Lord Angelo*—Meas V 76. *Gracious be the issue!*—Wint III 1 22.

GRACIOUSLY

Piously, righteously: *What he will do graciously, I will thankfully receive*—Per IV 6 65. By means of divine grace: *In nothing good, But graciously to know I am no better*—Meas II 4 76.

GRAFF (sb.)

(1) Graft; a scion: *This bastard graff shall never come to growth*—Lucr 1062.

(2) A twig, shoot: *The most just gods For every graff would send a caterpillar*—Per V 1 59.

GRAFF (vb.)

Graft: *I'll graff it with you*—As III 2 124. *A last year's pippin of my own graffing*—2 H4 V 3 2.

GRAFTER

The tree from which a scion is taken: [Shall] *Our scions . . . Spirt up so suddenly into the clouds, And overlook their grafters?*—H5 III 5 7.

GRAIN

(1) *Purple-in-grain*, dyed in kermes or scarlet grain: *Your purple-in-grain beard*—Mids I 2 96.

(2) Hence in grain, fast dyed; fig.: *'Tis in grain; Noah's flood could not do it*—Err III 2 108. *'Tis in grain, sir; 'twill endure wind and weather*—Tw I 5 255.

GRAINED[1]

Dyed in grain (see above), ineradicable: *Black and grained spots*—Hml III 4 90.

GRAINED[2]

Having tines or prongs, forked: *So slides he down upon his grained bat*—Compl 64.

GRAINED[3]

(1) Close grained: *Where against My grained ash an hundred times hath broke*—Cor IV 5 113.

(2) Showing the grain; fig., lined: *This grained face of mine*—Err V 311.

GRAMERCY

Thanks, thank you: Gob. *God bless your worship!* Bass. *Gramercy!*—Merch II 2 127. *Gramercy, fellow: there, drink that for me*—R3 III 2 108. In pl.: *Gramercies, Tranio, well dost thou advise*—Shr I 1 41. *Gramercies, good fool*—Tim II 2 69.

GRAND

With reference to physical magnitude, main, principal: *As petty . . . As is the morn-dew on the myrtle-leaf To his grand sea*—Ant III 12 8.

GRANT (sb.)

For matter of grant, as to anything to be granted: *That the King of France, having any occasion to write for matter of grant, shall . . .*—H5 V 2 364.

GRANT (vb.)

To consent, agree: *Before I would have granted to that act*—3 H6 I 1 245.

GRATE

To fret, vex: *Grating so harshly all his days of quiet*—Hml III 1 3. Att. *News, my good lord, from Rome.* Ant. *Grates me: the sum*—Ant I 1 18. *To grate on* or *upon,* to harass with importunities or exactions: *I have grated upon my good friends for three reprieves for you*—Wiv II 2 5. *What peer hath been suborn'd to grate on you?*—2 H4 IV 1 90.

GRATIFY

(1) To show gratitude to: *You must, as we do, gratify this gentleman, To whom we all rest generally beholding*—Shr I 2 273. To do so in a practical way, to reward, remunerate: *Antonio, gratify this gentleman*—Merch IV 1 406. *To gratify the good Andronicus*—Tit I 220. To reward (services, an action, &c.): *To gratify his noble service*—Cor II 2 44. *She did gratify his amorous works With that recognizance*—Oth V 2 213. *In these sear'd hopes, I barely gratify your love*—Cymb II 4 6.

(2) To render pleasing, grace: *To gratify the table with a grace*—LLL IV 2 161.

(3) To comply with (a request): *The which*

[request] *when any shall not gratify*—Per I 4 101.

GRATIS

Giving no fee, paying nothing: *Sin ne'er gives a fee, He gratis comes*—Lucr 913.

GRATULATE (adj.)

To be rejoiced at, gratifying: *There's more behind that is more gratulate*—Meas V 535.

GRATULATE (vb.)

(1) To welcome, hail: [To] *gratulate his safe return to Rome*—Tit I 221.

(2) To give pleasure to, gladden, cheer: *To gratulate the gentle princes*—R3 IV 1 10. *To gratulate thy plenteous bosom*—Tim I 2 131.

GRAVE (adj.)

(1) Of persons, influential, respected: *The generous and gravest citizens*—Meas IV 6 13. *Seem they grave and learned? Why, so didst thou*—H5 II 2 128. *Most reverend and grave elders*—Cor II 2 46. *Most potent, grave, and reverend signiors*—Oth I 3 76.

(2) Of advice, &c., weighty, authoritative: *Thy grave admonishments*—1 H6 II 5 98. *This land was famously enrich'd With politic grave counsel*—R3 II 3 19. *Your good advice, Which still hath been both grave and prosperous*—Mcb III 1 21.

(3) *This grave charm,* perh., deadly: *This grave charm . . . Like a right gipsy, hath . . . Beguiled me to the very heart of loss*—Ant IV 12 25.

GRAVE (vb.)

(1) To bury, inter: *Graved in the hollow ground*—R2 III 2 140. To swallow up as in a grave: *Ditches grave you all!*—Tim IV 3 166.

(2) To cut into: *Being steel'd, soft sighs can never grave it*—Ven 376.

GREASILY

Indecently: *You talk greasily; your lips grow foul*—LLL IV 1 139.

GREAT MORNING

Broad day: *It is great morning*—Troil IV 3 1; Cymb IV 2 61.

GREAT ONEYERS

Nobility and tranquillity, burgomasters and great oneyers—1 H4 II 1 84. App. a nonsensical nonce-formation from *great one,* to give a termination similar to that of *burgomasters,* so that the pair of words may form a parallel with *nobility and tranquillity.*

GREE

Agree: *How gree you now?*—Merch II 2 108. *This greed upon, To part with unhack'd edges*—Ant II 6 37.

GREEK

A roisterer, reveller; used with no very clearly defined meaning: *I prithee, foolish Greek, depart from me*—Tw IV 1 19.

GREEN

(1) Perh., new, fresh (sarcastically): *You may be jogging whiles your boots are green*—Shr III 2 213.

(2) *A green goose*, one fed up on grass; of a simpleton: LLL I 1 97; IV 3 75.

GREEN SLEEVES

A popular ditty, app. of a wanton nature: *They do no more adhere and keep place together than the Hundredth Psalm to the tune of 'Green Sleeves'*—Wiv II 1 62. *Let it thunder to the tune of Green Sleeves . . . let there come a tempest of provocation*—V 5 21.

GREET

(1) To gratify, please: *It greets me as an enterprise of kindness*—Per IV 3 38.

(2) *To greet together*, app., to greet (and remain on terms with) each other: *I cannot hope Cæsar and Antony shall well greet together*—Ant II 1 38.

GRIEF

(1) Disease, sickness: *My limbs, Weaken'd with grief*—2 H4 I 1 143.

(2) Physical pain: *Where lies thy grief?*—LLL IV 3 171. *Out of my grief and my impatience,* [I] *Answer'd neglectingly*—1 H4 I 3 51. [Can honour] *take away the grief of a wound?*—V 1 134.

(3) Mental suffering or distress: *Like patience on a monument, Smiling at grief*—Tw II 4 117. *With the same haviour that your passion bears Goes on my master's grief*—III 4 226. *This love . . . Doth add more grief to too much of mine own*—Rom I 1 194.

(4) A grievance, wrong: *The king hath sent to know The nature of your griefs*—1 H4 IV 3 41. *Be factious for redress of all these griefs*—Cæs I 3 118. *To enforce no further The griefs between ye*—Ant II 2 99. An expression of a sense of wrong done to one: *No more will I control thy griefs*—Tit III 1 260.

GRIEVANCE

(1) Oppression: [He will] *put upon you what restraint and grievance The law . . . Will give him cable*—Oth I 2 15.

(2) Trouble, distress: *If ever danger do environ thee, Commend thy grievance to my holy prayers*—Gent I 1 16. *I'll know his grievance, or be much denied*—Rom I 1 163. *Then can I grieve at grievances foregone*—Sonn 30 9.

GRIEVE

To regret, bemoan: *The effects of his fond jealousies so grieving*—Wint IV 1 18. *The nothing that I grieve*—R2 II 2 37.

GRIPE

A vulture: *Like a white hind under the gripe's sharp claws*—Lucr 543.

GRISE, GRIZE

A step, degree: Oli. *That's a degree to love.* Vio. *No, not a grize*—Tw III 1 134. *Every grise of fortune Is smooth'd by that below*—Tim IV 3 16. *As a grise or step*—Oth I 3 200.

GROOM

(1) A man, a 'fellow': *A bridegroom say you? 'tis a groom indeed, A grumbling groom*—Shr III 2 154. *You are gallant grooms*—Tit IV 2 164.

(2) A serving-man, male attendant: *You loggerheaded and unpolish'd grooms!*—Shr IV 1 128. *The surfeited grooms Do mock their charge with snores*—Mcb II 2 5.

GROSS (adj.)

(1) Big, stout: *A gross fat man*—1 H4 II 4 560. *The crows . . . Show scarce so gross as beetles*—Lr IV 6 13. Applied to an immaterial object, wide, far-reaching: *Not to strain my speech To grosser issues nor to larger reach Than to suspicion*—Oth III 3 218.

(2) Total, whole: *The gross band of the unfaithful*—As IV 1 199. *What is the gross sum that I owe thee?*—2 H4 II 1 91.

(3) Evident, palpable, striking: *To all sense 'tis gross*—All's I 3 178. *Gross as a mountain, open, palpable*—1 H4 II 4 250. *Examples gross as earth exhort me*—Hml IV 4 46.

(4) Lacking in perception, dull: *In gross brain little wots*—H5 IV 1 299. *Who's so gross, That seeth not this palpable device?*—R3 III 6 10.

GROSS (sb.)

(1) A total sum: *The gross Of full three thousand ducats*—Merch I 3 56.

(2) *By gross*, wholesale: *We that sell by gross*—LLL V 2 319. *In gross*, in a general way: *Which, to term in gross, Is an unlesson'd girl*—Merch III 2 160.

(3) *The gross and scope*, the general working, working on general lines: *In the gross and scope of my opinion*—Hml I 1 68.

GROSSLY

(1) Evidently, palpably: *With what poor judgement he hath now cast her off appears too grossly*—Lr I 1 293. *The purple pride . . . In my love's veins thou hast too grossly dyed*—Sonn 99 3.

(2) With want of clear perception, stupidly: *Grossly fear'st Thy death*—Meas III 1 18. *Though you . . . Are led so grossly by this meddling priest*—John III 1 162. *My woman's heart Grossly grew captive to his honey words*—R3 IV 1 79.

(3) Materially, as opposed to spiritually: *Whilst this muddy vesture of decay Doth grossly close it in* —Merch V 64. *[I] am in that dimension grossly clad Which from the womb I did participate*—Tw V 244. In a state of grossness or unspirituality: *He took my father grossly, full of bread*—Hml III 3 80.

(4) Clumsily, coarsely: *Let them say 'tis grossly done: so it be fairly done, no matter*—Wiv II 2 148. *It is apparent foul play; and 'tis shame That greatness should so grossly offer it*—John IV 2 93.

GROSSNESS

(1) Bulk, quantity: *Substance, Whose grossness little characters sum up*—Troil I 3 324.

(2) Obviousness, palpableness: *The grossness of the foppery*—Wiv V 5 131. *Such impossible passages of grossness*—Tw III 2 76 (for this last cf. *Passage* (3)).

GROUND

(1) The earth: *The wicked'st caitiff on the ground*—Meas V 53. *No man so potent breathes upon the ground But I will beard him*—1 H4 IV 1 11. *A nobler sir ne'er lived 'Twixt sky and ground*—Cymb V 5 145.

(2) A region, land, country: *The people 'twixt Philippi and this ground*—Cæs IV 3 204. *Friends to this ground*—Hml I 1 15.

(3) The theme on which a descant is raised (see *Descant* (sb.)). Fig.: *On that ground I'll build a holy descant*—R3 III 7 49. *An should the empress know This discord's ground, the music would not please*—Tit II 1 69.

GROUNDLING

A frequenter of the 'ground' or pit of a theatre: *To split the ears of the groundlings*—Hml III 2 11.

GROW

(1) To accrue, become due: *The sum that I do owe to you Is growing to me by Antipholus*—Err IV 1 7. *Knowing how the debt grows, I will pay it*—IV 4 124.

(2) To come by degrees *to*: *Say what the play treats on, then read the names of the actors, and so grow to a point*—Mids I 2 8.

(3) *To grow to*, to be an integral part of: *I lay aside that which grows to me!*—2 H4 I 2 99.

(4) *To grow upon*, to come to take liberties with (a superior): *Begin you to grow upon me?*—As I 1 90.

(5) In Merch II 2 17 (*My father did something smack, something grow to, he had a kind of taste*) prob. fig. from milk burnt and 'grown to' the bottom of the pan and so spoiled.

GRUDGE (sb.)

Unwillingness, discontent: *[I have] served Without or grudge or grumblings*—Tp I 2 248.

GRUDGE (vb.)

(1) To grumble, be discontented: *He eats his meat without grudging*—Ado III 4 89. *How will their grudging stomachs be provoked To wilful disobedience!*—1 H6 IV 1 141.

(2) *To grudge a thought*, to think an envious thought: *So perish they That grudge one thought against your majesty!*—1 H6 III 1 175.

GRUNT

To groan: *To grunt and sweat under a weary life*—Hml III 1 77.

GUARD (sb.)

(1) Keeping, custody: *He broke from those that had the guard of him* — Err V 149. *I'll take her to my guard*—Ant V 2 67.

(2) An ornamental border or trimming: *The damned'st body to invest and cover In prenzie guards*—Meas III 1 96. *The guards are but slightly basted on neither*—Ado I 1 289. *Rhymes are guards on wanton Cupid's hose*—LLL IV 3 58. *Velvet-guards*, velvet trimmings, meaning the female citizens wearing them: *Velvet-guards and Sunday-citizens*—1 H4 III 1 261.

(3) *The guards of the pole*, a name applied to the two 'pointers' of the Great Bear: *Seems to cast water on the burning bear, And quench the guards of the ever-fixed pole*—Oth II 1 14.

(4) *Stands at a guard with*, stands in a posture of defence against: *Lord Angelo . . . Stands at a guard with envy*—Meas I 3 50.

GUARD (vb.)

To trim, ornament: *The body of your discourse is sometime guarded with fragments*—Ado I 1 287. *Give him a livery More guarded than his fellows'* —Merch II 2 163. *To guard a title that was rich before*—John IV 2 10.

GUARDAGE

The state of being kept safe: *[Have] Run from her guardage to the sooty bosom Of such a thing as thou*—Oth I 2 70.

GUARDANT

A defender: *When my angry guardant stood alone, Tendering my ruin*—1 H6 IV 7 9. A sentinel: *A Jack guardant cannot office me from my son Coriolanus*—Cor V 2 67.

GUIDON

He who carries the guidon, a standard-bearer: *I stay but for my guidon*—H5 IV 2 60.

GUILDER

A Dutch coin; in pl. of money generally: *Wanting guilders to redeem their lives*—Err I 1 8. *I am bound To Persia and want guilders for my voyage*— IV 1 3.

GUILED

Endowed with guile, treacherous: *The guiled shore To a most dangerous sea*—Merch III 2 97.

GUILTY

Guilty to, responsible for: *The unthought-on accident is guilty To what we wildly do*—Wint IV 4 548.

GUINEA-HEN

A cant term of depreciation for a woman: *I would drown myself for the love of a guinea-hen*—Oth I 3 316.

GUISE

(1) Manner, way: *This is her very guise*—Mcb V 1 22. *This was thy father's guise*—Ven 1177.

(2) The custom or ways of the time: *Is this the guise, Is this the fashion in the court of England?*—2 H6 I 3 45. *How rarely does it meet with this time's guise, When man was wish'd to love his enemies!*—Tim IV 3 472. *To shame the guise o' the world*—Cymb V 1 32.

GULES

In heraldry, red; fig.: *With man's blood paint the ground, gules, gules*—Tim IV 3 59. *Head to foot Now is he total gules*—Hml II 2 478.

GULF

Applied to the gullet of a voracious animal: *Maw and gulf Of the ravin'd salt-sea shark*—Mcb IV I 23.

GULL¹

An unfledged bird: *That ungentle gull, the cuckoo's bird*—1 H4 V 1 60. *Lord Timon will be left a naked gull*—Tim II 1 31.

GULL²

A trick, deception: *I should think this a gull*—Ado II 3 123.

GUMMED

A gummed velvet, a piece of velvet stiffened with gum to make it sit well, and so wearing quickly: *He frets like a gummed velvet*—1 H4 II 2 2.

GUN-STONE

A cannon-ball, originally one of stone: *This mock of his Hath turn'd his balls (i.e.* the tennis-balls) *to gun-stones*—H5 I 2 281.

GUST (sb.)¹

Fig., an outbreak, outburst: *To kill, I grant, is sin's extremest gust*—Tim III 5 54.

GUST (sb.)²

Taste, inclination: *Mine eye well knows what with his gust is greeing*—Sonn 114 11.

GUST (vb.)

To taste; and hence, to perceive: *'Tis far gone, When I shall gust it last*—Wint I 2 218.

GUY, SIR

Sir Guy of Warwick, a knight of romance: *I am not Samson, nor Sir Guy, nor Colbrand*—H8 V 4 22.

H

H

Ado III 4 56. See *Ache.*

HABIT

Bearing, demeanour: *If I do not put on a sober habit, Talk with respect and swear but now and then*—Merch II 2 199. *I will speak to him like a saucy lackey and under that habit play the knave with him*—As III 2 313. *In the habit of some sir of note*—Tw III 4 81. *It is her habit only that is honest*—Tim IV 3 113. *My father, in his habit as (i.e.* as if) *he lived! i.e.* with the mien which was characteristic of him in life—Hml III 4 135.

HABITUDE

Constitution, character: *His real habitude gave life and grace To appertainings and to ornament*—Compl 114.

HACK

These knights will hack—Wiv II 1 52. Ex-plained as, to grow common; but this and other explanations offered are very doubtful.

HAGGARD, HAGGERD

A wild hawk captured for training after she has assumed her adult plumage: *Her spirits are as coy and wild As haggerds of the rock*—Ado III 1 35. *Another way I have to man my haggard, To make her come and know her keeper's call*—Shr IV 1 196. *Like the haggard, check at every feather*—Tw III 1 71. So as adj., of persons, wild, intractable: *If I do prove her haggard*—Oth III 3 260.

HAGGLE

To hack, mangle: *York, all haggled over, Comes to him*—H5 IV 6 11.

HAI

In fencing, a home-thrust: *Ah, the immortal passado! the punto reverso! the hai!*—Rom II 4 26.

HAIR

Kind, nature: *The quality and hair of our attempt*—1 H4 IV 1 61. *Against the hair*, contrary to the nature (*of* a thing), against the grain: *You go against the hair of your professions*—Wiv II 3 41. *He is melancholy without cause, and merry against the hair*—Troil I 2 27.

HALBERD

A long-handled battle-axe with a spear-head attached: *Guard with halberds!*—Err V 185. *Unless our halberds did shut up his passage*—3 H6 IV 3 20. *Advance thy halberd higher than my breast*—R3 I 2 40.

HALCYON

The kingfisher. It was believed that the body of a halcyon hung up, even indoors, by the bill would turn with the wind: *Renege, affirm, and turn their halcyon beaks With every gale and vary of their masters*—Lr II 2 84. Mention of a curious survival of the idea—the bird in this case being a woodpecker—will be found in the Letters of Edward FitzGerald, Letter to W. A. Wright of 20th January, 1872.

HALE

To haul, pull on (a rope): *Galling His kingly hands, haling ropes*—Per IV 1 54.

HALF-ACHIEVED

Half won: *I will not leave the half-achieved Harfleur*—H5 III 3 8.

HALF-CAP

A half-courteous salute, the cap being only slightly moved: *With certain half-caps and cold-moving nods*—Tim II 2 221.

HALF-CHECKED

Prob. = Half-cheeked, with only one of the cheeks or end rings left: *With a half-checked bit*—Shr III 2 57.

HALF-CHEEK

A face in profile: *Saint George's half-cheek in a brooch*—LLL V 2 620.

HALF-FACE

A face in profile; hence, a thin face: *Because he hath a half-face, like my father*—John I 92.

HALF-FACED

(1) With a profile stamped on it: *A half-faced groat*—John I 94. Hence, thin-faced: *This same half-faced fellow, Shadow*—2 H4 III 2 283.

(2) Half-visible: *Whose hopeful colours Advance our half-faced sun*—2 H6 IV 1 97. (Edward III adopted as his device the rays of the sun dispersing themselves out of a cloud.)

(3) Half-and-half: *Out upon this half-faced fellowship!*—1 H4 I 3 208.

HALF-KIRTLE

See *Kirtle*.

HALF-PART

Halves: *Half-part, mates, half-part*—Per IV 1 95.

HALF-SWORD

At half-sword, at close quarters: *I am a rogue, if I were not at half-sword with a dozen of them*—1 H4 II 4 182.

HALIDOM, HOLIDAME

A holy relic or other holy thing; hence, *by my halidom, holidame*, in asseverations: *By my halidom, I was fast asleep*—Gent IV 2 136. *Now, by my holidame, here comes Katharina!*—Shr V 2 99. *Now, by my holidame, What manner of man are you?*—H8 V 1 116. *And, by my holidame, The pretty wretch left crying*—Rom I 3 43.

HALL

A hall! a cry to make room for dancing: *A hall, a hall! give room! and foot it, girls*—Rom I 5 28.

HALLOWMAS

All Saints Day: *Whose father died at Hallowmas*—Meas II 1 128. *Like Hallowmas or short'st of day*—R2 V 1 80.

HALTING (ppl. adj.)

Shifty: *Not trusting to this halting legate here*—John V 2 174.

HALTING (sb.)

A using of shifts: *No further halting; satisfy me home What is become of her*—Cymb III 5 92.

HAND (sb.)

(1) *At hand*, at the start: *Horses hot at hand*—Cæs IV 2 23. *By hand: A lion foster'd up at hand*—John V 2 75.

(2) *To hold hand with*, to equal: *As she in beauty, education, blood, Holds hand with any princess of the world*—John II 493.

(3) *At, in, any hand, of all hands*, in any case: *All books of love, see that at any hand*—Shr I 2 147. *Let him fetch off his drum in any hand*—All's III 6 44. *Therefore of all hands must we be forsworn*—LLL IV 3 219.

(4) *Tall* or *proper of one's hands*, bold, active: *He is as tall a man of his hands as any is between this and his head*—Wiv I 4 26. *That I am a proper fellow of my hands*—2 H4 II 2 72.

HAND (vb.)

To handle, lay hands on: *We will not hand a rope more*—Tp I 1 25. *Let him that makes but trifles of his eyes First hand me*—Wint II 3 62. To put one's hand to, be occupied with (something): *When I was young And handed love as you do*—Wint IV 4 357.

HAND-FAST

(1) A contract (applied esp. to marriage): *To hold The hand-fast to her lord*—Cymb I 5 77.

(2) *In hand-fast*, in hold, under restraint: *If that shepherd be not in hand-fast, let him fly*—Wint IV 4 794.

HAND-IN-HAND

A hand-in-hand comparison, one in which the things compared are regarded as equal: *As fair and as good—a kind of hand-in-hand comparison*—Cymb I 4 75.

HANDKERCHER

A handkerchief: *Lend me a handkercher*—All's V 3 322. *I knit my handkercher about your brows*—John IV 1 42. *Scarfs and handkerchers*—Cor II 1 280.

HANDSAW

Prob. a corruption of Heronshaw, Heron: *I am but mad north-north-west: when the wind is southerly I know a hawk from a handsaw*—Hml II 2 396.

HANDSOME

Of language, apt, appropriate: *An honest method . . . by very much more handsome than fine, i.e.* aiming rather at aptness of expression than at ornament—Hml II 2 465.

HANDSOMELY

Conveniently, handily: *An if we miss to meet him handsomely*—Tit II 3 268.

HANDSOMENESS

Propriety, decency: *I will beat thee into handsomeness*—Troil II 1 16.

HANGER

The strap by which the sword was hung from the sword-belt: *Six French rapiers . . . with their assigns, as girdle, hangers, and so*—Hml V 2 156.

HANGMAN

An executioner in general: *The hangman's axe*—Merch IV 1 125. *As they had seen me with these hangman's (i.e.* bloody) *hands*—Mcb II 2 28.

HAPPILY

Haply, perchance: *Thy fortune . . . Might happily have proved far worse than his*—2 H6 III 1 305. *Which, happily, foreknowing may avoid*—Hml I 1 134.

HAPPY (adj.)

(1) Propitious, favourable: *Ports and happy havens*—R2 I 3 276. *The first and happiest hearers of the town*—H8 Prol 24. *And by the*

happy hollow of a tree Escaped the hunt—Lr II 3 2. Fortunate: *Disgraced me in my happy victories*—1 H4 IV 3 97. *Whether 'twas pride, Which . . . ever taints The happy man*—Cor IV 7 37.

(2) Well-endowed: *A happy gentleman in blood and lineaments*—R2 III 1 9.

HAPPY (vb.)

To make happy: *Which happies those that pay the willing loan*—Sonn 6 6.

HARBINGER

One sent on before to purvey lodgings for a royal train: *I'll be myself the harbinger*—Mcb I 4 45.

HARD

With an uneasy, wearisome movement: *[Time] trots hard with a young maid between the contract of her marriage and the day it is solemnized*—As III 2 331. See *Trot* (vb.).

HARDIMENT

(1) A deed of daring: *Like hardiment Posthumus hath To Cymbeline perform'd*—Cymb V 4 75. Changing hardiment, exchanging hard blows: *He did confound the best part of an hour In changing hardiment with great Glendower*—1 H4 I 3 100.

(2) Boldness: *Thus popp'd Paris in his hardiment*—Troil IV 5 28.

HARDINESS

Boldness, daring: *Let . . . our nation lose The name of hardiness*—H5 I 2 219. *Hardness ever Of hardiness is mother*—Cymb III 6 21.

HARDLY

Not easily, with difficulty: *These oracles are hardly attain'd, And hardly understood*—2 H6 I 4 74. *I was hardly moved to come to thee*—Cor V 2 78. *You shall see How hardly I was drawn into this war*—Ant V 1 73.

HARDNESS

Hardship, privation: *I do agnize A natural and prompt alacrity I find in hardness*—Oth I 3 232. *Hardness ever Of hardiness is mother*—Cymb III 6 21.

HARD-RULED

Hard to be ruled, difficult to manage: *Our hard-ruled king*—H8 III 2 101.

HARLOT

Applied to men of loose life as well as to women: *While she with harlots feasted in my house*—Err V 205. As adj.: *The harlot king*—Wint II 3 4.

HARLOTRY

(1) A harlot: *He sups to-night with a harlotry*—Oth IV 2 239.

10

(2) Without any connotation of lewdness, a hussy, baggage: *She is desperate here; a peevish self-will'd harlotry*—1 H4 III 1 198 (by Glendower of his daughter). *A peevish self-will'd harlotry it is*—Rom IV 2 14 (by Capulet of Juliet).

(3) In 1 H4 II 4 436 (*He doth it as like one of these harlotry players as ever I see!*) as adj., perh., ribald, profligate; but Mistress Quickly's language does not lend itself to exact definition.

HARP

To give voice to, to guess: *Thou hast harp'd my fear aright*—Mcb IV 1 74.

HARRY TEN SHILLINGS

Here's four Harry ten shillings in French crowns for you—2 H4 III 2 236. No pieces of this value appear to have been coined before the reign of Henry VII.

HATCH (sb.)

In pl., the deck of a ship: *I stood upon the hatches in the storm*—2 H6 III 2 103. *Who from my cabin tempted me to walk Upon the hatches*—R3 I 4 12. *Under hatches*, below deck: *The mariners all under hatches stow'd*—Tp I 2 230. So *beneath the hatches*: *We have a chest beneath the hatches*—Per III 1 71.

HATCH (vb.)¹

To close (a door): *'Twere not amiss to keep our door hatched*—Per IV 2 36.

HATCH (vb.)²

To lay strips of gold or silver on (a surface) by way of ornament; so perh. fig. in Troil I 3 65 (*Venerable Nestor, hatch'd in silver*) of Nestor decked with silver hair.

HATEFUL

Full of hate, malignant: *Little office The hateful commons will perform for us*—R2 II 2 137. *Hide thee from their hateful looks*—2 H6 II 4 23. *The most despiteful gentle greeting, The noblest hateful love*—Troil IV 1 32.

HATEFULLY

Malignantly: *Hatefully at random dost thou hit*—Ven 940.

HAUGHT

Haughty: *Thou haught insulting man*—R2 IV 254. *The haught Northumberland*—3 H6 II 1 169. *The queen's sons and brothers [are] haught and proud*—R3 II 3 28.

HAUGHTY

Lofty, aspiring, high-spirited: *This haughty great attempt*—1 H6 II 5 79. *Whose humble means match not his haughty mind*—R3 IV 2 37. Of words: *These haughty words of hers*—1 H6 III 3 78.

HAUNT

Frequenting, resort: *This our life exempt from public haunt*—As II 1 15. [Who] *Should have kept short, restrain'd and out of haunt, This mad young man*—Hml IV 1 18. *Dido and her Æneas shall want troops, And all the haunt be ours*—Ant IV 14 53.

HAVE

(1) To go; in imperative (app. 1st pers. pl., but gen. sing. in sense), announcing the speaker's intention to go somewhere; *have after, through, to, with*: Mar. *Let's follow* . . . Hor. *Have after*—Hml I 4 88. *Have through the very middest of you!*—2 H6 IV 8 63. *Have to my widow!*—Shr IV 5 78. Cel. *Will you go, coz?* Ros. *Have with you*—As I 2 267. To attack a person, commence a subject, set to something; *have at, to*: *Have at you, then, affection's men at arms. Consider* . . .—LLL IV 3 290. *And therefore, Peter, have at thee with a downright blow!*—2 H6 II 3 92. *Have at it then, by leave*—Cymb V 5 315. *And then have to't afresh*—Shr I 1 143. Cf. *I'll venture one have-at-him*—H8 II 2 85.

(2) In drinking, *have to*, here's to: *Ha' to thee, lad!* [Drinks to Hortensio—Shr V 2 37.

HAVING

(1) Possessions, property: *The gentleman is of no having*—Wiv III 2 73. *My having is not much*—Tw III 4 379. *Our content Is our best having*—H8 II 3 22.

(2) Personal endowment or qualities: *Man, how dearly ever parted, How much in having, or without or in, Cannot* . . .—Troil III 3 96. A personal quality: *Whose rarest havings made the blossoms dote*—Compl 235.

HAVIOUR

Behaviour: *The lusty haviour of his son*—R2 I 3 77. *Thou mayst think my haviour light*—Rom II 2 99. *Put thyself Into a haviour of less fear*—Cymb III 4 8.

HAVOC (sb.)

To cry havoc, to give the signal for indiscriminate slaughter (orig. for plunder): *Cry, 'havoc!' kings; back to the stained field*—John I 357. *Cry 'Havoc', and let slip the dogs of war*—Cæs III 1 273. *This quarry cries on havoc*, exclaims against the slaughter; or perh. rather, cries 'havoc' (see *Cry* (vb.) (5) and (6))—Hml V 2 375.

HAVOC (vb.)

To make havoc of, destroy; *To tear and havoc more than she can eat*—H5 I 2 173.

HAWKING

Hawk-like, keen: *His hawking eye*—All's I 1 105.

HAY

A country dance with a winding movement: *Let them dance the hay*—LLL V 1 161.

HAZARD

(1) That which is risked: *I do not doubt . . . to . . . bring your latter hazard back again*—Merch I 1 149.

(2) In tennis, the side of the court into which the ball is served: *We will . . . play a set Shall strike his father's crown into the hazard*—H5 I 2 262.

HAZARDED

App., risked (and lost): *Of thee craves The circle of the Ptolemies for her heirs, Now hazarded to thy grace*—Ant III 12 17.

HE

As sb.: *The proudest he That stops my way in Padua*—Shr III 2 236. *The proudest he that holds up Lancaster*—3 H6 I 1 46. *Now let me see the proudest He, that dares most, but wag his finger at thee*—H8 V 3 130. *Mantua's law Is death to any he that utters them*—Rom V 1 66.

HEAD (sb.)

(1) An armed force: *A mighty and a fearful head they are*—1 H4 III 2 167. *A head Of gallant warriors*—IV 4 25. *Young Laertes, in a riotous head, O'erbears your officers*—Hml IV 5 101.

(2) *To make a head*, to raise a force: *If we without his help can make a head*—1 H4 IV 1 80. *When Tarquin made a head for (i.e. against) Rome*—Cor II 2 92. So *to gather head: The French have gather'd head*—1 H6 I 4 100. *To raise head: Who first raised head against usurping Richard*—H8 II 1 108.

(3) *To draw to head*, to collect into a body, bring together: *The powers that he already hath in Gallia Will soon be drawn to head*—Cymb III 5 24. So *to assemble in head: The act For which we have in head assembled them*—H5 II 2 17.

HEAD (vb.)

To behead (a person): *Heading and hanging*—Meas II 1 250.

HEADLAND

A strip left in ploughing at the end of the furrows and sometimes round the whole field, ploughed (and sown) after the rest: *Shall we sow the headland with wheat?*—2 H4 V 1 15.

HEALTH

(1) Wellbeing, welfare, safety: *We have been praying for our husbands' healths*—Merch V 114. *Have mind upon your health, tempt me no farther*—Cæs IV 3 36. *The safety and health of this whole state*—Hml I 3 21. *Importing Denmark's health*—V 2 21. Eternal wellbeing: *Be thou a*

spirit of health (i.e. one in a state of salvation) *or goblin damn'd*—Hml I 4 40.

(2) *To the state's best health*, app., to the extent of its utmost ability: *The senators.—Of whom, even to the state's best health, I have Deserved this hearing (i.e.* the granting of this request)—Tim II 2 205.

HEAP

(1) A crowd, cluster: *Amongst this princely heap*—R3 II 1 53.

(2) *On heaps*, in crowds: *Let us on heaps go offer up our lives*—H5 IV 5 18. *As doth a battle, when they charge on heaps The enemy flying*—Troil III 2 29. *Upon a heap*, in a cluster: *There were drawn Upon a heap a hundred ghastly women*—Cæs I 3 22.

HEARKEN

(1) To give ear to: *Hearkens my brother's suit*—Tp I 2 122.

(2) *To hearken after*, to enquire about: *Hearken after their offence*—Ado V 1 216. *He hearkens after prophecies and dreams*—R3 I 1 54.

(3) *To hearken for*, to hanker after, to wait for eagerly: *The youngest daughter whom you hearken for*—Shr I 2 260 (cf. *Old Gremio is hearkening still*—IV 4 53). *They did me too much injury That ever said I hearken'd for your death*—1 H4 V 4 51. So perh. *hearken at*, to await: *Well, hearken at the end*—2 H4 II 4 303.

HEARSE (sb.)

A bier; a coffin: *All the tears that should bedew my hearse*—2 H4 IV 5 114. *Your laments, Wherewith you now bedew King Henry's hearse*—1 H6 I 1 103. *If honour may be shrouded in a hearse*—R3 I 2 2. *Stand from the hearse, stand from the body*—Cæs III 2 169.

HEARSE (vb.)

(1) To lay on a bier or in a coffin: *Would she were hearsed at my foot, and the ducats in her coffin!*—Merch III 1 93. *Thy canonized bones, hearsed in death*—Hml I 4 47.

(2) To enclose as in a tomb: *Thy sea within a puddle's womb is hearsed*—Lucr 657.

HEARTED

Established in the heart: *My cause is hearted*—Oth I 3 373. *Yield up, O love, thy crown and hearted throne*—III 3 448.

HEART-OFFENDING

Harming or paining the heart: *Heart-offending groans*—2 H6 III 2 60.

HEAT (sb.)

The element itself, till seven years' heat, Shall not behold her face—Tw I 1 26, till after the race or course, or till after the heat or hot seasons of seven years (shall have passed); or, with the orig.

reading *year(e)s*, till heated through seven years. (For *heat* = heated cf. *The iron of itself, though heat red-hot*—John IV 1 61.)

HEAT (vb.)
To run over as in a race: *Ere With spur we heat an acre*—Wint I 2 95.

HEAVILY
Sadly, sorrowfully: *Help us to sigh and groan, Heavily, heavily*—Ado V 3 17. *Ye cannot reason almost with a man That looks not heavily and full of fear*—R3 II 3 39. *Heavily from woe to woe [I can] tell o'er The sad account of fore-bemoaned moan*—Sonn 30 10.

HEAVINESS
Sadness, grief: *Let us not burthen our remembrance with A heaviness that's gone*—Tp V 199. *The tender boy . . . Doth weep to see his grandsire's heaviness*—Tit III 2 48. *To-night she is mew'd up to her heaviness*—Rom III 4 11.

HEBENON
Identified variously, and quite uncertainly, with ebony (which does not appear to be poisonous), henbane, and yew: *With juice of cursed hebenon in a vial*—Hml I 5 62.

HEDGE
To hedge out, to exclude; hence, app., to put off: *Nay, this shall not hedge us out*—Troil III 1 65.

HEDGE-PIG
A hedgehog: *Thrice and once the hedge-pig whined*—Mcb IV 1 2.

HEED
That which one heeds: *That eye shall be his heed*—LLL I 1 82.

HEFT
A heave, strain: *He cracks his gorge, his sides, With violent hefts*—Wint II 1 44.

HEIR
(1) An heiress: *To steal away a lady, An heir*—Gent IV 1 48. *The heir and daughter of Lord Scales*—3 H6 IV 1 52.

(2) That which is begotten, offspring: *Thou art the midwife to my woe, And Bolingbroke my sorrow's dismal heir*—R2 II 2 62. *Unfather'd heirs and loathly births of nature*—2 H4 IV 4 122. *The first heir of my invention*—Ven Ded 4.

HELL
A cant name for a debtors' prison: *One that before the judgement carries poor souls to hell*—Err IV 2 40.

HELL-HATED
Hated as hell: *The hell-hated lie*—Lr V 3 147.

HELP (sb.)
(1) Auxiliary troops: *If the help of Norfolk and myself . . . Will but amount to five and twenty thousand*—3 H6 II 1 178.

(2) Remedy, tendance: *Let him be brought forth and borne hence for help*—Err V 160. *My gashes cry for help*—Mcb I 2 42. *Poor helpless help, the treasure stol'n away, To burn the guiltless casket where it lay!*—Lucr 1056. Cure: *[The wound] being green, there is great hope of help*—2 H6 III 1 287.

(3) *At help*, of the wind, in a favourable quarter: *The bark is ready, and the wind at help*—Hml IV 3 46.

HELP (vb.)
(1) To benefit, profit: *Though what they (i.e. words) do impart Help not at all, yet do they ease the heart*—R3 IV 4 130. *It will help me nothing To plead mine innocence*—H8 I 1 207.

(2) To cure, relieve: *I will help his ague*—Tp II 2 97. *To help him of his blindness*—Gent IV 2 47. *He that helps him take all my outward worth*—Lr IV 4 10.

HELPLESS
(1) Affording no help or remedy, unavailing: *Urging helpless patience*—Err II 1 39. *The helpless balm of my poor eyes*—R3 I 2 13. *As those poor birds that helpless berries saw*—Ven 604. *Poor helpless help*—Lucr 1056.

(2) Admitting no remedy: *[My eyes will] grave . . . Upon my cheeks what helpless shame I feel*—Lucr 755.

HENCHMAN
A page of honour: *I do but beg a little changeling boy, To be my henchman*—Mids II 1 120.

HENT (sb.)
A clutch, grasp; or perh., an intention, design: *Up, sword; and know thou a more horrid hent*—Hml III 3 88. Or, as the word occurs as a form of Hint, possibly it should be taken in the sense given under that word.

HENT (vb.)
(1) To lay hold of, grasp: *Merrily hent the stile-a*—Wint IV 3 133.

(2) To reach, arrive at: *The . . . citizens Have hent the gates*—Meas IV 6 13.

HERB-GRACE, HERB OF GRACE
Rue: *We may call it herb-grace o' Sundays*—Hml IV 5 182. *The sweet-marjoram of the salad, or rather, the herb of grace*—All's IV 5 17.

HERE
They are here with me, they are at me: *They're here with me already*—Wint I 2 217. *Here be with them, go at them*—Cor III 2 74.

HEREBY

Close by: Prin. . . . *Where is the bush That we must stand . . . in?* For. *Hereby, upon the edge of yonder coppice*—LLL IV 1 7. Also I 2 140 (Arm. *I will visit thee at the lodge.* Jaq. *That's hereby.* Arm. *I know where it is situate*) as Arm. takes it. Jaq. seems to mean, that's as it may happen.

HERE-REMAIN

See *Remain* (sb.)².

HERETO

Hitherto: *If he remember A kinder value of the people than He hath hereto prized them at*—Cor II 2 62.

HERMIT

Equivalent to *Beadsman* (2): *Begging hermits in their holy prayers*—Tit III 2 41. For . . . *the late dignities . . . We rest your hermits*—Mcb 1 6 18.

HEROD

It out-herods Herod—Hml III 2 15. Herod appeared in the Miracle Plays as a swaggering uproarious tyrant. Cf. *What a Herod of Jewry is this!*—Wiv II 1 20.

HEST

(1) A bidding, injunction: *Refusing her grand hests*—Tp I 2 274. *I have broke your hest to say so*—III 1 37. [How I would make him] *shape his service wholly to my hests!*—LLL V 2 65.

(2) A determination, resolve: *Such as we see when men restrain their breath On some great sudden hest*—1 H4 II 3 64.

HIDE FOX, AND ALL AFTER

Hide and seek; as an exclamation: Hml IV 2 32.

HIGH AND LOW

False dice loaded to throw high and low respectively: *High and low beguiles the rich and poor*—Wiv I 3 95.

HIGH-BATTLED

At the head of a great host: *High-battled Cæsar*—Ant III 13 29.

HIGH-LONE

Quite alône, without support: *Then she could stand high-lone*—Rom I 3 36 (the reading of the first two Quartos).

HIGHMOST

Highest: *Now is the sun upon the highmost hill Of this day's journey*—Rom II 5 9. *When from highmost pitch . . . he* (i.e. the sun) *reeleth from the day*—Sonn 7 9.

HIGH-SIGHTED

Having the sight directed aloft, supercilious: *High-sighted tyranny*—Cæs II 1 118.

HIGH-STOMACHED

Hot, impetuous: *High-stomach'd are they both, and full of ire*—R2 I 1 18.

HIGHT

To call oneself, be called: *This child of fancy that Armado hight*—LLL I 1 171. *This grisly beast, which Lion hight by name*—Mids V 140. *This maid Hight Philoten*—Per IV Prol 17.

HIGH-WITTED

Equivalent to *Witty* (2): *High-witted Tamora*—Tit IV 4 35.

HILD

Pa. pple. of To hold: *Let it not be hild Poor women's faults*—Lucr 1257.

HILDING (adj.)

Base, contemptible: *Some hilding fellow*—2 H4 I 1 57. *To purge this field of such a hilding foe*—H5 IV 2 29.

HILDING (sb.)

A good-for-nothing; applied to both sexes: *If your lordship find him not a hilding*—All's III 6 3. *Helen and Hero hildings and harlots*—Rom II 4 44. *A hilding for a livery*—Cymb II 3 128.

HILT

In pl. in the sense of the sing.: *Seven, by these hilts*—1 H4 II 4 229. *I'll run him up to the hilts*—H5 II 1 68. *Take thou the hilts*—Cæs V 3 43.

HINT

An occasion, an opportunity: *It is a hint That wrings mine eyes to't*—Tp I 2 134. *Our hint of woe Is common*—II 1 3. *When the best hint was given him, he not took't*—Ant III 4 9.

HIPPED

Apparently covered on the hips: *His horse hipped with an old mothy saddle*—Shr III 2 49.

HIREN

Have we not Hiren here?—2 H4 II 4 173 189, prob. from a lost play by Peele, *The Turkish Mahomet and Hiren* [Irene] *the Fair Greek.*

HISTORY (sb.)

A story represented dramatically, a drama: *Your honour's players . . . Are come to play a pleasant comedy . . . a kind of history*—Shr Ind 2 131. *Last scene of all, That ends this strange eventful history*—As II 7 163. *An index and obscure prologue to the history of lust*—Oth II 1 263.

HISTORY (vb.)

To record, narrate: *That may repeat and history his loss*—2 H4 IV 1 203.

HITHERTO

To this point (in space): *England, from Trent and Severn hitherto . . . is to my part assign'd*—1 H4 III 1 74.

HIVE

A head-covering of platted straw: *Upon her head a platted hive of straw*—Compl 8.

HOAR (adj.)

(1) Mouldy, musty: *Something stale and hoar*—Rom II 4 139.

(2) *Hoar leprosy*, white leprosy, elephantiasis: *Make the hoar leprosy adored*—Tim IV 3 35.

HOAR (vb.)

(1) To become mouldy: *When it hoars ere it be spent*—Rom II 4 146.

(2) To smite with hoar leprosy (see *Hoar* (adj.) (2)): *Hoar the flamen*—Tim IV 3 155.

HOBBY-HORSE

In the morris-dance, &c., the figure of a horse fastened about the waist of a performer; used as a term of disparagement: *Eight or nine wise words . . . which these hobby-horses must not hear*—Ado III 2 74. *Then say My wife's a hobby-horse*— —Wint I 2 275. '*The hobby-horse is forgot*', app. a phrase from an old ballad—LLL III 30; Hml III 2 144.

HOB, NOB

Have or have not; app., give or take: *Hob, nob, is his word; give't or take't*—Tw III 4 262.

HODGE-PUDDING

A pudding made of a medley of ingredients; applied to Falstaff: *What, a hodge-pudding? a bag of flax?*—Wiv V 5 159.

HOISE

To hoist, heave, raise aloft: *We'll quickly hoise Duke Humphrey from his seat*—2 H6 I 1 169. *He, mistrusting them, Hoised sail*—R3 IV 4 528. Past tense and pple. hoist: *There they hoist us*—Tp I 2 148. '*Tis the sport to have the enginer Hoist with his own petar*—Hml III 4 206.

HOLD

(1) To sustain, endure: *The ripest mulberry That will not hold the handling*—Cor III 2 79. *Many pocky corses . . . that will scarce hold the laying in*—Hml V 1 181. So *to hold out*: *Happy he whose cloak and cincture can Hold out this tempest*—John IV 3 155. *He cannot long hold out these pangs*—2 H4 IV 4 117.

(2) To keep unbroken, abide by: *You yet shall hold your word*—Wiv V 5 258.

(3) To wager, lay: *I'll hold thee any wager*—Merch III 4 62. *I hold you a penny*—Shr III 2 85.

(4) *To hold in*, to stand one's ground; or perh., to keep counsel: *I am joined with no foot landrakers, no . . . but with . . . such as can hold in*—1 H4 II 1 81.

(5) *Hold or cut bow-strings*, a phrase not satisfactorily explained, app. meaning whatever happens: Quin. *At the duke's oak we meet.* Bot. *Enough; hold or cut bow-strings*—Mids I 2 113.

HOLDING

(1) Consistency: *This has no holding*—All's IV 2 27.

(2) The burden of a song: *The holding every man shall bear as loud As his strong sides can volley*—Ant II 7 117.

HOLIDAME

See *Halidom.*

HOLP

Past tense and pple. of To help: *Sir Robert never holp to make this leg*—John I 240. *Blessedly [were we] holp hither*—Tp I 2 63.

HOLY-ALE

A church-ale, a periodical festive gathering held in connection with a church: *It hath been sung at festivals, On ember-eves and holy-ales*—Per Prol 5.

HOLY-ROOD DAY

Holy Cross day, Sept. 14th: *On Holy-rood day, the gallant Hotspur there, Young Harry Percy and brave Archibald . . . At Holmedon met*—1 H4 I 1 52.

HONEST

(1) Used of good and honourable character and conduct in general: *Once again I do receive thee honest*—Gent V 4 78. *Honest in nothing but in his clothes*—Meas V 263. *He only, in a general honest thought And common good to all, made one of them*—Cæs V 5 71.

(2) Chaste, virtuous: *Though she appear honest to me, yet . . .*—Wiv II 2 230. *Those that she makes fair she scarce makes honest*—As I 2 40. *I think my wife be honest and think she is not*—Oth III 3 384. *Honest slanders*, not affecting one's good name: *I'll devise some honest slanders To stain my cousin with*—Ado III 1 84.

HONESTY

(1) Used of good and honourable character and conduct in general: *He is of a noble strain, of approved valour and confirmed honesty*—Ado II 1 394. *A father . . . whose skill was almost as great as his honesty*—All's I 1 19. *Here's ado, To lock up honesty and honour from The access of gentle visitors!*—Wint II 2 9.

(2) Decency, decorum: *Have you no wit, manners, nor honesty?*—Tw II 3 94. *I hold it not honesty to have it thus set down*—Hml II 2 204.

(3) Chastity: *To lay an amiable siege to the honesty of this Ford's wife* — Wiv II 2 243. *Honesty coupled to beauty*—As III 3 30. *Could beauty, my lord, have better commerce than with honesty?*—Hml III 1 109.

(4) Liberality, hospitality: *Every man has his fault, and honesty is his*—Tim III 1 29.

HONEY-STALKS

The stalks of clover: *More sweet, and yet more dangerous, Than . . . honey-stalks to sheep*—Tit IV 4 90.

HONOUR

To do honour to (by some outward action), to worship: *Divinest creature . . . How shall I honour thee for this success?*—1 H6 I 6 4. *Gods above, Who freely give to every one that comes To honour them*—Per II 3 59. *Till I have honoured you with some graver labour*—Ven Dedic 4.

HONOURABLE

Decent, becoming: *Chides the dice In honourable terms*—LLL V 2 326. *Tell him from me . . . He bear himself with honourable action*—Shr Ind I 109.

HONOURABLY

Decently, becomingly: *Speaking honourably*—Ado III 4 29. *Do this message honourably*—Tit IV 4 104.

HONOURED

To be honoured, honourable: *A custom More honour'd in the breach than the observance*—Hml I 4 15. *In honour'd love*—Lr V 1 9. [Whilst they] *kiss The honour'd gashes whole*—Ant IV 8 10. Stately: *He comes To an honour'd triumph strangely furnished*—Per II 2 52.

HONOUR-OWING

Possessing honour, honourable: *His honour-owing wounds*—H5 IV 6 9. Cf. *Owe* (1).

HOOD

In falconry, to cover the hawk till flown to prevent her from bating (see *Bate* (vb.)²): *'Tis a hooded valour; and when it appears, it will bate*—H5 III 7 121. *Hood my unmann'd blood, bating in my cheeks*—Rom III 2 14.

HOODMAN

The blindfolded player in *Hoodman-blind* (q.v.): *Hoodman comes!*—All's IV 3 136.

HOODMAN-BLIND

Blindman's buff: *What devil was't That thus hath cozen'd you at hoodman-blind?*—Hml III 4 76.

HOODWINK

Fig., to cover up from sight, make as nothing: *The prize I'll bring thee to Shall hoodwink this mischance*—Tp IV 205.

HOOP

Whoop: *That admiration did not hoop at them*—H5 II 2 108. (So later issues of the Globe, following the Folios. The first issue has the conjecture *whoop*.) *Out of all hooping*, beyond the power of any exclamations of surprise to do the matter justice: *Wonderful and . . . out of all hooping!*—As III 2 202.

HOOT

To shout in wonder or applause: *The people fall a-hooting*—LLL IV 2 61. *The rabblement hooted and clapped their chopped hands*—Cæs I 2 245.

HOPE (sb.)

Expectation (without implication of desire): *By how much better than my word I am, By so much shall I falsify men's hopes*—1 H4 I 2 233. *The griefs are ended By seeing the worst, which late on hopes depended*—Oth I 3 202.

HOPE (vb.)

To expect (without implication of desire): *Some of them (i.e.* the stars on his friend's armour) *will fall to-morrow, I hope*—H5 III 7 77. *I cannot hope Cæsar and Antony shall well greet together*—Ant II 1 38 (said by an enemy).

HORN (sb.)

A horned animal, a deer: *My lady goes to kill horns*—LLL IV 1 113.

HORN (vb.)

To 'give horns to', cuckold: *'Tis thought you have a goodly gift in horning*—Tit II 3 67.

HORN-BOOK

A sheet of paper containing the alphabet, &c., protected by a plate of transparent horn: *He teaches boys the horn-book*—LLL V 1 49.

HORN-MAD

Stark mad (orig. of horned beasts, ready to horn any one): *If he had found the young man, he would have been horn-mad*—Wiv I 4 50. By wordplay, mad with rage at having been made a cuckold: *If I have horns to make one mad, let the proverb go with me; I'll be horn-mad*—Wiv III 5 153. *If this should ever happen (i.e.* if you should ever be married), *thou wouldst be horn-mad*—Ado I 1 271. Illustrating both senses: *Sure my master is horn-mad . . . I mean not cuckold-mad; But, sure, he is stark mad*—Err II 1 57.

HOSE

Breeches; pl.: Fal. *Their points being broken,*—Poins. *Down fell their hose*—1 H4 II 4 238.

Sing.: *A silken doublet! a velvet hose! a scarlet cloak!*—Shr V 1 68.   *Round hose,* breeches swelling out round the hips: *A round hose, madam, now's not worth a pin*—Gent II 7 55.   *I think he bought . . . his round hose in France*—Merch I 2 79.   See also *Doublet and Hose.*

HOSPITABLE

Belonging to a host: *I am your host: With robbers' hands my hospitable favours You should not ruffle thus*—Lr III 7 39.

HOST (sb.)

An inn; *to lie at host,* to lie in an inn: *Your goods that lay at host, sir, in the Centaur*—Err V 410.

HOST (vb.)

To be a guest; to lodge, put up: *Go bear it to the Centaur, where we host*—Err I 2 9.   *I will bring you Where you shall host*—All's III 5 96.

HOT-HOUSE

A bathing-house with hot baths, a bagnio: *Now she professes a hot-house, which, I think, is a very ill house too*—Meas II 1 66.

HOURLY

App., marking the hours: *The hourly dial*—Lucr 327.

HOUSE (sb.)

A gentleman of the very first house, perh., a scholar of the most famous fencing school: *A duellist; a gentleman of the very first house*—Rom II 4 24.

HOUSE (vb.)

To drive or pursue into a house: *Even now we housed him in the abbey here*—Err V 188.

HOUSEKEEPER

(1) One who stays indoors: *You are manifest house-keepers*—Cor I 3 54.

(2) A watch-dog: *The valued file Distinguishes the swift . . . The housekeeper, the hunter . . .*—Mcb III 1 95.

(3) *A good housekeeper,* one who keeps a good house: *An honest man and a good housekeeper*—Tw IV 2 10.

HOUSEKEEPING

The keeping of a hospitable house, hospitality: *I hear your grace hath sworn out house-keeping*—LLL II 104.   *Thy deeds, thy plainness and thy housekeeping, Hath won the greatest favour of the commons*—2 H6 I 1 191.

HOUSEWIFE, HUSWIFE

A hussy, baggage, drab: *The overscutched huswives*—2 H4 III 2 340.   *Doth fortune play the huswife with me now?*—H5 V 1 85.   *Let me rail so high, That the false housewife Fortune break her wheel*—Ant IV 15 43.

HOWEVER

(1) However much, although: *This challenge . . . However it is spread in general name, Relates in purpose only to Achilles*—Troil I 3 321.   *So is he now . . . however he puts on this tardy form*—Cæs I 2 301.   *Howe'er thou art a fiend, A woman's shape doth shield thee*—Lr IV 2 66.

(2) In any case, at any rate: *However, but a folly bought with wit*—Gent I 1 34.   *Howe'er, I charge thee . . . To tell me truly*—All's I 3 189.

HOWLET

An owl: *Lizard's leg and howlet's wing*—Mcb IV 1 17.

HOWSOEVER

(1) However much, although: *The man doth fear God, howsoever it seems not in him*—Ado II 3 204.   *You love him not so ill . . . howsoever you speak this*—H5 IV 1 129.   *Howsoever you have been his liar . . . you cannot pass*—Cor V 2 32.

(2) In any case, at any rate: *But, howsoever, strange and admirable*—Mids V 27.   *Howsoever, he shall pay for me ere he has me*—Troil III 3 297.   *Howsoe'er, My brother hath done well*—Cymb IV 2 146.

HOX

To hough, hamstring: *Thou art a coward, Which hoxes honesty behind*—Wint I 2 243.

HUE

Form, aspect: *A man in hue, all 'hues' in his controlling*—Sonn 20 7.   *Hues* is often printed between inverted commas on the supposition that a proper name (perh. *Hugh, Hews* or *Hughes*) is meant to be suggested.

HUG

To lie close, cuddle: *To hug with swine*—John V 2 142.

HULK

A large ship of burden or transport: *You have not seen a hulk better stuffed in the hold*—2 H4 II 4 69.   *Like as rigour of tempestuous gusts Provokes the mightiest hulk against the tide*—1 H6 V 5 5.   *Light boats sail swift, though greater hulks draw deep*—Troil II 3 277.

HULL

To lie a-hull, lie to: *I am to hull here a little longer*—Tw I 5 217.   *There they hull, expecting but the aid Of Buckingham*—R3 IV 4 438.   To float, drift: *Thus hulling in The wild sea of my conscience*—H8 II 4 199.

HUMAN, HUMANE

(1) Gentle, friendly, courteous: *Lie further off, in human modesty, Such separation as . . . Becomes*

a virtuous bachelor and a maid—Mids II 2 57. *In humane gentleness, Welcome to Troy!*—Troil IV 1 20. *The mere form of civil and humane seeming*—Oth II 1 243. *Humane principle*, principle of good breeding: *If I had a thousand sons, the first humane principle I would teach them should be . . .*—2 H4 IV 3 132.

(2) *Human* in the sense in which the word is now spelt humane: *I have used thee . . . with human care*—Tp I 2 345. *Touch'd with human gentleness and love*—Merch IV 1 25. *The milk of human kindness*—Mcb I 5 18.

HUMBLE

App., courteous: *This is not generous, not gentle, not humble*—LLL V 2 632.

HUMOROUS

(1) Moist, humid: *He hath hid himself . . . To be consorted with the humorous night*—Rom II 1 30 (with a play on sense (2)).

(2) Subject to, influenced by, or dependent on humour or mood, whimsical, capricious, humoursome: *A humorous sigh*—LLL III 177. *Her humorous ladyship*—John III 1 119 (of Fortune). *'Tis no marvel he (i.e.* the devil) *is so humorous*—1 H4 III 1 234. *As humorous as winter*—2 H4 IV 4 34. *A vain, giddy, shallow, humorous youth*—H5 II 4 28. *I am known to be a humorous patrician*—Cor II 1 51.

(3) Moody, ill-tempered: *The duke is humorous*—As I 2 278. *The humorous duke*—II 3 8.

(4) Displaying humours (in sense (4) below); of an actor, taking 'character' parts: *The humorous man shall end his part in peace*—Hml II 2 335. So perh. in As IV 1 10 (*I have neither the scholar's melancholy . . . nor the musician's . . . nor the . . . but it is a melancholy of mine own . . . the sundry contemplation of my travels, in which my often rumination wraps me in a most humorous sadness*), proper to one's 'humour', characteristic, individual.

HUMOUR

(1) Moisture, vapour: *The humours Of the dank morning*—Cæs II 1 262.

(2) A morbid fluid of an animal: D. Pedro. *What! sigh for the toothache?* Leon. *Where is but a humour or a worm*—Ado III 2 26. *That trunk of humours*—1 H4 II 4 495. *Through all thy veins shall run A cold and drowsy humour*—Rom IV 1 95.

(3) One of the four 'cardinal humours', the combination of which in varying proportions was supposed to determine one's nature: *black-oppressing humour*, of melancholy: *Besieged with sable-coloured melancholy, I did commend the black-oppressing humour to the most wholesome physic of thy health-giving air*—LLL I 1 233.

(4) Mood natural to one's temperament, habitual frame of mind (as in *Every Man in His Humour*), whence *Humorous* (4).

A prevailing abuse of this word is ridiculed in Nym's use of it. See his part in H5 and Wiv *passim*.

HUMPHREY HOUR

R3 IV 4 175. An unexplained expression.

'HUNDRED MERRY TALES', 'THE'

Of unknown authorship. First printed (so far as is known) in 1526: *That I had my good wit out of the 'Hundred Merry Tales'*—Ado II 1 134.

HUNGARIAN

Needy, beggarly (slang, with a play on Hungry): *O base Hungarian wight!*—Wiv I 3 23.

HUNGERLY (adj.)

Having a starved look, meagre: *His beard grew thin and hungerly*—Shr III 2 177.

HUNGERLY (adv.)

Hungrily, greedily: *I feed Most hungerly on your sight*—Tim I 1 261. *They eat us hungerly*—Oth III 4 105.

HUNGRY

Hungered for: *Their hungry prey*—1 H6 I 2 28.

HUNT

The game killed in the chase: *We'll go dress our hunt*—Cymb III 6 90.

HUNT'S-UP

A song or tune to awaken huntsmen; hence, one to rouse anyone: *Since arm from arm that voice (i.e.* the lark's) *doth us affray, Hunting thee hence with hunt's-up to the day*—Rom III 5 33.

HURRICANO

A waterspout (hardly to be distinguished from *Cataract*): *The dreadful spout Which shipmen do the hurricano call*—Troil V 2 171. *You cataracts and hurricanoes, spout*—Lr III 2 2.

HURRY

Commotion, tumult: *[The] quietness of the people, which before Were in wild hurry*—Cor IV 6 3.

HUSBAND (sb.)

(1) A husbandman: *This Davy . . . is your serving-man and your husband*—2 H4 V 3 11.

(2) The manager of a house, a housekeeper: *You will turn good husband now, Pompey; you will keep the house*—Meas III 2 73. In gen., *good husband, ill husband*, one who manages his house or affairs well or ill: *While I play the good husband at home, my son and my servant spend all at the university*—Shr V 1 70. *In that I deem you an ill husband*—H8 III 2 141.

HUSBAND (vb.)

(1) To cultivate: *Husbanded and tilled*—2 H4 IV 3 130.

(2) To manage, carry out: *Husband your device* —Wiv IV 6 52. *It will be pastime passing excellent, If it be husbanded with modesty*—Shr Ind 1 67.

HUSBANDRY

(1) Agricultural produce, crops: *All her husbandry doth lie on heaps*—H5 V 2 39.

(2) The management of a household: *I commit into your hands The husbandry and manage of my house*—Merch III 4 24. *If you suspect my husbandry*—Tim II 2 164. Management, administration, in gen.: *That he bears all things fairly, And shows good husbandry for the Volscian state*—Cor IV 7 21.

HUSWIFE

See *Housewife.*

HYEN

Hyena: *I will laugh like a hyen*—As IV 1 156.

HYSTERICA PASSIO

The scientific name for hysteria: *Hysterica passio, down, thou climbing sorrow!*—Lr II 4 57.

I

I

Aye, punning: *Say thou but 'I', And that bare vowel 'I' shall poison more Than the death-darting eye of cockatrice*—Rom III 2 45. The conceit is continued in 48–51.

ICELAND DOG

A shaggy, sharp-eared white dog: *Pish for thee, Iceland dog! thou prick-ear'd cur of Iceland!* —H5 II 1 44.

IDEA

(1) The mental image of something remembered: *The idea of her life shall sweetly creep Into his study of imagination*—Ado IV 1 226.

(2) A likeness, 'picture': *I did infer your lineaments, Being the right idea of your father*— R3 III 7 12.

IDLE

Light-headed, crazy. Prob. the word should be taken in this sense in Hml III 2 95 (*They are coming to the play; I must be idle*).

IDLE-HEADED

Foolish, silly: *The superstitious idle-headed eld* —Wiv IV 4 36.

IDLENESS

Folly, frivolity: [I] *will awhile uphold The unyoked humour of your idleness*—1 H4 I 2 218. *Apes of idleness*—2 H4 IV 5 123. *But that your royalty Holds idleness your subject, I should take you For idleness itself*—Ant I 3 91.

I' FECKS

See *Fecks.*

IGNOMY

Ignominy: *I blush to think upon this ignomy*— Tit IV 2 115.

IGNORANT

Used causatively: *The ignorant fumes that mantle Their clearer reason*—Tp V 67. *Imprison't not In ignorant concealment*—Wint I 2 396.

'ILD

See *Yield.*

ILL (adj.)

Of persons, morally evil, wicked: *The ill spirit* —Tp I 2 458. *His ill angel*—2 H4 I 2 186. *Ill spirit, I would hold more talk with thee*—Cæs IV 3 289. *Of his own body he was ill,* he was given to vicious indulgence of his passions—H8 IV 2 43.

ILL (sb.)

An evil deed, misdeed: *Be your eyes the witness of this ill*—R3 III 4 69. *I curse the day . . . Wherein I did not some notorious ill*—Tit V 1 125. *Our ills told us Is as our earing*—Ant I 2 114. *Under what colour he commits this ill*—Lucr 476.

ILL-ANNEXED

Added or joined for evil ends: *We have no good that we can say is ours, But ill-annexed Opportunity Or kills his life or else his quality*—Lucr 873.

ILL-ERECTED

Erected for evil ends, or with evil auspices: *Julius Cæsar's ill-erected tower*—R2 V 1 2.

ILL-INHABITED

Badly housed or lodged: *O knowledge ill-inhabited!*—As III 3 10.

ILLNESS

Unscrupulousness: [Thou] *Art not without ambition, but without The illness should attend it*— Mcb I 5 20.

ILL-TAKEN

Conceived without cause: *His ill-ta'en suspicion*—Wint I 2 460.

ILL-TEMPERED

Ill compounded, referring to the 'humours' (see *Humour* (3)): *When grief, and blood ill-temper'd, vexeth him*—Cæs IV 3 115.

ILLUSTRATE

Illustrious: [The] *most illustrate king Cophetua*—LLL IV 1 65. *This most gallant, illustrate, and learned gentleman*—V 1 128.

IMAGINARY

(1) Imaginative: *Foul imaginary eyes of blood Presented thee more hideous than thou art*—John IV 2 265. *Your imaginary forces*—H5 Prol 18. *My soul's imaginary sight*—Sonn 27 9.

(2) Of the nature of an image or representation: *Much imaginary work was there*—Lucr 1422.

(3) *Imaginary wiles*, wiles of the imagination: *Sure, these are but imaginary wiles*—Err IV 3 10.

IMAGINE

To devise, plot: *When I imagine ill Against my king*—2 H6 I 2 19.

IMAGINED

Imagined speed, wing, the speed, wing of imagination: *Bring them, I pray thee, with imagined speed*—Merch III 4 52. *Thus with imagined wing our swift scene flies*—H5 III Chor 1.

IMBAR

App., to bar in, secure: [They] *rather choose to hide them in a net Than amply to imbar their crooked titles*—H5 I 2 93.

IMBRUE, EMBREW

To stain; in pregnant sense (*with blood* understood): *Shall we have incision? shall we imbrue?*—2 H4 II 4 210. Of a weapon: *Come, blade, my breast imbrue*—Mids V 351. *Embrewed*, stained with blood: *Lord Bassianus lies embrewed here*—Tit II 3 222.

IMMANITY

Atrocious ferocity: *Such immanity and bloody strife*—1 H6 V 1 13.

IMMASK

To cover as with a mask, disguise: *To immask our noted outward garments*—1 H4 I 2 201.

IMMATERIAL

Flimsy, slight: *Thou idle immaterial skein of sleave-silk*—Troil V 1 35.

IMMEDIATELY

Expressly: *Our law Immediately provided in that case*—Mids I 1 44.

IMMOMENT

Of no moment, trivial: *Some lady trifles . . . Immoment toys*—Ant V 2 165.

IMMURE

A wall: *Troy, within whose strong immures The ravish'd Helen . . . sleeps*—Troil Prol 8.

IMP (sb.)

A child: *Why, sadness is one and the self-same thing, dear imp*—LLL I 2 4. *Great Hercules is presented by this imp*—V 2 592. *Most royal imp of fame!*—2 H4 V 5 46. *A lad of life, an imp of fame*—H5 IV 1 45.

IMP (vb.)

To engraft feathers in a hawk's wing so as to make good deficiencies: [If we shall] *Imp out our drooping country's broken wing*—R2 II 1 292.

IMPAIR

Prob., unsuitable, inappropriate: *Nor dignifies an impair thought with breath*—Troil IV 5 103. So later issues of the Globe following the Folios and the Quarto. The first issue has the conjecture *impure*.

IMPALE, EMPALE

To encircle, surround: *Until my mis-shaped trunk that bears this head Be round impaled with a glorious crown*—3 H6 III 2 170. *Empale him with your weapons round about*—Troil V 7 5.

IMPART

(1) With material object, to afford, supply: *This no slaughterhouse no tool imparteth*—Lucr 1039.

(2) *I impart toward you*, I impart myself, communicate whatever I can bestow: *With no less nobility of love Than that which dearest father bears his son, Do I impart toward you*—Hml I 2 110.

IMPEACH

An impeachment, accusation, calling in question: *What an intricate impeach is this!*—Err V 269. *Ten to one is no impeach of valour*—3 H6 I 4 60.

IMPEACHMENT

(1) Hindrance: [I] *could be willing to march on to Calais Without impeachment*—H5 III 6 150.

(2) Detriment: *Which would be great impeachment to his age, In having known no travel in his youth*—Gent I 3 15.

IMPERCEIVERANT

Undiscerning: *Yet this imperceiverant thing loves him in my despite*—Cymb IV 1 15.

IMPERIOUS

Imperial, majestic: *Most imperious Agamemnon*—Troil IV 5 172. *Imperious Cæsar*—Hml V 1 236. *Imperious supreme of all mortal things*—

Ven 996. Of animals and things: *An imperious lion*—Oth II 3 276. *The imperious seas*—Cymb IV 2 35.

IMPERIOUSLY

Majestically, proudly: *Imperiously he leaps, he neighs, he bounds*—Ven 265.

IMPLEACHED

Interwoven, entwined: *With twisted metal amorously impleach'd*—Compl 205.

IMPLORATOR

One who implores or supplicates: *Mere implorators of unholy suits*—Hml I 3 129.

IMPONE

To lay, wager: *The king, sir, hath wagered with him six Barbary horses; against the which he has imponed . . . six French rapiers*—Hml V 2 154. *Why is this 'imponed', as you call it?*—170.

IMPORT

Importance, moment: *Tell us, what occasion of import Hath all so long detain'd you from your wife?*—Shr III 2 104. *Some purpose of import*—Oth III 3 316.

IMPORTANCE

(1) An affair of consequence; with qualifying context, one of slight consequence: *It had been pity you should have been put together with so mortal a purpose . . . upon importance of so slight and trivial a nature*—Cymb I 4 43.

(2) Importunity, urgent request: *Maria writ The letter at Sir Toby's great importance*—Tw V 370. *At our importance hither is he come*—John II 7.

(3) Import, meaning: *The wisest beholder . . . could not say if the importance were joy or sorrow*—Wint V 2 18.

IMPORTANCY

Importance: *The importancy of Cyprus to the Turk*—Oth I 3 20.

IMPORTANT

Importunate, urgent: *If the prince be too important, tell him there is measure in every thing*—Ado II 1 73. *His important blood will nought deny That she'll demand*—All's III 7 21. *Great France My mourning and important tears hath pitied*—Lr IV 4 25.

IMPORTLESS

Signifying nothing: *Matter needless, of importless burden*—Troil I 3 71.

IMPORTUNE

To impel, give occasion: *We shall write to you, As time and our concernings shall importune*—Meas I 1 56.

IMPOSE (sb.)

Bidding, injunction: *According to your ladyship's impose*—Gent IV 3 8.

IMPOSE (vb.)

To subject (*to* a penalty): *Impose me to what penance your invention Can lay upon my sin*—Ado V 1 283.

IMPOSITION

(1) Imputation, accusation, charge: *Which else would stand under grievous imposition*—Meas I 2 193. *The imposition clear'd Hereditary ours*—Wint I 2 74.

(2) A charge or ordinance imposed upon one: *Your father's imposition depending on the caskets*—Merch I 2 114. *I do desire you Not to deny this imposition*—III 4 32. *Let death and honesty Go with your impositions, I am yours*—All's IV 4 28.

IMPOSSIBLE

Incredible: *His gift is in devising impossible slanders*—Ado II 1 143. *Huddling jest upon jest with such impossible conveyance upon me that . . .*—252. *Such impossible passages of grossness*—Tw III 2 76.

IMPRESE

A device, emblem: [Whilst you have] *From my own windows torn my household coat, Razed out my imprese*—R2 III 1 24.

IMPRESSURE

An impression: *The cicatrice and capable impressure*—As III 5 23. *The impressure her Lucrece, with which she uses to seal*—Tw II 5 103.

IMPUDENT

Wanting in shame or modesty, shameless, unblushing: *If you could find out a country where but women were that had received so much shame, you might begin an impudent nation*—All's IV 3 361. *Thy face is, visard-like, unchanging, Made impudent with use of evil deeds*—3 H6 I 4 116. *A woman impudent and mannish grown*—Troil III 3 217.

IMPUGN

To find fault with (a person): *The Venetian law Cannot impugn you*—Merch IV 1 178.

IMPUTATION

(1) Reputation: *Our imputation shall be oddly poised In this wild action*—Troil I 3 339.

(2) Import or meaning ascribed to acts: *If imputation and strong circumstances . . . Will give you satisfaction*—Oth III 3 406.

IN (vb.)

To harvest, garner: *To in the crop*—All's I 3 48.

IN (prep.)

Used where modern usage would require

(1) On: *In the beached margent of the sea*—Mids II 1 85. *With this rhyme in's forehead*—All's IV 3 263. *Gold strew'd i' the floor*—Cymb III 6 50.

(2) Into: *Let the sounds of music Creep in our ears*—Merch V 55. *I am crept in favour with myself*—R3 I 2 259. *He'll turn your current in a ditch*—Cor III 1 96.

INAIDIBLE

Irremediable: *Labouring art can never ransom nature From her inaidible estate*—All's II 1 121.

INCAPABLE

Incapable of, unable to contain: *Incapable of more, replete with you*—Sonn 113 13. Unable to realize: *Incapable of her own distress*—Hml IV 7 179.

INCENSE¹

(1) To set on fire, kindle: *Whose bosom burns With an incensed fire of injuries*—2 H4 I 3 13.

(2) To incite, instigate: *I will incense Page to deal with poison*—Wiv I 3 109. *Your brother incensed me to slander the Lady Hero*—Ado V 1 242. *Think you . . . [he] Was not incensed by his subtle mother To taunt and scorn you?*—R3 III 1 151. *What they may incense him to . . . wisdom bids fear*—Lr II 4 309.

INCENSE²

More commonly Insense; to inform: *I have Incensed the lords o' the council, that he is . . . A most arch heretic*—H8 V 1 42.

INCERTAIN

Uncertain: *Incertain thought*—Meas III 1 127. *Aids incertain*—2 H4 I 3 24. At a loss what to betake oneself to: *What dangers . . . May drop upon his kingdom and devour Incertain lookers on*—Wint V 1 27.

INCERTAINTY

Uncertainty: *To the hazard Of all incertainties himself commended*—Wint III 2 169. *Certain o'er incertainty*—Sonn 115 11.

INCH¹

At an inch, close at hand, closely: *I think we watch'd you at an inch*—2 H6 I 4 45.

INCH²

A small island: *Saint Colme's inch*—Mcb I 2 61.

INCHARITABLE

Uncharitable, unfeeling: *You bawling, blasphemous, incharitable dog!*—Tp I 1 43.

INCH-MEAL

By inch-meal, by inches: *Make him By inch-meal a disease!*—Tp II 2 2.

INCIDENCY

An incident, event: *[I conjure thee] that thou declare What incidency thou dost guess of harm Is creeping toward me*—Wint I 2 402.

INCISION

Let us make incision for your love—Merch II 1 6, alluding to a fashion among young gallants, who cut themselves in order to drink the healths, or to write the names of their mistresses in the blood.

INCIVIL

Uncivil, rude: *A most incivil [prince]*—Cymb V 5 292.

INCIVILITY

Want of good manners, ill-bred behaviour: Cour. *. . . Is not your husband mad?* Adr. *His incivility confirms no less*—Err IV 4 48.

INCLINATION

Natural disposition, character: *[They change] their gentle hearts To fierce and bloody inclination*—John V 2 157. *Bid him Report the feature of Octavia, her years, Her inclination*—Ant II 5 111.

INCLINING

A party, following: *Hold your hands, Both you of my inclining, and the rest*—Oth I 2 81.

INCLIP

To encircle, enclose: *Whate'er the ocean pales, or sky inclips*—Ant II 7 74.

INCLUDE

To conclude, end: *We will include all jars With triumphs*—Gent V 4 160.

INCOME

Advent, coming: *Pain pays the income of each precious thing*—Lucr 334.

INCOMPREHENSIBLE

Boundless, infinite: *The incomprehensible lies that this same fat rogue will tell us*—1 H4 I 2 209.

INCONTINENT

Forthwith: *Put on sullen black incontinent*—R2 V 6 48. *He says he will return incontinent*—Oth IV 3 12. With a play: *A pair of stairs to marriage which they will climb incontinent, or else be incontinent before marriage*—As V 2 41.

INCONVENIENCE

A mischief, misfortune: *Why gentle Peace Should not expel these inconveniences*—H5 V 2 65. *To intercept this inconvenience (i.e. the spying from the tower)*—1 H6 I 4 14.

INCONVENIENT

Unmeet, unbefitting: *It is not impossible to me, if it appear not inconvenient to you, to set her before your eyes to-morrow human as she is*—As V 2 72.

INCONY

Dainty, 'nice': *My sweet ounce of man's flesh! my incony Jew!*—LLL III 136. *Most incony vulgar wit!*—IV 1 144.

INCORPORAL

Incorporeal, immaterial: *With the incorporal air do hold discourse*—Hml III 4 118.

INCORPORATE

(1) United in one substance or body: *As if our hands, our sides, voices and minds, Had been incorporate*—Mids III 2 207. *My incorporate friends*—Cor I 1 134 (the belly to the other members). *Her arms do lend his neck a sweet embrace; Incorporate then they seem; face grows to face*—Ven 539. United closely with another: *To me, That, undividable, incorporate, Am better than thy dear self's better part*—Err II 2 123. Sim.: *It is Casca; one incorporate To our attempts*—Cæs I 3 135.

(2) Admitted a member of a corporation: *I am incorporate in Rome*—Tit I 462.

(3) Constituting or implying a close connection: *Their incorporate league*—H5 V 2 394. *Hard at hand comes the master and main exercise, the incorporate conclusion*—Oth II 1 268.

INCORPSED

Made into one body (*with* something): *Incorpsed and demi-natured With the brave beast*—Hml IV 7 88.

INCORRECT

Unchastened; and hence, taking up an improper attitude, not submissive: *A will most incorrect to heaven*—Hml I 2 95.

INCREASEFUL

The fruit of a plentiful increase or harvest, abundant: *To cheer the ploughman with increaseful crops*—Lucr 958.

INCREDULOUS

Incredible: *No incredulous or unsafe circumstance*—Tw III 4 88.

INCUR

To bring on, entail: *Thy heat of lust, fond Paris, did incur This load of wrath that burning Troy doth bear*—Lucr 1473.

INDENT

(1) To zigzag, double: *Then shalt thou see the dew-bedabbled wretch Turn, and return, indenting with the way*—Ven 703.

(2) To come to terms, compound: *Shall we buy treason? and indent with fears?*—1 H4 I 3 87.

INDEX

(1) An introduction, prologue: *I'll sort occasion, As index to the story we late talk'd of, To part the queen's proud kindred from the king*—R3 II 2 148. *What act, That roars so loud, and thunders in the index?*—Hml III 4 51. *An index and obscure prologue to the history of lust*—Oth II 1 263. In R3 IV 4 85 (*The flattering index of a direful pageant*) explained as referring to papers containing a brief account of the exhibition circulated among the spectators of a pageant.

(2) An argument, summary: *In such indexes, although small pricks To their subsequent volumes, there is seen The baby figure of the giant mass*—Troil I 3 343.

INDIFFERENCY

(1) Impartiality, equity: *This Commodity Makes it* (*i.e.* the world) *take head from all indifferency*—John II 578.

(2) Moderateness (of size): *An I had but a belly of any indifferency, I were simply the most active fellow in Europe*—2 H4 IV 3 22.

INDIFFERENT (adj.)

Not differing, the same: *Their blue coats brushed and their garters of an indifferent knit*—Shr IV 1 93.

INDIFFERENT (adv.)

Indifferently, tolerably: *It does indifferent well*—Tw I 3 143. *He'll fight indifferent well*—Troil I 2 242. *I am myself indifferent honest*—Hml III 1 123.

INDIFFERENTLY

Without determination either way: *He waved indifferently 'twixt doing them neither good nor harm*—Cor II 2 19.

INDIGEST (adj.)

Shapeless: *Monsters and things indigest*—Sonn 114 5.

INDIGEST (sb.)

A shapeless mass: *To set a form upon that indigest*—John V 7 26.

INDIGN

Unworthy, disgraceful: *All indign and base adversities*—Oth I 3 274.

INDIGNITY

Conduct involving disgrace, an unworthy act: *I shall make this northern youth exchange His glorious deeds for my indignities*—1 H4 III 2 145.

INDIRECTLY

(1) Wrongfully, unjustly: *We shall repent each drop of blood That hot rash haste so indirectly shed*—John II 48. *Your crown and kingdom, indirectly held From him the native and true challenger*—H5 II 4 94.

(2) Evasively: *This bald unjointed chat of his, my lord, I answer'd indirectly*—1 H4 I 3 65.

INDISTINGUISHABLE

Perh., of indeterminate form, deformed: *You whoreson indistinguishable cur*—Troil V 1 32.

INDITE

Misused for Invite: *He is indited to dinner to the Lubber's-head*—2 H4 II 1 30. *She will indite him to some supper*—Rom II 4 135.

INDIVIDABLE

Perh., observing the unity of place: *Scene individable, or poem unlimited*—Hml II 2 418.

INDRENCHED

Buried in water: *In how many fathoms deep They lie indrench'd*—Troil I 1 50.

INDUBITATE

Undoubted: *The pernicious and indubitate beggar Zenelophon*—LLL IV 1 66.

INDUCEMENT

(1) An inducing or moving by persuasion or influence: *My son corrupts a well-derived nature With his inducement*—All's III 2 90.

(2) A moving cause, incentive: *Now, what moved me to't, I will be bold with time and your attention: Then mark the inducement*—H8 II 4 167.

INDUCTION

An initial step, beginning: *These promises are fair . . . And our induction full of prosperous hope*—1 H4 III 1 1. *Plots have I laid, inductions dangerous*—R3 I 1 32. *A dire induction am I witness to*—IV 4 5.

INDUE

See *Endue.*

INDURANCE

Protraction of an existing condition; or perh., durance, imprisonment: *I look'd You would have given me your petition . . . to have heard you, Without indurance, further*—H8 V 1 117.

INDUSTRIOUS

Skilful: *As in a theatre, whence they gape and point At your industrious scenes and acts of death*—John II 375.

INDUSTRIOUSLY

Of set purpose, designedly: *If industriously I play'd the fool, it was my negligence, Not weighing well the end*—Wint I 2 256.

INDUSTRY

Skill, dexterity: *In his moan, the ship splits on the rock, Which industry and courage might have saved*—3 H6 V 4 10.

INEQUALITY

Difference of rank; or perh., (seeming) inconsistency: *Do not banish reason For inequality*—Meas V 64.

INEXECRABLE

O, be thou damn'd, inexecrable dog!—Merch IV 1 128. Explained as an intensive of Execrable, but prob. a misprint for *inexorable.*

INFAMONIZE

A perversion of Infamize; to render infamous: *Dost thou infamonize me among potentates?*—LLL V 2 684.

INFECTION

App. a latinism; *infection of a man,* an unfinished, and hence, a deformed man: *Defused infection of a man*—R3 I 2 78 (echoing *perfection* in 75).

INFER

To bring forward, adduce: *Inferring arguments of mighty force*—3 H6 II 2 44. *Infer the bastardy of Edward's children*—R3 III 5 75. *I did infer your lineaments, Being the right idea of your father*—III 7 12. To report, relate: *'Tis inferr'd to us, His days are foul*—Tim III 5 73. To bring in, imply: *That need must needs infer this principle*—John III 1 213. To make known, demonstrate: *This poor show doth better; this doth infer the zeal I had to see him*—2 H4 V 5 13.

INFEST

To vex, distress: *Do not infest your mind*—Tp V 246.

INFLUENCE

In astrology, the supposed flowing from the heavenly bodies of an ethereal fluid affecting things on earth: *Servile to all the skyey influences*—Meas III 1 9. *Each particular star in heaven and . . . all their influences*—Wint I 2 425. *From whom each lamp and shining star doth borrow The beauteous influence that makes him bright*—Ven 861.

INFORM

(1) To take form: *It is the bloody business which informs Thus to mine eyes*—Mcb II 1 48.

(2) To direct, instruct, bid: *I shall inform them*—Cor III 3 18 (in answer to instructions to give certain directions to the people). *Her tongue will not obey her heart, nor can Her heart inform her tongue*—Ant III 2 47.

(3) To apprise; absol., to give information, report: *Inform on that*—All's IV 1 103. *Who, were't so, Would have inform'd for preparation*—Mcb I 5 33.

(4) To make known, tell: *Haply thou mayst inform Something to save thy life*—All's IV 1 91.

He did inform the truth—Cor I 6 42. So *to inform* (a person a thing): *He would be drunk too; that let me inform you*—Meas III 2 135.

INFORMAL

Disordered in mind: *These poor informal women*—Meas V 236. Cf. *Formal* (1).

INFORTUNATE

Unfortunate: *Infortunate in nothing but in thee*—John II 178. *Though he be infortunate*—2 H6 IV 9 18.

INFUSE

(1) To shed, diffuse: *Those clear rays which she infused on me*—1 H6 I 2 85.

(2) To inspire, imbue (a person or thing *with* a quality): *Infused with a fortitude from heaven*—Tp I 2 154. *Infusing him with self and vain conceit*—R2 III 2 166. *Infuse his breast with magnanimity*—3 H6 V 4 41. *You shall find That heaven hath infused them with these spirits*—Cæs I 3 68.

INFUSION

Character infused by nature: [I take] *his infusion* [to be] *of such dearth and rareness, as . . .*—Hml V 2 122.

INGENER

Engineer; an inventor: [One that] *in the essential vesture of creation Does tire the ingener*—Oth II 1 64.

INGENIOUS

(1) Having high intellectual capacity, able, talented: *Bold, quick, ingenious, forward, capable*—R3 III 1 155.

(2) Of feeling, &c., intelligent, lively: *Thy most ingenious sense*—Hml V 1 271. *That I . . . have ingenious feeling Of my huge sorrows*—Lr IV 6 287.

(3) Used by confusion for Ingenuous, befitting a well-born person: *Here let us . . . institute A course of learning and ingenious studies*—Shr I 1 8.

INGENIOUSLY

Used by confusion for Ingenuously: *Thou art true and honest; ingeniously I speak*—Tim II 2 230.

INGENUOUS

Used by confusion for *Ingenious* (1): *If their sons be ingenuous, they shall want no instruction*—LLL IV 2 80.

INGRAFT

Engrafted; firmly settled: *One of an ingraft infirmity*—Oth II 3 145.

INGRATEFUL

Ungrateful: *That most ingrateful boy*—Tw V 80. *All germens . . . That make ingrateful man*—Lr III 2 8.

INGROSS

See *Engross*.

INHABIT

Perh., to stay at home (out of danger): *If trembling I inhabit then, protest me The baby of a girl*—Mcb III 4 105.

INHABITABLE

Not habitable: *The frozen ridges of the Alps, Or any other ground inhabitable*—R2 I 1 64.

INHEARSE

To lay in a coffin: fig.: *See, where he lies inhearsed in the arms Of the most bloody nurser of his harms!*—1 H6 IV 7 45. *That did my ripe thoughts in my brain inhearse*—Sonn 86 3.

INHERENT

Sticking in, fixed; fig., cleaving fast, permanently indwelling: *A most inherent baseness*—Cor III 2 123.

INHERIT

(1) *To inherit of*, to cause (one) to have: *It must be great that can inherit us So much as of a thought of ill in him*—R2 I 1 85.

(2) To obtain, win: *This, or else nothing, will inherit her*—Gent III 2 87. *Which with pain purchased doth inherit pain*—LLL I 1 73. *I have lived To see inherited my very wishes*—Cor II 1 214.

(3) To have, possess: *The great globe itself, Yea, all which it inherit*—Tp IV 153. *A grave, Whose hollow womb inherits nought but bones*—R2 II 1 82. *Even such delight . . . shall you this night Inherit at my house*—Rom I 2 28.

INHERITANCE

(1) Obtaining, winning: *For the inheritance of their loves*—Cor III 2 68.

(2) Possession, ownership: *He will sell the fee-simple of his salvation, the inheritance of it*—All's IV 3 311. *Which had return'd To the inheritance of Fortinbras*—Hml I 1 91.

INHERITOR

A possessor, owner: *The sole inheritor Of all perfections*—LLL II 5. *Be inheritor of thy desire*—R3 IV 3 34. *The very conveyances of his lands will hardly lie in this box; and must the inheritor himself have no more?*—Hml V 1 119.

INHOOP

To enclose in a hoop so as to compel to fight: *His quails ever Beat mine, inhoop'd, at odds*—Ant II 3 37.

INITIATE

Pertaining to an unpractised person: *The initiate fear that wants hard use*—Mcb III 4 143.

INJOINT

To unite, join: *Have there injointed them with an after fleet*—Oth I 3 35.

INJURIOUS

(1) Insulting, contumelious: *Injurious Hermia!* —Mids III 2 195. *Injurious Margaret!*—3 H6 III 3 78. *Call me their traitor! Thou injurious tribune!*—Cor III 3 69.

(2) Insolent or wanton in wrong-doing: *Injurious wasps, to feed on such sweet honey And kill the bees that yield it!*—Gent I 2 106. *A false traitor and injurious villain*—R2 I 1 91. *Till the injurious Romans did extort This tribute from us*—Cymb III 1 48.

INJURY

(1) Calumny: *For sealing The injury of tongues* —Wint I 2 337. An affront, insult: *Quickly will return an injury*—H5 IV 7 189. *What said Warwick to these injuries?*—3 H6 IV 1 107.

(2) A bodily wound or sore: *We thought not good to bruise an injury till it were full ripe*—H5 III 6 129.

(3) *Injuries*: 1 H4 III 3 181 (*If thy pocket were enriched with any other injuries but these, I am a villain*), app., articles the taking of which is complained of as a wrong.

INKLE

(1) A piece of inkle, a kind of linen tape: *What's the price of this inkle?*—LLL III 139. *Inkles, caddisses, cambrics, lawns*—Wint IV 4 208.

(2) Linen thread or yarn (properly that from which inkle is made): *Her inkle, silk, twin with the rubied cherry*—Per V Prol 8.

INLAND

The country near the centres of population as opposed to wilder parts; hence, as adj., of persons, accustomed to good society: *An . . . uncle of mine taught me to speak, who was in his youth an inland man*—As III 2 362. Sim. as adv., *inland bred: Yet am I inland bred And know some nurture*—As II 7 96.

INLY

Inwardly felt, heartfelt: *The inly touch of love* —Gent II 7 18. *Inly sorrow*—3 H6 I 4 171.

INQUIRE (sb.)

Inquiry: *To make inquire Of his behaviour*— Hml II 1 4. *Fame answering the most strange inquire*—Per III Prol 22.

INQUIRE (vb.)

To search for, seek out; with *forth*: *Go on before;*

I shall inquire you forth—Gent II 4 186. With *out*: *Inquire My lodging out*—Merch II 2 162. *My young lady bade me inquire you out*—Rom II 4 172. *Can you inquire him out?*—Oth III 4 14.

INSANE

Causing insanity: *Have we eaten on the insane root That takes the reason prisoner?*—Mcb I 3 84. Perh. deadly nightshade is the plant referred to.

INSANIE

Insanity: *It insinuateth me of insanie*—LLL V 1 27.

INSCONCE

See *Ensconce*.

INSCULP

To carve, engrave: *A coin that bears the figure of an angel Stamped in gold, but that's insculp'd upon*—Merch II 7 56.

INSCULPTURE

Something carved: *On his grave-stone this insculpture*—Tim V 4 67.

INSENSIBLE

Not perceptible by the senses: *Doth he feel it? no. Doth he hear it? no. 'Tis insensible, then?* —1 H4 V 1 139.

INSEPARATE

Indivisible: *A thing inseparate Divides more wider than the sky and earth*—Troil V 2 148.

INSINEWED

App., joined, allied: *All members of our cause . . . That are insinew'd to this action*—2 H4 IV 1 171.

INSINUATE

(1) Intr. for refl., to wheedle, ingratiate oneself: *I hardly yet have learn'd To insinuate, flatter, bow, and bend my limbs*—R2 IV 164. *I will practise the insinuating nod*—Cor II 3 106. *To see so great a lord Basely insinuate and send us gifts*— Tit IV 2 37. *With Death she humbly doth insinuate*—Ven 1012.

(2) App., to hint to, suggest to: *It insinuateth me of insanie*—LLL V 1 27.

INSISTURE

Perh., steady continuance in a course: *The heavens . . . the planets . . . Observe degree, priority and place, Insisture, course*—Troil I 3 85.

INSOMUCH

Inasmuch as, in that: *I speak not this that you should bear a good opinion of my knowledge, insomuch I say I know you are*—As V 2 59.

11

INSTALMENT

A place wherein one is installed, a stall: *Each fair instalment, coat, and several crest, With loyal blazon, evermore be blest!*—Wiv V 5 67.

INSTANCE

(1) A motive: *Gave thee no instance why thou shouldst do treason*—H5 II 2 119. *The instances that second marriage move*—Hml III 2 192. A cause, reason: *His fears are shallow, wanting instance*—R3 III 2 25. *Troy . . . had been down . . . But for these instances*—Troil I 3 75.

(2) A being present: *The examples Of every minute's instance*—2 H4 IV 1 82, *i.e.* those drawn from (the occurrences of) each minute as it becomes the present.

(3) A proof: *What instance of the contrary?* —Gent II 4 16. *Offer them instances*—Ado II 2 41. *I have received A certain instance that Glendower is dead*—2 H4 III 1 102. *What's the instance?* what is to be my proof?—All's IV 1 44. A sign, token: *Instances of infinite of love*—Gent II 7 70. *Before the . . . deep Gave any tragic instance of our harm*—Err I 1 64. *Blushing red no guilty instance gave*—Lucr 1511.

(4) A detail, circumstance: *Why should that gentleman . . . Give then such instances of loss?*— 2 H4 I 1 55. A sample: *Nature is fine in love, and where 'tis fine, It sends some precious instance of itself After the thing it loves*—Hml IV 5 161.

(5) In pl., assiduities: [He received me] *Not with such familiar instances . . . As he hath used of old*—Cæs IV 2 16.

INSTANT (adj.)

Now present, happening or presenting itself: *From the time of his remembrance to this very instant disaster*—All's IV 3 126. *Whose figure even this instant cloud puts on*—H8 I 1 225. *Take the instant way*—Troil III 3 153.

INSTANT (sb.)

At an instant, at the same moment: *We still have slept together, Rose at an instant*—As I 3 75. *We rose both at an instant*—1 H4 V 4 150. *In the instant*, on the instant, immediately: *In the instant came The fiery Tybalt*—Rom I 1 115.

INSTATE

To endow: *His possessions . . . We do instate and widow you withal*—Meas V 427.

INSTRUCTION

(1) Knowledge, information: [The queen] *Of thy intents desires instruction*—Ant V 1 54.

(2) The imparting of knowledge; hence, *without some instruction*, without intending to make something known: *Nature would not invest herself in such shadowing passion without some instruction* —Oth IV 1 40.

INSTRUMENTAL

Serviceable: *The hand* [is not] *more instrumental to the mouth Than is the throne of Denmark to thy father*—Hml I 2 48.

INSUFFICIENCE

Insufficiency; incapacity, incompetence: *Your senses, unintelligent of our insufficience*—Wint I 1 15.

INSULT

To vaunt, glory, triumph: *You insult, exult, and all at once, Over the wretched*—As III 5 36. *That proud insulting ship Which Cæsar and his fortune bare at once*—1 H6 I 2 138. *So he walks, insulting o'er his prey*—3 H6 I 3 14. *I will insult on him*—Tit III 2 71.

INSULTER

A triumphant foe: *Paying what ransom the insulter willeth*—Ven 550.

INSULTMENT

Triumph: *He on the ground, my speech of insultment ended*—Cymb III 5 144.

INSUPPRESSIVE

Insuppressible: *The insuppressive mettle of our spirits*—Cæs II 1 134.

INTELLECT

Meaning, purport; or perh., a sign-manual, signature: *I will look again on the intellect of the letter, for the nomination of the party writing*— LLL IV 2 137.

INTELLIGENCE

(1) Intercourse, communication: *If with myself I hold intelligence*—As I 3 49. *The very gods show'd me a vision—I fast and pray'd for their intelligence*—Cymb IV 2 346.

(2) The obtaining of information by spies: *Sought to entrap me by intelligence*—1 H4 IV 3 98. Spies: *Where hath our intelligence been drunk? Where hath it slept?*—John IV 2 116.

INTELLIGENCING

Playing the intelligencer: *A most intelligencing bawd!*—Wint II 3 68.

INTELLIGENT

Bringing intelligence, communicating information: *Do you know, and dare not? Be intelligent to me*—Wint I 2 377. *Which are to France the spies and speculations Intelligent of our state*—Lr III 1 24. *Our posts shall be swift and intelligent betwixt us*—III 7 11. *An intelligent party to the advantages of France*, taking part in the matter of (*i.e.* watching) chances favourable to the French king and communicating information regarding them—Lr III 5 12.

INTEND

(1) To hold out, offer: *If thou dost intend Never so little show of love to her*—Mids III 2 333.

(2) To proceed on, undertake (a journey): *If he should intend this voyage towards my wife, I would turn her loose to him*—Wiv II 1 188. *Tyre, I now look from thee then, and to Tarsus Intend my travel*—Per I 2 115. *Then my thoughts . . . Intend a zealous pilgrimage to thee*—Sonn 27 5.

(3) To pretend: *Intend a kind of zeal both to the prince and Claudio*—Ado II 2 35. *I intend That all is done in reverend care of her*—Shr IV 1 206. *I can counterfeit the deep tragedian . . . Tremble and start . . . Intending deep suspicion*—R3 III 5 5. *Intending other serious matters*—Tim II 2 219.

INTENDMENT

An intention, design: *That . . . you might stay him from his intendment*—As I 1 139. *[We] fear the main intendment of the Scot*—H5 I 2 144. *What I protest intendment of doing*—Oth IV 2 205.

INTENIBLE

Incapable of holding or containing: *This captious and intenible sieve*—All's I 3 208.

INTENT

Meaning, import, purport: *The intent and purpose of the law*—Merch IV 1 247. *New-dated letters . . . Their cold intent, tenour and substance thus*—2 H4 IV 1 8. *You may be pleased to catch at mine intent By what did here befal me*—Ant II 2 41.

INTENTION

Intensity of attention or desire: *She did so course o'er my exteriors with such a greedy intention*—Wiv I 3 72. *Affection! thy intention stabs the centre*—Wint I 2 138.

INTENTIVELY

With undistracted attention: *My pilgrimage . . . Whereof by parcels she had something heard, But not intentively*—Oth I 3 153.

INTERCEPT

(1) To interrupt: *Being intercepted in your sport*—Tit II 3 80. *They will not intercept my tale*—III 1 40.

(2) To hinder, prevent: *She that might have intercepted thee . . . From all the slaughters, wretch, that thou hast done*—R3 IV 4 137.

INTERCHAIN

To link one to another: *Two bosoms interchained with an oath*—Mids II 2 49.

INTERCHANGE

To exchange (one thing *for* another): *I shall interchange My waned state for Henry's regal crown*—3 H6 IV 7 3.

INTERESS

To invest with a right (*to* a thing): *To whose young love The vines of France and milk of Burgundy Strive to be interess'd*—Lr I 1 85.

INTEREST

(1) Right, title (*to* a thing): [You] *Acquainte a me with interest to this land*—John V 2 89. *He hath more worthy interest to the state Than thou*—1 H4 III 2 98.

(2) Injury, detriment: *In the interest of thy bed A stranger came, and on that pillow lay*—Lucr 1619.

INTERIM

(1) An interlude: *For interim to our studies*—LLL I 1 172.

(2) *By interims*, at intervals: *By interims . . . we have heard The charges of our friends*—Cor I 6 5.

INTERJOIN

To unite mutually: [Fellest foes shall] *interjoin their issues*—Cor IV 4 22.

INTERLACE

To introduce, insert: *Here and there the painter interlaces Pale cowards*—Lucr 1390.

INTERLUDE

A stage-play: *To play in our interlude before the duke*—Mids I 2 5. *I was one, sir, in this interlude*—Tw V 380. *An interlude!*—Lr V 3 89.

INTERMISSION

(1) Time elapsing before the commencement of an action, delay: *Cut short all intermission*—Mcb IV 3 232.

(2) Interruption: [He] *Deliver'd letters, spite of intermission, Which presently they read,* perh., did so although this involved an interruption of the speaker's business, or, in spite of protest on his part—Lr II 4 33.

(3) App., pastime: *You loved, I loved for intermission. No more pertains to me, my lord, than you*—Merch III 2 201 (but some put no stop after *intermission,* and explain the word in the usual sense.

INTERMISSIVE

Interrupted, suspended: *Their intermissive miseries*—1 H6 I 1 88.

INTERMIT

To interrupt (the course of a thing), to suspend, avert: *Pray to the gods to intermit the plague That needs must light on this ingratitude*—Cæs I 1 59.

INTERRUPTION

Hindrance, obstruction: *Bloody England into England gone, O'erbearing interruption*—John III 4 8.

INTERVALLUM

Interval: *A shall laugh without intervallums*— 2 H4 V 1 90.

INTIL

Into: *Hath shipped me intil the land*—Hml V 1 81.

INTIMATE

To suggest (the doing of something): *The spirit of humours intimate reading aloud to him!*—Tw II 5 93.

INTITLE

Entitle; to name: *That which in mean men we intitle patience*—R2 I 2 33.

INTITLED

Entitled; having a claim: *Neither intitled in the other's heart*—LLL V 2 822.

INTITULED

In heraldry, blazoned, displayed: *Beauty, in that white intituled*—Lucr 57. Cf. *Entitled.*

INTO

Unto, to: [I'll] *pray God's blessing into thy attempt*—All's I 3 260. *He enchants societies into him*—Cymb I 6 167.

INTREASURE

See *Entreasure.*

INTRENCHANT

Incapable of being cut: *The intrenchant air*—Mcb V 8 9.

INTRINSE

Intricate: *Bite the holy cords a-twain Which are too intrinse t'unloose*—Lr II 2 80.

INTRINSICATE

The same as the foregoing: *This knot intrinsicate Of life at once untie*—Ant V 2 307.

INTRUDE

To invade, enter forcibly: *Why should the worm intrude the maiden bud?*—Lucr 848.

INVESTMENTS

Robes, dress: *Whose white investments figure innocence*—2 H4 IV 1 45. *Not of that dye which their investments show*—Hml I 3 128.

INVINCIBLE

App., invisible: *His dimensions to any thick sight were invincible*—2 H4 III 2 336.

INVISED

App., invisible: *The diamond,—why, 'twas beautiful and hard, Whereto his invised properties did tend*—Compl 211.

INWARD (adj.)

(1) Intimate: *Who is most inward with the noble duke?*—R3 III 4 8.

(2) Private, secret: *Any inward impediment why you should not be conjoined*—Ado I 1 12. *For what is inward between us, let it pass*—LLL V 1 102.

(3) Of wars, civil: *Were these inward wars once out of hand*—2 H4 III 1 107.

INWARD (sb.)

An intimate: *I was an inward of his*—Meas III 2 138.

INWARDNESS

Intimacy: *My inwardness and love Is very much unto the prince and Claudio*—Ado IV 1 247.

IRRECONCILED

Not expiated, unatoned: *Die in many irreconciled iniquities*—H5 IV 1 160.

IRRECOVERABLE

Hopelessly bad, irreclaimable: *The fiend hath pricked down Bardolph irrecoverable*—2 H4 II 4 359.

IRREGULOUS

Unruly, lawless: *That irregulous devil, Cloten*—Cymb IV 2 315.

ISSUE

(1) An action, deed: *The cruel issue of these bloody men*—Cæs III 1 294. *You are a fool granted; therefore your issues, being foolish, do not derogate*—Cymb II 1 50.

(2) Luck, fortune: *'Gainst Cæsar; Whose better issue in the war, from Italy . . . drave them*—Ant I 2 96.

IT

Its; a form intermediate between the old genitive His and the modern Its: *It most innocent mouth*—Wint III 2 101. *It lifted up it head*—Hml I 2 216. *The corse they follow did . . . Fordo it own life*—V 1 243. *It had it head bit off by it young*—Lr I 4 236.

ITERATION

A citing of quotations or tags; the habit thereof: Prince. *Thou didst well; for wisdom cries out in the streets, and no man regards it.* Fal. *O, thou hast damnable iteration*—1 H4 I 2 99. *When their rhymes . . . Want similes, truth tired with iteration*—Troil III 2 181.

I WIS

Assuredly, of a truth: *There be fools alive, I wis, Silver'd o'er*—Merch II 9 68. *I wis it is not half way to her heart*—Shr I 1 62. *I wis your grandam had a worser match*—R3 I 3 102.

J

JACK¹

(1) Applied to persons by way of disparagement: *Braggarts, Jacks, milksops!*—Ado V 1 91. *A mad-cap ruffian and a swearing Jack*—Shr II 1 290. *The prince is a Jack*—1 H4 III 3 99. In apposition: *A Jack guardant*—Cor V 2 67. To *play the Jack*, to play the knave: *Your fairy . . . has done little better than played the Jack with us*—Tp IV 196.

(2) A figure which struck the bell on a clock: *I stand fooling here, his Jack o' the clock*—R2 V 5 60. *Like a Jack thou keep'st the stroke Betwixt thy begging and my meditation*—R3 IV 2 117.

(3) A key of a virginal (see *Virginal* (vb.)); properly a piece of wood working with the key, and fitted with a quill which plucked the string on the key's being pressed: [How oft] *Do I envy those jacks that nimble leap To kiss the tender inward of thy hand*—Sonn 128 5.

JACK²

A (leathern) jug or tankard: *Be the jacks fair within, the jills fair without?*—Shr IV 1 51 (with a play on the proper names).

JACK-A-LENT

(1) A figure of a man set up in Lent to be pelted: *See now how wit may be made a Jack-a-Lent!*—Wiv V 5 134.

(2) Transf., a puppet: *You little Jack-a-Lent, have you been true to us?*—Wiv III 3 27.

JACK-AN-APES

An ape, monkey: *I could . . . sit* [my horse] *like a jack-an-apes, never off*—H5 V 2 147.

JACKSAUCE

A saucy or impudent fellow: *His reputation is as arrant . . . a Jacksauce, as ever his black shoe trod upon God's ground*—H5 IV 7 147.

JADE (sb.)

Hollow pamper'd jades of Asia, Which cannot go but thirty mile a-day—2 H4 II 4 178. A parody of the opening lines of Act IV Sc. 3 of the Second Part of Marlowe's *Tamburlaine the Great*.

JADE (vb.)

(1) To make jades of, drive in disorder like jades: *The ne'er-yet-beaten horse of Parthia We have jaded out o' the field*—Ant III 1 33.

(2) To befool, jape: *I do not now fool myself, to let imagination jade me*—Tw II 5 178. *To be thus jaded by a piece of scarlet*—H8 III 2 280.

JADED

App., mean, contemptible: *The honourable blood of Lancaster Must not be shed by such a jaded groom*—2 H6 IV 1 51.

JAKES

A privy: *I will tread this unbolted villain into mortar, and daub the walls of a jakes with him*—Lr II 2 70.

JAR (sb.)

A tick (of the clock): *I love thee not a jar o' the clock behind What lady-she her lord*—Wint I 2 43.

JAR (vb.)

To tick: *My thoughts are minutes; and with sighs they jar Their watches on unto mine eyes, the outward watch*—R2 V 5 51.

JAUNCE

App., to cause to prance up and down: *I bear a burthen like an ass, Spurr'd, gall'd and tired by jauncing Bolingbroke*—R2 V 5 93.

JAUNT (sb.)

A fatiguing or troublesome journey: *What a jaunt have I had!*—Rom II 5 26.

JAUNT (vb.)

To trot or trudge about: *To catch my death with jaunting up and down*—Rom II 5 53.

JEALOUS

(1) Suspicious, apprehensive, fearful: *Our first merriment hath made thee jealous*—Shr IV 5 76. *Be not jealous on me*—Cæs I 2 71. *You are jealous now That this is from some mistress*—Oth III 4 185. *The unback'd breeder, full of fear, Jealous of catching, swiftly doth forsake him*—Ven 320. So *jealous of*, apprehensive on account of: *Your nobles, jealous of your absence, Seek through your camp to find you*—H5 IV 1 302.

(2) Doubtful, not believing: *That you do love me, I am nothing jealous*—Cæs I 2 162.

JEALOUS-HOOD

Explained as = Jealousy; *A jealous-hood, a jealous-hood!*—Rom IV 4 13. Prob. the true reading is *jealous hood, hood* being used to typify the female head, and so = woman.

JEALOUSY

Suspicion, apprehension: *Jealousy shall be called assurance*—Ado II 2 49. *Jealousy what might befall your travel*—Tw III 3 8. *So full of artless jealousy is guilt, It spills itself in fearing to be spilt*—Hml IV 5 19. *Oft my jealousy Shapes faults that are not*—Oth III 3 147. A suspicion: *Let not my jealousies be your dishonours*—Mcb IV 3 29. *All little jealousies . . . Would then be nothing*—Ant II 2 134.

JENNET, GENNET

A small Spanish horse or mare: *You'll have coursers for cousins and gennets for germans*—Oth I 1 113. *A breeding jennet, lusty, young and proud*—Ven 260.

JERKIN

A close-fitting jacket: *An old cloak makes a new jerkin*—Wiv I 3 18. *A buff jerkin*—1 H4 I 2 48. *Put on two leathern jerkins and aprons*—2 H4 II 2 189.

JESSES

In falconry, narrow strips of soft leather fastened round a hawk's legs and fitted with rings for attaching the leash: *Though that her jesses were my dear heart-strings*—Oth III 3 261.

JEST

To disport or amuse oneself; perh., to act in a masque or play: *As gentle and as jocund as to jest Go I to fight*—R2 I 3 95.

JET¹

To strut, swagger: *How he jets under his advanced plumes!*—Tw II 5 36. *The gates of monarchs Are arch'd so high that giants may jet through*—Cymb III 3 4. *Whose men and dames so jetted and adorn'd*—Per I 4 26.

JET²

To encroach: *Insulting tyranny begins to jet Upon the innocent and aweless throne*—R3 II 4 51. *Think you not how dangerous It is to jet upon a prince's right?*—Tit II 1 63.

JEWEL

Any article of value used for adornment: *He hath got the jewel that I loved*—Merch V 224 (a ring). *Wear this jewel for me, 'tis my picture*—Tw III 4 228. *Search for a jewel that too casually Hath left mine arm*—Cymb II 3 146 (a bracelet).

JIG (sb.)

(1) A comic entertainment at the end or in an interval of a play: *He's for a jig or a tale of bawdry*—Hml II 2 522.

(2) A humorous ballad; hence, *jig-maker*: Oph. *You are merry, my lord. . . .* Ham. *O God, your only jig-maker*—Hml III 2 129.

JIG (vb.)

(1) To sing in the style of a jig (*i.e.* a tune for the dance): *To jig off a tune at the tongue's end*—LLL III 11.

(2) *Jigging*, in contempt, of a versifier as a composer of jigs (in sense (2) given under *Jig* (sb.): *What should the wars do with these jigging fools?*—Cæs IV 3 137.

JIG-MAKER

See *Jig* (sb.) (2).

JILL

Gill; a drinking-vessel (properly one holding a gill); see the quotation under *Jack²*.

JOCKEY

A familiar by-form of Jack or John: *Jockey of Norfolk, be not too bold*—R3 V 3 304.

JOHN DRUM'S ENTERTAINMENT

Rough treatment; a thrusting of a person out of one's company: *If you give him not John Drum's entertainment, your inclining cannot be removed*—All's III 6 40.

JOINED-STOOL, JOINT-STOOL

A stool; properly one made by a regular joiner as opposed to one of more clumsy make: *Thy state is taken for a joined-stool*—1 H4 II 4 418. *[He] jumps upon joined-stools, and swears with a good grace*—2 H4 II 4 269. *Away with the joint-stools*—Rom I 5 7.

JOINTRESS

A woman holding jointly: *The imperial jointress to this warlike state*—Hml I 2 9.

JOINT-RING

A ring made of two separable halves: *I would not do such a thing for a joint-ring*—Oth IV 3 72.

JOINT-STOOL

See *Joined-stool.*

JOLLITY

Finery: *Needy nothing trimm'd in jollity*—Sonn 66 3.

JORDAN

A chamber-pot: *They will allow us ne'er a jordan*—1 H4 II 1 21. *Empty the jordan*—2 H4 II 4 37.

JOUL

See *Jowl.*

JOURNAL

Diurnal, daily: *Ere twice the sun hath made his journal greeting To the under generation*—Meas IV 3 92. *Stick to your journal course*—Cymb IV 2 10.

JOURNEY-BATED

Reduced in condition by travel: *So are the horses of the enemy In general, journey-bated and brought low*—1 H4 IV 3 25.

JOVIAL

Of or pertaining to Jove: *Our Jovial star reign'd at his birth*—Cymb V 4 105. Resembling what pertains to Jove: *His Jovial face*—Cymb IV 2 311.

JOWL, JOUL

To dash, thrust: *They may joul horns together* —All's I 3 58. *How the knave jowls it to the ground!*—Hml V 1 84.

JOY

(1) To gladden, delight: *Much it joys me too, To see you are become so penitent*—R3 I 2 220. *Joy'd are we that you are*—Cymb V 5 424.

(2) To enjoy: *Live thou to joy thy life*—2 H6 III 2 365. *Was ever king that joy'd an earthly throne, And could command no more content than I?*—IV 9 1. *Let her joy her raven-colour'd love* —Tit II 3 83.

(3) To rejoice at: *Often up and down my sons were toss'd, For me to joy and weep their gain and loss*—R3 II 4 58.

JUDAS

Judas's [hair]: Ros. *His very hair is of the dissembling colour* (*i.e.* red). Cel. *Something browner than Judas's* — As III 4 7. Judas was usually represented with red hair.

JUDICIOUS

(1) Prob., judicial: *His last offences to us Shall have judicious hearing*—Cor V 6 127.

(2) Prob., consonant with justice: *Judicious punishment! 'twas this flesh begot Those pelican daughters*—Lr III 4 76.

JUMP (sb.)

A venture, hazard: *Our fortune lies Upon this jump*—Ant III 8 5.

JUMP (vb.)

(1) To hazard: *Here, upon this bank and shoal of time, We'ld jump the life to come*—Mcb I 7 6. [You must] *jump the after inquiry on your own peril*—Cymb V 4 188.

(2) To apply a violent stimulus to: *To jump a body with a dangerous physic*—Cor III 1 154.

JUMP (adv.)

Exactly, precisely: *Jump at this dead hour*— Hml I 1 65. *So jump upon this bloody question* —V 2 386. [To] *bring him jump when he may Cassio find*—Oth II 3 392.

JUNKET

A sweetmeat, delicacy: *There wants no junkets at the feast*—Shr III 2 250.

JUST (adj.)

(1) Faithful, honourable: [She] *always hath been just and virtuous In any thing that I do know by her*—Ado V 1 312. *He was my friend, faithful and just to me*—Cæs III 2 90. *Horatio, thou art e'en as just a man As e'er my conversation coped withal*—Hml III 2 59.

(2) Accurate, true: *How blest am I In my just censure, in my true opinion!*—Wint II 1 36. *The things I speak are just*—2 H4 V 3 127. *My report is just and full of truth*—Tit V 3 115. *Making just report*—Lr III 1 37.

(3) Exact, precise: *A just pound*—Merch IV 1 327. *The just proportion that we gave them out*— 2 H4 IV 1 23. *To meet his grace just distance 'tween our armies*—226. *Bring me just notice of the numbers dead* —H5 IV 7 122. Punctual: *I return again, Just to the time*—Sonn 109 6.

JUST (adv.)

In replies and expressions of assent, just so, right: Claud. *Perpetual durance?* Isab. *Ay, just* —Meas III 1 67. Leon. . . . *God will send you no horns.* Beat. *Just, if he send me no husband*— Ado II 1 27. Laf. *Uncertain life, and sure death.* Par. *Just, you say well*—All's II 3 20.

JUSTICER

A judge: *Sit thou here, most learned justicer*— Lr III 6 23. *Some upright justicer*—Cymb V 5 214.

JUSTIFY

(1) With complementary object, to prove: *I here could . . . justify you traitors*—Tp V 127.

(2) To acknowledge: *Thou shalt . . . justify in knowledge She is thy very princess*—Per V 1 219.

JUSTLY

(1) Faithfully, honourably: *I will deal in this As secretly and justly as your soul Should with your body*—Ado IV 1 249. *I do not find that thou dealest justly with me*—Oth IV 2 173. *What thou justly seemest, thy honourable appearance: Just opposite to what thou justly seem'st*—Rom III 2 78.

(2) Accurately, truly: *Look you speak justly*— Meas V 298. *Justly to your grave ears I'll present How I did thrive*—Oth I 3 124.

(3) Exactly, precisely: *In cash most justly paid* —H5 II 1 120. *If both were justly weigh'd*—Per V 1 89.

JUTTY (sb.)

A projection: *No jutty, frieze, Buttress, nor coign of vantage, but . . .*—Mcb I 6 6.

JUTTY (vb.)

To project beyond, overhang: *As fearfully as doth a galled rock O'erhang and jutty his confounded base*—H5 III 1 12.

JUVENAL

A youth: *My tender juvenal*—LLL I 2 8. *Most brisky juvenal*—Mids III 1 97. *The juvenal, the prince your master*—2 H4 I 2 22.

K

KAM

Awry, cross from the purpose: *This is clean kam*—Cor III 1 304.

KECKSY

A name applied to various hollow-stemmed plants: *Hateful docks, rough thistles, kecksies, burs*—H5 V 2 52.

KEECH

A lump of congealed fat: *I wonder That such a keech can with his very bulk Take up the rays o' the beneficial sun*—H8 I 1 54 (the Cardinal was the son of a butcher). As proper name: *Goodwife Keech, the butcher's wife*—2 H4 II 1 101.

KEEL

To cool (the contents of a pot) by stirring, skimming, &c., to prevent boiling over: *While greasy Joan doth keel the pot*—LLL V 2 930.

KEEP (sb.)

Keeping, custody: *In Baptista's keep my treasure is*—Shr I 2 118.

KEEP (vb.)

To dwell, live: *These banish'd men that I have kept withal*—Gent V 4 152. *The most impenetrable cur That ever kept with men*—Merch III 3 18. *This place is famous for the creatures Of prey that keep upon't*—Wint III 3 12. *Where earth-delving conies keep*—Ven 687.

KEEPER

One who has charge of the sick: *As the* [sick] *wretch . . . breaks like a fire Out of his keeper's arms*—2 H4 I 1 140. *How oft when men are at the point of death Have they been merry! which their keepers call A lightning before death*—Rom V 3 88.

KEN (sb.)

(1) The distance that bounds the range of ordinary vision: *Within a ken our army lies*—2 H4 IV 1 151. *Thou wast within a ken*—Cymb III 6 6.

(2) Sight, view: *Losing ken of Albion's wished coast*—2 H6 III 2 113. *'Tis double death to drown in ken of shore*—Lucr 1114.

KEN (vb.)

(1) To descry, distinguish: *As far as I could ken thy chalky cliffs*—2 H6 III 2 101.

(2) To recognize: *'Tis he, I ken the manner of his gait*—Troil IV 5 14.

(3) To know: *I ken the wight*—Wiv I 3 40.

KERN

A foot soldier of Ireland or the Western Islands of Scotland, app. more lightly armed than the gallowglass: *Now for our Irish wars: We must supplant those rough rug-headed kerns*—R2 II 1 155. See also 2 H6 IV 9 25 and Mcb I 2 12, quoted under *Gallowglass*.

KERNEL

A seed, pip: *Sowing the kernels of it (i.e. the apple) in the sea, [he will] bring forth more islands*—Tp II 1 92. *For picking a kernel out of a pomegranate*—All's II 3 275. Of a boy: *This kernel, This squash, this gentleman*—Wint I 2 159.

KERSEY

(1) A kind of coarse woollen cloth; a piece of such cloth: *A list of an English kersey*—Meas I 2 34.

(2) Fig., plain, homely: *Russet yeas and honest kersey noes*—LLL V 2 413.

KETTLE

Short for Kettledrum: *Let the kettle to the trumpet speak*—Hml V 2 286.

KIBE

A chilblain, esp. one on the heel: *If 'twere a kibe, 'Twould put me to my slipper*—Tp II 1 276. Fal. *Well, sirs, I am almost out at heels.* Pist. *Why, then, let kibes ensue*—Wiv I 3 34. *The toe of the peasant comes so near the heel of the courtier, he galls his kibe*—Hml V 1 152. *If a man's brains were in's heels, were't not in danger of kibes?*—Lr I 5 8.

KICKSHAW, KICKSHAWS

(1) A fancy dish: *Any pretty little tiny kickshaws, tell William cook*—2 H4 V 1 29.

(2) An elegant trifle: *Art thou good at these kickshawses?*—Tw I 3 122.

KICKY-WICKY

A wife (in depreciation): *He wears his honour in a box unseen, That hugs his kicky-wicky here at home*—All's II 3 296.

KID-FOX

App., a young fox: *We'll fit the kid-fox with a pennyworth*—Ado II 3 44.

KILLINGWORTH

Kenilworth: *Retire to Killingworth*—2 H6 IV 4 39. *Away with us to Killingworth*—44.

KILN-HOLE

Prob., the fireplace used in making malt: *Creep into the kiln-hole*—Wiv IV 2 59. App., a time spent gossiping round it: *Is there not milking-time . . . or kiln-hole, to whistle off these secrets?*—Wint IV 4 246.

KIND (adj.)

(1) Natural; showing natural feelings: Leon. *Did he break out into tears?* Mess. *In great measure.* Leon. *A kind overflow of kindness*— Ado I 1 24. Giving an appearance of nature: *Much imaginary work was there (i.e.* in the picture): *Conceit deceitful, so compact, so kind, That . . .*—Lucr 1422.

(2) Having the natural (good) qualities well developed: *Were all thy children kind and natural* —H5 II Chor 19.

(3) Agreeable, pleasing: [You have] *Set a fair fashion on our entertainment, Which was not half so beautiful and kind*—Tim I 2 152. *Be, as thy presence is, gracious and kind*—Sonn 10 11 (with a play).

KIND (sb.)

(1) Natural disposition, nature: *If the cat will after kind*—As III 2 109. *Why birds and beasts* [change] *from quality and kind*—Cæs I 3 64. *We will unfold To creatures stern sad tunes, to change their kinds*—Lucr 1146. Of its own kind, by its own nature, of itself: *Nature should bring forth, Of it own kind, all poison*—Tp II 1 162. *To do one's kind,* to do what is natural to one: *You must think this, look you, that the worm will do his kind*—Ant V 2 263. *Their several kinds have done,* have done their parts to the extent of their natural abilities: *So, with good life . . . my meaner ministers Their several kinds have done*—Tp III 3 86.

(2) Nature in general: *In the doing of the deed of kind*—Merch I 3 86. *Unfrequented plots . . . Fitted by kind for rape and villany*—Tit II 1 115.

(3) Mode of action, manner, way: *Dumb jewels often in their silent kind More than quick words do move a woman's mind*—Gent III 1 90. *If the prince do solicit you in that kind, you know your answer*—Ado II 1 70. *He says they can do nothing in this kind*—Mids V 88.

KINDLE

To bring forth (young): [Native] *as the cony that you see dwell where she is kindled*—As III 2 357.

KINDLESS

Without natural feeling: *Treacherous, lecherous, kindless villain!*—Hml II 2 609.

KINDLY (adj.)

(1) Natural, existing in one by the laws of nature: *By that fatherly and kindly power That you have in her, bid her answer truly*—Ado IV 1 75.

(2) Innate: *'Tis lack of kindly warmth they are not kind*—Tim II 2 226.

KINDLY (adv.)

(1) In accordance with one's nature: *Shalt see thy other daughter will use thee kindly*—Lr I 5 14 (with a play).

(2) Properly, fittingly: *This do and do it kindly* —Shr Ind 1 66.

(3) Exactly: *Thou hast most kindly hit it*—Rom II 4 59.

KINGDOM

Sovereignty, kingship: *I must be married to my brother's daughter, Or else my kingdom stands on brittle glass*—R3 IV 2 61.

KINGDOMED

Constituted as a kingdom; fig.: *Kingdom'd Achilles in commotion rages*—Troil II 3 185.

KIRTLE

A woman's gown consisting of a jacket with a skirt attached: *What stuff wilt have a kirtle of?* —2 H4 II 4 297. *A kirtle Embroider'd all with leaves of myrtle*—Pilgr 363. In 2 H4 V 4 23 (*If you be not swinged, I'll forswear half-kirtles*) half-kirtle seems to denote either the jacket or the skirt. Possibly some kind of short cloak may be meant.

KISSING-COMFIT

A comfit for sweetening the breath: [Let it] *hail kissing-comfits*—Wiv V 5 22.

KITCHEN

To entertain in the kitchen: *There is a fat friend at your master's house, That kitchen'd me for you to-day at dinner*—Err V 414.

KNACK

A knick-knack, toy: *Knacks, trifles, nosegays*— Mids I 1 34. ['Tis] *A knack, a toy, a trick*—Shr IV 3 67. *I was wont To load my she with knacks* —Wint IV 4 358.

KNAP[1]

To knock, rap: *She knapped 'em o' the coxcombs with a stick*—Lr II 4 124.

KNAP[2]

To bite, nibble: *As lying a gossip . . . as ever knapped ginger*—Merch III 1 9.

KNAVE

(1) A servant: *A couple of Ford's knaves, his hinds*—Wiv III 5 99. *Not being Fortune, he's but Fortune's knave*—Ant V 2 3.

(2) Opposed to knight: Lady F. . . . *Thou*

most untoward knave. Bast. *Knight, knight, good mother*—John I 243.

(3) Used endearingly or jocularly: *Poor knave, I blame thee not*—Cæs IV 3 241. *How now, my pretty knave! how dost thou?*—Lr I 4 107.

KNAVERY

(1) A roguish or waggish trick: *This is a knavery of them to make me afeard*—Mids III 1 115. *I would we were well rid of this knavery*—Tw IV 2 72. *He was full of jests, and gipes, and knaveries*—H5 IV 7 51.

(2) Tricks of dress or adornment: [We will] *revel it as bravely as the best, With silken coats . . . With amber bracelets, beads and all this knavery*—Shr IV 3 54.

KNIT (sb.)

Style of knitting, texture: or perh., style of tying: *Their garters of an indifferent knit*—Shr IV 1 94.

KNIT (vb.)

To tie (a knot), to tie in or to tie up with a knot: *I'll knit it (i.e. her hair) up in silken strings*—Gent II 7 45. *He shall not knit a knot in his fortunes with the finger of my substance*—Wiv III 2 75. *I knit my handkercher about your brows*—John IV 1 42. *I'll have this knot knit up to-morrow morning*—Rom IV 2 24.

KNOT (sb.)

A laid-out garden plot: *Her knots disorder'd and her wholesome herbs Swarming with caterpillars*—R2 III 4 46.

KNOT (vb.)

To gather together or become closely joined as in a knot: *A cistern for foul toads To knot and gender in*—Oth IV 2 61.

KNOT-GRASS

A kind of creeping weed: *You minimus, of hindering knot-grass made*—Mids III 2 329. An infusion of it was supposed to stunt the growth.

KNOTTY-PATED

Blockheaded: *Thou knotty-pated fool*—1 H4 II 4 251.

KNOW

(1) To learn, ascertain: *Turn you the key, and know his business of him*—Meas I 4 8. *I beseech you . . . to know of the knight what my offence to him is*—Tw III 4 277. *Know of the duke if his last purpose hold*—Lr V 1 1. *Go know of Cassio where he supp'd to-night*—Oth V 1 117. To take cognizance: *Let but your honour know . . . Had time cohered with place . . . Whether you had not sometime in your life Err'd in this point*—Meas II 1 8. *Know of your youth, examine well your blood, Whether . . .*—Mids I 1 68.

(2) Of two persons, to be acquainted: *You and I have known, sir*—Ant II 6 85. *Sir, we have known together in Orleans*—Cymb I 4 36.

(3) *To know for,* to be aware of: *He might have more diseases than he knew for*—2 H4 I 2 5.

KNOWING

Something known, an experience: *This sore night Hath trifled former knowings*—Mcb II 43.

L

LABEL (sb.)

A narrow strip attached to a deed to carry the seal: *Ere this hand, by thee to Romeo seal'd, Shall be the label to another deed*—Rom IV 1 56. App., a piece of paper written upon: *When I waked, I found This label on my bosom*—Cymb V 5 429.

LABEL (vb.)

To detail by way of supplement: *It (i.e. her beauty) shall be inventoried, and every particle and utensil labelled to my will*—Tw I 5 263.

LABOUR (sb.)

Trouble or pains taken: *If it please you, take it for your labour*—Gent II 1 139. *There's for thy labour*—H5 III 6 167. *We thank you for your well-took labour*—Hml II 2 83. *To confess, and be hanged for his labour*—Oth IV 1 38.

LABOUR (vb.)

(1) To produce or bring about with labour: *If your love Can labour aught in sad invention*—Ado V 1 292. *To labour and effect one thing specially*—Shr I 1 120.

(2) To strive to effect: *Swore . . . That he would labour my delivery*—R3 I 4 252.

(3) To suffer the pains of childbirth: *My Muse labours, And thus she is deliver'd*—Oth II 1 128. App. of the offspring: *When great things labouring perish in their birth*—LLL V 2 521. *The birth of our own labouring breath*—Troil IV 4 40.

LABOURED

Wearied: *Your king, whose labour'd spirits . . . Crave harbourage*—John II 232.

LABOURSOME

(1) Laborious: *By laboursome petition*—Hml I 2 59.

(2) Elaborate: *Your laboursome and dainty trims*—Cymb III 4 167.

LACK

(1) To be wanting or missing: *Here lacks but your mother for to say amen*—Tit IV 2 44. *What so poor a man as Hamlet is May do . . . God willing, shall not lack*—Hml I 5 185.

(2) To perceive the want of, miss: *You are loved, sir; They that least lend it you shall lack you first*—All's I 2 67. *I shall be loved when I am lack'd*—Cor IV 1 15. *Your noble friends do lack you:*—Mcb III 4 84. *She'll run mad When she shall lack it*—Oth III 3 317.

LADE

To empty by ladling or baling: *Saying, he'll lade it (i.e.* the sea) *dry to have his way*—3 H6 III 2 139.

LADY-SHE

A lady: *I love thee not . . . behind What lady-she her lord*—Wint I 2 43. Cf. *She.*

LAG (adj.)

Late: *Came too lag to see him buried*—R3 II 1 90. *Lag of,* later than: *For that I am some twelve or fourteen moonshines Lag of a brother*—Lr I 2 5.

LAG (sb.)

The lowest class (in a community): *The common lag of people*—Tim III 6 90.

LAG-END

The fag end: *The lag-end of my life*—1 H4 V 1 24. *The lag end of their lewdness*—H8 I 3 35.

LAKIN

See *By'r lakin.*

LAMENTABLE

Expressing sorrow: *Why holds thine eye that lamentable rheum?*—John III 1 22.

LAMPASS

A swelling of the roof of the mouth in horses: *Troubled with the lampass*—Shr III 2 52.

LAND

See *Laund.*

LAND-DAMN

App., to maltreat in some way: *I would land-damn him*—Wint II 1 143. Prob. corrupt.

LANGUISH

(1) To be sick *of: What is it . . . the king languishes of?*—All's I 1 37.

(2) To pass (a period of time) in languishing: *To think that man . . . will his free hours languish for Assured bondage*—Cymb I 6 69.

LANGUOR

Affliction of spirit, sorrow: *My heart's deep languor and my soul's sad tears*—Tit III 1 13.

LANK

To become shrunken: *Thy cheek So much as lank'd not*—Ant I 4 70.

LAPSE

App., to pounce upon, apprehend: *For which, if I be lapsed in this place, I shall pay dear*—Tw III 3 36.

LAPSED

Lapsed in time and passion, prob., having neglected the due time of action by giving way to emotion: *Your tardy son . . . That, lapsed in time and passion, lets go by The important acting of your dread command*—Hml III 4 106.

LARD

(1) To make fat or greasy: *Falstaff sweats to death, And lards the lean earth as he walks along*—1 H4 II 2 115. *It is the pasture lards the rother's sides*—Tim IV 3 12.

(2) To garnish: *In which array . . . doth he lie, Larding the plain*—H5 IV 6 7. *Larded with sweet flowers*—Hml IV 5 37.

LARGE

(1) Lavish, prodigal: *The poor King Reignier, whose large style Agrees not with the leanness of his purse*—2 H6 I 1 111.

(2) Unrestrained: *Be large in mirth*—Mcb III 4 11. *The adulterous Antony, most large In his abominations*—Ant III 6 93.

(3) Licentious: *By some large jests he will make*—Ado II 3 205. *I never tempted her with word too large*—IV 1 53.

(4) *At large,* in full size: *The baby figure of the giant mass Of things to come at large*—Troil I 3 345. In totality: *A land itself at large, a potent dukedom*—As V 4 175.

LARGE-HANDED

Grasping, rapacious: *Large-handed robbers*—Tim IV 1 11.

LARGELY

Fully, in detail: *I'll tell you largely of fair Hero's death*—Ado V 4 69.

LASS-LORN

Forsaken by one's sweetheart: *Thy broom-groves, Whose shadow the dismissed bachelor loves, Being lass-lorn*—Tp IV 66.

LAST

(1) The latest part, the conclusion, end: *Sit still, and hear the last of our sea-sorrow*—Tp I 2 170.

(2) The last time: *The last that e'er I took her leave at court*—All's V 3 79.

(3) *In the last,* in the end, finally: *In the last, When he had carried Rome . . .*—Cor V 6 42.

LATCH¹

To seize, catch: *Words That would be howl'd out in the desert air, Where hearing should not latch them*—Mcb IV 3 193. *It (i.e. his eye) no form delivers to the heart Of bird, of flower, or shap, which it doth latch*—Sonn 113 5.

LATCH²

Leach; to wet, moisten: *Hast thou yet latch'd the Athenian's eyes With the love-juice?*—Mids III 2 36. But this word is not well authenticated for the period. Perh. the reference should be made to Latch (the vb. of this form still current) in the transferred sense to fasten, and hence, to restrain from free activity, constrain to a particular activity.

LATE (adj.)

(1) Lately appointed: K. Hen. . . *Who are the late commissioners?* Cam. *I one, my lord: Your highness bade me ask for it to-day*—H5 II 2 61.

(2) *Latest*, last: *Hear . . . the very latest counsel That ever I shall breathe*—2 H4 IV 5 183. *Their latest refuge Was to send him*—Cor V 3 11. *The latest of my wealth I'll share amongst you*—Tim IV 2 23.

LATED

Belated: *Now spurs the lated traveller apace*—Mcb III 3 6. *I am so lated in the world, that I Have lost my way for ever*—Ant III 11 3.

LATTEN

A mixed metal, identical with or resembling brass; attrib.: *This latten bilbo*—Wiv I 1 165.

LATTER-BORN

Later-born: *My wife, more careful for the latter-born*—Err I 1 79.

LAUND, LAND

An open space in a wood, a glade: *You nymphs . . . Leave your crisp channels and on this green land Answer your summons*—Tp IV 128. *Through this laund anon the deer will come*—3 H6 III 1 2. *Homeward through the dark laund runs apace*—Ven 813.

LAVISH

Unrestrained, licentious, impetuous: *When means and lavish manners meet together, O, with what wings shall his affections fly!*—2 H4 IV 4 64. *His lavish tongue*—1 H6 II 5 47. *Curbing his lavish spirit*—Mcb I 2 57.

LAVISHLY

Laxly, arbitrarily: *Some about him have too lavishly Wrested his meaning and authority*—2 H4 IV 2 57.

LAVOLTA, LAVOLT

A lively dance for two: *Teach lavoltas high and swift corantos*—H5 III 5 33. *I cannot sing, Nor heel the high lavolt*—Troil IV 4 87.

LAW-DAY

A court-day; hence, a court: *Keep leets and law-days and in session sit*—Oth III 3 140.

LAWFUL

(1) Permissible, allowable: *Is't lawful, pray you, To see her women?*—Wint II 2 11. *Is it not lawful . . . to tell how many is killed?*—H5 IV 8 122. *Be it lawful I take up what's cast away*—Lr I 1 256.

(2) In R3 IV 4 29 (*Rest thy unrest on England's lawful earth, Unlawfully made drunk with innocents' blood!*) the word seems to be used without definite meaning merely in view of *unlawfully* following.

LAY (sb.)

A stake: *My fortunes against any lay worth naming*—Oth II 3 329. A wager: Clif. *My soul and body on the action both!* York. *A dreadful lay!*—2 H6 V 2 26. *I will have it no lay*—Cymb I 4 159.

LAY (vb.)

(1) To watch, beset: [I] *durst not peep out, for all the country is laid for me*—2 H6 IV 10 4.

(2) *To lay to pawn, to gage*, to deposit in pawn or as a pledge: *I have been content, sir, you should lay my countenance to pawn*—Wiv II 2 4. *Lay their swords to pawn*—III 1 112. [He] *Pawn'd honest looks, but laid no words to gage*—Lucr 1351.

(3) *Lay by*, in nautical phrase = lay to; hence, stand: *Got with swearing 'Lay by'*—1 H4 I 2 40.

(4) *To lay off*, to take (one's fingers) *off* (something): *To my thinking, he was very loath to lay his fingers off it*—Cæs I 2 242.

(5) *To lay off*, to steer (a ship) away from the shore: *Set her two courses off to sea again; lay her off*—Tp I 1 52.

(6) To lie: *Down I laid to list the sad-tuned tale*—Compl 4.

LAZAR (adj.)

Affected with a loathsome disease: *The lazar kite of Cressid's kind*—H5 II 1 80. See Cressida.

LAZAR (sb.)

A poor diseased person, esp. a leper: *To relief of lazars and weak age*—H5 I 1 15. *If she that lays thee out says thou art a fair corse, I'll be sworn . . . upon't she never shrouded any but lazars*—Troil II 3 34. *To be the louse of a lazar*—V 1 72.

LAZAR-LIKE

Like what pertains to a leper: *A most instant tetter bark'd about, Most lazar-like . . . All my smooth body*—Hml I 5 71.

LEAD

To carry, bear: [He] *has led the drum before the English tragedians*—All's IV 3 298. Sim.: *If you will lead these graces to the grave*—Tw I 5 260.

LEADING

Generalship: *Being men of such great leading as you are*—1 H4 IV 3 17.

LEAK

(1) To make water: *We leak in your chimney*—1 H4 II 1 22.

(2) In passive, to have sprung a leak: *Leak'd is our bark*—Tim IV 2 19.

LEAPING-HOUSE

A brothel: *The signs of leaping-houses*—1 H4 I 2 9.

LEARN

To teach, instruct: *The red plague rid you For learning me your language!*—Tp I 2 364. *You learn me noble thankfulness*—Ado IV 1 31. *Hast thou not learn'd me how To make perfumes?*—Cymb I 5 12.

LEARNED

Having had instruction; and so, well educated, cultured: *Never schooled and yet learned*—As I 1 173. *Free, learn'd and valiant*—Tw I 5 279. *If you are learn'd, Be not as common fools*—Cor III 1 99.

LEARNING

(1) A lesson: [The king] *Puts to him all the learnings that his time Could make him the receiver of*—Cymb I 1 43.

(2) Information, intelligence: [I] *have my learning from some true reports*—Ant II 2 47.

(3) An acquirement: *I once did hold it . . . A baseness to write fair and labour'd much How to forget that learning*—Hml V 2 33.

LEASING

Lying, falsehood: *Now Mercury endue thee with leasing, for thou speakest well of fools!*—Tw I 5 105. A falsehood: *In his praise [I] Have almost stamp'd the leasing*—Cor V 2 21.

LEAST

In the least, as the least: *What, in the least, Will you require?*—Lr I 1 194.

LEATHER-COAT

A russet apple: *There's a dish of leather-coats for you*—2 H4 V 3 44.

LEAVE (sb.)

To give leave, with dative or absol., to leave alone or in private: *Sir Thurio, give us leave, I pray, awhile*—Gent III 1 1. *James Gurney, wilt thou give us leave awhile?*—John I 230. *Nurse, give leave awhile*—Rom I 3 7.

LEAVE (vb.)

(1) To abandon, forsake (a habit, practice, &c.): Beat. . . . *How long have you professed apprehension?* Marg. *Ever since you left it*—Ado III 4 67. [I'll] *leave sack, and live cleanly*—1 H4 V 4 168.

(2) To cease, desist from, stop; with obj. a sb.: *With purpose presently to leave this war*—John V 7 86. *To leave this keen encounter of our wits*—R3 I 2 115. *Come, leave your tears*—Cor IV 1 1. With obj. a gerund: *The pretty wretch left crying*—Rom I 3 44. *Where I left reading*—Cæs IV 3 274. [She] *Bids them leave quaking*—Ven 899. With infinitive: *I cannot leave to love*—Gent II 6 17. *Leave to afflict my heart*—2 H6 II 1 182. *Could you on this fair mountain leave to feed?*—Hml III 4 66. Absol.: *Let us not leave till all our own be won*—1 H4 V 5 44. *Where did I leave?*—Hml II 1 51. *Let us leave here, gentlemen*—Cymb I 4 109.

(3) To part with, give up: *It seems you loved not her, to leave her token*—Gent IV 4 79. *I dare be sworn for him he would not leave it (i.e. the ring)*—Merch V 172. *Now you have left your voices, I have no further with you*—Cor II 3 180.

(4) To neglect, omit (to do a thing): *What some men do, While some men leave to do!*—Troil III 3 132.

LEAVENED

A leavened choice, one allowed to work long in the mind; or perh., one formed after working in scrutiny through the whole of the object: *We have with a leaven'd and prepared choice Proceeded to you*—Meas I 1 52.

LECHER (sb.)

One given to lewdness: *I will now take the lecher*—Wiv III 5 146. *An old lecher's heart*—Lr III 4 117.

LECHER (vb.)

To commit lewdness: *The small gilded fly Does lecher in my sight*—Lr IV 6 114.

LECTURE

(1) That which is read: *All books of love . . . And see you read no other lectures to her*—Shr I 2 147.

(2) A lesson, instruction: *When in music we have spent an hour, Your lecture shall have leisure for as much*—Shr III 1 7. *His lecture will be done ere you have tuned*—23. *My former lecture and advice*—Hml II 1 67.

(3) A reading out: *Would it not shame thee in so fair a troop To read a lecture of them* (*i.e.* his offences)*?*—R2 IV 231.

LEER

Countenance, hue: *He hath a Rosalind of a better leer than you*—As IV 1 66. *Here's a young lad framed of another leer*—Tit IV 2 119.

LEESE

Lose: *Flowers distill'd . . . Leese but their show*—Sonn 5 13.

LEET

A manor court: *You would present her at the leet*—Shr Ind 2 89. *Keep leets and law-days and in session sit*—Oth III 3 140.

LEGERITY

Lightness, nimbleness: *The organs . . . newly move, With casted slough and fresh legerity*—H5 IV 1 21.

LEGITIMATION

Legitimacy: *Legitimation, name and all is gone*—John I 248.

LEIGER, LIEGER

An ambassador, an agent: *Lord Angelo, having affairs to heaven, Intends you for his swift ambassador, Where you shall be an everlasting leiger*—Meas III 1 56. *Shall quite unpeople her Of liegers for her sweet*—Cymb I 5 79.

LEISURE

(1) Freedom or opportunity to do or *for* something: *What I told you then, I hope I shall have leisure to make good*—Err V 374. *That so I may . . . Have leave and leisure to make love to her*—Shr I 2 135. *Your lecture shall have leisure for as much*—III 1 8. *By my good leisure,* by making good use of opportunity—Meas III 2 261.

(2) Duration of opportunity, time available before it is too late: *No leisure had he to enrank his men*—1 H6 I 1 115.

(3) *Spiritual leisure,* time taken from ordinary avocations and given to religious duties: *You have scarce time To steal from spiritual leisure a brief span To keep your earthly audit*—H8 III 2 139.

LEMAN

A lover, sweetheart: *His wife's leman*—Wiv IV 2 171. *I sent thee sixpence for thy leman*—Tw II 3 25. *Drink unto the leman mine*—2 H4 V 3 49.

LENDINGS

(1) Money advanced to soldiers when the regular pay could not be given: *Mowbray hath received eight thousand nobles In name of lendings for your highness' soldiers*—R2 I 1 88.

(2) Superfluities: *Off, off, you lendings! come,*

unbutton here. [Tearing off his clothes]—Lr III 4 113.

LENGTH

To lengthen: *Short, night, to-night, and length thyself to-morrow*—Pilgr 210.

L'ENVOY

An epilogue, postscript: *Come, thy l'envoy; begin*—LLL III 72. *Moth. . . . Is not l'envoy a salve?* *Arm. No, page: it is an epilogue or discourse, to make plain Some obscure precedence*—81.

LESS (adj.)

Used where the sense requires *more*: *I ne'er heard yet That any of these bolder vices wanted Less impudence to gainsay what they did Than to perform it first*—Wint III 2 55. *Her judgement, which . . . an easy battery might lay flat, for taking a beggar without less quality*—Cymb I 4 22.

LESS (adv.)

(1) Used where the sense requires *more*: Mar. . . . *Tullus Aufidius, is he within your walls?* First Sen. *No, nor a man that fears you less than he*—Cor I 4 13.

(2) *Nothing less,* anything rather (than the thing in question): Bushy. *'Tis nothing but conceit, my gracious lady.* Queen. *'Tis nothing less*—R2 II 2 33.

LET (sb.)

An impediment, hindrance: *That I may know the let, why gentle Peace Should not expel these inconveniences*—H5 V 2 65. *Thy kinsmen are no let to me*—Rom II 2 69. *My uncontrolled tide . . . swells the higher by this let*—Lucr 645.

LET (vb.)[1]

To hinder, prevent: *What lets but one may enter at her window?*—Gent III 1 113. *What lets it but he would be here?*—Err II 1 105. *If nothing lets to make us happy both But . . .*—Tw V 256. *I'll make a ghost of him that lets me!*—Hml I 4 85.

LET (vb.)[2]

(1) To allow to remain: *I'll give him my commission To let him there a month behind the gest*—Wint I 2 40.

(2) To omit, forbear: *Collatine unwisely did not let To praise the clear unmatched red and white*—Lucr 10.

(3) To cause to, make: *He lets me feed with his hinds*—As I 1 19. *If your name be Horatio, as I am let to know it is*—Hml IV 6 10.

LETHE

App., death, and hence, life-blood (perh. influenced by Lat. *Letum*): *Sign'd in thy spoil, and crimson'd in thy lethe*—Cæs III I 206.

LETHE'D

App., Lethean, causing oblivion: *That sleep and feeding may prorogue his honour Even till a Lethe'd dulness*—Ant II 1 26.

LETTER

The letter, alliteration: *I will something affect the letter, for it argues facility*—LLL IV 2 56.

LEVEL (adj.)

Equipoised, steady: *So sways she level in her husband's heart*—Tw II 4 32. *It is not a confident brow . . . can thrust me from a level consideration*—2 H4 II 1 121.

LEVEL (sb.)

(1) The aim of a missile weapon: *As if that name, Shot from the deadly level of a gun (i.e. from a gun aimed in deadly fashion), Did murder her*—Rom III 3 102. *Against the level of mine aim*, not in accordance with my real design: *I am not an impostor that proclaim Myself against the level of mine aim*—All's II 1 158.

(2) The line of fire; the range of the aim (the two senses sometimes difficult to distinguish): *The harlot king Is quite beyond mine arm, out of the blank And level of my brain*—Wint II 3 4. *My life stands in the level of your dreams*—III 2 82. *I stood i' the level Of a full-charged confederacy*—H8 I 2 2. *Bring me within the level of your frown*—Sonn 117 11. *Not a heart which in his level came Could 'scape the hail of his all-hurting aim*—Compl 309.

LEVEL (vb.)

(1) To guess: *Level at my affection*—Merch I 2 41. *She level'd at our purposes*—Ant V 2 339.

(2) To accord, be in keeping: *Such accommodation . . . As levels with her breeding*—Oth I 3 239.

LEVEL (adv.)

With direct aim: *Whose whisper . . . As level as the cannon to his blank, Transports his poison'd shot*—Hml IV 1 41. *It shall as level to your judgement pierce As day does to your eye*—IV 5 151.

LEVY

To levy offence, app. suggested by the phrase *to levy war*: *Never did thought of mine levy offence*—Per II 5 52.

LEWD

(1) Ill-mannered: [*He*] *Cannot be quiet scarce a breathing-while, But you must trouble him with lewd complaints*—R3 I 3 60.

(2) Wicked, unprincipled, given to evil courses: *We'll talk with Margaret, How her acquaintance grew with this lewd fellow (i.e. Borachio, who has just confessed his villainy)*—Ado V 1 341. *You have been so lewd and so much engraffed to Falstaff*—2 H4 II 2 66.

(3) Of things, mean, sorry, unworthy: *This [cap] was moulded on a porringer; A velvet dish: fie, fie! 'tis lewd and filthy*—Shr IV 3 64. *The which (i.e. the money) he hath detain'd for lewd employments*—R2 I 1 90. *Such poor, such bare, such lewd, such mean attempts*—1 H4 III 2 13.

LEWDLY

Wickedly, evilly: *A sort of naughty persons, lewdly bent*—2 H6 II 1 167

LEWDNESS

Folly: *There . . . They may . . . wear away The lag end of their lewdness and be laugh'd at*—H8 I 3 33.

LEWDSTER

A lecherous man: *Against such lewdsters . . . Those that betray them do no treachery*—Wiv V 3 23.

LEWD-TONGUED

Speaking with ill manners, foul-spoken: *Thy lewd-tongued wife*—Wint II 3 172.

LIABLE

(1) Subject, subservient: *All that we upon this side the sea . . . Find liable to our crown*—John II 488. *Reason to my love is liable*—Cæs II 2 104.

(2) Attached: *Who else but I, And such as to my claim are liable, Sweat in this business?*—John V 2 100.

(3) Suitable, apt: *The posterior of the day . . . is liable, congruent and measurable for the afternoon*—LLL V 1 96. *Apt, liable to be employ'd in danger*—John IV 2 226.

LIBBARD

Leopard: *With libbard's head on knee*—LLL V 2 551.

LIBEL

A leaflet or pamphlet publicly circulated: *Plots have I laid . . . By drunken prophecies, libels and dreams*—R3 I 1 32.

LIBERAL

(1) Large-minded, gentlemanly: *The people liberal, valiant, active, wealthy*—2 H6 IV 7 68. *They are soldiers, Witty, courteous, liberal, full of spirit*—3 H6 I 2 42.

(2) Such as should weigh with a gentleman; compatible with good taste: *All liberal reason I will yield unto*—LLL II 168. *Most delicate carriages, and of very liberal conceit*—Hml V 2 159.

(3) Unrestrained by decorum: *To excuse . . . The liberal opposition of our spirits*—LLL V 2 742. *Parts that become thee happily enough . . .*

But where thou art not known, why, there they show Something too liberal—Merch II 2 191. *With a liberal tongue*—R2 II 1 229. As adv., *I will speak as liberal as the north*—Oth V 2 220.

(4) Licentious: *Most like a liberal villain*—Ado IV 1 93. *Is he not a most profane and liberal counsellor?*—Oth II 1 164.

LIBERAL-CONCEITED

Tastefully designed: *Three liberal-conceited carriages*—Hml V 2 169. Cf. *Conceited* (3).

LIBERTY

(1) Unrestrained action, licence: *Liberty plucks justice by the nose*—Meas I 3 29. *The flesh'd soldier . . . In liberty of bloody hand shall range*—H5 III 3 11. *Lust and liberty*—Tim IV 1 25. *Such wanton, wild and usual slips As are companions . . . To youth and liberty*—Hml II 1 22. *Liberties of sin*, app., unbridled evil-doers: *Prating mountebanks, And many such-like liberties of sin*—Err I 2 101.

(2) One's domain: *Should he wrong my liberties in my absence?*—Per I 2 112.

(3) *The law of writ and the liberty*—Hml II 2 420. See *Writ* (2).

LID

See *God's lid*.

LIE

(1) To sojourn, dwell: *I know she will lie at my house*—All's III 5 33. *When I lay at Clement's Inn*—2 H4 III 2 299. *I sometime lay here in Corioli At a poor man's house*—Cor I 9 82.

(2) *Lie for you*, be imprisoned in your stead: *I will deliver you, or else lie for you*—R3 I 1 115.

LIEF, LIEVE

(1) Dear, beloved: *My liefest liege*—2 H6 III 1 164.

(2) Pleasing, acceptable; *had as lief, lieve,* would hold equally pleasing; and so, would as willingly: *Had as lieve hear the devil as a drum*—1 H4 IV 2 19. *She . . . had as lief see a toad*—Rom II 4 214. *I had as lief the town-crier spoke my lines*—Hml III 2 4.

LIEGER

See *Leiger*.

LIEN

Pa. pple. of To lie: *Many a poor man's son would have lien still*—John IV 1 50. *An Egyptian That had nine hours lien dead*—Per III 2 84.

LIEU OF, IN

(1) In return for: *That he, in lieu o' the premises . . . Should presently extirpate me and mine*—Tp I 2 123. *In lieu whereof* (i.e. of his services), *Three thousand ducats . . . We freely cope your courteous pains withal*—Merch IV 1 410. *A rotten*

tree, That cannot so much as a blossom yield In lieu of all thy pains—As II 3 63.

(2) App., in virtue of, presenting as one's credential: *That same scrubbed boy . . . In lieu of this last night did lie with me*—Merch V 261. Cf. *By this ring the doctor lay with me*—259.

LIEUTENANTRY

(1) Lieutenancy, the office of a lieutenant: *If such tricks as these strip you out of your lieutenantry*—Oth II 1 172.

(2) Lieutenancy, delegation of command: *He alone Dealt on lieutenantry*—Ant III 11 38. See *Deal* (vb.) (2).

LIEVE

See *Lief.*

LIFE

That which sustains life, one's living: *For competence of life I will allow you*—2 H4 V 5 70.

LIFTER

A thief (with a play): Pan. . . . *Yet will he, within three pound, lift as much as his brother Hector.* Cres. *Is he so young a man and so old a lifter?*—Troil I 2 125.

LIGGENS

Possibly a perversion of Lifekins (cf. *Bodykins*): *By God's liggens*—2 H4 V 3 69.

LIGHT

Light of ear, credulous of evil, ready to receive malicious reports: *False of heart, light of ear, bloody of hand*—Lr III 4 95.

LIGHT

Pa. pple. of To light, to fall: *You are light into my hands*—Per IV 2 77.

LIGHTLY

(1) In no great measure, slightly: *They love his grace but lightly*—R3 I 3 45.

(2) Commonly, often: *Short summers lightly have a forward spring*—R3 III 1 94.

LIGHTNESS

App., lightheadedness: *Fell into a sadness . . . Thence to a lightness*—Hml II 2 147.

LIGHTNING

Lightening, a shedding of light; and so, an exhilaration or revival (of the spirits): *How oft when men are at the point of death Have they been merry! which their keepers call A lightning before death*—Rom V 3 88.

LIGHT O' LOVE

An old dance-tune: *Best sing it to the tune of 'Light o' love'*—Gent I 2 83. *Clap's into 'Light o' love' . . . do you sing it, and I'll dance it*—Ado III 4 44.

LIKE (adj.)

Likely: *O, that it were as like as it is true!*—Meas V 104. *Is't like that lead contains her?*—Merch II 7 49. *'Tis most like The sovereignty will fall upon Macbeth*—Mcb II 4 29.

LIKE (sb.)

Likelihood, probability: *Say that he thrive, as 'tis great like he will*—2 H6 III 1 379.

LIKE (vb.)¹

To liken: *When the prince broke thy head for liking his father to a singing-man*—2 H4 II 1 96. To make like: *Like me to the peasant boys of France*—1 H6 IV 6 48.

LIKE (vb.)²

(1) To please, suit: *That that likes not you pleases me best* — Troil V 2 102. *This likes me well*—Hml V 2 276. *If aught . . . Or all of it . . . may fitly like your grace*—Lr I 1 201.

(2) To be in good bodily condition, thrive: *That lived, that loved, that liked, that look'd with cheer*—Mids V 299. *You like well and bear your years very well*—2 H4 III 2 92.

LIKE (adv.)

(1) In a like degree, equally: *My fellow-ministers Are like invulnerable* — Tp III 3 65. *The enterprise whereof Shall be to you, as us, like glorious*—H5 II 2 182. *Subtle as the fox for prey, Like warlike as the wolf for what we eat*—Cymb III 3 40.

(2) As well as, as also: *Ghastly looks Are at my service, like enforced smiles*—R3 III 5 8.

LIKELIHOOD

(1) A semblance, similitude: *By a . . . loving likelihood*—H5 V Chor 29.

(2) An indication, sign: *Many likelihoods informed me of this before*—All's I 3 128. *What of his heart perceive you in his face By any likelihood he show'd to-day?*—R3 III 4 56.

(3) The quality of offering a prospect of success, promise: *A fellow of no mark nor likelihood*—1 H4 III 2 45.

LIKELY

Likely of, giving signs of, promising: *Our hopes, yet likely of fair birth*—2 H4 I 3 63.

LIKING

Bodily condition: *As long as I have an eye to make difference of men's liking*—Wiv II 1 56. Esp. good bodily condition: *I'll repent, and that suddenly, while I am in some liking*—1 H4 III 3 5.

LILY-LIVERED

Cowardly: *Thou lily-liver'd boy*—Mcb V 3 15. *A lily-livered, action-taking knave*—Lr II 2 18. See *Liver* (3).

LIMBECK

Alembic; a retort: *Memory . . . Shall be a fume, and the receipt of reason A limbeck only*—Mcb I 7 65. *Siren tears, Distill'd from limbecks foul as hell within*—Sonn 119 1.

LIMBER

Limp, flaccid; fig.: *You put me off with limber vows*—Wint I 2 47.

LIMB-MEAL

Limb by limb: *O, that I had her here, to tear her limb-meal!*—Cymb II 4 147.

LIMBO, LIMBO PATRUM

(1) A region on the border of hell, the abode of the just who died before Christ's coming and of unbaptized infants; used gen. for hell: *Talked of Satan and of Limbo and of Furies*—All's V 3 261. *As far from help as Limbo is from bliss*—Tit III 1 149.

(2) Of a prison: *He's in Tartar limbo, worse than hell*—Err IV 2 32. *I'll have some of 'em in Limbo Patrum*—H8 V 4 67.

LIMBS OF LIMEHOUSE

See *Tribulation of Tower-hill*.

LIMIT (sb.)

(1) A prescribed period: *The dateless limit of thy dear exile*—R2 I 3 151. *Dispatch; the limit of your lives is out*—R3 III 3 8. *Strength of limit*, strength gained in the prescribed period of rest after child-bearing: *Hurried Here to this place, i' the open air, before I have got strength of limit*—Wint III 2 105.

(2) A time fixed for an event: *Between which time of the contract and limit of the solemnity, her brother Frederick was wrecked at sea*—Meas III 1 223.

(3) A region, tract: *Buried in highways out of all sanctified limit*—All's I 1 152. *The arch-deacon hath divided it Into three limits very equally*—1 H4 III 1 72. *Within this limit is relief enough*—Ven 235. *Brought From limits far remote*—Sonn 44 3.

LIMIT (vb.)

(1) To fix, assign: *How may I do it, having the hour limited?*—Meas IV 2 175. *I'll limit thee this day To seek thy life by beneficial help*—Err I 1 151. *As you answer, I do know the scope And warrant limited unto my tongue*—John V 2 122. *'Tis my limited service*—Mcb II 3 57. To appoint (a person *to* an office): [I'll] *Limit each leader to his several charge*—R3 V 3 25.

(2) *Limited professions*, those under some restraint (and so outwardly respectable): *There is boundless theft In limited professions*—Tim IV 3 430.

12

LIMITATION

An appointed time: *You have stood your limitation*—Cor II 3 146.

LINE (sb.)[1]

(1) Position, station: *To show the line and the predicament Wherein you range*—1 H4 I 3 168. *In that very line, Harry, standest thou*—III 2 85.

(2) App., a pedigree: *He sends you this most memorable line, In every branch truly demonstrative; Willing you overlook this pedigree*—H5 II 4 88.

(3) *With full line*, with the full extent: *Upon his place, And with full line of his authority, Governs Lord Angelo*—Meas I 4 55.

LINE (sb.)[2]

Lind; the linden or lime: *Come, hang them (i.e. the 'glistering apparel, &c.') on this line*—Tp IV 193 (or perh. a clothes-line is meant).

LINE (vb.)[1]

To draw: *All the pictures fairest lined Are but black to Rosalind*—As III 2 97.

LINE (vb.)[2]

(1) To strengthen, reinforce: *I fear my brother Mortimer . . . hath sent for you To line his enterprize*—1 H4 II 3 84. *To line and new repair our towns of war*—H5 II 4 7. *[He] did line the rebel With hidden help*—Mcb I 3 112.

(2) To cover, overlay: *Now doth Death line his dead chaps with steel*—John II 352. To pad: *Pluck the lined crutch from thy old limping sire*—Tim IV 1 14.

LINEAL

Lineal of, lineally descended from: *Queen Isabel . . . Was lineal of the Lady Ermengare*—H5 I 2 81.

LINE-GROVE

A grove of lindens: *The line-grove which weather-fends your cell*—Tp V 10. See *Line* (sb.)[2].

LINGER

To prolong, protract: *Death, Who gently would dissolve the bands of life, Which false hope lingers in extremity*—R2 II 2 70. *Unless his abode be lingered here by some accident*—Oth IV 2 230. To defer or put off the accomplishment of: *She lingers my desires*—Mids I 1 4.

LINK

A torch, used to smoke and smarten up a hat: *There was no link to colour Peter's hat*—Shr IV 1 137.

LINSEY-WOOLSEY

A mixed material of flax and wool; fig., a medley, nonsense: *What linsey-woolsey hast thou to speak to us again?*—All's IV 1 13.

LINSTOCK

A staff holding a gunner's match: *The nimble gunner With linstock now the devilish cannon touches*—H5 III Chor 32.

LIQUID

Clear, bright: *The liquid drops of tears that you have shed*—R3 IV 4 321. *The morn and liquid dew of youth*—Hml I 3 41.

LIQUOR

A liquid in general: *One vial full of Edward's sacred blood . . . Is crack'd, and all the precious liquor spilt*—R2 I 2 17. *[How] changes fill the cup of alteration With divers liquors*—2 H4 III 1 52. *The fire that mounts the liquor till't run o'er*—H8 I 1 144.

LIST

(1) A strip of cloth: *A kersey boot-hose . . . gartered with a red and blue list*—Shr II 2 68.

(2) A limit, bound: *You have restrained yourself within the list of too cold an adieu*—All's II 1 52. *I am bound to your niece, sir; I mean, she is the list of my voyage*—Tw I 1 85. *The ocean, overpeering of his list*—Hml IV 5 99. *Confine yourself but in a patient list*—Oth IV 1 76.

LISTEN

To listen after, to endeavour to hear or to hear of: *My servant Travers, whom I sent . . . to listen after news*—2 H4 I 1 28. *I will follow Eleanor, And listen after Humphrey, how he proceeds*—2 H6 I 3 151.

LITHER

Yielding: *Winged through the lither sky*—1 H6 IV 7 21.

LITIGIOUS

App., doubtful, precarious: *Tyrus stands In a litigious peace*—Per III 3 2.

LITTLE (adj.)

A little: *Hold little faith, though thou hast too much fear*—Tw V 174. *Which to his former strength may be restored With good advice and little medicine*—2 H4 III 1 42.

LITTLE (sb.)

(1) *In little*, in miniature: *His picture in little*—Hml II 2 383. In small compass: *The quintessence of every sprite Heaven would in little show*—As III 2 147. So *drawn in little*, brought together in small compass: *If all the devils of hell be drawn in little*—Tw III 4 94.

(2) *In a little*, in a few words, briefly: *I'll tell you in a little*—H8 II 1 11.

LIVELIHOOD

Liveliness, animation: *The tyranny of her sorrows takes all livelihood from her cheek*—All's I 1 57. *His sweating palm, The precedent of pith and livelihood*—Ven 25.

LIVELY (adj.)

(1) Living, alive: *Had I but seen thy picture in this plight, It would have madded me: what shall I do Now I behold thy lively body so?*—Tit III 1 103. *To blush through lively veins*—Sonn 67 10. Undying: *A dateless lively heat, still to endure*—Sonn 153 6.

(2) Resembling the life, lifelike: *Some lively touches of my daughter's favour*—As V 4 27. *Artificial strife Lives in these touches, livelier than life*—Tim I 1 37.

LIVELY (adv.)

In a lifelike manner, to the life: *Which I so lively acted with my tears That . . .*—Gent IV 4 174. *As lively painted as the deed was done*—Shr Ind 2 58. *To see the life as lively mock'd as ever Still sleep mock'd death*—Wint V 3 19. *Thou counterfeit'st most lively*—Tim V 1 85.

LIVER

The seat or a seat

(1) Of passion in general: *You do measure the heat of our livers with the bitterness of your galls*—2 H4 I 2 197.

(2) Of anger: *I will inflame thy noble liver, And make thee rage*—2 H4 V 5 33.

(3) Of courage: *[Cowards] Who, inward search'd, have livers white as milk*—Merch III 2 86. *To awake your dormouse valour, to put fire in your heart, and brimstone in your liver*—Tw III 2 20.

(4) Of love: *If ever love had interest in his liver*—Ado IV 1 233. *To wash your liver . . . that there shall not be one spot of love in't*—As III 2 442.

LIVER-VEIN

The style of a man in love: *This is the liver-vein, which makes flesh a deity*—LLL IV 3 74. Cf. *Liver* (4).

LIVERY (sb.)

To sue one's livery, of an heir on coming of age, to sue for possession of lands held by the Court of Wards: *By his attorneys-general to sue His livery*—R2 II 1 203. *I am denied to sue my livery here*—II 3 129. *He came but . . . To sue his livery*—1 H4 IV 3 61.

LIVERY (vb.)

To array in a livery; fig.: *Did livery falseness in a pride of truth*—Compl 105.

LIVING (ppl. adj.)

Living art, the art of which we shall give a living proof: *Our court shall be a little Academe, Still and contemplative in living art*—LLL I 1 13.

LIVING (sb.)

(1) Duration of life, lifetime: *To spend her living in eternal love*—Compl 238.

(2) Property, possessions: *Within a mile where my land and living lies*—Wint IV 3 104. *Life, living, all is Death's*—Rom IV 5 40. *If I gave them all my living, I'ld keep my coxcombs myself*—Lr I 4 120. In pl.: *I might in virtues, beauties, livings, friends, Exceed account*—Merch III 2 158.

LIZARD

Their softest touch as smart as lizards' stings—2 H6 III 2 325. *Venom toads, or lizards' dreadful stings*—3 H6 II 2 138. Like the blind-worm the harmless lizard appears to have been thought poisonous in Shakespeare's time. Cf. *Blind-worm.*

LOADEN

Pa. pple. of To load: *A post from Wales loaden with heavy news*—1 H4 I 1 37. *Loaden with honour*—Cor V 3 164. *When thy car is loaden with their heads*—Tit V 2 53.

LOATHLY

With abhorrence: *Seeing how loathly opposite I stood To his unnatural purpose*—Lr II 1 51.

LOB (sb.)

A lout: *Thou lob of spirits*—Mids II 1 16.

LOB (vb.)

To allow to hang heavily: *Their poor jades Lob down their heads*—H5 IV 2 46.

LOCKRAM

A kind of linen originally made at Locronan in Brittany: *The kitchen malkin pins Her richest lockram 'bout her reechy neck*—Cor II 1 224.

LOCUST

The fruit of the carob tree; a locust-bean: *As luscious as locusts*—Oth I 3 354.

LODGE

To harbour, entertain (a feeling): *I well might lodge a fear*—2 H4 IV 5 208. *If ever any grudge were lodged between us*—R3 II 1 65. *A lodged hate*, one harboured (and grown inveterate): *I give no reason . . . More than a lodged hate . . . I bear Antonio*—Merch IV 1 59.

LODGING

(1) A room: *Empty lodgings and unfurnish'd walls*—R2 I 2 68. *The lodging where I first did swoon*—2 H4 IV 5 234. *Retire with me to my lodging*—Lr I 2 183. *To conduct These knights unto their several lodgings*—Per II 3 109.

(2) Material to lie or sleep on: *Hard lodging and thin weeds*—LLL V 2 811.

LOGGATS

A game in which the players threw sticks to lie as near a mark as possible: *Did these bones cost no*

more the breeding, but to play at loggats with 'em?
—Hml V 1 99.

LONDON-STONE

Strikes his staff on London-stone—2 H6 IV 6 (Stage Dir). *Sitting upon London-stone*—2. Now built into the street wall of St. Swithin's Church, Cannon Street, but formerly standing on the south side of the street; supposed to have been the Roman *Milliarium* or central milestone.

LONG

Belong: *No ceremony that to great ones longs*—Meas II 2 59. *An honour longing to our house*—All's IV 2 42.

LONG-ENGRAFFED

Engrafted, inveterate: *The imperfections of long-engraffed condition*—Lr I 1 300.

LONGLY

For a long while: *You look'd so longly on the maid*—Shr I 1 170.

LONG OF

Owing to, through: *All this coil is long of you*—Mids III 2 339. *All this is long of you*—Cor V 4 31. *Long of her it was That we meet here so strangely*—Cymb V 5 271.

LONG PURPLE

A local name for various species of Orchis: *Crow-flowers, nettles, daisies, and long purples*—Hml IV 7 170.

LONG-STAFF SIXPENNY STRIKERS

Ruffians with long cudgels who rob poor passengers: *I am joined with . . . no long-staff sixpenny strikers*—1 H4 II 1 81.

LOOF

Luff; to bring the head of (a ship) nearer to the wind: *She once being loof'd . . . Antony Claps on his sea-wing, and . . . flies after her*—Ant III 10 18.

LOOK

(1) To look to, examine: *I must go look my twigs*—All's III 6 115.

(2) To look for, expect: *The gifts she looks from me*—Wint IV 4 368.

(3) To seek, search for: *I will look some linen for your head*—Wiv IV 2 83. *He hath been all this day to look you*—As II 5 33. *That we may wander o'er this bloody field To look our dead*—H5 IV 7 75.

(4) To tend to, promise to: *That is there which looks With us to break his neck*—Cor III 3 29.

(5) The imperative prefixed to *what, when*, forming indefinite relatives = *whatever, whenever: Look when I serve him so, he takes it ill*—Err II 1 12.

Look what will serve is fit—Ado I 1 320. *Look what I speak, or do, or think to do, You are still crossing it*—Shr IV 3 194. *Look what I speak, my life shall prove it true*—R2 I 1 87. *Look when he fawns, he bites*—R3 I 3 290. *Look what is best, that best I wish in thee*—Sonn 37 13. It seems better to print this idiomatic expression without the comma commonly inserted after *Look*. In 'Look when his infant fortune came to age'—1 H4 I 3 253, the quotation begins, as here printed, at *Look*, and not, as generally printed, at *when*.

(6) *To look back*, to look back to: *Looking back what I have left behind*—Ant III 11 53.

(7) *To look beyond*, to misjudge: *You look beyond him quite*—2 H4 IV 4 67.

(8) *To look on*, to hold in esteem, respect: *Yet I am not look'd on in the world*—3 H6 V 7 22.

(9) *To look up*, to cheer up, take heart: *Dear, look up*—Wint V 1 215. *My sovereign lord, cheer up yourself, look up*—2 H4 IV 4 113. *Then I'll look up; My fault is past*—Hml III 3 50.

(10) *To look upon*, to be a spectator: *All of you that stand and look upon*—R2 IV 237. *Why stand we . . . Wailing our losses, whiles the foe doth rage; And look upon, as if the tragedy Were play'd in jest*—3 H6 II 3 25. *He is my prize; I will not look upon* (i.e. will not stand idly by while the other fights)—Troil V 6 10.

(11) *Looks o'er the crown*, explained as, looks on it with the aspiration to place himself over it, to become master of it: *Richmond aims At young Elizabeth . . . And, by that knot, looks proudly o'er the crown*—R3 IV 3 40.

LOON, LOWN

(1) A low fellow; a rogue, scamp: *The devil damn thee black, thou cream-faced loon!*—Mcb V 3 11. *With that he call'd the tailor lown*—Oth II 3 95.

(2) A man of low birth: *Both lord and lown*—Per IV 6 19.

LOOP

A loophole, opening: *[We must] stop all sight-holes, every loop*—1 H4 IV 1 71.

LOOPED

Full of holes: *Poor naked wretches . . . How shall . . . Your loop'd and window'd raggedness defend you?*—Lr III 4 28.

LOOSE

The act of discharging an arrow; *at the very loose*, at the last moment: *Often at his very loose [time] decides That which long process could not arbitrate*—LLL V 2 752.

LOP

The smaller branches of trees: *We take From every tree lop, bark, and part o' the timber*—H8 I 2 95.

LORD

To lord with, to make (one) the master of, endow (him) with: *He being thus lorded, Not only with what my revenue yielded, But what my power might else exact*—Tp I 2 97.

LORDING

(1) A lord: *Lordings, farewell*—2 H6 I 1 145. *A lording's daughter*—Pilgr 211.

(2) As a diminutive: *You were pretty lordings then?*—Wint I 2 62.

LORD'S SAKE

For the Lord's sake, the language in which prisoners for debt begged from passengers: *All great doers in our trade, and are now 'for the Lord's sake'*—Meas IV 3 20.

LOSE

(1) To destroy, bring to destruction, be the ruin of: *Methought her eyes had lost her tongue*—Tw II 2 21. *[Shall we] indent with fears, When they have lost and forfeited themselves?*—1 H4 I 3 87. To ruin in estimation: *Though not to have it Hath lost me in your liking*—Lr I 1 235.

(2) To forget: *My mind did lose it*—Mids I 1 114. *Hear what I say, and then go home and lose me*—H8 II 1 57. *The lesson is but plain, And once made perfect, never lost again*—Ven 407.

LOSS

Perdition, destruction, misfortune: *In the loss that may happen, it concerns you something to know it*—All's I 3 124. *Pitying My father's loss . . . Restored me to my honours*—H8 II 1 112. *Weigh what loss your honour may sustain*—Hml I 3 29. *His life, With thine . . . Stand in assured loss*—Lr III 6 100. *Beguiled me to the very heart of loss*—Ant IV 12 29.

LOTTERY

(1) A drawing of lots; decision by drawing of lots: *Make a lottery; And, by device, let blockish Ajax draw The sort*—Troil I 3 374. *'Tis put to lottery*—II 1 140. *Till each man drop by lottery*—Cæs II 1 119 (alluding to decimation; or perh. the meaning is, by chance, as chance picks him out).

(2) Something which comes by fortune: *Octavia is A blessed lottery to him*—Ant II 2 247.

LOUSE

To be infested with lice: *The head . . . shall louse*—Lr III 2 29.

LOVE

A friend: *Bid her be judge Whether Bassanio had not once a love*—Merch IV 1 276 (said by Antonio of himself).

LOVE-DAY

A day for settling disputes: *This day shall be a love-day*—Tit I 491.

LOVE-FEAT

An act of courtship: *Every one his love-feat will advance Unto his several mistress*—LLL V 2 123. Cf. *Feat* (sb.) (1).

LOVE-IN-IDLENESS

The common pansy or heartsease: *A little western flower, Before milk-white, now purple with love's wound, And maidens call it love-in-idleness*—Mids II 1 166.

LOVELY (adj.)

Loving, affectionate: *A lovely kiss*—Shr III 2 125. Amorous: *Sweet Cytherea . . . Did court the lad with many a lovely look*—Pilgr 43.

LOVELY (adv.)

Beautifully, lovably: *I framed to the harp Many an English ditty lovely well*—1 H4 III 1 123. *Thou weed, Who art so lovely fair*—Oth IV 2 67.

LOVER

A friend: *How dear a lover of my lord your husband*—Merch III 4 7 (of Antonio). *I tell thee, fellow, The general is my lover*—Cor V 2 13 (said by Menenius). *Romans, countrymen, and lovers!*—Cæs III 2 13.

LOVE-SPRING

A love-shoot: *Shall . . . Even in the spring of love, thy love-springs rot?*—Err III 2 2. Cf. *Spring.*

LOWER CHAIR

A low or easy chair: *He, sir, sitting, as I say, in a lower chair*—Meas II 1 132.

LOWLY

App., lying low (in death): *As looks the mother on her lowly babe When death doth close his tender dying eyes*—1 H6 III 3 47.

LOWN

See *Loon.*

LOWT

More commonly Lout; to treat with contumely, mock: *I am lowted by a traitor villain*—1 H6 IV 3 13.

LOYALTY

Conjugal faithfulness: *This minion stood upon her chastity, Upon her nuptial vow, her loyalty*—Tit II 3 124. *The oath of loyalty*—Cymb I 6 102.

LOZEL

A scoundrel: *Lozel, thou art worthy to be hang'd*—Wint II 3 109.

LUCE

A pike: *They may give the dozen white luces in their coat*—Wiv I 1 16.

LUCRE

Lucre of, gain or profit to be derived from (something): *Shall I, for lucre of the rest unvanquish'd, Detract so much from that prerogative, As to be call'd but viceroy of the whole?*—1 H6 V 4 141.

LUD'S-TOWN

London: *Made Lud's town with rejoicing fires bright*—Cymb III 1 32. *On the gates of Lud's-town* [I'll] *set your heads*—IV 2 99.

LUMPISH

Low-spirited, dull: *She is lumpish, heavy, melancholy*—Gent III 2 62.

LUNE

In pl., fits of frenzy, mad freaks or tantrums: *Your husband is in his old lunes again*—Wiv IV 2 21. *These dangerous unsafe lunes i' the king*—Wint II 2 30. [They] *watch His pettish lunes*—Troil II 3 138.

LURCH

(1) To lurk, skulk: [I] *am fain to shuffle, to hedge and to lurch*—Wiv II 2 25.

(2) *To lurch of*, to be beforehand with in securing: *In the brunt of seventeen battles since He lurch'd all swords of the garland*—Cor II 2 104.

LURE

A sham bird with a bait (consisting of food and known as a train) attached, used to attract back an erring hawk: *Till she stoop she must not be full-gorged, For then she never looks upon her lure*—Shr IV 1 194. *As falcon to the lure, away she flies*—Ven 1027. Cf. *Train* (sb.) and (vb.).

LUSH

Succulent, luxuriant: *How lush and lusty the grass looks!*—Tp II 1 52.

LUST

(1) Pleasure, delight: *Whose eyes do never give*

But thorough lust and laughter—Tim IV 3 491. *Gazing upon the Greeks with little lust*—Lucr 1384.

(2) (One's) desire, (one's) good pleasure; *I'll answer to my lust*, to my satisfaction, so as to take my fill of it: *When I am hence, I'll answer to my lust*—Troil IV 4 133.

LUST-BREATHED

Inspired by lust, or breathing lust: *Lust-breathed Tarquin*—Lucr 3.

LUST-DIETED

Feeding on lust, voluptuous: *The superfluous and lust-dieted man*—Lr IV 1 70.

LUSTY

Lustful: *As once Europa did* [rejoice] *at lusty Jove, When he would play the noble beast in love*—Ado V 4 46. *I do suspect the lusty Moor Hath leap'd into my seat*—Oth II 1 304.

LUXURIOUS

Lascivious, unchaste: *She knows the heat of a luxurious bed*—Ado IV 1 42. *The dissembling luxurious drab*—Troil V 4 8. *O most insatiate and luxurious woman!*—Tit V 1 88. *I grant him bloody, Luxurious, avaricious*—Mcb IV 3 57.

LUXURIOUSLY

Lasciviously: *Besides what hotter hours . . . you have Luxuriously pick'd out*—Ant III 13 118.

LUXURY

Lasciviousness, lust: *His hateful luxury, And bestial appetite in change of lust*—R3 III 5 80. *How the devil Luxury . . . tickles these together!*—Troil V 2 55. *A couch for luxury and damned incest*—Hml I 5 83. *To't, luxury, pell-mell! for I lack soldiers*—Lr IV 6 119.

LYM

A lyam-hound, bloodhound: *Hound or spaniel, brach or lym*—Lr III 6 72.

M

MAD

To be or become mad: *When* [Ascanius] *to madding Dido would unfold His father's acts*—2 H6 III 2 117.

MADE-UP

Consummate, perfect: *A made-up villain*—Tim V 1 101.

MAGNANIMITY

Courage, fortitude: *Infuse his breast with magnanimity*—3 H6 V 4 41.

MAGNANIMOUS

Courageous, valiant: *Be magnanimous in the enterprise and go on*—All's III 6 70. *As valiant as the wrathful dove or most magnanimous mouse*—2 H4 III 2 170. *Valiant and magnanimous deeds*—Troil II 2 200.

MAGNIFICO

A Venetian magnate: *The duke himself, and the magnificoes Of greatest port*—Merch III 2 283. *The magnifico is much beloved*—Oth I 2 12.

MAGNUS' CORNER, SAINT

By the Church of St. Magnus the Martyr, Fish Street (*q.v.*), destroyed in the Great Fire and rebuilt by Wren: *Up Fish Street! down Saint Magnus' Corner!*—2 H6 IV 8 1.

MAGOT-PIE

Magpie: *Augurs . . . have By magot-pies and choughs and rooks brought forth The secret'st man of blood*—Mcb III 4 124.

MAID

A man who has always abstained from sexual intercourse: *You are betroth'd both to a maid and man*—Tw V 270.

MAID MARIAN

Robin Hood's mistress; a character in the morris-dance (see *Morris, Morris-dance*), generally represented by a clown or a strumpet: *For womanhood, Maid Marian may be the deputy's wife of the ward to thee*—1 H4 III 3 129.

MAIL (sb.)

A piece of mail-armour: *To have done is to hang Quite out of fashion, like a rusty mail*—Troil III 3 151.

MAIL (vb.)

To wrap up, envelop: *Methinks I should not thus be led along, Mail'd up in shame, with papers on my back*—2 H6 II 4 30.

MAIM

A disablement, injury: *A dearer merit, not so deep a maim . . . Have I deserved*—R2 I 3 156. *Your father's sickness is a maim to us*—1 H4 IV 1 42. *Humphrey . . . [is] scarce himself, That bears so shrewd a maim*—2 H6 II 3 40.

MAIN (adj.)

(1) Important, momentous: *He might . . . in a main danger fail you*—All's III 6 16. *What cross devil Made me put this main secret in the packet?*—H8 III 2 214.

(2) Pre-eminent, foremost: *His son; who . . . stands up For the main soldier*—Ant I 2 196.

(3) General, that of all or the majority: *By the main assent Of all these learned men she was divorced*—H8 IV 1 31. *If he were foil'd, Why then, we did our main opinion crush In taint of our best man*—Troil I 3 372. *No further Than the main voice of Denmark goes withal*—Hml I 3 27.

(4) Fixed, strongly held: *The main opinion he held once Of fantasy, of dreams and ceremonies*—Cæs II 1 196.

(5) *The main flood*, high water: *You may as well go stand upon the beach And bid the main flood bate his usual height*—Merch IV 1 71.

(6) *Main chance.* See under that heading.

MAIN (sb.)[1]

(1) Strength, force; *with all our main of power*, with the full strength of our power: *To-morrow We must with all our main of power stand fast*—Troil II 3 272.

(2) Mainland, land: *Swell the curled waters 'bove the main*—Lr III 1 6.

(3) A broad expanse: *Nativity, once in the main of light, Crawls to maturity*—Sonn 60 5.

(4) The chief matter, principal thing: *I doubt it is no other but the main; His father's death, and our o'erhasty marriage*—Hml II 2 56. The chief or principal part: *Goes it against the main of Poland, sir, Or for some frontier?*—Hml IV 4 15.

MAIN (sb.)[2]

In the game of hazard, a number called by the 'caster' before the throwing of the dice, and forming the main factor determining his fortunes; fig., of something at hazard: *[Were it good] to set so rich a main On the nice hazard of one doubtful hour?*—1 H4 IV 1 47. See also *Main Chance.*

MAIN (vb.)

Maim: *Thereby is England mained*—2 H6 IV 2 171.

MAIN CHANCE

Equivalent to *Main* (sb.)[2]; fig., the general probability with regard to a future event: *There is a history in all men's lives . . . The which observed, a man may prophesy, With a near aim, of the main chance of things*—2 H4 III 1 80. *To look to the main* or *to the main chance*, to use one's best endeavours (for some object): Sal. *Then let's make haste away, and look unto the main.* War. *Unto the main! O father, Maine is lost . . . Main chance, father, you meant; but I meant Maine*—2 H6 I 1 208.

MAIN-COURSE

The mainsail: Tp I 1 38. See *Try* (vb.).

MAINLY

(1) Violently, vigorously: *These four . . . mainly thrust at me*—1 H4 II 4 222.

(2) In a high degree: *By your safety, wisdom, all things else, You mainly were stirr'd up*—Hml IV 7 8. Entirely: *I am mainly ignorant What place this is*—Lr IV 7 65. *So mainly*, so much: *I do not call your faith in question So mainly as my merit*—Troil IV 4 86.

MAINTAIN

(1) To bear the expense of, afford: *What 'cerns it you if I wear pearl and gold? . . . I am able to maintain it*—Shr V 1 77.

(2) App., to represent (a character): *This side is Hiems . . . this Ver . . . the one maintained by the owl, the other by the cuckoo*—LLL V 2 901.

MAINTENANCE

Bearing, behaviour: *I saw him hold Lord Percy at the point With lustier maintenance than I did look for*—1 H4 V 4 21.

MAJORITY

Superiority, pre-eminence: *Whose . . . great name in arms Holds from all soldiers chief majority* —1 H4 III 2 108.

MAKE

To do, be about: *What makes he here?*—As III 2 234. *What makest thou in my sight?*— R3 I 3 164. *What make you from Wittenberg?*— Hml I 2 164. *What make you from home?*—Oth III 4 169.

MAKELESS

Mateless: *The world will wail thee, like a makeless wife*—Sonn 9 4.

MAKING

Bodily form, make: *Stigmatical in making, worse in mind*—Err IV 2 22. *I mistake your shape and making quite*—Mids II 1 32.

MALE

A male parent, a father: *I, the hapless male to one sweet bird* (*i.e.* his son)—3 H6 V 6 15.

MALICE

(1) Harmfulness, harmful action: *Our cannons' malice vainly shall be spent*—John II 251. *Bend Your sharpest deeds of malice on this town*—379.

(2) A malicious act: *To report otherwise, were a malice*—Cor II 2 36.

(3) *In strength of malice*, perh., with strength as great as would be that of malice: *Our arms, in strength of malice . . . do receive you in With all kind love*—Cæs III 1 174. But the line is probably corrupt.

MALICIOUSLY

Violently: *A lingering dram that should not work Maliciously like poison*—Wint I 2 320. *I will be treble-sinew'd, hearted, breathed, And fight maliciously*—Ant III 13 178.

MALIGN

To envy, look grudgingly upon: *You malign our senators for that They are not such as you*— Cor I 1 117. *Wayward fortune did malign my state*—Per V 1 90.

MALKIN

A slut, slattern: *The kitchen malkin pins Her richest lockram 'bout her reechy neck*—Cor II 1 224. *Ours was blurted at and held a malkin*— Per IV 3 34.

MALL

(1) A diminutive of Mary: *Loved Mall, Meg and Marian*—Tp II 2 50.

(2) *Mistress Mall's picture*, prob. merely typically of a lady's portrait: *Are they like to take dust, like Mistress Mall's picture?*—Tw I 3 135.

MALMSEY

A strong sweet wine originally from the neighbourhood of Monemvasia (whence, by corruption, the name) in the Morea: *Metheglin, wort, and malmsey*—LLL V 2 233. *Malmsey-butt: We will chop him in the malmsey-butt in the next room*—R3 I 4 160. *Malmsey-nose*, red-nosed: *That arrant malmsey-nose knave, Bardolph*—2 H4 II 1 42.

MALT-HORSE

A maltster's horse; as a term of abuse: *Mome, malt-horse . . . idiot, patch!*—Err III 1 32. *You whoreson malt-horse drudge!*—Shr IV 1 132.

MALT-WORM

A lover of beer, toper: *None of these mad mustachio purple-hued malt-worms*—1 H4 II 1 82. *Lucifer's privy-kitchen, where he doth nothing but roast malt-worms*—2 H4 II 4 360.

MAMMER

To vacillate, waver: *I wonder . . . What you would ask me, that I should deny, Or stand so mammering on*—Oth III 3 68.

MAMMET

A doll, puppet: *This is no world To play with mammets*—1 H4 II 3 94. *A wretched puling fool, A whining mammet*—Rom III 5 185.

MAMMOCK

To tear into pieces: *He did so . . . tear it; O . . . how he mammocked it!*—Cor I 3 70.

MAN

(1) To provide with a servant: *I was never manned with an agate till now*—2 H4 I 2 18.

(2) Of a hawk, to make tractable: *Another way I have to man my haggard*—Shr IV 1 196.

(3) App. = *Manage* (vb.) (2): *Man but a rush against Othello's breast, And he retires*—Oth V 2 270.

MANAGE (sb.)

(1) The training and managing of horses: [I heard thee] *Speak terms of manage to thy bounding steed*—1 H4 II 3 52. *Whether the horse by him became his deed, Or he his manage by the well-doing steed*—Compl 111. The action and paces taught; the discipline enforced: [His horses] *are taught their manage*—As I 1 13. *Those that tame wild horses . . . spur 'em Till they obey the manage* —H8 V 3 21. *She's not paced yet: you must take some pains to work her to your manage*—Per IV 6 68. A feat of horsemanship: *Full merrily Hath this brave manage . . . been run*—LLL V 2 481.

Control (of horses): *Glistering Phaethon, Wanting the manage of unruly jades*—R2 III 3 178.

(2) A wielding (of a weapon); hence app., a wielding or employing (against each other of things regarded as weapons): *Which now the manage of two kingdoms must With fearful bloody issue arbitrate*—John I 37.

(3) Administration, management: *To him put The manage of my state*—Tp I 2 69. *I commit into your hands The . . . manage of my house*—Merch III 4 24. *Their negotiations all must slack, Wanting his manage*—Troil III 3 24. Arrangements: *Expedient manage must be made*—R2 I 4 39. Conduct, course: *I can discover all The unlucky manage of this fatal brawl*—Rom III 1 147.

MANAGE (vb.)

(1) To put (a horse) through the exercises of the manage (see *Manage* (sb.) (1)): *He will not manage her, although he mount her*—Ven 598.

(2) To wield, handle (a weapon): *Hope is a lover's staff; walk hence with that And manage it against despairing thoughts*—Gent III 1 246. *Distaff-women manage rusty bills*—R2 III 2 118. *Manage me your caliver*—2 H4 III 2 292. *Put up thy sword, Or manage it to part these men*—Rom I 1 75. To wield (authorities): *Idle old man, That still would manage those authorities That he hath given away!*—Lr I 3 16.

(3) To carry on (a quarrel): *To manage private and domestic quarrel, In night!*—Oth II 3 215.

MANAGER

One who wields or uses (a weapon, &c.): *Rust, rapier! be still, drum! for your manager is in love*—LLL I 2 187.

MANDRAGORA, MANDRAKE

A plant with narcotic properties, the root of which was thought to resemble the human form, and was fabled to utter a deadly shriek when torn up: *Thou whoreson mandrake*—2 H4 I 2 16 (said to the little page). *The whores called him mandrake*—III 2 338. *Would curses kill, as doth the mandrake's groan*—2 H6 III 2 310. *Shrieks like mandrakes' torn out of the earth*—Rom IV 3 47. *Not poppy, nor mandragora, Nor all the drowsy syrups of the world*—Oth III 3 330.

MAN-ENTERED

See *Enter* (1).

MANKIND

Infuriated, mad: *A mankind witch! Hence with her*—Wint II 3 67. *Are you mankind?*—Cor IV 2 16.

MANNER¹

In manner, in a manner, in some sort: *You have in manner . . . Made a divorce betwixt his queen and him*—R2 III 1 11.

MANNER²

Mainour; the stolen thing which is found in a thief's possession when he is arrested; *to be taken with the manner*, of a thief, to be taken with the stolen thing in his possession: *Thou stolest a cup of sack eighteen years ago, and wert taken with the manner*—1 H4 II 4 345. Also, to be taken in the act of doing something unlawful: *The manner of it is, I was taken with the manner (i.e.* in company with a woman contrary to the edict)—LLL I 1 204. Not very intelligibly used by the Clown in Wint IV 4 749 (*Your worship had like to have given us one (i.e.* app., to have told them a lie), *if you had not taken yourself with the manner*), app. meaning that Autolycus would have told them a lie, if he had not caught himself in the act, and made the retractation *but we pay them, &c.*, in his (no doubt purposely) obscure speech immediately preceding.

MANNINGTREE

In Essex, famous for its fat oxen and fairs: *That roasted Manningtree ox with the pudding in his belly*—1 H4 II 4 498.

MAN-QUELLER

A slayer of men: *Thou art a honey-seed* [meaning homicide], *a man-queller, and a woman-queller*—2 H4 II 1 57.

MANSIONRY

Perh., mansions or dwellings collectively: *The temple-haunting martlet does approve, By his loved mansionry, that the heaven's breath Smells wooingly here*—Mcb I 6 4.

MANTLE

The green vegetable scum on standing water: [Poor Tom that] *drinks the green mantle of the standing pool*—Lr III 4 138.

MANURE

To till, cultivate: *To have it (i.e.* the garden) *sterile with idleness, or manured with industry*—Oth I 3 327.

MAPPERY

In contempt, making of maps, mere bookish theory: *They call this bed-work, mappery, closet-war*—Troil I 3 205.

MARGENT

(1) Margin: *Writ o' both sides the leaf, margent and all*—LLL V 2 8. *The beached margent of the sea*—Mids II 1 85. *A river . . . Upon whose weeping margent she was set*—Compl 38.

(2) A commentary (originally in the margin): *I knew you must be edified by the margent ere you had done*—Hml V 2 162. Fig.: *His face's own margent did quote such amazes*—LLL II 246. *What obscured in this fair volume lies Find written in the margent of his eyes*—Rom I 3 85.

MARK[1]

(1) Marking, noting: *The strong statutes Stand . . . As much in mock as mark*—Meas V 322. *The contemplation, mark, and denotement of her parts and graces*—Oth II 3 322.

(2) *God bless the mark, God save the mark*, an exclamation used by way of apology for introducing something: *My master, who, God bless the mark, is a kind of devil*—Merch II 2 24. *I saw the wound . . .—God save the mark!—here on his manly breast*—Rom III 2 52. To add emphasis: *He . . . must his lieutenant be, And I—God bless the mark!—his Moorship's ancient*—Oth I 1 32.

MARK[2]

A money of account = 13*s.* 4*d.*: *Unless a thousand marks be levied, To quit the penalty*—Err I 1 22. *There's a franklin . . . hath brought three hundred marks with him in gold*—1 H4 II 1 59. *Give her an hundred marks*—H8 V 1 170.

MARKET

The marketing of a commodity; the manner of disposing of it: *What is a man, If his chief good and market of his time Be but to sleep and feed?*—Hml IV 4 33.

MARK-MAN

Marksman: *A right good mark-man!*—Rom I 1 212.

MARMOSET

A small monkey, without restriction, as at present, to any particular species: *[I will] instruct thee how To snare the nimble marmoset*—Tp II 2 173.

MARROW

The pith of plants, the pulp of fruit: *[Common mother], Dry up thy marrows, vines, and plough-torn leas*—Tim IV 3 193.

MARRY

Originally Mary, an exclamation of asseveration, surprise, &c.: *Marry, And I am glad of it with all my heart*—1 H4 III 1 127. *Marry, God forfend!*—2 H6 III 2 30. *God forgive me, Marry, and amen*—Rom IV 5 7.

MARSHAL

To point out (the way): *Thou marshall'st me the way that I was going*—Mcb II 1 42. *When these mutualities so marshal the way*—Oth II 1 267.

MARSHALSEA

A prison in High Street, Southwark, so called as pertaining to the Marshals of England: *I'll find A Marshalsea shall hold ye play these two months*—H8 V 4 89. It stood a little north of St. George's Church.

MART (sb.)

Trafficking: *Foreign mart for implements of war*—Hml I 1 74. A bargain: *[I] venture madly on a desperate mart*—Shr II 329.

MART (vb.)

(1) To traffic: *If he shall think it fit, A saucy stranger in his court to mart As in a Romish stew*—Cymb I 6 150.

(2) To traffic in: *You have let him go And nothing marted with him*—Wint IV 4 361. *To sell and mart your offices for gold*—Cæs IV 3 11.

MARTIAL

Resembling what pertains to Mars: *His Martial thigh*—Cymb IV 2 310.

MARTLEMAS

Martinmas; applied to Falstaff in allusion to the practice of slaughtering fat cattle at Martinmas for salting: *How doth the martlemas, your master?*—2 H4 II 2 110. Cf. *My sweet beef*—1 H4 III 3 199.

MARTYR

To wound, mutilate, disfigure: *Speak, gentle sister, who hath martyr'd thee?*—Tit III 1 81. *That face Which . . . Immodestly lies martyr'd with disgrace*—Lucr 800. *Her martyred signs*, those to which her mutilation compels her to resort: *I can interpret all her martyr'd signs*—Tit III 2 36.

MARY-BUD

The bud of a marigold: *Winking Mary-buds begin To ope their golden eyes*—Cymb II 3 26.

MASTER

To possess, own: *For the wealth That the world masters*—Merch V 173. *As if he master'd there a double spirit Of teaching and of learning instantly*—1 H4 V 2 64. *You'll find a difference . . . Between the promise of his greener days And these he masters now*—H5 II 4 134. *Such a beauty as you master now*—Sonn 106 8.

MASTERLY

Gave you such a masterly report, gave such an account of your master-like proficiency—Hml IV 7 97.

MASTER OF FENCE

One who has taken his master's (the highest) degree in the art: *Playing at sword and dagger with a master of fence*—Wiv I 1 294.

MASTIC

A doubtful word; possibly formed from μάστιξ, a whip, with the sense scourging, vituperative: *When rank Thersites opes his mastic jaws*—Troil I 3 73.

MATCH (sb.)

(1) An opponent, antagonist: *Match to match I have encounter'd him*—2 H6 V 2 10.

(2) A (fair) matching of adversaries against each other: *It were no match, your nail against his horn*—Troil IV 5 46.

(3) An agreement, bargain: *A match! 'tis done* —Shr V 2 74. *This is a match, And made between's by vows*—Wint V 3 137. [*We*] *Will play the cook and servant; 'tis our match*—Cymb III 6 30. A device: *What cunning match have you made with this jest?*—1 H4 II 4 101. An appointment: *The hour is fixed; the match is made*—Wiv II 2 303. *To set a match*, to make an appointment: *Now shall we know if Gadshill have set a match*—1 H4 I 2 118. *I'll make my match to live*, prob., will make such bargains as I may live by, as may bring me profit—Troil IV 5 37.

(4) *To cry a match*, app., to cry victory: *Switch and spurs; or I'll cry a match*—Rom II 4 73.

MATCH (vb.)

(1) To associate, join together: *God match me with a good dancer!*—Ado II 1 111. *A sharp wit match'd with too blunt a will*—LLL II 49. *Such inordinate and low desires . . . As thou art match'd withal and grafted to*—1 H4 III 2 12.

(2) To meet in combat, fight *with*: *Blows have answer'd blows; Strength match'd with strength*—John II 329.

(3) To speak of as being on an equality *with*: *To match us in comparisons with dirt*—Troil I 3 194.

(4) To procure as a match: *Here comes another of the tribe: a third cannot be matched, unless the devil himself turn Jew*—Merch III 1 80.

MATE¹

To vie or cope with: *That in the way of loyalty and truth . . . Dare mate a sounder man than Surrey can be*—H8 III 2 272.

MATE²

(1) To baffle, nonplus: *That is good deceit Which mates him first that first intends deceit*—2 H6 III 1 264. To render nugatory: *Her more than haste is mated with delays*—Ven 909.

(2) To confound, daunt: *My mind she has mated*—Mcb V 1 86. To stupefy, bewilder: *I think you are all mated or stark mad*—Err V 281.

MATERIAL

(1) Forming the material or substance of a thing: *She that herself will sliver and disbranch From her material sap*—Lr IV 2 34.

(2) Full of matter: *A material fool!*—As III 3 32.

MATIN

Morning: *The glow-worm shows the matin to be near*—Hml I 5 89.

MAUGRE

In spite of: *Maugre all thy pride*—Tw III 1 163. *Maugre all the world*—Tit IV 2 110. *Maugre thy strength*—Lr V 3 131.

MAUND

A wicker basket: *A thousand favours from a maund she drew*—Compl 36.

MAY

Can: *Whom stripes may move, not kindness*— —Tp I 2 345. *If any man may* [win her], *you may as soon as any*—Wiv II 2 245. *Cutting a smaller hair than may be seen*—LLL V 2 258. *Which till to-night I ne'er might say before*—Oth II 3 235.

MAZZARD

The head: *Knocked about the mazzard with a sexton's spade*—Hml V 1 97. *I'll knock you o'er the mazzard*—Oth II 3 155.

MEACOCK

Effeminate, cowardly: *How tame . . . A meacock wretch can make the curstest shrew*—Shr II 314.

MEAL

To spot, stain: *Were he meal'd with that Which he corrects, then were he tyrannous*—Meas IV 2 86.

MEAN (sb.)

(1) In music, the tenor or alto: *There wanteth but a mean to fill your song*—Gent I 2 95. *He can sing A mean most meanly*—LLL V 2 327. One who takes the 'mean' part: *Three-man-song-men all . . . but they are most of them means and bases*—Wint IV 3 44.

(2) Something intervening or interposed: *I chide the means that keeps me from it*—3 H6 III 2 141. Something interposed as a bond of union: *Far better might we Have loved without this mean, if on both parts This be not cherish'd*—Ant II 2 31 (said by Cæsar to Antony of Octavia, the former's sister and the latter's wife).

(3) A means: *They have devised a mean How he her chamber-window will ascend*—Gent III 1 38. *A mean to draw the Moor Out of the way*— Oth III 1 39. *A swifter mean Shall outstrike thought*—Ant IV 6 35. An opportunity: *Many a man would take you at your word, And go indeed, having so good a mean*—Err I 2 17. *To make means*, to take steps, use efforts: *To make such means for her as thou hast done And leave her*— Gent V 4 137. *What means do you make to him* (*i.e.* to the king for a reconciliation)?—Cymb II 4 3.

MEAN (vb.)

To lament: *And thus she means, videlicet*— Mids V 330.

MEANLY

Moderately, slightly: *My wife, not meanly proud of two such boys*—Err I 1 59.

MEASURABLE

App., suitable, apt: LLL V 1 97 (quoted under *Liable* (3)).

MEASURE

(1) That which is adequate; *with measure*, adequately, creditably: *He cannot but with measure fit the honours*—Cor II 2 127. That which satisfies one's wishes: [Till] *fortune* [hath] *given me measure of revenge*—3 H6 II 3 32. *These particulars are not my measure*—Sonn 91 7.

(2) Moderation: *If the prince be too important, tell him there is measure in every thing*—Ado II 1 73. *In measure rein thy joy*—Merch III 2 113. *My poor heart no measure keeps in grief*—R2 III 4 8.

(3) A tune, accompaniment: *Shall braying trumpets . . . be measures to our pomp?*—John III 1 303.

MECHANIC

Suited to a handicraftsman, vulgar: *To stand On mere mechanic compliment*—Ant IV 4 31.

MECHANICAL (adj.)

Earning one's living by manual labour: *Being mechanical, you ought not walk . . . without the sign Of your profession*—Cæs I 1 3. Mean, base: *Mechanical salt-butter rogue!*—Wiv II 2 290. *Haled thither By most mechanical and dirty hand*—2 H4 V 5 37.

MECHANICAL (sb.)

A handicraftsman, artisan: *Rude mechanicals, That work for bread upon Athenian stalls*—Mids III 2 9. *Base dunghill villain and mechanical*—2 H6 I 3 196.

MEDAL

A metal disc bearing a figure worn as a trinket; *her medal*, one with her portrait: *He that wears her favour like her medal, hanging About his neck*—Wint I 2 307.

MEDDLE

(1) To mingle: *More to know Did never meddle with my thoughts*—Tp I 2 21.

(2) To mingle in fight, to fight: *Meddle you must, that's certain, or forswear to wear iron about you*—Tw III 4 275.

MEDICINE¹

Of drugs and preparations used for other than remedial purposes; for philtres: *If the rascal have not given me medicines to make me love him, I'll be hanged*—1 H4 II 2 18. *She is . . . corrupted By spells and medicines bought of mountebanks*—

Oth I 3 60. For poisons: *Reg. Sick, O, sick! Gon. [Aside] If not, I'll ne'er trust medicine*—Lr V 3 95. Fig. of poisoning the mind: *Work on, My medicine, work!*—Oth IV 1 45 (said by Iago when Othello falls into the trance). In alchemy: *The tinct and multiplying medicine*—All's V 3 102.

MEDICINE²

A physician, healer: *I have seen a medicine That's able to breathe life into a stone*—All's II 1 75. *Camillo . . . The medicine of our house, how shall we do?*—Wint IV 4 595. *Meet we the medicine of the sickly weal*—Mcb V 2 27.

MEED

(1) A gift: *No meed, but he repays Sevenfold above itself*—Tim I 1 288.

(2) Merit, excellence, worth: *Each one already blazing by our meeds*—3 H6 II 1 36. *My meed hath got me fame*—IV 8 38. *In his meed he's unfellowed*—Hml V 2 149.

MEEK

Gentle, courteous: *What hath broach'd this tumult but thy pride? Hadst thou been meek, our title still had slept*—3 H6 II 2 159. *Courteous destroyers, affable wolves, meek bears*—Tim III 6 105. *Pardon me . . . That I am meek and gentle with these butchers!*—Cæs III 1 254. As adv.: *This Duncan Hath borne his faculties so meek*—Mcb I 7 16.

MEERED

Perh., sole, only; or, marked out or designated by meres or boundaries: *He being The meered question*—Ant III 13 9.

MEET (adj.)

To be meet, to be quits: *He'll be meet with you*—Ado I 1 47.

MEET (vb.)

(1) To light upon, find (a thing): *When in the streets he meets such golden gifts*—Err III 2 188. *God knows . . . By what by-paths . . . I met this crown*—2 H4 IV 5 184.

(2) To come to or be present at a meeting, to keep an appointment: *'Tis past the hour, sir, that Sir Hugh promised to meet*—Wiv II 3 4. *Much upon this time have I promised here to meet*—Meas IV 1 17. *As you love Rosalind, meet*—As V 2 128.

(3) *To meet with*, to agree or accord with: *How rarely does it meet with this time's guise, When man was wish'd to love his enemies!*—Tim IV 3 472. To encounter, oppose (an enemy): *We must prepare to meet with Caliban*—Tp IV 166. *At Shrewsbury . . . The king . . . Meets with Lord Harry*—1 H4 IV 4 10. *I must go and meet with danger there, Or it will seek me in another place*—2 H4 II 3 48.

MEETLY

Pretty good, passable: *You can do better yet; but this is meetly*—Ant I 3 81.

MEINY

A retinue, train: *They summon'd up their meiny, straight took horse*—Lr II 4 35.

MELL

To associate, have intercourse: *Men are to mell with, boys are not to kiss*—All's IV 3 257.

MEMORABLE

App., commemorative: *I wear it (i.e.* the Welsh leek*) for a memorable honour*—H5 IV 7 109. *A memorable trophy of predeceased valour*—V 1 75.

MEMORIZE

To cause to be remembered, make memorable: *Some blessing to this land, which shall In it be memorized*—H8 III 2 51. [To] *memorize another Golgotha*—Mcb I 2 40.

MEMORY

(1) A memento, memorial: *You memory Of old Sir Rowland*—As II 3 3. *That surname; a good memory, And witness of the malice and displeasure Which thou shouldst bear me*—Cor IV 5 77. *These weeds are memories of those worser hours*—Lr IV 7 7.

(2) *Of memory*, remembered, not forgotten: *I have some rights of memory in this kingdom*—Hml V 2 400.

MEND (sb.)

In pl., remedy: *She has the mends in her own hands*—Troil I 1 68.

MEND (vb.)

(1) To make amends or reparation for: *You have been too rough . . . You must return and mend it*—Cor III 2 25.

(2) To adjust: *He will look upon his boot and sing; mend the ruff and sing*—All's III 2 6. *Your crown's awry; I'll mend it*—Ant V 2 321.

(3) To supplement, make up the deficiency of: *We'll mend our dinner here?*—Err IV 3 60. *To mend the petty present*—Ant I 5 45.

(4) To grow better in quality, improve: *What think you of this fool, Malvolio? doth he not mend?* —Tw I 5 79. *Still he mends; But this is not the best*—Ant I 3 82. *To mend upon the world,* to improve with time: *They are people such That mend upon the world*—Cymb II 4 25.

MERCATANTE

A merchant: *Tra. What is he, Biondello? Bion. Master, a mercatante, or a pedant*—Shr IV 2 62. An Italian word.

MERCHANDISE

Traffic, trading: *Were he out of Venice, I can make what merchandise I will*—Merch III 1 133.

MERCHANDIZE

To make merchandise of, traffic in: *That love is merchandized whose rich esteeming The owner's tongue doth publish every where*—Sonn 102 3.

MERCHANT

(1) A trading vessel, merchantman: *Every day some sailor's wife, The masters of some merchant and the merchant Have just our theme of woe*—Tp II 1 4. The second *merchant* seems to refer to a shipper of goods.

(2) A 'customer', fellow: *This is a riddling merchant for the nonce*—1 H6 II 3 57. *What saucy merchant was this?*—Rom II 4 153.

MERCURIAL

Resembling what pertains to Mercury: *His foot Mercurial*—Cymb IV 2 310.

MERCY

(1) *I cry you mercy,* see Cry (vb.) (8).

(2) *By mercy,* app., by your leave: *To kill, I grant, is sin's extremest gust; But, in defence, by mercy, 'tis most just*—Tim III 5 54.

MERE (adj.)

Absolute, sheer: *His mere enemy*—Merch III 2 265. *The mere despair of surgery*—Mcb IV 3 152. *The mere perdition of the Turkish fleet*—Oth II 2 3. *To thy mere confusion*—Cymb IV 2 92.

MERE (adv.)

Absolutely: *Dia. . . . Think you it is so? Hel. Ay, surely, mere the truth*—All's III 5 57.

MERELY

Absolutely, entirely, simply: *We are merely cheated of our lives*—Tp I 1 59. *To live in a nook merely monastic*—As III 2 440. [We are] *merely our own traitors*—All's IV 3 25. *The horse were merely lost*—Ant III 7 9.

MERIT

(1) That which is deserved, a reward: *A dearer merit . . . Have I deserved*—R2 I 3 156.

(2) The condition or fact of deserving (good or evil), character with respect to desert (of good or evil): *It was not altogether your brother's evil disposition made him seek his (i.e.* Gloucester's*) death; but a provoking merit (i.e.* demerit on Gloucester's part*)*—Lr III 5 6. *So to use them As we shall find their merits and our safety May equally determine*—V 3 43. *When we (i.e.* the greatest ones*) fall, We answer others' merits in our name*—Ant V 2 177.

MERMAID

Used as = Siren: *Train me not, sweet mermaid, with thy note*—Err III 2 45. *I'll stop mine ears against the mermaid's song*—169. *I'll drown more sailors than the mermaid shall*—3 H6 III 2 186.

MERRIMENT

(1) A jest, a piece of fooling: *Our first merriment hath made thee jealous*—Shr IV 5 76. *He will drive you out of your revenge and turn all to a merriment*—2 H4 II 4 323. A comic device or entertainment: *Here was a consent, Knowing aforehand of our merriment, To dash it*—LLL V 2 460. [We] *met your loves In their own fashion, like a merriment*—793.

(2) An act of merry-making: [You] *rather proved the sliding of your brother A merriment than a vice*—Meas II 4 115. *Stir up the Athenian youth to merriments*—Mids I 1 12.

(3) Entertainment, amusement: *You all are bent To set against me for your merriment*—Mids III 2 145.

MERRY

(1) Of a place or country, pleasant, delightful to dwell in; proverbially: *It was never merry world since . . .*—Meas III 2 6; Tw III 1 109; 2 H6 IV 2 9. (So originally in 'Merry England'.)

(2) Of a wind, favourable: *The merry wind Blows fair from land*—Err IV 1 90.

MERVAILOUS

A form of Marvellous, but app. used without any definite meaning: Nym. . . . *I would have you solus.* Pist. . . . *The 'solus' in thy most mervailous face*—H5 II 1 47.

MESH

Mash; to brew: *Tears, Brew'd with her sorrow, mesh'd upon her cheeks*—Tit III 2 37.

MESS

(1) A dish of food: *Our feasts In every mess have folly*—Wint IV 4 10. *He that makes his generation messes To gorge his appetite*—Lr I 1 119. *I will chop her into messes*—Oth IV 1 211.

(2) A quantity required for a dish: *Coming in to borrow a mess of vinegar*—2 H4 II 1 103.

(3) A group sitting together at a banquet: *Your traveller, He and his toothpick at my worship's mess*—John I 189.

(4) A company of four, orig. the number of each group at a banquet: *You three fools lack'd me fool to make up the mess*—LLL IV 3 207. *A mess of Russians left us but of late*—V 2 361. *Where are your mess of sons to back you now?*—3 H6 I 4 73 (naming four).

(5) *Lower messes*, inferiors (orig. those sitting in an inferior position): *Lower messes Perchance are to this business purblind?*—Wint I 2 227.

METAL

Mettle; the material of which man is figured to be made: *Let there be some more test made of my metal*—Meas I 1 49. *Not till God make men of some other metal than earth*—Ado II 1 62. *I am made Of the self-same metal that my sister is*—Lr I 1 70.

METAPHYSICAL

Supernatural: *The golden round, Which fate and metaphysical aid doth seem To have thee crown'd withal*—Mcb I 5 29.

METE

To measure distances for shooting; hence, to aim: *Let the mark have a prick in't, to mete at*—LLL IV 1 134.

METE-YARD

A measuring rod: *Give me thy mete-yard, and spare not me*—Shr IV 3 153.

METHEGLIN

A spiced kind of mead: *Given to . . . sack and wine and metheglins*—Wiv V 5 166. *Metheglin, wort, and malmsey*—LLL V 2 233.

METHOD

A scheme or summary of the contents of a book set forth in a table: Oli. . . . *Where lies your text?* . . . *In what chapter of his bosom?* Vio. *To answer by the method, in the first of his heart*—Tw I 5 240.

METHOUGHTS

Past tense of Methinks: *Methoughts I did recoil Twenty-three years*—Wint I 2 154. *Methoughts that I had broken from the Tower*—R3 I 4 9. *Methoughts, a legion of foul fiends Environ'd me about*—58.

MICHER

A truant: *Shall the blessed sun of heaven prove a micher?*—1 H4 II 4 449.

MICHING MALLECHO

Of uncertain meaning; explained as sneaking or stealthy (miche = to sneak, skulk) mischief (Sp. malhecho, misdeed): *This is miching mallecho; it means mischief*—Hml III 2 147.

MICKLE

Great, much: *The one ne'er got me credit, the other mickle blame*—Err III 1 45. *Mickle age*—2 H6 V 1 174. *Mickle is the powerful grace that lies In herbs*—Rom II 3 15.

MIDDLE-EARTH

The earth as being between heaven and hell, or as occupying the centre of the universe: *I smell a man of middle-earth*—Wiv V 5 84.

MIGHT

Bodily strength: *I have a man's mind, but a woman's might*—Cæs II 4 8.

MIGHT

Takes it in might, not merit, app., regards the might-have-been rather than the actual desert: *What poor duty cannot do, noble respect Takes it in might, not merit*—Mids V 91.

MIGHTINESS

Unchanged in plural: *Your mightiness on both parts best can witness*—H5 V 2 28.

MILCH

Giving milk; fig. of weeping eyes: *Would have made milch the burning eyes of heaven*—Hml II 2 540.

MILE-END

A manor and hamlet of Stepney Parish, east of Whitechapel: *He had the honour to be the officer at a place there* (*i.e.* in England) *called Mile-end, to instruct for the doubling of files*—All's IV 3 301. *Mile-end Green*, now Stepney Green: *I remember at Mile-end Green . . . there was a little quiver fellow*—2 H4 III 2 298. Mile-end was a mustering place for the city train-bands.

MILK-LIVERED

Spiritless: *Milk-liver'd man!*—Lr IV 2 50. See *Liver* (3).

MILLIOND

Prob. a form of Million (and to be printed thus, not *million'd*): *Time, whose milliond accidents Creep in 'twixt vows*—Sonn 115 5.

MILL-SIXPENCE

One coined in a mill as opposed to one struck with the hammer: *Seven groats in mill-sixpences*—Wiv I 1 158. The mill was first used in the English mint in 1561.

MIMIC

A mime, burlesque actor: *Anon his Thisbe must be answered, And forth my mimic comes*—Mids III 2 18.

MIND

(1) To remind: *Let me be punish'd, that have minded you Of what you should forget*—Wint III 2 226. *I do thee wrong to mind thee of it*—H5 IV 3 13. *I minded him how royal 'twas to pardon*—Cor V 1 18.

(2) To call to mind, think of: *Minding true things by what their mockeries be*—H5 IV Chor 53.

(3) To perceive, notice: *I'll fall flat; Perchance he will not mind me*—Tp II 2 16. To attend to, mark: *My lord, you nod; you do not mind the play*—Shr I 1 254.

(4) To be inclined, purpose, intend: *I mind to tell him plainly what I think*—3 H6 IV 1 8. *I shortly mind to leave you*—64. *The most high gods not minding longer To withhold the vengeance*—Per II 4 3.

MINERAL

(1) A mine, or a vein in a mine: *Like some ore Among a mineral of metals base*—Hml IV 1 25.

(2) A mineral preparation or poison: *Thou hast . . . Abused her delicate youth with drugs or minerals*—Oth I 2 73. *The thought whereof Doth, like a poisonous mineral, gnaw my inwards*—II 1 305. *She had For you a mortal mineral*—Cymb V 5 49.

MINGLE

A mixture: *O heavenly mingle!*—Ant I 5 59. A mingling of sounds: *Make mingle with our rattling tabourines*—IV 8 37.

MINIKIN

Dainty, or perh., shrill: *One blast of thy minikin mouth*—Lr III 6 45.

MINIMUS

A very small creature: *You dwarf, You minimus*—Mids III 2 328.

MINION

A favoured person, favourite (without any implication of contempt): *Fortune shall cull forth Out of one side her happy minion*—John II 391. *Sweet Fortune's minion and her pride*—1 H4 I 1 83. *Valour's minion*—Mcb I 2 19. *The minions of their race*, the most highly prized: *Duncan's horses . . . Beauteous and swift, the minions of their race*—Mcb II 4 14.

MINISTER

(1) To prompt, suggest: *Though sometimes you do blench from this to that, As cause doth minister*—Meas IV 5 5.

(2) To administer (something healing): *You gave me bitter pills, And I must minister the like to you*—Gent II 4 149. *Present medicine must be minister'd*—John V 1 15. Absol.: *Canst thou not minister to a mind diseased?*—Mcb V 3 40.

(3) To dispense justice: *Pluck the . . . senate from the bench, And minister in their steads!*—Tim IV 1 5. To perform (a rite): *Before All sanctimonious ceremonies may . . . be minister'd*—Tp IV 15.

(4) *Minister communication of A most poor issue*—H8 I 1 86, app., give an opportunity for a conference leading to a poor result.

MINUTE-JACK

A time server; or perh., a fickle person: *Cap and knee slaves, vapours, and minute-jacks!*—Tim III 6 107.

MINUTELY

Happening every minute: *Minutely revolts upbraid his faith-breach*—Mcb V 2 18.

MINUTE WHILE

A minute: *That walk'd about me every minute while*—1 H6 I 4 54.

MIRABLE

Wonderful, marvellous: *Not Neoptolemus so mirable*—Troil IV 5 142.

MIRACLE

Refl., to partake of the marvellous, be incomprehensible: *Who this should be, Doth miracle itself*—Cymb IV 2 28.

MIRE

To sink in mire: *Paint till a horse may mire upon your face*—Tim IV 3 147.

MIRTH

A diversion, entertainment; or perh., a jest: *To give a kingdom for a mirth*—Ant I 4 18.

MISADVENTURED

Unfortunate: *Misadventured piteous overthrows*—Rom Prol 7.

MISANTHROPOS

Misanthrope: *I am Misanthropos, and hate mankind*—Tim IV 3 53.

MISCARRY

(1) To come to harm, perish: *Frederick the great soldier who miscarried at sea*—Meas III 1 217. *I would not have him miscarry for the half of my dowry*—Tw III 4 69. *If a son . . . do sinfully miscarry upon the sea*—H5 IV 1 154. *All that have miscarried By underhand corrupted foul injustice*—R3 V 1 5. In pass.: *Our sister's man is certainly miscarried*—Lr V 1 5.

(2) Of a child, to be born prematurely: *An the child I now go with do miscarry*—2 H4 V 4 10. *I pray God the fruit of her womb miscarry!*—15.

(3) Of natural productions, to fail: *If horns that year miscarry*—LLL IV 1 114.

MISCONCEIVED

Having a misconception or wrong idea: *No, misconceived!*—1 H6 V 4 49.

MISCREATE

Improperly framed, illegitimate: *Titles miscreate*—H5 I 2 16.

MIS-DREAD

Dread of evil: *The passions of the mind That have their first conception by mis-dread*—Per I 2 11.

MISER

A miserable or wretched person: *Decrepit miser! base ignoble wretch!*—1 H6 V 4 7.

MISERY

(1) A despicable condition; *noble misery*, condition despicable in a nobleman: *This is a lord! O noble misery!*—Cymb V 3 64.

(2) Miserliness, niggardliness: *He covets less Than misery itself would give*—Cor II 2 130.

MISGOVERNED

Unruly, ill-behaved: *Rude misgovern'd hands*—R2 V 2 5.

MISGOVERNING

Misconduct: *Black lust, dishonour, shame, misgoverning*—Lucr 654.

MISGOVERNMENT

Misconduct: *I am sorry for thy much misgovernment*—Ado IV 1 100.

MISGRAFFED

Grafted amiss; fig., badly matched: *Misgraffed in respect of years*—Mids I 1 137.

MISORDERED

Disordered, deranged: *The time misorder'd*—2 H4 IV 2 33.

MISPRISION[1]

Undervaluing: *Proud scornful boy . . . That dost in vile misprision shackle up My love and her desert*—All's II 3 158.

MISPRISION[2]

Mistaking, a mistake: *There is some strange misprision in the princes*—Ado IV 1 187. *Of thy misprision must perforce ensue Some true love turn'd*—Mids III 2 90. *Misprision in the highest degree!*—Tw I 5 61 (app. with a play on misprision of treason, an offence or misdemeanour akin to treason, but involving a lesser degree of guilt). *Envy, therefore, or misprision Is guilty of this fault*—1 H4 I 3 27.

MISPRIZE,[1] MISPRISE[1]

To contemn, undervalue, slight: *Disdain and scorn ride sparkling in her eyes, Misprising what they look on*—Ado III 1 51. *The misprising of a maid too virtuous For the contempt of empire*—All's III 2 33. *Misprizing The knight opposed*—Troil IV 5 74.

MISPRIZE,[2] MISPRISE[2]

To mistake; *misprised*, mistaken: *You spend your passion on a misprised mood*—Mids III 2 74.

MISPROUD

Wrongly proud, arrogant: *Misproud York*—3 H6 II 6 7.

MISQUOTE

To construe unfavourably: *Look how we can . . . Interpretation will misquote our looks*—1 H4 V 2 12.

MISS (sb.)

A misdeed, wrong-doing: *He saith she is immodest, blames her miss*—Ven 53.

MISS (vb.)

To lack: *What I can help thee to thou shalt not miss*—All's I 3 262. To do without: *As 'tis, We cannot miss him*—Tp I 2 310. To be missed, to.

be missing, not found: *Thy record never can be miss d*—Sonn 122 8.

MISSINGLY

With a feeling of loss: *I have missingly noted, he is of late much retired from court*—Wint IV 2 35.

MISSIVE

A messenger: *Came missives from the king, who all-hailed me " Thane of Cawdor"*--Mcb I 5 6. *With taunts Did gibe my missive out of audience* —Ant II 2 73.

MISTAKE

(1) To misjudge a person in respect of his character: *I am sorry To hear this of him; and could wish he were Something mistaken in't*—H8 I 1 193. *Your rage mistakes us*—III 1 101. *Thyself thou gavest, thy own worth then not knowing, Or me, to whom thou gavest it, else mistaking*—Sonn 87 9.

(2) To commit an error in regard to: *This letter is mistook, it importeth none here*—LLL IV 1 57. *Thou hast mistaken his letter*—108.

MISTEMPERED

(1) Ill compounded: *This inundation of mistemper'd humour*—John V 1 12. Cf. *Humour* (3).

(2) Tempered to evil ends: *Throw your mistemper'd weapons to the ground*—Rom I 1 94.

MISTHINK

To think ill of: *How will the country for these woful chances Misthink the king!* — 3 H6 II 5 107. *We . . . are misthought For things that others do*—Ant V 2 176.

MISTREADING

A mis-step, misdeed: *Mark'd For . . . the rod of heaven To punish my mistreadings*—1 H4 III 2 9.

MISTRESS

In bowling, the jack: *Rub on, and kiss the mistress*—Troil III 2 52.

MISTRUSTFUL

Inspiring mistrust or suspicion: *In some mistrustful wood*—Ven 826.

MISUSE (sb.)

(1) Ill-usage, abuse: *Upon whose dead corpse there was such misuse . . . By those Welshwomen done*—1 H4 I 1 43.

(2) Wrong conduct: *How have I been behaved, that he might stick The small'st opinion on my least misuse?*—Oth IV 2 108.

MISUSE (vb.)

(1) To revile, slander: *She misused me past the endurance of a block! . . . She told me . . .*—

Ado II 1 246. *You have simply misused our sex in your love-prate*—As IV 1 205. *With twenty such vile terms, As had she studied to misuse me so*—Shr II 159.

(2) To speak falsely of, misrepresent: *My vows are oaths but to misuse thee . . . For I have sworn deep oaths of thy deep kindness, Oaths of thy love, thy truth*—Sonn 152 7.

(3) To mislead, deceive: *Proof enough to misuse the prince*—Ado II 2 28.

MOAN

A state of grief, grief: *Thy mirth shall turn to moan*—1 H6 II 3 44. *This mutual heavy load of moan*—R3 II 2 113. *Thou hast finish'd joy and moan*—Cymb IV 2 273. *The sad account of forebemoaned moan*—Sonn 30 11.

MOBLE

To muffle one's head or face: *But who, O, who had seen the mobled queen*—Hml II 2 524.

MOCK

To deal in a spirit of mockery with (a matter), to trifle with another in regard to (it): *I long till Edward fall by war's mischance, For mocking marriage with a dame of France*—3 H6 III 3 254. *Bid him yield; Being so frustrate, tell him he mocks The pauses that he makes*—Ant V 1.

MOCKWATER

App. a nonsense word coined by the Host referring to the mode of diagnosis mentioned under *Cast* (vb.) (5): *A word, Mounseur Mockwater*— Wiv II 3 59 (said to Dr. Caius).

MODEL

(1) A plan or a set of plans: *When we mean to build, We first survey the plot, then draw the model*—2 H4 I 3 41. *I'll draw the form and model of our battle*—R3 V 3 24. Fig.: *Will it serve for any model to build mischief on?*—Ado I 3 48.

(2) A copy, likeness, 'image': *Thy wretched brother . . . Who was the model of thy father's life* —R2 I 2 27. *The model of our chaste loves, his young daughter*—H8 IV 2 132. *My father's signet . . . Which was the model of that Danish seal*—Hml V 2 49.

(3) A mould, something that envelops closely: *That small model of the barren earth Which serves as paste and cover to our bones*—R2 III 2 153. *O England! model to thy inward greatness*—H5 II Chor 16.

MODERN

Everyday, ordinary, commonplace: *Wise saws and modern instances*—As II 7 156. *To make modern and familiar, things supernatural and causeless*—All's II 3 2. *Which modern lamentation might have moved*—Rom III 2 120. *Things of such dignity As we greet modern friends withal* —Ant V 2 166.

13

MODEST

Reasonable, becoming, not exaggerated: *Give me modest assurance if you be the lady of the house* —Tw I 5 192. *Resolve me, with all modest haste, which way Thou mightst deserve . . . this usage*— Lr II 4 25. *All my reports go with the modest truth*—IV 7 5. Of persons, moderate: *Reverence to your calling makes me modest*—H8 V 3 69.

MODESTLY

Without exaggeration, in fitting terms: *Modestly I think, The fall of every Phrygian stone will cost A drop of Grecian blood*—Troil IV 5 222. [I] *Will modestly discover to yourself That of yourself which you yet know not of*—Cæs I 2 69.

MODESTY

Moderation, self-control, freedom from exaggeration: *It will be pastime passing excellent, If it be husbanded with modesty* — Shr Ind 1 67. *I am doubtful of your modesties; Lest . . . You break into some merry passion* — 94. *The enemies of Cæsar shall say this; Then, in a friend, it is cold modesty*—Cæs III 1 212. *An excellent play . . . set down with as much modesty as cunning*—Hml II 2 459. *With this special observance, that you o'erstep not the modesty of nature* (*i.e.* the bounds of propriety implied in an adherence to nature)— III 2 20.

MODULE

An image, counterfeit: *Bring forth this counterfeit module*—All's IV 3 113. *All this thou seest is but a clod And module of confounded royalty*— —John V 7 57.

MOE

More: *Keep me company but two years moe*— Merch I 1 108. *Many moe Of noble blood*—R2 II 1 239. *Send out moe horses*—Mcb V 3 35.

MOIETY

(1) One's portion or share: *My moiety . . . In quantity equals not one of yours*—1 H4 III 1 96. *Curiosity in neither can make choice of either's moiety*—Lr I 1 6. *By their verdict is determined The clear eye's moiety and the dear heart's part*— Sonn 46 11.

(2) A small part: *A moiety of my rest Might come to me again* — Wint II 3 8. *Whereof this pamphlet . . . is but a superfluous moiety*—Lucr Dedic 1.

MOIST (adj.)

Liquid: *My tears, The moist impediments unto my speech*—2 H4 IV 5 139. *The two moist elements* (*i.e.* the humid air and the liquid water)— Troil I 3 41.

MOIST (vb.)

To moisten: *Write till your ink be dry, and with your tears Moist it again*—Gent III 2 75.

No more The juice of Egypt's grape shall moist this lip—Ant V 2 284.

MOLDWARP

A mole: *Telling me of the moldwarp and the ant*—1 H4 III 1 149.

MOLESTATION

A vexed condition, turmoil: *I never did like molestation view On the enchafed flood*—Oth II 1 16.

MOME

A blockhead, dolt: *Mome, malt-horse . . . idiot, patch!*—Err III 1 32.

MOMENT

Cause, motive: *I have seen her die twenty times upon far poorer moment*—Ant I 2 146.

MOMENTANY

Momentary, transitory: *Momentany as a sound* —Mids I 1 143.

MONARCHO

The nickname of a crack-brained Italian living about the Court who fancied himself to be the sovereign of the world: *This Armado is a Spaniard, that keeps here in court; A phantasime, a Monarcho* —LLL IV 1 100.

MONSTER

(1) To make monstrous: *Her offence Must be of such unnatural degree, That monsters it*—Lr I 1 221.

(2) To represent as wonderful: *I had rather . . . than idly sit And hear my nothings monster'd*— Cor II 2 79.

MONSTROUS

Unnatural: *Why all these things change . . . To monstrous quality*—Cæs I 3 66. *Monstrous lust*, Per V 3 86. Of persons: *Monstrous friends*—Tim IV 2 46.

MONSTRUOSITY

Monstrosity, abnormality: *This is the monstruosity in love, lady, that the will is infinite and the execution confined*—Troil III 2 87.

MONTANT

In fencing, a downright thrust: *To see thee pass thy punto, thy stock . . . thy montant*—Wiv II 3 26.

MONUMENT

(1) A sepulchre: *Which, like a taper in some monument, Doth shine upon the dead man's earthy cheeks*—Tit II 3 228. *In that dim monument where Tybalt lies*—Rom III 5 203. *Our monuments Shall be the maws of kites*—Mcb III 4 72.

(2) A portent: *Some wondrous monument, Some comet or unusual prodigy*—Shr III 2 97.

(3) A carved figure, statue: *Or else for ever be confixed here, A marble monument*—Meas V 232. *You are no maiden, but a monument*—All's IV 2 6. *Be her sense but as a monument, Thus in a chapel lying!*—Cymb II 2 32.

(4) *Monuments of conquered France*, app. referring to the conquered towns to be given up on the marriage, regarded as monuments of English prowess: *Defacing monuments of conquer'd France, Undoing all, as all had never been*—2 H6 I 1 102.

(5) App., remembrance: *He shall live no longer in monument than the bell rings*—Ado V 2 80.

MONUMENTAL

Serving as a memento: *He hath given her his monumental ring*—All's IV 3 20.

MOOD

Anger: *Who, in my mood, I stabb'd unto the heart*—Gent IV 1 51. *Thou art as hot a Jack in thy mood as any in Italy, and as soon moved to be moody*—Rom III 1 12. *You are but now cast in his mood*—Oth II 3 273.

MOODY

Angry: Rom III 1 14 (quoted under *Mood*). So *moody-mad*: *Moody-mad and desperate stags*—1 H6 IV 2 50.

MOON-CALF

A misshapen birth, monstrosity: *How camest thou to be the siege of this moon-calf?*—Tp II 2 110. *I hid me under the dead moon-calf's gaberdine*—115. (In both cases of Caliban.)

MOOR-DITCH

An unsavoury ditch encompassing the part of the old London Wall fronting Moorfields (*q.v.*): *What sayest thou* [for a simile] *to . . . the melancholy of Moor-ditch?*—1 H4 I 2 87. *Moor-ditch melancholy* appears to have been a current phrase.

MOORFIELDS

A moor lying to the north of the old London Wall, a mustering place for the city train-bands: *Is this Moorfields to muster in?*—H8 V 4 33. Finsbury Square and Circus, the City Road, &c., now cover the site. See *Finsbury*.

MOP

A grimace; in phrase *mop and mow*: *Each one, tripping on his toe, Will be here with mop and mow*—Tp IV 46.

MOPE

To move or act without the guidance of thought: *Even in a dream were we divided from them And were brought moping hither*—Tp V 239. *What a . . . peevish fellow is this king of England, to mope . . . so far out of his knowledge!*—H5 III 7 142. *But a sickly part of one true sense Could not so mope*—Hml III 4 80.

MOPPING

Grimacing; in phrase *mopping and mowing*: *Flibbertigibbet* [prince] *of mopping and mowing*—Lr IV 1 64.

MORAL (adj.)

(1) Moralizing, enunciating moral precepts: *'Tis all men's office to speak patience To those that wring under the load of sorrow, But no man's virtue nor sufficiency To be so moral when he shall endure The like himself*—Ado V 1 27. *Thou, a moral fool, sit'st still*—Lr IV 2 58. *A moral medicine*, a remedy consisting in moralizing: *I wonder that thou . . . goest about to apply a moral medicine to a mortifying mischief*—Ado I 3 11.

(2) Of paintings, allegorical, emblematical: *A thousand moral paintings I can show*—Tim I 1 90. Sim. *a moral meaning*, a hidden meaning—Ado III 4 80 (quoted under *Moral* (sb.) (1)).

MORAL (sb.)

(1) A hidden meaning: Beat. *Benedictus! why Benedictus? you have some moral in this Benedictus.* Marg. *Moral! . . . I have no moral meaning*—Ado III 4 77. Bion. *. . .* [He] *has left me here behind, to expound the meaning or moral of his signs and tokens.* Luc. *I pray thee, moralize them*—Shr IV 4 78.

(2) A symbolical figure: *Fortune (i.e.* as represented in the manner described) *is an excellent moral*—H5 III 6 40.

MORAL (vb.)

To moralize: *When I did hear The motley fool thus moral on the time*—As II 7 28.

MORALER

A moralist: *You are too severe a moraler*—Oth II 3 301.

MORALIZE

To interpret, expound—Shr IV 4 81 (quoted under *Moral* (sb.) (1)). So, to explain to oneself, realize the meaning of: *Nor could she moralize his wanton sight*—Lucr 104.

MORE

(1) With substantives of condition, action, &c., greater in degree or extent: *A thousand more mischances than this one*—Gent V 3 3. *To make a more requital to your love*—John I 34. *Her best is better'd with a more delight*—Ven 78.

(2) Greater in importance; *more and less*, high and low: *The more and less came in with cap and knee*—1 H4 IV 3 68. *More and less do flock to follow him*—2 H4 I 1 209.

MORE ABOVE

Moreover: *This . . . hath my daughter shown me, And more above, hath his solicitings . . . All given to mine ear*—Hml II 2 125.

MORISCO

A morris-dancer: *I have seen Him caper upright like a wild Morisco*—2 H6 III 1 364. See *Morris*, *Morris-dance*.

MORRIS

The nine men's morris, a piece of turf marked like an imperfect chess-board on which a game resembling chess or draughts was played by two players each with nine men: *The nine men's morris is fill'd up with mud*—Mids II 1 98.

MORRIS, MORRIS-DANCE

A grotesque dance performed on festival occasions, such as May-day and Whitsuntide, by persons in fancy costume usually representing characters from the Robin Hood legend: [As fit as] *a morris for May-day*—All's II 2 25. *With no more* [show of fear] *than if we heard that England Were busied with a Whitsun morris-dance*—H5 II 4 24.

MORRIS-PIKE

A kind of pike said to have been of Moorish origin: *To do more exploits with his mace than a morris-pike*—Err IV 3 27.

MORROW

Morning: *I shall say good night till it be morrow*—Rom II 2 186. *She looks for night, and then she longs for morrow*—Lucr 1571.

MORT

The note sounded on a horn at the death of the deer: *To sigh, as 'twere The mort o' the deer*—Wint I 2 117. But perh. here rather to be taken as = death, the reference being to the sighs of the dying deer.

MORTAL

Perh., abounding *in*: *As all is mortal in nature, so is all nature in love mortal in folly*—As II 4 55. Cf. a 'mort' = a great deal.

MORTALITY

Death (of individuals): *Mortality and mercy in Vienna Live in thy tongue and heart*—Meas I 1 45. *I beg mortality, Rather than life preserved with infamy*—1 H6 IV 5 32.

MORTALLY

After the manner of mortals: *I was mortally brought forth*—Per V 1 105.

MORTIFIED

(1) Dead to the world, ascetic: *Dumain is mortified*—LLL I 1 28. *Their dear causes Would to the bleeding and the grim alarm Excite the mortified man*—Mcb V 2 3.

(2) Dead, killed: *His wildness, mortified in him, Seem'd to die too*—H5 I 1 26.

(3) Deadened, numbed: *Thou, like an exorcist, hast conjured up My mortified spirit*—Cæs II 1

323. *Their numb'd and mortified bare arms*—Lr II 3 15.

MORTIFYING

Deadly: *A mortifying mischief*—Ado I 3 13. *Mortifying groans*—Merch I 1 82 (or perh. here deadening, sapping vitality).

MOSE IN THE CHINE

Of a horse, prob., to suffer from some disease akin to glanders: *Like to mose in the chine*—Shr III 2 51.

MOST

Greatest: *Always resolute in most extremes*—1 H6 IV 1 38. *With most gladness*—Ant II 2 169. Longest: *I have possess'd him my most stay Can be but brief*—Meas IV 1 44.

MOT

A motto: *Tarquin's eye may read the mot afar*—Lucr 830.

MOTHER

The popular name for hysteria: *How this mother swells up toward my heart!*—Lr II 4 56.

MOTION (sb.)

(1) Power of movement as a property of an animate body: *This sensible warm motion to become A kneaded clod*—Meas III 1 120 (meaning here the body endowed with the power). *Vile earth, to earth resign; end motion here*—Rom III 2 59.

(2) Bodily exertion: *When in your motion you are hot and dry*—Hml IV 7 158.

(3) An inward prompting or impulse: *The wanton stings and motions of the sense*—Meas I 4 59. *The motions of his spirit are dull as night*—Merch V 86. *Between the acting of a dreadful thing And the first motion*—Cæs II 1 63. *We have reason to cool our raging motions, our carnal stings, our unbitted lusts*—Oth I 3 334. Impulses collectively: *You sway the motion of Demetrius' heart*—Mids I 1 193.

(4) Specifically, the sexual impulse: *Sense, sure, you have, Else could you not have motion*—Hml III 4 71. [Thou hast] *Abused her delicate youth with drugs or minerals That waken motion*—Oth I 2 74 (reading the conjecture *waken* for *weaken*, the reading of most modern texts: the Quartos and Folios read *weakens*). *A maiden . . . Of spirit so still and quiet, that her motion Blush'd at herself*—I 3 94.

(5) A proposal: *I have a motion much imports your good*—Meas V 541. *I'll make the motion*—Tw III 4 316. *How doth your grace affect their motion?*—1 H6 V 1 7. A request: *Meanwhile must be an earnest motion Made to the queen to call back her appeal*—H8 II 4 233.

(6) Prompting, urging, using of influence: *He gives her folly motion and advantage*—Wiv III

2 35. *We in your motion turn and you may move us*—Err III 2 24. *We do request . . . Your loving motion toward the common body, To yield what passes here*—Cor II 2 56. *I do know but one That unassailable holds on his rank, Unshaked of motion*—Cæs III 1 68.

(7) A motive: *From sincere motions*—H8 I 1 153. *Hasty . . . upon too trivial motion*—Cor II 1 55.

(8) Perception, intuition: *An outward man, That the great figure of a council frames By self-unable motion*—All's III 1 11. [Thou hast] *Abused her delicate youth with drugs or minerals That weaken motion*—Oth I 2 74. *I see it in My motion, have it not in my tongue*—Ant II 3 13.

(9) In pl., app. = doings: *I knew of their going to bed, and of other motions, as promising her marriage*—All's V 3 263.

(10) A puppet-show: *He compassed a motion of the Prodigal Son*—Wint IV 3 102. *The eye interprets to the ear The heavy motion that it doth behold*—Lucr 1325. A puppet: *O excellent motion! O exceeding puppet!*—Gent II 1 100. Perh. attrib., *a motion generative*, a (mere) puppet (or seeming) begetter, *i.e.* no begetter, impotent: *He is a motion generative; that's infallible*—Meas III 2 119 (cf. *This ungenitured agent*—184).

MOTION (vb.)

To propose: *One that still motions war and never peace*—1 H6 I 3 63.

MOTIVE

(1) A mover, instigator: *Nor are they living Who were the motives that you first went out*—Tim V 4 26.

(2) A moving or inciting cause: *Am I the motive of these tears?*—Oth IV 2 43. [Fulvia] *made wars here; For which myself, the ignorant motive, do . . . ask pardon*—Ant II 2 95.

(3) An agent: *It hath fated her to be my motive And helper to a husband*—All's IV 4 20. An instrument: *My teeth shall tear The slavish motive of recanting fear* (*i.e.* his tongue)—R2 I 1 192. *I did admit it* (*i.e.* the gold) *as a motive The sooner to effect what I intended*—H5 II 2 156.

(4) A moving organ or limb: *Her wanton spirits look out At every joint and motive of her body*—Troil IV 5 56.

MOTLEY

(1) A particoloured dress, the regular attire of a professional fool or jester: *I* (*i.e.* the Clown) *wear not motley in my brain*—Tw I 5 63. *The sweet and bitter fool Will presently appear; The one in motley here, The other found out there*—Lr I 4 158.

(2) Hence, a fool, jester: *Will you be married, motley?*—As III 3 79. [I have] *made myself a motley to the view*—Sonn 110 2. So *a motley fool*: *I met a fool i' the forest, A motley fool*—As II

7 12. So also *motley-minded*: *This is the motley-minded gentleman*—As V 4 40.

MOUGHT

Might, could: *More he spoke . . . That mought not be distinguish'd*—3 H6 V 2 43. Cf. *May*.

MOULD

Men of mould, men made of earth, mortal men: *Be merciful, great duke, to men of mould*—H5 III 2 23.

MOULTEN

Having moulted: *A clip-wing'd griffin and a moulten raven*—1 H4 III 1 152.

MOUNT

(1) To elevate, cause to rise: *What power is it which mounts my love so high* (*i.e.* to Bertram)*?*—All's I 1 235. *Though his affections are higher mounted than ours, yet, when they stoop, they stoop with the like wing*—H5 IV 1 110. *The fire that mounts the liquor till't run o'er*—H8 I 1 144. *Mounted*, elevated in situation: *Where castles mounted stand*—2 H6 I 4 40.

(2) To erect: *Hedgehogs which . . . mount Their pricks at my footfall*—Tp II 2 10.

MOUNTAIN

Prob., of more than ordinary proportions: *His mountain sire, on mountain standing*—H5 II 4 57.

MOUNTANT

Mounting, rising: *Hold up, you sluts, Your aprons mountant*—Tim IV 3 134.

MOUNTANTO

Signior Mountanto—Ado I 1 30, Beatrice's name for Benedick; prob. formed sportively from *Montant* (q.v.), as who should say 'Mr. Thruster'.

MOUNTEBANK

To get by mountebank persuasion: *I'll mountebank their loves, Cog their hearts from them*—Cor III 2 132.

MOUSE

To tear, bite: *Well moused, Lion*—Mids V 274. *Now* [Death] *feasts, mousing the flesh of men*—John II 354.

MOUSE-HUNT

A hunter of mice (meaning women): *You have been a mouse-hunt in your time*—Rom IV 4 11.

MOUTH

To join lips *with*, kiss: *He would mouth with a beggar*—Meas III 2 193.

MOUTHED

Gaping: *Mouthed wounds*—1 H4 I 3 97. *Mouthed graves*—Sonn 77 6.

MOVE

(1) To urge, make a proposal or request to: *The Florentine will move us For speedy aid*—All's I 2 6. *I could divide myself and go to buffets, for moving such a dish of skim milk with so honourable an action!*—1 H4 II 3 34. *To this effect, Achilles, have I moved you*—Troil III 3 216. *We have had no time to move our daughter*—Rom III 4 2.

(2) To commence (war, &c.): *His fellowship i' the cause against your city, In part for his sake moved*—Tim V 2 12.

(3) To bring forward: *We dare not move the question of our place*—Troil II 3 89. To deal with in discourse: *To me she speaks; she moves me for her theme*—Err II 2 183. To prefer (a suit): *If I do find him fit, I'll move your suit*—Oth III 4 166. To put (a question): *Let me but move one question to your daughter*—Ado IV 1 74. To impel to (a course of action): *The instances that second marriage move*—Hml III 2 192.

MOVER

(1) A cause: *Poisonous compounds, Which are the movers of a languishing death*—Cymb I 5 8.

(2) Prob., an active, stirring fellow (ironically): *See here these movers that do prize their hours At a crack'd drachma!*—Cor I 5 5.

MOW (sb.)

A grimace: *Those that would make mows at him*—Hml II 2 381. *Apes and monkeys . . . would . . . Contemn with mows the other*—Cymb I 6 39. In phrase *mop and mow*: Tp IV 47 (quoted under *Mop*).

MOW (vb.)

To make grimaces: *Apes that mow and chatter at me*—Tp II 2 9. *Mowing*, grimacing, in phrase *mopping and mowing*: Lr IV 1 64 (quoted under *Mopping*).

MOY

An imaginary name of a coin evolved by Pistol from a misunderstanding of the Fr. *Moi*: Fr. Sol. *. . . Ayez pitié de moi!* Pist. *Moy shall not serve; I will have forty moys*—H5 IV 4 12. Fr. Sol. *O pardonnez moi!* Pist. *. . . Is that a ton of moys?* —22.

MUCH (adj.)

Great: *Thanks . . . for thy much goodness*—Meas V 534. *I am sorry for thy much misgovernment*—Ado IV 1 100. *His fault is much*—Lr II 2 148.

MUCH (adv.)

Very: *I confess me much guilty*—As I 2 196. *I am much ill*—2 H4 IV 4 111. *Seems much unequal*—Ant II 5 101.

MUFFLER

(1) A sort of scarf worn by women in the 16th and 17th centuries, covering part of the face and neck: *He might put on a hat, a muffler and a kerchief, and so escape*—Wiv IV 2 73. *There's her thrummed hat and her muffler too*—80.

(2) A bandage for blindfolding: *Fortune is painted blind, with a muffler afore her eyes*—H5 III 6 32.

MULETER

Muleteer: *Base muleters of France!*—1 H6 III 2 68. *Your mariners are muleters*—Ant III 7 36.

MULL

To dull, stupefy: *Peace is a very apoplexy, lethargy; mulled, deaf, sleepy*—Cor IV 5 238.

MULTITUDINOUS

Belonging to the multitude: *The multitudinous tongue*—Cor III 1 156.

MUMBLE-NEWS

A tale-bearer: *Some carry-tale, some please-man . . . Some mumble-news*—LLL V 2 463.

MUMBUDGET

Equivalent to Mum (perh. orig. the name of some children's game); divided to serve as a password: *I . . . cry 'mum'; she cries 'budget'*—Wiv V 2 6. *I . . . cried 'mum', and she cried 'budget'*—V 5 209.

MUMMY

(1) A preparation of the substance of dead bodies; app. not merely of Egyptian mummies: *Scale of dragon, tooth of wolf, Witches' mummy*—Mcb IV 1 22. *It was dyed in mummy which the skilful Conserved of maidens' hearts*—Oth III 4 74.

(2) Used jocularly for dead flesh: *The water swells a man . . . I should have been a mountain of mummy*—Wiv III 5 16.

MUNIMENTS

Things with which one is provided; of parts of the body: *The leg, the tongue . . . With other muniments and petty helps In this our fabric*—Cor I 1 121.

MUNITION

Ammunition: *I'll to the Tower . . . To view the artillery and munition*—1 H6 I 1 167.

MURAL

A wall: *Now is the mural down between the two neighbours*—Mids V 208.

MURDERING-PIECE

A small cannon or mortar from which case-shot was often fired: *This, Like to a murdering-piece, in many places Gives me superfluous death*—Hml IV 5 94.

MURE

A wall: *The incessant care and labour of his mind Hath wrought the mure that should confine it in So thin that . . .*—2 H4 IV 4 118.

MURMUR

Rumour: *Then 'twas fresh in murmur . . . That . . .*—Tw I 2 32.

MURRAIN

Plague, pestilence in general; in imprecations: *A murrain on your monster!*—Tp III 2 88. *A murrain on't!*—Cor I 5 3.

MURRION

Equivalent to Murrain in the still current sense, a disease in cattle; attrib., *the murrion flock*, the pestilence-stricken flock: *Crows are fatted with the murrion flock*—Mids II 1 97.

MUSCADEL

A sweet wine made from muscat grapes: *Quaff'd off the muscadel*—Shr III 2 174.

MUSE

(1) To wonder: *I muse your majesty doth seem so cold*—John III 1 317. *I muse you make so slight a question*—2 H4 IV 1 167. *I muse my mother Does not approve me further*—Cor III 2 7. *Do not muse at me*—Mcb III 4 85.

(2) To wonder at: *I cannot too much muse Such shapes, such gesture and such sound*—Tp III 3 36.

(3) To murmur, complain: *Well, I will muse no further*—Wiv V 5 253.

MUSET

A gap in a fence or hedge through which hares habitually pass: *The many musets through the which he goes*—Ven 683.

MUSIC

(1) A band of musicians: Page. *The music is come, sir.* Fal. *Let them play. Play, sirs*—2 H4 II 4 245. *Bid the music leave*—H8 IV 2 94. *I would this music would come*—Cymb II 3 12.

(2) Attrib. = musical: *The honey of his music vows*—Hml III 1 164.

MUSS

A scramble: *When I cried 'Ho!' Like boys unto a muss, kings would start forth*—Ant III 13 90.

MUSTER

(1) To enlist, enroll: *We being not known, not muster'd Among the bands*—Cymb IV 4 10.

(2) Perh., to set an example of: *They wear themselves in the cap of the time, there do muster true gait*—All's II 1 54.

MUTINE (sb.)

A turbulent person: *Do like the mutines of Jerusalem*—John II 378. A mutineer: *Methought*

I lay Worse than the mutines in the bilboes—Hml V 2 5.

MUTINE (vb.)

To mutiny: *Rebellious hell, If thou canst mutine in a matron's bones*—Hml III 4 82.

MUTINER

A mutineer: *Worshipful mutiners, Your valour puts well forth*—Cor I 1 254.

MUTINY (sb.)

A state of discord, a dispute, quarrel: *A man . . . whom right and wrong Have chose as umpire of their mutiny*—LLL I 1 169. *You do not well . . . To raise a mutiny betwixt yourselves*—1 H6 IV 1 128. *There is a mutiny in's mind*—H8 III 2 120. *In mutiny*, at variance: *So with herself is she in mutiny*—Lucr 1153.

MUTINY (vb.)

To contend, quarrel: *Where will doth mutiny with wit's regard*—R2 II 1 28. *My very hairs do mutiny; for the white Reprove the brown for rashness*—Ant III 11 13.

MUTTON

(1) A sheep: *Flesh of muttons, beefs, or goats*—Merch I 3 168. *The grease of a mutton*—As III 2 57.

(2) Food for lust, loose women: *The duke . . . would eat mutton on Fridays. He's not past it yet*—Meas III 2 191. *A laced (i.e. prob., ornamented, braided) mutton*, a loose woman: *I, a laced mutton, gave your letter to her, a laced mutton*—Gent I 1 101.

MUTUAL

(1) Of intercourse, intimate: *The stealth of our most mutual entertainment*—Meas I 2 158. *The mutual conference that my mind hath had . . . With you*—2 H6 I 1 25.

(2) *Mutual ranks*, ranks in which all are united in a common cause: *[We] Shall now, in mutual well-beseeming ranks, March all one way and be no more opposed Against acquaintance*—1 H4 I 1 14.

MUTUALITY

An act of intimacy: *When these mutualities so marshal the way, hard at hand comes the master and main exercise*—Oth II 1 267.

MUTUALLY

In return: *The dear love I bear to fair Anne Page, Who mutually hath answer'd my affection*—Wiv IV 6 9.

MYSTERY

(1) An occupation, calling: *He will discredit our mystery*—Meas IV 2 29. *Not to have us thrive*

in our mystery—Tim IV 3 457. *Your mystery, your mystery* (*i.e.* do the office of your calling)—Oth IV 2 30.

(2) Skill, art: *If you think your mystery in stratagem can bring this instrument of honour again into his native quarter*—All's III 6 68.

N

NAKED

(1) Without weapons or armour, unarmed: *Make him, naked, foil a man at arms*—3 H6 V 4 42. *Naked as I am, I will assault thee*—Oth V 2 258. *The poor soldier . . . whose naked breast Stepp'd before targes of proof*—Cymb V 5 3.

(2) *Naked bed*, with reference to the custom of sleeping without clothing on the person: *Who sees his true-love in her naked bed . . . But . . .?*—Ven 397.

NAME

To utter (a word), to say (it): Dum. *Will you vouchsafe with me to change a word?* Mar. *Name it*—LLL V 2 238. *What's worse than murderer, that I may name it?*—3 H6 V 5 58. *If Marcus did not name the word of hands*—Tit III 2 33.

NAPKIN

A pocket-handkerchief: *He sends this bloody napkin*—As IV 3 94. [They would] *dip their napkins in his sacred blood*—Cæs III 2 138. *Here, Hamlet, take my napkin, rub thy brows*—Hml V 2 299. *I am glad I have found this napkin: This was her first remembrance from the Moor*—Oth III 3 290.

NATIVE

(1) Connected by birth or race, closely related: *The mightiest space in fortune nature brings To join like likes and kiss like native things*—All's I 1 237. *Choice breeds A native slip to us from foreign seeds*—I 3 151. *The head is not more native to the heart*—Hml I 2 47.

(2) Entitled to a position by birth, rightful: *Her native king*—R2 III 2 25. *The native and true challenger*—H5 II 4 95.

(3) Natural: *No pulse Shall keep his native progress*—Rom IV 1 96.

NATURAL

(1) Equivalent to Native (2): *His natural king*—3 H6 I 1 82.

(2) Connected by actual consanguinity: *A secret and villanous contriver against me his natural brother*—As I 1 150. *Myself . . . They take for natural father*—Cymb III 3 106.

NATURALIZE

To naturalize in, to familiarize with: *I will return perfect courtier; in the which, my instruction shall serve to naturalize thee*—All's I 1 221.

NATURE

Births of nature, app., natural, *i.e.* spontaneous or seemingly so: *Unfather'd heirs and loathly births of nature*—2 H4 IV 4 122.

NAUGHT (adj.)

(1) Morally bad; wicked, naughty: *All forsworn, all naught, all dissemblers*—Rom III 2 87. *You are naught, you are naught: I'll mark the play*—Hml III 2 157. *Thy sister's naught*—Lr II 4 136. *She was naught*—Cymb V 5 271. *It was not she that call'd him all-to naught*—Ven 993. But as *all-to* (*q.v.*) regularly precedes a verb or participle, it is better in the last quotation to read *all to* (as in the original edition). The quotation then comes under Head (1) of *Naught* (sb.).

(2) Of a title, invalid: [His title] *was corrupt and naught*—H5 I 2 73.

(3) Lost, ruined: *Be gone, away! All will be naught else*—Cor III 1 230. *Naught, naught, all naught!*—Ant III 10 1.

NAUGHT (sb.)

(1) Nothing, nought; hence, *to call all to naught*, to abuse vehemently: *It was not she that call'd him all to naught*—Ven 993. (With reference to this see under *Naught* (adj.) (1).) *To be naught*, to efface oneself, withdraw: *Marry, sir, be better employed, and be naught awhile*—As I 1 38.

(2) Wickedness: *He that doth naught with her*—R3 I 1 99. So *a thing of naught: A paramour is, God bless us, a thing of naught*—Mids IV 2 13.

NAUGHTY

(1) Good for nothing, worthless: *Thou naughty gaoler*—Merch III 3 9. *He's a good drum, my lord, but a naughty orator*—All's V 3 253. Morally bad, wicked: *So shines a good deed in a naughty world*—Merch V 91. *A sort of naughty persons, lewdly bent*—2 H6 II 1 167.

(2) Of weather, bad, nasty: *'Tis a naughty night to swim in*—Lr III 4 115.

NAVE

App., the navel: *He unseam'd him from the nave to the chaps*—Mcb I 2 22.

NAVIGATION

Vessels collectively, shipping: *Though the yesty waves Confound and swallow navigation up*—Mcb IV 1 53.

NAYWARD

To the nayward, towards disbelief: *You would believe my saying, Howe'er you lean to the nayward*—Wint II 1 63.

NAYWORD

(1) A watchword, password: *Have a nay-word, that you may know one another's mind, and the boy never need to understand any thing*—Wiv II 2 131. *We have a nay-word how to know one another*—V 2 5.

(2) A byword; *Let me alone with him: if I do not gull him into a nayword . . . do not think . . .*—Tw II 3 145.

NE

Nor: *All perishen of man, of pelf, Ne aught escapen but himself*—Per II Prol 35.

NEAF

See *Neif*.

NEAR

As comparative: *Nor near nor farther off*—R2 III 2 64. *Better far off than near*, [and] *be ne'er the near*—V 1 88. *The near in blood, The nearer bloody*—Mcb II 3 146.

NEAR-LEGGED

Near-legged before, going with the fore-legs close together: *Near-legged before and with a half-checked bit*—Shr III 2 57.

NEAT

Spruce, smart: *A certain lord, neat, and trimly dress'd, Fresh as a bridegroom*—1 H4 I 3 33. *You neat slave*—Lr II 2 45.

NEB

The bill of a bird; hence applied to the mouth of a person: *How she holds up the neb, the bill to him!*—Wint I 2 183.

NECESSARY

Of servants, functionaries, &c., rendering useful services: *You are . . . a perfecter giber for the table than a necessary bencher in the Capitol*—Cor II 1 90.

NECESSITIED

Brought into necessity: *If her fortunes ever stood Necessitied to help*—All's V 3 84.

NECESSITY

(1) A necessary act or piece of business: *These should be hours for necessities, Not for delights*—H8 V 1 2. *It must omit Real necessities*—Cor III 1 146.

(2) Something unavoidable: *One of these two must be necessities*—Wint IV 4 38. *Are these things then necessities? Then let us meet them like necessities*—2 H4 III 1 92.

NECK

In the neck of that, immediately thereafter: [He] *deprived* [the king] *of his life; And in the neck of that, task'd the whole state*—1 H4 IV 3 91.

NEEDFUL

Standing in need; *this needful war*, clamant in needs, calling for reinforcements: *With aid of soldiers to this needful war*—3 H6 II 1 147.

NEEDLESS

Not in need or want: *Weeping into the needless stream*—As II 1 46.

NEEDLY

Of necessity; *needly will*, needs must: *If sour woe delights in fellowship And needly will be rank'd with other griefs*—Rom III 2 116.

NEEDY

Needful, necessary: *Stored with corn to make your needy bread*—Per I 4 95.

NEELD

Needle: *With her neeld composes Nature's own shape*—Per V Prol 5.

NEEZE

To sneeze: [They] *waxen in their mirth and neeze and swear A merrier hour was never wasted there*—Mids II 1 56.

NEGATIVE

Making denial: [If thou wilt] *be impudently negative, To have nor eyes nor ears nor thought*—Wint I 2 274.

NEGLECT

To cause (a thing) to be neglected: *I hope My absence doth neglect no great designs*—R3 III 4 24.

NEGLECTINGLY

Negligently, carelessly: [I] *Answer'd neglectingly I know not what*—1 H4 I 3 52.

NEGLECTION

Negligence, neglect: *Sleeping neglection doth betray to loss The conquest of our scarce cold conqueror*—1 H6 IV 3 49. *This neglection of degree*—Troil I 3 127. *If neglection Should therein make me vile*—Per III 3 20.

NEIF, NEAF

A fist: *Give me your neaf, Mounsieur Mustardseed*—Mids IV 1 20. *Sweet knight, I kiss thy neif*—2 H4 II 4 200.

NEPHEW

(1) A cousin: *Henry the Fourth . . . Deposed his nephew Richard* [II]—1 H6 II 5 63 (they were cousins-german). *There is among the Greeks A lord of Trojan blood, nephew to Hector; They call*

him Ajax—Troil I 2 12 (cf. Hect. [to Ajax]
Thou art, great lord, my father's sister's son—IV
5 120).

(2) A grandson: *You'll have your daughter
covered with a Barbary horse; you'l' have your
nephews neigh to you*—Oth I 1 111.

NERVE

A sinew or tendon: *Thy nerves are in their
infancy again And have no vigour in them*—Tp I
2 484. *My fate cries out, And makes each petty
artery in this body As hardy as the Nemean lion's
nerve*—Hml I 4 81. [He] *Strains his young
nerves and puts himself in posture That acts my
words*—Cymb III 3 94.

NERVY

Sinewy, vigorous: *Death . . . in's nervy arm
doth lie*—Cor II 1 177.

NETHER-STOCK

See *Stock*.²

NEW-BEGOT

Lately won: *Let not sloth dim your honours
new-begot*—1 H6 I 1 79. Cf. *Beget* (1).

NEW-TROTHED

Lately betrothed: *So says the prince and my
new-trothed lord*—Ado III 1 38.

NEXT

(1) *The next way*, the shortest or most direct
way: *I speak the truth the next way*—All's I 3 62.
Home, home, the next way—Wint III 3 128. *'Tis
the next way to turn tailor*—1 H4 III 1 264.

(2) Immediately preceding: *Each following day
Became the next day's master, till the last Made
former wonders its*—H8 I 1 16.

NICE

(1) Wanton, loose-mannered: *These betray nice
wenches, that would be betrayed without these*—
—LLL III 23. *When mine hours Were nice and
lucky, men did ransom lives Of me for jests*—Ant
III 13 179.

(2) Coy, prudish: *Since you are strangers and
come here by chance, We'll not be nice: take hands*
—LLL V 2 218. *Upholding the nice fashion of
your country in denying me a kiss*—H5 V 2 299.
To make nice of, to make a scruple in regard to:
*He that stands upon a slippery place Makes nice of
no vile hold to stay him up*—John III 4 137.

(3) Unimportant, trivial: *Every idle, nice and
wanton reason*—2 H4 IV 1 191. *Bade him bethink How nice the quarrel was*—Rom III 1 158.
The letter was not nice but full of charge—V 2 18.
*It is not meet That every nice offence should bear
his comment*—Cæs IV 3 7.

(4) Critical, doubtful: *To set so rich a main On
the nice hazard of one doubtful hour*—1 H4 IV 1
47.

(5) Thin, unsubstantial: *That policy may . . .
feed upon such nice and waterish diet*—Oth III 3
14.

(6) Effeminate, unmanly: *Hence, therefore, thou
nice crutch!*—2 H4 I 1 145.

NICELY

(1) Subtly, fantastically: *They that dally nicely
with words may quickly make them wanton*—Tw
III 1 16 (with suggestion of sense wantonly; cf.
Nice (1)). *Can sick men play so nicely with their
names?*—R2 II 1 84. With excess of subtlety:
*God forbid . . . That you should . . . nicely charge
your understanding soul With opening titles miscreate*—H5 I 2 13.

(2) With insistence on detail, strictly: *When
articles too nicely urged be stood on*—H5 V 2 94.

NICELY-GAWDED

Daintily adorned: *Their nicely-gawded cheeks*—
Cor II 1 233.

NICENESS

Coyness, reserve: [Change] *fear and niceness—
The handmaids of all women . . . —into a waggish courage*—Cymb III 4 158.

NICE-PRESERVED

Carefully guarded: *That nice-preserved honesty
of yours*—Tit II 3 135.

NICETY

Equivalent to *Niceness* (q.v.): *Lay by all nicety
and prolixious blushes*—Meas II 4 162.

NICHOLAS, SAINT

(1) The patron saint of school-boys and scholars:
Speed. . . . *Come; try me in thy paper.* Launce.
There; and Saint Nicholas be thy speed!—Gent
III 1 299.

(2) Prob. = 'Old Nick': *I know thou worship-
pest Saint Nicholas*—1 H4 II 1 70 (to Gadshill,
the highwayman). *Saint Nicholas' clerks*, high-
waymen: *If they meet not with Saint Nicholas'
clerks, I'll give thee this neck*—67.

NICK (sb.)

A notch cut for keeping a score; hence *out of
all nick*, beyond all reckoning: *He loved her out of
all nick*—Gent IV 2 76.

NICK (vb.)

(1) To cut in nicks or notches; of the hair:
With scissors nicks him like a fool—Err V 175.

(2) To cut into, cut short: *The itch of his affection should not then Have nick'd his captainship*—
Ant III 13 7.

NICKNAME

To mention by mistake: *You nickname virtue;
vice you should have spoke*—LLL V 2 349.

NIECE

A grand-daughter: Duch. [of York]. *Who meets us here? my niece Plantagenet* (*i.e.* Margaret, daughter of Clarence, the speaker's son)—R3 IV 1 1.

NIGGARD

(1) To act in a niggardly fashion: [Thou] *makest waste in niggarding*—Sonn I 12.

(2) To put off *with* a small allowance: *Nature must obey necessity; Which we will niggard with a little rest*—Cæs IV 3 227.

NIGHT-CROW

A bird not certainly identified; perh. the night-heron: *The night-crow cried, aboding luckless time*—3 H6 V 6 45.

NIGHT-GOWN

A loose gown worn at night (but not in bed); a dressing-gown: *I saw the Duchess of Milan's gown . . . 'Ti]s but a night-gown in respect of yours*—Ado III 4 15. *Get on your nightgown, lest occasion call us, And show us to be watchers*—Mcb II 2 70. *I have seen her rise from her bed, throw her nightgown upon her*—V I 4. *Shall I go fetch your night-gown?*—Oth IV 3 34.

NIGHT-RAVEN

Prob. the same as *Night-crow* (q.v.): *I pray God his bad voice bode no mischief. I had as lief have heard the night-raven*—Ado II 3 83.

NIGHT-RULE

Order of the night, night-revel: *What night-rule now about this haunted grove?*—Mids III 2 5. Cf. *Rule.*

NILL

To be unwilling, not to will: *I nill relate, action may Conveniently the rest convey*—Per III Prol 55. *In scorn or friendship, nill I construe whether*—Pilgr 188.

NINE-FOLD

An attendant set of nine: *He met the night-mare, and her nine-fold* (*i.e.* her nine familiars)—Lr III 4 126.

NINE MEN'S MORRIS

See *Morris.*

NINE WORTHIES, THE

Generally considered to be Joshua, David, Judas Maccabæus, Hector, Alexander, Julius Cæsar, Arthur, Charlemagne, and Godfrey of Bouillon: *I say [no show] so fit as to present the Nine Worthies*—LLL V 1 129. [Thou art] *ten times better than the Nine Worthies*—2 H4 II 4 238. In LLL, however, Hercules and Pompey are included.

NOB

A diminutive of Robert: *I would not be Sir Nob in any case*—John I 147, referring to Sir Robert, his putative father. See 139. *Sir Robert's his* in that line appears to be a double genitive.

NOBLE

(1) App., the nobles: *Hath he not pass'd the noble and the common?*—Cor III 1 29.

(2) A gold coin = 6s. 8d.: *Mowbray hath received eight thousand nobles*—R2 I 1 88. Nym. *I shall have my eight shillings I won of you at betting?* Pist. *A noble shalt thou have*—H5 II 1 110. *I gave a noble to the priest*—1 H6 V 4 23. There appears to have been also a coin, known in Shakespeare's day as an 'old noble', worth 10s. This seems to be the coin meant in the passage in H5.

NOBODY

The picture of Nobody, referring to some engraving of the time which cannot now be identified: *This is the tune of our catch, played by the picture of Nobody*—Tp III 2 135.

NOD

Noddy; a fool (with a play): Pan. . . . *You shall see him nod at me.* Cres. *Will he give you the nod?*—Troil I 2 211. (*The rich shall have more*—214 = you will be still more of a fool.)

NO HAD?

Had I not? K. John. . . . *Thou hadst [no cause] to kill him.* Hub. *No had, my lord! why, did you not provoke me?*—John IV 2 206.

NOISE (sb.)

(1) Rumour, report: *The noise goes, this [was his cause of anger]*—Troil I 2 12. *Tom, away! Mark the high noises*—Lr III 6 117. *Cleopatra, catching but the least noise of this, dies instantly*—Ant I 2 144.

(2) Of agreeable or musical sounds: *The isle is full of noises, Sounds and sweet airs*—Tp III 2 144. *What noise is this?* [Hautboys—Mcb IV 1 106. [Music of the hautboys . . . Fourth Sold. *Peace! what noise?*—Ant IV 3 12.

(3) A company or band of musicians: *See if thou canst find out Sneak's noise*—2 H4 II 4 12.

NOISE (vb.)

To noise it, to clamour, raise turmoil: *A trull, That noises it against us*—Ant III 6 95.

NOLE

The head, noddle: *An ass's nole I fixed on his head*—Mids III 2 17

NOMINATE

(1) To name, entitle: *Thy young days, which we may nominate tender*—LLL I 2 15. *Who is intituled, nominated, or called, Don Adriano*—V 1 8.

(2) To mention or specify by name: *Can you nominate in order now the degrees of the lie?*—As V 4 92. *Sight may distinguish of colours, but suddenly to nominate them all, it is impossible*—2 H6 II 1 129.

(3) To appoint, set down: *Let the forfeit Be nominated for an equal pound Of your fair flesh*—Merch I 3 149. *Is it so nominated in the bond?*—IV 1 259.

NOMINATION

(1) A mentioning or specifying by name: *I will look . . . for the nomination of the party writing*—LLL IV 2 137. *What imports the nomination of this gentleman?*—Hml V 2 133.

(2) A specifying or appointing: Hast. . . . *When is the royal day?* Buck. *Are all things fitting for that royal time?* Der. *It is, and wants but nomination*—R3 III 4 3.

NONCE

For the nonce, for a particular purpose, for the purpose: *I have cases of buckram for the nonce*—1 H4 I 2 200. *I'll have prepared him A chalice for the nonce*—Hml IV 7 160. As a tag, with no special meaning: *This is a riddling merchant for the nonce*—1 H6 II 3 57.

NON-REGARDANCE

Disregard, contempt: *Since you to non-regardance cast my faith*—Tw V 124.

NOOK-SHOTTEN

Running out into corners or angles: *That nook-shotten isle of Albion*—H5 III 5 14.

NORTH

The north wind: *I will speak as liberal as the north*—Oth V 2 220. *The tyrannous breathing of the north*—Cymb I 3 36.

NOSE-HERB

A herb for smelling at: *They are not herbs, you knave; they are nose-herbs*—All's IV 5 19.

NOT

Not only: *It is not my consent, But my entreaty too*—Meas IV 1 67. *You may salve so, Not what is dangerous present, but the loss Of what is past*—Cor III 2 70. [He has] *Given hostile strokes, and that not in the presence Of dreaded justice, but on the ministers That do distribute it*—III 3 97. *Not your knowledge, your personal pain, but even Your purse, still open*—Per III 2 46.

NOTE (sb.)

(1) A strain of music, melody, tune: *Train me not, sweet mermaid, with thy note*—Err III 2 45. *I'll give you a verse to this note that I made yesterday*—As II 5 48. *Cause the musicians play me*

that sad note I named my knell—H8 IV 2 78. *Sing him to the ground, As once our mother; use like note and words*—Cymb IV 2 236. Fig.: *That is the very note of it*—Wiv I 1 171.

(2) A mark: *Some natural notes about her body*—Cymb II 2 28. A sign, token: *The greatest note of it is his melancholy*—Ado III 2 54. *A note infallible Of breaking honesty*—Wint I 2 287. *Upon his royal face there is no note How dread an army hath enrounded him*—H5 IV Chor 35. *My windpipe's dangerous notes*, the indications showing where the windpipe, the point of danger, is: *I should fear to drink at meals; Lest they should spy my windpipe's dangerous notes*—Tim I 2 51.

(3) A stigma, brand: *The more to aggravate the note, With a foul traitor's name stuff I thy throat*—R2 I 1 43. *My posterity, shamed with the note*—Lucr 208. *A perjured note*, a brand of perjury: *Ill, to example ill, Would from my forehead wipe a perjured note*—LLL IV 3 124.

(4) A remark, observation: *A good note; that keeps you from the blow of the law*—Tw III 4 168.

(5) Observation; *upon the warrant of my note*, on the strength of my observation (of your character): [I] *dare, upon the warrant of my note, Commend a dear thing to you*—Lr III 1 18. Sim. *take this note*, mark this: *Therefore I do advise you, take this note*—Lr IV 5 29.

(6) A thing observed: *Nine changes of the watery star hath been The shepherd's note since . . .*—Wint I 2 1.

(7) Information, knowledge: *She that from Naples Can have no note*—Tp II 1 247. *His picture I will send far and near, that all the kingdom May have due note of him*—Lr II 1 83. *To come to note*, to become known: *He shall conceal it Whiles you are willing it shall come to note*—Tw IV 3 28. Notice, intimation: *Rouse him and give him note of our approach*—Troil IV 1 43.

(8) A bill or account: *Here is now the smith's note for shoeing and plough-irons*—2 H4 V 1 19.

(9) *Out of my note*, not among the things which I have to bear in mind: *Dates?—none, that's out of my note*—Wint IV 3 49. *The note of expectation*, the list of guests expected: *The rest That are within the note of expectation Already are i' the court*—Mcb III 3 9.

(10) *By note*, by written warrant: *I come by note, to give and to receive*—Merch III 2 141 (referring to the scroll from the casket).

NOTE (vb.)

(1) To stigmatize: *You have condemn'd and noted Lucius Pella*—Cæs IV 3 2.

(2) To indicate, show: [That you never shall] *note That you know aught of me*—Hml I 5 178.

(3) *Noted*, known: *Cases of buckram . . . to immask our noted outward garments*—1 H4 I 2 201. *So well noted*: *The antique and well noted face Of plain old form*—John IV 2 21.

NOTION

Understanding, intellect: *His own notion . . . shall join To thrust the lie unto him*—Cor V 6 107. [I told] *all things else that might To half a soul and to a notion crazed Say ' Thus did Banquo '*—Mcb III 1 82. *His notion weakens, his discernings Are lethargied*—Lr I 4 248.

NOTORIOUS

Egregious, having the qualities of the kind in a high degree: *You have done me wrong, Notorious wrong*—Tw V 336. *I curse the day . . . Wherein I did not some notorious ill*—Tit V 1 125. *The Moor's abused by some most villanous knave, Some base notorious knave*—Oth IV 2 139. *'Tis a notorious villain*—V 2 239 (of Iago, whose villainy has just become known).

NOTORIOUSLY

Egregiously, in a high degree: *There was never man so notoriously abused*—Tw IV 2 94. *He hath been most notoriously abused*—V 388.

NOT-PATED

Having the head close cropped (*not* = close cropped): *Wilt thou rob this leathern jerkin, crystal-button, not-pated* [fellow]*?*—1 H4 II 4 77.

NOUNS

'Od's nouns. See *'Od's.*

NOURISH

A nurse; fig.: [When] *Our isle* [shall] *be made a nourish of salt tears*—1 H6 I 1 50.

NOUSLE

To bring *up*, nurture: *Those mothers who, to nousle up their babes, Thought nought too curious*—Per I 4 42.

NO-VERBS

A nonsense word coined by the Host: *He gives me the proverbs and the no-verbs*—Wiv III 1 106.

NOVUM

More fully *Novum Quinque*, a game at dice in which the principal throws were nine and five: *Abate* [a] *throw at novum*—LLL V 2 547.

NOYANCE

An aphetic form of *Annoyance*; in sense (1) given under that word: *To keep itself from noyance*—Hml III 3 13.

NUMBER

App., to put into numbers or verse: *Hearts, tongues . . . poets, cannot Think, speak . . . number, ho! His love to Antony*—Ant III 2 16.

NUMBERED

Perh., abounding in numbers (of stones): *The twinn'd stones Upon the number'd beach*—Cymb I 6 35.

NUNCIO

A messenger: *She will attend it better in thy youth Than in a nuncio's of more grave aspect*—Tw I 4 27.

NUNCLE

A variant of uncle; app. a usual address of a fool to his superiors: *How now, nuncle! Would I had two coxcombs and two daughters!*—Lr I 4 117. *If thou wert my fool, nuncle, I'ld . . .*—I 5 45. *Cry to it, nuncle*—II 4 123.

NURSERY

(1) Nursing, tender care: *I loved her most, and thought to set my rest On her kind nursery*—Lr I 1 125.

(2) That which is reared, a crop: *The seeded pride . . . must or now be cropp'd, Or, shedding, breed a nursery of like evil*—Troil I 3 316.

NUTHOOK

A hooked stick used in nutting; applied to beadles, &c.: *If you run the nuthook's humour on me*—Wiv I 1 170. *Nut-hook, nut-hook, you lie*—2 H4 V 4 8 (addressed to the beadle).

O

O

Of anything circular; of the marks of smallpox: *O that your face were not so full of O's!*—LLL V 2 45. Of the heavenly bodies: *All yon fiery oes and eyes of light*—Mids III 2 188. Of the theatres of the time: *May we cram Within this wooden O the very casques That did affright the air at Agincourt?*—H5 Prol 12. Of the earth: *The little O, the earth*—Ant V 2 81. Of a halter: Mal. . . . *A should follow, but O does.* Fab. *And O shall end, I hope*—Tw II 5 142.

OATHABLE

Fit to be sworn, oath-worthy: *You are not oathable*—Tim IV 3 135.

OB.

Abbreviation of Obolus (which was applied to various European coins of small value); used to denote a halfpenny: *Item, Bread, ob.*—1 H4 II 4 590.

OBJECT (sb.)

(1) The presentation (of something) to the eye

or perception : *Reason flies the object of all harm*—Troil II 2 41. *The object of our misery is as an inventory to particularize their abundance*—Cor I 1 20.

(2) *Swear against objects*, perh., renounce (the hearing and sight of) objects (in so far as they might move to pity); explained by the following lines : Tim IV 3 122.

OBJECT (vb.)

(1) To bring forward, propose : *Good Master Vernon, it is well objected*—1 H6 II 4 43 (referring to the proposal just made).

(2) To bring forward as a charge or accusation : *What dost thou object Against the Duke of Norfolk?*—R2 I 1 28. [I] *Purpose to answer what thou canst object*—1 H6 III 1 7. *To object* a thing *to* one, to cast it in his teeth : *The saying did not hold In him that did object the same to thee*—R3 II 4 16.

OBJECTION

A charge or accusation : *You do not well To bear with their perverse objections*—1 H6 IV 1 128. *As for your spiteful false objections, Prove them, and I lie open to the law*—2 H6 I 3 158. *I dare your worst objections*—H8 III 2 307.

OBLIGED

Pledged : *To keep obliged faith unforfeited*—Merch II 6 7.

OBLIQUE

Of a bull, possibly referring to the crooked shape of the horns : *The bull,—the primitive statue, and oblique memorial of cuckolds*—Troil V 1 60.

OBSCENE

Foul, abominable (without connotation of indecency) : *That obscene and most preposterous event*—LLL I 1 244. *So heinous, black, obscene a deed*—R2 IV 131.

OBSCURE

Frequenting the darkness : *The obscure bird Clamour'd the livelong night*—Mcb II 3 64 (no doubt the owl; cf. II 2 3 and 16).

OBSEQUIES

Commemorative rites : *The obsequies that I for thee will keep Nightly shall be to strew thy grave and weep*—Rom V 3 16.

OBSEQUIOUS

(1) Prompt to serve or please, dutiful (without connotation of servility) : *I see you are obsequious in your love, and I profess requital*—Wiv IV 2 2. *The general, subject to a well-wish'd king . . . in obsequious fondness Crowd to his presence*—Meas II 4 27. *Let me be obsequious in thy heart, And take thou my oblation*—Sonn 125 9.

(2) Proper to obsequies, mourning, funereal :

Uncle, draw you near, To shed obsequious tears upon this trunk—Tit V 3 151. *To do obsequious sorrow*—Hml I 2 92. *Many a holy and obsequious tear*—Sonn 31 5. Dutiful in manifesting regard for the dead : *So obsequious will thy father be . . . As Priam was for all his valiant sons*—3 H6 II 5 118.

OBSEQUIOUSLY

With due manifestation of regard for the dead : *Whilst I awhile obsequiously lament The untimely fall of virtuous Lancaster*—R3 I 2 3.

OBSERVANCE

(1) An ordinance, rule : *There are other strict observances*—LLL I 1 36. *Degrees, observances, customs, and laws*—Tim IV 1 19.

(2) Reverential attention, homage : *Adoration, duty, and observance*—As V 2 102. With *of* : *With due observance of thy godlike seat*—Troil I 3 31. *To do observance*, to do homage : *Do observance to my mercy*—2 H4 IV 3 16. Regard, respect ; with *of* : *Without observance or respect of any*—Troil II 3 175. Dutiful service : [I] *ever shall With true observance seek to eke out that Wherein toward me my homely stars have fail'd*—All's II 5 78. *Observances, attentions* : *We must think men are not gods, Nor of them look for such observances As fit the bridal*—Oth III 4 148.

(3) Observant care, heed : *Suit the action to the word, the word to the action ; with this special observance, that . . .*—Hml III 2 19. So, minute attention to detail in workmanship : *Sweet observance in this work (i.e.* the picture) *was had*—Lucr 1385.

OBSERVANT

An obsequious attendant : *Silly ducking observants*—Lr II 2 109.

OBSERVATION

(1) An observance, rite : *Now our observation is perform'd*—Mids IV 1 108.

(2) Courteous regard or attention : *He is but a bastard to the time That doth not smack of observation*—John I 207.

(3) Observant care, heed : [With] *observation strange my meaner ministers Their several kinds have done*—Tp III 3 87.

OBSERVE

To treat with respectful attention, humour, gratify : *He is gracious, if he be observed*—2 H4 IV 4 30. *Let his very breath, whom thou'lt observe, Blow off thy cap*—Tim IV 3 212. *Must I observe you? must I stand and crouch Under your testy humour?*—Cæs IV 3 45.

OBSERVING

Compliant, obsequious : [They] *underwrite in an observing kind His humorous predominance*—Troil II 3 137.

OBSTRUCT

A conjectural emendation for *abstract*, to mean obstruction, in Ant III 6 61 (*Being an obstruct 'tween his lust and him*). The word is not otherwise known.

OCCASION

(1) An opportunity (of fault-finding): *That the time's enemies may not have this To grace occasions*—John IV 2 61.

(2) The course of events or circumstances: *Withhold thy speed, dreadful occasion! . . . till I have pleased My discontented peers*—John IV 2 125. [We] *are enforced from our most quiet there By the rough torrent of occasion*—2 H4 IV 1 71.

(3) Something occasioned or caused: *That woman that cannot make her fault her husband's occasion, let her never nurse her child herself*—As IV 1 177 (or perh. the word should be taken in sense (1), *i.e.* an opportunity (of fault-finding) against her husband).

(4) A personal need or requirement: *My extremest means Lie all unlock'd to your occasions*—Merch I 1 138. *My occasions have found time to use 'em toward a supply of money*—Tim II 2 200. *If his occasion were not virtuous, I should not urge it half so faithfully*—III 2 45. *A page so kind . . . So tender over his occasions*—Cymb V 5 86. *He married but his occasion*, he married merely to suit his interests: *Antony will use his affection where it is: he married but his occasion here*—Ant II 6 138.

(5) *Quarrelling with occasion*, setting oneself at variance with what the occasion calls for, answering perversely: *Yet more quarrelling with occasion!*—Merch III 5 60.

OCCUPATION

(1) Mechanical employment, handicraft: *Now the red pestilence strike all trades in Rome, And occupations perish!*—Cor IV 1 13. *You that stood so much Upon the voice of occupation and The breath of garlic-eaters*—IV 6 96.

(2) *A man of any occupation*, a worker or doer (and not a mere talker): *An I had been a man of any occupation, if I would not have taken him at a word, I would I might go to hell*—Cæs I 2 268.

OCCUPY

These villains will make the word as odious as the word 'occupy'; which was an excellent good word before it was ill sorted—2 H4 II 4 160. The word fell into disrepute about the end of the 16th century, and was little in good use in the 17th and most of the 18th centuries, probably because it was vulgarly employed in an indecent sense (*occupare amplexu*) now quite lost. Cf. Rom II 4 105, the only other passage where the word occurs.

OCCURRENCE

That which has occurred, course of events: *All the occurrence of my fortune since Hath been between this lady and this lord*—Tw V 264.

OCCURRENT

An occurrence, event: *So tell him, with the occurrents, more and less, Which have solicited*—Hml V 2 368.

ODD

(1) Remarkable, wonderful: *Stood* (*i.e.* in the picture) *many Trojan mothers . . . And to their hope they such odd action yield, That through their light joy seemed to appear*—Lucr 1431.

(2) Situated apart, out of the way: *Whom I left . . . In an odd angle of the isle*—Tp I 2 222.

(3) At variance or strife: *The general state, I fear, Can scarce entreat you to be odd with him*—Troil IV 5 264.

ODD-CONCEITED

Fantastically devised: *Twenty odd-conceited true-love knots*—Gent II 7 46. Cf. *Conceited* (3).

ODD-EVEN

At this odd-even . . . watch o' the night, perh., the time when one cannot say whether it is night or morning, the dead of night—Oth I 1 124.

ODDLY

Unequally, disadvantageously as compared with the other side: *Our imputation shall be oddly poised In this wild action*—Troil I 3 339.

ODDS

Contention, a quarrel: *I desire Nothing but odds with England*—H5 II 4 128. *Thou . . . that put'st odds Among the rout of nations*—Tim IV 3 42. *I cannot speak Any beginning to this peevish odds*—Oth II 3 184.

'OD'S

God's, in various asseverations, such as *'Od's nouns*, God's wounds—Wiv IV 1 25. *'Ods pittikins*, God's dear pity—Cymb IV 2 293. And in others, without much meaning, originating by some confusion from such expressions; *e.g.*, *Od's me*—Wiv I 4 64. *'Od's my little life*—As III 5 43. *'Od's my will*—IV 3 17.

ŒILLADE

An amorous glance, ogle: [Who] *examined my parts with most judicious œillades*—Wiv I 3 67. *She gave strange œillades and most speaking looks To noble Edmund*—Lr IV 5 25.

O'ER-

See words in *Over-*.

OF

(1) Used in various senses where modern usage would require (a) By: *Finding yourself desired of such a person*—Meas II 4 91. *A night of groans*

Endured of her—R3 IV 4 303.   *This dreaded sight, twice seen of us*—Hml I 1 25.   (b) Concerning, about: *'Tis pity of him*—Ant I 4 71.   *Bring us what she says, And how you find of her*—V 1 67.   (c) During: *Not [to] be seen to wink of all the day*—LLL I 1 43.   *Did I never speak of all that time?*—Shr Ind 2 84.   (d) For: *I have no mind of feasting forth to-night*—Merch II 5 37.   (e) From: *One that I brought up of a puppy*—Gent IV 4 2.   *Being of so young days brought up with him*—Hml II 2 11.   (f) From being: *Henry . . . Is of a king become a banish'd man*—3 H6 III 3 24.   (g) In: *Thy mistress is o' the brothel*—Tim IV 1 13.   (h) In the person of: *You shall find of the king a husband*—All's I 1 7.   (i) On: *A box of the ear*—Merch I 2 86.   *A plague of all drums!*—All's IV 3 331.   *To keep one's eyes of either side's nose*—Lr I 5 22.   (j) Over: *The sovereign power you have of us*—Hml II 2 27.   (k) With: *I am provided of a torch-bearer*—Merch II 4 24.   *You are as well provided of both as any prince in the world*—H5 III 7 9.

(2) In adjurations; *of all loves*: *Mistress Page would desire you to send her your little page, of all loves*—Wiv II 2 118.   *Speak, of all loves!*—Mids II 2 154.   *Of charity*: *Of charity, what kin are you to me?*—Tw V 237.

(3) *Of a fool*, in aggravation of thy folly: *That did but show thee, of a fool, inconstant*—Wint III 2 187.

OFF

Beside the mark, not to the purpose: *That's off; I would you rather had been silent*—Cor II 2 64.

OFFENCE

(1) Harm, injury: *Worm nor snail, do no offence*—Mids II 2 23.   *To do offence and scath in Christendom*—John II 75.   *So shall he waste his means, weary his soldiers, Doing himself offence*—Cæs IV 3 200.   *I had rather have this tongue cut from my mouth Than it should do offence to Michael Cassio*—Oth II 3 221.

(2) Pain, trouble: *You have some sick offence within your mind*—Cæs II 1 268.

(3) Disfavour, disgrace: *I am now so far in offence with my niece that I cannot . . .*—Tw IV 2 74.

(4) A thing that causes disgust: *Methinks, thou art a general offence*—All's II 3 269.

(5) The fruits of an offence: *May one be pardon'd and retain the offence?*—Hml III 3 56.   Cf. *Theft.*

OFFEND

(1) To harm, injure: *Thou but offend'st thy lungs to speak so loud*—Merch IV 1 140.   [She] *was in mine eye The dust that did offend it*—All's V 3 54.   *This last surrender of his will but offend us*—Lr I 1 309.

(2) To give (physical) pain or annoyance to:

I have a salt and sorry rheum offends me—Oth III 4 51.

(3) To trespass against, wrong: *Who have you offended, masters, that you are thus bound?*—Ado V 1 232.   *Till you do live to see a son of mine Offend you and obey you, as I did*—2 H4 V 2 105.   *I never did Offend you in my life*—Oth V 2 58.   To transgress (the law or the course of law): *He hath offended the law*—Meas III 2 16.   *Not a man Shall . . . offend the stream Of regular justice*—Tim V 4 59.

OFFER

(1) To take the offensive, offer assault: *We of the offering side*—1 H4 IV 1 69.   *His power, like to a fangless lion, May offer, but not hold*—2 H4 IV 1 218.

(2) To venture, presume: *To offer to get your living by the copulation of cattle*—As III 2 84.   *What are you that offer to beat my servant?*—Shr V 1 65.   *All that offer to defend him*—Lr III 6 101.

OFFICE (sb.)

(1) A service, benefit: *I will no more enforce mine office on you*—All's II 1 129.   *Little office The hateful commons will perform for us*—R2 II 2 137.   Pains taken on another's behalf: *Since then my office hath so far prevail'd That . . .*—H5 V 2 29.

(2) A bodily or mental function: *Whom I with all the office of my heart Entirely honour*—Oth III 4 113.   [That] *bent all offices to honour her*—Per II 5 48.

OFFICE (vb.)

(1) To perform in the way of service: *Although The air of paradise did fan the house And angels officed all*—All's III 2 127.

(2) To appoint to an office: *So stands this squire Officed with me*—Wint I 2 171.

(3) To drive away or expel by virtue of one's office: *A Jack guardant cannot office me from my son Coriolanus*—Cor V 2 67.

OFFICED

Having a particular function: *My speculative and officed instruments*—Oth I 3 271.

OFFICIOUS

Active in service: *Be every one officious To make this banquet*—Tit V 2 202.

OFT

Frequent: *By oft predict that I in heaven find*—Sonn 14 8.

OLD (adj.)

In colloq. use, plentiful, abundant, 'grand': *Here will be an old abusing of God's patience*—Wiv I 4 4.   *Yonder's old coil at home*—Ado V 2 98.   *We shall have old swearing*—Merch IV 2 15.

If a man were porter of hell-gate, he should have old turning the key—Mcb II 3 1.

OLD (sb.)

Wold: *S. Withold footed thrice the old*—Lr III 4 125.

OLD (adv.)

In ancient times, long ago: *To sing a song that old was sung*—Per Prol 1.

OMEN

App., an event portended: *As harbingers preceding still the fates And prologue to the omen coming on*—Hml I 1 122.

OMIT

(1) To pass over, leave disregarded: *What if we do omit This reprobate till he were well inclined?*—Meas IV 3 77. *Therefore omit him not; blunt not his love*—2 H4 IV 4 27. *Wherefore grieve I at an hour's poor loss, Omitting Suffolk's exile?*—2 H6 III 2 381.

(2) To forbear or cease to retain: *The gutter'd rocks . . . do omit Their mortal natures*—Oth II 1 69.

OMITTANCE

Omission (to inflict something): *Omittance is no quittance*—As III 5 133.

ON

Used where modern usage would require Of: *We are such stuff As dreams are made on*—Tp IV 156. *One on's father's moods*—Cor I 3 72. *I' the very throat on me*—Mcb II 3 43. *The bird is dead That we have made so much on*—Cymb IV 2 197.

ONCE

(1) Once for all: *To be once in doubt Is once to be resolved*—Oth III 3 179. Hence, to speak in a word, in short: *Once, if he do require our voices, we ought not to deny him*—Cor II 3 1. So *Once this,—your long experience of her wisdom, Her sober virtue . . . Plead on her part*—Err III 1 89. *'Tis once, thou lovest*—Ado I 1 320. So also *at once: My lords, at once: the care you have of us . . .*—2 H6 III 1 66. *My lords, at once: the cause why we are met Is . . .*—R3 III 4 1.

(2) Nay, positively: *What we oft do best, By sick interpreters, once weak ones, is Not ours, or not allow'd*—H8 I 2 81.

(3) For once: *O, once tell true*—Mids III 2 68. *Once in my days I'll be a madcap*—1 H4 I 2 159.

(4) Some time or other: *Once to-night Give my sweet Nan this ring*—Wiv III 4 103. One day: *Meditating that she must die once*—Cæs IV 3 191.

(5) Ever, at any time: *If idle talk will once be necessary*—Ant V 2 50.

(6) Once when: *Once we stood up about the corn, he himself stuck not to . . .*—Cor II 3 16.

ONE-TRUNK-INHERITING

Possessing but one trunk: [A] *one-trunk-inheriting slave*—Lr II 2 20. Cf. *Inherit* (3).

ONEYERS

See *Great Oneyers.*

ONSET

A beginning: *To give the onset to thy good advice*—Gent III 2 94. *For an onset . . . Lavinia will I make my empress*—Tit I 238. *In the onset come*—Sonn 90 11.

OPEN (sb.)

Open, unconcealed condition; *in open*, in public: *The Lady Anne . . . This day was view'd in open as his queen*—H8 III 2 402.

OPEN (vb.)

(1) To disclose, make known, set forth: *I command thee to open thy affair*—Wint IV 4 762. *Causes now in hand, Which I have open'd to his grace at large*—H5 I 1 77. *But she spoke it dying, I would not Believe her lips in opening it*—Cymb V 5 41. *The petty wrens of Tarsus will fly hence, And open this to Pericles*—Per IV 3 22.

(2) To explain, expound: *God forbid . . . That you should . . . nicely charge your understanding soul With opening titles miscreate*—H5 I 2 13.

OPENER

One who reveals and interprets: *The very opener and intelligencer Between the grace, the sanctities of heaven And our dull workings*—2 H4 IV 2 20.

OPERANT

(1) Operative, active: *My operant powers their functions leave to do*—Hml III 2 184.

(2) Powerful in effect: *Thy most operant poison*—Tim IV 3 25.

OPINION

(1) Favourable estimate of oneself; self-conceit, arrogance: *Learned without opinion*—LLL V 1 5. *Pride, haughtiness, opinion and disdain*—1 H4 III 1 185. *A plague of opinion!*—Troil III 3 265. In good sense, self-confidence: *To steel a strong opinion to themselves*—Troil I 3 353. *Let us rear The higher our opinion*—Ant II 1 35.

(2) The estimation in which one stands, reputation, credit: *Thou hast redeem'd thy lost opinion*—1 H4 V 4 48. *In the trial much opinion dwells*—Troil I 3 336. *Opinion that so sticks on Marcius*—Cor I 1 275. *His silver hairs Will purchase us a good opinion*—Cæs II 1 144.

(3) App., an imputation of fault: *How have I been behaved, that he might stick The small'st opinion on my least misuse?*—Oth IV 2 108.

OPPORTUNITY

Erroneously used as = Importunity: *If oppor-*

14

tunity and humblest suit Cannot attain it—Wiv
III 4 20.

OPPOSE

To expose: *Opposing freely The beauty of her
person to the people*—H8 IV 1 67.

OPPOSITE (adj.)

Antagonistic, adverse: *Be opposite with a kinsman*—Tw II 5 162. *A stubborn opposite intent*
—2 H6 III 2 251. *To be thus opposite with
heaven*—R3 II 2 94. *Seeing how loathly opposite
I stood To his unnatural purpose*—Lr II 1 51.

OPPOSITE (sb.)

An adversary, enemy: *His opposite . . . bears
. . . no great presage of cruelty*—Tw III 2 68.
*'Tis not enough our foes are this time fled, Being
opposites of such repairing nature*—2 H6 V 3 21.
[He] *leaves nothing undone that may fully discover
him their opposite*—Cor II 2 22. *The captives
That were the opposites of this day's strife*—Lr V
3 41.

OPPOSITION

(1) A setting opposite (as, *e.g.*, for combat):
The opposition of your person in trial—Hml V 2
178.

(2) That which counterbalances or is put in the
opposite scale: *Your whole plot* [is] *too light for
the counterpoise of so great an opposition*—1 H4 II
3 13.

(3) Encounter, combat: *In single opposition,
hand to hand*—1 H4 I 3 99. *Swords out . . . In
opposition bloody*—Oth II 3 183. *More remarkable
in single oppositions*—Cymb IV 1 14.

OPPRESS

To put down, suppress: *The mutiny he there
hastes t' oppress*—Per III Prol 29.

OPULENCY

Opulence: *The infinite flatteries that follow
youth and opulency*—Tim V 1 37.

OR

Sooner than, rather than: *He'll grant the tribute
. . . Or look upon our Romans*—Cymb II 4 13.

ORB

(1) A circle, ring: *I serve the fairy queen, To
dew her orbs* (*i.e.* fairy rings) *upon the green*—
Mids II 1 8.

(2) Equivalent to Sphere (q.v.): *You seem to me
as Dian in her orb*—Ado IV 1 58. *The inconstant
moon, That monthly changes in her circled orb*—
Rom II 2 109. *My good stars . . . Have empty
left their orbs*—Ant III 13 145.

(3) Fig., sphere of action, rank, station: [Will
you] *move in that obedient orb again Where you
did give a fair and natural light?*—1 H4 V 1 17.

After this strange starting from your orbs—Cymb
V 5 371. *In our orbs we'll live so round and safe,
That . . .*—Per I 2 122.

(4) The earth: *Foolery, sir, does walk about the
orb like the sun*—Tw III 1 43. *A silence in the
heavens . . . : and the orb below As hush as death*
—Hml II 2 506. *When he meant to quail and
shake the orb*—Ant V 2 85.

ORDER

(1) Ordering, conduct: *The Duke of Gloucester,
to whom the order of the siege is given*—H5 III 2
69.

(2) An arrangement: *Shall we, upon the footing
of our land, Send fair-play orders and make com-
promise?*—John V 1 66. *Having our fair order
written down*—V 2 4. *Shall we divide our right
According to our threefold order ta'en?*—1 H4 III
1 70. *Worthy Macduff and we Shall take upon's
what else remains to do, According to our order*—
Mcb V 6 4.

(3) *To take order*, to take measures, make
arrangements: *Therefore this order hath Baptista
ta'en, That none shall have access unto Bianca*—
Shr I 2 126. *I'll order take my mother shall not
hear*—All's IV 2 55. *To take some privy order,
To draw the brats of Clarence out of sight*—R3 III
5 106. *His mouth is stopp'd; Honest Iago hath
ta'en order for't*—Oth V 2 71.

(4) The manner in which a thing has happened:
The manner and true order of the fight—2 H4 IV
4 100. *The order of his death*—2 H6 III 2 129.

ORDINANCE

(1) The same as Ordnance: *By the compulsion
of their ordinance* (*i.e.* the French cannon)—John
II 218.

(2) Ordained or appointed course or condition:
By custom and the ordinance of times—H5 II 4 83.
*Why all these things change from their ordinance
. . . To monstrous quality*—Cæs I 3 66. *That
which is ordained: Let ordinance Come as the gods
foresay it*—Cymb IV 2 145.

(3) Rank, order: [To] *be still and wonder, When
one but of my ordinance stood up*—Cor III 2 11.

ORDINANT

Ordering, arranging: *Why, even in that was
heaven ordinant*—Hml V 2 48.

ORGAN

A musical instrument generally: *There is much
music, excellent voice, in this little organ* (*i.e.* the
recorder)—Hml III 2 384.

ORGULOUS

Proud, haughty: *The princes orgulous, their high
blood chafed*—Troil Prol 2.

ORIFEX

An orifice, opening: *No orifex for a point*—
Troil V 2 151.

ORIGINAL

(1) Origin, originator: *We are their parents and original*—Mids II 1 117.

(2) Origin, origination: *It hath it original from much grief*—2 H4 I 2 131.

ORPHAN

Prob. = *Unfathered* (q.v.): *Fairies, black, grey, green, and white . . . You orphan heirs of fixed destiny*—Wiv V 5 41.

ORT

A fragment, scrap: *The fractions of her faith, orts of her love*—Troil V 2 158. *It is some poor fragment, some slender ort of his remainder*—Tim IV 3 400. *A beggar's orts*—Lucr 985.

ORTHOGRAPHY

App. an error of some kind for Orthographer: *Now is he turned orthography*—Ado II 3 21.

OSTENT

Appearance, display: *Like one well studied in a sad ostent*—Merch II 2 205. *Fair ostents of love*—II 8 44. *Giving full trophy, signal and ostent Quite from himself to God*—H5 V Chor 21.

OSTENTATION

(1) Manifestation, appearance, display: *Maintain a mourning ostentation*—Ado IV 1 207. *Make good this ostentation, and you shall Divide in all with us*—Cor I 6 86. *[No] hatchment o'er his bones, No noble rite nor formal ostentation*—Hml IV 5 214. *[You] have prevented The ostentation of our love*—Ant III 6 51.

(2) A spectacular exhibition: *The king would have me present the princess . . . with some delightful ostentation, or show, or pageant*—LLL V 1 116.

OTHER

As plural: *He awaking when the other do*—Mids IV 1 69. *In noble eminence enthroned and sphered Amidst the other*—Troil I 3 90. *Call Claudius and some other of my men*—Cæs IV 3 242. *Other of your insolent retinue*—Lr I 4 221.

OTHERGATES

In another way, otherwise: *If he had not been in drink, he would have tickled you othergates than he did*—Tw V 197.

OTHERWHILES

At times, now and then: *Otherwhiles the famish'd English . . . Faintly besiege us one hour in a month*—1 H6 I 2 7.

OUCH

Applied vaguely to various ornaments; a necklace, bracelet, buckle or the like: *Your brooches, pearls, and ouches*—2 H4 II 4 53.

OUGHT

Past tense of To owe: *[He] said this other day you ought him a thousand pound*—1 H4 III 3 151.

OUNCE

Applied vaguely to various feline beasts: *Be it ounce, or cat, or bear, Pard, or boar with bristled hair*—Mids II 2 30.

OUPHE

A variant of Oaf; properly, a goblin child, a changeling; app. = hobgoblin, elf: *We'll dress [them] Like urchins, ouphes and fairies*—Wiv IV 4 48. *Strew good luck, ouphes, on every sacred room*—V 5 61.

OUSEL

The blackbird: *The ousel cock so black of hue*—Mids III 1 128. Applied to a person: Shal. . . . *[How doth] my god-daughter Ellen?* Sil. *Alas, a black ousel*—2 H4 III 2 7.

OUT (adv.)

(1) Completely, fully: *Then thou wast not Out three years old*—Tp I 2 40. *The word is too good to paint out her wickedness*—Ado III 2 112. *Thou hast beat me out Twelve several times*—Cor IV 5 127. *So right out: Swears he will . . . be a boy right out*—Tp IV 100.

(2) *I'll ne'er out*, I'll not give in: *I am not so well as I should be, but I'll ne'er out*—Ant II 7 35. *Will not out*, will not fail you: *The knave will stick by thee . . . A will not out*—2 H4 V 3 69.

OUT (prep.)

(1) Out of: *Those that bawl out the ruins of thy linen*—2 H4 II 2 26 (app. referring to bastard children). *When you have pushed out your gates the very defender of them*—Cor V 2 41.

(2) Outside, without: *The Athenians both within and out that wall*—Tim IV 1 38.

OUTBREATHED

Put out of breath: *Wearied and outbreathed*—2 H4 I 1 108.

OUT-CRAFTY

To outwit: *That drug-damn'd Italy hath outcraftied him*—Cymb III 4 15.

OUT-DWELL

To tarry beyond (a time): *It is marvel he outdwells his hour*—Merch II 6 3.

OUTFACE

To brazen (a matter) out: *Outfacing faults in love*—Pilgr 8.

OUTJEST

To drive out by jesting: *The fool; who labours to outjest His heart-struck injuries*—Lr III 1 16.

OUTLIVE

To survive, remain alive: *Let not this wasp out-live, us both to sting*—Tit II 3 132.

OUTLOOK

To stare down, outstare: *To outlook conquest*—John V 2 115.

OUT-PEER

To excel, surpass: [Great men] *Could not out-peer these twain*—Cymb III 6 87.

OUTPRIZE

To exceed in value: *Your unparagoned mistress is . . . outprized by a trifle*—Cymb I 4 87.

OUTRAGE

Outbreak of fury, loud or extravagant expression of passion: *I fear some outrage, and I'll follow her*—John III 4 106. *Are you not ashamed With this immodest clamorous outrage To trouble and disturb the king and us?*—1 H6 IV 1 125. *My charity is outrage*—R3 I 3 277. *Seal up the mouth of outrage for a while*—Rom V 3 216. Disorder, tumult: *The conquerors Make war upon themselves . . . O, preposterous And frantic outrage, end thy damned spleen*—R3 II 4 61.

OUTSELL

To sell for more than; hence, to exceed in value: *Her pretty action did outsell her gift*—Cymb II 4 102. *She, of all compounded, Outsells them all*—III 5 73.

OUT-SPEAK

Out-speaks possession of a subject, goes beyond the value of what a subject ought to possess: *Which (i.e. the plate, &c.) I find at such proud rate, that it out-speaks Possession of a subject*—H8 III 2 126.

OUTSTAND

To stay beyond (one's time): *I have outstood my time*—Cymb I 6 207.

OUTSTRETCH

To stretch to its limit: *Timon is dead, who hath outstretch'd his span*—Tim V 3 3.

OUTWARD

An outward man, an outsider: *A common and an outward man*—All's III 1 11.

OUTWORK

To excel in workmanship: *O'er-picturing that Venus where we see The fancy outwork nature*—Ant II 2 205.

OUTWORTH

To exceed in value, surpass: *A beggar's book Outworths a noble's blood*—H8 I 1 122.

OVERBLOW

To blow away: *Whiles yet the . . . wind of grace O'erblows the . . . clouds Of heady murder*—H5 III 3 30.

OVERBULK

To surpass in bulk, overtower: *A nursery of like evil, To overbulk us all*—Troil I 3 319.

OVERBUY

To pay too much for: [He] *overbuys me Almost the sum he pays*—Cymb I 1 146.

OVERCOME

(1) To dominate, possess: *A worthy officer i' the war; but insolent, O'ercome with pride*—Cor IV 6 30. To obtain sway over: *She purposed . . . to O'ercome you with her show*—Cymb V 5 52.

(2) To overrun, cover: *The trees . . . O'ercome with moss and baleful mistletoe*—Tit II 3 94.

(3) To come over suddenly: *Can such things be, And overcome us like a summer's cloud, Without our special wonder?*—Mcb III 4 110.

OVER-COUNT

To outnumber: Ant. . . . *At land, thou know'st How much we do o'er-count thee.* Pom. *At land, indeed, Thou dost o'er-count me of my father's house*—Ant II 6 25 (app. in the second occurrence the word = to do out of).

OVER-CROW

To crow or exult over; hence, to overpower: *The potent poison quite o'er-crows my spirit*—Hml V 2 364.

OVER-DYED

Dyed over with a second colour; and so, sophisticated: *False As o'er-dyed blacks*—Wint I 2 131.

OVER-EAT

To eat or nibble all over or on all sides; fig.: *Her o'er-eaten faith*—Troil V 2 160.

OVER-EYE

To observe, mark, notice: *Like a demigod here sit I in the sky, And wretched fools' secrets heedfully o'er-eye*—LLL IV 3 79. *Over-eyeing of his odd behaviour*—Shr Ind 1 95.

OVERFLOURISH

To cover with blossom or verdure: *Empty trunks o'erflourish'd by the devil*—Tw III 4 404.

OVERGO

To go beyond, surpass: *What cause have I . . . To overgo thy plaints and drown thy cries!*—R3 II 2 59. *Look in your glass, and there appears a face That over-goes my blunt invention quite*—Sonn 103 6.

OVERGONE

Overpowered, oppressed: *Sad-hearted men, much overgone with care*—3 H6 II 5 123.

OVER-GREEN

To cover with verdure; hence, to cover (a defect) so as to conceal it; fig.: *What care I . . . So you o'er-green my bad?*—Sonn 112 3.

OVERGROWN

Covered (with hair): *Yourself So out of thought, and thereto so o'ergrown, Cannot be question'd*—Cymb IV 4 32. Cf. *A wretched ragged man, o'ergrown with hair*—As IV 3 107.

OVERHEAR

To hear told over: *I stole into a neighbour thicket by, And overheard what you shall overhear*—LLL V 2 94.

OVERHOLD

To overestimate: *If he overhold his price so much, We'll none of him*—Troil II 3 142.

OVERLOOK

(1) To examine, survey: *Catesby, o'erlook the walls*—R3 III 5 17. *Let your cares o'erlook What shipping and what lading's in our haven*—Per I 2 48. To peruse, read: *I would I had o'erlooked the letter*—Gent I 2 50. *Willing you overlook this pedigree*—H5 II 4 90. *I find it (i.e.* the letter) *not fit for your o'er-looking*—Lr I 2 39.

(2) To look upon with the evil eye, bewitch: *Thou wast o'erlook'd even in thy birth*—Wiv V 5 87. *Beshrew your eyes, They have o'erlook'd me*—Merch III 2 14.

OVERMASTER

To dominate, to hold in one's power or possession: *Would it not grieve a woman to be over-mastered with a piece of valiant dust?*—Ado II 1 63. *The crown that thou o'ermasterest*—John II 109.

OVER-NAME

To name in succession, enumerate: *I pray thee, over-name them (i.e.* the suitors)—Merch I 2 39.

OVERPARTED

Cast for too difficult a part: *For Alisander . . .* [he is] *a little o'erparted*—LLL V 2 587.

OVERPASS

To pass, spend (time): [Thou hast] *like a hermit overpass'd thy days*—1 H6 II 5 117.

OVER-PERCH

To fly over and perch beyond: *With love's light wings did I o'er-perch these walls*—Rom II 2 66.

OVER-POST

To get over (a matter) easily: *You may thank the unquiet time for your quiet o'er-posting that action*—2 H4 I 2 170.

OVER-PRIZE

To exceed in value: *That which . . . O'er-prized all popular rate*—Tp I 2 91.

OVER-RAUGHT

See *Over-reach.*

OVER-REACH

(Past tense and pple. Over-raught.)

(1) To overtake: *Certain players We o'er-raught on the way*—Hml III 1 16.

(2) To cheat: *The villain is o'er-raught of all my money*—Err I 2 96.

OVERSCUTCHED

Perh., worn out in the service: *Sung those tunes to the overscutched huswives that he heard the carmen whistle*—2 H4 III 2 340.

OVERSEE

To bewitch: *How was I overseen!*—Lucr 1206. Cf. *Overlook* (2).

OVER-SIZE

To cover over as with size: *O'er-sized with coagulate gore*—Hml II 2 484.

OVERSLIP

To pass unnoticed by, escape the notice of: *When that hour o'erslips me in the day Wherein I sigh not, Julia, for thy sake*—Gent II 2 9. *Which all this time hath overslipp'd her thought*—Lucr 1576.

OVERSTINK

Perh., to flow stinkingly over: *I left them I' the filthy-mantled pool . . . There dancing up to the chins, that the foul lake O'erstunk their feet*—Tp IV 181.

OVERSWAY

(1) To overrule, overmaster, overpower: *So perttaunt-like would I o'ersway his state*—LLL V 2 67. *Thus he that overruled I oversway'd*—Ven 109. *Sad mortality o'er-sways their power*—Sonn 65 2.

(2) To prevail over by superior authority: *But that great command o'ersways the order*—Hml V 1 251.

(3) To lead into a course of action, prevail upon: *If he be so resolved, I can o'ersway him*—Cæs II 1 202.

OVER-TEEMED

Exhausted by child-bearing: *Her lank and all o'er-teemed loins*—Hml II 2 531.

OVERTURE

(1) A disclosure: *It was he That made the overture of thy treasons to us*—Lr III 7 88.

(2) App., publicity: *I wish, my liege, You had only in your silent judgment tried it, Without more overture*—Wint II 1 170.

(3) *Overture of war*, app., a declaration of war: *I bring no overture of war, no taxation of homage*—Tw I 5 224.

OVERWATCH

To pass too much of (a night) in sitting up: *I fear we shall out-sleep the coming morn As much as we this night have overwatch'd*—Mids V 372.

OVER-WEATHERED

Battered by violent weather: *With over-weather'd ribs and ragged sails*—Merch II 6 18.

OVERWHELM

To overhang: *Let the brow o'erwhelm it* (*i.e.* the eye) *As fearfully as . . .*—H5 III 1 11. *His louring brows o'erwhelming his fair sight*—Ven 183.

OVERWHELMING

Overhanging: *With overwhelming brows*—Rom V 1 39.

OWE

(1) To be the owner of, to own, possess: *Thou dost here usurp The name thou owest not*—Tp I 2 453. *That blood which owed the breadth of all this isle*—John IV 2 99. *The prince that owed that crown*—R3 IV 4 142. *Those infirmities she owes*—Lr I 1 205.

(2) *One time will owe another*, will bring us as our due another (and a better)—Cor III 1 242. *The great danger Which this man's life did owe you*, would have exposed you to as if your due—Cor V 6 138.

OXLIP

A natural hybrid between the cowslip and primrose: *Where oxlips and the nodding violet grows*—Mids II 1 250. *Bold oxlips and The crown imperial*—Wint IV 4 125.

P

PACE

A step as of stairs: *This neglection of degree it is That by a pace goes backward, with a purpose It hath to climb*—Troil I 3 127. *Every step, Exampled by the first pace that is sick Of his superior*—131.

PACK (sb.)

An underhand design, plot: *There's a knot, a ging, a pack, a conspiracy against me*—Wiv IV 2 123.

PACK (vb.)

(1) To plot, conspire: *Go pack with him, and give the mother gold*—Tit IV 2 155. Something at any rate of this sense may be seen in Hml III 4 211 (*This man* (*i.e.* Polonius whom he has just killed) *shall set me packing*).

(2) *Packing*, plotting: *Here's packing . . . to deceive us all!*—Shr V 1 121. A plot: *Snuffs and packings of the dukes*—Lr III 1 26. *Packed*, confederate: *That goldsmith there, were he not pack'd with her, Could witness it*—Err V 219. *Margaret, Who I believe was pack'd in all this wrong*—Ado V 1 308.

(3) To arrange (cards) with a view to cheating; *to pack cards with*, to make a cheating arrangement with: *She, Eros, has Pack'd cards with Cæsar, and false-play'd my glory*—Ant IV 14 18.

PADDOCK

A toad: [Who] *Would from a paddock, from a bat, a gib, Such dear concernings hide?*—Hml III 4 190. A familiar spirit in the shape of a toad: *Paddock calls*—Mcb I 1 9.

PAGAN

A person of heathenish character; specifically, a woman of loose habits: Page. *None, my lord, but . . . Mistress Doll Tearsheet.* Prince. *What pagan may that be?*—2 H4 II 2 166.

PAGEANT (sb.)

The pageants of the sea, of Antonio's argosies, alluding to large machines of various shapes drawn about the streets in ancient pageants—Merch I 1 11.

PAGEANT (vb.)

To imitate as in a pageant or play, mimic: *With ridiculous and awkward action . . . He pageants us*—Troil I 3 149.

PAIN (sb.)

(1) A penalty: *His offence is . . . Accountant to the law upon that pain*—Meas II 4 85. Punishment: *She that makes me sin awards me pain*—Sonn 141 14.

(2) Trouble, toil: *With pain purchased*—LLL I 1 73. *Take pain To allay with some cold drops of modesty Thy skipping spirit*—Merch II 2 194. *To refresh the mind of man After his studies or his usual pain*—Shr III 1 11. *Her presence Shall quite strike off all service I have done, In most accepted pain*—Troil III 3 28. *The toil o' the war, A pain that only seems to seek out danger*—Cymb III 3 49.

(3) Solicitude: *Of all* (*i.e.* of children and grandchildren alike) [there is] *one pain, save for a night of groans Endured of her, for whom you bid like sorrow*—R3 IV 4 303 (*i.e.* the mother's solicitude is greater only on account of the pangs she endured). See the second *Bid*.

PAIN (vb.)

To put to trouble: *Give me pardon, That I, your vassal, have employ'd and pain'd Your unknown sovereignty!*—Meas V 390.

PAINFUL

(1) Toilsome, laborious: *There be some sports are painful*—Tp III 1 1. *If it had been painful, I would not have come*—Ado II 3 260. *Painful service*—Cor IV 5 74.

(2) Enduring toil: *The painful warrior famoused for fight*—Sonn 25 9.

PAINFULLY

With toil, painstakingly: *Painfully to pore upon a book*—LLL I 1 74. *Us your lawful king, Who painfully . . . Have brought a countercheck*—John II 222. *Thou hast painfully discover'd*—Tim V 2 1.

PAINT

To flatter with specious words: *Nay, never paint me now: Where fair is not, praise cannot mend the brow*—LLL IV 1 16.

PAINTED CLOTH

Canvas used for hangings on which figures, devices, mottoes, &c., were painted: *You will be scraped out of the painted cloth for this*—LLL V 2 578. *I answer you right painted cloth, from whence you have studied your questions*—As III 2 290. *As ragged as Lazarus in the painted cloth*—1 H4 IV 2 27.

PAJOCK

Prob. a form of Peacock: *And now reigns here A very, very—pajock*—Hml III 2 294.

PALABRAS

See *Pallabris*.

PALATE

App., to resemble in flavour: *Both your voices blended, the great'st taste Most palates theirs*—Cor III 1 103.

PALE (sb.)[1]

Paleness, pallor: *The red blood reigns in the winter's pale*—Wint IV 3 4. *Whereat a sudden pale . . . Usurps her cheek*—Ven 589. *Nor ashy pale* [showed] *the fear that false hearts have*—Lucr 1512.

PALE (sb.)[2]

A fence, paling: *Too unruly deer, he breaks the pale*—Err II 1 100. *Thy wisdom, Which, like a bourn, a pale, a shore, confines Thy . . . parts*—Troil II 3 259. *Within the circuit of this ivory pale*—Ven 230.

PALE (vb.)

To encircle, surround: *Will you pale your head in Henry's glory* (*i.e.* the crown)*?*—3 H6 I 4 103. To encircle, enclose: *Whate'er the ocean pales, or sky inclips*—Ant II 7 74.

PALL

(1) To fail, miss of the intended effect: *Our indiscretion sometimes serves us well, When our deep plots do pall*—Hml V 2 8.

(2) To impair, depress: *I'll never follow thy pall'd fortunes more*—Ant II 7 88

PALLABRIS

Paucas pallabris (Sp. *Pocas palabras*), few words: *Therefore paucas pallabris; let the world slide*—Shr Ind 1 5. So *palabras* alone: *Palabras, neighbour Verges*—Ado III 5 18.

PALLIAMENT

A robe: *This palliament of white and spotless hue*—Tit I 182.

PANG

To afflict, torment: *A sufferance panging As soul and body's severing*—H8 II 3 15. *How thy memory Will then be pang'd by me*—Cymb III 4 97.

PANTALOON

The Venetian character in Italian comedy, represented as a lean and foolish old man; hence applied to an old dotard: *The sixth age shifts Into the lean and slipper'd pantaloon*—As II 7 157. *That we might beguile the old pantaloon*—Shr III 1 36.

PANTLER

The officer of a household who supplied the bread and had charge of the pantry: *She was both pantler, butler, cook*—Wint IV 4 56. *A would have made a good pantler, a would ha' chipped bread well*—2 H4 II 4 257. *A hilding for a livery, a squire's cloth, A pantler, not so eminent*—Cymb II 3 128.

PAPER

To inscribe the name of (a person) in a letter or writ: *His own letter . . . Must fetch him in he papers*—H8 I 1 78.

PARAGON

(1) To compare: *If thou with Cæsar paragon again My man of men*—Ant I 5 71.

(2) To excel: *A maid That paragons description*—Oth II 1 61.

(3) To set forth as a paragon or model: *The primest creature That's paragon'd o' the world*—H8 II 4 229.

PARALLEL

(1) To make parallel, bring into conformity: *His life is parallel'd Even with the stroke and line of his great justice*—Meas IV 2 82.

(2) To adduce as a parallel case: *My young remembrance cannot parallel A fellow to it*—Mcb II 3 67.

PARAQUITO

Parakeet; a bird of the parrot kind: *Come, come, you paraquito, answer me Directly*—1 H4 II 3 88.

PARCEL (sb.)

(1) An item, detail, particular: *Between these main parcels of dispatch* [I have] *effected many nicer needs*—All's IV 3 103. *I sent your grace The parcels and particulars of our grief*—2 H4 IV 2 35. *An inventory, thus importing; The several parcels of his plate*—H8 III 2 124. *To your audit comes Their distract parcels in combined sums* — Compl 230. App., items collectively: *His (i.e.* the drawer's) *eloquence* [is] *the parcel of a reckoning*—1 H4 II 4 113.

(2) A company or group of persons: *A holy parcel of the fairest dames*—LLL V 2 160. *This parcel of wooers*—Merch I 2 118. *This youthful parcel Of noble bachelors*—All's II 3 58.

PARCEL (vb.)

No doubt = *Piece* (vb.) (1): *What a wounding shame is this . . . that mine own servant should Parcel the sum of my disgraces by Addition of his envy!*—Ant V 2 159.

PARCELLED

App., particular: *Their woes are parcell'd, mine are general*—R3 II 2 81.

PARD

A panther or leopard: *More pinch-spotted make them Than pard or cat o' mountain*—Tp IV 261. *Be it ounce, or cat, or bear, Pard, or boar with bristled hair*—Mids II 2 30. *Bearded like the pard*—As II 7 150. [As false as] *Pard to the hind*—Troil III 2 201.

PARDON (sb.)

Leave, permission: *My thoughts and wishes . . . bow them to your gracious leave and pardon*—Hml I 2 55. *First asking your pardon thereunto*—IV 7 46. *I begg'd His pardon for return*—Ant III 6 59.

PARDON (vb.)

To remit (a penalty): *I pardon thee thy life before thou ask it*—Merch IV 1 369. *I pardon that man's life*—Lr IV 6 111.

PAREL

Apparel: *I'll bring him the best parel that I have*—Lr IV 1 51.

PARIS-GARDEN

A manor or liberty on the Bankside in Southwark in which Paris-garden Theatre, a circus for bull and bear baiting, was erected: *Do you take the court for Paris-garden?*—H8 V 4 2.

PARISH-TOP

A large whipping-top kept in villages for exercise in cold weather: *He's a coward . . . that will not drink to my niece till his brains turn o' the toe like a parish-top*—Tw I 3 42.

PARITOR

An apparitor or summoning officer of an ecclesiastical court: [Dan Cupid,] *Sole imperator and great general Of trotting paritors*—LLL III 187 (app. referring to citations for fornication).

PARLE (sb.)

(1) Speech, conversation: *The fair resort of gentlemen That every day with parle encounter me*—Gent I 2 4.

(2) A parley: *Our trumpet call'd you to this gentle parle*—John II 205. *This is the latest parle we will admit*—H5 III 3 2. *Go, trumpet, to the walls, and sound a parle*—3 H6 V 1 16. *In an angry parle*—Hml I 1 62.

PARLE (vb.)

To speak, converse: *Their purpose is to parle, to court and dance*—LLL V 2 122. *She, that never coped with stranger eyes, Could pick no meaning from their parling looks*—Lucr 99.

PARLOUS

A syncopated form of Perilous: *Thou art in a parlous state, shepherd*—As III 2 45. Terrible, 'shocking': *By'r lakin, a parlous fear*—Mids III 1 14. *A parlous knock*—Rom I 3 54. Dangerously clever: *A parlous boy: go to, you are too shrewd*—R3 II 4 35. *O, 'tis a parlous boy*—III 1 154.

PARMACETI

A corruption of Spermaceti: *The sovereign'st thing on earth Was parmaceti for an inward bruise*—1 H4 I 3 57.

PART (sb.)

(1) A piece of conduct, an act, deed: [We] *Set this device against Malvolio here, Upon some stubborn and uncourteous parts We had conceived against him (i.e.* in consequence of some conduct which they conceived to be stubborn, &c., and put down against him)—Tw V 368. *This part of his conjoins with my disease*—2 H4 IV 5 64. *If not for any parts in him . . . yet, more to move you, Take my deserts to his, and join 'em both*—Tim III 5 76. *My parts, my title and my perfect soul Shall manifest me rightly*—Oth I 2 31.

(2) A function, duty: *I conjure thee, by all the*

parts of man Which honour does acknowledge—Wint I 2 400.

(3) A party, body of adherents, faction: *Banding themselves in contrary parts*—1 H6 III 1 81. *Throw in the frozen bosoms of our part Hot coals of vengeance!*—2 H6 V 2 35. *I'll fight Against the part I come with*—Cymb V 1 24. *Parts*, app., adherents, partisans: *Uncurable discomfit Reigns in the hearts of all our present parts*—2 H6 V 2 86.

(4) *Of the part of*, on the side of: Bast. . . . *Who art thou?* Hub. *Of the part of England*—John V 6 2. *On the part of*, on the side of, as an adherent of: *My father . . . Came on the part of York*—3 H6 II 5 65. *On part and part*, on one side and the other: *Came more and more and fought on part and part*—Rom I 1 121.

(5) Respect: *Though in general part we were opposed*—Tim V 2 7.

(6) *Parts*, in heraldry, the places in a shield on which armorial devices are borne: *Whether beauty, birth, or wealth, or wit . . . Entitled in thy parts do crowned sit*—Sonn 37 5.

PART (vb.)

(1) Of two or more persons, to divide or share between or among themselves: *Let's part the word*—LLL V 2 249. *Let's away, To part the glories of this happy day*—Cæs V 5 80. *This coronet part betwixt you*—Lr I 1 141. Sim. *to part a thing with* another: *The fellow that . . . parts bread with him*—Tim I 2 47.

(2) To depart from, leave: *Since presently your souls must part your bodies*—R2 III 1 3. *When we with tears parted Pentapolis*—Per V 3 38.

PARTAKE

(1) Of food, &c., take some of, take: *One may drink, depart, And yet partake no venom*—Wint II 1 40.

(2) To share in (something imparted), be informed of (it): *Thy bosom shall partake The secrets of my heart*—Cæs II 1 305.

(3) To impart, communicate: *Your exultation Partake to every one*—Wint V 3 131. *Our mind partakes Her private actions to your secrecy*—Per I 1 152.

(4) To take part, take a side: *When I against myself with thee partake*—Sonn 149 2.

PARTAKER

A supporter, confederate: *Your partaker Pole*—1 H6 II 4 100.

PARTED

Endowed with parts (of such and such a kind): *Man, how dearly ever parted*—Troil III 3 96.

PARTICIPATE (ppl. adj.)

Participating: *The other instruments . . . mutually participate, did minister Unto . . . the whole body*—Cor I 1 104.

PARTICIPATE (vb.)

App., to receive or have as part of one: [I] *am in that dimension grossly clad Which from the womb I did participate* (*i.e.* received as his material part)—Tw V 244. See *Grossly* (3).

PARTICLE

A part: [My beauty] *shall be inventoried, and every particle and utensil labelled to my will*—Tw I 5 264.

PARTI-COATED

Having a particoloured or motley coat: *Which parti-coated presence of loose love*—LLL V 2 776.

PARTICULAR (adj.)

Individual, personal: *I will have it in a particular ballad else*—2 H4 IV 3 52. Ham. *Ay, madam, it is common.* Queen. *If it be, Why seems it so particular with thee?*—Hml I 2 74. *Domestic and particular broils*—Lr V 1 30.

PARTICULAR (sb.)

(1) Personal relation, intimacy: *Your hand and heart . . . Should . . . As 'twere in love's particular, be more To me, your friend, than any*—H8 III 2 186. *Who loved him In a most dear particular*—Cor V 1 2.

(2) Personal interest or concern: *As far as toucheth my particular*—Troil II 2 9. *Him that, his particular to foresee, Smells from the general weal*—Tim IV 3 159.

(3) *On my particular*, in the matter of my personal duties: *My course, Which . . . does* [not] *The ministration and required office On my particular*—All's II 5 63. *For one's particular*, as far as regards one personally: *I wish, sir,—I mean for your particular,—you had not . . .*—Cor IV 7 12. *For his particular, I'll receive him gladly*—Lr II 4 295. So *in one's own particular*: *Forgive me in thine own particular*—Ant IV 9 20. *My more particular*, what is more especially my own personal reason: *My more particular . . . Is Fulvia's death*—Ant I 3 54.

(4) An individual person; *by particulars*, individually: *He's to make his requests by particulars*—Cor II 3 47.

(5) A statement or enumeration of details; *with every course in his particular*, with the process of each event set down in the detail appropriate to it: *The manner how this action hath been borne Here . . . may your highness read, With every course in his particular*—2 H4 IV 4 88. Sim.: *Let me answer to the particular of the inter'gatories*—All's IV 3 206.

PARTICULARITY

(1) A personal or individual matter: *Let the general trumpet blow his blast, Particularities and petty sounds To cease!*—2 H6 V 2 43.

(2) A detail: *In the derivation of my birth, and in other particularities*—H5 III 2 141.

PARTICULARLY

Personally, individually: *Who hath done To thee particularly and to all the Volsces Great hurt* —Cor IV 5 71. *Halts not particularly*, does not stop at any single character: *My free drift Halts not particularly*—Tim I 1 45.

PARTISAN

A long-handled spear with a blade having cutting projections: *Clubs, bills, and partisans! strike! beat them down!*—Rom I 1 80. *Shall I strike at it with my partisan?*—Hml I 1 140. *I had as lief have a reed that will do me no service as a partisan I could not heave*—Ant II 7 13. *[Let us] make him with our pikes and partisans A grave*—Cymb IV 2 399.

PARTLET

Dame Partlet, a name given to a hen (*e.g.* in Chaucer's Nuns' Priest's Tale): *Thou art woman-tired, unroosted By thy dame Partlet here*—Wint II 3 74. *How now, Dame Partlet the hen!*— 1 H4 III 3 60.

PARTY

Part, side: *Upon the right and party of her son* —John I 34. *All your southern gentlemen [are] in arms Upon his party*—R2 III 2 202. *Which on thy royal party granted once*—III 3 115. *Were . . . he Upon my party*—Cor I 1 237.

PARTY-VERDICT

One's share of a joint decision: *Thy son is banish'd upon good advice, Whereto thy tongue a party-verdict gave*—R2 I 3 233.

PASH (sb.)

The head: *Thou want'st a rough pash . . . To be full like me*—Wint I 2 128.

PASH (vb.)

To strike violently, batter: *With my armed fist I'll pash him o'er the face*—Troil II 3 212. *The pashed corses of the kings*—V 5 10.

PASS (sb.)

(1) The act of passing, passage: *Charming the narrow seas To give you gentle pass*—H5 II Chor 38. *To give quiet pass Through your dominions for this enterprise*—Hml II 2 77.

(2) A course of action: *I perceive your grace . . . Hath look'd upon my passes*—Meas V 374.

(3) Reputation, estimation: *Common speech Gives him a worthy pass*—All's II 5 57.

(4) Event, issue: *To no other pass my verses tend*—Sonn 103 11.

(5) In fencing, a lunge, thrust: *You stand on distance, your passes, stoccadoes, and I know not what*—Wiv II 1 233. *A pass of practice*—Hml IV 7 139. Applied to the thrusting of combatants at each other: *'Tis dangerous when the baser nature* comes *Between the pass and fell incensed points Of mighty opposites*—Hml V 2 60. A round or bout: *I had a pass with him, rapier, scabbard and all*— Tw III 4 302. A dozen passes between yourself and him—Hml V 2 172. Fig. *pass of pate*, a stroke of wit: *[It] is an excellent pass of pate*— Tp IV 244.

PASS (vb.)

(1) To die: *Let him pass peaceably*—2 H6 III 3 25. *Thus might he pass indeed*—Lr IV 6 47.

(2) To excel, surpass: *She passes praise*—LLL IV 3 241. *I have that within which passeth show* —Hml I 2 85. To exceed description, 'beat everything': *The women have so cried and shrieked at it, that it passed*—Wiv I 1 309. *Why, this passes, Master Ford*—IV 2 127. *All the rest so laughed, that it passed*—Troil I 2 181.

(3) To care, reck: *As for these silken-coated slaves, I pass not*—2 H6 IV 2 136.

(4) In fencing, to make (a lunge): *To see thee pass thy punto, thy stock*—Wiv II 3 26. To lunge: *Pass with your best violence*—Hml V 2 309. Fig.: *Nay, an thou pass upon me, I'll no more with thee* —Tw III 1 48.

(5) To leave unnoticed, disregard, omit: *He shall not pass you*—Meas IV 6 12. *If you fondly pass our proffer'd offer*—John II 258. *Please you That I may pass this doing*—Cor II 2 142. *You should have . . . pass'd him unelected*—II 3 206.

(6) To effect, carry through: *We'll pass the business privately and well*—Shr IV 4 57.

(7) To penetrate, enter: *No villanous bounty yet hath pass'd my heart*—Tim II 2 182.

(8) To give, hand over: *[That you will] pass my daughter a sufficient dower*—Shr IV 4 45.

(9) App., to perform, take the part of: *This swain . . . shall pass Pompey*—LLL V 1 134.

(10) *To pass upon*, to impose upon, befool: *This practice hath most shrewdly pass'd upon thee* —Tw V 360.

PASSADO

In fencing, a forward thrust, one foot being advanced at the same time: *The passado he respects not*—LLL I 2 184. *Ah, the immortal passado!*—Rom II 4 26. *Come, sir, your passado* —III 1 88.

PASSAGE

(1) The time when people are passing: *Now in the stirring passage of the day*—Err III 1 99. People passing: *What, ho! no watch? no passage?* —Oth V 1 37.

(2) Death: *Would some part of my young years Might but redeem the passage of your age!*—1 H6 II 5 107. *When he is fit and season'd for his passage*—Hml III 3 86. *For his passage, The soldiers' music and the rites of war Speak loudly for him*—V 2 409.

(3) Something which passes, an incident, proceeding, step: *In thy passages of life*—1 H4 III 2 8. [You] *oft have hinder'd, oft, The passages made toward it*—H8 II 4 164. *Passages of proof,* see *Proof* (sb.)(3). Occurrence: *No act of common passage*—Cymb III 4 94. *Passages of grossness,* obvious proceedings, *i.e.*, palpable absurdities: *No Christian, that means to be saved by believing rightly, can ever believe such impossible passages of grossness*—Tw III 2 75. Cf. *Gross* (adj.) (3) and *Grossness* (2).

(4) An expression: *O, that 'had'! how sad a passage 'tis!*—All's I 1 20.

(5) Process, course: *Thou Shalt feel our justice, in whose easiest passage Look for no less than death* —Wint III 2 90. *The passage and whole carriage of this action*—Troil II 3 140. *The fearful passage of their death-mark'd love*—Rom Prol 9.

(6) The course by which a title passes: [The] *passages Of his true titles to some certain dukedoms* —H5 I 1 86.

(7) *Foreign passages,* wanderings abroad: *Must I not serve a long apprenticehood To foreign passages?*—R2 I 3 271.

PASSANT

In heraldry, of a beast, walking, with the dexter fore-paw raised: *The dozen white louses do become an old coat well; it agrees well, passant*—Wiv I 1 19.

PASSING

Surpassing, transcendent: *'Tis a passing shame* —Gent I 2 17. *Her passing deformity*—II 1 81. *O passing traitor!*—3 H6 V 1 106.

PASSION (sb.)

(1) The sufferings of Christ; allusively in asseverations: *Got's will, and his passion of my heart!*—Wiv III 1 62. *Cock's passion,* God's passion: *Cock's passion, silence! I hear my master* —Shr IV 1 121 (see *Cock*³). Sim. *Cox my passion: Cox my passion! give me your hand*—All's V 2 42.

(2) Suffering, affliction in gen.: *Give her what comforts The quality of her passion shall require*— Ant V 1 62.

(3) A disorder or disease; of mental disorder: *Till this afternoon his passion Ne'er brake into extremity of rage*—Err V 47. An access of a disorder or disease: *If much you note him, You shall offend him and extend his passion*—Mcb III 4 56. *In passion,* in an access of a disorder: *At your birth Our grandam earth, having this distemperature, In passion shook*—1 H4 III 1 33.

(4) A passionate speech or outburst: *This passion* (referring to Pyramus's speech), *and the death of a dear friend, would go near to make a man look sad*—Mids V 293. *Here she comes; and her passion ends the play*—320. *I never heard a passion so confused . . . As the dog Jew did utter in the streets*—Merch II 8 12. *Your passion draws ears hither*—Troil V 2 181.

PASSION (vb.)

To show or be affected by sorrow: *Shall not myself, One of their kind, that relish all as sharply, Passion as they, be kindlier moved than thou art?* —Tp V 22. *Ariadne passioning For Theseus' perjury*—Gent IV 4 172. *I passion to say wherewith* —LLL I 1 263. *Dumbly she passions*—Ven 1059.

PASSIONATE (adj.)

Sad, sorrowful: *Poor forlorn Proteus, passionate Proteus*—Gent I 2 124. *She is sad and passionate at your highness' tent*—John II 544.

PASSIONATE (vb.)

To express with passion: [We] *cannot passionate our tenfold grief*—Tit III 2 6.

PASSY MEASURES PAVIN

Italian *Passemezzo Pavana,* app., a variety of the Pavan, a grave and stately dance: *He* (*i.e.* Dick [the] surgeon) *'s a rogue, and a passy measures pavin: I hate a drunken rogue*—Tw V 206. No doubt we are to figure Dick to ourselves as, at any rate when sober, a grave and solemn person to whom the expression would be applicable. The reading *pavin* is from the Second Folio: the First (which the Globe follows) reads *panyn,* which is unintelligible.

PAST PROPORTION

Immeasurableness, immensity: *Will you with counters sum The past proportion of his infinite?* —Troil II 2 28.

PASTRY

A room in which pastry is made: *They call for dates and quinces in the pastry*—Rom IV 4 2.

PATCH

Said to have been the nickname of Cardinal Wolsey's fool; hence, a domestic fool, jester: *Thou scurvy patch!*—Tp III 2 71 (addressed to Trinculo the Jester). A fool, dolt: *Coxcomb, idiot, patch!* —Err III 1 32. *What patch is made our porter?*— 36. *A crew of patches, rude mechanicals*—Mids III 2 9. *What soldiers, patch?*—Mcb V 3 15.

PATCHED FOOL

A fool in a particoloured coat: *Man is but a patched fool, if he will offer to say what methought I had*—Mids IV 1 214.

PATCHERY

Roguery, knavery: *Here is such patchery, such juggling and such knavery!*—Troil II 3 77. *You hear him cog, see him dissemble, Know his gross patchery*—Tim V 1 98.

PATENT

Privilege or authority to do something; *my virgin patent,* the liberty which I enjoy as a maid: *So will I grow, so live, so die, my lord, Ere I will yield my virgin patent up Unto his lordship*—Mids I 1 79.

PATH

To go as in a path, take one's way: *If thou path, thy native semblance on*—Cæs II 1 83.

PATHETICAL

(1) Exciting tender emotion or affection: *Sweet invocation of a child; most pretty and pathetical!*—LLL I 2 102. *It is a most pathetical nit!*—IV 1 150.

(2) App., dreadful, shocking: *I will think you the most pathetical break-promise*—As IV 1 195.

PATIENCE

(1) *Patience perforce*, patience upon compulsion: *Patience perforce with wilful choler meeting Makes my flesh tremble in their different greeting*—Rom I 5 91.

(2) Leave, permission; hence *by your patience*, by your leave: *By your patience, no*—Tw II 1 3. *Sir, by your patience, I hold you but a subject of this war*—Lr V 3 59. So *under your patience*: *Under your patience, gentle empress, 'Tis thought . . .*—Tit II 3 66. *With your patience*: *With your patience, that we may Taste of your wine*—1 H6 II 3 78. *Stay upon your patience*, await your permission to come in: Ham. . . . *Be the players ready? Ros. Ay, my lord; they stay upon your patience*—Hml III 2 111. (Cf. *Stay* (vb.) (1)).

PATIENT

Refl., to calm oneself, be patient: *Patient yourself, madam, and pardon me*—Tit I 121.

PATINE

Paten; the plate on which the bread is laid at the celebration of the Eucharist; a thin circular plate of metal or anything resembling one: *Look how the floor of heaven Is thick inlaid with patines of bright gold*—Merch V 58.

PATRONAGE

To protect, uphold: *As an outlaw in a castle keeps And useth it to patronage his theft*—1 H6 III 1 47. *As well as you dare patronage The envious barking of your saucy tongue*—III 4 32.

PATTERN (sb.)

(1) Something formed after a model: *The patterns that by God and by French fathers Had twenty years been made*—H5 II 4 61.

(2) A signal instance or example: *Behold this pattern of thy butcheries*—R3 I 2 54.

(3) An instance appealed to, a precedent: *We could find some pattern of our shame*—John III 4 16. *A pattern, precedent, and lively warrant*—Tit V 3 44.

PATTERN (vb.)

(1) To be a precedent for, to justify by a precedent: *Let mine own judgement pattern out my death*—Meas II 1 30. *Pattern'd by thy fault, foul sin may say . . .*—Lucr 629. To prefigure: *Such a place there is . . . Pattern'd by that the poet here describes*—Tit IV 1 55.

(2) To match, parallel: *More Than history can pattern*—Wint III 2 36.

PAUL'S

St. Paul's Cathedral, a constant place of resort for business: *I bought him (i.e. Bardolph) in Paul's, and he'll buy me a horse in Smithfield*—2 H4 I 2 58. A place for legal announcements: *That it (i.e. the indictment of Hastings) may be this day read o'er* (prob. by the City Recorder) *in Paul's*—R3 III 6 3.

PAUNCH

To stab or wound in the paunch: *With a log* [thou mayst] *Batter his skull, or paunch him with a stake*—Tp III 2 97.

PAUSE

Refl., to make a pause: [We] *pause us, till these rebels, now afoot, Come underneath the yoke of government*—2 H4 IV 4 9.

PAVED

Having a pebbly bottom: *By paved fountain or by rushy brook*—Mids II 1 84.

PAWN (sb.)

(1) A pledge or gage of battle: *If guilty dread have left thee so much strength As to take up mine honour's pawn, then stoop*—R2 I 1 73. *There is my honour's pawn; Engage it to the trial, if thou darest*—IV 55.

(2) A stake: *My life I never held but as a pawn To wage against thy enemies*—Lr I 1 157.

PAWN (vb.)

(1) To stake, wager, risk: *If two gods should . . . on the wager lay two earthly women, And Portia one, there must be something else Pawn'd with the other*—Merch III 5 84. *I'll pawn the little blood which I have left To save the innocent*—Wint II 3 166. *I dare thereupon pawn the moiety of my estate to your ring*—Cymb I 4 118.

(2) App., to forfeit, give up: *The garter, blemish'd,* [hath] *pawn'd his knightly virtue*—R3 IV 4 370. *Boys, who, being mature in knowledge, Pawn their experience to their present pleasure*—Ant I 4 31.

PAX

A tablet bearing a representation of the Crucifixion or other sacred subject kissed by the celebrant at Mass and passed to the people to be kissed: *He hath stolen a pax, and hanged must a be*—H5 III 6 42.

PEAK

(1) To make a mean figure, mope: *The peaking Cornuto her husband*—Wiv III 5 71. [I] *peak, Like John-a-dreams, unpregnant of my cause, And can say nothing*—Hml II 2 594.

(2) To droop in health and spirits, waste away: *Weary se'nnights nine times nine Shall he dwindle, peak and pine*—Mcb I 3 22.

PEASCOD

App., a peascod-branch, the *cods* being the pods: *The wooing of a peascod instead of her, from whom I took two cods*—As II 4 51.

PEAT

A pet, darling: *A pretty peat!*—Shr I 1 78.

PECK

A variant of *Pick* (q.v.): *I'll peck you o'er the pales else*—H8 V 4 94.

PECULIAR

(1) Of possessions, private, appropriated to an individual: *Groping for trouts in a peculiar river* —Meas I 2 91. *There's millions now alive That nightly lie in those unproper beds Which they dare swear peculiar*—Oth IV 1 68.

(2) Individual, personal: [He] *carries on the stream of his dispose . . . In will peculiar*—Troil II 3 174. *The single and peculiar life*—Hml III 3 11. *For my peculiar end*—Oth I 1 60. *So much For my peculiar care*—Cymb V 5 82.

PEDANT

A schoolmaster, tutor: *A domineering pedant o'er the boy*—LLL III 179. *Wrangling pedant*— Shr III 1 4 (addressed to Lucentio in his supposed character of teacher of languages). *Like a pedant that keeps a school i' the church*—Tw III 2 80.

PEDASCULE

Vocative of a supposed Latin word *Pedasculus* (app. to = a diminutive of Pedant (*q.v.*)): *Pedascule, I'll watch you better yet*—Shr III 1 50.

PEELED

Tonsured: *Peel'd priest*—1 H6 I 3 30.

PEEP

To protrude (the head): *There is not a dangerous action can peep out his head but I am thrust upon it*—2 H4 I 2 238.

PEER

To cause to appear: *Who o'er the white sheet peers her whiter chin*—Lucr 472.

PEEVISH

(1) Silly, senseless, foolish: *His worst fault is, that he is given to prayer; he is something peevish that way*—Wiv I 4 13. *'Tis but a peevish boy*— As III 5 110. *What a wretched and peevish fellow*

is this king of England!—H5 III 7 142. *I cannot speak Any beginning to this peevish odds*—Oth II 3 184. *Desire My man's abode where I did leave him: he Is strange and peevish*—Cymb I 6 52.

(2) Of a thing, slight, trifling: *I will not so presume To send such peevish tokens to a king*—1 H6 V 3 185.

(3) Malignant: *What wilt thou do, thou peevish officer? Hast thou delight to see a wretched man Do outrage . . . to himself?*—Err IV 4 117.

(4) Perverse, refractory, headstrong: *A peevish girl, That flies her fortune when it follows her*— Gent V 2 49. *Run after that same peevish messenger . . . he left this ring behind him, Would I or not*—Tw I 5 319. *Being wrong'd as we are by this peevish town*—John II 402. *Why should we in our peevish opposition Take it to heart?*—Hml I 2 100.

PEEVISHLY

Perversely, in a headstrong manner: *Come, sir, you peevishly threw it* (*i.e.* the ring referred to in I 5 320 quoted under *Peevish* (4) above) *to her*— Tw II 2 14.

PEG-A-RAMSEY

The name of a tune: *Malvolio's a Peg-a-Ramsey* —Tw II 3 81. Two tunes of the name were known in Shakespeare's time. The application of the word here is unexplained.

PEISE, PEIZE

(1) To keep in equilibrium, balance: *The world, who of itself is peised well*—John II 575. Fig., to keep suspended, delay the course of: *I speak too long; but 'tis to peize the time*—Merch III 2 22.

(2) To burden, oppress: *Lest leaden slumber peise me down to-morrow*—R3 V 3 105.

PELF

Property, goods: *All perishen of man, of pelf*— Per II Prol 35. Applied to a recompense or compensation: *Shadows like myself, As take the pain, but cannot pluck the pelf*—Pilgr 191.

PELICAN

Referring to the fable according to which the young of the pelican fed on their parents' blood: *To his good friends thus wide I'll ope my arms; And like the kind, life-rendering pelican, Repast them with my blood*—Hml IV 5 145. *'Twas this flesh begot Those pelican daughters*—Lr III 4 76.

PELLET

(1) To form into pellets: *The brine That season'd woe had pelleted in tears*—Compl 17.

(2) To send in the form of pellets: *The discandying of this pelleted storm*—Ant III 13 165.

PELT

To throw out angry words: *Another smother'd seems to pelt and swear*—Lucr 1418.

PELTING

Paltry, petty, insignificant: *Every pelting, petty officer*—Meas II 2 112. *Like to a tenement or pelting farm*—R2 II 1 60. *We have had pelting wars, since you refused The Grecians' cause*—Troil IV 5 267. *Poor pelting villages*—Lr II 3 18.

PENDULOUS

Held suspended overhead: *All the plagues that in the pendulous air Hang fated o'er men's faults*—Lr III 4 69.

PENITENT

Undergoing penance: *We that know what 'tis to fast and pray Are penitent for your default to-day*—Err I 2 51.

PENSIONER

(1) One of a body of gentlemen, instituted by Henry VIII, attached to the sovereign as a body-guard: *And yet there has been earls, nay, which is more, pensioners*—Wiv II 2 77.

(2) In gen., an attendant, retainer: *The cowslips tall her pensioners be*—Mids II 1 10.

PENSIVED

App., rendered pensive, saddened: *Pensived and subdued desires*—Compl 219.

PENURIOUS

Needy, poverty-stricken: *The want whereof doth daily make revolt In my penurious band*—Tim IV 3 91.

PERCEIVE

To get, obtain: *I could perceive nothing at all from her; no, not so much as a ducat*—Gent I 1 144.

PERDIE, PERDY

French *par dieu*; by God, verily: *Perdie, your doors were lock'd*—Err IV 4 74. *My lady is unkind, perdy*—Tw IV 2 81. *Then, belike, he likes it not, perdy*—Hml III 2 305.

PERDITION

Loss, diminution, lessening: *Not so much perdition as an hair Betid to any creature*—Tp I 2 30. *The perdition of th' athversary hath been very great*—H5 III 6 103. *His definement suffers no perdition in you*—Hml V 2 117.

PERDU

A soldier placed in a position of special danger, and hence regarded as virtually lost: *To watch—poor perdu!—With this thin helm*—Lr IV 7 35.

PERDY

See *Perdie*.

PEREGRINATE

Foreign-fashioned: *Too affected, too odd, as it were, too peregrinate*—LLL V 1 14.

PEREMPTORY

(1) Resolved, determined (to do a thing). *Not Death himself In mortal fury* [is] *half so peremptory, As we to keep this city*—John II 453. *We are peremptory to dispatch This viperous traitor*—Cor III 1 286. Having one's mind made up: *To-morrow be in readiness to go: Excuse it not, for I am peremptory*—Gent I 3 70.

(2) Positive, final: *We will suddenly Pass our accept and peremptory answer*—H5 V 2 81.

PERFECT (adj.)

(1) Fully informed, certain: *Thou art perfect then, our ship hath touch'd upon The deserts of Bohemia?*—Wint III 3 1. *I am perfect That the Pannonians . . . are now in arms*—Cymb III 1 73. *Bel. What hast thou done? Gui. I am perfect what: cut off one Cloten's head*—IV 2 117.

(2) Of a notion, &c., accurate, correct: *Bast. Hubert, I think? Hub. Thou hast a perfect thought*—John V 6 6. *A perfect guess That great Northumberland . . . Would . . .*—2 H4 III 1 88.

(3) Completely satisfied, contented: *Might we but have that happiness . . . we should think ourselves for ever perfect*—Tim I 2 86. *Then comes my fit again: I had else been perfect*—Mcb III 4 21.

PERFECT (vb.)

To instruct or acquaint completely: *Being once perfected how to grant suits*—Tp I 2 79. *Her cause and yours I'll perfect him withal*—Meas IV 3 145.

PERFECTION

(1) Accomplishment, carrying out: *Vowing more than the perfection of ten and discharging less than the tenth part of one*—Troil III 2 93. *No perfection in reversion shall have a praise in present*—99. *Is your perfection*, perh., typifies your fulfilment of obligations: *Smoke and luke-warm water Is your perfection*—Tim III 6 99.

(2) The condition of being accomplished or carried out, realization: *I trust it will grow to a most prosperous perfection*—Meas III 1 271. *I, a drone-like bee, Have no perfection of my summer left*—Lucr 836.

PERFORCE

(1) By actual physical force, by violence, forcibly: *He rush'd into my house and took perforce My ring away*—Err IV 3 95. *What he hath taken away from thy father perforce, I will render thee again in affection*—As I 2 20. *He that perforce robs lions of their hearts*—John I 268. So *force perforce*: [*Why thou dost*] *force perforce Keep Stephen Langton, chosen archbishop Of Canterbury, from that holy see?*—John III 1 142. *The king . . . Was force perforce compell'd to banish him*—2 H4 IV 1 115. *Force perforce I'll make him yield the crown*—2 H6 I 1 258.

(2) *Patience perforce.* See *Patience* (1).

PERFORM

To carry to completion, finish: *A piece* (*i.e.* the statue) *many years in doing and now newly performed*—Wint V 2 104.

PERIAPT

A charm worn on the person, an amulet: *Now help, ye charming spells and periapts*—1 H6 V 3 2.

PERIL

Like *Danger* (sb.) (1): *Without the peril of the Athenian law*—Mids IV 1 157.

PERIOD (sb.)

(1) Finish, consummation: *This is the period of my ambition*—Wiv III 3 47. *There wanteth now our brother Gloucester here, To make the perfect period of this peace*—R3 II 1 43. Fitting ending: *There would be no period to the jest, should he not be publicly shamed*—Wiv IV 2 236.

(2) Highest point, acme: *This would have seem'd a period To such as love not sorrow*—Lr V 3 204. *Time is at his period*—Ant IV 14 107.

(3) End to be attained, goal: *There's his period, To sheathe his knife in us*—H8 I 2 209. *My point and period will be throughly wrought, Or well or ill, as this day's battle's fought*—Lr IV 7 97.

PERIOD (vb.)

To bring to an end: *Which failing, Periods his comfort*—Tim I 1 98.

PERISH

To destroy: *Because thy flinty heart . . . Might in thy palace perish Margaret*—2 H6 III 2 99.

PERJURE (sb.)

A perjurer: *He comes in like a perjure, wearing papers*—LLL IV 3 47. Perjurers undergoing punishment wore a paper expressing the crime.

PERJURE (vb.)

To make perjured: *Want will perjure The ne'er-touch'd vestal*—Ant III 12 30.

PERORATION

A speech, harangue: *What means this passionate discourse, This peroration with such circumstance?*—2 H6 I 1 104.

PERPEND

To consider, ponder: *Ford, perpend*—Wiv II 1 119. *Learn of the wise, and perpend*—As III 2 68. *Therefore perpend, my princess, and give ear*—Tw V 307. Trans.: *Perpend my words*—H5 IV 4 8.

PERPLEXED

Troubled, distressed: *Leaving his spoil perplex'd in greater pain*—Lucr 733.

PERSEVER

A form of Persevere.

(1) In the still current sense: *I'll say as they say and persever so*—Err II 2 217. *Ay, do, persever, counterfeit sad looks*—Mids III 2 237. *Persever not, but hear me, mighty kings*—John II 421.

(2) Of things, to continue, endure: *My love as it begins shall so persever*—All's IV 2 37.

PERSISTED

App. = persisted in: *Our most persisted deeds*—Ant V 1 30.

PERSON

Bodily presence, presence in person: *How say'st thou, that Macduff denies his person At our great bidding?*—Mcb III 4 128.

PERSONAGE

Bodily frame, figure, personal appearance: *With her personage, her tall personage, Her height, forsooth, she hath prevail'd with him*—Mids III 2 292. *Of what personage and years is he?*—Tw I 5 164.

PERSONAL

Present or engaged in person: *When he was personal in the Irish war*—1 H4 IV 3 88.

PERSONATE

(1) To represent, describe: *Some obscure epistles of love; wherein . . . he shall find himself most feelingly personated*—Tw II 3 168. *One do I personate* (*i.e.* in the poem) *of Lord Timon's frame*—Tim I 1 69.

(2) To stand for, symbolize: *The lofty cedar, royal Cymbeline, Personates thee*—Cymb V 5 453.

PERSONATING

A representation or description: *It must be a personating of himself; a satire against the softness of prosperity*—Tim V 1 35.

PERSPECTIVE

(1) An optical instrument for looking through contrived to produce fantastic effects, *e.g.* by distortion of images: *Contempt his scornful perspective did lend me, Which warp'd the line of every other favour*—All's V 3 48.

(2) A picture or figure made so as to appear distorted or confused except from one point of view: *Like perspectives, which rightly gazed upon Show nothing but confusion, eyed awry Distinguish form*—R2 II 2 18. See *Rightly*.

(3) With a reference, not easily defined, to some such optical illusion: *One face, one voice, one habit, and two persons, A natural perspective, that is and is not!*—Tw V 223. (*Glass* in 272 (*If this be so, as yet the glass seems true*) seems to refer to the 'perspective'.)

(4) In Sonn 24 4 (*Perspective it is best painter's art*) prob., the science of perspective.

PERSPECTIVELY

As through a perspective (in sense (1) above): *You see them* (*i.e.* the French cities) *perspectively, the cities turned into a maid*—H5 V 2 347.

PERSUADE

(1) To plead with, advise or counsel strongly: *Sir Hugh, persuade me not*—Wiv I 1 1. [My conscience] *is even now at my elbow, persuading me not to kill the duke*—R3 I 4 149. *Has almost charmed me from my profession, by persuading me to it*—Tim IV 3 454.

(2) To use persuasion, plead: *Cease to persuade, my loving Proteus*—Gent I 1 1. *How I persuaded, how I pray'd, and kneel'd*—Meas V 93. With *with: The duke himself, and the magnificoes . . . have all persuaded with him*—Merch III 2 283.

(3) To advise or recommend (a course of action): *Sends me a paper to persuade me patience*—3 H6 III 3 176. *Hadst thou thy wits, and didst persuade revenge, It could not move thus*—Hml IV 5 168.

(4) *To persuade from*, to advise against (a course), dissuade from (it): *You shall not entreat him to a second, that have so mightily persuaded him from a first*—As I 2 217. *Thrice I led him off, Persuaded him from any further act*—2 H6 V 3 9.

PERSUASION

Something tending to induce a state of mind, an argument: Her. . . . *Then let us teach our trial patience, Because* . . . Lys. *A good persuasion*—Mids I 1 152.

PERT

Lively, brisk: *Awake the pert and nimble spirit of mirth*—Mids I 1 13.

PERTLY

Briskly, smartly: *Appear, and pertly!*—Tp IV 58.

PERTTAUNT-LIKE

An unexplained word, no doubt a corruption: *So perttaunt-like would I o'ersway his state*—LLL V 2 67.

PERUSAL

Survey, scrutiny: *He falls to such perusal of my face As he would draw it*—Hml II 1 90.

PERUSE

To survey, scrutinize: *I'll view the manners of the town, Peruse the traders, gaze upon the buildings*—Err I 2 12. *Peruse them* (*i.e.* the 'youthful parcel of noble bachelors') *well*—All's II 3 67. *He, being remiss* . . . *Will not peruse the foils*—Hml IV 7 135.

PERVERT

To turn aside, divert; *Let's follow him, and pervert the present wrath He hath against himself*—Cymb II 4 151.

PESTER

To obstruct by crowding: *Dissentious numbers pestering streets*—Cor IV 6 7.

PETAR

Petard; a small engine of war charged with powder used to blow in gates, &c.: *'Tis the sport to have the enginer Hoist with his own petar*—Hml III 4 206.

PETITIONARY

Of persons, suppliant, entreating: *Thy petitionary countrymen*—Cor V 2 82.

PEW-FELLOW

A companion, associate: *Makes her pew-fellow with others' moan*—R3 IV 4 58.

PHANTASIME

A fantastic fellow: *This Armado is a Spaniard . . . A phantasime*—LLL IV 1 100. *I abhor such fanatical phantasimes*—V 1 19.

PHEEZE

To drive off, frighten away; hence, *I'll pheeze*, vaguely as a threat, I'll do for, settle: *I'll pheeze you, in faith*—Shr Ind I 1. *An a be proud with me, I'll pheeze his pride*—Troil II 3 215.

PHILIP

(1) *Philip and Jacob*, the feast of Saints Philip and James, May 1st: *His child is a year and a quarter old, come Philip and Jacob*—Meas III 2 213.

(2) *Philip*, a name for a sparrow: Gur. *Good leave, good Philip.* Bast. *Philip! sparrow*—John I 231.

PHILIPPAN

His sword Philippan, alluding to Antony's prowess at the battle of Philippi: [I] *put my tires and mantles on him, whilst I wore his sword Philippan*—Ant II 5 22.

PHRASE

A word: '*Steal!' foh! a fico for the phrase!*—Wiv I 3 32. *Good phrases are . . . very commendable. Accommodated! . . . very good; a good phrase*—2 H4 III 2 76. *Is not pig great? the pig, or the great, or the mighty . . . are all one reckonings, save the phrase is a little variations*—H5 IV 7 16. *That's an ill phrase, a vile phrase; 'beautified' is a vile phrase*—Hml II 2 111. *The phrase* (*i.e.* 'carriages') *would be more german to the matter, if . . .*—V 2 165.

PHRASELESS

App., which there is no phrase to describe: *Advance of yours that phraseless hand*—Compl 225.

PHYSICAL

Curative, remedial: *The blood I drop is rather physical Than dangerous to me* — Cor I 5 19. Wholesome: *Is it physical To walk unbraced and suck up the humours Of the dank morning?* — Cæs II 1 261.

PIA MATER

One of the coverings of the brain and spinal cord; applied to the brain itself: *These [i.e.* forms, figures, &c.] *are . . . nourished in the womb of pia mater*—LLL IV 2 70. *One of thy kin has a most weak pia mater*—Tw I 5 122. *His pia mater is not worth the ninth part of a sparrow*—Troil II 1 77.

PICK

A collateral form of Pitch; to throw: *As high As I could pick my lance*—Cor I 1 203. Cf. *Peck.*

PICKED

Exquisite, finical, precise: *He is too picked, too spruce, too affected*—LLL V 1 14. *My picked man of countries*—John I 193. *The age is grown so picked that . . .*—Hml V 1 151.

PICKERS AND STEALERS

The hands, referring to the phrase *To keep my hands from picking and stealing* in the Church Catechism: *So I do still, by these pickers and stealers*—Hml III 2 348.

PICKING

Trifling, trivial: *The king is weary Of dainty and such picking grievances*—2 H4 IV 1 197.

PICK-THANK

One who 'picks a thank', *i.e.* plays the syco-phant or tale-bearer; a tale-bearer, tell-tale: *Smiling pick-thanks and base newsmongers* — 1 H4 III 2 25.

PICKT-HATCH

A noted haunt of harlots and disorderly people: *To your manor of Pickt-hatch! Go*—Wiv II 2 18. It lay by Goswell Street (now the southern part of Goswell Road).

PIECE (sb.)

(1) Of a person in whom a quality is exemplified or realized: *Thy mother was a piece of virtue*— Tp I 2 56. *A piece of beauty*—Wint IV 4 32. *The piece of virtue (i.e.* Octavia), *which is set Betwixt us*—Ant III 2 28. The sense seems to be similar in H8 V 5 26 (*All princely graces, That mould up such a mighty piece as this (i.e.* the infant Elizabeth) *is*), the speaker using the present tense, but looking to the future.

(2) A cask of wine: *The lees and dregs of a flat tamed piece*—Troil IV 1 62.

PIECE (vb.)

(1) To complete or increase, as by adding a piece or pieces: *Shall we thither and with our company piece the rejoicing?*—Wint V 2 116. *I* ['ll have] *twice five hundred* [voices] *and their friends to piece 'em*—Cor II 3 220. *If aught within that little seeming substance, Or all of it, with our displeasure pieced . . . may fitly like your grace*— Lr I 1 201. *I will piece Her opulent throne with kingdoms*—Ant I 5 45. So *to piece out: Thus must I piece it out*—Cæs II 1 51. *I will piece out the comfort with what addition I can*—Lr III 6 2.

(2) *To piece up in oneself,* app., to make one's own: *Let him . . . have power To take off so much grief from you as he Will piece up in himself*— Wint V 3 54.

PIGEON-LIVERED

Spiritless: *I am pigeon-liver'd and lack gall*— Hml II 2 605. See *Liver* (3).

PIGHT

Pa. pple. of To pitch.

(1) Of tents: *You vile abominable tents, Thus proudly pight upon our Phrygian plains*—Troil V 10 23.

(2) Determined, resolved: *When I . . . found him pight to do it*—Lr II 1 66.

PIKE

The spike in the centre of a buckler: *Marg. . . . We have bucklers of our own. Bene. If you use them, Margaret, you must put in the pikes with a vice*—Ado V 2 18.

PILCHER

A scabbard: *Will you pluck your sword out of his pilcher?*—Rom III 1 83.

PILE

Two pile and a half: Yonder's my lord your son with a patch of velvet on's face . . . his left cheek is a cheek of two pile and a half—All's IV 5 99. Cf. *Three-pile.*

PILED

Meas I 2 35. See under *Three-piled.*

PILL

(1) To plunder, despoil: *The commons hath he pill'd with grievous taxes*—R2 II 1 246.

(2) To commit depredation or extortion: *Large-handed robbers your grave masters are, And pill by law*—Tim IV 1 11.

(3) To take by force: *That which you have pill'd from me*—R3 I 3 159.

PILLICOCK

Pillicock sat on Pillicock-hill—Lr III 4 78. A reminiscence of an old ballad. *Pillicock (=* penis) was used as a term of endearment; but the exact meaning here is quite uncertain.

15

PIN

(1) A peg or stud in the centre of a target: *Cleaving the pin*—LLL IV 1 138. *The very pin of his heart cleft with the blind bow-boy's butt-shaft*—Rom II 4 15.

(2) *Pin and web*, a disease of the eye: [Wishing] *all eyes Blind with the pin and web but theirs*—Wint I 2 290. So *the web and the pin*: *He (i.e. the foul fiend Flibbertigibbet) gives the web and the pin*—Lr III 4 122.

(3) *A pin-buttock*, a narrow or sharp one: *A barber's chair that fits all buttocks, the pin-buttock . . . or any buttock*—All's II 2 17.

PINCH (sb.)

A seizure with the teeth, bite: *If we be English deer, be then in blood; Not rascal-like, to fall down with a pinch*—1 H6 IV 2 48.

PINCH (vb.)

(1) To seize with the teeth: *As a bear, encompass'd round with dogs, Who having pinch'd a few . . .*—3 H6 II 1 15.

(2) To reduce to straits, 'put in a tight place': *What, have I pinch'd you, Signior Gremio?*—Shr II 373.

(3) *A pinched thing*, possibly a doll or puppet pinched out of clouts: *I Remain a pinch'd thing; yea, a very trick For them to play at will*—Wint II 1 50. Cf. *Trick* (sb.) (3).

PINE

(1) To afflict, distress: *Where shivering cold and sickness pines the clime*—R2 V 1 77.

(2) To emaciate, cause to waste away: *As poor birds, deceived with painted grapes, Do surfeit by the eye and pine the maw*—Ven 601. *Her pale and pined cheek*—Compl 32.

PINFOLD

A pound for securing stray animals: *I mean the pound,—a pinfold*—Gent I 1 113. *If I had thee in Lipsbury pinfold, I would make thee care for me*—Lr II 2 9 (of *Lipsbury* nothing is known).

PINKED

Ornamented with perforations: *Her pinked porringer*—H8 V 4 50.

PINK EYNE

Small eyes, winking or half-shut eyes: *Plumpy Bacchus with pink eyne!*—Ant II 7 121. Cf. *Eyne.*

PIONED, TWILLED

Thy banks with pioned and twilled brims—Tp IV 64. Very obscure words, perh. signifying agricultural operations for repairing the brims or edges of the banks. *Pioned* may be from Pion, to dig, trench. *Twilled* may be connected with Fr.

Touiller (interpreted by Cotgrave as to bedurt, besmear) and refer to refacing the edges with mire from the trenches.

PIONER

Pioneer.

(1) In the military sense: *Have you quit the mines? have the pioners given o'er?*—H5 III 2 91. *The general camp, Pioners and all*—Oth III 3 345.

(2) Gen., a digger, miner: *Well said, old mole. canst work i' the earth so fast? A worthy pioner!*—Hml I 5 162.

PIPE-WINE

Wine from the wood (with a play on the musical pipe and a reference to the dance canary (see *Canary*) (sb.) (1)): Host. . . . *I will to my honest knight Falstaff, and drink canary with him.* [Exit. Ford. [Aside] *I think I shall drink in pipe-wine first with him; I'll make him dance*—Wiv III 2 88.

PISMIRE

An ant: *I am whipp'd and scourged with rods, Nettled and stung with pismires*—1 H4 I 3 239.

PISS HIS TALLOW

Said of a buck growing lean after rutting-time: *Send me a cool rut-time, Jove, or who can blame me to piss my tallow?*—Wiv V 5 15.

PISSING CONDUIT

On Cornhill: *I charge and command that . . . the pissing-conduit run nothing but claret wine*—2 H6 IV 6 2.

PIT

A hole dug in the ground for a dead body, a grave: *And soon lie Richard in an earthy pit!*—R2 IV 219. *A pit of clay for to be made For such a guest is meet*—Hml V 1 104.

PITCH (sb.)

(1) In falconry, the height to which a hawk soars before stooping (see the second *Stoop*): *Between two hawks, which flies the higher pitch*—1 H6 II 4 11. *What a pitch she flew above the rest!*—2 H6 II 1 6. Fig.: *How high a pitch his resolution soars!*—R2 I 1 109. *These growing feathers pluck'd from Cæsar's wing Will make him fly an ordinary pitch*—Cæs I 1 77.

(2) Height in gen.: *Were the whole frame here, It is of such a spacious lofty pitch, Your roof were not sufficient to contain't*—1 H6 II 3 54. *The pitch and height of all his thoughts*—R3 III 7 188. Value: *Of what validity and pitch soe'er*—Tw I 1 12. Importance: *Enterprises of great pitch and moment*—Hml III 1 86. App., height, dignity: *All men's honours Lie like one lump before him, to be fashion'd Into what pitch he please*—H8 II 2 48.

PITCH (vb.)

(1) *Pitch and pay*, to pay ready money: *The word is 'Pitch and Pay': Trust none*—H5 II 3 51.

(2) Of a price, to set, fix: *Whose vulture thought doth pitch the price so high, That . . .*—Ven 551.

PITEOUS

Full of pity, compassionate: *Tell your piteous heart There's no harm done*—Tp I 2 14. *In thy piteous heart plant thou thine ear*—R2 V 3 126.

PITTANCE

A scanty meal: *At so slender warning, You are like to have a thin and slender pittance*—Shr IV 4 60.

PITTIKINS

'Ods pittikins. See *'Od's.*

PLACE

(1) A dwelling-place, residence: *This is no place; this house is but a butchery*—As II 3 27. *Love lack'd a dwelling, and made him her place*—Compl 82.

(2) Of a hawk, her pitch (see *Pitch* (sb.) (1)): *A falcon, towering in her pride of place*—Mcb II 4 12.

(3) Standing, precedency: *These fix'd evils sit so fit in him, That they take place, when virtue's steely bones Look bleak i' the cold wind*—All's I 1 113. *I crave fit disposition for my wife, Due reference of place*—Oth I 3 237.

(4) *In place*, present: *Here's one in place I cannot pardon*—Meas V 504. *I have heard that she was there in place*—3 H6 IV 1 103. *Let me blame your grace, For choosing me when Clarence is in place*—IV 6 30.

(5) *Upon his place*, in his stead: *Upon his place . . . Governs Lord Angelo*—Meas I 4 55.

PLACKET

(1) An article of feminine attire not certainly identified, app. having relation to some particular part: [Dan Cupid,] *Dread prince of plackets, king of codpieces*—LLL III 186. *Is there no manners left among maids? will they wear their plackets where they should bear their faces?*—Wint IV 4 244. *You might have pinched a placket, it was senseless*—620. *Keep thy foot out of brothels, thy hand out of plackets*—Lr III 4 99.

(2) The wearer of a placket, a woman: *Those that war for a placket*—Troil II 3 22.

PLAGUE

In the plague of custom, app., exposed to the disabilities inflicted by custom: *Wherefore should I Stand in the plague of custom?*—Lr I 2 2.

PLAIN¹

To make plain, explain: *What's dumb in show I'll plain with speech*—Per III Prol 14.

PLAIN²

To lament on account of, bewail: *Making just report Of how unnatural and bemadding sorrow The king hath cause to plain*—Lr III 1 37.

PLAINING

Crying, lamentation: [The] *piteous plainings of the pretty babes*—Err I 1 73. *After our sentence plaining comes too late*—R2 I 3 175. *His heart granteth No penetrable entrance to her plaining*—Lucr 558.

PLAIN-SONG

A simple melody or theme: *An honest country lord . . . may bring his plain-song And have an hour of hearing*—H8 I 3 44. Attrib.: *The plain-song cuckoo gray*—Mids III 1 134. *The very plain-song of it, the plain truth of it: The humour of it is too hot, that is the very plain-song of it*—H5 III 2 5.

PLAINTFUL

Mournful: *A plaintful story*—Compl 2.

PLANCHED

Made of boards: *To that vineyard is a planched gate*—Meas IV 1 30.

PLANET

In the Old Astronomy, a heavenly body having an apparent motion of its own among the fixed stars; hence including the sun and moon: *The glorious planet Sol*—Troil I 3 89. *The fleeting moon No planet is of mine*—Ant V 2 240.

PLANT

The sole of the foot (with a play): *Some o' their plants are ill-rooted already*—Ant II 7 1.

PLANTAGE

Vegetation, herbage: *As true as steel, as plantage to the moon*—Troil III 2 184 (alluding to a supposed influence of the moon on the growth of vegetation).

PLANTAIN

The herb of the name, the leaf of which was considered to be efficacious in healing wounds: *O, sir, plantain, a plain plantain! . . . no salve, sir, but a plantain!*—LLL III 74. So *plantain-leaf*: Rom. *Your plantain-leaf is excellent for that.* Ben. *For what, I pray thee?* Rom. *For your broken shin*—Rom I 2 52.

PLANTATION

Settling, colonizing: *Had I plantation of this isle*—Tp II 1 143.

PLATE (sb.)

A piece of silver money, a silver coin: *Realms and islands were As plates dropp'd from his pocket* —Ant V 2 91.

PLATE (vb.)

To clothe in plate-armour; fig.: *Plate sin with gold, And the strong lance of justice hurtless breaks* —Lr IV 6 169. *Plated*, wearing plate-armour: *Plated in habiliments of war*—R2 I 3 28. *Plated Mars*—Ant I 1 4.

PLATFORM

A scheme, design: [To] *lay new platforms to endamage them*—1 H6 II 1 77.

PLAUSIBLY

With applause, by acclamation: *The Romans plausibly did give consent To Tarquin's everlasting banishment*—Lucr 1854.

PLAUSIVE

(1) Pleasing, winning: *His plausive words*—All's I 2 53 (or perh. here, worthy of commendation, noteworthy): *Some habit that too much o'erleavens The form of plausive manners*—Hml I 4 29.

(2) Plausible: *It must be a very plausive invention that carries it*—All's IV 1 29.

PLAY (sb.)

A game: *All hid, all hid; an old infant play*— LLL IV 3 78. *Primo, secundo, tertio, is a good play*—Tw V 39. *If I make my play*, perh., if I may choose my game: Anne. *You are a merry gamester, My Lord Sands.* Sands. *Yes, if I make my play*—H8 I 4 45.

PLAY (vb.)

To play off, in drinking, to toss off: *When you breathe in your watering, they cry ' hem!' and bid you play it off*—1 H4 II 4 17.

PLEA

That which is demanded by pleading, a claim: *The plea of no less weight Than Aquitaine*—LLL II 7. *None can drive him from the envious plea Of forfeiture, of justice and his bond*—Merch III 2 285. *Though justice be thy plea, consider this*— IV 1 198.

PLEACHED

Of a bower, formed by the pleaching or intertwisting of boughs: *Bid her steal into the pleached bower*—Ado III 1 7. So *thick-pleached*: *Walking in a thick-pleached alley*—Ado I 2 9. Of the arms, folded: *Wouldst thou . . . see Thy master thus with pleach'd arms*—Ant IV 14 72.

PLEAD

To plead for, crave: *Know then, I here . . . Plead a new state* (i.e. a renewed interest or title) *in thy unrival'd merit*—Gent V 4 142. *When*

good will is show'd . . . The actor may plead pardon —Ant II 5 8.

PLEASANCE

Enjoyment, merriment: *Joy, pleasance, revel and applause*—Oth II 3 293. *Youth is full of pleasance, age is full of care*—Pilgr 158.

PLEASANT

Jocular, facetious: *You are pleasant, sir, and speak apace*—Meas III 2 120. *He's returned; and as pleasant as ever he was*—Ado I 1 37. *Take it not unkindly, pray, That I have been thus pleasant with you both*—Shr III 1 57. *We are glad the Dauphin is so pleasant with us*—H5 I 2 259.

PLEASANTLY

As by way of pleasantry: *Think'st thou to catch my life so pleasantly?*—Troil IV 5 249.

PLEASE-MAN

One who curries favour: *Some carry-tale, some please-man, some slight zany*—LLL V 2 463.

PLEASING (ppl. adj.)

App., having pleasure, merry: *Relish your nimble notes to pleasing ears*—Lucr 1126.

PLEASING (sb.)

Pleasingness: *The lascivious pleasing of a lute* —R3 I 1 13.

PLENTY

Following a sb., in plenty, in large quantity: *Earth's increase, foison plenty*—Tp IV 110.

PLIANT

Apt, suitable: *Which I observing, Took once a pliant hour*—Oth I 3 150.

PLUME

To plume up, to prank up; and hence, to gratify: *To plume up my will In double knavery*—Oth I 3 399.

PLUMMET

Is a plummet o'er me, perh., is higher than I am by the length of a sounding-line: *Ignorance itself is a plummet o'er me*—Wiv V 5 172.

PLURISY

Superabundance, excess: *Goodness, growing to a plurisy, Dies in his own too much*—Hml IV 7 118.

POINT (sb.)

(1) A jot, whit; *no point*, not a bit: Biron. *Will you prick 't with your eye?* Ros. *No point, with my knife*—LLL II 189. *Dumain was at my service . . . No point, quoth I*—V 2 276.

(2) A short strain of melody; *a point of war*, a

trumpet-call: [Turning] *your tongue divine To a loud trumpet and a point of war*—2 H4 IV 1 51. Hence *points*, directions, orders: *Tullus Aufidius . . . obeys his points As if he were his officer*—Cor IV 6 124.

(3) A tagged lace for attaching the hose to the doublet: *With two broken points*—Shr III 2 48. *For a silken point I'll give my barony*—2 H4 I 1 53. *To flatter Cæsar, would you mingle eyes With one that ties his points?*—Ant III 13 156. With a play: Clo. *. . . I am resolved on two points.* Mar. *That if one break, the other will hold*—Tw I 5 24. Fal. *Their points (i.e.* the points of their swords) *being broken,*— Poins. *Down fell their hose*—1 H4 II 4 238. App., a lace worn to indicate military rank: *God's light, with two points on your shoulder?*—2 H4 II 4 142.

(4) In falconry, of a hawk, the action of rising vertically in the air: *What a point, my lord, your falcon made!*—2 H6 II 1 5.

(5) *A point of . . .*, something showing . . . : *'Tis a point of friendship*—1 H4 V 1 122. *Do so, it is a point of wisdom*—R3 I 4 99.

(6) *At point, at a point*, in readiness, prepared: *To let him keep At point a hundred knights*—Lr I 4 346. *Old Siward . . . Already at a point, was setting forth*—Mcb IV 3 134. *At point to do a thing*, on the point of doing it: *You are at point to lose your liberties*—Cor III 1 194. *Who was once at point . . . to master Cæsar's sword*—Cymb III 1 30.

(7) *At point, at all points*, completely: *Armed at point exactly*—Hml I 2 200. Mar. *. . . Is Harry Hereford arm'd?* Aum. *Yea, at all points*—R2 I 3 1. So *at ample point: I do enjoy At ample point all that I did possess*—Troil III 3 88.

(8) *To point, to the point*, completely, exactly: *Hast thou, spirit, Perform'd to point the tempest that I bade thee?*—Tp I 2 193. *Agree with his demands to the point*—Meas III 1 254.

(9) *At the point*, at the sword's point: *I saw him hold Lord Percy at the point*—1 H4 V 4 21.

(10) *Come we to full points here?* are we to stop here and have nothing further?—2 H4 II 4 198.

POINT (vb.)

Aphetic form of Appoint: *I'll not be tied to hours nor pointed times*—Shr III 1 19. *He'll woo a thousand, point the day of marriage*—III 2 15. *Whoever plots the sin, thou point'st the season*—Lucr 879. *Nor can I fortune to brief minutes tell, Pointing to each his thunder, rain and wind*—Sonn 14 5.

POINT-DEVICE, POINT-DEVISE

Precise, particular: *I abhor such . . . point-devise companions*—LLL V 1 19. *You are rather point-device in your accoutrements*—As III 2 401. As adv., completely, in every point: *I will be point-devise the very man*—Tw II 5 177.

POISE (sb.)

(1) Weight, importance: *Occasions . . . of some poise*—Lr II 1 122. *It (i.e.* her suit) *shall be full of poise and difficult weight*—Oth III 3 82.

(2) Forcible impact, momentum: *The great swing and rudeness of his poise (i.e.* that of the battering-ram)—Troil I 3 207.

POISE (vb.)

(1) To weigh, estimate: [To] *poise the cause in justice' equal scales*—2 H6 II 1 204. *Our imputation shall be oddly poised In this wild action*—Troil I 3 339. To weigh (one thing *with* another): *Herself poised with herself in either eye*—Rom I 2 100. To put in as a weight: *We, poising us in her defective scale, Shall weigh thee to the beam*—All's II 3 161.

(2) To counterbalance: *If the balance of our lives had not one scale of reason to poise another of sensuality*—Oth I 3 330.

POKE

A pocket: *He drew a dial from his poke*—As II 7 20.

POKING-STICK

A rod for stiffening the plaits of ruffs: *Pins and poking-sticks of steel*—Wint IV 4 228.

POLACK

A Pole: *He smote the sledded Polacks on the ice*—Hml I 1 63. The king of Poland: *A preparation 'gainst the Polack*—II 2 63. *The Polack never will defend it*—IV 4 23. As adj., Polish: *The Polack wars*—V 2 387.

POLE

The pole-star: *The guards of the ever-fixed pole*—Oth II 1 15. Fig.: *The soldier's pole is fall'n*—Ant IV 15 65.

POLE-CLIPT

Pole-clipt vineyard, so called because the vines clip or embrace the poles (see *Clip*): [Leave] *thy pole-clipt vineyard*—Tp IV 68. Also explained as, hedged in by poles.

POLICY

(1) Political science: *Turn him to any cause of policy*—H5 I 1 45.

(2) A device, stratagem: *Is there no military policy, how virgins might blow up men?*—All's I 1 132. *The city gates . . . Through which our policy must make a breach*—1 H6 III 2 1. *Search out thy wit for secret policies*—III 3 12.

POLITIC

Dealing with statecraft: *I will read politic authors*—Tw II 5 175.

POLITICIAN

A schemer, intriguer: *Policy I hate: I had as lief be a Brownist as a politician*—Tw III 2 33. *This vile politician, Bolingbroke*—1 H4 I 3 241. *Like a scurvy politician, seem To see the things thou dost not*—Lr IV 6 175.

POLL (sb.)

(1) A unit in numbering (like Head unchanged for pl.): *The muster-file . . . amounts not to fifteen thousand poll*—All's IV 3 189.

(2) Number ascertained by counting, muster: *We are the greater poll*—Cor III 1 134.

(3) *By the poll*, by the head, man by man: *A catalogue Of all the voices that we have procured Set down by the poll*—Cor III 3 8.

POLL (vb.)

To clip, shear the hair of (a person or animal); fig.: *He will mow all down before him, and leave his passage polled*—Cor IV 5 214.

POMANDER

A scent-ball; also a case, often in the shape of an apple or orange, in which a scent-ball was carried: *I have sold all my trumpery . . . not a ribbon, glass, pomander . . . [left]*—Wint IV 4 607. It is uncertain in which sense the word is here to be taken.

POMEWATER

A large juicy kind of apple: *Ripe as the pomewater*—LLL IV 2 4.

POMGARNET

Pomegranate; as the name of a room: *Look down into the Pomgarnet, Ralph*—1 H4 II 4 41.

POMP

A ceremonial or splendid procession or show: *This unlook'd for, unprepared pomp*—John II 560. *Shall braying trumpets . . . be measures to our pomp?*—III 1 303. *This funeral pomp*—Tit I 1 176. *What need these feasts, pomps and vainglories?*—Tim I 2 248.

POMPOUS

Which ought to be treated with ceremony: *To undeck the pompous body of a king*—R2 IV 250.

PONDEROUS

Weighty, important: *Your more ponderous and settled project*—Wint IV 4 534.

PONTIC SEA

The Black Sea: *The Pontic sea, Whose icy current . . . Ne'er feels retiring ebb*—Oth III 3 453.

POOP

To cozen, beguile: *She quickly pooped him, she made him roast-meat for worms*—Per IV 2 25.

POOR-JOHN

Hake salted and dried: *He smells like a fish . . . a kind of not of the newest Poor-John*—Tp II 2 26. *'Tis well thou art not fish; if thou hadst, thou hadst been poor John*—Rom I 1 36.

POPERIN PEAR

So called from Poperingue, near Ypres: Rom II 1 38.

POPINJAY

A parrot; of a person in disparagement: *To be so pester'd with a popinjay*—1 H4 I 3 50.

POPULAR

Of lowly birth, plebeian: *Art thou officer? Or art thou base, common and popular?*—H5 IV 1 37. *The popular throngs*—Cor II 1 230.

POPULARITY

Intercourse with common people: *[There was] never noted in him . . . any sequestration From open haunts and popularity*—H5 I 1 57.

POPULOUS

Many in number: *The dust . . . Raised by your populous troops*—Ant III 6 48.

PORING

The poring dark, the darkness brooding on the earth: *Creeping murmur and the poring dark Fills the wide vessel of the universe*—H5 IV Chor 2.

PORPENTINE

Porcupine: *A sharp-quill'd porpentine*—2 H6 III 1 363. *Like quills upon the fretful porpentine*—Hml I 5 20. As the name of an inn: *Bring it, I pray you, to the Porpentine*—Err III 1 116. *He dined with her there, at the Porpentine*—V 275.

PORPUS

Porpoise: *When I saw the porpus how he bounced and tumbled*—Per II 1 26.

PORRIDGE

Pottage or soup made with vegetables or meat: *That at dinner they (i.e. his hair) should not drop in his porridge*—Err II 2 99. *Your date is better in your pie and your porridge than in your cheek*—All's I 1 172. *They want their porridge and their fat bull-beeves*—1 H6 I 2 9. *Chaff and bran! porridge after meat!*—Troil I 2 262.

PORRINGER

A cap resembling a porringer: *Her pinked porringer fell off her head*—H8 V 4 50. Cf. *Why, this [cap] was moulded on a porringer*—Shr IV 3 64.

PORT¹

A gate: *Golden care! That keep'st the ports of slumber open wide*—2 H4 IV 5 23. *At the port, lord, I'll give her to thy hand*—Troil IV 4 113.

Him I accuse The city ports by this hath enter'd— —Cor V 6 5. *A thousand . . . at the port expect you*—Ant IV 4 21.

PORT²

Style of living: *A more swelling port Than my faint means would grant continuance*—Merch I 1 124. *Keep house and port and servants, as I should*—Shr I 1 208. Social position: *The magnificoes Of greatest port*—Merch III 2 283.

PORTABLE

Bearable, endurable: *All these* [vices] *are portable, With other graces weigh'd*—Mcb IV 3 89. *How light and portable my pain seems now*—Lr III 6 115.

PORTAGE¹

A mariner's venture which he was allowed to put on board and trade with on his own account; fig. (suggested by the child's birth at sea): *Even at the first Thy loss is more than can thy portage quit, With all thou canst find here,* already thy loss is so great that thou canst not hope to make good thy venture, *i.e.* thy being born (see *Quit* (vb.) (7))—Per III 1 34. *Here* seems to mean, in the world.

PORTAGE²

Provision of port-holes; fig.: *Let it* (*i.e.* the eye) *pry through the portage of the head Like the brass cannon*—H5 III 1 10.

PORTANCE

Conduct, bearing: *Your loves . . . took from you The apprehension of his present portance*—Cor II 3 230. [My] *portance in my travels' history*— Oth I 3 139.

PORTLY

Of good demeanour or bearing: *He bears him like a portly gentleman*—Rom I 5 68.

POSIED

Bearing a *Posy* (q.v.): *Many a ring of posied gold and bone*—Compl 45.

POSITION

Affirmation; *in position,* positively: *I do not in position Distinctly speak of her*—Oth III 3 234.

POSSESS

(1) To seize, take possession of: *Remember First to possess his books*—Tp III 2 99. *This* [is] *the regal seat: possess it, York*—3 H6 I 1 26. To obtain, get, win: *Tell me how long you would have her after you have possessed her*—As IV 1 143. *The moveables The which you promised I should possess*—R3 IV 2 93.

(2) *To possess of,* to put in possession of: *I will possess you of that ship and treasure*—Ant III 11 21.

(3) To inform: *I have possess'd him my most stay Can be but brief*—Meas IV 1 44. *Possess the people in Messina here How innocent she died*— Ado V 1 291. [I'll] *by the way possess thee what she is*—Troil IV 4 114. *Is the senate possessed of this?*—Cor II 1 145. With *with: Some reasons . . . I have possess'd you with*—John IV 2 40.

POSSET

To curdle: *It doth posset . . . The thin and wholesome blood*—Hml I 5 68.

POST (sb.)¹

(1) The door-post of a tavern used for keeping a reckoning: *I from my mistress come to you in post; If I return, I shall be post indeed, For she will score your fault upon my pate*—Err I 2 63.

(2) *A sheriff's post,* a post at the sheriff's door on which proclamations, &c., were fixed: *He'll stand at your door like a sheriff's post*—Tw I 5 156. Cf. *Myself on every post Proclaim'd a strumpet* —Wint III 2 102.

POST (sb.)²

(1) A courier, messenger: *I long to see Quick Cupid's post*—Merch II 9 99. *Your native town you enter'd like a post*—Cor V 6 50. *Ere I was risen . . . came there a reeking post*—Lr II 4 29.

(2) A post-horse: *I have foundered nine score and odd posts*—2 H4 IV 3 39. *To take post,* to start on a journey with post-horses: [I] *presently took post to tell it you*—Rom V 1 21.

(3) *In post,* with all speed: *I from my mistress come to you in post*—Err I 2 63. *I have dispatch'd in post . . . Cleomenes and Dion*—Wint II 1 182. *Away with me in post to Ravenspurgh*—R2 II 1 296. *In all post: The mayor towards Guildhall hies him in all post*—R3 III 5 73. *In such post,* in such haste: *Why comest thou in such post?*— 3 H6 I 2 48.

POST (vb.)

(1) To convey swiftly: *The swiftest harts have posted you by land*—Cymb II 4 27.

(2) *To post over,* to slur over: *His guilt should be but idly posted over*—2 H6 III 1 255. *To post off,* to put off: [I have not] *posted off their suits with slow delays*—3 H6 IV 8 40.

POSTER

One who travels swiftly: *The weird sisters . . . Posters of the sea and land*—Mcb I 3 32.

POSTURE

Perh., direction, disposition: *The posture of your blows are yet unknown*—Cæs V 1 33.

POSY

A motto inscribed within a ring: *A paltry ring . . . whose posy was . . .*—Merch V 147. *Is this a prologue, or the posy of a ring?*—Hml III 2 162.

POT

To the pot, so as to be cut in pieces like meat for the pot, to destruction: First Sol. *See, they have shut him in* (*i.e.* within the hostile gates). All. *To the pot, I warrant him*—Cor I 4 47.

POTATO

The tuber of the plant *Batatas edulis*, now distinguished as the Sweet or Spanish Potato; supposed to have aphrodisiac qualities: *Let the sky rain potatoes . . . let there come a tempest of provocation*—Wiv V 5 20. Cf. *How the devil Luxury, with his . . . potato-finger, tickles these together!*—Troil V 2 55.

POTCH

To make a stab or thrust: *I'll potch at him some way Or wrath or craft may get him*—Cor I 10 15.

POTENT

A potentate: *Cry, 'havoc!' kings; back to the stained field, You equal potents*—John II 357.

POTENTATE

A person of rank: *This gentleman is come to me, With commendation from great potentates*—Gent II 4 78. *Dost thou infamonize me among potentates?*—LLL V 2 684.

POTENTIAL

Powerful, commanding: *Pregnant and potential spurs*—Lr II 1 78. *A voice potential*—Oth I 2 13. *O most potential love!*—Compl 264.

POTTING

Drinking, tippling: *They are most potent in potting*—Oth II 3 79.

POTTLE

A two-quart pot: *I'll give you a pottle of burnt sack*—Wiv II 1 222. *Go brew me a pottle of sack finely*—III 5 29. Loosely, a drinking-vessel: *Ere the next pottle can be filled*—Oth II 3 87. So *pottle-pot*: Shal. . . . *You'll crack a quart together, ha! will you not, Master Bardolph?* Bard. *Yes, sir, in a pottle-pot*—2 H4 V 3 66. Cf. *Is't such a matter to get a pottle-pot's maidenhead* (*i.e.* a tavern-maid's)?—2 H4 II 2 83.

POTTLE-DEEP

To the bottom of the pottle (see *Pottle*): *Potations pottle-deep*—Oth II 3 56.

POULTER

A poulterer: *Hang me up by the heels for . . . a poulter's hare*—1 H4 II 4 479.

POUNCET-BOX

App., a pounced (*i.e.* perforated) box for carrying perfumes: *'Twixt his finger and his thumb he held A pouncet-box, which ever and anon He gave his nose*—1 H4 I 3 37.

POWDER

(1) To salt: *I'll give you leave to powder me and eat me too*—1 H4 V 4 112.

(2) Humorously, with a reference to the next word and to the treatment of venereal disease mentioned under *Tub*: *Ever your fresh whore and your powdered bawd*—Meas III 2 61.

POWDERING-TUB

A salting-tub; with a reference to the treatment of the tub as under *Powder* (2): *The powdering-tub of infamy*—H5 II 1 79.

POWER

(1) A fighting force, army: *Our navy is address'd, our power collected*—2 H4 IV 4 5. *A holy prophetess . . . Is come with a great power to raise the siege*—1 H6 I 4 102. *Our power is ready*—Mcb IV 3 236. *Can he be there in person? 'tis impossible; Strange that his power should be*—Ant III 7 57. Collectively, forces: *For us to levy power Proportionable to the enemy Is all unpossible*—R2 II 2 124. So in pl.: *I'll send those powers o'er to your majesty*—John III 3 70. *Whose powers are these?*—Hml IV 4 9.

(2) For *Deal in her command without her power*—Tp V 271, see *Deal* (vb.) (2).

POX

In imprecations; no doubt referring to the small-pox: *A pox o' your throat!*—Tp I 1 43. *A pox of that jest!*—LLL V 2 46. *A pox on't*—All's III 6 48.

PRABBLES

Leave your prabbles, 'oman—Wiv IV 1 52. See *Pribbles and Prabbles*.

PRACTIC

Practical: *The art and practic part of life*—H5 I 1 51.

PRACTICE

(1) Machination, treachery: *Thou art suborn'd against his honour In hateful practice*—Meas 106. *Your son Will . . . be caught With cautelous baits and practice*—Cor IV 1 31. *A pass of practice*—Hml IV 7 139. *This is practice, Gloucester*—Lr V 3 151.

(2) A plot, stratagem: *This needs must be a practice*—Meas V 123. *I overheard him and his practices*—As II 3 26. *This practice hath most shrewdly pass'd upon thee*—Tw V 360. *On whose foolish honesty My practices ride easy*—Lr I 2 197.

PRACTISANT

A plotter, contriver; or perh., a performer of a stratagem: *Here enter'd Pucelle and her practisants*—1 H6 III 2 20.

PRACTISE

(1) To use stratagems or artifices, plot: *Banished For practising to steal away a lady*—Gent IV 1 47. *He will practise against thee by poison*—As I 1 156. *Let them practise and converse with spirits* —1 H6 II 1 25. *Have practised dangerously against your state*—2 H6 II 1 171. *To practise on* or *upon*, to use stratagems or artifices against: *I . . . will so practise on Benedick that . . .*—Ado II 1 397. *You have . . . practised upon the easy-yielding spirit of this woman*—2 H4 II 1 124. *Caitiff, to pieces shake, That . . . Hast practised on man's life*—Lr III 2 55. *Practising upon his peace and quiet*—Oth II 1 319.

(2) Trans., to plot, contrive: *I doubt My uncle practises more harm to me*—John IV 1 19.

PRÆMUNIRE

More fully *Præmunire facias*, a writ charging the sheriff to summon an offender against the Statute of Præmunire (16th Richard II), directed against the assertion of papal jurisdiction in England: *All those things you have done of late, By your power legatine, within this kingdom, Fall into the compass of a præmunire*—H8 III 2 338.

PRAISE (sb.)

(1) Praiseworthiness, merit: *How many things by season season'd are To their right praise and true perfection!*—Merch V 107. *The prescript praise and perfection of a good . . . mistress*—H5 III 7 49. *To be valiant is no praise at all*—Troil II 2 145. *Being fond on praise, which makes your praises worse*—Sonn 84 14.

(2) An object of praise: *That praise which Collatine doth owe*—Lucr 82.

PRAISE (vb.)

To appraise, value: *Were you sent hither to praise me?*—Tw I 5 267. *Praise us as we are tasted*—Troil III 2 97.

PRAY

(1) To invite (to a feast or the like): *I pray you home to dinner with me*—Meas II 1 292.

(2) *To pray in aid*, in legal phrase, to ask help from another person interested in one's case; hence, to make suit to another as having a common interest, as an ally, not a subject: *You shall find A conqueror that will pray in aid for kindness*—Ant V 2 26.

PREAMBULATE

To walk or go before: *Arts-man, preambulate, we will be singuled from the barbarous*—LLL V 1 85.

PRECEDENCE

Something said before: *An epilogue or discourse, to make plain Some obscure precedence*—LLL III 82. *I do not like ' But yet', it does allay The good precedence*—Ant II 5 50.

PRECEDENT

(1) The original from which a copy is made: *Let this be copied out . . . Return the precedent to these lords again*—John V 2 1. *This is the indictment . . . Eleven hours I spent to write it over . . . The precedent was full as long a-doing*—R3 III 6 1.

(2) A sign, token: *His sweating palm, The precedent of pith and livelihood*—Ven 25.

PRECEPTIAL

Preceptual, consisting of precepts: *Would give preceptial medicine to rage*—Ado V 1 24.

PRECIOUS

(1) Sensitive: *Any annoyance in that precious sense (i.e. the eye)*—John IV 1 94. *The most precious square of sense*—Lr I 1 76. *Can we not Partition make with spectacles so precious 'Twixt fair and foul?*—Cymb I 6 36.

(2) Touching one nearly: *Such a precious loss* —Troil IV 4 10.

(3) *Precious winners*, app., winners of what is precious, of what was desired: *Go together, You precious winners all*—Wint V 3 130.

PRECIOUSLY

As a thing of value: *The time 'twixt six and now Must by us both be spent most preciously*—Tp I 2 240.

PRECIPITATE

To fall headlong: *So many fathom down precipitating*—Lr IV 6 50.

PRECIPITATION

Steep descent, precipitousness: [Let them] *pile ten hills on the Tarpeian rock, That the precipitation might down stretch Below the beam of sight*— Cor III 2 3.

PRE-CONTRACT

A pre-existing contract (of marriage): *He is your husband on a pre-contract*—Meas IV 1 72.

PRECURRER

A forerunner: *Foul precurrer of the fiend*— Phœn 6.

PRECURSE

A heralding, foretokening: *The like precurse of fierce events*—Hml I 1 121.

PREDICT

A prediction: *By oft predict that I in heaven find*—Sonn 14 8.

PREDOMINANCE

Spherical predominance, in astrology, the ascendency or controlling influence of the heavenly bodies in their spheres: *Knaves, thieves, and treachers, by spherical predominance*—Lr I 2 133.

PREDOMINANT

In astrology, having ascendency or controlling influence: *When he (i.e.* Mars) *was predominant* —All's I 1 211. *It is a bawdy planet, that will strike Where 'tis predominant*—Wint I 2 201.

PREDOMINATE

In astrology, to have ascendency or controlling influence: *I will awe him with my cudgel: it shall hang like a meteor o'er* [him] . . . *I will predominate over the peasant*—Wiv II 2 291.

PREFER

(1) To introduce or recommend: *If you . . . know any such, Prefer them hither*—Shr I 1 95. *If Messala will prefer me to you*—Cæs V 5 62. *My book preferr'd me to the king*—2 H6 IV 7 77. *Who lets go by no vantages that may Prefer you to his daughter*—Cymb II 3 50.

(2) To put before any one for acceptance, to offer, present. This may be the meaning in *The short and the long is, our play is preferred*—Mids IV 2 39 (but the usual meaning suits the context better, although it involves an inconsistency; see V 32 and foll.). Of a person, refl., to present himself: *Who is the first that doth prefer himself?*— Per II 2 17.

(3) To forward, promote (an affair, &c.): *I have access my own love to prefer*—Gent IV 2 4. *So shall you have a shorter journey to your desires by the means I shall then have to prefer them*—Oth II 1 284.

PREFERMENT

(1) A giving of preference: *Nor is your firm resolve unknown to me, In the preferment of the eldest sister*—Shr II 93.

(2) *Hath a preferment in't,* implies what would amount to (future) advancement: *I speak against my present profit, but my wish hath a preferment in't*—Cymb V 4 214.

PREGNANCY

Readiness, quickness: *Pregnancy is made a tapster, and hath his quick wit wasted in giving reckonings*—2 H4 I 2 192.

PREGNANT[1]

Clear, obvious: *'Tis very pregnant, The jewel that we find, we stoop and take't*—Meas II 1 23. *If ever truth were pregnant by circumstance*—Wint V 2 33. *The profits of my death Were very pregnant and potential spurs To make thee seek it*—Lr II 1 77. *It is a most pregnant and unforced position*—Oth II 1 239. *Were't not that we stand up against them all, 'Twere pregnant they should square between themselves*—Ant II 1 44. *O, 'tis pregnant, pregnant!*—Cymb IV 2 325.

PREGNANT[2]

(1) Versed: *The nature of our people, Our city's institutions . . . you're as pregnant in As . . .*—

Meas I 1 10. Resourceful: *The pregnant enemy* —Tw II 2 29. Apt: *How pregnant sometimes his replies are!*—Hml II 2 212.

(2) Apt to receive or be influenced, receptive, inclined, ready: *My matter hath no voice, lady, but to your own most pregnant and vouchsafed ear* —Tw III 1 99. *Fair virtues all, To which the Grecians are most prompt and pregnant*—Troil IV 4 89. *The pregnant hinges of the knee*—Hml III 2 66. *A most poor man . . . Who . . . Am pregnant to good pity*—Lr IV 6 225. *The pregnant instrument of wrath*—Per IV Prol 44.

PREGNANTLY

Clearly, cogently: *That shall demonstrate these quick blows of Fortune's More pregnantly than words*—Tim I 1 91.

PREMEDITATION

A consideration of something beforehand: *A cold premeditation for my purpose!*—3 H6 III 2 133.

PREMISED

Sent before their time: [Let] *the premised flames of the last day Knit earth and heaven together!*— 2 H6 V 2 41.

PRENOMINATE (adj.)

Before-named, above-named: *The prenominate crimes*—Hml II 1 43.

PRENOMINATE (vb.)

To name beforehand: *To prenominate in nice conjecture Where thou wilt hit me dead*—Troil IV 5 250.

PRENZIE

Claud. *The prenzie Angelo!* Isab. *O, 'tis the cunning livery of hell, The damned'st body to invest and cover In prenzie guards!*—Meas III 1 94. A doubtful word, prob. corrupt. It is explained as prim, demure.

PRE-ORDINANCE

Previously established ordinance or rule: *These couchings . . . Might . . . turn pre-ordinance and first decree Into the law of children*—Cæs III 1 36.

PREPARATION

(1) A fighting force, armament: *Defences, musters, preparations, Should be maintain'd, assembled and collected*—H5 II 4 18. *These three lead on this preparation*—Cor I 2 15. *The Turkish preparation makes for Rhodes*—Oth I 3 14.

(2) An accomplishment: *Generally allowed for your many war-like, court-like, and learned preparations*—Wiv II 2 236.

PREPARE

Preparation: *Go levy men, and make prepare for war*—3 H6 IV 1 131.

PREROGATIVE

Precedence: *Give me leave to have prerogative*—Shr III 1 6.

PRESCRIPT

Prescribed, regular: *The prescript praise and perfection of a good and particular mistress*—H5 III 7 49.

PRESENCE

(1) Person, personality: *Lord of thy presence and no land beside*—John I 137. *In us, that are our own great deputy, and bear possession of our person here, Lord of our presence, Angiers, and of you*—II 365. *Your royal presences be ruled by me*—377. *Thus did I keep . . . My presence, like a robe pontifical, Ne'er seen but wonder'd at*—1 H4 III 2 55.

(2) Persons present, an assembly, company: *Here is like to be a good presence of Worthies*—LLL V 2 536. *In such a presence here to plead my thoughts*—Mids I 1 61. *This presence knows . . . how I am punish'd With sore distraction*—Hml V 2 239. *You wrong this presence*—Ant II 2 111.

(3) A presence-chamber: [Suppose] *The grass whereon thou tread'st the presence strew'd* (*i.e.* with rushes)—R2 I 3 289. *The two great cardinals Wait in the presence*—H8 III 1 16. Sometimes used as a dining-room: *Her beauty makes This vault a feasting presence full of light*—Rom V 3 85.

PRESENT (adj.)

(1) Immediate: *I will give him a present shrift*—Meas IV 2 223. *A present remedy*—Ado I 3 9. *Marcius is worthy Of present death*—Cor III 1 211. *The present death of Hamlet*—Hml IV 3 67.

(2) *Present money*, money in hand, ready money: *I am not furnish'd with the present money*—Err IV 1 34. *If he had The present money to discharge the Jew*—Merch III 2 275.

PRESENT (sb.)

A matter in hand: *What present hast thou there?*—LLL IV 3 189. [I beseech you] *that you not delay the present*—Cor I 6 60. One's present store: *I'll make division of my present with you*—Tw III 4 380. *From the present*, not to the point: *This is from the present*—Ant II 6 30.

PRESENT (vb.)

(1) To represent, symbolize: *The image of the king whom I presented*—2 H4 V 2 79. *The other* (*i.e.* the white rose) *his pale cheeks, methinks, presenteth*—3 H6 II 5 100. To represent, act, play the part of: *When I presented Ceres*—Tp IV 167. *To-night . . . Must my sweet Nan present the Fairy Queen*—Wiv IV 6 19. *You shall present before her the Nine Worthies*—LLL V 1 124. *The quick comedians . . . will . . . present Our Alexandrian revels*—Ant V 2 216.

(2) To charge, sue: [You would] *say you would present her at the leet*—Shr Ind 2 89.

PRESENTATION

(1) A semblance: *The presentation of but what I was*—R3 IV 4 84.

(2) Cover, show: *He uses his folly like a stalking-horse and under the presentation of that he shoots his wit*—As V 4 111.

PRESENTLY

Immediately: [That he] *Should presently extirpate me and mine Out of the dukedom*—Tp I 2 125. *When you fasted, it was presently after dinner*—Gent II 1 29. *Do it presently*—Cor V 6 121. *The queen would speak with you, and presently*—Hml III 2 391.

PRESENTMENT

Presentation (of a book) to a patron: Pain. *. . . When comes your book forth?* Poet. *Upon the heels of my presentment*—Tim I 1 26.

PRESS

(1) To oppress: *As if it press'd her heart*—Lr IV 3 28. *I have this while with leaden thoughts been press'd*—Oth III 4 177. *I had my load before, now press'd with bearing*—Ven 430. *He with her plenty press'd, she faint with dearth*—545.

(2) With allusion to the *peine forte et dure* inflicted by pressure of a heavy weight on persons indicted who refused to plead: *Pressing to death, whipping, and hanging*—Meas V 528. [She would] *press me to death with wit*—Ado III 1 76.

PRESSURE

An impression, an image: *All forms, all pressures past, That youth and observation copied there* (*i.e.* in his memory)—Hml I 5 100. [To show] *the very age and body of the time his form and pressure*—III 2 26.

PREST

Ready: *I am prest unto it*—Merch I 1 160. *Cursed Dionyza hath The pregnant instrument of wrath Prest for this blow*—Per IV Prol 43.

PRESTER JOHN

Presbyter or Priest John, an alleged Christian priest and king, generally identified with the King of Ethiopia or Abyssinia: [I will] *bring you the length of Prester John's foot*—Ado II 1 275.

PRESUPPOSE

To presuppose upon, app., to suggest to or put before in way of deception: [Thou camest in] *in such forms which here were presupposed Upon thee in the letter*—Tw V 358. Cf. *Suppose* (3).

PRETENCE

A design, purpose: *Love of you . . . Hath made me publisher of this pretence*—Gent III 1 46. *The pretence whereof being by circumstances partly laid open*—Wint III 2 18. *To keep your great pretences veil'd*—Cor I 2 20. *A very pretence and purpose of unkindness*—Lr I 4 75. *Pretence of danger,* harmful design: *To no further pretence of danger* —Lr I 2 94.

PRETEND

(1) To offer, proffer: *Reward not hospitality With such black payment as thou hast pretended*—Lucr 575.

(2) To claim to have (a title): *Why shall we fight, if you pretend no title?*—3 H6 IV 7 57.

(3) To assert: *In the Capitol and senate's right, Whom you pretend to honour and adore*—Tit I 41.

(4) To intend, purpose, plan: *I'll give her father notice Of their disguising and pretended flight*—Gent II 6 36. *Such as shall pretend Malicious practices against his state*—1 H6 IV 1 6. To propose to oneself: *What good could they pretend?* —Mcb II 4 24.

(5) To portend, presage: *Doth this churlish superscription Pretend some alteration in good will?* —1 H6 IV 1 53.

PRETTY

Ingeniously made, artful: *[We have] pretty traps to catch the petty thieves*—H5 I 2 177.

PREVAIL

To avail: *If wishes would prevail with me*—H5 III 2 16. *It helps not, it prevails not: talk no more*—Rom III 3 60.

PREVAILMENT

Power, influence: *Messengers Of strong prevailment in unharden'd youth*—Mids I 1 34.

PREVENT

To anticipate: *I would have stay'd till I had made you merry, If worthier friends had not prevented me*—Merch I 1 60. *He comes armed in his fortune and prevents the slander of his wife*—As IV 1 60. *Both the degrees prevent my curses* —2 H4 I 2 259. *So shall my anticipation prevent your discovery*—Hml II 2 304.

PREVENTION

(1) The action of baffling or stopping another person in the execution of a design: *The prevention of poor Bolingbroke About his marriage*—R2 II 1 167. *Nor never seek prevention of thy foes*—2 H6 II 4 57. *Casca, be sudden, for we fear prevention*—Cæs III 1 19.

(2) A precaution, defensive measure: *Achievements, plots, orders, preventions*—Troil I 3 181.

PREYFUL

Prone to prey: *The preyful princess*—LLL IV 2 58.

PRIBBLES AND PRABBLES

Petty disputation, vain chatter: *If we leave our pribbles and prabbles*—Wiv I 1 56. [Given to] *swearings and starings, pribbles and prabbles*—V 5 168.

PRICE, PRIZE

(1) Estimation, regard: *Our rash faults Make trivial price of serious things we have*—All's V 3 60. *Nought enters there . . . But falls into abatement and low price*—Tw I 1 11. *Held in idle price*, rated as folly: *How I have ever . . . held in idle price to haunt assemblies*—Meas I 3 8.

(2) Value, worth: *She is a pearl, Whose price hath launch'd above a thousand ships*—Troil II 2 81. *If he overhold his price so much, We'll none of him*—II 3 142. *I know my price*—Oth I 1 11. *Her own price Proclaims how she esteem'd him* —Cymb I 1 51. *Of price*, worth much: *Happy news of price*—2 H4 V 3 100.

(3) In form *Prize*, valuation, appraisement: *Cæsar's no merchant, to make prize with you Of things that merchants sold*—Ant V 2 183. The value assigned to something (= sense (2)): *Then had my prize Been less, and so more equal ballasting To thee*—Cymb III 6 77.

PRICK (sb.)

(1) A prickle: *Hedgehogs which . . . mount Their pricks at my footfall*—Tp II 2 10. A skewer: *Bedlam beggars, who . . . Strike in their . . . arms Pins, wooden pricks, nails*—Lr II 3 14.

(2) A point on the dial of a clock: *Now Phaëthon hath . . . made an evening at the noontide prick*—3 H6 I 4 33. *Ere he (i.e. the sun) arrive his weary noon-tide prick*—Lucr 781.

(3) The bull's eye of a target: *Let the mark have a prick in't, to mete at*—LLL IV 1 134.

(4) A mere point: *In such indexes, although small pricks To their subsequent volumes*—Troil I 3 343.

PRICK (vb.)

(1) To fasten with a pin or the like: *An old hat and 'the humour of forty fancies' pricked in't for a feather*—Shr III 2 69.

(2) To mark (a name) in a list: *Prick him (i.e. Mouldy, one of the men from whom the recruits were to be selected)*—2 H4 III 2 121 (in using the word in the next line Mouldy seems merely to echo Falstaff without any particular meaning). *Will you be prick'd in number of our friends?*—Cæs III 1 216. *These many, then, shall die; their names are prick'd*—IV 1 1. In gen., to choose, pick out: *She prick'd thee out for women's pleasure*—Sonn 20 13.

(3) To attire, dress up: *If he had been a man's tailor, he'ld ha' pricked you*—2 H4 III 2 163.

PRICKET

A male fallow deer in his second year: *'Twas

a pricket that the princess killed—LLL IV 2 48.
*The preyful princess pierced and prick'd a pretty
pleasing pricket*—58.

PRICK-SONG

Harmony written or pricked down: *He fights
as you sing prick-song*—Rom II 4 21.

PRIDE

(1) Splendid adornment or ornamentation: *The
madams . . . did almost sweat to bear The pride
upon them*—H8 I 1 23. *New unfolding his (i.e.
the wardrobe's) imprison'd pride* — Sonn 52 12.
Why is my verse so barren of new pride?—76 1.
(2) The highest point, prime: *In the very heat
And pride of their contention*—1 H4 I 1 59. *And
there died . . . in his pride*—1 H6 IV 7 15. *A
falcon towering in her pride of place*—Mcb II 4 12.
(3) Mettle, fire: *Now their (i.e. the horses')
pride and mettle is asleep*—1 H4 IV 3 22. *Wert
thou the unicorn, pride and wrath would confound
thee*—Tim IV 3 338. *The colt that's back'd and
burden'd being young Loseth his pride*—Ven 419.
(4) Lust: *His hand . . . Smoking with pride*—
Lucr 437. *Wooing his purity with her foul pride*
—Sonn 144 8. *In pride*, in heat: *As salt as wolves
in pride*—Oth III 3 404.
(5) Love of display, extravagance: *Ambitions,
covetings, change of prides* [are the woman's]—
Cymb II 5 25. [He] *leaves it (i.e. his gold) to
be master'd by his young; Who in their pride do
presently abuse it*—Lucr 863.
(6) Honour, glory: *Fight by thy father's side;
And . . . let's die in pride*—1 H6 IV 6 56.

PRIEST

Applied to a priestess: *Should he make me* (re-
ferring to Imogen) *Live like Diana's priest*—Cymb
I 6 132. *When my maiden priests are met together*
—Per V 1 243.

PRIME

(1) Original, given at the beginning: *Who ever
but his approbation added, Though not his prime
consent*—Per IV 3 26.
(2) Lustful: *As prime as goats, as hot as monkeys*
—Oth III 3 403.

PRIMERO

A gambling card-game: *I never prospered since
I forswore myself at primero*—Wiv IV 5 103. [I]
left him at primero—H8 V 1 7. It seems to have
been a complicated game, but not much is known
of the rules.

PRIMOGENITIVE

Primogeniture: *The primogenitive and due of
birth*—Troil I 3 106.

PRIMY

In its spring: *A violet in the youth of primy
nature*—Hml I 3 7.

PRINCIPAL

A main rafter of a house: *The very principals
did seem to rend*—Per III 2 16.

PRINCIPALITY

An angel of a high order: *If not divine, Yet let
her be a principality*—Gent II 4 151.

PRINCOX

A pert, forward youth: *You are a princox; go*
—Rom I 5 88.

PRINT

In print, in a precise and perfect manner, to
a nicety: *All this I speak in print, for in print
I found it*—Gent II 1 175. *I will do it, sir, in
print*—LLL III 173. *We quarrel in print, by
the book*—As V 4 94.

PRISCIAN

Priscian a little scratched, said of an unimportant error in Latin, in allusion to the saying that
anyone guilty of bad Latinity broke the head
of Priscian, the celebrated Roman sixth-century
grammarian (*diminuere Prisciani caput*): *Bon,
bon, fort bon! Priscian a little scratched, 'twill
serve*—LLL V 1 31. With the present reading
in 30 (which is that of the Quarto and of the
Folios) it is not easy to say what error Holofernes
professes to detect.

PRISER

A prize-fighter: *The bonny priser of the humorous
duke*—As II 3 8.

PRIVATE

(1) A private person: *What have kings, that
privates have not too?*—H5 IV 1 255.
(2) An intimate, favourite: Ham. *Then you
live . . . in the middle of her (i.e. Fortune's)
favours?* Guil. *'Faith, her privates we*—Hml II
2 236.
(3) Privacy: *Let me enjoy my private: go off*—
Tw III 4 99.
(4) A private communication: *The Count Melun
. . . Whose private with me of the Dauphin's love
Is much more general than these lines import*—
John IV 3 15.

PRIVILEGE

(1) A circumstance to which one owes a favour
or immunity: *My patience, more than thy desert,
Is privilege for thy departure hence*—Gent III 1
159. *Your virtue is my privilege*—Mids II 1 220.
(2) An advantage yielded, pre-eminence: *I
would see his heart out, ere the priest Should ever
get that privilege of me*—1 H6 III 1 120.

PRIZE (sb.)[1]

A contest: *Like one of two contending in a
prize*—Merch III 2 142. *To play a prize*, to

engage in a contest or match; fig.: *So, Bassianus, you have play'd your prize*—Tit I 399.

PRIZE (sb.)²

(1) An advantage, privilege: *It is war's prize to take all vantages*—3 H6 I 4 59. *'Tis prize enough to be his son*—II 1 20.

(2) For sense valuation, appraisement, see *Price* (3).

PRIZE (vb.)

(1) To estimate, rate: *What we have we prize not to the worth Whiles we enjoy it*—Ado IV 1 220. *If you prized my lady's favour at any thing more than contempt*—Tw II 3 130. [I] *prize me at her worth*—Lr I 1 72. To account, reckon: *Having so swift and excellent a wit As she is prized to have*—Ado III 1 89. *Prized by their masters*, rated according to the esteem in which their owners are held: *Things of like value differing in the owners Are prized by their masters*—Tim I 1 170.

(2) With negative, to care nothing for, not to heed: *My love . . . Prizes not quantity of dirty lands*—Tw II 4 84. *She prizes not such trifles as these are*—Wint IV 4 367. *I would not prize them Without her love*—385. *Not prizing her poor infant's discontent*—Sonn 143 8.

PRIZER

One who estimates or rates: [Value] *holds his estimate . . . As well wherein 'tis precious of itself As in the prizer*—Troil II 2 54.

PROBABLE

Such as to approve or commend itself to the mind, worthy of acceptance or belief: *Single I'll resolve you, Which to you shall seem probable, of every These happen'd accidents*—Tp V 248. *With what apology you think May make it probable need*—All's II 4 51. *The least of all these signs were probable*—2 H6 III 2 178. *It is spoke freely out of many mouths*—*How probable I do not know—that . . .*—Cor IV 6 64.

PROBAL

Probable (in the above sense): *This advice is free I give and honest, Probal to thinking*—Oth II 3 343.

PROBATION

(1) Testing, examination: *There is no consonancy in the sequel; that suffers under probation*—Tw II 5 141.

(2) Proof, demonstration: *What he with his oath And all probation will make up full clear*—Meas V 156. *Of the truth herein This present object made probation*—Hml I 1 155. *So prove it, That the probation bear no hinge nor loop To hang a doubt on*—Oth III 3 364. *Which for more probation I can with ease produce*—Cymb V 5 362.

To pass in probation, to go through in way of proof: [I] *pass'd in probation with you, How you were borne in hand*—Mcb III 1 80.

PROCEEDING

One's course, career: *My dear dear love To your proceeding bids me tell you this*—Cæs II 2 102.

PROCESS

(1) Drift, tenor: *Witness the process of your speech, wherein You told how . . .*—Troil IV 1 8.

(2) A relation, narrative: *To set the needless process by, How I persuaded, how . . .*—Meas V 92. *The whole ear of Denmark Is by a forged process of my death Rankly abused*—Hml I 5 36. *Such was the process*—Oth I 3 142.

(3) A command, mandate: *Thou mayst not coldly set Our sovereign process*—Hml IV 3 64. *Where's Fulvia's process?*—Ant I 1 28.

(4) Course of law: *Proceed by process*—Cor III 1 314.

PROCREANT

One who procreates: *Leave procreants alone and shut the door*—Oth IV 2 28.

PROCURE

(1) To bring about, cause: *I am sorry that such sorrow I procure*—Meas V 479. *Proceed, Solinus, to procure my fall*—Err I 1 1. *All these could not procure me any scathe*—2 H6 II 4 62. *To wilful men, The injuries that they themselves procure Must be their schoolmasters*—Lr II 4 305. With subordinate clause: *Procure That Lady Margaret do vouchsafe to come*—1 H6 V 5 88.

(2) To induce, get: *That you'll procure the vicar To stay for me at church*—Wiv IV 6 48. *Send me word to-morrow, By one that I'll procure to come to thee*—Rom II 2 144. With adv. of place, to cause to come, bring: *What unaccustom'd cause procures her hither?*—Rom III 5 68.

PRODIGIOUS

Of the nature of a prodigy, portentous, ominous: *Mole, hare lip, nor scar, Nor mark prodigious*—Mids V 418. *It is prodigious, there will come some change*—Troil V 1 100. [A man] *prodigious grown And fearful, as these strange eruptions are*—Cæs I 3 77.

PRODIGIOUSLY

App., by monstrous births: *Let wives with child Pray that their burthens may not fall this day, Lest that their hopes prodigiously be cross'd*—John III 1 89.

PRODITOR

A betrayer: *Thou most usurping proditor, And not protector, of the king or realm*—1 H6 I 3 31.

PROFACE

A formula of welcome to a meal; much good may it do you: *Good master page, sit. Proface!—* —2 H4 V 3 29.

PROFESS

To declare friendship: *A man which ever Profess'd to him*—Wint I 2 455. So refl.: *If you know That I profess myself in banqueting To all the rout*—Cæs I 2 76.

PROFESSED

Making professions: *To your professed bosoms I commit him*—Lr I 1 275.

PROFIT (sb.)

(1) Progress, improvement: *My brother Jaques he keeps at school, and report speaks goldenly of his profit*—As I 1 5. *No profit grows where is no pleasure ta'en: In brief, sir, study what you most affect*—Shr I 1 39.

(2) Something tending to one's improvement or advantage: *Profits of the mind, study and fast*—Meas I 4 61. *To be direct and honest is not safe. I thank you for this profit*—Oth III 3 378.

PROFIT (vb.)

To make progress, improve: *My son profits nothing in the world at his book*—Wiv IV 1 14. *Their daughters profit very greatly under you*—LLL IV 2 77.

PROFITED

Proficient: *Exceedingly well read, and profited In strange concealments*—1 H4 III 1 166.

PROFITLESS

Making no profit: *Profitless usurer, why dost thou use So great a sum of sums, yet canst not live?* —Sonn 4 7.

PROFOUND

App., of the full size compatible with adhesion, and so ready to fall: *Upon the corner of the moon There hangs a vaporous drop profound*—Mcb III 5 23.

PROGENY

(1) Parentage, descent: *Doubting thy birth and lawful progeny*—1 H6 III 3 61.

(2) Stock, race: *Issued from the progeny of kings*—1 H6 V 4 38. *The Hector That was the whip of your bragg'd progeny*—Cor I 8 11.

PROJECT (sb.)

An idea, notion: *She cannot love, Nor take no shape nor project of affection*—Ado III 1 54. *Flattering himself in project of a power*—2 H4 I 3 29.

PROJECT (vb.)

To set forth, set out: *I cannot project mine own cause so well To make it clear*—Ant V 2 121.

PROLIXIOUS

Retarding the fulfilment of a design: *Lay by all nicety and prolixious blushes*—Meas II 4 162.

PROLONG

To defer, postpone: *This wedding-day Perhaps is but prolong'd*—Ado IV 1 255. *I myself am not so well provided As else I would be, were the day prolong'd*—R3 III 4 46.

PROMPT (adj.)

Ready in mind, inclined: *Fair virtues all, To which the Grecians are most prompt and pregnant* —Troil IV 4 89. Ready or prepared (to do a thing): *I am prompt To lay my crown at's feet*— Ant III 13 75.

PROMPT (vb.)

(1) To put (one) in mind: *Soft and delicate desires, All prompting me how fair young Hero is* —Ado I 1 305.

(2) To suggest; with direct and dative of indirect object: *The matter which your heart prompts you*—Cor III 2 54.

PROMPTED

Ready, eager: *My prompted sword Falling on Diomed*—Troil V 2 175.

PRONE

(1) Ready, eager: *I never saw one so prone (i.e. to die)*—Cymb V 4 207. *O, that prone lust should stain so pure a bed!*—Lucr 684.

(2) Perh. unforced, natural: *In her youth There is a prone and speechless dialect, Such as move men* —Meas I 2 187.

PROOF (adj.)

Impenetrable: *Fight With hearts more proof than shields*—Cor I 4 24.

PROOF (sb.)

(1) Of armour, impenetrability: *Add proof unto mine armour with thy prayers*—R2 I 3 73. *Mars's armour forged for proof eterne*—Hml II 2 512. Hence *of proof*: *He need not fear the sword; for his coat is of proof*—2 H6 IV 2 64 (app. playing on the meaning well tried, well worn). *Targes of proof*—Cymb V 5 5. *To the proof*: Bap. . . . *Be thou arm'd for some unhappy words.* Pet. *Ay, to the proof*—Shr II 140.

(2) Proof armour: *Ten thousand soldiers Armed in proof*—R3 V 3 218. *That Bellona's bridegroom, lapp'd in proof*—Mcb I 2 54.

(3) A passing through or having experience of something, experience: *This is an accident of hourly proof*—Ado II 1 188. *I do pronounce him in that very shape He shall appear in proof*—H8 I 1 196. *Alas, that love . . . Should be so tyrannous and rough in proof!*—Rom I 1 175. *Who knows By history, report, or his own proof, What woman*

is—Cymb I 6 69. *A bliss in proof, and proved, a very woe*—Sonn 129 11. *By proof*, as matter of experience: *By proof we see The waters swell before a boisterous storm*—R3 II 3 43. *Passages of proof*, incidents of (daily) experience: *I see, in passages of proof, Time qualifies the spark and fire of it* (*i.e.* of love)—Hml IV 7 113 (cf. *Passage* (3)).

(4) An experience: *We have ten proofs to one that blood hath the victory*—Ado II 3 171. *'Tis a vulgar proof, That very oft we pity enemies*—Tw III 1 135. *'Tis a common proof, That lowliness is young ambition's ladder*—Cæs II 1 21.

(5) Knowledge gained from experience, experience: *Out of your proof you speak*—Cymb III 3 27. *Nor gives it satisfaction to our blood, That we must curb it upon others' proof*—Compl 162.

(6) Result, fulfilment: *There's never none of these demure boys come to any proof*—2 H4 IV 3 96. *To no proof*, in vain: *All my pains is sorted to no proof*—Shr IV 3 43.

(7) *One's just proof*, proof that one is just or honourable: *When false opinion . . . In thy just proof, repeals and reconciles thee*—Lr III 6 119.

PROPAGATION

Augmentation, increase: *For propagation of a dower*—Meas I 2 154.

PROPEND

To incline: *I propend to you* (*i.e.* I incline to your opinion) *In resolution to keep Helen still*—Troil II 2 190.

PROPENSION

Inclination, impulse: *Your full consent Gave wings to my propension*—Troil II 2 132.

PROPER

(1) (One's) own: *Men hang and drown Their proper selves*—Tp III 3 59. *The mere effusion of thy proper loins*—Meas III 1 30. *My proper life*—Hml V 2 66. *Though our proper son Stood in your action*—Oth I 3 69. Innate, natural: *Proper deformity*—Lr IV 2 60.

(2) Handsome, good-looking: *A sweet-faced man*; *a proper man*—Mids I 2 88. *Three proper young men*—As I 2 129. *As proper men as ever trod upon neat's leather*—Cæs I 1 28. *Cassio's a proper man*—Oth I 3 398. So *a proper man of person*: *He's one o' the soundest judgements in Troy . . . and a proper man of person*—Troil I 2 207.

(3) Of good character, respectable: *An advertisement to a proper maid in Florence*—All's IV 3 240. *A proper gentlewoman*—2 H4 II 2 169.

(4) *Proper of one's hands*, see *Hand* (sb.) (4).

PROPER-FALSE

Handsome and deceitful: *How easy is it for the proper-false In women's waxen hearts to set their forms!*—Tw II 2 30.

PROPERLY

Personally, as one's own: *The matter, The loss, the gain . . . is all Properly ours*—Wint II 1 168. *I owe My revenge properly*—Cor V 2 89.

PROPERTIED

Endowed with qualities indicated by the context: *His voice was propertied As all the tuned spheres*—Ant V 2 83.

PROPERTY (sb.)

(1) Personality, individuality: *A king, Upon whose property and most dear life A damn'd defeat was made*—Hml II 2 597. *Property was thus appalled*—Phœn 37.

(2) Characteristic quality, nature: *The property of rain is to wet*—As III 2 27. *Sweet love, I see, changing his property, Turns to the sourest and most deadly hate*—R2 III 2 135. *He comes too short of that great property Which still should go with Antony*—Ant I 1 58.

(3) A mere accessory or instrument: *'Tis a thing impossible I should love thee but as a property*—Wiv III 4 9. *Do not talk of him, But as a property*—Cæs IV 1 39.

(4) *In property of*, app., in anything appertaining to: *If I . . . flinch in property Of what I spoke, unpitied let me die*—All's II 1 190. *Property of blood*, app., identity of blood: *I disclaim all my paternal care, Propinquity and property of blood*—Lr I 1 115.

PROPERTY (vb.)

(1) To treat as a mere piece of property: *They have here propertied me; keep me in darkness*—Tw IV 2 99. To make a tool of: *I am too high-born to be propertied*—John V 2 79.

(2) To make (a thing) one's own property: *His large fortune . . . Subdues and properties to his love and tendance All sorts of hearts*—Tim I 1 55.

PROPONTIC

The Sea of Marmora: *Whose icy current . . . keeps due on To the Propontic*—Oth III 3 454.

PROPORTION (sb.)

(1) The action of proportioning, proportionate reckoning or adjustment: *Would thou hadst less deserved, That the proportion both of thanks and payment Might have been mine!* (*i.e.* might have been in his power)—Mcb I 4 18.

(2) Metrical rhythm: First Gent. *What, in metre?* Lucio. *In any proportion or in any language*—Meas I 2 22.

(3) Size, magnitude: *Northumberland, Whose power was in the first proportion*—1 H4 IV 4 14. *The just proportion that we gave them out*—2 H4 IV 1 23. *A second Hector, for his grim aspect, And large proportion of his strong-knit limbs*—1 H6 II 3 20.

(4) *Proportions*, preparations for war, contin-

gents: *We must . . . lay down our proportions to defend Against the Scot*—H5 I 2 136. *Let our proportions for these wars Be soon collected*—304. *The levies, The lists and full proportions*—Hml I 2 31.

PROPORTION (vb.)

To hold proportion with: *His ransom; which must proportion the losses we have borne*—H5 III 6 133.

PROPOSE

(1) To suppose, imagine: *Make the case yours; Be now the father and propose a son*—H4 V 2 91.

(2) To set before one's mind as something to be expected, to look for, anticipate: *I propose not merely to myself The pleasures such a beauty brings with it*—Troil II 2 146. Hence, to be ready to face or confront: *A thousand deaths Would I propose to achieve her whom I love*—Tit II 1 79.

(3) To set forth (the terms of a question to be answered or an oath to be taken): *Kneel thou, Whilst I propose the selfsame words to thee, Which, traitor, thou wouldst have me answer to*—3 H6 V 5 19. *Propose the oath, my lord*—Hml I 5 152.

(4) To carry on a discussion, converse, talk: *There shalt thou find my cousin Beatrice Proposing with the prince and Claudio*—Ado III 1 2. *The bookish theoric, Wherein the toged consuls can propose As masterly as he*—Oth I 1 24.

PROPOSER

One who sets forth the terms of an appeal: *Let me conjure you, by the rights of our fellowship, by . . . by . . . and by what more dear a better proposer could charge you withal*—Hml II 2 293.

PROPOSITION

(1) A putting forward for acceptance: *The ample proposition that hope makes In all designs*—Troil I 3 3.

(2) A question proposed: *It is as easy to count atomies as to resolve the propositions of a lover*—As III 2 245.

PROPRIETY

Individuality; *to strangle one's propriety*, to deny one's identity: *It is the baseness of thy fear That makes thee strangle thy propriety*—Tw V 149. The state proper to a thing: *Silence that dreadful bell: it frights the isle From her propriety*—Oth II 3 175.

PROPUGNATION

Defence, protection: *What propugnation is in one man's valour?*—Troil II 2 136.

PROROGUE

(1) To defer, postpone: *My life were better ended by their hate, Than death prorogued, wanting of thy love*—Rom II 2 77. *I hear thou must, and nothing may prorogue it, On Thursday next be*

married—IV 1 48. *To prorogue his honour*, prob., to delay the exertion of his sense of honour: *That sleep and feeding may prorogue his honour Even till a Lethe'd dulness*—Ant II 1 26.

(2) To protract: [He hath not] *taken sustenance But to prorogue his grief*—Per V 1 25.

PROSECUTION

The action of pursuing, pursuit, chase; fig.: *When I should see behind me The inevitable prosecution of Disgrace and horror*—Ant IV 14 64.

PROSPECT

The appearance presented by anything, aspect: *Would you . . . Behold her topp'd? . . . It were a tedious difficulty, I think, To bring them to that prospect*—Oth III 3 395.

PROTEST

(1) To declare publicly, proclaim, publish: *Do me right, or I will protest your cowardice*—Ado V 1 148. *Protest me The baby of a girl*—Mcb III 4 105. *Protest their first of manhood*, take their places as men for the first time: *Many unrough youths that even now Protest their first of manhood*—Mcb V 2 10.

(2) To vow: *I here protest, By this white glove . . . Henceforth my wooing mind shall be express'd In . . .*—LLL V 2 410. *On Diana's altar to protest For aye austerity and single life*—Mids I 1 89.

(3) In Tim IV 3 437 (*Do villany, do, since you protest to do't, Like workmen*), the sense profess, make a thing one's profession, seems to be required.

PROTESTER

One who professes friendship: *To stale with ordinary oaths my love To every new protester*—Cæs I 2 73.

PROTRACT

To defer, postpone: *Let us bury him, And not protract with admiration what Is now due debt*—Cymb IV 2 231.

PROTRACTIVE

Lengthening out, delaying: *The protractive trials of great Jove*—Troil I 3 20.

PROUD

(1) Sensually excited: *The flesh being proud, Desire doth fight with Grace*—Lucr 712. Of female animals, in heat: *A breeding jennet, lusty, young and proud*—Ven 260.

(2) *He is grown Too proud to be so valiant*, too proud (for our safety) for one of his valour: Cor I 1 262.

PROUD-PIED

Splendidly variegated: *Proud-pied April*—Sonn 98 2.

PROVAND

Provender: *Camels in the war, who have their provand Only for bearing burdens*—Cor II 1 267.

PROVE

(1) To experience, to know by experience: *'Tis too much proved, that with 'devotion's visage . . . we do sugar o'er The devil himself*—Hml III 1 47. *You have seen and proved a fairer former fortune Than that which is to approach*—Ant I 2 33. *A bliss in proof, and proved, a very woe*—Sonn 129 11.

(2) To try, attempt: *The steed is stalled up, and even now To tie the rider she begins to prove*—Ven 39. *She hath assay'd as much as may be proved*—608.

PROVIDE

(1) To prepare, make preparation, get ready; absol.: *We must to horse again. Go, go, provide*—All's V 1 37. *My cook and I'll provide*—Tim III 4 119. With infin.: *You must provide to bottom it on me*—Gent III 2 53. *Let us in, and with all speed provide To see her coronation be perform'd*—2 H6 I 1 73. Trans. with vbl. sb.: *Provide your going*, make your preparations for going—Ant III 4 36.

(2) Refl., to make one's preparations: *You, niece, provide yourself*—As I 3 89. *We will ourselves provide*—Hml III 3 7.

PROVINCIAL

(1) Of an ecclesiastic, subject to the authorities of a particular province: *His subject am I not, Nor here provincial*—Meas V 317.

(2) *Provincial (i.e. Provençal) roses*, by an error applied to roses of Provins, a town in north-east France: *With two Provincial roses on my razed shoes*—Hml III 2 287. A ribbon gathered in the form of a rose was worn on shoes.

PROVOKE

To incite, impel: *Beauty provoketh thieves sooner than gold*—As I 3 112. *As rigour of tempestuous gusts Provokes the mightiest hulk against the tide*—1 H6 V 5 5. *Not provoked by any suitor else*—R3 I 3 64. *The bloody spur cannot provoke him on*—Sonn 50 9.

PROVOST

An officer charged with the apprehension, custody and punishment of offenders: *Here comes Signior Claudio, led by the provost to prison*—Meas I 2 118. *The provost hath A warrant for his execution*—I 4 73. And *passim* in the play.

PRUNE

Of a bird, to trim or dress (the feathers) with the beak: *His royal bird Prunes the immortal wing . . . As when his god is pleased*—Cymb V 4 117. Refl. and fig.: *Which makes him prune himself, and bristle up The crest of youth against your dignity*—1 H4 I 1 98. Of a person, refl., to trim or dress himself up: *When shall you see me . . . spend a minute's time In pruning me?*—LLL IV 3 181.

PSALTERY

A stringed instrument resembling the dulcimer, but played with the fingers or a plectrum: *Trumpets, sackbuts, psalteries and fifes*—Cor V 4 52.

PUBLISH

To make an open declaration as to (a person) to an effect stated: *Thus far I will boldly publish her; she bore a mind that envy could not but call fair*—Tw II 1 29. To denounce: *How will this grieve you . . . that You thus have publish'd me!*—Wint II 1 96.

PUGGING

Of uncertain meaning; generally explained as thieving, thievish: *The white sheet bleaching on the hedge . . . Doth set my pugging tooth on edge*—Wint IV 3 5.

PUISNY

Puny; insignificant, paltry: *A puisny tilter*—As III 4 46.

PUISSANCE

Equivalent to *Power* (1) (q.v.): *Cousin, go draw our puissance together*—John III 1 339. *Let us deliver Our puissance into the hand of God, Putting it straight in expedition*—H5 II 2 189.

PUKE-STOCKING

A stocking of a puke colour, *i.e.* prob., a bluish-black or inky colour; attrib.: *Wilt thou rob this leathern jerkin, crystal-button . . . puke-stocking [fellow]?*—1 H4 II 4 77.

PUMPION

Pompion, Pumpkin: *This unwholesome humidity, this gross watery pumpion (i.e. Falstaff)*—Wiv III 3 42.

PUN

Pound: *He would pun thee into shivers with his fist*—Troil II 1 42.

PUNK

A strumpet: *This punk is one of Cupid's carriers*—Wiv II 2 141. *She may be a punk; for many of them are neither maid, widow, nor wife*—Meas V 179. *As fit as . . . your French crown for your taffeta punk*—All's II 2 22.

PUNTO

In fencing, a stroke or thrust with the point: *To see thee pass thy punto, thy stock, thy reverse*—Wiv II 3 26. *Punto reverso*, a back-handed stroke or thrust: *Ah, the immortal passado! the punto reverso!*—Rom II 4 26.

PURBLIND

Blind: *This wimpled, whining, purblind, wayward boy* (*i.e.* Cupid)—LLL III 181 (cf. *The blind bow-boy*—Rom II 4 16). *Lower messes Perchance are to this business purblind?*—Wint I 2 227. *Purblind Argus, all eyes and no sight*—Troil I 2 31. *Her* (*i.e.* Venus's) *purblind son and heir, Young Adam Cupid*—Rom II 1 12. This sense seems to be pretty certain for the first, third and fourth quotations. In the second the word may be taken in the still current sense, dim-sighted.

PURCHASE (sb.)

(1) Acquisition, gaining: *The difference Is purchase of a heavy curse from Rome*—John III 1 204. *I sought the purchase of a glorious beauty*—Per I 2 72. Gain, profit: *The purchase is to make men glorious*—Per Prol 9.

(2) Booty, spoil: *Thou shalt have a share in our* (*i.e.* the thieves') *purchase*—1 H4 II 1 100. *A . . . widow . . . Made prize and purchase of his lustful eye*—R3 III 7 185. App. with a play on this sense and sense (1): *They will steal any thing, and call it purchase*—H5 III 2 44.

PURCHASE (vb.)

(1) To exert oneself for the attainment of an object: *How unluckily it happened, that I should purchase the day before for a little part, and undo a great deal of honour!*—Tim III 2 51.

(2) To bring about, produce, procure: *Lest it make you choleric and purchase me another dry basting*—Err II 2 63. *His silver hairs Will purchase us a good opinion*—Cæs II 1 144. *One poor retiring minute in an age Would purchase thee a thousand thousand friends*—Lucr 962.

(3) To procure for oneself, acquire, obtain: *Your accent is something finer than you could purchase in so removed a dwelling*—As III 2 359. *Now were I happy, if . . . I could . . . Purchase the sight again of dear Sicilia*—Wint IV 4 518. *Say I sent thee forth to purchase honour*—R2 I 3 282.

(4) In legal phrase, of a thing coming to the owner otherwise than through operation of law by descent: *What in me was purchased* (*i.e.* the crown which he had seized), *Falls upon thee in a more fairer sort* (*i.e.* by inheritance)—2 H4 IV 5 200. *Hereditary, Rather than purchased*—Ant I 4 13.

PURELY

So as to make pure: *Faith and troth, Strain'd purely from all hollow bias-drawing*—Troil IV 5 168.

PURLIEU

A tract of land on the border of a forest: *Where in the purlieus of this forest stands A sheep-cote*—As IV 3 77.

PURPLE-IN-GRAIN

See *Grain* (1).

PURPOSE

(1) That which one propounds, a proposition, proposal: *In the morning early shall my uncle Bring him our purposes*—1 H4 IV 3 110. *Your purpose is both good and reasonable*—1 H6 V 1 36. *We'll execute your purpose*—Troil III 3 50. *Therefore have we Our written purposes before us sent*—Ant II 6 3.

(2) Import, effect: *He bade me take a trumpet, And to this purpose speak*—Troil I 3 263.

(3) Discourse, conversation: *There will she hide her, To listen our purpose*—Ado III 1 11.

(4) Matter, subject; *of this war's purpose*, as touching the matter of this war: *What have you dream'd of late of this war's purpose?*—Cymb IV 2 345.

PURVEYOR

An officer charged with the purveyance of necessaries, lodging, &c., for the sovereign or some other great personage: *We coursed him at the heels, and had a purpose To be his purveyor*—Mcb I 6 21.

PUSH (sb.)

An attack, onset: *To . . . stand the push Of every beardless vain comparative*—1 H4 III 2 66. *To stand the push and enmity of those This quarrel would excite*—Troil II 2 137. *Sudden push gives them the overthrow*—Cæs V 2 5.

PUSH (int.)

Pish, Tush: *Push! did you see my cap?*—Tim III 6 119. *To make a push at*, to speak contemptuously of: *However they have . . . made a push at chance and sufferance*—Ado V 1 37.

PUSH-PIN

A child's game in which each player pushed his pin to cross that of another: [To see] *Nestor play at push-pin with the boys*—LLL IV 3 169.

PUT

(1) To cause, to compel: *I am put to know that . . .*—Meas I 1 5. *Had I first been put to speak my mind*—2 H6 III 1 43. *You put me to forget a lady's manners*—Cymb II 3 110.

(2) To affirm, assert: *I love my country, and am not One that rejoices in the common wreck, As common bruit doth put it*—Tim V 1 194.

(3) *To put back*, to repulse, reject: *Petitioners for blood thou ne'er put'st back*—3 H6 V 5 80. *When my indisposition put you back*—Tim II 2 139. *Coming from thee, I could not put him back*—Lucr 843.

(4) *To put by*, to desist from: *Put by this barbarous brawl*—Oth II 3 172.

(5) *To put in*, to intercede: *They had gone down*

too, but that a wise burgher put in for them—Meas I 2 102.

(6) *To put off*, to dismiss, discard: *The clothiers . . . have put off The spinsters, carders, fullers*—H8 I 2 31. *What cause Hath my behaviour given to your displeasure, That thus you should proceed to put me off?*—II 4 19.

(7) *To put on*, (a) to incite, instigate: *Say, you ne'er had done't . . . but by our putting on*—Cor II 3 259. (b) To incite to (a thing): *When devils will the blackest sins put on*—Oth II 3 357. *Gods! if you Should have ta'en vengeance on my faults, I never Had lived to put on this*—Cymb V 1 7. *One that . . . did justly put on the vouch of very malice itself,* was justified in calling upon malice itself to testify to her worth—Oth II 1 146. (c) To bring about, promote: *Deaths put on by cunning and forced cause*—Hml V 2 394. *That you protect this course, and put it on By your allowance*—Lr I 4 227. (d) App., to put to the test: *He was likely, had he been put on, To have proved most royally*—Hml V 2 408.

(8) *To put over*, to refer: *For the certain knowledge of that truth I put you o'er to heaven and to my mother*—John I 61.

(9) *To put to*, to go to work, set to: [A] *flaxwench that puts to Before her troth-plight*—Wint I 2 277.

(10) *To put up*, to submit to, endure tamely: *Be dishonour'd openly, And basely put it up without revenge?*—Tit I 432. *To put up in peace what already I have foolishly suffered*—Oth IV 2 181.

PUTTER-ON

An inciter, instigator: *You are abused and by some putter-on That will be damn'd for't*—Wint II 1 141. *On you, as putter on Of these exactions*—H8 I 2 24.

PUTTER-OUT

A putter-out of five for one, a traveller who staked a sum to be repaid fivefold if he returned and to be forfeited if he was lost: *Which* [wonders] *now we find Each putter-out of five for one will bring us Good warrant of*—Tp III 3 47.

PUTTOCK

A kite: *Who finds the partridge in the puttock's nest, But may imagine how the bird was dead?*—2 H6 III 2 191. *To be a dog . . . an owl, a puttock . . . I would not care*—Troil V 1 66. *I chose an eagle, and did avoid a puttock*—Cymb I 1 139.

PUZZEL

A form of Pucelle; used to denote a drab, a slut: *Pucelle or puzzel . . . Your hearts I'll stamp out with my horse's heels*—1 H6 I 4 107.

PUZZLE

To cause (a person) to be at a loss what to do or how to turn, to put to a non-plus, confound: *There is no darkness but ignorance; in which thou art more puzzled than the Egyptians in their fog*—Tw IV 2 46. *Your presence needs must puzzle Antony*—Ant III 7 11.

PYRAMIS

Pyramid: *A statelier pyramis to her I'll rear Than Rhodope's*—1 H6 I 6 21. Pl. *Pyramises: I have heard the Ptolemies' pyramises are very goodly things*—Ant II 7 39. *Pyramides: Make My country's high pyramides my gibbet*—Ant V 2 60.

Q

QUAIL (sb.)

A loose woman: *Here's Agamemnon, an honest fellow enough, and one that loves quails*—Troil V 1 56.

QUAIL (vb.)

(1) To flag, slacken: *Let not search and inquisition quail*—As II 2 20.

(2) To destroy: *O Fates, come, come . . . Quail, crush, conclude, and quell!*—Mids V 290. To daunt: *When he meant to quail and shake the orb*—Ant V 2 85.

QUAINT

(1) Of persons, knowing, skilled: *The quaint musician, amorous Licio*—Shr III 2 149. *To show how quaint an orator you are*—2 H6 III 2 274. Dainty, charming: *Fine apparition! My quaint Ariel*—Tp I 2 317. *Quaint in green she shall be loose enrobed*—Wiv IV 6 41. *The clamorous owl that . . . wonders At our quaint spirits*—Mids II 2 6.

(2) Of dress, fine, elegant: *A fine, quaint, graceful and excellent fashion*—Ado III 4 22. *I never saw a better-fashion'd gown, More quaint, more pleasing*—Shr IV 3 101.

(3) Of devices, &c., clever, ingenious: *Quaint lies*—Merch III 4 69. *With forged quaint conceit*—1 H6 IV 1 102. *Quaint mazes, intricate: The quaint mazes in the wanton green*—Mids II 1 99.

QUAINTLY

(1) Elegantly, tastefully: *The lines are very quaintly writ*—Gent II 1 128. *'Tis vile, unless it may be quaintly order'd*—Merch II 4 6.

(2) Skilfully, with ingenious art (with a view to the production of something): *A ladder quaintly made of cords*—Gent III 1 117. *To carve out dials quaintly*—3 H6 II 5 24.

(3) Skilfully, ingeniously (with a view to the accomplishment of something): *Breathe his faults so quaintly That they may seem . . .*—Hml II 1 31. *Time . . . With your fine fancies quaintly eche*—Per III Prol 12.

QUAKE

To cause to quake, frighten: *Where ladies shall be frighted, And, gladly quaked, hear more*—Cor I 9 5.

QUALIFICATION

Temper, character: *Even out of that will I cause these of Cyprus to mutiny; whose qualification shall come into no true taste again but by the displanting of Cassio*—Oth II 1 281.

QUALIFIED

Endowed with qualities indicated by the context: *So qualified as may beseem The spouse of any noble gentleman*—Shr IV 5 66. *With thoughts so qualified as your charities Shall best instruct you*—Wint II 1 113.

QUALIFY

(1) To appease, pacify (a person): *Your discontenting father strive to qualify*—Wint IV 4 542.

(2) To bring into a proper condition, regulate: *This inundation of mistemper'd humour Rests by you only to be qualified*—John V 1 12. *Is your blood So madly hot that no discourse of reason . . . Can qualify the same?*—Troil II 2 115.

QUALITY

(1) Good natural gifts: *The Grecian youths are full of quality*—Troil IV 4 78.

(2) An accomplishment: *I have bred her . . . In qualities of the best*—Tim I 1 124. *A quality Wherein, they say, you shine*—Hml IV 7 73.

(3) Profession, occupation: *A man of such perfection As we do in our quality much want*—Gent IV 1 57. *What quality are they of?*—Meas II 1 59. *What is thy name? I know thy quality*—H5 III 6 146. Office, function: *Attend your office and your quality*—Wiv V 5 44. A fraternity, one's fellows: *To thy strong bidding task Ariel and all his quality*—Tp I 2 192. The theatrical profession: *Will they pursue the quality no longer than they can sing?*—Hml II 2 362. *A taste of your quality*, a specimen of your professional skill: *Come, give us a taste of your quality; come, a passionate speech*—Hml II 2 451.

(4) Party, side: *Because you are not of our quality*—1 H4 IV 3 36.

(5) Manner, style: *Hate counsels not in such a quality*—Merch III 2 6. *Thou'lt not believe With how depraved a quality*—O Regan!—Lr II 4 138.

(6) Nature with reference to origin; hence, cause, occasion: *Give him note of our approach,*

With the whole quality wherefore—Troil IV 1 43. *Know you the quality of Lord Timon's fury?*—Tim III 6 117.

QUANTITY

(1) Relative or proportional size or amount, proportion: *Women's fear and love holds quantity*—Hml III 2 177. *Holding no quantity*, deformed (= disproportioned in Tp V 290 (*He is as disproportion'd in his manners As in his shape*)): *Things base and vile, holding no quantity, Love can transpose to form and dignity*—Mids I 1 232 (*things*, of course, referring to personal appearance). Cf. *To disproportion me in every part*—3 H6 III 2 160.

(2) A small piece or amount, fragment: *Thou rag, thou quantity, thou remnant*—Shr IV 3 112. *Retaining but a quantity of life*—John V 4 23. *If I were sawed into quantities*—2 H4 V 1 69.

QUARREL

(1) A ground or occasion of complaint or dispute: *Against whom comest thou? and what's thy quarrel?*—R2 I 3 33. *Thrice is he arm'd that hath his quarrel just*—2 H6 III 2 233. *Since the quarrel Will bear no colour for the thing he is*—Cæs II 1 28. *To have a quarrel to* (a person): *I am sure no man hath any quarrel to me*—Tw III 4 247. *Had we no quarrel else to Rome*—Cor IV 5 133.

(2) One's cause in a contest: *[He hath] put his cause and quarrel To the disposing of the cardinal*—John V 7 91. *The best quarrels, in the heat, are cursed*—Lr V 3 56. *In quarrel of*, in the cause of: *In quarrel of the house of York The worthy gentleman did lose his life*—3 H6 III 2 6. *To fight in quarrel of the house of Lancaster*—R3 I 4 209. So *in Rome's quarrel: All my blood in Rome's great quarrel shed*—Tit III 1 4.

(3) Quarrelling, quarrelsomeness: *He'll be as full of quarrel and offence As my young mistress' dog*—Oth II 3 52.

(4) App. = quarreller: *That quarrel, fortune*—H8 II 3 14.

QUARRELOUS

Quarrelsome: *As quarrelous as the weasel*—Cymb III 4 162.

QUARRY

A heap made of the deer killed at a hunting: *To relate the manner, Were, on the quarry of these murder'd deer, To add the death of you*—Mcb IV 3 205. Applied to slain men: *I'ld make a quarry With thousands of these quarter'd slaves*—Cor I 1 202. *This quarry cries on havoc*—Hml V 2 375.

QUART D'ÉCU

An old French silver coin = ¼ of the gold écu: *For a quart d'écu he will sell the fee-simple of his salvation*—All's IV 3 311. *There's a quart d'écu for you*—V 2 35.

QUARTER

(1) A part of an army or camp: *Had all your quarters been as safely kept As that whereof I had the government*—1 H6 II 1 63.

(2) *To keep good quarter*, to keep good watch: *Keep good quarter and good care to-night*—John V 5 20.

(3) The place where soldiers are lodged: *Within her quarter and mine own precinct I was employ'd* —1 H6 II 1 68. *Not a man Shall pass his quarter* —Tim V 4 59. Cf. *If you think your mystery in stratagem can bring this instrument of honour* (*i.e.* the captured drum) *again into his native quarter* —All's III 6 68.

(4) Assigned position; *as far as we have quarter*, to the limit of our bounds: *Follow the noise so far as we have quarter*—Ant IV 3 22.

(5) Relations, conduct: *So he would keep fair quarter with his bed*—Err II 1 108. *Friends all but now, even now, In quarter and in terms like bride and groom*—Oth II 3 179.

QUARTERED

In or belonging to military quarters: *Their quarter'd fires*—Cymb IV 4 18.

QUAT

A pimple or pustule; applied to a person: *I have rubb'd this young quat almost to the sense*— Oth V 1 11.

QUATCH-BUTTOCK

Of uncertain meaning: *A barber's chair that fits all buttocks . . . the quatch-buttock . . . or any buttock*—All's II 2 17.

QUEAN

Equivalent to Woman, but used vaguely as a term of abuse: *A witch, a quean, an old cozening quean!*—Wiv IV 2 180. [As fit] *as a scolding quean to a wrangling knave*—All's II 2 27. *Throw the quean in the channel*—2 H4 II 1 51.

QUEASY

Hazardous; *of a queasy question*, involving hazardous considerations: *I have one thing, of a queasy question, Which I must act*—Lr II 1 19.

QUELL (sb.)

A slaying: *Who shall bear the guilt Of our great quell*—Mcb I 7 71.

QUELL (vb.)

To slay: *O Fates, come, come . . . Quail, crush, conclude, and quell!*—Mids V 290.

QUENCH

Of a person, to cool down: *Dost thou think in time She will not quench?*—Cymb I 5 46.

QUERN

A hand-mill: [That] *sometimes labour in the quern*—Mids II 1 36.

QUEST

(1) An official enquiry: *Crowner's quest law*— Hml V 1 24.

(2) The persons holding a quest, a jury: *What lawful quest have given their verdict up?*—R3 I 4 189. *To 'cide this title is impanneled A quest of thoughts*—Sonn 46 9.

(3) A person employed in searching or a body of searchers: *The senate hath sent about three several quests To search you out*—Oth I 2 46.

QUESTANT

A seeker: *When The bravest questant shrinks, find what you seek*—All's II 1 15.

QUESTION (sb.)

(1) Consideration, discussion: *This haste was hot in question*—1 H4 I 1 34. *The scambling and unquiet time Did push it out of farther question*—H5 I 1 4. *I'ld have it come to question* —Lr I 3 13. *Of thy beauty do I question make*— Sonn 12 9. *To call in question*, to discuss (a thing), make (it) one's subject: [Do not] *call the giddiness of it in question*—As V 2 6. *'Tis the way To call hers* (*i.e.* her beauty) *exquisite, in question more*—Rom I 1 234. *Now sit we close . . . And call in question our necessities*—Cæs IV 3 164.

(2) Talk, discourse, conversation: *I met the duke yesterday and had much question with him*— As III 4 38. *After some question with him*—V 4 167. *Make the trial of it in any constant question* —Tw IV 2 52. [We will] *have some question with the shepherd*—Wint IV 2 54. In pl.: *I will not stay thy questions*—Mids III 1 235. *In the loss of question*, in idle talk: *I subscribe not that, nor any other, But in the loss of question*—Meas II 4 89.

(3) *In question*, under judicial examination: Bora. *We are like to prove a goodly commodity, being taken up of these men's bills.* Con. *A commodity in question*—Ado III 3 190 (with a play). *Camillo . . . who now Has these poor men in question*—Wint V 1 197. *He that was in question for the robbery?*—2 H4 I 2 68.

(4) *First in question*, mentioned first: *Old Escalus, Though first in question, is thy secondary* —Meas I 1 46. *In contempt of question*, without doubt: *It is, in contempt of question, her hand*— Tw II 5 97. *With more facile question*, with less formidable questioning of, (*i.e.*, opposition to), his proceedings: *So may he with more facile question bear it*—Oth I 3 23.

QUESTION (vb.)

(1) To hold discourse, discuss, dispute: *Question, my lords, no further of the case*—1 H6 II 1 72. *Let your reason with your choler question What 'tis you go about*—H8 I 1 130. *Had I not . . . I grant*

We were to question further (*i.e.* with the sword) —Cymb II 4 50. *Long he questioned With modest Lucrece*—Lucr 122. To make inquiry: *'T is safer to Avoid what's grown than question how 'tis born* —Wint I 2 432.

(2) To inquire about, investigate: *Lest that our king Come here himself to question our delay*—H5 II 4 141. [Let us] *question this most bloody piece of work*—Mcb II 3 134. In pass. construction: *Thou hast found mine; But how, is to be question'd*—Wint V 3 138.

QUESTIONABLE

Lending itself to question; or (like conversable) lending itself to discourse (see *Question* (vb.) (1)): *Thou comest in such a questionable shape That I will speak to thee*—Hml I 4 43. Or perh. the meaning may be, inciting to question, suggesting inquiry (the ghost being in arms. Cf. *My father's spirit in arms! all is not well*—I 2 255).

QUESTRIST

One who goes in quest: *Some five or six and thirty of his knights, Hot questrists after him*—Lr III 7 16.

QUICK

(1) Pregnant, with child: *She's quick*—LLL V 2 682. *Then shall Hector be whipped for Jaquenetta that is quick by him*—686.

(2) Of a spring, running, flowing: *I'll not show him Where the quick freshes are*—Tp III 2 74.

(3) Of air, sharp, piercing: *The air is quick there, And it pierces and sharpens the stomach*— Per IV 1 28.

QUICKEN

To recover life, revive: *Quicken with kissing*— —Ant IV 15 39.

QUIETUS

Discharge, acquittance: *Her audit, though delay'd, answer'd must be, And her quietus is to render thee*—Sonn 126 13. Discharge or release from life: *When he himself might his quietus make With a bare bodkin*—Hml III 1 75.

QUILL

In the quill, in a body: *Then we may deliver our supplications in the quill*—2 H6 I 3 3.

QUILT

A soft bed; applied to a person: *How now, blown Jack! how now, quilt!*—1 H4 IV 2 53.

QUINTAIN

A mark to be tilted at or thrown at with darts as an exercise of skill: *But a quintain, a mere lifeless block*—As I 2 263.

QUIRE (sb.)

A company: *Then the whole quire hold their hips and laugh*—Mids II 1 55.

QUIRE (vb.)

To sing or sound in concert: *Still quiring to the young-eyed cherubins* — Merch V 62. *My throat of war . . . Which quired with my drum* —Cor III 2 112.

QUIRK

(1) Turn of mind, temper: *Belike this is a man of that quirk*—Tw III 4 268.

(2) A sudden stroke, shock: *I have felt so many quirks of joy and grief, That . . .*—All's III 2 51.

QUIT (adj.)

Quit with, of, even with: *Hortensio will be quit with thee by changing*—Shr III 1 92. *To be full quit of those my banishers*—Cor IV 5 89.

QUIT (vb.)

(1) To release, set free: *Your master quits you* —Tw V 329.

(2) To free, rid: *Quitting thee thereby of ten thousand shames*—2 H6 III 2 218. *God safely quit her of her burthen!*—H8 V 1 70. Refl.: *Now quit you of great shames*—H5 III 5 47.

(3) To clear, acquit: *Till thou canst quit thee by thy brother's mouth Of what we think against thee*—As III 1 11. *Here I quit him*—All's V 3 300. To free from the consequences of crime: *God quit you in his mercy!*—H5 II 2 166. To clear oneself from: *I would I could Quit all offences with as clear excuse As . . .*—I H4 III 2 18.

(4) To remit: *To quit the fine for one half of his goods*, to remit the fine as touching one half (and so to leave that half to the offender): *So please my lord the duke . . . To quit the fine for one half of his goods, I am content*—Merch IV 1 380. To pardon: *For those earthly faults, I quit them all*— Meas V 488.

(5) To repay, requite, pay out (a person): *Well, Angelo, your evil quits you well*—Meas V 501. *Is't not perfect conscience, To quit him with this arm?*—Hml V 2 67. *God quit you!*—Ant III 13 124. *He has Hipparchus . . . whom He may at pleasure whip, or hang, or torture, As he shall like, to quit me*—148. Absol.: *If Hamlet give the first or second hit, Or quit in answer of the third exchange*—Hml V 2 279. *To quit oneself of*, to be revenged upon: *They shall find . . . Both strength of limb and policy of mind . . . To quit me of them throughly*—Ado IV 1 199.

(6) To repay, requite, make a return for (something): *To quit their griefs, Tell thou the lamentable tale of me*—R2 V 1 43. *Unless the Lady Bona quit his pain*—3 H6 III 3 128. *Be trusty, and I'll quit thy pains*—Rom II 4 204. *Enkindle all the sparks of nature, To quit this horrid act*—Lr III 7 86.

(7) To be a return or equivalent for, balance: *Like doth quit like*—Meas V 416. *Plantagenet doth quit Plantagenet*—R3 IV 4 20. *The other*

Edward [is] *dead, to quit my Edward*—64. *Even at the first Thy loss is more than can thy portage quit*—Per III 1 34.

(8) To pay up, clear off: *Unless a thousand marks be levied, To quit the penalty*—Err I 1 22.

QUITTAL

Requital: *In revenge or quittal of such strife*—Lucr 236.

QUITTANCE (sb.)

Return: *Rendering faint quittance, wearied and outbreathed, To Harry Monmouth*—2 H4 I 1 108. Recompense: [We] *shall forget the office of our hand, Sooner than quittance of desert and merit*—H5 II 2 33. *Use of quittance*, usual requital: *No gift to him, But breeds the giver a return exceeding All use of quittance*—Tim I 1 289.

QUITTANCE (vb.)

To repay, requite: *To quittance their deceit*—1 H6 II 1 14.

QUIVER

Active, nimble: *A little quiver fellow*—2 H4 III 2 300.

QUOIF

A close-fitting cap: *Golden quoifs and stomachers, For my lads to give their dears*—Wint IV 4 226. *A sickly quoif*, one worn by an invalid: *Hence, thou sickly quoif!*—2 H4 I 1 147.

QUOTE

(1) To give the reference to (a passage in a book); fig.: *His face's own margent did quote such amazes*—LLL II 246.

(2) To note down: *A fellow by the hand of nature mark'd, Quoted and sign'd to a deed of shame*—John IV 2 221.

(3) To observe, mark, scrutinize: *I have with exact view perused thee, Hector, And quoted joint by joint*—Troil IV 5 232. *Note how she quotes the leaves*—Tit IV 1 50. *What care I What curious eye doth quote deformities?*—Rom I 4 30. *I am sorry that with better heed and judgement I had not quoted him*—Hml II 1 111.

(4) To set down, look upon (as being something): *Her amber hair for foul hath amber quoted*—LLL IV 3 87. Dum. *Our letters, madam, show'd much more than jest* . . . Ros. *We did not quote them so*—V 2 795. *He's quoted for a most perfidious slave*—All's V 3 205.

R

R

Rom. . . . *Both* [begin] *with an R.* Nurse. *Ah, mocker! that's the dog's name*—Rom II 4 221. R was called the dog's letter from its resemblance in sound to the snarling of a dog.

RABATO

A kind of stiff collar: *Troth, I think your other rabato were better*—Ado III 4 6.

RABBIT-SUCKER

A sucking rabbit, young rabbit: *Hang me up by the heels for a rabbit-sucker*—1 H4 II 4 479.

RACE¹

The course of time: *If the midnight bell Did* . . . *Sound on into the drowsy race of night*—John III 3 37.

RACE²

(1) A stud or herd (of horses): [A] *race of youthful and unhandled colts*—Merch V 72.

(2) An individual's nature derived from the race, one's natural disposition: *Thy vile race . . . had that in't which good natures Could not abide to be with*—Tp I 2 358. *My sensual race*, that part of my nature which is sensual, my lust: *Now I give my sensual race the rein*—Meas II 4 160. So perh. in Ant I 3 36 (*None our parts so poor, But was a race of heaven*) *a race of heaven* = an in-

dividual trait derived from the race, and that race heavenly.

RACE,³ RAZE

A root (of ginger): *A race or two of ginger*—Wint IV 3 50. *A gammon of bacon and two razes of ginger*—1 H4 II 1 26.

RACK (sb.)

Clouds moving in the upper air: *As we often see . . . A silence in the heavens, the rack stand still*—Hml II 2 505. *That which is now a horse, even with a thought The rack dislimns*—Ant IV 14 9. In Tp IV 155 (*And, like this insubstantial pageant faded,* [shall] *Leave not a rack behind*) *rack* seems to be used in the sense of a single cloud or a fragment of cloud; but such a use lacks analogy.

RACK (vb.)¹

Of clouds, to drift with the wind: *Three glorious suns . . . Not separated with the racking clouds*—3 H6 II 1 26.

RACK (vb.)²

(1) To stretch or raise beyond the normal: *Then we rack the value*—Ado IV 1 222. *My credit . . . shall be rack'd, even to the uttermost*—Merch I 1 180.

(2) App., to rack or strain oneself, toil: *A pair of tribunes that have rack'd for Rome*—Cor V 1 16.

RAGE (sb.)

Madness, insanity: *The reason that I gather he is mad, Besides this present instance of his rage, Is . . .*—Err IV 3 87. *The great rage, You see, is kill'd in him*—Lr IV 7 78. Of a poet's inspiration: *Your true rights* [should] *be term'd a poet's rage*—Sonn 17 11.

RAGE (vb.)

(1) To be frenzied, rave: *Doth he (i.e.* the sick king) *still rage?*—John V 7 11. *When one so great begins to rage, he's hunted Even to falling*—Ant IV 1 7.

(2) To enrage: *Young hot colts being raged do rage the more*—R2 II 1 70.

RAGING-WOOD

Raging mad: *The young whelp of Talbot's, raging-wood*—1 H6 IV 7 35. See *Wood.*

RAISINS OF THE SUN

Sun-dried grapes: *Four pound of prunes, and as many of raisins o' the sun*—Wint IV 3 51.

RAKE UP

To cover with something brought together: *Here, in the sands, Thee I'll rake up*—Lr IV 6 280.

RAMPALLIAN

A ruffian, scoundrel; applied to a woman: *Away, you scullion! you rampallian!*—2 H4 II 1 65.

RAMPING

Rearing on the hind legs in a threatening posture; an epithet of beasts: *A couching lion and a ramping cat*—1 H4 III 1 153. *The ramping lion*—3 H6 V 2 13.

RAMPIRE

To strengthen or block up (a gate) against attack: *Set but thy foot Against our rampired gates, and they shall ope*—Tim V 4 46.

RAMPS

Perh. = Romps; *vaulting variable ramps*, cutting all sorts of capers: *Whiles he is vaulting variable ramps, In your despite*—Cymb I 6 134. See *Variable.*

RANGE

A rank, file: *That great face of war, whose several ranges Frighted each other*—Ant III 13 5.

RANK (adj.)

(1) Lustful, in heat: *The ewes being rank*—Merch I 3 81. *Lust and rank thoughts*—Cymb II 5 24. *In the rank garb,* app., with tales of lewd conduct: [I'll] *Abuse him to the Moor in the rank garb*—Oth II 1 315 (see *Garb*).

(2) High in amount: *Nor will it yield to Norway or the Pole A ranker rate, should it be sold in fee*—Hml IV 4 21.

(3) Excessively great or large, swollen, puffed up: *To diet rank minds sick of happiness*—2 H4 IV 1 64. *I know not . . . Who else must be let blood, who else is rank*—Cæs III 1 151. *Which, rank of goodness, would by ill be cured*—Sonn 118 12.

(4) In Tw II 5 135 (*Sowter will cry upon't for all this, though it be as rank as a fox*) the second *it* seems to refer to a scent crossing and foiling the true scent.

RANK (sb.)

Movement in line or file: *It is the right butter-women's rank to market*—As III 2 103. *I do know but one That unassailable holds on his rank, Unshaked of motion*—Cæs III 1 68.

RANK (adv.)

Completely: *How rank soever rounded in with danger*—Troil I 3 196.

RANKED

Surrounded with ranks or rows: *The base o' the mount Is rank'd with all deserts, all kind of natures*—Tim I 1 64.

RANKLE

To cause a painful festering: *Fell sorrow's tooth doth never rankle more Than when he bites, but lanceth not the sore*—R2 I 3 302. *His venom tooth will rankle to the death*—R3 I 3 291.

RANSACK

To carry off as prey: *The ransack'd queen*—Troil II 2 150.

RANSOM (sb.)

A means of expiating a fault, a penalty: *If hearty sorrow Be a sufficient ransom for offence*—Gent V 4 74. *Lowly words were ransom for their fault*—2 H6 III 1 127. *The ransom (i.e.* the penalty in case of failure) *of my bold attempt Shall be this cold corpse on the earth's cold face*—R3 V 3 265. *My ransom's death*—Cymb V 3 80.

RANSOM (vb.)

To expiate, atone for: *Those tears . . . ransom all ill deeds*—Sonn 34 13. [My trespass] *ransoms yours*—120 14.

RAP

To transport, carry away (with some emotion): *What, dear sir, Thus raps you?*—Cymb I 6 50.

RAPINE

Rape, ravishment; as proper name: *So thou destroy Rapine and Murder there*—Tit V 2 59. *When thou find'st a man that's like thyself . . . Good Rapine, stab him; he's a ravisher*—99.

RAPTURE

(1) Violent seizing: *Spite of all the rapture of the sea*—Per II 1 161.

(2) A paroxysm, fit: *Your prattling nurse Into a rapture lets her baby cry*—Cor II 1 222.

RASCAL (adj.)

Of things, worthless, base: *When Marcus Brutus grows so covetous, To lock such rascal counters from his friends*—Cæs IV 3 79.

RASCAL (sb.)

A worthless deer: *The noblest deer hath them* (*i.e.* horns) *as huge as the rascal*—As III 3 57. Of a person: *Thou rascal, that art worst in blood to run*—Cor I 1 163.

RASCAL-LIKE

Like a rascal in the above sense: *If we be English deer, be then in blood; Not rascal-like, to fall down with a pinch*—1 H6 IV 2 48.

RASH

(1) Operating quickly and strongly: *With no rash potion, But with a lingering dram*—Wint I 2 319. *Though it do work as strong As aconitum or rash gunpowder*—2 H4 IV 4 47.

(2) Urgent, pressing: *I scarce have leisure to salute you, My matter is so rash*—Troil IV 2 61.

(3) Hasty, sudden: [*Why I*] *would not rather Make rash remonstrance of my hidden power Than let him so be lost*—Meas V 396. *The reason of this rash alarm to know*—Lucr 473.

RASH-LEVIED

Hastily got together: *Buckingham and his rash-levied army*—R3 IV 3 50.

RATE (sb.)

(1) A total computed number: *I judge their number Upon or near the rate of thirty thousand*—2 H4 IV 1 21.

(2) Estimated value or worth: *That which . . . O'er-prized all popular rate*—Tp I 2 91. *Stones whose rates are either rich or poor As fancy values them*—Meas II 2 150. *She reckon'd it At her life's rate*—All's V 3 90. *Which* (*i.e.* the plate, &c.) *I find at such proud rate, that . . .*—H8 III 2 126.

(3) Estimation, way of thinking: *My son is lost and, in my rate, she too*—Tp II 1 109.

(4) The price (of a single thing): *Purchased At a superfluous rate*—H8 I 1 98. *Nor will it yield to Norway or the Pole A ranker rate, should it be sold in fee*—Hml IV 4 21.

(5) Style of living: *To be abridged From such a noble rate*—Merch I 1 126.

RATE (vb.)

(1) To assign (one his share): [*That*] *we had not rated him His part o' the isle*—Ant III 6 25.

(2) To reckon, calculate: *Then must we rate the cost of the erection*—2 H4 I 3 44.

(3) App., to equal in worth: *Fall not a tear, I say; one of them rates All that is won and lost*—Ant III 11 69.

RATED

(Highly) rated or valued: *Who with them was a rated sinew too*—1 H4 IV 4 17.

RATHER

The rather, (all) the more quickly, (all) the sooner: *When Duncan is asleep—Whereto the rather shall his day's hard journey Soundly invite him*—Mcb I 7 61.

RATO-LORUM

By confusion for (*Custos*) *Rotulorum*: Wiv I 1 8. See under *Custalorum*.

RATTLE

To berattle: *Another* [drum] *shall As loud as thine rattle the welkin's ear*—John V 2 171.

RAUGHT

See *Reach*.

RAVEL

To become entangled: *As you unwind her love from him, Lest it should ravel . . . You must . . .*—Gent III 2 51.

RAVIN (adj.)

Ravenous: *Better 'twere I met the ravin lion when he roar'd*—All's III 2 119.

RAVIN (vb.)

Raven; to devour: *Like rats that ravin down their proper bane*—Meas I 2 133. *Thriftless ambition, that wilt ravin up Thine own life's means!*—Mcb II 4 28.

RAVINED

Ravenous; or perh., glutted: *Maw and gulf Of the ravin'd salt-sea shark*—Mcb IV 1 23.

RAVISH

(1) To spoil, corrupt: *With rotten damps ravish the morning air*—Lucr 778.

(2) To tear away: *These hairs which thou dost ravish from my chin*—Lr III 7 38.

RAW

Unripe, immature: *I tender you my service, Such as it is, being tender, raw and young; Which elder days shall ripen*—R2 II 3 41.

RAWLY

Without due provision; or perh., at an immature age (cf. *Raw*): *Some* [crying] *upon their children rawly left*—H5 IV 1 147.

RAWNESS

In that rawness, so abruptly, without due provision: *Why in that rawness left you wife and child?*—Mcb IV 3 26.

RAY

To beray, befoul: *Rayed with the yellows*—Shr III 2 54 (or perh. here = arrayed, from Array, to afflict, distress). *Was ever man so rayed?*—IV I 3.

RAZE (sb.)

See *Race*[3].

RAZE (vb.)

(1) To scratch, tear: *He dreamt to-night the boar had razed his helm*—R3 III 2 11. *Stanley did dream the boar did raze his helm*—III 4 84.

(2) To scrape out, erase: *That* [commandment] *he razed*—Meas I 2 11. *Razing the characters of your renown*—2 H6 I 1 101. [Canst thou not] *Raze out the written troubles of the brain?*—Mcb V 3 42. *From the book of honour razed quite*—Sonn 25 11.

RAZED

Slashed: *With two Provincial roses on my razed shoes*—Hml III 2 287.

RAZURE

Obliteration, effacement: *The tooth of time And razure of oblivion*—Meas V 12.

REACH

(Past tense and pple. Raught.)

(1) To attain, get possession of: *This staff of honour raught, there let it stand*—2 H6 II 3 43.

(2) To seize, take hold of: *The hand of death hath raught him*—Ant IV 9 30.

READ

To teach (something *to* a person): *What will you read to her?*—Shr I 2 154 (addressed to Lucentio in his supposed character of teacher of languages). *Give me leave to read philosophy*—III I 13 (said by Lucentio). *Where is he living . . . Which calls me pupil, or hath read to me?*—1 H4 III 1 44.

READY

Dressed, having finished one's toilet: *Enter . . . the Bastard of Orleans, Alençon, and Reignier, half ready, and half unready*—1 H6 II 1 38 (Stage Dir). *Lady . . . What's your lordship's pleasure?* Clo. *Your lady's person: is she ready?*—Cymb II 3 85.

RE-ANSWER

To meet, be an equivalent for: *The losses we have borne, the subjects we have lost . . . which in weight to re-answer, his pettiness would bow under*—H5 III 6 134.

REAR

To bring into existence, cause to appear: *From their ashes shall be rear'd A phœnix that shall make all France afeard*—1 H6 IV 7 92.

REASON (sb.)

(1) A statement: [The king] *foreseeing those fell mischiefs Our reasons laid before him, hath commanded . . .*—H8 V 1 49. A saying, observation, remark: *Your reasons at dinner have been sharp and sententious*—LLL V 1 2. *Thy words are too precious to be cast away upon curs; throw some of them at me; come, lame me with reasons*—As I 3 4. *Your reasons are too shallow and too quick*—R3 IV 4 361. Talk, discourse: *Feed yourselves with questioning; That reason wonder may diminish*—As V 4 144. *Flesh stays no farther reason*— Sonn 151 8. Reasoning: *She hath prosperous art When she will play with reason and discourse, And well she can persuade*—Meas I 2 189. *My reasonable part produces reason How I may be deliver'd of these woes*—John III 4 54.

(2) Satisfaction, justice; in phrase *to do reason*: [I am] *resolved withal To do myself this reason and this right*—Tit I 278.

(3) Possibility of action or occurrence: *When I look on her perfections, There is no reason but I shall be blind*—Gent II 4 211. *I see no reason but supposed Lucentio Must get a father*—Shr II 409.

(4) App., an assertion (more or less) agreeable to reason: *His reasons are as two grains of wheat hid in two bushels of chaff*—Merch I 1 114.

REASON (vb.)

(1) To talk, discuss, discourse: *I reason'd with a Frenchman yesterday*—Merch II 8 27. *I will not reason what is meant hereby*—R3 I 4 94. *Reason with the fellow . . . where he heard this*—Cor IV 6 51. *I am not very sick, Since I can reason of it*—Cymb IV 2 13. To discuss, bring forward (a matter): *Reason not the need*—Lr II 4 267. *Why is this reason'd?*—V 1 28.

(2) To support, urge (as by reasoning): *This boy . . . Does reason our petition with more strength Than thou hast to deny't*—Cor V 3 174.

REASONABLE

(1) Requiring the use of reason: *Is not your father grown incapable Of reasonable affairs?*—Wint IV 4 407.

(2) *The reasonable shore*, the shore of reason: *Their understanding Begins to swell, and the approaching tide Will shortly fill the reasonable shore*—Tp V 79. *Reasonable swiftness*, speed consistent with due caution: [Let] *all things* [be] *thought upon That may with reasonable swiftness add More feathers to our wings*—H5 I 2 305.

REASONING

Talk: *This reasoning is not in the fashion to choose me a husband*—Merch I 2 22.

REBATE

To blunt, make dull: [One who] *doth rebate and blunt his natural edge With profits of the mind*—Meas I 4 60.

REBECK

An early form of the fiddle, having three strings; as proper name: *What say you, Hugh Rebeck?*—Rom IV 5 135.

REBUKE (sb.)

A check: *Thus ever did rebellion find rebuke*—1 H4 V 5 1. Correction: *For living murmurers There's places of rebuke*—H8 II 2 131.

REBUKE (vb.)

To check, force back, repress: *To rebuke the usurpation Of thy unnatural uncle*—John II 9. *We could have rebuked him at Harfleur*—H5 III 6 128. *Under him My Genius is rebuked*—Mcb III 1 55.

RECEIPT

(1) Reception, accommodation; *such receipt of learning*, the reception of such (men of) learning: *The most convenient place . . . For such receipt of learning is Black-Friars*—H8 II 2 138.

(2) A receptacle: *The receipt of reason* [shall be] *A limbeck only*—Mcb I 7 66.

(3) Capability of receiving, capacity: *In things of great receipt with ease we prove Among a number one is reckon'd none*—Sonn 136 7.

(4) That which is received: *Three parts of that receipt I had for Calais Disbursed I duly*—R2 I 1 126. *The discontented members, the mutinous parts That envied his receipt*—Cor I 1 115. *Drunken Desire must vomit his receipt*—Lucr 703.

RECHEAT

A series of notes sounded on a horn to call the hounds together or at the close of the hunt: *That I will have a recheat winded in my forehead (i.e. on the horns of cuckoldom) . . . all women shall pardon me*—Ado I 1 242.

RECKLESS

Neglectful of duty: *So flies the reckless shepherd from the wolf*—3 H6 V 6 7.

RECKON

To take into consideration, make account of: *Reckoning time, whose milliond accidents Creep in 'twixt vows and change decrees of kings*—Sonn 115 5.

RECKONING

Estimation, repute: *Of honourable reckoning are you both*—Rom I 2 4.

RECLAIM

(1) To restrain, hold back: *Beauty that the tyrant oft reclaims*—2 H6 V 2 54.

(2) Of a hawk, to reduce to obedience, tame; hence of a person: *My heart is wondrous light, Since this same wayward girl is so reclaim'd*—Rom IV 2 46. Of conquests in war: *This arm that hath reclaim'd To your obedience fifty fortresses . . . Beside five hundred prisoners*—1 H6 III 4 5.

RECOGNIZANCE

(1) A bond or obligation for securing a debt: *His statutes, his recognizances, his fines*—Hml V 1 113.

(2) A badge, token: *That recognizance and pledge of love Which I first gave her*—Oth V 2 214.

RECOIL

(1) To degenerate: *A good and virtuous nature may recoil In an imperial charge*—Mcb IV 3 19. *You Recoil from your great stock*—Cymb I 6 127.

(2) To go back in memory: *Methoughts I did recoil Twenty-three years*—Wint I 2 154.

RECOLLECT

(1) To collect, gather: [How] *These fishers . . . from their watery empire recollect All that may men approve or men detect!*—Per II 1 53.

(2) *Recollected terms*, perh., picked, refined: *Recollected terms Of these most brisk and giddy-paced times*—Tw II 4 5.

RECOMFORTED

Inspired with fresh spirit: *Ne'er through an arch so hurried the blown tide, As the recomforted through the gates*—Cor V 4 50.

RECOMFORTURE

Consolation, comfort: *They shall breed Selves of themselves, to your recomforture*—R3 IV 4 424.

RECOMMEND

(1) To give in charge, commit: *Mine own purse, Which I had recommended to his use*—Tw V 93. *We recommend to you, tribunes of the people, Our purpose to them*—Cor II 2 155.

(2) To inform: *Signior Montano . . . With his free duty recommends you thus*—Oth I 3 39.

RECORD (sb.)

(1) A witness: *Heaven be the record to my speech!*—R2 I 1 30.

(2) Remembrance, recollection: *That record is lively in my soul*—Tw V 253.

RECORD (vb.)

(1) To sing, warble: *She sung, and made the night-bird mute, That still records with moan*—Per IV Prol 26. To render in song: *Here can I . . . to the nightingale's complaining notes Tune my distresses and record my woes*—Gent V 4 4.

(2) To bear witness, attest: *How proud I am of thee and of thy gifts Rome shall record*—Tit I 254. To bear witness to (a person): *Let me be*

recorded by the righteous gods, I am as poor as you
—Tim IV 2 4.

RECORDATION

(1) Commemoration: *To rain upon remembrance with mine eyes, That it may grow . . . For recordation to my noble husband*—2 H4 II 3 59.

(2) A recording: *To make a recordation to my soul Of every syllable that here was spoke*—Troil V 2 116.

RECORDER

A wind instrument of the flute kind: *He hath played on his prologue like a child on a recorder*—Mids V 122. *Come, some music! come, the recorders!*—Hml III 2 302.

RECOUNTMENT

A narrative, relation: [When] *Tears our recountments had most kindly bathed*—As IV 3 141.

RECOURSE

(1) A recurring flow: *Their eyes o'ergalled with recourse of tears*—Troil V 3 55.

(2) Access, admission: *That no man hath recourse to her by night*—Gent III 1 112. *I'll give you a pottle of burnt sack to give me recourse to him*—Wiv II 1 222. *That no manner of person At any time have recourse unto the princes*—R3 III 5 108.

RECOVER

(1) To bring back into friendship: *There are ways to recover the general again*—Oth II 3 272.

(2) To obtain, get possession of: *If I cannot recover your niece, I am a foul way out*—Tw II 3 200. *Take you this weapon, Which I have here recover'd from the Moor*—Oth V 2 239.

(3) To reach, gain: *Ere I could recover the shore*—Tp III 2 16. *If we recover that (i.e. the forest), we are sure enough*—Gent V 1 12.

(4) To rescue: *If you will not . . . kill him whom you have recovered (i.e. from the sea)*—Tw II 1 38.

RECOVERABLE

Capable of being retraced: *A prodigal course Is like the sun's; but not, like his, recoverable*—Tim III 4 12.

RECOVERY

See *Fine* (sb.) (3).

RECREATION

A refection, repast: *We will to our recreation (i.e. to dinner)*—LLL IV 2 172.

RECTIFY

To restore to a sound or healthy condition: *I meant to rectify my conscience,—which I then did feel full sick, and yet not well*—H8 II 4 203.

RECTOR

A governor: *Her death itself . . . was faithfully confirmed by the rector of the place*—All's IV 3 67.

RECTORSHIP

Government, rule: *Against the rectorship of judgement*—Cor II 3 213.

RECURE

To cure, remedy: *Which to recure, we heartily solicit Your gracious self to take on you the charge . . . of this your land*—R3 III 7 130. *A smile recures the wounding of a frown*—Ven 465. *Until life's composition be recured*—Sonn 45 9.

RED

(1) Applied to diseases marked by evacuation of blood or cutaneous eruptions: *The red plague rid you!*—Tp I 2 364. *A red murrain o' thy jade's tricks!*—Troil II 1 20. *The red pestilence strike all trades in Rome!*—Cor IV 1 13.

(2) *Red wheat*, a spring (or late sown) variety: Davy. . . . *Shall we sow the headland with wheat?* Shal. *With red wheat, Davy*—2 H4 V 1 15. Cf. *Headland.*

REDE

Counsel: *Himself the primrose path of dalliance treads, And recks not his own rede*—Hml I 3 50.

REDEEM

(1) To go in exchange for: *Would some part of my young years Might but redeem the passage of your age!*—1 H6 II 5 107.

(2) To make up to oneself for, repay: *I will redeem all this on Percy's head*—1 H4 III 2 132.

RE-DELIVER

To report: *Shall I re-deliver you e'en so?*—Hml V 2 186.

RED LATTICE

A window of lattice-work painted red marking an alehouse: *A calls me e'en now, my lord, through a red lattice*—2 H4 II 2 85. Attrib.: *Your red-lattice phrases*—Wiv II 2 28.

REDOUBTED

Redoubtable, dread: *These assume but valour's excrement To render them redoubted!*—Merch III 2 87. *My most redoubted lord*—R2 III 3 198. *My most redoubted father*—H5 II 4 14.

REDRESS (sb.)

Assistance, aid: *I defy all counsel, all redress*—John III 4 23. *The proffer'd means of succour and redress*—R2 III 2 32. *No way canst thou turn thee for redress*—1 H6 IV 2 25. *Then music . . . With speedy help doth lend redress*—Rom IV 5 145. *Past redress*, beyond the possibility of remedy: *Things past redress are now with me past care*—R2 II 3 171.

REDRESS (vb.)

To mend, repair: *Broken glass no cement can redress*—Pilgr 178.

REDUCE

To bring back: *Which to reduce into our former favour You are assembled*— H5 V 2 63. *All springs reduce their currents to mine eyes*—R3 II 2 68. *Traitors . . . That would reduce these bloody days again*—V 5 35.

REECHY

Smoky, dirty, stinking: *Like Pharaoh's soldiers in the reechy painting*— Ado III 3 142. *Her reechy neck*— Cor II 1 225. *A pair of reechy kisses*—Hml III 4 184.

REEK

Of vapour, &c., to be emitted or exhaled, to rise, emanate: *In some perfumes is there more delight Than in the breath that from my mistress reeks*—Sonn 130 7. Fig.: [I] *Saw sighs reek from you*—LLL IV 3 140. *The sun shall . . . draw their honours reeking up to heaven*—H5 IV 3 100.

REEKY

Stinking: *Reeky shanks and yellow chapless skulls*—Rom IV 1 83.

REELING RIPE

See *Ripe*.

REELS

Revels, revelry: *Drink thou; increase the reels*—Ant II 7 100. See also *Up-spring*.

REFEL

To refute, confute: *How he refell'd me, and how I replied*—Meas V 94.

REFER

Refl., to commit or entrust oneself: [She] *hath referr'd herself Unto a poor but worthy gentleman*—Cymb I 1 6. To appeal: *I do refer me to the oracle*—Wint III 2 116. *I'll refer me to all things of sense, If . . .*—Oth I 2 64. To have recourse: *Refer yourself to this advantage*—Meas III 1 255.

REFERENCE

(1) Assignment: *I crave fit disposition for my wife, Due reference of place and exhibition*—Oth I 3 237.

(2) A committing or entrusting oneself: *Make your full reference freely to my lord*—Ant V 2 23.

REFLECT

(1) To shine: *Whose virtues will . . . Reflect on Rome as Titan's rays on earth*—Tit I 225. *Whether it is that she reflects so bright, That dazzleth them*—Lucr 376.

(2) Of a person, to throw or cast (the expression of some feeling *on* another): *Reflect I not on thy baseness court-contempt?*—Wint IV 4 757.

(3) To bestow regard: *To whose kindnesses· l am most infinitely tied. Reflect upon him accordingly*—Cymb I 6 23.

REFLECTION

Shining: *Whence the sun gins his reflection*——Mcb I 2 25. *I have seen small reflection of her wit*—Cymb I 2 33.

REFLEX

To throw or cast (beams): *May never glorious sun reflex his beams Upon the country where you make abode*—1 H6 V 4 87.

REFRAIN

To keep oneself from (an action): *Scarce I can refrain The execution of my big-swoln heart Upon that Clifford*—3 H6 II 2 110.

REFUGE (sb.)

A resource: *Their latest refuge Was to send him*—Cor V 3 11. *Must I be his last refuge?*—Tim III 3 11.

REFUGE (vb.)

To shelter; hence, to comfort: *Silly beggars Who sitting in the stocks refuge their shame, That many have and others must sit there*—R2 V 5 25.

REFUSE

(1) To renounce, disown, cast off: *Refuse me, hate me, torture me to death!*— Ado IV 1 186. *We have had pelting wars, since you refused The Grecians' cause*—Troil IV 5 267. *Deny thy father and refuse thy name*—Rom II 2 34. *In wholesome wisdom He might not but refuse you*—Oth III 1 49.

(2) To decline to meet (an opponent): *No disgrace Shall fall you for refusing him at sea*—Ant III 7 39.

REGARD (sb.)

(1) An object of sight: *Till we make the main and the aerial blue An indistinct regard*—Oth II 1 39.

(2) Perh., intention, purpose: *The king is full of grace and fair regard*—H5 I 1 22. *Our reasons are so full of good regard That were you, Antony, the son of Cæsar, You should be satisfied*—Cæs III 1 224.

(3) Repute, estimation, account: *Virtue is of so little regard in these costermonger times that . . .*—2 H4 I 2 190. *A toy, a thing of no regard*—1 H6 IV 1 145. *What things there are Most abject in regard and dear in use!*—Troil III 3 127. *In one's regard*, in one's estimation: *Your worth is very dear in my regard*—Merch I 1 62. *And that, in my regard, Of the unworthiest siege*—Hml IV 7 76. *Wit's regard*, that which the understanding holds in estimation or approves of: *Where will doth mutiny with wit's regard*—R2 II 1 28.

(4) Consideration, deliberation: *Sad pause and deep regard beseem the sage*—Lucr 277. *They all rate his ill, Which drives the creeping thief to some regard*—304. *The mild glance that sly Ulysses lent Show'd deep regard*—1399.

(5) Care, heed: *Your loss is great, so your regard* (*i.e.* to secure his safety) *should be*—1 H6 IV 5 22.

(6) Something taken into account, a consideration: *Enterprises . . . With this regard their currents turn awry*—Hml III 1 86. *Love's not love When it is mingled with regards that stand Aloof from the entire point*—Lr I 1 241. *On such regards, on such conditions: On such regards of safety and allowance As therein are set down*—Hml II 2 79 (*of safety and allowance* app. = providing for the security of the country and the regulation of the passage of the troops).

(7) *In regard of*, out of consideration for: *I thank my liege, that in regard of me He shortens four years of my son's exile*—R2 I 3 216. On account of, by reason of: *In regard of causes now in hand*—H5 I 1 77. Sim.: *In which regard . . . I must show out a flag and sign of love*—Oth I 1 154. *In regard*, since, inasmuch as: *In regard King Henry gives consent*—1 H6 V 4 124.

REGARD (vb.)

(1) To look to, tend: *Ere we go, regard this dying prince*—1 H6 III 2 86.

(2) With *that*, to consider, take into account: [Not] *regarding that she is my child*—Gent III 1 70.

REGENERATE

Re-born, brought anew into existence: *O thou, the earthly author of my blood, Whose youthful spirit, in me regenerate, Doth . . .*—R2 I 3 69.

REGENT

A ruler, lord: *Dan Cupid, Regent of love-rhymes*—LLL III 182. *Wert thou regent of the world*—R2 II 1 109.

REGIMENT

Rule, sway: [Antony] *gives his potent regiment to a trull*—Ant III 6 95.

REGION

The air, heaven: *Her eyes in heaven Would through the airy region stream so bright That birds would sing*— Rom II 2 20. *Anon the dreadful thunder Doth rend the region*—Hml II 2 508. Attrib.: *The region kites*—Hml II 2 607. *The region cloud*—Sonn 33 12.

REGREET (sb.)

(1) A return of a greeting: [Shall these hands] *Unyoke this seizure and this kind regreet?*—John III 1 241.

(2) In pl., greetings: *From whom he bringeth sensible regreets*—Merch II 9 89.

REGREET (vb.)

(1) To greet again: *Till twice five summers have enrich'd our fields* [you] *Shall not regreet our fair dominions*—R2 I 3 141.

(2) To greet: *I regreet The daintiest last*—R2 I 3 67. [You] *never* [shall] *write, regreet, nor . . .*—186.

REGUERDON (sb.)

Recompense, reward: *In reguerdon of that duty done*—1 H6 III 1 170.

REGUERDON (vb.)

To recompense, reward: *Never have you . . . been reguerdon'd with so much as thanks*—1 H6 III 4 22.

REJOICE

To feel joy on account of: *Which I in sufferance heartily will rejoice*—H5 II 2 159. *Ne'er mother Rejoiced deliverance more*—Cymb V 5 369.

REJOINDURE

Joining, union: *Injury of chance . . . rudely beguiles our lips Of all rejoindure*—Troil IV 4 35.

REJOURN

To adjourn: *And then rejourn the controversy . . . to a second day of audience*—Cor II 1 79.

RELAPSE

Relapse of mortality, perh. a falling into a second state of deadliness: *Abounding valour in our English, That being dead . . . Break out into a second course of mischief, Killing in relapse of mortality*—H5 IV 3 104.

RELATION

(1) *Relations*, the (secret or mystical) relations between things: *Augurs and understood relations have . . . brought forth The secret'st man of blood*—Mcb III 4 124.

(2) *Hath full relation to*, clearly applies to: *The intent and purpose of the law Hath full relation to the penalty*—Merch IV 1 247.

RELATIVE

Positive, definite: *I'll have grounds More relative than this*—Hml II 2 632.

RELENT

(1) To dissolve: *Stone at rain relenteth*—Ven 200. Cf. *He, a marble to her tears, is washed with them, but relents not*—Meas III 1 238.

(2) To give up a previous determination, yield: Fal. . . . *You will not do it, you!* Pist. *I do relent*—Wiv II 2 29. *Relent, sweet Hermia: and, Lysander, yield Thy crazed title*—Mids I 1 91. *Will ye relent, And yield to mercy?*—2 H6 IV 8 11.

RELENTING

Pitiful, compassionate: *As the mournful crocodile With sorrow snares relenting passengers*—2 H6 III 1 226. *Do not steep thy heart In such relenting dew of lamentations*—Lucr 1828.

RELIEF

(1) Entertainment, sport: *Within this limit is relief enough*—Ven 235.

(2) App., deliverance from danger, safety: *Away, for your relief!*—2 H6 V 2 88.

RELIEVE

To lift or raise up: *The shore, that o'er his waveworn basis bow'd, As stooping to relieve him*—Tp II 1 120.

RELIGION

Conscientiousness, fidelity: [I will keep my promise] *with no less religion than if thou wert indeed my Rosalind*—As IV 1 201. *When the devout religion of mine eye Maintains such falsehood, then turn tears to fires!*—Rom I 2 93.

RELIGIOUSLY

Solemnly, ceremoniously: [I] *Do in his (i.e.* the Pope's) *name religiously demand Why . . .*—John III 1 140.

RELINQUISH

To give up as incurable: *To be relinquished of the artists*—All's II 3 10.

RELISH (sb.)

An individual taste or liking: *We have some old crab-trees here at home that will not Be grafted to your relish (i.e.* so as to bear fruit to his taste)—Cor II 1 205.

RELISH (vb.)[1]

(1) To taste (a thing): *Take a taste of my finding him, and relish it with good observance*—As III 2 246.

(2) To feel: *Myself, One of their kind, that relish all as sharply*—Tp V 22.

(3) To appreciate, understand: [If you] *cannot or will not Relish a truth like us*—Wint II 1 166.

(4) To find acceptance: *It would not have relished among my other discredits* — Wint V 2 132.

RELISH (vb.)[2]

To sing, warble: *To relish a love-song, like a robin-redbreast*—Gent II 1 20. *Relish your nimble notes to pleasing ears*—Lucr 1126.

REMAIN (sb.)[1]

That which remains to be done: *All the remain is 'Welcome!'*—Cymb III 1 87.

REMAIN (sb.)[2]

Stay: *Let's fetch him off, or make remain alike (i.e.* share his fate)—Cor I 4 62. *Since my here-remain in England*—Mcb IV 3 148.

REMAIN (vb.)

To have one's abode, dwell: *Vouchsafe my prayer May know if you remain upon this island*—Tp I 2 422. *Where remains he?*—As III 2 235. K. Hen. *Where did you dwell when I was King of England?* Sec. Keep. *Here in this country, where we now remain*—3 H6 III 1 74. *For my mistress, I nothing know where she remains*—Cymb IV 3 13.

REMEDIATE

App., remedial: *Be aidant and remediate In the good man's distress!*—Lr IV 4 17.

REMEMBER

(1) To mention, say: *We will accite, As I before remember'd, all our state*—2 H4 V 2 141. To make mention of: *Thy ignominy sleep with thee in the grave, But not remember'd in thy epitaph!*—1 H4 V 4 100. To commemorate: *The ditty does remember my drown'd father*—Tp I 2 405.

(2) *To be remembered*, to remember, bethink oneself: *You being then, if you be remembered, cracking the stones*—Meas II 1 109. *And, now I am remember'd,* [he] *scorn'd at me*—As III 5 131. *If I had been remember'd*—R3 II 4 23. *Remembered*, prob., remembering: *Thy sting is not so sharp As friend remember'd not*—As II 7 188. So *to remember oneself: Now I remember me, They say . . . he's much distract*—Tw V 286. *I have remember'd me, thou's (i.e.* thou shalt) *hear our counsel*—Rom I 3 9. *Thyself remember,* think of thy sins and make thy peace with heaven: *Thou old unhappy traitor, Briefly thyself remember*—Lr IV 6 232.

(3) To remind: *Let me remember thee what thou hast promised*—Tp I 2 243. *I'll not remember you of my own lord*—Wint III 2 231. *It doth remember me the more of sorrow*—R2 III 4 14. *Thou but rememberest me of mine own conception*—Lr I 4 72.

(4) To recognize (something known before as appearing in something seen now): *I do remember in this shepherd boy Some lively touches of my daughter's favour*—As V 4 26.

REMEMBRANCE

(1) The faculty of remembering: *This lord of weak remembrance*—Tp II 1 232. *Unkind remembrance! thou . . .* [hast] *done me shame (i.e.* in his failure to recognize the Bastard)—John V 6 12.

(2) A memorial inscription: *Tombless, with no remembrance over them*—H5 I 2 229.

(3) A reminder: *I do commit into your hand The unstained sword . . . With this remembrance*—2 H4 V 2 113.

REMISS

Indifferent, unobservant: *He, being remiss, Most generous and free from all contriving, Will not peruse the foils*—Hml IV 7 135.

REMIT

To give up, resign: Prin. . . . *Will you have me, or your pearl again?* Biron. *Neither of either; I remit both twain*—LLL V 2 458.

REMONSTRANCE

Manifestation: [Why I] *would not rather Make rash remonstrance of my hidden power*—Meas V 396.

REMORSE

(1) Pity, relenting, tender feeling: [You] *Expell'd remorse and nature*—Tp V 76. [This shall Change slander to remorse*—Ado IV 1 213. *Thy mercy and remorse*—Merch IV 1 20. *A servant that he bred, thrill'd with remorse, Opposed against the act*—Lr IV 2 73.

(2) *Without remorse*, without intermission: *That ye squeak out your coziers' catches without any mitigation or remorse of voice*—Tw II 3 96.

(3) A solemn obligation: *To obey shall be in me remorse*—Oth III 3 468.

REMORSEFUL

Compassionate, tender-hearted: *Thou art a gentleman . . . Valiant, wise, remorseful*—Gent IV 3 11. *The gaudy, blabbing and remorseful day*—2 H6 IV 1 1. *These eyes, which never shed remorseful tear*—R3 I 2 156.

REMOTION

(1) Remoteness, keeping aloof: *All thy safety were remotion and thy defence absence*—Tim IV 3 345.

(2) A removal, departing: *This remotion of the duke and her Is practice only*—Lr II 4 115.

REMOVE

(1) A removing by death: *Your son gone; and he most violent author Of his own just remove*—Hml IV 5 80 (no doubt meant to be taken by the Queen in sense (3)).

(2) The raising of a siege: *For the remove Bring up your army*—Cor I 2 28.

(3) A removal, departing: *The night before there was no purpose in them Of this remove*—Lr II 4 3. *Our pleasure . . . requires Our quick remove from hence*—Ant I 2 201. A stage in a journey: *Here's a petition from a Florentine, Who hath for four or five removes come short To tender it herself*—All's V 3 130.

(4) A removal or shifting (of a thing): *Change you favours too; so shall your loves Woo contrary, deceived by these removes*—LLL V 2 134. *There a nay is placed without remove*—Pilgr 256.

(5) A period of absence: *In our remove be thou at full ourself*—Meas I 1 44.

REMOVED

(1) Remote, retired, secluded: *I have ever loved the life removed*—Meas I 3 8. *Your accent is something finer than you could purchase in so removed a dwelling*—As III 2 359. *It waves you to a more removed ground*—Hml I 4 61.

(2) Separated by time: [He] *grew a twenty years removed thing While one would wink*—Tw V 92.

(3) *Removed time*, time of absence: *This time removed was summer's time*—Sonn 97 5. *Any soul removed*, a stranger: *To lay so dangerous and dear a trust On any soul removed*—1 H4 IV 1 34.

REMOVEDNESS

One's (doings in) absence: *I have eyes under my service which look upon his removedness*—Wint IV 2 40.

RENDER (sb.)

(1) A surrender: *Mutual render, only me for thee*—Sonn 125 12.

(2) A rendering of an account: *Take No stricter render of me than my all*—Cymb V 4 16.

(3) A statement, confession: *Newness Of Cloten's death . . . may drive us to a render Where we have lived*—Cymb IV 4 9. An acknowledgment of wrong-doing: [The public body] *send forth us, to make their sorrow'd render*—Tim V 1 152.

RENDER (vb.)

(1) To represent as, give out to be: *He did render him the most unnatural That lived amongst men*—As IV 3 123. *The desperate languishings whereof The king is render'd lost*—All's I 3 235.

(2) To declare, state: *Render to me some corporal sign about her*—Cymb II 4 119. *My boon is, that this gentleman may render Of whom he had this ring*—V 5 135.

RENDEZVOUS

(1) A retreat, refuge: *A rendezvous, a home to fly unto*—1 H4 IV 1 57. *News have I, that my Nell is dead . . . And there my rendezvous is quite cut off*—H5 V 1 86.

(2) A last resort or shift: *I will do as I may: that is my rest, that is the rendezvous of it*—H5 II 1 17.

RENEGE

(1) To renounce: *His captain's heart . . . reneges all temper*—Ant I 1 6.

(2) To deny: *Renege, affirm . . . Knowing nought, like dogs, but following*—Lr II 2 84.

RENOWN (sb.)

(1) Reputation (of a specified kind): *A young gentlewoman . . . of a most chaste renown*—All's IV 3 17. *That dignifies the renown of a bawd*—Per IV 6 42. Good name, reputation: *By wounding his belief in her renown*—Cymb V 5 202.

17

(2) Report: *This famous Duke of Milan, Of whom so often I have heard renown*—Tp V 192.

RENOWN (vb.)

To make famous: *The things of fame That do renown this city*—Tw III 3 23. *The blood and courage that renowned them*—H5 I 2 118.

RENT

To rend, tear: *Will you rent our ancient love asunder?*—Mids III 2 215. *In top of rage the lines she rents*—Compl 55.

RENY

To renounce, abjure: *Heart's renying, Causer of this*—Pilgr 251.

REPAIR (sb.)

A going or coming: *A repair i' the dark*—Meas IV 1 43. *All senses to that sense did make their repair*—LLL II 240. *Where slept our scouts . . . That we could hear no news of his repair?*—3 H6 V 1 19. *I will forestal their repair hither*—Hml V 2 228.

REPAIR (vb.)¹

To return: Prin. *Will they return?* Boyet. *They will . . . Therefore change favours; and, when they repair, Blow like sweet roses*—LLL V 2 289. *If I might beseech you, gentlemen, to repair some other hour*—Tim III 4 68.

REPAIR (vb.)²

To revive, recreate (a person): *Repair me with thy presence, Silvia!*—Gent V 4 11. *It much repairs me To talk of your good father*—All's I 2 30.

REPAST

To feed, nourish: *Like the kind life-rendering pelican, [I'll] Repast them with my blood*—Hml IV 5 146.

REPASTURE

A repast, food: *Food for his rage, repasture for his den*—LLL IV 1 95.

REPEAL (sb.)

Recall from banishment, reversal of sentence of banishment: *When she for thy repeal was suppliant*—Gent III 1 234. *If the time thrust forth A cause for thy repeal*—Cor IV 1 40. *Their people Will be as rash in the repeal, as hasty To expel him thence*—IV 7 31. *I sue for exiled majesty's repeal*—Lucr 640. *Freedom of repeal*, an unconditional recall: *Desiring thee that Publius Cimber may Have an immediate freedom of repeal*—Cæs III 1 53.

REPEAL (vb.)

(1) To recall from banishment: *[I] repeal thee home again*—Gent V 4 143. *The banish'd Bolingbroke repeals himself*—R2 II 2 49. *I will*

repeal thee, or, be well assured, Adventure to be banished myself*—2 H6 III 2 349. *Unshout the noise that banish'd Marcius, Repeal him*—Cor V 5 4. Fig.: *This healthful hand, whose banish'd sense Thou hast repeal'd*—All's II 3 54.

(2) To restore to favour: *When false opinion . . . In thy just proof, repeals and reconciles thee*—Lr III 6 119. To try to get (a person) restored to favour: *I'll pour this pestilence into his ear, That she repeals him for her body's lust*—Oth II 3 362.

REPENT

To grieve, regret: *Repent but you that you shall lose your friend, And he repents not that he pays your debt*—Merch IV 1 278. *Let him repent Thou wast not made his daughter*—Ant III 13 134. *[She] repented The evils she hatch'd were not effected*—Cymb V 5 59. To grieve at: *I repent my fault more than my death*—H5 II 2 152.

REPETITION

All repetition, app., all reverting to what is past: *We are reconciled, and the first view shall kill All repetition*—All's V 3 21.

REPINE

Discontent: *Had not his [eyes] clouded with his brow's repine*—Ven 490.

REPINING

Grudging in admission: *What the repining enemy commends, That breath fame blows*—Troil I 3 243.

REPLENISHED

(1) Furnished with what is fitting: *His intellect is not replenished*—LLL IV 2 27.

(2) Full, perfect: *The most replenish'd villain in the world*—Wint II 1 79. *The most replenished sweet work of nature*—R3 IV 3 18.

REPORT (sb.)

(1) Reputation, repute, fame: *A gentlewoman of mine, Who . . . Hath blister'd her report*—Meas II 3 10. *Signior Benedick . . . Goes foremost in report through Italy*—Ado III 1 95. *Report of valour*—Tw III 2 41. *Without any further deed to have them at all into their estimation and report*—Cor II 2 30.

(2) Testimony, commendation: *Much too little of that good I saw Is my report to his great worthiness*—LLL II 62. *Therefore have I slept in your report (i.e.* in commending her)—Sonn 83 5.

(3) App. = reporter, informant: *[I] have my learning from some true reports, That drew their swords with you*—Ant II 2 47.

REPORT (vb.)

To give an account of, describe (a person): *He shall know you better, sir, if I may live to report you*—Meas III 2 171. *If you report him truly*—Cor V 4 27. *Report me and my cause aright To the unsatisfied*—Hml V 2 350. Refl.: *Never saw I figures So likely to report themselves*—Cymb II 4 82.

REPORTINGLY

By report or hearsay: *Others say thou dost deserve, and I Believe it better than reportingly*—Ado III 1 115.

REPOSE

To rely, confide: *Upon whose faith and honour I repose*—Gent IV 3 26. *Lest, reposing too far in his virtue . . . he might . . . fail you*—All's III 6 14. Refl., to settle oneself with confidence *on*: *On thy fortune I repose myself*—3 H6 IV 6 47.

REPRISAL

A prize: *I am on fire To hear this rich reprisal is so nigh And yet not ours*—1 H4 IV 1 117.

REPROACH (sb.)

A verbal insult: *In confutation of which rude reproach . . . I crave the benefit of law of arms*—1 H6 IV 1 98.

REPROACH (vb.)

To bring reproach or discredit upon: *Else imputation . . . might reproach your life*—Meas V 425.

REPROACHFUL

Abusive: *O monstrous! what reproachful words are these?*—Tit I 308. *Not I, till I have . . . Thrust these reproachful speeches down his throat*—II 1 53.

REPROACHFULLY

Shamefully, ignominiously: *And shall I then be used reproachfully?*—2 H6 II 4 97.

REPROOF

(1) App. = punishment: *Those enemies . . . Whom you yourselves shall set out for reproof Fall and no more*—Tim V 4 56.

(2) Refutation, disproof: *In the reproof of this lies the jest*—1 H4 I 2 213. *In reproof of many tales devised*—III 2 23. *A malice, that, giving itself the lie, would pluck reproof and rebuke from every ear*—Cor II 2 36. Overcoming, making of no effect: *In the reproof of chance Lies the true proof of men*—Troil I 3 33.

REPROVE

To refute, disprove: *'Tis so, I cannot reprove it*—Ado II 3 240. *Reprove my allegation, if you can*—2 H6 III 1 40. *What have you urged that I cannot reprove?*—Ven 787.

REPUGN

To resist, withstand: *When stubbornly he did repugn the truth*—1 H6 IV 1 94.

REPUGNANCY

Resistance, opposition: *And let the foes quietly cut their throats, Without repugnancy*—Tim III 5 44.

REPURE

To purify again: *Love's thrice repured nectar*—Troil III 2 23.

REPUTE

To repute of, to think highly of: *Reputing of his high descent*—2 H6 III 1 48.

REQUIRE

To ask for, request: *The satisfaction I would require is likewise your own benefit*—Meas III 1 156. *If he do require our voices, we ought not to deny him*—Cor II 3 1. *In best time We will require her welcome*—Mcb III 4 5. *To lend me arms and aid when I required them*—Ant II 2 88. To ask permission: *He salutes thee, and Requires to live in Egypt*—Ant III 12 11. To ask (a person) to do something; with subordinate clause: *I require your highness, That it shall please you to declare . . . whether . . .*—H8 II 4 144. With ellipse of infinitive: *He will require them, As if he did contemn what he requested*—Cor II 2 160.

REQUIT

Pa. pple. of To requite: *You three . . . Exposed unto the sea, which hath requit it, Him and his innocent child*—Tp III 3 69.

RERE-MOUSE

A bat: *Some war with rere-mice for their leathern wings*—Mids II 2 4.

RESEMBLANCE

A likelihood, probability: *Not a resemblance, but a certainty*—Meas IV 2 203.

RESERVATION

A keeping to oneself: *I . . . beseech your lordship to make some reservation of your wrongs*—All's II 3 259. A keeping for one's own use: *He will'd me In heedfull'st reservation to bestow them*—All's I 3 230.

RESERVE

(1) To keep in one's possession: *She reserves it evermore about her*—Oth III 3 295. *Reserve them for my love, not for their rhyme*—Sonn 32 7.

(2) To guard, preserve: *Kind Rome, that hast thus lovingly reserved The cordial of mine age*—Tit I 165. *No reason I . . . should reserve My crack'd [life] to more care*—Cymb IV 4 48. *Reserve That excellent complexion*—Per IV 1 40.

RESIST

To repel, be distasteful to: *These cates resist me, she but thought upon*—Per II 3 29.

RESOLUTE

A desperado: *A list of lawless resolutes*—Hml I 1 98.

RESOLUTION

Certainty, freedom from doubt: *I would unstate myself, to be in a due resolution*—Lr I 2 108.

RESOLVE

(1) To dissolve, melt; trans.: *The sea's a thief, whose liquid surge resolves The moon into salt tears*—Tim IV 3 442. *His passion . . . Even there resolved my reason into tears*—Compl 295. Intrans.: *Even as a form of wax Resolveth from his figure 'gainst the fire*—John V 4 24.

(2) To dissipate, dispel (fears): *Until our fears, resolved, Be by some certain king purged and deposed*—John II 371.

(3) To free from doubt or perplexity, bring to certainty, satisfy: *This shall absolutely resolve you*—Meas IV 2 225. *I cannot joy, until I be resolved Where our right valiant father is become*—3 H6 II 1 9. *That Antony May . . . be resolved How Cæsar hath deserved to lie in death*—Cæs III 1 130. With *of: Single I'll resolve you . . . of every These happen'd accidents*—Tp V 248. *We would be resolved . . . of some things of weight*—H5 I 2 4. To give a positive answer to: *I am now going to resolve him*—Meas III 1 194. *May it please your highness to resolve me now*—3 H6 III 2 19. *I will resolve your grace immediately*—R3 IV 2 26. *Resolve me whether you will or no*—120. To inform, tell: *These letters will resolve him of my mind*—R3 IV 5 19. *Resolve me . . . which way Thou mightst deserve . . . this usage*—Lr II 4 25. *Resolve your angry father, if . . .*—Per II 5 68. To convince, satisfy: *Long since we were resolved of your truth*—1 H6 III 4 20. *I am resolved That Clifford's manhood lies upon his tongue*—3 H6 II 2 124. *To resolve on,* to be convinced or satisfied of: *Resolve on this, thou shalt be fortunate, If thou receive me for thy warlike mate*—1 H6 I 2 91.

(4) Refl., to make up one's mind: *Resolve thee, Richard*—3 H6 I 1 49. *Resolve yourselves apart*—Mcb III 1 138. *I have myself resolved upon a course*—Ant III 11 9.

(5) *Resolved,* determined upon: *A resolved and honourable war*—John II 585. *Resolved correction*—2 H4 IV 1 213.

RESOLVEDLY

So as to satisfy, clearly: *Of that . . . Resolvedly more leisure shall express*—All's V 3 331.

RESPECT (sb.)

(1) *In respect of,* in comparison with: *[It]'s but a night-gown in respect of yours*—Ado III 4 18. *Hector was but a Troyan in respect of this*—LLL V 2 639. *He does deny him, in respect of his (i.e. of his resources), What charitable men afford to beggars*—Tim III 2 81. *In respect of a fine workman, I am but . . . a cobbler*—Cæs I 1 10. *In respect,* in comparison: *He was a man; this, in respect, a child*—3 H6 V 5 56.

(2) *In respect of,* in view of, because of: *She is not to be kissed fasting, in respect of her breath*—Gent III 1 326. *I could be well contented to be there, in respect of the love I bear your house*—1 H4 II 3 1. *Your lordship may minister the potion of imprisonment to me in respect of poverty*—2 H4 I 2 145.

(3) Relationship, reference; *without respect,* absolutely, independently of circumstances: *Nothing is good, I see, without respect*—Merch V 99.

(4) A consideration: *My respects are better than they seem*—All's II 5 71. *When such profound respects do pull you on*—John III 1 318. *There's the respect That makes calamity of so long life*—Hml III 1 68. *Respects of fortune are his love*—Lr I 1 251.

(5) Rank, station: *Many of the best respect in Rome*—Cæs I 2 59. *Such things else of quality and respect As doth import you*—Oth I 3 283.

(6) Estimation, worth: *I never heard a man of his place . . . so wide of his own respect*—Wiv III 1 57. *A place of high respect with me*—Mids II 1 209. *This ring, Whose high respect and rich validity Did lack a parallel*—All's V 3 191. *Of a good respect,* well spoken of: *Thou art a fellow of a good respect*—Cæs V 5 45.

(7) Consideration, deliberation: *Reason and respect Make livers pale and lustihood deject*—Troil II 2 49. *The icy precepts of respect*—Tim IV 3 258. A considering: *Full of respects, yet nought at all respecting*—Ven 911. *Upon respect,* deliberately: *Dangerous majesty, when perchance it frowns More upon humour than advised respect*—John IV 2 213. *'Tis worse than murder, To do upon respect such violent outrage*—Lr II 4 23.

RESPECT (vb.)

(1) To consider: *Respect your end*—Err IV 4 44. *Full of respects, yet nought at all respecting*—Ven 911.

(2) To consider, look upon *as: She respects me as her only son*—Mids I 1 160.

(3) *Respecting,* considering, bearing in mind: *There is none worthy, Respecting her that's gone*—Wint V 1 34. *Respecting what a rancorous mind he bears*—2 H6 III 1 24. *Whether our daughter were legitimate, Respecting this our marriage with the dowager*—H8 II 4 179.

(4) To esteem, prize, value: *If you respect them, best to take them up*—Gent I 2 134. *What should it be that he respects in her But I can make respective in myself?*—IV 4 199. *Lest thou . . . shouldst . . . six or seven winters more respect Than a perpetual honour*—Meas III 1 75. *That more than all the world I did respect her*—LLL V 2 437.

RESPECTIVE

(1) Careful: *You should have been respective and have kept it*—Merch V 156.

(2) Discriminating: *Away to heaven, respective lenity!*—Rom III 1 128.

(3) Courteous, considerate: *New-made honour doth forget men's names; 'Tis too respective and too sociable*—John I 187.

(4) Worthy of esteem, to be prized: Gent IV 4 200 (quoted under *Respect* (vb.) (4)).

RESPECTIVELY

With becoming respect: *You are very respectively welcome*—Tim III 1 7.

RESPITE

(1) Delay, stay: *Ourself . . . After some respite will return to Calais*—1 H6 IV 1 169.

(2) *This All-Souls' day . . . Is the determined respite of my wrongs*, the day ending the appointed period during which punishment of my evil deeds has been delayed—R3 V 1 18.

RESPONSIVE

Corresponding, suited: *Three of the carriages . . . are . . . very responsive to the hilts*—Hml V 2 158.

REST (sb.)¹

(1) Restored vigour: *The better part of* [our horses] *are full of rest*—1 H4 IV 3 27. *We, lying still, Are full of rest, defence, and nimbleness*—Cæs IV 3 201.

(2) Abiding, stay: [I entreat you] *That you vouchsafe your rest here in our court Some little time*—Hml II 2 13. *In Tarsus was not best Longer for him to make his rest*—Per II Prol 25.

(3) *In rest*, in peaceful possession: *If what in rest you have in right you hold*—John IV 2 55.

REST (sb.)²

At primero, a stake kept in reserve the loss of which ended the game; fig.: *When I cannot live any longer, I will do as I may: that is my rest*—H5 II 1 16. *To set up one's rest*, to stake it; hence, fig., to be resolved or determined, make up one's mind: *He that sets up his rest to do more exploits with his mace than a morris-pike*—Err IV 3 27. *As I have set up my rest to run away*—Merch II 2 110. *Since you set up your rest 'gainst remedy*—All's II 1 138. *The County Paris hath set up his rest, That you shall rest but little*—Rom IV 5 6. To take up one's abode: *Here Will I set up my everlasting rest*—Rom V 3 109. *To set one's rest on*, to stake one's happiness on, make it consist in: *I loved her most, and thought to set my rest On her kind nursery*—Lr I 1 125.

REST (vb.)¹

(1) To remain as a course open to one: *Nought rests for me in this tumultuous strife But . . .*—1 H6 I 3 70. *There rests no other shift but this*—II 1 75. *What then? what rests?*—Hml III 3 64.

(2) To remain as a thing requiring to be done: *Here it rests, that you'll procure the vicar To stay for me*—Wiv IV 6 48. *One thing more rests*—Shr I 1 250. *While you are thus employ'd, what resteth more, But . . .?*—3 H6 I 2 44.

REST (vb.)²

God rest you merry, God give you peaceful continuance in that state, God keep you so: As V 1 65. So [God] *rest you merry*, &c.: *Rest you merry!*—Rom I 2 86. *Rest you fair, good signior*—Merch I 3 60. *Rest you happy!*—Ant I 1 62.

REST (vb.)

Aphetic form of Arrest: *He is rested on the case*—Err IV 2 42. *The man, sir, that, when gentlemen are tired . . . rests them*—IV 3 23. *So much money . . . as I am rested for*—IV 4 2.

RESTING

Remaining stationary: *The northern star, Of whose true-fix'd and resting quality There is no fellow in the firmament*—Cæs III 1 60.

RESTRAIN

(1) To withhold: *That thou restrain'st from me the duty which To a mother's part belongs*—Cor V 3 167. *Restraining aid to Timon*—Tim V 1 151. App. extended to confiscation: *You having lands . . . They would restrain* [them]—R3 V 3 321.

(2) To forbid: *To put metal in restrained means*—Meas II 4 48.

(3) To draw tightly: *A head-stall of sheep's leather which, being restrained to keep him from stumbling, hath been often burst*—Shr III 2 58.

RESTY

Sluggish, indolent: *Resty sloth*—Cymb III 6 34. *Rise, resty Muse*—Sonn 100 9.

RESUME

App., to take (care): [He] *resumes no care Of what is to continue*—Tim II 2 4.

RETENTION

Detention, confinement: *To send the . . . king To some retention and appointed guard*—Lr V 3 46.

RETENTIVE

Confining, restraining: *Must my house Be my retentive enemy, my gaol?*—Tim III 4 81. [Not] *strong links of iron Can be retentive to the strength of spirit*—Cæs I 3 94.

RETIRE (sb.)

(1) Return: [She conjures him] *That to his borrow'd bed he make retire*—Lucr 573.

(2) Retreat in war: *When English measure backward their own ground In faint retire*—John

V 5 3. *Neither foolish in our stands, Nor cowardly in retire*—Cor I 6 2. *Then began A stop i' the chaser, a retire*—Cymb V 3 39. A withdrawing to or from a place: *All his behaviours did make their retire To the court of his eye*—LLL II 234. *With a blessed and unvex'd retire . . . We will bear home that lusty blood again*—John II 253.

RETIRE (vb.)

(1) To return: *He'll say in Troy when he retires, The Grecian dames . . .*—Troil I 3 281. *Back [she] retires to rate the boar for murther*—Ven 906. *One poor retiring minute in an age*—Lucr 962.

(2) To draw back, cause to move back: *The locks . . . Each one by him enforced retires his ward*—Lucr 302.

RETORT

(1) To repay (a loan): *I will retort the sum in equipage*—Wiv II 2 3. (So the first two Quartos).

(2) To throw back upon an adversary: *With one hand beats Cold death aside, and with the other sends It back to Tybalt, whose dexterity Retorts it*—Rom III 1 166.

(3) To radiate (heat which had been imparted): *When his virtues shining upon others Heat them and they retort that heat again*—Troil III 3 100.

(4) To reject: *The duke's unjust, Thus to retort your manifest appeal*—Meas V 302.

RETROGRADE

Contrary, repugnant (*to* something): *It is most retrograde to our desire*—Hml I 2 114.

RETURN (sb.)

An answer: *If my father render fair return, It is against my will*—H5 II 4 127.

RETURN (vb.)

(1) To send back (a person): *Say that Marcius Return me . . . Unheard*—Cor V 1 41. *I returned you an empty messenger*—Tim III 6 40.

(2) To fall *to*: *I would have put my wealth into donation, And the best half should have return'd to him*—Tim III 2 90. *Against the which, a moiety competent Was gaged by our king; which had return'd To the inheritance of Fortinbras, Had he been vanquisher*—Hml I 1 90.

REVERB

To reverberate, re-echo: *Nor are those empty-hearted whose low sound Reverbs no hollowness*—Lr I 1 155.

REVERBERATE

Reverberating, re-echoing: *[I would] Halloo your name to the reverberate hills*—Tw I 5 291.

REVERSE

In fencing, a back-handed stroke or cut: *To see thee pass thy punto, thy stock, thy reverse*—Wiv II 3 26.

REVIEW

To see again: *I shall review Sicilia*—Wint IV 4 679.

REVOKEMENT

Revocation: *That through our intercession this revokement And pardon comes*—H8 I 2 106.

REVOLT (sb.)[1]

A revolter, rebel: *You degenerate, you ingrate revolts*—John V 2 151. *Lead me to the revolts of England here*—V 4 7. *Barbarous and unnatural revolts*—Cymb IV 4 6.

REVOLT (sb.)[2]

Revulsion of appetite: *That suffer surfeit, cloyment and revolt*—Tw II 4 102.

REVOLT (vb.)

To return to one's allegiance: *The king is merciful, if you revolt*—2 H6 IV 2 133.

RHAPSODY

A medley or string (of words): *Such a deed As . . . sweet religion makes A rhapsody of words*—Hml III 4 45.

RHEUM

(1) The watery secretion of the mucous glands or membranes; of tears: *An hour in clamour and a quarter in rheum*—Ado V 2 84. *The north-east wind . . . Awaked the sleeping rheum, and so by chance Did grace our hollow parting with a tear*—R2 I 4 6. Of saliva: *You, that did void your rheum upon my beard*—Merch I 3 118. *The valleys, whose low vassal seat The Alps doth spit and void his rheum upon*—H5 III 5 51. Of discharge from the nose; app. this is meant in Err III 2 131.

(2) *Altering rheums*, prob., changes in the secretions: *Is he not stupid With age and altering rheums?*—Wint IV 4 408.

RHEUMATIC

(1) Suffering from a morbid defluxion of rheum (see above): *Were I hard-favour'd . . . despised, rheumatic and cold*—Ven 133.

(2) Of a disease, characterized by such a defluxion: *Rheumatic diseases do abound*—Mids II 1 105.

(3) Of weather, &c., inducing such defluxions: *In your doublet and hose this raw rheumatic day!*—Wiv III 1 46.

RHEUMY

Equivalent to *Rheumatic* (3): *The rheumy and unpurged air*—Cæs II 1 266.

RIBAUDRED

An unexplained word, no doubt a corruption: *Yon ribaudred nag of Egypt*—Ant III 10 10.

RICHED

Enriched: *All these bounds . . . With shadowy forests and with champains rich'd*—Lr I 1 64.

RID

(1) To remove, take away: *Rid me these villains from your companies*—Tim V 1 104. *Kill me outright with looks and rid my pain*—Sonn 139 14.

(2) To remove by violence, destroy: *The red plague rid you!*—Tp I 2 364. *I am the king's friend, and will rid his foe*—R2 V 4 11. *You have rid this sweet young prince*—3 H6 V 5 67. With double object: *This Gloucester should be quickly rid the world*—2 H6 III 1 233.

(3) To dispatch, get through; *to rid way*, to cover ground, move ahead: *Willingness rids way*—3 H6 V 3 21.

RIDICULOUS

(1) Characterized by laughter: *This spleen ridiculous*—LLL V 2 117.

(2) Derisive, mocking: *The heaving of my lungs provokes me to ridiculous smiling*—LLL III 77.

RIGGISH

Wanton, lewd: *The holy priests Bless her when she is riggish*—Ant II 2 244.

RIGHT (sb.)

(1) *In right of, in the right of*, in support of the claim of, in defence of: *In her right we came*—John II 548. *Accept this scroll . . . Which in the right of Richard Plantagenet We do exhibit*—1 H6 III 1 149. *Slain manfully in arms, In right and service of their noble country*—Tit I 196. So *upon the right of*: *Till she had kindled France . . . Upon the right and party of her son*—John I 33. *This right hand, whose protection Is most divinely vow'd upon the right Of him it holds*—II 236.

(2) *Right for right*, explained as, justice answering to the claims of justice: *Right for right Hath dimm'd your infant morn to aged night*—R3 IV 4 15.

(3) *To do one right*; by combat: *Do me right, or I will protest your cowardice*—Ado V 1 148. By pledging in drinking: *Why, now you have done me right* [To Silence, seeing him take off a bumper—2 H4 V 3 76.

RIGHT (adv.)

Exactly, just: *Here begins his morning story right*—Err V 356. *I will tell you every thing, right as it fell out*—Mids IV 2 31. *'Tis Nestor right*—Troil I 3 170. *Right now*, just now: *Came he right now to sing a raven's note?*—2 H6 III 2 40.

RIGHTEOUSLY

Rightly, in a fitting manner: *If the truth of thy love to me were so righteously tempered as mine is to thee*—As I 2 13.

RIGHT-HAND FILE

The patricians: *Do you two know how you are censured here in the city, I mean of us o' the right-hand file?*—Cor II 1 24.

RIGHTLY

Directly, straight: *.Perspectives, which rightly gazed upon Show nothing but confusion*—R2 II 2 18.

RIGOL

A ring or circle: *About the mourning and congealed face Of that black blood a watery rigol goes*—Lucr 1744. So, a crown: *This is a sleep That from this golden rigol hath divorced So many English kings*—2 H4 IV 5 35.

RIM

Rim [of the belly], the peritoneum: *I will fetch thy rim out at thy throat In drops of crimson blood*—H5 IV 4 15.

RING

Pray God, your voice, like a piece of uncurrent gold, be not cracked within the ring—Hml II 2 447. Referring to a ring surrounding the sovereign's head on coins. If a crack extended further inwards than the ring the coin was not current.

RING-CARRIER

A go-between: Wid. *Marry, hang you!* Mar. *And your courtesy, for a ring-carrier!*—All's III 5 94.

RINGLET

A dance in a ring: *To dance our ringlets to the whistling wind*—Mids II 1 86.

RIPE

In a state in which one may be expected to do something, about to do something; *reeling ripe*: *Trinculo is reeling ripe*—Tp V 279. *Sinking-ripe*: *The sailors . . . left the ship, then sinking-ripe, to us*—Err I 1 77. *Weeping-ripe*: *The king was weeping-ripe for a good word*—LLL V 2 274. *What, weeping-ripe, my Lord Northumberland?*—3 H6 I 4 172.

RIPELY

The time being ripe, urgently: *It fits us therefore ripely Our chariots and our horsemen be in readiness*—Cymb III 5 22.

RIVAGE

A shore, coast: *Do but think You stand upon the rivage*—H5 III Chor 13.

RIVAL

A partner, comrade: *If you do meet Horatio and Marcellus, The rivals of my watch, bid them make haste*—Hml I 1 12. The word (in the second occurrence) may be taken in this sense in *You both are rivals, and love Hermia; And now both rivals, to mock Helena*—Mids III 2 155.

RIVALITY

Partnership: *Cæsar . . . presently denied him rivality*—Ant III 5 7.

RIVE

Of cannon, app., to discharge them crammed to the bursting point: *To rive their dangerous artillery Upon . . . Talbot*—1 H6 IV 2 29.

RIVELLED

Wrinkled: *The rivelled fee-simple of the tetter*—Troil V 1 26.

RIVO

A Bacchanalian exclamation of uncertain origin and meaning: *'Rivo!' says the drunkard*—1 H4 II 4 124.

ROAD

(1) A spell of riding, journey: *At last, with easy roads, he came to Leicester*—H8 IV 2 17.

(2) An inroad, incursion: *The Scot, who will make road upon us With all advantages*—H5 I 2 138. *Ready, when time shall prompt them, to make road Upon's again*—Cor III 1 5.

ROARER

A blustering bully; applied to waves: *What cares these roarers for the name of king?*—Tp I 1 17.

ROB

(1) To steal, carry off: *When's god's asleep, he'll rob his bottle*—Tp II 2 155. *To fashion a carriage to rob love from any*—Ado I 3 30. *The jewel of life . . . was robb'd and ta'en away*—John V 1 40.

(2) To cut off (*from* something): *Thy sentence . . . Which robs my tongue from breathing native breath*—R2 I 3 172

ROGUE

A vagrant or vagabond: *Having flown over many knavish professions, he settled only in rogue*—Wint IV 3 105. *To hovel thee with swine, and rogues forlorn*—Lr IV 7 39.

ROGUING

Vagrant: *These roguing thieves serve the great pirate Valdes*—Per IV 1 97.

ROGUISH

Characteristic of a vagrant: *Let's . . . get the Bedlam . . . his roguish madness Allows itself to any thing*—Lr III 7 103.

ROISTING

Roistering: *I have a roisting challenge sent*—Troil II 2 208.

ROMAGE

Rummage; a bustle, turmoil: *This post-haste and romage in the land*—Hml I 1 107.

RONDURE

A round, circle: *All things rare That heaven's air in this huge rondure hems*—Sonn 21 7.

RONYON

A mangy creature: *You polecat, you ronyon!*—Wiv IV 2 194. *'Aroint thee, witch!' the rump-fed ronyon cries*—Mcb I 3 6.

ROOK

Refl., to crouch, cower: *The raven rook'd her on the chimney's top*—3 H6 V 6 47.

ROOKY

Full of rooks; or perh., misty, foggy (rook, roke = mist, fog): *The crow Makes wing to the rooky wood*—Mcb III 2 50.

ROOM

A particular place assigned to a person: *Go thou, and fill another room in hell*—R2 V 5 108.

ROPERY

Knavish waggery: *What saucy merchant was this, that was so full of his ropery?*—Rom II 4 153.

ROPE-TRICK

Perh. a punning or illiterate distortion of Rhetoric: *An he begin once, he'll rail in his rope-tricks*—Shr I 2 112.

ROPING

Forming filaments: *Like roping icicles Upon our houses' thatch*—H5 III 5 23.

ROTE

To learn by rote: *Such words that are but roted in Your tongue*—Cor III 2 55.

ROTHER

An ox: *It is the pasture lards the rother's sides*—Tim IV 3 12.

ROUND (adj.)

(1) Plain, straightforward: *I will a round unvarnish'd tale deliver*—Oth I 3 90.

(2) Perh., circling in the due paths: *In our orbs we'll live so round and safe*—Per I 2 122.

ROUND (vb.)[1]

We are such stuff As dreams are made on, and our little life Is rounded with a sleep—Tp IV 156, like dreams we exist only in the mind of a (higher) being; our life is rounded off by, begins and ends with, a phase of that mind typified as sleep.

ROUND (vb.)[2]

To whisper: *Whispering, rounding ' Sicilia is a so-forth '*—Wint I 2 217. To address in a whisper: *Rounded in the ear With that same purpose-changer*—John II 566. *She will not stick to round me i' the ear, To teach my tongue to be so long*—Pilgr 349.

ROUND (adv.)

Openly, in a straightforward manner: *I went round to work*—Hml II 2 139.

ROUNDEL

A dance in a circle: *Come, now a roundel and a fairy song*—Mids II 2 1.

ROUNDLY

Fluently, glibly: *This tongue that runs so roundly in thy head*—R2 II 1 122.

ROUNDURE

A round, circle: *The roundure of your old-faced walls*—John II 259.

ROUSE (sb.)

(1) A bumper: *They have given me a rouse already*—Oth II 3 66.

(2) A revel, intemperate mirth: *The king's rouse the heavens shall bruit again*—Hml I 2 127. *The king doth wake to-night and takes his rouse*—I 4 8. *There o'ertook in's rouse*—II 1 58.

ROUSE (vb.)

(1) To raise, make erect: *Being mounted and both roused in their seats*—2 H4 IV 1 118. Refl.: *Here . . . He rouseth up himself and makes a pause*—Lucr 540.

(2) To rouse oneself: *Whiles night's black agents to their preys do rouse*—Mcb III 2 53. To become erect, stand up: *My fell of hair Would at a dismal treatise rouse and stir*—Mcb V 5 11.

ROUT

An uproar, tumult: *Give me to know How this foul rout began, who set it on*—Oth II 3 209.

ROW

A line or verse: *The first row of the pious chanson will show you more*—Hml II 2 438.

ROYAL

A gold coin = 10*s.*; referred to: Groom. *Hail, royal prince!* K. Rich. *Thanks, noble peer; The cheapest of us is ten groats too dear*—R2 V 5 67 (with a play on the Noble (see *Noble* (2)). *Thou camest not of the blood royal, if thou darest not stand for ten shillings*—1 H4 I 2 156. Host. . . . *There is a nobleman of the court at door . . .*

Prince. *Give him as much as will make him a royal man*—II 4 317 (with a play as in the first quotation). See also 2 H4 I 2 23.

ROYALTIES

The property and privileges belonging to a member of the royal house: *Seek you to seize . . . The royalties and rights of banish'd Hereford?*—R2 II 1 189. *My rights and royalties Pluck'd from my arms perforce and given away*—II 3 120. *His coming hither hath no further scope Than for his lineal royalties*—III 3 112.

ROYNISH

Scurvy, mangy: *The roynish clown . . . is also missing*—As II 2 8. Explained also as, obtrusive, troublesome.

RUB (sb.)

In bowling, the deflection of a running bowl from its course: Lady. *Madam, we'll play at bowls.* Queen. *'Twill make me think the world is full of rubs*—R2 III 4 3 (with a reference to the derived sense). Hence, an impediment, hindrance: *Shall blow each dust, each straw, each little rub, Out of the path*—John III 4 128. *Every rub is smoothed on our way*—H5 II 2 188. *This so dishonour'd rub, laid falsely I' the plain way of his merit*—Cor III 1 60. A roughness, unevenness: *To leave no rubs nor botches in the work*—Mcb III 1 134.

RUB (vb.)

In bowling, of a running bowl, to be deflected from its course: Cost. . . . *Challenge her to bowl.* Boyet. *I fear too much rubbing*—LLL IV 1 140. *Rub on*, app., go ahead, obstacles and all: *Rub on, and kiss the mistress*—Troil III 2 52. Hence, to hinder, cross: *Whose disposition . . . Will not be rubb'd nor stopp'd*—Lr II 2 160.

RUBIOUS

Ruby-red: *Diana's lip Is not more smooth and rubious*—Tw I 4 31.

RUDDOCK

The robin-redbreast: *The ruddock would, With charitable bill . . . bring thee all this*—Cymb IV 2 224.

RUDESBY

A rude, blustering fellow: *A mad-brain rudesby full of spleen*—Shr III 2 10. *Rudesby, be gone!*—Tw IV 1 55.

RUE

To pity: *In thy closet pent up, rue my shame*—2 H6 II 4 24. *Rue the tears I shed*—Tit I 105.

RUFF

The top of a boot turned over and hanging loosely down: *He will look upon his boot and sing; mend the ruff and sing*—All's III 2 6.

RUFFLE (sb.)

Stir, bustle: *A blusterer, that the ruffle knew Of court, of city*—Compl 58.

RUFFLE (vb.)

To swagger, play the bully: *One fit . . . To ruffle in the commonwealth of Rome*—Tit I 312. Of winds, to be boisterous: *The bleak winds Do sorely ruffle*—Lr II 4 303. *Ruffling*, of clothes, fluttering; or perh., rustling: *The tailor stays thy leisure, To deck thy body with his ruffling treasure* —Shr IV 3 59.

RUINATE

To ruin, subvert: *I will not ruinate my father's house*—3 H6 V 1 83. *To order well the state, That like events may ne'er it ruinate*—Tit V 3 203. *To ruinate proud buildings with thy hours* —Lucr 944.

RUINOUS

Of a person, ruined, decayed: *Is yond despised and ruinous man my lord?*—Tim IV 3 465.

RULE

Course of proceeding, conduct: *Of a strange nature is the suit you follow; Yet in such rule that the Venetian law Cannot impugn you as you do proceed*—Merch IV 1 177. *You would not give means for this uncivil rule*—Tw II 3 131.

RUMOUR

(1) A confused noise, din: *Bear me hence From forth the noise and rumour of the field*—John V 4 44. *I heard a bustling rumour, like a fray*—Cæs II 4 18.

(2) Fame, reputation: *Great is the rumour of this dreadful knight*—1 H6 II 3 7.

RUMOURER

A spreader of reports: *Go see this rumourer whipp'd*—Cor IV 6 47.

RUMP-FED

Variously explained as, fed on offal; fed on the best joints; fat-rumped: *'Aroint thee, witch!' the rump-fed ronyon cries*—Mcb I 3 6.

RUNAGATE

(1) A renegade, apostate: *White-liver'd runagate, what doth he there?*—R3 IV 4 465 (or perh. sense (2) is meant). *More noble than that runagate to your bed*—Cymb I 6 137.

(2) A vagabond, fugitive: *In Mantua, Where that same banish'd runagate doth live*—Rom III 5 89. *I cannot find those runagates*—Cymb IV 2 62.

RUNAWAY

Spread thy close curtain, love-performing night, That runaways' (or *runaway's*) *eyes may wink*— Rom III 2 5. A much disputed word, probably corrupt. It has been (quite unsatisfactorily) explained as meaning Fame or Rumour, night, day, Cupid (cf. *Winking Cupids*—Cymb II 4 89), busy-bodies, &c.

RURAL

Rustic: *Here is a rural fellow*—Ant V 2 233.

RUSH (sb.)

A rush ring: [As fit] as *Tib's rush for Tom's forefinger*—All's II 2 24.

RUSH (vb.)

To rush aside, to thrust aside: *The kind prince, Taking thy part, hath rush'd aside the law*—Rom III 3 25.

RUSSET

Gray or ash-colour; *russet-pated*: *Russet-pated choughs*—Mids III 2 21.

RUTH

Pity: *The venom'd vengeance . . . Spur them to ruthful work, rein them from ruth*—Troil V 3 47. *Would the nobility lay aside their ruth, And let me use my sword*—Cor I 1 201. *Looking with pretty ruth upon my pain*—Sonn 132 4.

RUTHFUL

Piteous, pitiable: *O that my death would stay these ruthful deeds!*—3 H6 II 5 95. Troil V 3 48 (quoted under *Ruth*). *Villanies Ruthful to hear* —Tit V 1 65.

S

SABA

The Queen of Sheba: *Saba was never More covetous of wisdom*—H8 V 5 24.

SABLES

Nay then, let the devil wear black, for I'll have a suit of sables—Hml III 2 137. Prob., a robe richly trimmed with sable fur (as in IV 7 81 (*Settled age* [becomes] *his sables and his weeds*)) as opposed to a mourning habit. *Sable* is explained also as a material of a cream colour (Fr. *Isabelle*).

SACK

The name given to various white wines imported from Spain and the Canaries: *A pottle of burnt sack*—Wiv II 1 221. *Will't please your lordship drink a cup of sack?*—Shr Ind 2 2. *Unless hours were cups of sack and minutes capons*

—1 H4 I 2 7. *I'll steep this letter in sack and make him eat it*—2 H4 II 2 147. See also *Sherris.*

SACKBUT

A wind instrument resembling the trombone: *Trumpets, sackbuts, psalteries and fifes*—Cor V 4 52.

SACKERSON

A celebrated bear kept at Paris-garden: *I have seen Sackerson loose twenty times*—Wiv I 1 307.

SACRAMENT

To take the sacrament, to receive Communion as a confirmation of one's word: [That we] *May know wherefore we took the sacrament And keep our faiths firm and inviolable*—John V 2 6. *You shall . . . take the sacrament To bury mine intents*—R2 IV 328. *Ten thousand French have ta'en the sacrament To* [slay Talbot]—1 H6 IV 2 28. So *to receive the sacrament*: *Thou didst receive the holy sacrament, To fight in quarrel of the house of Lancaster*—R3 I 4 208.

SACRED

Accursed, damned (jocularly): *Our empress, with her sacred wit*—Tit II 1 120.

SACRING BELL

The bell rung at Mass at the elevation of the Host; in post-Reformation times also a bell rung to summon to morning prayer; in the quotation following probably the latter, in spite of the anachronism: *I'll startle you Worse than the sacring bell, when the brown wench Lay kissing in your arms*—H8 III 2 294.

SAD

(1) Serious, grave; of persons: Bene. *Gallants, I am not as I have been.* Leon. *So say I: methinks you are sadder*—Ado III 2 15. *Where is Malvolio? he is sad and civil*—Tw III 4 5. *The sad and solemn priests*—H5 IV 1 318. Of discourse, bearing, &c.: *What sad talk was that Wherewith my brother held you in the cloister?*—Gent I 3 1. *Speak you this with a sad brow?*—Ado I 1 185. *Like one well studied in a sad ostent To please his grandam*—Merch II 2 205. *I sent for thee upon a sad occasion*—Tw III 4 20. *My father and the gentlemen are in sad talk*—Wint IV 4 316.

(2) Morose, gloomy: *That sad dog That brings me food*—R2 V 5 70.

SAD-EYED

Grave in aspect: *The sad-eyed justice*—H5 I 2 202.

SADLY

Seriously: *This can be no trick: the conference was sadly borne*—Ado II 3 228. *But sadly tell me who*—Rom I 1 207.

SADNESS

Seriousness: *This merry inclination Accords not with the sadness of my suit*—3 H6 III 2 76. *In sadness, in good sadness,* seriously: *Tell me in sadness, who is that you love*—Rom I 1 205. *In good sadness, sir, I am sorry that for my sake you have suffered all this*—Wiv III 5 125. *In good sadness, I do not know*—All's IV 3 230.

SAFE (adj.)

(1) Mentally or morally sound or sane: *Nor do I think the man of safe discretion That does affect it*—Meas I 1 72. *On a safer judgement all revoke Your ignorant election*—Cor II 3 226. *The safer sense will ne'er accommodate His master thus*—Lr IV 6 81. *Are his wits safe?*—Oth IV 1 280. Sim.: *In all safe reason He must have some attendants*—Cymb IV 2 131. This seems to be the meaning in Per I 2 122 (*In our orbs we'll live so round and safe*).

(2) *Your safest haste,* the haste which is your best safety, the sooner the better for you: *Mistress, dispatch you with your safest haste*—As I 3 42.

SAFE (vb.)

To take away from a thing any appearance of its involving dangerous consequences: *That which most with you should safe my going, Is Fulvia's death*—Ant I 3 55. To conduct to safety, safeguard: *Best you safed the bringer Out of the host*—Ant IV 6 26.

SAFETY

(1) Safe-keeping, custody: *Deliver him to safety*—John IV 2 158. *Hold him in safety, till the prince come hither*—Rom V 3 183.

(2) A means of safety: *Let not my jealousies be your dishonours, But mine own safeties*—Mcb IV 3 29.

SAFFRON

A snipt-taffeta fellow there, whose villanous saffron would have made all the . . . youth of a nation in his colour—All's IV 5 1. Alluding to a fashion of wearing ruffs, &c., stiffened with yellow starch.

SAGITTARY

(1) A centaur-bowman mentioned by Lydgate and others as fighting for the Trojans: *The dreadful Sagittary Appals our numbers*—Troil V 5 14.

(2) An inn with this centaur or the centaur of the zodiac as a sign: *Lead to the Sagittary the raised search*—Oth I 1 159. *Send for the lady to the Sagittary*—I 3 115.

SAID

Well said, well done: *Now, masters, draw.* [They shoot.] *O, well said, Lucius!*—Tit IV 3 63. [A chair brought in.] *O, that's well said; the chair*—Oth V 1 98. *Come, give me that: this way; well said*—Ant IV 4 28.

SAIN

Pa. pple. of To say: [A] *discourse, to make plain Some obscure precedence that hath tofore been sain* —LLL III 82.

SAINT

To live a saintly life: *Think women still to strive with men, To sin and never for to saint*— Pilgr 341.

SALE-WORK

Ready-made goods: *I see no more in you than in the ordinary Of nature's sale-work*—As III 5 42.

SALLET¹

Salad: *To see if I can . . . pick a sallet*—2 H6 IV 10 8. [Poor Tom that] *eats cow-dung for sallets*—Lr III 4 137. Fig.: *One said there were no sallets in the lines to make the matter savoury*— Hml II 2 462.

SALLET²

A light globular headpiece: *Many a time, but for a sallet, my brain-pan had been cleft*—2 H6 IV 10 12.

SALT¹

Lewd, lecherous: *Whose salt imagination yet hath wrong'd Your well defended honour*—Meas V 406. *His salt and most hidden loose affection*— Oth II 1 244. *As salt as wolves in pride*—III 3 404. *Salt Cleopatra*—Ant II 1 21.

SALT²

Pungent, stinging: *The pride and salt scorn of his eyes*—Troil I 3 371.

SALUTATION

Excitement, quickening: *Why should others' false adulterate eyes Give salutation to my sportive blood?*—Sonn 121 5.

SALUTE

(1) To pay one's respects to: *Don Alphonso . . . [is] journeying to salute the emperor*—Gent I 3 39. *If the prince do live, let us salute him*—Per II 4 27.

(2) To excite, affect: *Would I had no being, If this salute my blood a jot*—H8 II 3 102.

SALVE

To remedy, make good: *You may salve so . . . the loss Of what is past*—Cor III 2 70. To palliate, soften down: *I would have salved it with a longer treatise*—Ado I 1 317. *Salving thy amiss, Excusing thy sins*—Sonn 35 7.

SAMINGO

San (Saint) Domingo, app. looked upon as the patron of topers: *Do me right, And dub me knight: Samingo*—2 H4 V 3 77.

SAMPHIRE

Sea-fennel, a plant growing on sea-cliffs, used in pickles: *Half way down* [the cliff] *Hangs one that gathers samphire*—Lr IV 6 14.

SAMPLE

An example, pattern: *A sample to the youngest* —Cymb I 1 48.

SANCTIMONIOUS

Holy, sacred: *Before All sanctimonious ceremonies may With full and holy rite be minister'd* —Tp IV 15.

SANCTIMONY

Piety, holiness: *Which holy undertaking with most austere sanctimony she accomplished*—All's IV 3 58. *If sanctimony be the gods' delight*—Troil V 2 140. A sacred thing: *If vows be sanctimonies* —Troil V 2 139.

SANCTUARIZE

To shelter as a sanctuary does: *No place, indeed, should murder sanctuarize*—Hml IV 7 128.

SANDAL SHOON

Sandals: *By his cockle hat and staff, And his sandal shoon*—Hml IV 5 25. Cf. *Shoon*.

SAND-BLIND

Purblind, dim-sighted: *This is my true-begotten father! who, being more than sand-blind . . . knows me not*—Merch II 2 36. *I am sand-blind; I know you not*—77.

SANDED

Of a sandy colour: *My hounds are bred out of the Spartan kind, So flew'd, so sanded*—Mids IV 1 123.

SANGUINE

Prob., red-faced: *This sanguine coward, this bed-presser*—1 H4 II 4 268. Prob., pink-skinned as opposed to black: *Ye sanguine, shallow-hearted boys! Ye white-limed walls!*—Tit IV 2 97 (contrasting them with the black infant).

SANS

Without: *A confidence sans bound*—Tp I 2 97. *Sans intermission*—As II 7 32. *Sans check*— Troil I 3 94. *Ears without hands or eyes, smelling sans all*—Hml III 4 79.

SAP

A fluid of any kind: *If with the sap of reason you would quench, Or but allay, the fire of passion* —H8 I 1 148.

SARUM

Salisbury: *If I had you upon Sarum plain*— Lr II 2 89.

SATIRE

A satirist: *Be a satire to decay, And make Time's spoils despised every where*—Sonn 100 11.

SAUCY

Wanton, prurient: *O strange men! That can such sweet use make of what they hate, When saucy trusting of the cozen'd thoughts Defiles the pitchy night*—All's IV 4 21.

SAVAGERY

Wild growth: *The coulter rusts That should deracinate such savagery*—H5 V 2 46.

SAVOUR

To relish, take pleasure in: *Filths savour but themselves*—Lr IV 2 39.

SAVOY

Now go some and pull down the Savoy—2 H6 IV 7 1. A house or palace in the Strand built in 1245 by Peter, Earl of Savoy and Richmond, and destroyed by Wat Tyler in 1381. It was rebuilt by Henry VII for a hospital. The hospital was dissolved in 1702, and the buildings were gradually swept away. The (restored) chapel remains.

SAWN

Pa. pple. of To sow: *On his visage was in little drawn What largeness thinks in Paradise was sawn*—Compl 90.

SAY (sb.)[1]

A kind of serge: *Thou say, thou serge, nay, thou buckram lord!*—2 H6 IV 7 27.

SAY (sb.)[2]

A taste, flavour: *Thy tongue some say of breeding breathes*—Lr V 3 143.

SAY (vb.)

Assay; to try: *Of all say'd yet, mayst thou prove prosperous! Of all say'd yet, I wish thee happiness!*—Per I 1 59.

'SBLOOD

[By] God's blood: *'Sblood, I am as melancholy as a gib cat*—1 H4 I 2 82. *'Sblood, there is something in this more than natural*—Hml II 2 384. *'Sblood, but you will not hear me*—Oth I 1 4.

SCALD (adj.), SCAULD

Scabby, scurvy: *The rascally, scauld, beggarly ... knave*—H5 V 1 5. *Scald rhymers* [will] *Ballad us out o' tune*—Ant V 2 215.

SCALD (vb.)

(1) To burn (of other agents than water): *A rich armour worn in heat of day, That scalds with safety*—2 H4 IV 5 30. *Summer's scalding heat*—3 H6 V 7 18.

(2) In Tim II 2 71 (*She's e'en setting on water to scald such chickens as you are. Would we could see you at Corinth!*) there is an allusion to the treatment mentioned under *Tub*.

SCALED

Weighed, measured; or perh., deprived of scales, and so, exposed: *By this is . . . the poor Mariana advantaged, and the corrupt deputy scaled*—Meas III 1 263.

SCAMBLE

To scramble, struggle: *England now is left To tug and scamble*—John IV 3 145. *The scambling and unquiet time*—H5 I 1 4. *I get thee with scambling*—V 2 217. *Scambling*, perh., pushing: *Scambling, out-facing, fashion-monging boys*—Ado V 1 94.

SCAMEL

Sometimes I'll get thee Young scamels from the rock—Tp II 2 175. A doubtful word; explained as a limpet, and also as a species of bird, the bar-tailed godwit.

SCANDAL

To defame, throw scandal upon: [You] *Scandal'd the suppliants for the people*—Cor III 1 44. *That I do fawn on men . . . And after scandal them*—Cæs I 2 75. *Sinon's weeping Did scandal many a holy tear*—Cymb III 4 61.

SCANDALED

Scandalous, disgraceful: *Her blind boy's scandal'd company*—Tp IV 90.

SCANDALIZED

Disgraced, infamous: *It will make me scandalized*—Gent II 7 61. [We] *Live scandalized and foully spoken of*—1 H4 I 3 154.

SCANDALOUS

Disgraced, infamous: [It] *will ignoble make you, Yea, scandalous to the world*—Wint II 3 120.

SCANT

Scarcely, hardly: *She shall scant show well that now shows best*—Rom I 2 104.

SCANTLING

A pattern, sample: *The success, Although particular, shall give a scantling Of good or bad unto the general*—Troil I 3 340.

SCANTLY

Grudgingly: *Spoke scantly of me*—Ant III 4 6.

SCAPE

An escapade, misdemeanour: *I can read waiting-gentlewoman in the scape*—Wint III 3 73. *Day . . . night's scapes doth open lay*—Lucr 747.

SCATTERED

Divided, disunited: *From France there comes a power Into this scatter'd kingdom*—Lr III 1 30.

SCHEDULE

A paper, note: *The portrait of a blinking idiot, Presenting me a schedule!*—Merch II 9 54. *Take . . . this schedule, For this contains our general grievances*—2 H4 IV 1 168. *Hail, Cæsar! read this schedule*—Cæs III 1 3. *By this short schedule (i.e. her letter) Collatine may know Her grief*—Lucr 1312.

SCHOOL

(1) A university: *Your (i.e. Hamlet's) intent In going back to school in Wittenberg*—Hml I 2 112. No doubt also in As I 1 5 (*My brother Jaques he keeps at school*).

(2) Learning: *Wisdom's warrant and the help of school*—LLL V 2 71.

SCONCE (sb.)

(1) A fort: *Sconce call you it? so you would leave battering, I had rather have it a head*—Err II 2 35. *Where services were done; at such and such a sconce*—H5 III 6 75.

(2) A covering for the head, a helmet: *I must get a sconce for my head*—Err II 2 37.

SCONCE (vb.)

Refl., to ensconce, conceal oneself: *I'll sconce me even here*—Hml III 4 4.

SCOPE

(1) An aim, purpose: *His coming hither hath no further scope Than for his lineal royalties*—R2 III 3 112.

(2) A wide range of action; and so, an aberration: *Every scope by the immoderate use Turns to restraint*—Meas I 2 131. *No scope of nature, no distemper'd day*—John III 4 154. *To scope*, so as to show a wide range (of imagination): *'Tis conceived to scope*—Tim I 1 72.

SCORE

Perh., to set a mark of disgrace on, brand: *Have you scored me?*—Oth IV 1 130.

SCORN (sb.)

(1) A mock, scoff: *If sickly ears . . . Will hear your idle scorns*—LLL V 2 873. *Some are yet ungotten and unborn That shall have cause to curse the Dauphin's scorn (i.e. the sending of the tennis-balls)*—H5 I 2 287. *After many scorns, many foul taunts*—3 H6 II 1 64. *The fleers, the gibes, and notable scorns, That dwell in every region of his face*—Oth IV 1 83.

(2) Mockery, derision: [*That a man*] *will, after he hath laughed at such shallow follies in others, become the argument of his own scorn*—Ado II 3 10. *They may jest Till their own scorn return*

to them unnoted—All's I 2 33. *Good beauties, let me sustain no scorn*—Tw I 5 186. *Here's thy hand, in scorn to thee sent back*—Tit III 1 238.

(3) An object of derision: *To make a loathsome abject scorn of me*—Err IV 4 106. *These oaths and laws will prove an idle scorn*—LLL I 1 311. *Thou comest not to be made a scorn in Rome*—Tit I 265. *To become the geck and scorn O' th' other's villany*—Cymb V 4 67.

(4) *To take, think scorn*, to disdain: *Your majesty takes no scorn to wear the leek*—H5 IV 7 106. *I think scorn to sigh*—LLL I 2 66.

SCORN (vb.)

(1) To mock, deride: *Did not her kitchen-maid rail, taunt and scorn me?*—Err IV 4 77. *To join with men in scorning your poor friend*—Mids III 2 216. [*He hath*] *laughed at my losses, mocked at my gains, scorned my nation*—Merch III 1 57. *To taunt and scorn you thus opprobriously*—R3 III 1 153.

(2) To scoff or jeer *at*: *And, now I am remember'd*, [*he*] *scorn'd at me*—As III 5 131. *Why scorn'st thou at sir Robert?*—John I 228. *To fleer and scorn at our solemnity*—Rom I 5 59.

SCORNFUL

(1) Mocking, derisive: *Sing a scornful rhyme*—Wiv V 5 95. *Scornful Lysander!*—Mids I 1 95. *Shall's have a play of this? Thou scornful page, There lie thy part*—Cymb V 5 228.

(2) Provoking scorn or contempt: *Thy surviving husband shall remain The scornful mark of every open eye*—Lucr 519.

SCRIMER

A fencer: *The scrimers of their nation*—Hml IV 7 101.

SCRIPPAGE

The contents of a scrip: *Though not with bag and baggage, yet with scrip and scrippage*—As III 2 170.

SCRIPTURE

A writing; of a letter (with a play): *What is here? The scriptures of the loyal Leonatus, All turn'd to heresy?*—Cymb III 4 82.

SCROWL

Perh. a misprint for scrawl: *See, how with signs and tokens she can scrowl*—Tit II 4 5.

SCROYLE

A scrofulous fellow, wretch: *These scroyles of Angiers flout you, kings*—John II 373.

SCRUBBED

Scrubby, stunted: *A kind of boy, a little scrubbed boy*—Merch V 162. *That same scrubbed boy, the doctor's clerk*—261.

SCRUPULOUS

Perh., standing on and disputing about trifles: *Equality of two domestic powers Breed scrupulous faction*—Ant I 3 47.

SCULL

A school or shoal of fish: *Like scaled sculls Before the belching whale*—Troil V 5 22.

'SDEATH

[By] God's death: *'Sdeath! The rabble should have first unroof'd the city, Ere so prevail'd with me*—Cor I 1 221.

SEA-COAL

Pit-coal as distinguished from charcoal, so called because it was brought by sea: *At the latter end of a sea-coal fire*—Wiv I 4 9. *Sitting . . . by a sea-coal fire*—2 H4 II 1 94.

SEALED QUARTS

Quart-measures officially stamped as holding the proper quantity: *Because she brought stone jugs and no seal'd quarts*—Shr Ind 2 90.

SEA-LIKE

In sea-going trim: *Our sever'd navy . . . fleet, threatening most sea-like*—Ant III 13 170.

SEAM

Fat, grease: *The proud lord That bastes his arrogance with his own seam*—Troil II 3 194.

SEA-MONSTER

The virgin tribute paid by howling Troy To the sea-monster—Merch III 2 56. Hesione, daughter of Laomedon, King of Troy, was in accordance with an oracle to be devoured by a monster by whom Troy was vexed. She was rescued by Hercules (called Alcides in 55). In Lr I 4 281 (*Ingratitude . . . More hideous when thou show'st thee in a child Than the sea-monster!*) perh. the reference is vaguely to some such monster.

SEAR

Cere; to wrap in a cerecloth; fig.: *Sear up my embracements from a next With bonds of death!*—Cymb I 1 116.

SEARCH

A body of searchers: *Lead to the Sagittary the raised search*—Oth I 1 159.

SEASON (sb.)

(1) *Of season*, when in season: *We kill the fowl of season*—Meas II 2 85. *Of the season*, in season: *Buck, and of the season too*—Wiv III 3 169. *A day of season*, app., a day of settled weather proper to a particular season: *I am not a day of season, For thou mayst see a sunshine and a hail In me at once*—All's V 3 32.

(2) That which keeps a thing fresh, a preserva-

tive: [I] *Corrupt with virtuous season*—Meas II 2 168. *Salt too little which may season give To her foul-tainted flesh*—Ado IV 1 144. *The season of all natures, sleep*—Mcb III 4 141.

SEASON (vb.)

(1) To keep fresh, apply a preservative to: *'Tis the best brine a maiden can season her praise in*—All's I 1 55. *To season A brother's dead love, which she would keep fresh*—Tw I 1 30.

(2) To gratify, tickle: *Let their palates Be season'd with such viands*—Merch IV 1 96.

SECOND (adj.)

(1) Subordinate, secondary: *Being the agents, or base second means*—1 H4 I 3 165. *In second voice*, by the mouth of a subordinate: *In second voice we'll not be satisfied*—Troil II 3 149.

(2) Helpful, aiding: *Be second to me*—Wint II 3 27.

SECOND (sb.)

(1) A supporter: *Now the gates are ope: now prove good seconds*—Cor I 4 43. *No seconds? all myself?*—Lr IV 6 198. *A Roman, Who had not now been drooping here, if seconds Had answer'd him*—Cymb V 3 89. A supporting, aiding: *your condemned seconds*, your damnable (because undesired) aid: *You have shamed me In your condemned seconds*—Cor I 8 14. An alternative project: *This project Should have a back or second*—Hml IV 7 153.

(2) *Seconds*, an inferior kind of flour; fig.: *Take thou my oblation, poor but free, Which is not mix'd with seconds*—Sonn 125 10.

SECONDED

Confirmed: *The slave's report is seconded*—Cor IV 6 62.

SECT¹

Sex: Host. *Sick of a calm* (meaning a qualm) . . . Fal. *So is all her sect*—2 H4 II 4 40.

SECT²

A cutting, scion: *Whereof I take this that you call love to be a sect or scion*—Oth I 3 336.

SECURE (adj.)

Unsuspecting, heedless, confiding: *Though Page be a secure fool*—Wiv II 1 241. *This happy night the Frenchmen are secure, Having all day caroused*—1 H6 II 1 11. *Upon my secure hour thy uncle stole*—Hml I 5 61. *Wear your eye thus, not jealous nor secure*—Oth III 3 198.

SECURE (vb.)

To make heedless or confident: *Our means secure us, and our mere defects Prove our commodities*—Lr IV 1 22. *I do not so secure me in the error*—Oth I 3 10. To set at rest: *Secure thy heart*—Tim II 2 185.

SECURELY

(1) Surely, certainly: *Securely I espy Virtue with valour couched in thine eye*—R2 I 3 97.

(2) Heedlessly, confidently: *And yet we strike not* [sail], *but securely perish*—R2 II 1 266. *'Tis done like Hector; but securely done*—Troil IV 5 73. *She securely gives good cheer . . . to her princely guest*—Lucr 89.

SECURITY

Heedlessness, confidence: *Bolingbroke, through our security, Grows strong*—R2 III 2 34. *That's mercy, but too much security*—H5 II 2 44. *Security gives way to conspiracy*—Cæs II 3 8. *Security Is mortals' chiefest enemy*—Mcb III 5 32.

SEE

(1) To see one another, meet: *How have ye done Since last we saw in France?*—H8 I 1 1. *When shall we see again?*—Troil IV 4 59.

(2) To see to, look after: *Bid him repair to us to Ely House To see this business*—R2 II 1 216. *First will I see the coronation*—3 H6 II 6 96.

SEEDNESS

Sowing: *As blossoming time That from the seedness the bare fallow brings To teeming foison*—Meas I 4 41.

SEEING

Like *Seeming* (sb.), fair appearance: *Why should false painting . . . steal dead seeing of his living hue?*—Sonn 67 5.

SEEL

Of a newly-taken hawk, to close the eyes by drawing a fine silken thread through the eyelids, in order to make her endure the hood; fig. of persons: *When light-wing'd toys Of feather'd Cupid seel . . . My speculative . . . instruments*—Oth I 3 269. *To seel her father's eyes up close as oak*—III 3 210. *The wise gods seel our eyes*—Ant III 13 112. Of day personified: *Come, seeling night, Scarf up the tender eye of pitiful day*—Mcb III 2 46.

SEEMING (adj.)

Having a specious appearance: [I will] *pluck the borrowed veil of modesty from the so seeming Mistress Page*—Wiv III 2 41. *If aught within that little seeming substance . . . may fitly like your grace*—Lr I 1 201.

SEEMING (sb.)

Appearance: *We will both our judgements join In censure of his seeming*—Hml III 2 91. *He hath a kind of honour sets him off, More than a mortal seeming*—Cymb I 6 170. Fair appearance: *These keep Seeming and savour all the winter long*—Wint IV 4 74. False appearance: *Seeming, seeming! I will proclaim thee, Angelo!*—Meas II 4 150. *She that, so young, could give out such a seeming*—Oth III 3 209.

SEEMING (adv.)

Becomingly: *Bear your body more seeming, Audrey*—As V 4 72.

SELD

Seldom: *Seld I have the chance*—Troil IV 5 150. *Goods lost are seld or never found*—Pilgr 175.

SELD-SHOWN

Seldom seen: *Seld-shown flamens*—Cor II 1 229.

SELF

(1) One's own: *Who . . . by self and violent hands Took off her life*—Mcb V 8 70.

(2) Same: *That self chain about his neck Which he forswore . . . to have*—Err V 10. *To shoot another arrow that self way Which you did shoot the first*—Merch I 1 148. *That self bill is urged*—H5 I 1 1. *One self mate and mate could not beget Such different issues*—Lr IV 3 36. *That self exhibition Which your own coffers yield*—Cymb I 6 122.

SELF-ABUSE

A misdirection of one's powers; an abnormal state accompanying this: *My strange and self-abuse Is the initiate fear that wants hard use*—Mcb III 4 142.

SELF-ADMISSION

Self-approbation, self-satisfaction: [He] *carries on the stream of his dispose . . . In will peculiar and in self-admission*—Troil II 3 174.

SELF-AFFECTED

In love with oneself, full of self-love: [What a vice were it in Ajax if he were] *strange, or self-affected!*—Troil II 3 250.

SELF-ASSUMPTION

In self-assumption, in one's own conceit: *In self-assumption greater Than in the note of judgement*—Troil II 3 133.

SELF-BORN

Indigenous, home-sprung: [To] *fright our native peace with self-born arms*—R2 II 3 80.

SELF-BOUNTY

Innate generosity: *I would not have your free and noble nature, Out of self-bounty, be abused*—Oth III 3 199.

SELF-CHARITY

Care of oneself: *Unless self-charity be sometimes a vice*—Oth II 3 202.

SELF-COVERED

Thou self-covered thing, thou that hast been covering up thy true (fiendish) self: *Thou changed and self-cover'd thing, for shame, Be-monster not thy feature*—Lr IV 2 62.

SELF-DOING

Committed by oneself: *To you it doth belong Yourself to pardon of self-doing crime*—Sonn 58 11.

SELF-DRAWING

Formed by drawing out of oneself: *Spider-like, Out of his self-drawing web, he . . .*—H8 I 1 62.

SELF-EXAMPLE

A precedent furnished by oneself: *By self-example mayst thou be denied!*—Sonn 142 14.

SELF-EXPLICATION

The power of giving an account of oneself: *A thing perplex'd Beyond self-explication*—Cymb III 4 7.

SELF-FIGURED

Formed by oneself: *To knit their souls . . . in self-figured knot*—Cymb II 3 122.

SELF-GRACIOUS

Voluntarily, or perh. innately gracious: *[Which] his majesty, out of a self-gracious remembrance, did first propose*—All's IV 5 77.

SELF-METTLE

One's own ardour: *A full-hot horse, who being allow'd his way, Self-mettle tires him*—H8 I 1 133.

SELF-REPROVING

Confutation of oneself: *He's full of alteration And self-reproving*—Lr V 1 3.

SELF-SOVEREIGNTY

Sovereignty in oneself: *Do not curst wives hold that self-sovereignty Only for praise sake?*—LLL IV 1 36.

SELF-SUBSTANTIAL

Consisting in one's own substance: *[Thou] Feed'st thy light's flame with self-substantial fuel*—Sonn 1 6.

SELF-UNABLE

Powerless in itself: *Like a common . . . man, That the great figure of a council-frames By self-unable motion*—All's III 1 11.

SEMBLABLE

Similar, like: *The semblable coherence of his men's spirits and his*—2 H4 V 1 72. *Thousands more Of semblable import*—Ant III 4 2. As sb.: *His semblable, yea, himself, Timon disdains*—

Tim IV 3 22. *His semblable is his mirror*—Hml V 2 124.

SEMBLABLY

In like manner: *Semblably furnish'd like the king himself*—1 H4 V 3 21.

SEMBLANCE

(Fair) outward appearance: *Let there be no honour Where there is beauty; truth, where semblance*—Cymb II 4 108.

SEMBLATIVE

App., in appearance: *All is semblative a woman's part*—Tw I 4 34.

SENIORY

See *Signory*.

SENNET

A particular set of notes on a trumpet or cornet—Cæs I 2 24 (Stage Dir). *Sennet sounded*—Mcb III 1 10 (Stage Dir).

SENOYS

The Sienese, the people of Siena: *The Florentines and Senoys are by the ears*—All's I 2 1. Cf. *Syenna*.

SENSE

(1) Sexual passion: *The wanton stings and motions of the sense*—Meas I 4 59. *Can it be That modesty may more betray our sense Than woman's lightness?*—II 2 168. *My sanctity Will to my sense bend no licentious ear*—Per V 3 29.

(2) *To the sense*, to the quick: *I have rubb'd this young quat almost to the sense*—Oth V 1 11.

(3) Unchanged in pl.: *My adder's sense To critic and to flatterer stopped are*—Sonn 112 10.

SENSELESS

(1) Not perceived by the senses: *My good name, that senseless reputation*—Lucr 820.

(2) *My senseless conjuration*, an adjuration addressed to an object void of sense: *Mock not my senseless conjuration (i.e. that which he has just addressed to the earth)*—R2 III 2 23.

SENSIBLE

(1) Derived from the senses: *The sensible and true avouch Of mine own eyes*—Hml I 1 57.

(2) In a moral sense, deeply felt: *With affection wondrous sensible He wrung Bassanio's hand*—Merch II 8 48. *My woe too sensible thy passion maketh More feeling-painful*—Lucr 1678.

(3) Capable of sensation or perception: *Thou art sensible in nothing but blows*—Err IV 4 28. *The wall, methinks, being sensible, should curse again*—Mids V 183. *I would your cambric were sensible as your finger*—Cor I 3 94. Sensitive: *Who are of such sensible and nimble lungs that they always use to laugh at nothing*—Tp II 1 174.

18

(4) Perceptible; and so, substantial: *He bring-eth sensible regreets, To wit . . . Gifts of rich value*—Merch II 9 89.

SENSIBLY

(1) Feelingly: Moth. *I will tell you sensibly.* Cost. *Thou hast no feeling of it, Moth*—LLL III 114. [I] *am most sensibly in grief for it*—Hml IV 5 150.
(2) (Though) having sensation: *O noble fellow! Who sensibly outdares his senseless sword*—Cor I 4 52. Perh., as a sentient creature: *He is your brother, lords, sensibly fed Of that self-blood that first gave life to you*—Tit IV 2 122.

SENTENCE

A saw, maxim: *Quips and sentences and these paper bullets of the brain*—Ado II 3 249. *Good sentences and well pronounced*—Merch I 2 11. *Let me . . . lay a sentence, Which . . . may help these lovers Into your favour*—Oth I 3 199. *Who fears a sentence or an old man's saw*—Lucr 244.

SENTINEL

To watch, guard: *Time's glory is . . . To wake the morn and sentinel the night*—Lucr 939.

SEPARABLE

Separating: *A separable spite*—Sonn 36 6.

SEPTENTRION

The north: *As opposite . . . as the south* [is] *to the septentrion*—3 H6 I 4 134.

SEQUENT (adj.)

Consequent, following: *What to this was sequent*—Hml V 2 54. *Nature finds itself scourged by the sequent effects*—Lr I 2 114. Successive: *A dozen sequent messengers*—Oth I 2 41.

SEQUENT (sb.)

A follower: *A sequent of the stranger queen's*—LLL IV 2 142.

SEQUESTER

Separation, withdrawal: *This hand of yours requires A sequester from liberty*—Oth III 4 39.

SEQUESTRATION

Separation, withdrawal: *Sequestration From open haunts and popularity*—H5 I 1 58. Division, rupture: *Thou shalt see an answerable sequestration*—Oth I 3 350. Seclusion: *Since Henry Monmouth first began to reign . . . This loathsome sequestration* (i.e. in the Tower) *have I had*—1 H6 II 5 23.

SERE

The sear of a gun, a pivoted piece in the lock which holds the hammer at full or half cock; fig., *tickle o' the sere*, easily going off (in laughter): *The clown shall make those laugh whose lungs are tickle o' the sere*—Hml II 2 336.

SERGEANT

A bailiff: *If any hour meet a sergeant, a turns back for very fear*—Err IV 2 56. *This fell sergeant, death, Is strict in his arrest*—Hml V 2 347.

SERPIGO

Herpes, a tetter on the skin: *Do curse the gout, serpigo, and the rheum*—Meas III 1 31. *The dry serpigo on the subject!*—Troil II 3 80.

SERVANT (sb.)

A professed lover: Val. *Madam and mistress, a thousand good-morrows . . .* Sil. *Sir Valentine and servant, to you two thousand*—Gent II 1 102. *Though you respect not aught your servant doth*—V 4 20 (Proteus to Silvia). *Dumain was at my service, and his sword: No point, quoth I; my servant straight was mute*—LLL V 2 276.

SERVANT (vb.)

To subject, subordinate: *My affairs Are servanted to others*—Cor V 2 88.

SESSA

App. an exhortation to do something at once or with speed: *Let the world slide: sessa!*—Shr Ind I 5. *Sessa! let him trot by*—Lr III 4 104. *Sessa! come march to wakes and fairs*—III 6 77.

SET

(1) To stake, hazard: *To set the exact wealth of all our states All at one cast*—1 H4 IV 1 46. *I have set my life upon a cast*—R3 V 4 9. *To set Upon one battle all our liberties*—Cæs V 1 75. To challenge (properly by laying down stakes): *Who sets me else?*—R2 IV 57.
(2) To estimate, value: *The man that mocks at it and sets it light*—R2 I 3 293. *I do not set my life at a pin's fee*—Hml I 4 65. *When thou shalt be disposed to set me light*—Sonn 88 1. *Coldly set*, to slight, treat with indifference: *Thou mayst not coldly set Our sovereign process*—Hml IV 3 64. *To set nothing, little by*, to think nothing, little of: *I think you set nothing by a bloody coxcomb*—Tw V 194. [I set] *As little by such toys as may be possible*—Gent I 2 82.
(3) *To be set*, to be seated: Val. *. . . I stand affected to her.* Speed. *I would you were set, so your affection would cease*—Gent II 1 90. *I was set at work Among my maids*—H8 III 1 74. *Here come and sit . . . And being set, I'll smother thee with kisses*—Ven 17. *A river . . . Upon whose weeping margent she was set*—Compl 38. *Is set him down*, has sat down: *The king by this is set him down to sleep* (in conformity with his vow not to lie down)—3 H6 IV 3 2.
(4) *To be set*, to have set out (on a journey): *The king is set from London*—H5 II Chor 34. *To set on*, to set in motion: *Bid him set on his powers betimes before*—Cæs IV 3 308. *Set our battles on*—3 108. To march, go on: *Shall we go draw our*

numbers and set on?—2 H4 I 3 109. *Set on; and leave no ceremony out*—Cæs I 2 11.

(5) *To set down*, of the pegs of a musical instrument, to let down, lower: *I'll set down the pegs that make this music*— Oth II 1 203. To take up a position, encamp: *If they set down before's, for the remove Bring up your army*—Cor I 2 28. *Before proud Athens he's set down by this*—Tim V 3 9. *To set off*, to put out of account: *Every thing set off That might so much as think you enemies*—2 H4 IV 1 145. *To set to*, to set (a broken limb): *Can honour set to a leg?*—1 H4 V 1 133.

SETTER

One who does the office of a setter-dog for thieves: *'Tis our setter: I know his voice*—1 H4 II 2 53 (of Gadshill, the highwayman).

SEVERAL (adj.)

(1) Various, divers: *With strange and several noises*—Tp V 232. *The rest have worn me out With several applications*—All's I 2 73. *He sings several tunes faster than you'll tell money*—Wint IV 4 184.

(2) Private, not common: *Why should my heart think that a several plot Which my heart knows the wide world's common place?*—Sonn 137 9. A portion of a common enclosed and allotted to a private owner was called a several; so in LLL II 223 (*My lips are no common, though several they be*) Maria seems to mean that her lips are no common, though, being several (*i.e.* parted), they may, by a play on the word, be called a field.

SEVERAL (sb.)

(1) A particular person, individual: *Not noted, is't, But . . . by some severals Of head-piece extraordinary?*—Wint I 2 225.

(2) That which belongs to an individual: *All our abilities . . . Severals and generals of grace exact*—Troil I 3 179.

(3) *Severals*, particulars: *The severals and unhidden passages Of his true titles*—H5 I 1 86.

SEWER

An officer charged with the service of the table: *Enter a* Sewer, *and divers* Servants *with dishes and service*—Mcb I 7 (Stage Dir).

'SFOOT

[By] God's foot: *'Sfoot, I'll learn to conjure and raise devils*—Troil II 3 6.

SHAG

Shaggy, hairy: *Fetlocks shag and long*—Ven 295.

SHAG-HAIRED

Having shaggy hair: *A shag-hair'd crafty kern*—2 H6 III 1 367. *Thou liest, thou shag-hair'd villain!*—Mcb IV 2 83.

SHAKE

To shake the head, app., to nod: [Hast thou not] thought thee happy when I shook my head?*—2 H6 IV 1 55.

SHALE

A shell, husk: *Leaving them but the shales and husks of men*—H5 IV 2 18.

SHAME

To be ashamed: *Thou shamest to acknowledge me in misery*—Err V 322. *I do not shame To tell you what I was*—As IV 3 136. *How he did prevail I shame to speak*—John I 104. *Shamest thou to show thy dangerous brow by night?*—Cæs II 1 78.

SHAPELESS

Effecting nothing, futile; or perh., aimless: [To] *Wear out thy youth with shapeless idleness*—Gent I 1 8.

SHARD

(1) A potsherd: *Shards, flints and pebbles should be thrown on her*—Hml V 1 254.

(2) The wing-case of a beetle: *They are his shards, and he their beetle*—Ant III 2 20.

SHARD-BORNE

Borne by shards (in sense (2)); more properly by the wings: *The shard-borne beetle*—Mcb III 2 42.

SHARDED

Having shards (in sense (2)): *The sharded beetle*—Cymb III 3 20.

SHARE

To receive or take as a share, gain: *I would not lose so great an honour As one man more, methinks, would share from me*—H5 IV 3 31. *The least of you shall share his part thereof*—R3 V 3 268. *What glory our Achilles shares from Hector*—Troil I 3 367.

SHARK UP

To get together by shifts: [He hath] *Shark'd up a list of lawless resolutes*—Hml I 1 98.

SHARP-LOOKING

Hungry-looking: *A needy, hollow-eyed, sharp-looking wretch*—Err V 240.

SHE

As sb.: *You are the cruell'st she alive*—Tw I 5 259. *I was wont To load my she with knacks*—Wint IV 4 358. *The shes of Italy*—Cymb I 3 29. *I think my love as rare As any she belied with false compare*—Sonn 130 13.

SHEAL

To shell: *A shealed peascod*—Lr I 4 219.

SHEARMAN

One who shears cloth, *i.e.*, clips the nap: *Thy father was a plasterer; And thou thyself a shearman, art thou not?*—2 H6 IV 2 140.

SHEAVED

Made of straw: *Her sheaved hat*—Compl 31.

SHEEP-BITER

An ill-trained sheep-dog who snaps at the sheep; hence, a betrayer of trust, and app. used vaguely as a term of abuse: *The niggardly rascally sheepbiter*—Tw II 5 5.

SHEEP-BITING

App. used in a derived sense similar to that given under the preceding word: *Show your sheepbiting face*—Meas V 359.

SHEEP-COTE

An enclosure for sheep containing a cottage: *At our sheepcote now . . . there is nothing That you will feed on*—As II 4 84. *A sheep-cote fenced about with olive trees*—IV 3 78. *Draw our throne into a sheep-cote!*—Wint IV 4 807. *Poor pelting villages, sheep-cotes, and mills*—Lr II 3 18.

SHEER

(1) Pure, clear: *Thou sheer, immaculate and silver fountain!*—R2 V 3 61.

(2) By itself, alone: *Fourteen pence on the score for sheer ale*—Shr Ind 2 24.

SHELVING

App., sloping outwards: *Her chamber is . . . built so shelving that one cannot climb it*—Gent III 1 114.

SHEND

To reprove, abuse: *We shall all be shent*—Wiv I 4 38. *I am shent for speaking to you*—Tw IV 2 112. *He shent our messengers*—Troil II 3 86. *How in my words soever she be shent*—Hml III 2 416.

SHERRIS

Sherry, the wine of Xeres: *The second property of your excellent sherris*—2 H4 IV 3 110; and *passim* in the speech. So *sherris-sack*, *i.e.* sack of Xeres: *A good sherris-sack hath a two-fold operation in it*—2 H4 IV 3 103. Cf. *Sack*.

SHIELD

To forfend, forbid: *Heaven shield my mother play'd my father fair!*—Meas III 1 141. *God shield you mean it not!*—All's I 3 174 (with a redundant negative). *God shield I should disturb devotion!*—Rom IV 1 41.

SHIPPING

A going by ship, voyage (jocularly): *I have seen them in the church together: God send 'em good shipping!*—Shr V 1 42.

SHIP-TIRE

A head-dress resembling a ship; or perh., one adorned with streamers——Wiv III 3 60 (quoted under *Tire* (sb.)².

SHIVE

A slice: *Easy it is Of a cut loaf to steal a shive*—Tit II 1 86.

SHOCK

To meet with force and drive back: *Come the three corners of the world in arms, And we shall shock them*—John V 7 116.

SHOG

To move off, go: *Will you shog off?*—H5 II 1 47. *Shall we shog?*—II 3 47.

SHOON

Pl. of Shoe: *Such as go in clouted shoon*—2 H6 IV 2 195. See also *Sandal shoon*.

SHOOT

(1) A shot: *A stand where you may make the fairest shoot*—LLL IV 1 10. *A shot a fine shoot*—2 H4 III 2 49. *So my shoot is lost*—3 H6 III 1 7. *End thy ill aim before thy shoot be ended*—Lucr 579.

(2) *Shoots*, app., horns (figuratively): *Thou want'st . . . the shoots that I have, To be full like me*—Wint I 2 128.

SHORE (sb.)

A form of Sewer: *Empty . . . common shores of filth*—Per IV 6 185.

SHORE (vb.)

To set on shore: *If he think it fit to shore them again*—Wint IV 4 867.

SHORE

Pa. pple. of To shear: *Since you have shore With shears his thread of silk*—Mids V 347.

SHORT (adj.)

To keep short, to keep within bounds: *Us, whose providence Should have kept short . . . This mad young man*—Hml IV 1 17.

SHORT (vb.)

(1) To come short of: *I shall short my word By lengthening my return*—Cymb I 6 200.

(2) To be short: *Short, night, to-night, and length thyself to-morrow*—Pilgr 210.

SHOT

Collectively, shooters, marksmen: *A guard of chosen shot*—1 H6 I 4 53.

SHOTTEN

Of a herring, that has shed its roe and so is worth little: *If manhood . . . be not forgot . . . then am I a shotten herring*—1 H4 II 4 140.

SHOUGH

A kind of shaggy dog: Mcb III 1 94.

SHOULDER-SHOTTEN

Sprained in the shoulder: *Swayed in the back and shoulder-shotten*—Shr III 2 56.

SHOVE-GROAT, SHOVEL-BOARD

A game consisting in pushing pieces of money on a board to reach certain marks; *a shove-groat shilling, an Edward shovel-board* (a shilling of Edward VI), coins used in the game: *Quoit him down, Bardolph, like a shove-groat shilling*—2 H4 II 4 206. *Two Edward shovel-boards, that cost me two shilling and two pence a-piece*—Wiv I 1 159.

SHREW

As a minor imprecation like Beshrew (q.v.): *Shrew my heart*—Wint I 2 281. *Shrew me*—Cymb II 3 147.

SHREWD

(1) Of persons, ill-tempered, virulent, malicious: *Thou wilt never get thee a husband, if thou be so shrewd of thy tongue*—Ado II 1 19. *A shrewd unhappy gallows*—LLL V 2 12. *When she's angry, she is keen and shrewd*—Mids III 2 323. *Her elder sister is so curst and shrewd*—Shr I 1 185. *Thy eyes' shrewd tutor, that hard heart of thine*—Ven 500.

(2) Of things, bad, evil, vexatious, destructive: *There is shrewd construction made of her*—Wiv II 2 232. *There are some shrewd contents in yon same paper*—Merch III 2 246. *This young maid might do her A shrewd turn*—All's III 5 70. *To lift shrewd steel against our golden crown*—R2 III 2 59. *This last day was A shrewd one to's*—Ant IV 9 4.

(3) Remarkable of its kind: *A fit or two o' the face; but they are shrewd ones*—H8 I 3 7.

SHREWDLY

(1) Sharply, keenly: *The air bites shrewdly; it is very cold*—Hml I 4 1.

(2) In a high degree: *He's shrewdly vexed at something*—All's III 5 92. *You boggle shrewdly, every feather starts you*—V 3 232. *This practice hath most shrewdly pass'd upon thee*—Tw V 360. *My fame is shrewdly gored*—Troil III 3 228.

SHRIEVE

Sheriff: *Getting the shrieve's fool with child*—All's IV 3 212.

SHRILL-GORGED

Shrill-throated, having a high-pitched note: *The shrill-gorged lark*—Lr IV 6 58.

SHRINE

The image of a saint or goddess: *To kiss this shrine, this mortal-breathing saint*—Merch II 7 40. *For feature laming The shrine of Venus*—Cymb V 5 163.

SHROW

Shrew: *I beshrew all shrows*—LLL V 2 46.

SHROWD

Shelter, protection: *[That] you had . . . put yourself under his shrowd*—Ant III 13 70.

SHUT UP

Concluded; or perh., retired to rest: *[The king] shut up In measureless content*—Mcb II 1 16.

SICK

To sicken, fall ill: *A little time before . . . Edward sick'd and died*—2 H4 IV 4 127.

SICKEN

To impoverish, impair: *Kinsmen of mine . . . that have By this so sicken'd their estates, that . . .*—H8 I 1 81.

SICKLY

To give a sickly appearance to: *Sicklied o'er with the pale cast of thought*—Hml III 1 85.

SIDE (adj.)

Long, wide; *side sleeves*, long and wide hanging sleeves, forming ornamental appendages to the sleeves actually covering the arms: [It (*i.e.* the Duchess of Milan's gown)] *'s but a night-gown in respect of yours: cloth o' gold, and cuts, and laced with silver, set with pearls down sleeves, side sleeves, and skirts*—Ado III 4 18. (Printing no comma after *pearls* seems to be the better course.)

SIDE (vb.)

To take the side of: *[They'll] side factions*—Cor I 1 197.

SIEGE

(1) A seat: *Upon the very siege of justice*—Meas IV 2 101.

(2) A rank, class: *Of the unworthiest siege*—Hml IV 7 77. *I fetch my life and being From men of royal siege*—Oth I 2 21.

(3) Excrement: *How camest thou to be the siege of this moon-calf? can he vent Trinculos?*—Tp II 2 110.

SIEVE

A basket for scraps: *The remainder viands We do not throw in unrespective sieve*—Troil II 2 70.

SIGHT

App., insight: *Through the sight I bear in things to love*—Troil III 3 4.

SIGHTLESS

(1) Invisible: *You murdering ministers, Wherever in your sightless substances You wait on nature's mischief*—Mcb I 5 49. *The sightless couriers of the air*—I 7 23.

(2) Unsightly: *Unpleasing blots and sightless stains*—John III 1 45.

(3) In which one cannot see: *Sightless night*—Lucr 1013.

SIGN (sb.)

She's a good sign, she has a good outward appearance (referring to the signs marking houses and inns): *She's a good sign, but I have seen small reflection of her wit*—Cymb I 2 32.

SIGN (vb.)

(1) To mark, denote: *A fellow by the hand of nature . . . sign'd to do a deed of shame*—John IV 2 221. *You sign your place and calling . . . With meekness and humility*—H8 II 4 108. *Here thy hunters stand, Sign'd in thy spoil*—Cæs III 1 205.

(2) To augur, bode: First Sold. *Music i' the air. . . .* Fourth Sold. *It signs well, does it not?*—Ant IV 3 13.

SIGNAL

A sign, token: *Giving full trophy, signal and ostent Quite from himself to God*—H5 V Chor 21. *In signal of my love to thee . . . Will I . . . wear this rose*—1 H6 II 4 121. *Hold up thy hand, make signal of thy hope*—2 H6 III 3 28. *The weary sun . . . Gives signal of a goodly day to-morrow*—R3 V 3 19.

SIGNIFICANT

An indication, token: *In dumb significants proclaim your thoughts*—1 H6 II 4 26. Affectedly of a letter: *Bear this significant* [giving a letter] *to . . . Jaquenetta*—LLL III 131.

SIGNORY, SIGNIORY, SENIORY

(1) Seniority: *Give mine the benefit of seniory*—R3 IV 4 36.

(2) A principality: *Through all the signories it* (*i.e.* Milan) *was the first*—Tp I 2 71. A lordship, domain: *Whilst you have fed upon my signories*—R2 III 1 22. *All the Duke of Norfolk's signories*—2 H4 IV 1 111.

(3) The governing body, senate, of an Italian state: *My services which I have done the signiory*—Oth I 2 18.

SILLY

(1) Helpless, weak, inoffensive: *Outrages On silly women or poor passengers*—Gent IV 1 71. *While as the silly owner of the goods Weeps over them*—2 H6 I 1 225. *Had I been there, which am a silly woman*—3 H6 I 1 243. *Shepherds looking on their silly sheep*—II 5 43. *The wolf would . . . never fright the silly lamb that day*—Ven 1097.

(2) Plain, simple: *It is silly sooth*—Tw II 4 47. Of clothes, such as are worn by peasants: *A fourth man, in a silly habit*—Cymb V 3 86.

(3) Poor, insufficient: *A pedigree Of threescore and two years; a silly time To make prescription for a kingdom's worth*—3 H6 III 3 92.

SIMULAR

(1) Feigning: *Thou simular man of virtue That art incestuous*—Lr III 2 54.

(2) Feigned, fabricated: *Simular proof enough To make the noble Leonatus mad*—Cymb V 5 200.

SINCE

When: *Thou rememberest Since once I sat upon a promontory*—Mids II 1 148. *This fellow I remember, Since once he play'd a farmer's eldest son*—Shr Ind 1 83. *Remember since you owed no more to time Than I do now*—Wint V 1 219. *Do you remember since we lay all night in the windmill?*—2 H4 III 2 206. *We know the time since he was mild and affable*—2 H6 III 1 9.

SINEW (sb.)

A nerve: *This rest might yet have balm'd thy broken sinews*—Lr III 6 105. *A second fear through all her sinews spread*—Ven 903.

SINEW (vb.)

To knit together, join: *So shalt thou sinew both these lands together*—3 H6 II 6 91.

SINGLE (adj.)

(1) Of small account, weak, feeble: Pros. . . . *What wert thou, if the King of Naples heard thee?* Fer. *A single thing, as I am now*—Tp I 2 431 (with a play). *Whiles he thought to steal the single ten, The king was slily finger'd from the deck!*—3 H6 V 1 43. *My thought . . . Shakes so my single state of man that . . .*—Mcb I 3 139. *All our service . . . Were poor and single business*—I 6 14.

(2) *A single bond*, prob., one without a surety: *Go with me to a notary, seal me there Your single bond*—Merch I 3 145.

SINGLE (vb.)

As a term of art in woodcraft, to segregate the hart to be hunted: *Now, Clifford, I have singled thee alone*—3 H6 II 4 1. *Single you thither then this dainty doe*—Tit II 1 117.

SINGLY

Uniquely: *Thou singly honest man*—Tim IV 3 530.

SINGULARITY

In what fashion more than his singularity, with what accompaniment to himself: *Let's hence, and hear . . . in what fashion, More than his singularity, he goes*—Cor I 1 280.

SINGULE

To single out, separate: *We will be singuled from the barbarous*—LLL V 1 85.

SINK-A-PACE

See *Cinque pace.*

SINKING-RIPE

See *Ripe.*

SIR

(1) A sovereign: *Sole sir o' the world*—Ant V 2 120. A gentleman: *A loyal sir To him thou follow'st*—Tp V 69. *In the habit of some sir of note*—Tw III 4 81. *Which . . . you are most apt to play the sir in*—Oth II 1 175. *A lady to the worthiest sir that ever Country call'd his*—Cymb I 6 160.

(2) A title given to priests (originally to those who had taken a bachelor's degree): *Sir Oliver Martext, the vicar of the next village*—As III 3 43. *Sir Topas the curate*—Tw IV 2 2. *I thank thee, good Sir John*—R3 III 2 111 (to the Priest).

(3) *Sirs*, used in addressing women: *Ah, women, women, look, Our lamp is spent, it's out! Good sirs, take heart*—Ant IV 15 84.

SIRRAH

Used in addressing a woman: *Sirrah Iras, go*—Ant V 2 229.

SIR-REVERENCE

A corruption of save-reverence (*salva reverentia*): *Such a one as a man may not speak of without he say ' Sir-reverence'*—Err III 2 91.

SISTER

(1) To resemble closely: *Her art sisters the natural roses*—Per V Prol 7.

(2) *Sistering*, neighbouring: *A sistering vale*—Compl 2.

SITH (adv.)

Since: *Being of so young days brought up with him, And sith so neighbour'd to his youth and haviour*—Hml II 2 11.

SITH (conj.)

Since, seeing that: *Sith 'twas my fault to give the people scope*—Meas I 3 35. *So call it, Sith nor the exterior nor the inward man Resembles that it was*—Hml II 2 5. *I'll love no friend, sith love breeds such offence*—Oth III 3 380. *The world will hold thee in disdain, Sith in thy pride so fair a hope is slain*—Ven 761. So *sith that*: *'Tis no sin, Sith that the justice of your title to him Doth flourish the deceit*—Meas IV 1 73. *Sith that both charge and danger Speak 'gainst so great a number*—Lr II 4 242.

SITH (prep.)

Since: *I come to tell you things sith then befall'n*—3 H6 II 1 106.

SITHENCE (adv.)

Since: *Have you inform'd them sithence?*—Cor III 1 47.

SITHENCE (conj.)

Since, seeing that: *Sithence . . . it concerns you something to know it*—All's I 3 124.

SIZE

(1) An allowance: *'Tis not in thee . . . to scant my sizes*—Lr II 4 176.

(2) A portion allotted, share: *Our size of sorrow, Proportion'd to our cause, must be as great As that which makes it*—Ant IV 15 4.

SKAINS-MATE

I am none of his flirt-gills; I am none of his skains-mates—Rom II 4 161. A doubtful word; explained from skein (of thread) as a sempstress, with connotation of bad character; from skain, a dagger, as a swaggerer.

SKILL (sb.)

(1) Reason, cause: Per . . . *I might fear . . . You woo'd me the false way.* Flo. *I think you have As little skill to fear as I have purpose To put you to't*—Wint IV 4 150. But perhaps the word is better taken here in the usual modern sense, referring to Perdita's innocence and ignorance of the ways of the world.

(2) Discriminating faculty, mind: *All the skill I have Remembers not these garments*—Lr IV 7 66.

SKILL (vb.)

It skills not, it matters not: *I am to get a man,—whate'er he be, It skills not much*—Shr III 2 133. *As a madman's epistles are no gospels, so it skills not much when they are delivered*—Tw V 294. *It skills not greatly who impugns our doom*—2 H6 III 1 281.

SKILLET

A pot, saucepan: *Let housewives make a skillet of my helm*—Oth I 3 273.

SKIMBLE-SKAMBLE

Confused, disconnected: *Such a deal of skimble-skamble stuff As puts me from my faith*—1 H4 III 1 154.

SKIPPER

A flighty, thoughtless person: *Skipper, stand back*—Shr II 341.

SKIRR

Scour; intr.: *We will come to them, And make them skirr away*—H5 IV 7 63. Trans.: *Skirr the country round*—Mcb V 3 35.

SKOGAN

I see him (*i.e.* Falstaff) *break Skogan's head at the court-gate*—2 H4 III 2 32. It is impossible to say who is alluded to. There appear to have been two Skogans of some note, Henry, a poet, about the time of Henry IV, and John, a jester, about the time of Edward IV. If either is meant it is probably the latter, in spite of the anachronism.

SLAB

Thick, viscous: *Make the gruel thick and slab*—Mcb IV 1 32.

SLAKE

To become less, abate: *No flood by raining slaketh*—Lucr 1677.

SLANDER (sb.)

(1) Disgrace, reproach: *Free from these slanders and this open shame*—Err IV 4 70. *He The sacred honour of himself, his queen's . . . betrays to slander*—Wint II 3 83. *Thou hast wrought A deed of slander . . . Upon my head*—R2 V 6 34. *My blood shall wash the slander of mine ill*—Lucr 1207. *Partial slander*, the reproach of partiality: *A partial slander sought I to avoid*—R2 I 3 241. *That which brings disgrace: This slander of his blood*—R2 I 1 113. *You must learn to know such slanders of the age*—H5 III 6 83. *Thou slander of thy mother's heavy womb!*—R3 I 3 231.

(2) Bad report, ill repute: *This well carried shall on her behalf Change slander to remorse*—Ado IV 1 212. *You shall not find me . . . After the slander of most stepmothers, Evil-eyed unto you*—Cymb I 1 70.

SLANDER (vb.)

To discredit, disgrace: *Tax not so bad a voice To slander music*—Ado II 3 46. *I would not . . . Have you so slander any moment leisure, As to . . .*—Hml I 3 132. *Throwing favours on The low Posthumus slanders so her judgement That . . .*—Cymb III 5 75. *Slandering creation with a false esteem*—Sonn 127 12.

SLANDEROUS

(1) Bringing disgrace: *Ugly and slanderous to thy mother's womb*—John III 1 44.

(2) Disgraceful, degraded: *Such an office . . . As slanderous deathsman to so base a slave*—Lucr 1000.

SLAVE

To enslave, subject to one's will: *The . . . lust-dieted man That slaves your ordinance*—Lr IV 1 70.

SLEAVE

Matted, unspun silk: *Sleep that knits up the ravell'd sleave of care*—Mcb II 2 37. So *sleave-silk*: *Thou idle immaterial skein of sleave-silk*—Troil V 1 35.

SLEDDED

Sleigh-borne, going on sledges: *The sledded Polacks*—Hml I 1 63.

SLEEVE

Worn as a favour: Tro. . . . *Wear this sleeve.* Cres. *And you this glove*—Troil IV 4 72. *Here, Diomed, keep this sleeve*—V 2 66. *That sleeve is mine that he'll bear on his helm*—169. *Diomed has got that same . . . young knave's sleeve of Troy there in his helm*—V 4 3. No doubt 'side sleeves' are meant. See *Side* (adj.).

SLEEVE-HAND

A wristband, cuff: *You would think a smock were a she-angel, he so chants to the sleeve-hand . . . on't*—Wint IV 4 210.

SLEIDED

Unwoven, untwisted: *When she weaved the sleided silk*—Per IV Prol 21. *With sleided silk . . . Enswathed*—Compl 48.

'SLID

[By] God's lid (*i.e.* eyelid): *'Slid, 'tis but venturing*—Wiv III 4 24. *'Slid, I'll after him again*—Tw III 4 426.

SLIGHT

To throw, pitch: *The rogues slighted me into the river*—Wiv III 5 9.

'SLIGHT

[By] God's light: *'Slight, I could so beat the rogue!*—Tw II 5 38. *'Slight, will you make an ass o' me?*—III 2 14.

SLIP

A counterfeit coin: Rom. . . . *What counterfeit did I give you?* Mer. *The slip, sir, the slip*—Rom II 4 49. *Which purchase if thou make, for fear of slips Set thy seal-manual on my wax-red lips*—Ven 515. In both cases with a play. Cf. Troil II 3 27 (*If I could have remembered a gilt counterfeit, thou wouldst not have slipped out of my contemplation*).

SLIPPER

Slippery: *A slipper and subtle knave*—Oth II 1 246.

SLOBBERY

Muddy, sloppy: *A slobbery and a dirty farm*—H5 III 5 13.

SLOP

Loose trousers: *Rhymes are guards on wanton Cupid's hose: Disfigure not his slop*—LLL IV 3 58. *There's a French salutation to your French slop*—Rom II 4 46. In pl.: *A German from the waist downward, all slops*—Ado III 2 35. *The satin for my short cloak and my slops*—2 H4 I 2 34.

SLUBBER

To slur over, do carelessly: *Slubber not business for my sake*—Merch II 8 39.

SLUT

A wanton: *Hold up, you sluts, Your aprons mountant*—Tim IV 3 134 (to the courtesans).

SLUTTISH

Wanton: *Set them down For sluttish spoils of opportunity And daughters of the game*—Troil IV 5 61.

SMART

Accompanied by smarting: *Poison be their drink! ... Their softest touch as smart as lizards' stings*—2 H6 III 2 321.

SMATCH

A smack, taste: *Thy life hath had some smatch of honour in it*—Cæs V 5 46.

SMATTER

To chatter: *Smatter with your gossips, go*—Rom III 5 172.

SMILE

To smile at: *Smile you my speeches, as I were a fool?*—Lr II 2 88.

SMOKE

(1) To find out (a person): *He was first smoked by the old lord Lafeu*—All's III 6 111. *They begin to smoke me*—IV 1 30.
(2) To beat, dust: *I'll smoke your skin-coat, an I catch you right*—John II 139. To suffer from ill-treatment or violence: *Some of you shall smoke for it in Rome*—Tit IV 2 111.

SMOOTH

To use flattering words or cajoleries: *I cannot flatter and speak fair ... smooth, deceive and cog*—R3 I 3 47. *I can smooth and fill his aged ear With golden promises*—Tit IV 4 96. *The sinful father Seem'd not to strike, but smooth*—Per I 2 77. Trans., to flatter, humour: *Every grise of fortune Is smooth'd by that below*—Tim IV 3 16. *Such smiling rogues ... smooth every passion That in the natures of their lords rebel*—Lr II 2 79. To pronounce caressingly: *What tongue shall smooth thy name?*—Rom III 2 98.

SMOOTHING

Flattering, cajoling: *Let not his smoothing words Bewitch your hearts*—2 H6 I 1 156. *My tongue could never learn sweet smoothing words*—R3 I 2 169.

SMOOTH-PATE

Much the same as the later Roundhead: *The whoreson smooth-pates do now wear nothing but high shoes*—2 H4 I 2 43.

SMOTHER

Thick, stifling smoke: *Thus must I from the smoke into the smother*—As I 2 299.

SMUG

Neat, trim: *The smug and silver Trent*—1 H4 III 1 102.

SNATCH

(1) A catching (of the voice): *The snatches in his voice, And burst of speaking*—Cymb IV 2 105.
(2) A shuffling answer: *Leave me your snatches, and yield me a direct answer*—Meas IV 2 6.

SNEAK-CUP

One who sneaks from or shirks his cup: *The prince is a Jack, a sneak-cup*—1 H4 III 3 99.

SNEAP (sb.)

A reprimand, snub: *I will not undergo this sneap without reply*—2 H4 II 1 133.

SNEAP (vb.)

Of frost, &c., to nip, pinch: *An envious sneaping frost*—LLL I 1 100. *That may blow No sneaping winds at home*—Wint I 2 12. *The sneaped birds*—Lucr 333.

SNECK UP

Go hang: *We did keep time, sir, in our catches. Sneck up!*—Tw II 3 100.

SNIPT-TAFFETA

Wearing snippings of *Taffeta* (q.v.): *Your son was misled with a snipt-taffeta fellow*—All's IV 5 1.

SNUFF[1]

A charred wick; as an object of contempt or disgust: *Let me not live ... After my flame lacks oil, to be the snuff Of younger spirits*—All's I 2 58. *My snuff and loathed part of nature*—Lr IV 6 39.

SNUFF[2]

(1) An offence-taking, huff: *Snuffs and packings of the dukes*—Lr III 1 26.
(2) Hence *to take in snuff*, to take offence at: *You'll mar the light by taking it in snuff*—LLL V 2 22. *A pouncet-box, which ever and anon He gave his nose ... Who therewith angry ... Took it in snuff*—1 H4 I 3 38. So *to be in snuff*, to be offended: *He dares not come there (i.e. into the lanthorn) for the candle; for, you see, it is already in snuff*—Mids V 253. In all three cases with a play.

SOFTLY-SPRIGHTED

Perh., of a gentle spirit or nature: *A softly-sprighted man, is he not?*—Wiv I 4 25.

SOIL

To stall-feed with green food: *The fitchew, nor the soiled horse, goes to't With a more riotous appetite*—Lr IV 6 124.

SOILURE

Stain, defilement: *Not making any scruple of her soilure*—Troil IV 1 56.

SOLA

Holloa! LLL IV 1 151; Merch V 39.

SOLACE (sb.)

Happiness, delight: *With his soul fled all my worldly solace*—2 H6 III 2 151. *Sorrow changed to solace, solace mix'd with sorrow*—Pilgr 203.

SOLACE (vb.)

(1) To delight, amuse: *We will with some strange pastime solace them*—LLL IV 3 377.

(2) To take delight, amuse oneself: *This sickly land might solace as before*—R3 II 3 30. *But one thing to rejoice and solace in*—Rom IV 5 47. *To . . . solace I' the dungeon by a snuff*—Cymb I 6 86.

SOLE

(1) Unmatched, unique: *This, so sole and so unmatchable*—John IV 3 52. *Though it alter not love's sole effect*—Sonn 36 7. *The bird of loudest lay, On the sole Arabian tree*—Phœn 1.

(2) Mere: *This tyrant, whose sole name blisters our tongues*—Mcb IV 3 12.

SOLELY

(1) Completely, wholly: *A great way fool, solely a coward*—All's I 1 112.

(2) Alone, by oneself: *Leave me solely*—Wint II 3 17.

SOLEMN

Pertaining to a holiday, festive: *A solemn hunting is in hand*—Tit II 1 112.

SOLEMNITY

Festivity: *We will include all jars With triumphs, mirth and rare solemnity*—Gent V 4 160. *A fortnight hold we this solemnity, In nightly revels and new jollity*—Mids V 376. A festival: *Dares the slave Come hither, cover'd with an antic face, To fleer and scorn at our solemnity?*—Rom I 5 57.

SOLICIT

To incite, move: *The part I had in Woodstock's blood Doth more solicit me than your exclaims*—R2 I 2 1. *Solicit Henry with her wondrous praise*—1 H6 V 3 190. *The occurrents, more and less, Which have solicited*—Hml V 2 368.

SOLICITING

An incitement, prompting: *This supernatural soliciting Cannot be ill, cannot be good*—Mcb I 3 130.

SOLIDARE

App., a small coin of some description: *Here's three solidares for thee*—Tim III 1 46.

SOLVE

A solution, explanation: *The solve is this, that thou dost common grow*—Sonn 69 14.

SOMETIME

(1) Sometimes, at times: *A savage jealousy That sometime savours nobly*—Tw V 122. *Sometime he angers me*—1 H4 III 1 148. *Lear's i' the town; Who sometime . . . remembers What we are come about*—Lr IV 3 40. *Sometime too hot the eye of heaven shines*—Sonn 18 5.

(2) Once upon a time, on a certain occasion: *Henry the Fifth did sometime prophesy, 'If once . . .'*—1 H6 V 1 31. *Therefore present to her,—as sometime Margaret Did to thy father . . . A handkerchief*—R3 IV 4 274. *I sometime lay here in Corioli At a poor man's house*—Cor I 9 82. *Belarius whom you sometime banish'd*—Cymb V 5 333.

(3) Formerly, in other times: *I will . . . myself present As I was sometime Milan*—Tp V 85. *This was sometime a paradox, but now the time gives it proof*—Hml III 1 114. *The ruin speaks that sometime It was a worthy building*—Cymb IV 2 354. *Sometime lofty towers I see down-razed*—Sonn 64 3. As adj.: *Our sometime sister, now our queen*—Hml I 2 8. *My sometime daughter*—Lr I 1 122.

SOMETIMES

Formerly, in other times: *Sometimes from her eyes I did receive fair speechless messages*—Merch I 1 163. *The dowager, Sometimes our brother's wife*—H8 II 4 180. *That fair and warlike form In which the majesty of buried Denmark Did sometimes march*—Hml I 1 47. As adj.: *Thy sometimes brother's wife*—R2 I 2 54. *My sometimes royal master's face*—V 5 75.

SONANCE

A sound, call: *Let the trumpets sound The tucket sonance and the note to mount*—H5 IV 2 34.

SONTIES

App. a corruption of Saints or Sanctities: *By God's sonties, 'twill be a hard way to hit*—Merch II 2 47.

SOON

With expressions of time, app. conveying a notion of indefiniteness; *soon at night: We'll have a posset for't soon at night*—Wiv I 4 8. *I shall be sent for soon at night*—2 H4 V 95. *Say if I shall see you soon at night*—Oth III 4 198. *Soon at five o'clock: Soon at five o'clock . . . I'll meet with you*—Err I 2 26. *Soon at supper, sup-*

per-time, after-supper: *Soon at supper shalt thou see Lorenzo*—Merch II 3 5. *Soon at supper-time I'll visit you*—Err III 2 179. *Come to me, Tyrrel, soon at after-supper*—R3 IV 3 31 (the hyphen seems to be required here; see *After-supper*).

SOON-SPEEDING

Quickly destroying: *A dram of poison, such soon-speeding gear As will . . .*—Rom V 1 60. See *Speed* (vb.).

SOOTH

Cajolery, flattery: *That e'er this tongue of mine, That laid the sentence . . . On yon proud man, should take it off again With words of sooth!*—R2 III 3 133. Personified: *When Signior Sooth here does proclaim a peace, He flatters you*—Per I 2 44.

SOOTHE

(1) To assent to, humour: *Is 't good to soothe him in these contraries?*—Err IV 4 82. *In soothing them, we nourish 'gainst our senate The cockle of rebellion*—Cor III 1 69. *Soothe him; let him take the fellow*—Lr III 4 182. *Shrill-tongued tapsters . . . Soothing the humour of fantastic wits*—Ven 849. To cajole, flatter: *You soothed not, therefore hurt not*—Cor II 2 77. With *up*: *Thou art perjured too, And soothest up greatness*—John III 1 120.

(2) To smooth over: *To soothe your forgery and his*—3 H6 III 3 175.

SOOTHER

A flatterer: *I do defy The tongues of soothers*—1 H4 IV 1 6.

SOOTHING (ppl. adj.)

Flattering, cajoling: *Love's best habit is a soothing tongue*—Pilgr 11.

SOOTHING (sb.)

Flattery: *Let courts and cities be Made all of false-faced soothing!*—Cor I 9 43.

SOP

(1) *Quaff'd off the muscadel And threw the sops all in the sexton's face*—Shr III 2 174. At weddings cakes, wafers, &c., were blessed and put in wine.

(2) *Sop o' the moonshine*, prob. an allusion to a dish called eggs in moonshine, made of eggs cooked in oil: *I'll make a sop o' the moonshine of you*—Lr II 2 34.

SOPHISTER

A sophist, subtle arguer: *A subtle traitor needs no sophister*—2 H6 V 1 191.

SOPHY

The Shah of Persia: *This scimitar That slew the Sophy*—Merch II 1 24. *A pension of thousands to be paid from the Sophy*—Tw II 5 197. *They say he has been fencer to the Sophy*—III 4 306.

SORE

A male fallow deer in his fourth year: *The preyful princess pierced and prick'd a pretty pleasing pricket; Some say a sore . . . put L to sore, then sorel jumps from thicket*—LLL IV 2 58.

SOREL

A male fallow deer in his third year—LLL IV 2 60 (quoted under the preceding word).

SORROW

To feel sorrow over, grieve for; hence *sorrowed*, sorrowful, regretful: *[The public body] send forth us, to make their sorrow'd render*—Tim V 1 152.

SORRY

Sore, painful: *I have a salt and sorry rheum offends me*—Oth III 4 51.

SORT (sb.)

(1) A lot: *Let blockish Ajax draw The sort to fight with Hector*—Troil I 3 375.

(2) Rank, quality: *Few of any sort, and none of name*—Ado I 1 7. *It may be his enemy is a gentleman of great sort*—H5 IV 7 141. *What prisoners of good sort are taken?*—IV 8 80. High rank: *Give notice to such men of sort and suit as are to meet him*—Meas IV 4 19. *There was none such in the army of any sort*—Ado I 1 32. *Of sorts*, of various ranks: *They have a king and officers of sorts*—H5 I 2 190.

(3) A set, crew: *The shallowest thick-skin of that barren sort*—Mids III 2 13. *A sort of traitors*—R2 IV 246. *Here I stand to answer thee, Or any he the proudest of thy sort*—3 H6 II 2 96. *A sort of vagabonds, rascals, and runaways*—R3 V 3 316. *Many in sort*, many together: *Russet-pated choughs, many in sort*—Mids III 2 21.

(4) Manner, way: *You do look, my son, in a moved sort*—Tp IV 146. *Unless you may be won by some other sort than your father's imposition*—Merch I 2 113. *Express yourself in a more comfortable sort*—Cor I 3 1. *[He] smiles in such a sort As if he mock'd himself*—Cæs I 2 205. *In sort, in a sort, in some sort*, in a way, to some extent: *Am I yourself But, as it were, in sort or limitation?*—Cæs II 1 282. *Is not, sir, my doublet as fresh as the first day I wore it? I mean, in a sort*—Tp II 1 102. *I have heard in some sort of thy miseries*—Tim IV 3 76.

SORT (vb.)

(1) To ordain, dispose: *God sort all!*—Merch V 132. *If God sort it so*—R3 II 3 36.

(2) To select, pick out: *Let us into the city presently To sort some gentlemen well skill'd in music*—Gent III 2 91. *To help me sort such needful ornaments As you think fit*—Rom IV 2 34.

(3) To arrange, contrive: *All my pains is sortea to no proof*—Shr IV 3 43. *I will sort a pitchy day for thee*—3 H6 V 6 85. *I'll sort occasion . . . To part the queen's proud kindred from the king*—R3 II 2 148. *When wilt thou sort an hour great strifes to end?*—Lucr 899. So *to sort out*: [Thy father] *Hath sorted out a sudden day of joy*—Rom III 5 110.

(4) To class, cause to associate: *I will not sort you with the rest of my servants*—Hml II 2 274. *Sorted*, associated: King [reads]. '*sorted and consorted . . . with . . .* Cost. *With a wench*—LLL I 1 261. *The word 'occupy'; which was an excellent good word before it was ill sorted*—2 H4 II 4 161.

(5) To adapt, make conformable: *My will is something sorted with his wish*—Gent I 3 63. *Sort thy heart to patience*—2 H6 II 4 68. [The maid] *sorts a sad look to her lady's sorrow*—Lucr 1221.

(6) To chance, turn out: *If it sort not well, you may conceal her*—Ado IV 1 242. *I am glad that all things sort so well*—V 4 7. *So far am I glad it so did sort*—Mids III 2 352. *Sort how it will, I shall have gold for all*—2 H6 I 2 107.

(7) To associate, consort: [The hare] *sometime sorteth with a herd of deer*—Ven 689.

(8) To suit, be fitting: *Why then it sorts, brave warriors, let's away*—3 H6 II 1 209. *This woman's answer sorts*—Troil I 1 109. *Well may it sort that this portentous figure Comes armed through our watch*—Hml I 1 109. With *with*: *Not sorting with a nuptial ceremony*—Mids V 55. *It sorts well with your fierceness*—H5 IV 1 63.

SORTANCE

Agreement, conformity: *With such powers As might hold sortance with his quality*—2 H4 IV 1 10.

SOT

A fool, dolt: *Without them (i.e. his books) He's but a sot, as I am*—Tp III 2 100. *Have you make-a de sot of us?*—Wiv III 1 118. *Of the loyal service of his son, When I inform'd him, then he call'd me sot*—Lr IV 2 7. *His description Proved us unspeaking sots*—Cymb V 5 177.

SOTTISH

Foolish: *Patience is sottish*—Ant IV 15 79.

SOUD

App. an imitative word to represent an exclamation by a tired person: Shr IV 1 145.

SOUL-FEARING

Soul-terrifying: *Their soul-fearing clamours (i.e. of the cannon)*—John II 383. See *Fear* (vb.) (1).

SOUND

Of the voice, not yet cracked: *Thy small pipe Is as the maiden's organ, shrill and sound*—Tw I 4 32.

SOUR

Used where we should rather say bitter: *You Pilates Have here deliver'd me to my sour cross*—R2 IV 240 (cf. 1 H4 I 1 25: *Those blessed feet Which . . . were nail'd . . . on the bitter cross*). *Heart's discontent and sour affliction*—2 H6 III 2 301. *Let me embrace thee, sour adversity*—3 H6 III 1 24. *Farewell sour annoy!*—V 7 45.

SOURLY

So as to cause a feeling of bitterness: *That sweet thief which sourly robs from me*—Sonn 35 14. Cf. the preceding word.

SOUSE

Of a bird of prey, to swoop down on: *Like an eagle o'er his aery towers, To souse annoyance that comes near his nest*—John V 2 149.

SOUSED

Pickled: *If I be not ashamed of my soldiers, I am a soused gurnet*—1 H4 IV 2 12.

SOUTH

The south wind: *Like foggy south puffing with wind and rain*—As III 5 50. *Tempest of commotion, like the south Borne with black vapour*—2 H4 II 4 392. Sim. *south-west*: *A south-west blow on ye!*—Tp I 2 323.

SOWL

To pull, haul: *He'll go, he says, and sowl the porter of Rome gates by the ears*—Cor IV 5 213.

SOWTER

A cobbler; as the name of a hound: *Sowter will cry upon't for all this*—Tw II 5 135. The application is not clear.

SPAN-COUNTER

A game in which one player threw a counter which the opponent won if he could throw another so as to hit it or to lie within a span of it: *Henry the Fifth, in whose time boys went to span-counter for French crowns*—2 H6 IV 2 165.

SPAVIN

A disease of horses affecting the hock-joint: *One would take it . . . the spavin Or springhalt reign'd among 'em*—H8 I 3 11. In pl.: *Sped with spavins*—Shr III 2 53.

SPEAK

(1) To speak of, describe (a person): *If thy rare qualities . . . could speak thee out*—H8 II 4 137. *I speak my good lord cardinal to this point*—166. *I cannot speak him home*—Cor II 2 107. *You speak him far*—Cymb I 1 24.

(2) App., to speak to, call upon: *The occasion speaks thee*—Tp II 1 207.

(3) To bespeak: *We have not spoke us (i.e. for ourselves) yet of torchbearers, we have not yet*

bespoken our torchbearers—Merch II 4 5. For the *of* cf. Merch IV 1 402 (*I humbly do desire your grace of pardon*); As V 4 56 (*I desire you of the like*).

SPECIALTY

(1) Essence, principle: *The specialty of rule hath been neglected*—Troil I 3 78.

(2) A deed or instrument, properly one under seal: *The packet is not come Where that and other specialties are bound*—LLL II 164. *Let specialties be therefore drawn between us*—Shr II 127.

SPECTACLES

Organs of vision, eyes: [I] *bid mine eyes be packing with my heart And call'd them blind and dusky spectacles*—2 H6 III 2 111. *Can we not Partition make with spectacles so precious 'Twixt fair and foul?*—Cymb I 6 36.

SPECULATION

(1) Looking on: *Though we . . . Took stand for idle speculation*—H5 IV 2 30.

(2) Vision, faculty of sight: *Speculation turns not to itself, Till it . . . is mirror'd there Where it may see itself*—Troil III 3 109. *Thou hast no speculation in those eyes*—Mcb III 4 95.

(3) An observer: *Servants . . . Which are to France the spies and speculations Intelligent of our state*—Lr III 1 23.

SPECULATIVE

Seeing, having the faculty of sight: *My speculative and officed instruments*—Oth I 3 271.

SPEED (sb.)

A speeder, helping power: *Saint Nicholas be thy speed!*—Gent III 1 300. *Hercules be thy speed!*—As I 2 222. *Good manners be your speed!*—1 H4 III 1 190. *Saint Francis be my speed!*—Rom V 3 121.

SPEED (vb.)

To dispatch, do for: *So be gone: you are sped*—Merch II 9 72. *Sped with spavins*—Shr III 2 53. *We three are married, but you two are sped*—V 2 185. *A plague o' both your houses! I am sped*—Rom III 1 94.

SPEKEN

Speak: *Where each man Thinks all is writ he speken can*—Per II Prol 11.

SPERR

To shut, bar: [The gates] *Sperr up the sons of Troy*—Troil Prol 19.

SPHERE

One of the transparent concentric shells supposed to surround the earth and carry the heavenly bodies with them in their revolution: *Yonder Venus in her glimmering sphere*—Mids III 2 61.

Two of the fairest stars . . . do entreat her eyes To twinkle in their spheres till they return—Rom II 2 15. *As the star moves not but in his sphere*—Hml IV 7 15.

SPHERED

(1) Set in his sphere: *Therefore is the glorious planet Sol In noble eminence enthroned and sphered Amidst the other*—Troil I 3 89.

(2) Rounded: *Thy sphered bias cheek*—Troil IV 5 8.

SPHERY

Starry: *Hermia's sphery eyne*—Mids II 2 99.

SPILL

To mar, destroy: *So full of artless jealousy is guilt, It spills itself in fearing to be spilt*—Hml IV 5 19. *All germens spill at once, That make ingrateful man!*—Lr III 2 8.

SPILTH

Spilling, effusion: *Drunken spilth of wine*—Tim II 2 169.

SPINSTER

A person who spins: *The spinsters and the knitters in the sun*—Tw II 4 45. *The spinsters, carders, fullers, weavers*—H8 I 2 33. *Nor the division of a battle knows More than a spinster*—Oth I 1 23.

SPIRT

To sprout, shoot: [Shall] *Our scions, put in wild and savage stock, Spirt up so suddenly into the clouds*—H5 III 5 7.

SPITAL

A hospital: *To the spital go*—H5 II 1 78. *My Nell is dead i' the spital*—V 1 86.

SPITAL-HOUSE

The same as the foregoing: *She, whom the spital-house and ulcerous sores Would cast the gorge at*—Tim IV 3 39.

SPITE

(1) Injury or insult inflicted: *I'll find Demetrius and revenge this spite*—Mids III 2 420. *The tears have got small victory by that; For it* (*i.e.* her face) *was bad enough before their spite*—Rom IV 1 30. *Kill me with spites*—Sonn 40 14.

(2) Vexation, mortification: *This is the deadly spite that angers me*—1 H4 III 1 192. *The time is out of joint: O cursed spite, That ever I was born to set it right!*—Hml I 5 189. *'Tis the spite of hell, the fiend's arch-mock*—Oth IV 1 71.

(3) *In spite of,* in contempt or scorn of, so as to mortify: *To fashion this false sport, in spite of me*—Mids III 2 194. *Old Montague is come, And flourishes his blade in spite of me*—Rom I 1 84. So *in his master's spite: Him will I tear out of*

that cruel eye, Where he sits crowned in his master's spite—Tw V 130.

(4) *In spite of spite, spite of spite,* in spite of everything, come what come may: *Faulconbridge, In spite of spite, alone upholds the day*—John V 4 4. *Spite of spite needs must I rest awhile*—3 H6 II 3 5.

SPIT WHITE

Spitting white was said to be a consequence of inflaming the stomach with liquor: [If] *I brandish any thing but a bottle, I would I might never spit white again*—2 H4 I 2 236.

SPLAY

To spay, castrate (a female): *Does your worship mean to geld and splay all the youth of the city?*—Meas II 1 242.

SPLEEN

(1) Supposed to be a seat of strong emotions; (a) Of fierceness, pugnacity: *With ladies' faces and fierce dragons' spleens*—John II 68. *Such things as might offend the weakest spleen To fight for and maintain*—Troil II 2 128. (b) Of anger: *You shall digest the venom of your spleen, Though it do split you*—Cæs IV 3 47. (c) Of laughter: *Such fantastic tricks . . . As make the angels weep; who, with our spleens, Would all themselves laugh mortal*—Meas II 2 121.

(2) Hence used of moods and acts supposed to proceed from the spleen; (a) Fire, impetuosity: *I am scalded with my violent motion, And spleen of speed to see your majesty*—John V 7 49. *The unruly spleen Of Tybalt deaf to peace*—Rom III 1 162. (b) Ill-will, resentment: *Take good heed You charge not in your spleen a noble person*—H8 I 2 173. *I have no spleen against you*—II 4 89. (c) Violent mirth: *With such a zealous laughter . . . That in this spleen ridiculous appears . . . passion's solemn tears*—LLL V 2 116. *Haply my presence May well abate the over-merry spleen*—Shr Ind 1 136. *If you desire the spleen, and will laugh yourselves into stitches, follow me*—Tw III 2 72. (d) Caprice: *That same wicked bastard of Venus that was . . . conceived of spleen and born of madness*—As IV 1 216. *A weasel hath not such a deal of spleen As you are toss'd with*—1 H4 II 3 81. *Base inclination and the start of spleen*—III 2 125. (e) Passion: *Patience; Or I shall say you are all in all in spleen*—Oth IV 1 88. (f) A sudden fit: *The lightning . . . That, in a spleen, unfolds both heaven and earth*—Mids I 1 145. An impulse: *A thousand spleens bear her a thousand ways*—Ven 907.

SPLEENFUL

Hot, impetuous: *Their spleenful mutiny*—2 H6 III 2 128. *Let my spleenful sons this trull deflour*—Tit II 3 191.

SPLEENY

Headstrong, fervent: *I know her for A spleeny Lutheran*—H8 III 2 98.

SPLENITIVE

Hasty, passionate: *Though I am not splenitive and rash*—Hml V 1 284.

SPLINTER

To bind up in splints; fig.: *The broken rancour of your high-swoln hearts, But lately splinter'd, knit, and join'd together*—R3 II 2 117. *This broken joint between you and her husband entreat her to splinter*—Oth II 3 328.

SPOIL (sb.)

Ravage, destruction: *Old age . . . can do no more spoil upon my face*—H5 V 2 248. *Death doth front thee with apparent spoil*—1 H6 IV 2 26. *Yonder is the wolf that makes this spoil*—3 H6 V 4 80. *Who his* (*i.e.* Time's) *spoil of beauty can forbid?*—Sonn 65 12. Ruin of character: *Villanous company hath been the spoil of me*—1 H4 III 3 11. An act of ravage or rapine: *Fit for treasons, stratagems and spoils*—Merch V 85. App., blood: *Here thy hunters stand, Sign'd in thy spoil*—Cæs III 1 205.

SPOIL (vb.)

(1) To destroy, undo: *In, or we are spoil'd!*—Err V 37. *Disorder, that hath spoil'd us, friend us now!*—H5 IV 5 17. *Take good heed You . . . spoil* [not] *your nobler soul*—H8 I 2 173. *I am spoil'd, undone by villains!*—Oth V 1 54.

(2) To carry off as spoil: *His that spoils her young before her face*—3 H6 II 2 14.

SPORT

Amorous dallying, wantonness: *Being intercepted in your sport*—Tit III 3 80. *When the blood is made dull with the act of sport*—Oth II 1 229.

SPORTFUL

Amorous, wanton: *Let Kate be chaste and Dian sportful!*—Shr II 263. *Sportful Edward*—3 H6 V 1 18.

SPORTIVE

The same as the preceding word: *I, that am not shaped for sportive tricks*—R3 I 1 14. *Why should others' false adulterate eyes Give salutation to my sportive blood?*—Sonn 121 5.

SPOT

Prob., a pattern: *What are you sewing here? A fine spot, in good faith*—Cor I 3 55.

SPOUSAL

Espousal: *So be there 'twixt your kingdoms such a spousal, That . . .*—H5 V 2 390.

SPRAG

Smart, quick: *He is a good sprag memory*—Wiv IV 1 84.

SPRIGHT

Spirit; mind, soul: *Adonis, with a lazy spright . . . cries . . .*—Ven 181. *Intending weariness with heavy spright*—Lucr 121.

SPRIGHTFUL

High-spirited: *Spoke like a sprightful noble gentleman*—John IV 2 177.

SPRIGHTFULLY

With high spirit: *The Duke of Norfolk, sprightfully and bold, Stays but the summons*—R2 I 3 3.

SPRING

A sprout, shoot: *This canker that eats up Love's tender spring*—Ven 656. *To dry the old oak's sap and cherish springs*—Lucr 950.

SPRINGHALT

Stringhalt; a disorder of horses, consisting in a convulsive movement of the hind legs: *One would take it . . . the spavin Or springhalt reign'd among 'em*—H8 I 3 11.

SPRITE (sb.)

Spirit; mind, soul: *The quintessence of every sprite Heaven would in little show*—As III 2 147. *Her contrite sighs unto the clouds bequeathed Her winged sprite*—Lucr 1727. *One's sprites,* one's spirits: *Cheer we up his sprites*—Mcb IV 1 127.

SPRITE (vb.)

To haunt: *I am sprited with a fool*—Cymb II 3 144.

SPRITELY

Ghost-like, spectral: *Spritely shows Of mine own kindred*—Cymb V 5 428.

SPY

(1) An advanced guard, forerunner: *When sorrows come, they come not single spies, But in battalions*—Hml IV 5 78.

(2) *The perfect spy of the time,* perh., (the result of) an exact discovery or determination of the (fitting) time to do the deed: *[I will] Acquaint you with the perfect spy o' the time*—Mcb III 1 130.

SQUANDER

(1) To scatter, disperse: *Other ventures he hath, squandered abroad*—Merch I 3 21.

(2) To go at random: *The squandering glances of the fool*—As II 7 57.

SQUARE (adj.)

Square to, truly representing: *If report be square to her*—Ant II 2 189.

SQUARE (sb.)

(1) The yoke (of a smock): *You would think a smock were a she-angel, he so chants to . . . the work about the square on't*—Wint IV 4 210.

(2) *The most precious square of sense,* the most exquisitely sensitive part of sensibility: *All other joys, Which the most precious square of sense possesses*—Lr I 1 75. Cf. *Precious* (1).

SQUARE (vb.)

(1) To adjust one's estimate of, measure: *Critics apt . . . to square the general sex By Cressid's rule*—Troil V 2 131.

(2) To quarrel: *Now they never meet . . . But they do square*—Mids II 1 28. *Are you such fools To square for this?*—Tit II 1 99. *'Twere pregnant they should square between themselves*—Ant II 1 45. *Mine honesty and I begin to square*—III 13 41.

SQUARER

A quarreller, brawler: *Is there no young squarer now that will make a voyage with him to the devil?*—Ado I 1 82.

SQUASH

An unripe peascod: *I pray you (i.e.* Peaseblossom), *commend me to Mistress Squash, your mother, and to Master Peascod, your father*—Mids III 1 190. *As a squash is before 'tis a peascod*—Tw I 5 166. Of a boy: *This kernel, This squash, this gentleman*—Wint I 2 159.

SQUIER

Square; a rule, measure: *Do not you know my lady's foot by the squier?*—LLL V 2 474. *Jumps twelve foot and a half by the squier*—Wint IV 4 347. *If I travel but four foot by the squier further*—1 H4 II 2 12.

SQUINY

To look asquint: *Dost thou squiny at me?*—Lr IV 6 140.

STABLISH

Establish: *[To] stablish quietness on every side*—1 H6 V 1 10.

STABLISHMENT

Establishment; a settled government: *Unto her He gave the stablishment of Egypt*—Ant III 6 8.

STAFF

(1) A spear-shaft, a spear: *No plume in any English crest That is removed by a staff of France*—John II 317. *Their armed staves in charge*—2 H4 IV 1 120. *Amaze the welkin with your broken staves!*—R3 V 3 341. *Wretched kerns, whose arms Are hired to bear their staves*—Mcb V 7 17.

(2) A stanza: *Let me hear a staff, a stanze, a verse*—LLL IV 2 107.

STAGGERS

Perplexities, bewilderment: *I will throw thee . . . Into the staggers . . . Of youth and ignorance*—All's II 3 169.

STAID

In a state of calmness, not excited: *Ere wildness Vanquish my staider senses*—Cymb III 4 9.

STAIN

A trace, tinge: *You have some stain of soldier in you*—All's I 1 122. *Nor [hath] any man an attaint but he carries some stain of it*—Troil I 2 26.

STALE (sb.)[1]

(1) A bait, decoy: *Bring it hither, For stale to catch these thieves*—Tp IV 186. *To cast thy wandering eyes on every stale*—Shr III 1 90. A mask, a cover for a loose life: *Poor I am but his stale*—Err II 1 101.

(2) A dupe, laughing-stock: *Is it your will To make a stale of me amongst these mates?*—Shr I 1 57. *Had he none else to make a stale but me?*—3 H6 III 3 260. *Was there none else in Rome to make a stale, But Saturnine?*—Tit I 304.

STALE (sb.)[2]

A harlot: *A contaminated stale*—Ado II 2 25. *To link my dear friend to a common stale*—IV 1 66.

STALE (sb.)[3]

Urine (of horses): *Thou didst drink The stale of horses*—Ant I 4 61.

STALE (vb.)

To make common or cheap: *This thrice worthy . . . lord Must not so stale his palm, nobly acquired*—Troil II 3 200. *Did [I] use To stale with ordinary oaths my love To every new protester*—Cæs I 2 72. *Out of use and staled by other men*—IV 1 38. *Age cannot wither her, nor custom stale Her infinite variety*—Ant II 2 240. To tell to the common ear: *I will venture To stale't (i.e.* the tale*) a little more*—Cor I 1 94.

STALKING-HORSE

A real or artificial horse under cover of which a sportsman stole up to game: *He uses his folly like a stalking-horse*—As V 4 111.

STALL

(1) To install, invest: *[Mayst thou] see another . . . Deck'd in thy rights, as thou art stall'd in mine!*—R3 I 3 205. To place, set: *Stall this in your bosom*—All's I 3 131.

(2) Equivalent to *Single* (vb.) (*q.v.*): *When as thine eye hath . . . stall'd the deer that thou shouldst strike*—Pilgr 299.

(3) To dwell: *We could not stall together In the whole world*—Ant V 1 39.

STAMP

A coin: *I found thee of more value Than stamps in gold*—Wiv III 4 15. *Hanging a golden stamp about their necks*—Mcb IV 3 153. *'Tween man and man they weigh not every stamp*—Cymb V 4 24.

STANCH

To quench, allay: *Let my tears stanch the earth's dry appetite*—Tit III 1 14.

STANCHLESS

Unquenchable, insatiate: *A stanchless avarice*—Mcb IV 3 78.

STAND (vb.)

(1) To resist, stand up to: *An she stand him but a little*—Shr I 2 113. *None durst stand him*—1 H6 I 1 123. *The villain would not stand me*—Cymb I 2 15. *Who dares not stand his foe*—V 3 60.

(2) *To stand on, upon,* to concern, be of consequence to: *Consider how it stands upon my credit*—Err IV 1 68. *It stands me much upon, To stop all hopes whose growth may damage me*—R3 IV 2 59. *It only stands Our lives upon to use our strongest hands*—Ant II 1 50. To be incumbent upon: *It stands your grace upon to do him right*—R2 II 3 138. *Does it not, thinks't thee, stand me now upon . . . To quit him with this arm?*—Hml V 2 63. To make it incumbent upon: *My state Stands on me to defend, not to debate*—Lr V 1 68. To be in a position calling for: *O, let us hence; I stand on sudden haste*—Rom II 3 93.

STANDARD

He who bears the standard, an ensign: *Thou shalt be my lieutenant, monster, or my standard*—Tp III 2 17.

STANDING

(1) Existence, duration: *His folly . . . [which] will continue The standing of his body*—Wint I 2 429.

(2) *How this grace Speaks his own standing!* how clearly in this graceful embodiment (*i.e.* that in the picture) does (the grace of) its attitude appear—Tim I 1 30.

STANDING-BED

A bed on legs: *There's his chamber . . . his standing-bed and truckle-bed*—Wiv IV 5 6.

STANDING-TUCK

See *Tuck.*

STANIEL

A kestrel, a worthless kind of hawk: *With what wing the staniel checks at it!*—Tw II 5 124.

STANZE, STANZO

Stanza: *Let me hear a staff, a stanze, a verse*—LLL IV 2 107. *Come, more; another stanzo*—As II 5 18.

STAR

(1) One's sphere or fortune; *out of thy star,* above thee in fortune: *Lord Hamlet is a prince, out of thy star*—Hml II 2 141. Cf. *In my stars I am above thee*—Tw II 5 155.

(2) *The seven stars,* the Pleiades: *We that take purses go by the moon and the seven stars*—1 H4 I 2 15. *The reason why the seven stars are no more than seven*—Lr I 5 37.

STARE

To stand on end: *That makest my blood cold and my hair to stare*—Cæs IV 3 280.

STARTING-HOLE

A loophole, evasion: *What starting-hole canst thou now find out?*—1 H4 II 4 290.

STARTINGLY

Abruptly, impetuously: *Why do you speak so startingly and rash?*—Oth III 4 79.

STATE

(1) A mode of standing, an attitude: *When shall you hear that I Will praise a hand, a foot . . . A gait, a state?*—LLL IV 3 183.

(2) Settled order: *Grievous crimes Committed . . . Against the state and profit of this land*—R2 IV 223.

(3) Estate, fortune: *My state being gall'd with my expense*—Wiv III 4 5. *I told you My state was nothing*—Merch III 2 261. *Were it good To set the exact wealth of all our states All at one cast?*—1 H4 IV 1 45.

(4) Station, rank: [All] *Shall share the good of our returned fortune According to the measure of their states*—As V 4 180. *I'll have thy beauty . . . made More homely than thy state*—Wint IV 4 435. *I would the college of the cardinals Would choose him pope . . . That were a state fit for his holiness* —2 H6 I 3 64. *Had he match'd according to his state*—3 H6 II 2 152. Condition of king, king-ship: *To-day . . . O'erthrows thy* (i.e. King Richard's) *joys, friends, fortune and thy state*— R2 III 2 71. *The skipping king . . . carded his state, Mingled his royalty with capering fools*— 1 H4 III 2 60. *By my state I* (i.e. King Edward) *swear to thee*—3 H6 III 2 03. *State of law,* legal status as king: *Thy* (i.e. King Richard's) *state of law is bondslave to the law*—R2 II 1 114.

(5) Political science: *The state, wherein I studied, Is . . . Grown . . . tedious*—Meas II 4 7. *An affectioned ass, that cons state without book*— Tw II 3 160.

(6) A canopy of state: *A small table under a state for the* Cardinal—H8 I 4 (Stage Dir). So *cloth of state: The King takes place under the cloth of state*— H8 I 4 (Stage Dir). A seat of state or dignity: *Sitting in my state*—Tw II 5 50. *This chair shall be my state*—1 H4 II 4 415. *He sits in his state, as a thing made for Alexander*—Cor V 4 22. So *chair of state: Look where the sturdy rebel sits, Even in the chair of state*—3 H6 I 1 50. *Her grace sat down To rest awhile . . . In a rich chair of state*—H8 IV 1 65.

(7) Dignitaries, notables: *Our coronation done, we will accite . . . all our state*—2 H4 V 2 141. *Your greatness and this noble state*—Troil II 3 118. *Hail, all you state of Greece!*—IV 5 65. In pl.: *How like you this wild counsel, mighty states?* —John II 395. *Kings, queens and states . . . This viperous slander enters*—Cymb III 4 39. So *general state: Priam and the general state of Troy*—Troil IV 2 69. *State of war,* council of war: [Ajax] *rails on our state of war*—Troil I 3 191. *Please it our great general To call together all his state of war*—II 3 270.

(8) *The state of floods,* the majestic body of the ocean: *The tide of blood in me . . . Now doth . . . turn and ebb back to the sea, Where it shall mingle with the state of floods*—2 H4 V 2 129.

(9) App., a body of considerations: *The question did at first so stagger me, Bearing a state of mighty moment in't*—H8 II 4 212.

STATION

An attitude: *A station like the herald Mercury* —Hml III 4 58. Standing: *Her motion and her station are as one*—Ant III 3 22.

STATIST

A statesman, politician: *I once did hold it, as our statists do, A baseness to write fair*—Hml V 2 33. *Statist though I am none*—Cymb II 4 16.

STATUA

Statue: *Like dumb statuas or breathing stones*— R3 III 7 25. *She dreamt to-night she saw my statua*—Cæs II 2 76. *The base of Pompey's statua* —III 2 192.

STATUTE

(1) A bond, mortgage; a particular mode of recognizance, the debt becoming a charge on the party's lands (see *Recognizance* (1)): *His statutes, his recognizances, his fines*—Hml V 1 113. *The statute of thy beauty thou wilt take, Thou usurer* —Sonn 134 9.

(2) *Statutes,* articles of agreement: *You three . . . Have sworn . . . to keep those statutes*—LLL I 1 15.

STATUTE-CAPS

Woollen caps which citizens and the lower orders were under obligation to wear on certain days under a statute of Elizabeth for the encouragement of the woollen industry: *Better wits have worn plain statute-caps*—LLL V 2 281.

STAY (sb.)

An obstacle, check: *Here's a stay*—John II 455.

19

STAY (vb.)

(1) To await, wait for: *My father stays my coming*—Gent II 2 13. *The Duke of Norfolk . . . Stays but the summons*—R2 I 3 3. *Say either* [good or bad], *and I'll stay the circumstance*—Rom II 5 36. So *to stay upon: I have a servant comes with me along, That stays upon me*—Meas IV 1 46. *Our throats are sentenced and stay upon execution*—Cor V 4 8. *To stay upon one's leisure, will,* &c.: *Worthy Macbeth, we stay upon your leisure*—Mcb I 3 148. *He stays upon your will*—Ant I 2 119. *They stay upon your patience*—Hml III 2 112.

(2) To keep, detain: [He] *stays me here at home unkept*—As I 1 8. *A great suspicion; stay the friar too*—Rom V 3 187. *Calpurnia here, my wife, stays me at home*—Cæs II 2 75.

(3) To face, encounter: *She will not stay the siege of loving terms*—Rom I 1 218. *They basely fly and dare not stay the field*—Ven 894.

STEAD

(1) To help, serve: *Rich garments, linens . . . Which since have steaded much*—Tp I 2 164. *Can you so stead me As bring me to the sight of Isabella?*—Meas I 4 17. *My intercession likewise steads my foe*—Rom II 3 54. *I could never better stead thee than now*—Oth I 3 344.

(2) *To stead up,* to keep or fulfil instead of another: *We shall advise this wronged maid to stead up your appointment*—Meas III 1 259.

STEALTH

(1) Theft: *Ingratitude makes it worse than stealth*—Tim III 4 27. *Hog in sloth, fox in stealth*—Lr III 4 95.

(2) A secret going: *I told him of your stealth unto this wood*—Mids III 2 310. *Fair Helen told me of their stealth*—IV 1 164. Imperceptible motion or progress: *I feel this youth's perfections With an invisible and subtle stealth To creep in at mine eyes*—Tw I 5 315. *Thy dial's shady stealth*—Sonn 77 7.

STEELY

Unyielding (in rectitude): *Virtue's steely bones*—All's I 1 114.

STEEP-DOWN

Steep, precipitous: *Steep-down gulfs of liquid fire*—Oth V 2 280.

STEEP-UP

Steep, precipitous: *The steep-up heavenly hill*—Sonn 7 5. *Her stand she takes upon a steep-up hill*—Pilgr 121.

STELL

To set, place: *A face where all distress is stell'd*—Lucr 1444. *Mine eye hath play'd the painter and hath stell'd Thy beauty's form in table of my heart*—Sonn 24 1.

STELLED

Stellated, starry; or perh., set in their spheres (see *Sphere* and *Stell*): *The sea . . . would have buoy'd up, And quench'd the stelled fires*—Lr III 7 59.

STERNAGE

To sternage of, astern of, so as to follow: *Grapple your minds to sternage of this navy*—H5 III Chor 18.

STEW

(1) App., a stew-pan: *I have seen corruption boil and bubble Till it o'er-run the stew*—Meas V 320.

(2) A brothel: *He would unto the stews, And from the common'st creature pluck a glove*—R2 V 3 16. *An I could get me but a wife in the stews*—2 H4 I 2 59. *If he shall think it fit, A saucy stranger in his court to mart As in a Romish stew*—Cymb I 6 150.

STICKLER-LIKE

In the manner of a stickler, *i.e.* an umpire who watched a duel and stopped it when he considered that the combatants had fought enough: *The dragon wing of night o'erspreads the earth, And, stickler-like, the armies separates*—Troil V 8 17.

STIGMATIC

One branded with deformity: *Foul stigmatic*—2 H6 V 1 215. *Like a foul mis-shapen stigmatic*—3 H6 II 2 136.

STIGMATICAL

Branded with deformity: *Unkind, Stigmatical in making, worse in mind*—Err IV 2 21.

STILL (adj.)

Continual, constant: *Still use of grief makes wild grief tame*—R3 IV 4 229. *By still practice [I will] learn to know thy meaning*—Tit III 2 45.

STILL (adv.)

Constantly, always: *Love is still most precious in itself*—Gent II 6 24. *Pardon is still the nurse of second woe*—Meas II 1 298. *This thy counten-ance, still lock'd in steel, I never saw till now*—Troil IV 5 195. *Thou still hast been the father of good news*—Hml II 2 42. *Still the house-affairs would draw her thence*—Oth I 3 147. *Still and anon,* every now and then: *Still and anon [I] cheer'd up the heavy time*—John IV 1 47. *Still an end,* constantly: *A slave, that still an end turns me to shame!*—Gent IV 4 67.

STILL-BREEDING

Continually propagating: *These two beget A generation of still-breeding thoughts*—R2 V 5 7.

STILL-CLOSING

Continually closing: *The still-closing waters*—Tp III 3 64.

STILL-GAZING

Continually gazing: *In silent wonder of still-gazing eyes*—Lucr 84.

STILLITORY

A still, alembic: *From the stillitory of thy face excelling Comes breath perfumed*—Ven 443.

STILLNESS

(1) Silence, taciturnity: *There are a sort of men . . . [who] do a wilful stillness entertain*—Merch I 1 88. *Modest stillness and humility*—H5 III 1 4.

(2) Well-regulated behaviour: *The gravity and stillness of your youth*—Oth II 3 191.

STILL-PEERING

App. a corruption; perh. *still-piecing*, i.e. continually closing, should be read: *You leaden messengers . . . Fly with false aim; move the still-peering air, That sings with piercing*—All's III 2 111.

STILL-VEXED

Continually agitated or disturbed: *The still-vex'd Bermoothes*—Tp I 2 229.

STINT

(1) To cause to cease, check: *We must not stint Our necessary actions*—H8 I 2 76. *The combatants being kin Half stints their strife before their strokes begin*—Troil IV 5 92. *He can at pleasure stint their melody*—Tit IV 4 86. *[I will] make peace stint war*—Tim V 4 83.

(2) To cease: *Pretty fool, it stinted and said 'Ay'*—Rom I 3 48. *And stint thou too, I pray thee, nurse, say I*—58. *[She] swears she'll never stint*—Per IV 4 42.

STITHY (sb.)

An anvil; and hence, a smithy: *My imaginations are as foul As Vulcan's stithy*—Hml III 2 88.

STITHY (vb.)

To forge: *The forge that stithied Mars his helm*—Troil IV 5 255.

STOCCADO

Italian; in fencing, a lunge, thrust: *You stand on distance, your passes, stoccadoes, and I know not what*—Wiv II 1 233.

STOCCATA

The same as the foregoing: *Alla stoccata* (perh. better *a la stoccata*, *la stoccata* being taken as a single word, with the English indefinite article prefixed) *carries it away*—Rom III 1 77.

STOCK¹

In the same sense as *Stoccado*: *To see thee pass thy punto, thy stock, thy reverse*—Wiv II 3 26.

STOCK²

A stocking: *What need a man care for a stock (i.e. a portion) with a wench, when she can knit him a stock?*—Gent III 1 311. *With a linen stock on one leg*—Shr III 2 67. *In a flame-coloured stock*—Tw I 3 144. So *nether-stock*: *Ere I lead this life long, I'll sew nether stocks*—1 H4 II 4 129. *When a man's over-lusty at legs, then he wears wooden nether-stocks*—Lr II 4 9.

STOCK-FISH

A fish (commonly cod) cured by splitting and drying hard without salt: *Some [report] that he was begot between two stock-fishes*—Meas III 2 116. *You starveling, you elf-skin . . . you stock-fish!*—1 H4 II 4 270. *To make a stock-fish of*, to beat as a stock-fish is beaten before it is cooked in order to soften it: *I'll turn my mercy out o' doors and make a stock-fish of thee*—Tp III 2 78.

STOCKISH

Blockish, insensible: *Nought so stockish . . . But music for the time doth change his nature*—Merch V 81.

STOLE

A long vest: *There my white stole of chastity I daff'd*—Compl 297.

STOMACH (sb.)

(1) As a seat of strong emotions: *Losers will have leave To ease their stomachs with their bitter tongues*—Tit III 1 233. *I should answer From a full-flowing stomach*—Lr V 3 73.

(2) Hence applied to (a) Anger: *That you might kill your stomach on your meat And not upon your maid*—Gent I 2 68. *The winds grow high; so do your stomachs, lords*—2 H6 II 1 54. (b) Courage, spirit: *Which raised in me An undergoing stomach, to bear up Against what should ensue*—Tp I 2 156. *The bloody Douglas . . . Gan vail his stomach*—2 H4 I 1 127. *Some enterprise That hath a stomach in't*—Hml I 1 99. (c) Pride, haughtiness: *Vail your stomachs, for it is no boot*—Shr V 2 176. *A man Of an unbounded stomach, ever ranking Himself with princes*—H8 IV 2 33.

STOMACH (vb.)

To resent: *Believe not all; or, if you must believe, Stomach not all*—Ant III 4 11.

STOMACHING

Ill-feeling: *'Tis not a time For private stomaching*—Ant II 2 8.

STONE

To turn to stone: *Thou dost stone my heart*—Oth V 2 63.

STONE-BOW

A cross-bow for shooting stones: *O, for a stone-bow, to hit him in the eye!*—Tw II 5 51.

STONISHED

Astonished: *Stonish'd as night-wanderers often are*—Ven 825.

STOOP

Perh. as adj., stooping: Dum. *As upright as the cedar.* Biron. *Stoop, I say; Her shoulder is with child*—LLL IV 3 89.

STOOP

Of a hawk, to swoop down from her pitch (see *Pitch* (sb.) (1)) upon her prey: *My falcon now is sharp and passing empty; And till she stoop she must not be full-gorged*—Shr IV 1 193 (with a play). *Though his affections are higher mounted than ours, yet, when they stoop, they stoop with the like wing*—H5 IV 1 110. Of an eagle: *They fly Chickens, the way which they stoop'd eagles*—Cymb V 3 41. *The holy eagle Stoop'd, as to foot us*—V 4 115.

STORE

Increase, breeding: *Those whom Nature hath not made for store*—Sonn 11 9. *Truth and beauty shall together thrive, If from thyself to store thou wouldst convert*—14 11.

STORY

To narrate, give an account of: [She] *stories His victories, his triumphs and his glories*—Ven 1013. *He stories to her ears her husband's fame*—Lucr 106. To describe (a person): *Rather than story him in his own hearing*—Cymb I 4 34.

STOUP

A drinking-vessel: *Marian, I say! a stoup of wine!*—Tw II 3 14. *Fetch me a stoup of liquor*—Hml V 1 68. *Set me the stoups of wine upon that table*—V 2 278. *I have a stoup of wine*—Oth II 3 30.

STOUT

Proud, haughty: *I will be strange, stout*—Tw II 5 185. *As stout and proud as he were lord of all*—2 H6 I 1 187. *Correcting thy stout heart*—Cor III 2 78.

STOUTNESS

Pride, haughtiness: *Thy dangerous stoutness*—Cor III 2 127. *His stoutness When he did stand for consul*—V 6 27.

STOVER

Fodder: *Flat meads thatch'd with stover*—Tp IV 63.

STRACHY

An unexplained word, no doubt a corruption: *The lady of the Strachy married the yeoman of the wardrobe*—Tw II 5 44.

STRAIGHT-PIGHT

Straight-fixed, erect: *Straight-pight Minerva*—Cymb V 5 164. See *Pight*.

STRAIN (sb.)¹

(1) Disposition, nature: *I would all of the same strain were in the same distress*—Wiv III 3 196. *You have shown to-day your valiant strain*—Lr V 3 40.

(2) A trait, tendency: *Unless he know some strain in me, that I know not myself*—Wiv II 1 90. *Love is full of unbefitting strains*—LLL V 2 770. *Praise his most vicious strain, And call it excellent*—Tim IV 3 213. *A strain of rareness*, a trait not easily to be matched: [Thou] *shalt hereafter find It is no act of common passage, but A strain of rareness*—Cymb III 4 93.

STRAIN (sb.)²

(1) Stretch, pitch: *If it did infect my blood with joy, Or swell my thoughts to any strain of pride*—2 H4 IV 5 170.

(2) A strain on the feelings, a pang: *Measure his woe the length and breadth of mine And let it answer every strain for strain*—Ado V 1 11. *Other strains of woe*—Sonn 90 13.

(3) *The fine strains of honour*, honour strained to a fine point, the niceties or refinements of honour: *Thou hast affected the fine strains of honour, To imitate the graces of the gods*—Cor V 3 149.

(4) *Make no strain but that*, make no difficulty about thinking that: *Make no strain, But that Achilles . . . will . . .*—Troil I 3 326.

STRAIN (vb.)

(1) To urge, press: *If your lady strain his entertainment*—Oth III 3 250.

(2) Perh., to swerve from the right path: *I appeal To your own conscience . . . With what encounter so uncurrent I Have strain'd to appear thus*—Wint III 2 46.

(3) Perh., to produce in a constrained manner: *It is the lark that sings so out of tune, Straining harsh discords*—Rom III 5 27.

STRAIT

(1) Tight: *You rode . . . in your strait strossers*—H5 III 7 56.

(2) Miserly, niggardly: *I beg cold comfort; and you are so strait . . . you deny me that*—John V 7 42.

STRAITED

Put to difficulty, at a loss: *If your lass Interpretation should abuse . . . you were straited For a reply*—Wint IV 4 362.

STRANGE

(1) Foreign, of another country: *One of the strange queen's lords*—LLL IV 2 133. *Look you lisp and wear strange suits*—As IV 1 33. *Desire My man's abode where I did leave him: he Is strange and peevish*—Cymb I 6 52. *I am something curious, being strange, To have them in safe stowage*—191. Perh. also Wint II 3 179 (quoted under *Strangely* (1)) (the child being regarded as the offspring of an alien).

(2) Unacquainted, not understanding: *To put a strange face on his own perfection*—Ado II 3 49. *In thy fortunes [I] am unlearn'd and strange*—Tim IV 3 56. *You make me strange Even to the disposition that I owe*—Mcb III 4 112.

(3) Like a stranger: *You grow exceeding strange*—Merch I 1 67. *I will acquaintance strangle and look strange*—Sonn 89 8. As adv.: *Why look you strange on me? you know me well*—Err V 295. *Why do you look so strange upon your wife?*—All's V 3 168. Distant, not familiar: *I will be strange, stout*—Tw II 5 185. *You throw a strange regard upon me*—V 219. Nest. *What a vice were it in Ajax now,—* Ulyss. *If he were proud,— . . .* Dio. *Or strange*—Troil II 3 246. *I'll prove more true Than those that have been cunning to be strange*—Rom II 2 100. Reserved, retiring: *Till strange love, grown bold, Think true love acted simple modesty*—Rom III 2 15.

(4) Used to mark a thing as worthy of high commendation or as otherwise noteworthy or remarkable: [With] *observation strange my meaner ministers Their several kinds have done*—Tp III 3 87. *Impossible be strange attempts to those That weigh their pains in sense*—All's I 1 239. *He hath laid strange courtesies . . . upon me*—Ant II 2 157. *Fame answering the most strange inquire*—Per III Prol 22.

(5) *To make it strange*, to seem to be shocked: *She makes it strange; but she would be best pleased To be so anger'd with another letter*—Gent I 2 102. To think too much of the difficulty of a thing: *Why makest thou it so strange? She is a woman, therefore may be woo'd*—Tit II 1 81.

STRANGE-ACHIEVED

Perh., gained in foreign lands or by unusual methods: *The canker'd heaps of strange-achieved gold*—2 H4 IV 5 72.

STRANGELY

(1) As an alien: *As by strange fortune It (i.e.* the babe) *came to us, I . . . charge thee . . . That thou commend it strangely to some place Where chance may nurse or end it*—Wint II 3 179. See *Strange* (1).

(2) In the manner of a stranger, in a distant or reserved manner: *You all look strangely on me*—2 H4 V 2 63. *Please it our general to pass strangely by him*—Troil III 3 39. *They pass by strangely*—71. *Against that time when thou shalt strangely pass And scarcely greet me*—Sonn 49 5.

(3) In a way worthy of high commendation or otherwise noteworthy or remarkable: *Thou Hast strangely stood the test*—Tp IV 6. *O mischief strangely thwarting!*—Ado III 2 135. *The herds Were strangely clamorous to the frighted fields*—1 H4 III 1 39.

STRANGENESS

Distant behaviour, reserve: *Ungird thy strangeness and tell me what I shall vent to my lady*—Tw IV 1 16. *The strangeness of his alter'd countenance*—2 H6 III 1 5. *Worthier than himself Here tend the savage strangeness he puts on*—Troil II 3 134. *He shall in strangeness stand no further off Than in a politic distance*—Oth III 3 12.

STRANGER (adj.)

Strange: *You, that did . . . foot me as you spurn a stranger cur*—Merch I 3 118. *She, that never coped with stranger eyes*—Lucr 99. Foreign, of another country: *New friends and stranger companies*—Mids I 1 219. *Swearing allegiance . . . To stranger blood*—John V 1 10. *The stranger paths of banishment*—R2 I 3 143.

STRANGER (vb.)

To estrange, alienate: *Dower'd with our curse, and stranger'd with our oath*—Lr I 1 207.

STRAPPADO

A military punishment consisting in raising the culprit to a height by means of a rope and suddenly letting him fall half-way with a jerk: *An I were at the strappado, or all the racks in the world*—1 H4 II 4 261.

STRATAGEM

A dreadful deed: *The man that hath no music in himself . . . Is fit for treasons, stratagems and spoils*—Merch V 83. *What stratagems, how fell, how butcherly . . . This deadly quarrel daily doth beget!*—3 H6 II 5 89. A calamity: *Every minute now Should be the father of some stratagem*—2 H4 I 1 7.

STRAY (sb.)

(1) A wandering, aberration: *I would not from your love make such a stray*—Lr I 1 212.

(2) Collectively, stragglers: *Pursue the scatter'd stray*—2 H4 IV 2 120.

STRAY (vb.)

To lead astray: *Hath not else his eye Stray'd his affection in unlawful love?*—Err V 50.

STREAK

To rub: *With the juice of this I'll streak her eyes*—Mids II 1 257.

STRENGTH

A fighting force: *Dissever your united strengths, And part your mingled colours*—John II 388. *That he should draw his several strengths together . . . Need not be dreaded*—2 H4 I 3 76. *Thou princely leader of our English strength*—1 H6 IV 3 17. *Then from Ireland come I with my strength*—2 H6 III 1 380.

STREWMENTS

Things strewed: *She is allow'd . . . Her maiden strewments*—Hml V 1 255.

STRICT

(1) Tight, close: *Their strict embrace* — Ven 874.

(2) Hard to make good: *You undergo too strict a paradox*—Tim III 5 24.

(3) Restricted: *Take No stricter render of me than my all*—Cymb V 4 16.

STRICTURE

Strictness: *A man of stricture and firm abstinence*—Meas I 3 12.

STRIKE

(1) Of malefic influences, to blast or destroy: *It is a bawdy planet, that will strike Where 'tis predominant*—Wint I 2 201. *With a sudden re-inforcement struck Corioli like a planet*—Cor II 2 117. *Then no planets strike* — Hml I 1 162. *Strike her young bones, You taking airs, with lameness!*—Lr II 4 165.

(2) Of a cask, to tap: *Strike the vessels, ho! Here is to Cæsar!*—Ant II 7 103.

(3) Of a battle, to deliver, fight: *When Cressy battle fatally was struck*—H5 II 4 54.

STRONG

Resolute, determined (in a bad sense): *O heinous, strong and bold conspiracy!*—R2 V 3 59. *Strong and fasten'd villain!*—Lr II 1 79.

STROSSERS

Trousers: *You rode . . . your French hose off, and in your strait strossers*—H5 III 7 56.

STROY

To destroy: *What I have left behind Stroy'd in dishonour*—Ant III 11 53.

STUBBORN

(1) Rough, rugged: *I fear these stubborn lines lack power to move*—LLL IV 3 55. *Therefore was I created with a stubborn outside*—H5 V 2 243. *You must therefore be content to slubber the gloss of your new fortunes with this more stubborn and boisterous expedition*—Oth I 3 226.

(2) Harsh, rude: *She sends him on purpose, that I may appear stubborn to him*—Tw III 4 73. *Some stubborn and uncourteous parts*—V 369. *You bear too stubborn and too strange a hand Over your friend that loves you*—Cæs I 2 35.

(3) Perverse, of evil disposition: *Thou art said to have a stubborn soul*—Meas V 485. *It is the stubbornest young fellow of France*—As I 1 148. *Stubborn critics*—Troil V 2 131.

STUBBORNNESS

Harshness, roughness: *The stubbornness of fortune*—As II 1 19. *His stubbornness, his checks, his frowns*—Oth IV 3 20.

STUCK

Equivalent to *Stock*[1]: *He gives me the stuck in*—Tw III 4 303. *If he by chance escape your venom'd stuck*—Hml IV 7 162.

STUDIED

(1) Having disposed one's mind in a particular way: *[I] am well studied for a liberal thanks Which I do owe you*—Ant II 6 48. Given, inclined: *A prince should not be so loosely studied*—2 H4 II 2 9.

(2) *Studied in*, having taken pains in regard to: *Like one well studied in a sad ostent*—Merch II 2 205. *Studied to do something*, having taken pains in regard to doing it: *As one that had been studied in his death To throw away the dearest thing he owed*—Mcb I 4 9.

STUDY

His study of (*i.e.* consisting in) *imagination*, his imaginative contemplation: *The idea of her life shall sweetly creep Into his study of imagination*—Ado IV 1 226.

STUFFED

Filled, stored: *Stuffed with all honourable virtues*—Ado I 1 56. *Stuff'd, as they say, with honourable parts*—Rom III 5 183. *Of stuffed sufficiency*, of ample ability: *Cleomenes and Dion, whom you know Of stuff'd sufficiency*—Wint II 1 184.

STURDY

Overbearing, overweening: *Look where the sturdy rebel sits, Even in the chair of state*—3 H6 I 1 50.

SUBDUEMENT

A conquest, victory: *Despising many forfeits and subduements*—Troil IV 5 187.

SUBJECT

Subjects, people: *The greater file of the subject held the duke to be wise*—Meas III 2 144. *A gallant child; one that indeed physics the subject*—Wint I 1 42. *The subject of the land*—Hml I 1 72. *The levies . . . are all made Out of his subject*—I 2 31.

SUBJECTION

A subject's duty: *To whom . . . I do bequeath my faithful services And true subjection everlastingly*—John V 7 103. *I dare be bound he's true and shall perform All parts of his subjection loyally*—Cymb IV 3 18. *Proportion of subjection*, service regularly and lawfully due: *The king . . . whom to disobey were against all proportion of subjection*—H5 IV 1 152.

SUBSCRIBE

(1) To sign (away); and so, to resign: *The king gone to-night! subscribed his power! Confined to exhibition!*—Lr I 2 24.

(2) To write down or characterize as: *I will subscribe him a coward*—Ado V 2 58.

(3) To grant, assent to: *I subscribe not that, nor any other*—Meas II 4 89. *Will you subscribe his thought, and say he is?*—Troil II 3 156. With *to* in a sim. sense: *Thy unrival'd merit, To which I thus subscribe*—Gent V 4 144. *When I had subscribed To mine own fortune*, when I had owned how matters stood with me—All's V 3 96.

(4) To submit, yield: *To your pleasure humbly I subscribe*—Shr I 1 81. *If I have fewest, I subscribe in silence*—1 H6 II 4 44. *I will subscribe and say I wrong'd the duke*—2 H6 III 1 38. *Hector in his blaze of wrath subscribes to tender objects*—Troil IV 5 105. *We will all subscribe to thy advice*—Tit IV 2 130. *My love looks fresh, and Death to me subscribes*—Sonn 107 10. *All cruels else subscribed*, all cruel deeds making to the contrary being remitted: *If wolves had at thy gate howl'd that stern time, Thou shouldst have said 'Good porter, turn the key', All cruels else subscribed*—Lr III 7 63.

(5) *To subscribe for*, to become surety for, go bail for: *I know thou'rt valiant; and, to the possibility of thy soldiership, will subscribe for thee*—All's III 6 88 (*to the possibility of thy soldiership* = so far as your soldierly qualities can advance the matter). *I will subscribe for thee, thou art both knave and fool*—IV 5 34.

(6) *To subscribe a person*, to put his name down: *They shall subscribe them for large sums of gold*—R2 I 4 50.

SUBSCRIPTION

Submission, obedience: *You owe me no subscription*—Lr III 2 18.

SUBSTRACTOR

App., a detractor: *They are scoundrels and substractors that say so of him*—Tw I 3 36.

SUBTLE

Smooth, even: *Like to a bowl upon a subtle ground*—Cor V 2 20.

SUCCEED

(1) To come to pass: *The effects he writes of succeed unhappily*—Lr I 2 156. To proceed,

result: *Hope succeeding from so fair a tree As your fair self*—Per I 1 114.

(2) To take up, inherit: *If . . . only he Owe and succeed thy weakness*—Meas II 4 122.

(3) To come down by order of succession, devolve: *A ring . . . That downward hath succeeded in his house From son to son*—All's III 7 22. *Seize upon the fortunes of the Moor, For they succeed on you*—Oth V 2 366.

SUCCEEDING

Consequence, result: *A most harsh [language], and not to be understood without bloody succeeding*—All's II 3 198.

SUCCESS

Succession: *Our parents' noble names, In whose success* (*i.e.* in virtue of our succession from whom) *we are gentle*—Wint I 2 393. Something succeeding; *success of mischief*, one mischief succeeding another: *So success of mischief shall be born*—2 H4 IV 2 47.

SUCCESSANTLY

Variously explained as without delay, in succession, successfully: *Then go successantly, and plead to him*—Tit IV 4 113.

SUCCESSION

Successors, heirs: *For him And his succession granted Rome a tribute*—Cymb III 1 7. Those who come after: *Example . . . cannot . . . dissuade succession*—All's III 5 23. Futurity: *Slander lives upon succession*—Err III 1 105. *Their own succession*, that to which they must themselves come: *Their writers do them* (*i.e.* the child actors) *wrong, to make them exclaim against their own succession*—Hml II 2 366.

SUCCESSIVE

(1) Entitled to succeed: *Next the king he was successive heir*—2 H6 III 1 49. *Now is black beauty's successive heir*—Sonn 127 3.

(2) Giving a right to succeed: *Plead my successive title with your swords*—Tit I 4.

SUCCESSIVELY

By right of inheritance: *Thou the garland wear'st successively*—2 H4 IV 5 202. *To take on you the . . . kingly government . . . as successively from blood to blood*—R3 III 7 131.

SUDDEN

(1) Speedy: *Then let us both be sudden*—Tp II 1 306. *The winds [are] thy sighs; Who . . . Without a sudden calm, will overset Thy tempest-tossed body*—Rom III 5 135. *Casca, be sudden, for we fear prevention*—Cæs III 1 19. *[She hath] returned me expectations . . . of sudden respect and acquaintance*—Oth IV 2 191.

(2) Hasty, rash, violent: *Jealous in honour, sudden and quick in quarrel*—As II 7 151. *As*

sudden As flaws congealed in the spring of day— 2 H4 IV 4 34. *Revoke Your sudden approbation* —Cor II 3 258. *He is rash and very sudden in choler—*Oth II 1 279.

SUDDEN-BOLD

Hasty and bold: *Pardon me, I am too sudden-bold—*LLL II 107.

SUDDENLY

Speedily, immediately: *Mistress Ford desires you to come suddenly—*Wiv IV 1 5. *When time is ripe, which will be suddenly, I'll . . .—*1 H4 I 3 294. *I'll repent, and that suddenly—*III 3 5. *I will leave him, and suddenly contrive the means of meeting between him and my daughter—*Hml II 2 215.

SUFFER

(1) To perish: *An islander, that hath lately suffered by a thunderbolt—*Tp II 2 37. *Let the frame of things disjoint, both the worlds suffer—*Mcb III 2 16.

(2) To acquiesce in or endure whatever is proposed: *Such suffering souls That welcome wrongs* —Cæs II 1 130. *Thou hast no weapon, and perforce must suffer—*Oth V 2 256.

(3) *Suffered*, left alone, allowed scope: *Being suffer'd in that harmful slumber—*2 H6 III 2 262. [A cur] *Who, being suffer'd with the bear's fell paw* (*i.e.* allowed to engage with it), *Hath clapp'd his tail between his legs—*V 1 153. *A little fire is quickly trodden out; Which, being suffer'd, rivers cannot quench—*3 H6 IV 8 7.

SUFFERANCE

(1) Suffering, pain: *Thy unkindness shall his death draw out To lingering sufferance—*Meas II 4 166. *The poor beetle . . . In corporal sufferance finds a pang as great As when a giant dies—*III 1 79. *'Tis a sufferance panging As soul and body's severing—*H8 II 3 15. *The mind much sufferance doth o'erskip—*Lr III 6 113.

(2) Damage, loss: *A grievous wreck and sufferance On most part of their fleet—*Oth II 1 23.

(3) Dying, death: *God be thanked for prevention* (*i.e.* in the execution of his intended crime); *Which I in sufferance heartily will rejoice—*H5 II 2 158.

(4) Forbearance: *England shall repent his folly, see his weakness, and admire our sufferance—*H5 III 6 131.

SUGGEST

(1) To prompt, incite: [He] *suggests the king . . . To this last costly treaty—*H8 I 1 164. *Two loves I have of comfort and despair, Which like two spirits do suggest me still—*Sonn 144 1. To suggest to in an underhand way: *We must suggest the people in what hatred He still hath held them—*Cor II 1 261.

(2) To prompt or incite to evil, tempt, seduce: *Tender youth is soon suggested—*Gent III 1 34. *I give thee not this to suggest thee from thy master—*All's IV 5 46. *That he did plot the Duke of Gloucester's death, Suggest his soon-believing adversaries* —R2 I 1 100. *Other devils that suggest by treasons* —H5 II 2 114. *When devils will the blackest sins put on, They do suggest at first with heavenly shows* —Oth II 3 357. *Perchance his boast of Lucrece' sovereignty Suggested this proud issue of a king—* Lucr 36.

SUGGESTION

(1) Prompting or incitement to evil, temptation: *The strong'st suggestion Our worser genius can—* Tp IV 26. *Suggestions are to other as to me—* LLL I 1 159. *Arthur, whom they say is kill'd to-night On your suggestion—*John IV 2 165. *Misled by your suggestion—*1 H4 IV 3 51. *I'ld turn it all To thy suggestion, plot, and damned practice—*Lr II 1 74.

(2) Indirect or crafty action: *One that, by suggestion, Tied all the kingdom—*H8 IV 2 35.

SUIT (sb.)

(1) Service due to a feudal superior: *Give notice to such men of sort and suit as are to meet him—* Meas IV 4 19. *Out of suits with*, turned out of the service of: *Wear this for me, one out of suits with fortune—*As I 2 258.

(2) Followers, suite: [A nun] *Which late her noble suit in court did shun—*Compl 234.

SUIT (vb.)

To dress, array: *Were it not better . . . That I did suit me all points like a man?—*As I 3 116. *Description cannot suit itself in words—*H5 IV 2 53. [I'll] *suit myself As does a Briton peasant—* Cymb V 1 23. *Suited*, dressed: *How oddly he is suited!—*Merch I 2 79. *So went he suited to his watery tomb—*Tw V 241. *The lark at IV 7 6.* In Merch III 5 70 (*O dear discretion, how his words are suited!*) app., either tricked out, or matched (meaning ill-matched) with the matter.

SULLEN

(1) Dark, gloomy: *Like bright metal on a sullen ground—*1 H4 I 2 235. *Why are thine eyes fix'd to the sullen earth?—*2 H6 I 2 5. *The lark at break of day arising From sullen earth—*Sonn 29 11.

(2) Sad, inspiring or indicating sorrow or melancholy: *Sullen sorrow—*R2 I 3 227. *Put on sullen black—*V 6 48. *A sullen bell Remember'd tolling a departing friend—*2 H4 I 1 102. *Our solemn hymns to sullen dirges change—*Rom IV 5 88.

SUMLESS

Incalculable, inestimable: *Sunken wreck and sumless treasuries—*H5 I 2 165.

SUMMERED

Kept through the summer: *Maids, well summered and warm kept, are like flies at Bartholomew-tide*—H5 V 2 335.

SUMMER-SEEMING

Like summer, and so, transitory; or perh., proper to the (short) summer of life: *Summer-seeming lust*—Mcb IV 3 86.

SUMPTER

A pack-horse; and so, a bearer of burdens, a drudge: *Persuade me rather to be slave and sumpter To this detested groom*—Lr II 4 219.

SUN-EXPELLING

Keeping off the sun (cf. *Expel*): *Her sun-expelling mask*—Gent IV 4 158.

SUPERFLUOUS

(1) Overflowing, running over: *That their hot blood may spin in English eyes, And dout them with superfluous courage*—H5 IV 2 10. *The love I dedicate to your lordship . . . whereof this pamphlet . . . is but a superfluous moiety*—Lucr Ded 1.

(2) Having more than enough: *Cold wisdom waiting on superfluous folly*—All's I 1 116. *Our basest beggars Are in the poorest thing superfluous*—Lr II 4 267. *The superfluous and lust-dieted man*—IV 1 70. *Superfluous riots*, noisy feastings in the midst of superfluities—Per I 4 54.

(3) Too great, excessive: *Purchased At a superfluous rate*—H8 I 1 98.

(4) Doing something uncalled for: *I see no reason why thou shouldst be so superfluous to demand the time of the day*—1 H4 I 2 11.

SUPERFLUX

Superfluity: *Expose thyself to feel what wretches feel, That thou mayst shake the superflux to them*—Lr III 4 34.

SUPERSCRIPT

The superscription or address of a letter: *I will overglance the superscript: 'To the . . .'*—LLL IV 2 135.

SUPERSERVICEABLE

Over-officious; or perh., above one's work: [A] *superserviceable, finical rogue*—Lr II 2 19.

SUPERSTITIOUS

Idolatrously devoted: [Have I] *Been, out of fondness, superstitious to him?*—H8 III 1 131.

SUPERVISE (sb.)

A looking over, reading: [A command] *That, on the supervise . . . My head should be struck off*—Hml V 2 23.

SUPERVISE (vb.)

To look over, read: *Let me supervise the canzonet*—LLL IV 2 124.

SUPERVISOR

A spectator, looker-on: *Would you, the supervisor, grossly gape on?*—Oth III 3 395.

SUPPLIANCE

That which fills up, a gratification: *The perfume and suppliance of a minute*—Hml I 3 9.

SUPPLY (sb.)

Reinforcement: *Looks he not for supply?*—1 H4 IV 3 3. *The Earl of Salisbury craveth supply*—1 H6 I 1 159. A reinforcing body of troops: *The great supply That was expected by the Dauphin here, Are wreck'd*—John V 3 9. *The Roman legions, all from Gallia drawn, Are landed on your coast, with a supply Of Roman gentlemen*—Cymb IV 3 24. Sim. in pl.: *Our supplies live largely in the hope Of great Northumberland*—2 H4 I 3 12. *'Tis their fresh supplies*—Cymb V 2 16.

SUPPLY (vb.)

(1) To gratify, content: *This is the body That . . . did supply thee at thy garden-house*—Meas V 210. *Who having, by . . . voluntary dotage of some mistress, Convinced or supplied them*—Oth IV 1 26.

(2) To reinforce: [Macdonwald] *from the western isles Of kerns and gallowglasses is supplied*—Mcb I 2 12.

SUPPLYANT

Reinforcing, auxiliary: *Whereunto your levy Must be supplyant*—Cymb III 7 13.

SUPPLYMENT

(Continuance of) supply: *I will never fail Beginning nor supplyment*—Cymb III 4 181.

SUPPORTANCE

Maintenance, support: *For the supportance of his vow*—Tw III 4 329. *Give some supportance to the bending twigs*—R2 III 4 32.

SUPPOSAL

An opinion, notion: *Holding a weak supposal of our worth*—Hml I 2 18.

SUPPOSE

(1) Expectation: *We come short of our suppose*—Troil I 3 11.

(2) Presumption, conjecture: *Lose not so noble a friend on vain suppose*—Tit I 440.

(3) App., something suggested to or put before a person in way of deception: *While counterfeit supposes blear'd thine eyne*—Shr V 1 120. Cf. *Presuppose.*

SUPPOSED

Pretended, supposititious: *Let the supposed fairies pinch him sound*—Wiv IV 4 61. *Supposed Lucentio Must get a father, called 'supposed Vincentio'*—Shr II 409. *This supposed distress of his*—Tim V 1 15. *Edmund, supposed Earl of Gloucester*—Lr V 3 112.

SUR-ADDITION

A new or other name: *Gain'd the sur-addition Leonatus*—Cymb I 1 33. Cf. *Addition* (1).

SURANCE

Assurance: *Give some surance that thou art Revenge*—Tit V 2 46.

SURCEASE (sb.)

A ceasing, cessation: *If the assassination Could . . . catch With his surcease success*—Mcb I 7 2.

SURCEASE (vb.)

To cease: *Lest I surcease to honour mine own truth*—Cor III 2 121. *No pulse Shall keep his native progress, but surcease*—Rom IV 1 96. *If they surcease to be that should survive*—Lucr 1766.

SURE

(1) Out of danger, safe: *The forest is not three leagues off; If we recover that, we are sure enough*—Gent V 1 11. *The lords at Pomfret . . . Were jocund, and supposed their state was sure*—R3 III 2 85. *[Doors] must be employ'd Now to guard sure their master*—Tim III 3 39.

(2) Indissolubly united: *She and I . . . Are now so sure that nothing can dissolve us*—Wiv V 5 236. *Dumain is mine, as sure as bark on tree*—LLL V 2 285. *You and you are sure together*—As V 4 141.

SURLY

Sad, inspiring melancholy: *That surly spirit, melancholy*—John III 3 42. *The surly sullen bell*—Sonn 71 2.

SURMISE

Thought, reflection: *Tarquin answers with surmise, In silent wonder of still-gazing eyes*—Lucr 83. *Being from the feeling of her own grief brought By deep surmise of others' detriment*—1578.

SURMOUNT

To surpass, excel: *This Hector far surmounted Hannibal*—LLL V 2 677. *[Your presence] far surmounts our labour to attain it*—R2 II 3 64. *Her virtues that surmount*—1 H6 V 3 191. *I all other in all worths surmount*—Sonn 62 8.

SURPRISE

To seize, capture: *The prisoners, Which he in this adventure hath surprised*—1 H4 I 1 92. *Is the traitor Cade surprised?*—2 H6 IV 9 8.

SUR-REINED

Overridden, overstrained: *A drench for sur-rein'd jades*—H5 III 5 19.

SURVEY

To perceive, observe: *The Norweyan lord surveying vantage*—Mcb I 2 31.

SUSPECT

Suspicion: *[You] draw within the compass of suspect The unviolated honour of your wife*—Err III 1 87. *To draw me in these vile suspects*—R3 I 3 89. *In whose breast Doubt and suspect, alas, are placed too late*—Tim IV 3 518. *If some suspect of ill mask'd not thy show*—Sonn 70 13.

SUSPICION

Hath not the world one man but he will wear his cap with suspicion, i.e. suspicion among his friends that the cap conceals a cuckold's horns?—Ado I 1 199.

SUSPIRATION

The act of drawing breath: *Windy suspiration of forced breath*—Hml I 2 79.

SUSPIRE

To breathe: *Did he suspire, that light and weightless down Perforce must move*—2 H4 IV 5 33. To receive breath, come into being: *Since the birth of Cain . . . To him that did but yesterday suspire*—John III 4 79.

SUSTAINING

On their sustaining garments not a blemish—Tp I 2 218, either, which bore them up (in the water), or, enduring (the drenching of the sea) without injury.

SUTTON CO'FIL'

Sutton Coldfield in Warwickshire: *We'll to Sutton Co'fil' to-night*—1 H4 IV 2 3.

SWAG-BELLIED

Having a large overhanging belly: *Your swag-bellied Hollander*—Oth II 3 80.

SWARTH

A swath: *That cons state without book and utters it by great swarths*—Tw II 3 161.

SWASHER

A blusterer, bully: *I have observed these three swashers*—H5 III 2 29.

SWASHING

(1) Smashing: *Remember thy swashing blow*—Rom I 1 69.

(2) Blustering, dashing: *We'll have a swashing and a martial outside*—As I 3 122.

SWATH

A swaddling-band: *Hadst thou, like us from our first swath, proceeded*—Tim IV 3 252.

SWATHLING CLOTHES

Swaddling clothes: *Mars in swathling clothes*—1 H4 III 2 112.

SWAY (sb.)

(1) *The sway of earth*, the established order, or perh., the balanced swing of the earth: *All the sway of earth Shakes like a thing unfirm*—Cæs I 3 3.

(2) App., that which sways: *This sway of motion, this Commodity*—John II 578.

SWAY (vb.)

To be directed: *The mind I sway by*—Mcb V 3 9. *To sway on*, to swing on in steady motion: *Let us sway on and face them in the field*—2 H4 IV 1 24.

SWAYED

Strained and weakened: *Swayed in the back and shoulder-shotten*—Shr III 2 56.

SWEAR

(1) To swear by: *Thou hast sworn against religion, By what thou swear'st against the thing thou swear'st*—John III 1 280. *Thou swear'st thy gods in vain*—Lr I 1 163.

(2) *To swear out*, to renounce solemnly: *I hear your grace hath sworn out house-keeping*—LLL II 104.

SWEAT (sb.)

The sweating-sickness, a febrile epidemic disease which visited England at various times: *What with the war, what with the sweat . . . I am custom-shrunk*—Meas I 2 83.

SWEAT (vb.)

Alluding to a process for the cure of venereal disease: *I'll sweat and seek about for eases*—Troil V 10 56. See *Tub*.

SWEET

Perfumed: *A pair of sweet gloves*—Wint IV 4 253. *Call for sweet water, wash thy hands*—Tit II 4 6. *Thy bridal bed . . . Which with sweet water nightly I will dew*—Rom V 3 12.

SWEET AND TWENTY

A term of endearment, my sweet lass of twenty: *Then come kiss me, sweet and twenty*—Tw II 3 52.

SWEET-COMPLAINING

Sweetly lamenting: *The night's dead silence Will well become such sweet-complaining grievance*—Gent III 2 85. See *Complain* (1).

SWEETMEATS

Perfumed sugar-plums used as kissing-comfits (see *Kissing-comfit*): *Because their breaths with sweetmeats tainted are*—Rom I 4 76. No doubt this is the meaning also in Mids I 1 34 (*Knacks, trifles, nosegays, sweetmeats*).

SWEET-SUGGESTING

Sweetly tempting: *Sweet-suggesting Love*—Gent II 6 7. See *Suggest* (2).

SWELTER

To cause to exude: *Toad, that under cold stone Days and nights has thirty one Swelter'd venom sleeping got*—Mcb IV 1 6.

SWILL

To wash, drench: *His* (i.e. the rock's) *confounded base, Swill'd with the wild and wasteful ocean*—H5 III 1 13.

SWINGE-BUCKLER

A swash-buckler, roisterer: *You had not four such swinge-bucklers in all the inns o' court again*—2 H4 III 2 24.

SWOOPSTAKE

Taking all the stakes; and so, indiscriminately: *Is't writ in your revenge, That, swoopstake, you will draw both friend and foe?*—Hml IV 5 141.

SWORD-AND-BUCKLER

Keeping low company, the sword and buckler being the weapons proper to serving-men; or perh. nothing more is meant than roistering, swaggering: *That same sword-and-buckler Prince of Wales*—1 H4 I 3 230.

SWOUND

Swoon: *I swounded at the sight*—Rom III 2 56. *I swound to see thee*—Tim IV 3 373. *Here manly Hector faints, here Troilus swounds*—Lucr 1486.

'SWOUNDS

[By] God's wounds: *'Swounds, I should take it*—Hml II 2 604. *'Swounds, show me what thou'lt do*—V 1 297.

SYENNA

Siena, i.e. the ruler thereof: *Bold Iachimo, Syenna's brother*—Cymb IV 2 340. Cf. *Senoys*.

SYMPATHIZE

(1) To be of like nature *with*: *The men do sympathize with the mastiffs in robustious and rough coming on*—H5 III 7 158.

(2) To participate in: [All] *That by this sympathized one day's error Have suffer'd wrong*—Err V 397.

(3) To answer to, tally with: *The senseless brands will sympathize The heavy accent of thy moving tongue*—R2 V 1 46. *True sorrow then is feelingly sufficed When with like semblance it is sympathized*—Lucr 1112. *Thou truly fair wert truly sympathized In true plain words by thy true-telling friend*—Sonn 82 11.

(4) To contrive with suitable adaptation: *A message well sympathized; a horse to be ambassador for an ass*—LLL III 52.

SYMPATHY

Conformity, correspondence: *You are not young, no more am I; go to then, there's sympathy*—Wiv II 1 6. *What a sympathy of woe is this!*—Tit III 1 148. *Just in her case! O woful sympathy!*—Rom III 3 85. *Sympathy in years, manners and beauties*—Oth II 1 232. *The action of my life is like it, which I'll keep, if but for sympathy*—Cymb V 4 150. Of equality of rank: *If that thy valour stand on sympathy*—R2 IV 33.

T

TABLE (sb.)

(1) That on which a picture is drawn or painted: *To sit and draw His arched brows . . . In our heart's table*—All's I 1 104. *Myself Drawn in the flattering table of her eye*—John II 502. *Mine eye hath play'd the painter and hath stell'd Thy beauty's form in table of my heart*—Sonn 24 1.

(2) A tablet for writing on, a note-book: *The table wherein all my thoughts Are visibly character'd*—Gent II 7 3. *The table of my memory*—Hml I 5 98. In pl.: *Look, whether. . . his man be not lisping to his master's old tables, his note-book*—2 H4 II 4 288. *My tables,—meet it is I set it down*—Hml I 5 107. *Thy gift, thy tables, are within my brain*—Sonn 122 1. Of a letter: *You clasp young Cupid's tables*—Cymb III 2 39.

(3) In palmistry, the palm: *If any man in Italy have a fairer table . . .*—Merch II 2 166.

(4) *Tables*, backgammon: *When he plays at tables, chides the dice In honourable terms*—LLL V 2 326.

TABLE (vb.)

To set out in tabular form: *Though the catalogue of his endowments had been tabled by his side*—Cymb I 4 5.

TABLE-BOOK

A note-book: *Not a . . . table-book, ballad, knife . . . [left]*—Wint IV 4 608. *If I had play'd the desk or table-book*—Hml II 2 136.

TABOR

A small drum: *Then I beat my tabor*—Tp IV 175. *Now had he rather hear the tabor and the pipe*—Ado II 3 15. *The shepherd knows not thunder from a tabor More than I know . . .*—Cor I 6 25.

TABORER

One who plays on the tabor: *I would I could see this taborer*—Tp III 2 160.

TABOURINE

A side-drum: *Beat loud the tabourines*—Troil

IV 5 275. *Make mingle with our rattling tabourines*—Ant IV 8 37.

TAFFETA

A silk fabric, worn in Shakespeare's time by both men and women: *The tailor make thy doublet of changeable taffeta*—Tw II 4 76. *A fair hot wench in flame-coloured taffeta*—1 H4 I 2 10.

TAG

The rabble: *Will you hence, Before the tag return?*—Cor III 1 247.

TAILOR

An unexplained exclamation: *Down topples she, And 'tailor' cries*—Mids II 1 53.

TAINT (sb.)

Disgrace, discredit: *We did our main opinion crush In taint of our best man*—Troil I 3 373.

TAINT (vb.)

(1) To tincture, imbue: *A pure unspotted heart, Never yet taint with love*—1 H6 V 3 182. *Nero will be tainted with remorse*—3 H6 III 1 40.

(2) To disgrace, discredit, throw a slur upon: *My age was never tainted with such shame*—1 H6 IV 5 46. *We come not by the way of accusation, To taint that honour*—H8 III 1 54. *Brought him forward, As a man sorely tainted, to his answer*—IV 2 13. *To anger Cassio . . . by . . . tainting his discipline*—Oth II 1 274.

(3) To be tinctured or imbued: *I cannot taint with fear*—Mcb V 3 3.

TAINTURE

Defilement: *See here the tainture of thy nest*—2 H6 II 1 188.

TAKE

(1) To catch, come upon (a person): *I thought to have ta'en you at the Porpentine*—Err III 2 172. *Though I take thee in the king's company*—H5 IV 1 236.

(2) To bewitch, infect: *He blasts the tree and takes the cattle*—Wiv IV 4 32. *No fairy takes*—

Hml I 1 163. *Strike her young bones, You taking airs, with lameness!*—Lr II 4 165. *Bless thee from whirlwinds, star-blasting, and taking!*—III 4 60. *Now the witch take me, if I meant it thus!*—Ant IV 2 37.

(3) *To take haste*, to make haste: *Let him take his haste*—Tim V 1 213.

(4) *To take order*, to take measures: *I'll order take my mother shall not hear*—All's IV 2 55. *Until the duke take order for his burial*—R3 I 4 288. *His mouth is stopp'd; Honest Iago hath ta'en order for't*—Oth V 2 71.

(5) *To take scorn*, see *Scorn* (sb.) (4).

(6) *To take a truce* (see *Truce*), *to take peace*, to make peace: *With my vex'd spirits I cannot take a truce*—John III 1 17. *Offences . . . that I cannot take peace with*—H8 II 1 84. So *to take reconciliation*, to effect it: *His present reconciliation take*—Oth III 3 47.

(7) *To take in*, to conquer, subdue: *Affliction may subdue the cheek, But not take in the mind*—Wint IV 4 586. *Take in that kingdom, and enfranchise that*—Ant I 1 23.

(8) *To take off*, to kill: *The deep damnation of his taking-off*—Mcb I 7 20. *Let her . . . devise His speedy taking off*—Lr V 1 64. So *took off her life: Who . . . by self and violent hands Took off her life*—Mcb V 8 70.|

(9) *To take on*, to pretend: *Take on as you would follow*—Mids III 2 258. So *to take on* or *upon oneself: I told him you were sick; he takes on him to understand so much, and therefore comes to speak with you*—Tw I 5 148. *'How comes that?' says he, that takes upon him not to conceive*—2 H4 II 2 123. *She takes upon her to spy a white hair on his chin*—Troil I 2 153.

(10) *To take out*, to copy: *I'll have the work ta'en out*—Oth III 3 296. *Take me this work out*—III 4 180.

(11) *To take up*, (a) to make up, settle (a quarrel): *How was that [quarrel] ta'en up?*—As V 4 50. *I have his horse to take up the quarrel*—Tw III 4 320. (b) To get goods on credit: *If a man is through with them in honest taking up*—2 H4 I 2 45. With a play: *We are like to prove a goodly commodity, being taken up of these men's bills*—Ado III 3 190. *When shall we go to Cheapside and take up commodities upon our bills?*—2 H6 IV 7 134. (c) To rebuke, rate: *I was taken up for laying them down*—Gent I 2 135. *Yet art thou good for nothing but taking up*—All's II 3 217 (with a play). *A whoreson jackanapes must take me up for swearing*—Cymb II 1 4. (d) To cope with, engage: *Perforce a third [division] Must take up us*—2 H4 I 3 72. *I could myself Take up a brace o' the best of them*—Cor III 1 243. (e) Of soldiers, to levy: *You are to take soldiers up in counties as you go*—2 H4 II 1 199. *You have ta'en up . . . The subjects of . . . my father*—IV 2 26.

(12) *To take a thing upon one's honour*, salva-tion, &c., to pledge one's honour, &c., in the matter: *I took't upon mine honour thou hadst it not*—Wiv II 2 12. *They take it already upon their salvation, that . . .*—1 H4 II 4 9. *I'll take it upon my death, I gave him this wound*—V 4 154. Sim. *to take one's death: I will take my death, I never meant him any ill*—2 H6 II 3 90. *To take the sacrament*, see *Sacrament*.

(13) *To take a person with one*, to make him follow one's meaning: *I would your grace would take me with you*—1 H4 II 4 506. *Take me with you, wife*—Rom III 5 142.

(14) *He's bravely taken*, he is accepted or looked upon as brave; or perh., has a fine reputation—All's III 5 55. *I can take*, app., I can take fire, go off: *I can take, and Pistol's cock is up*—H5 II 1 55.

TALENT[1]

Talon; with a play: Nath. *A rare talent!* Dull. [Aside] *If a talent be a claw, look how he claws him with a talent*—LLL IV 2 64.

TALENT[2]

App. used of a precious possession in general: *You, which I account his beyond all talents*—Cymb I 6 80. *Behold these talents of their hair*—Compl 204.

TALL

Stout, lusty: *He's as tall a man as any's in Illyria*—Tw I 3 20. *Many a good tall fellow*—1 H4 I 3 62. *Much tall youth*—Ant II 6 7. Of ships, large and stout: *Where the carcases of many a tall ship lie buried*—Merch III 1 6. *His tall ship*—Oth II 1 79. For *Tall of one's hands* see *Hand* (sb.) (4).

TALLOW-CATCH

An obscure word, possibly a tub in which tallow is caught or collected: *Thou whoreson, obscene, greasy tallow-catch*—1 H4 II 4 252.

TAMED

Of wine, app., vapid, flat: *The lees and dregs of a flat tamed piece*—Troil IV 1 62.

TANGLE

To ensnare, trap: *I think she means to tangle my eyes too!*—III 5 44. *Fly thou how thou canst, they'll tangle thee*—2 H6 II 4 55. *My king is tangled in affection to A creature of the queen's*—H8 III 2 35.

TANLING

One tanned by the sun: *To be still hot summer's tanlings*—Cymb IV 4 29.

TARDY

To delay in carrying out (an order): *The good mind of Camillo tardied My swift command*—Wint III 2 163.

TARGE

A target, shield: *With targe and shield*—LLL V 2 556. [To] *bear back Our targes undinted*— Ant II 6 38. *Whose naked breast Stepp'd before targes of proof*—Cymb V 5 4.

TARRE

To set on, incite: *Like a dog . . . [will] Snatch at his master that doth tarre him on*—John IV 1 116. *Pride alone Must tarre the mastiffs on*— Troil I 3 391. *The nation holds it no sin to tarre them to controversy*—Hml II 2 370.

TARTAR

Tartarus: *He's in Tartar limbo, worse than hell* —Err IV 2 32. Mar. . . . *Follow me.* Sir To. *To the gates of Tartar*—Tw II 5 225. *He might return to vasty Tartar back*—H5 II 2 123.

TASK

(1) To tax: [He] *task'd the whole state*—1 H4 IV 3 92.

(2) To lay a charge upon; applied to a challenge: Wor. *The Prince of Wales . . . challenged you to single fight.* Hot. . . . *How show'd his tasking?* —1 H4 V 2 46. So *task me to my word,* challenge me to make my word good: *Nay, task me to my word; approve me, lord*—1 H4 IV 1 9.

TASSEL-GENTLE

Tercel-gentle; the male of the peregrine falcon: *O, for a falconer's voice, To lure this tassel-gentle back again!*—Rom II 2 159 (of Romeo).

TASTE (sb.)

(1) A trial, test: *Till that the nobles . . . Have of their puissance made a little taste*—2 H4 II 3 51. *An essay or taste of my virtue*—Lr I 2 47.

(2) *In some taste,* in a way, to some extent: *In some taste, is Lepidus but so*—Cæs IV 1 34.

TASTE (vb.)

(1) To try, test: *Men that put quarrels purposely on others, to taste their valour*—Tw III 4 266. *Praise us as we are tasted*—Troil III 2 97.

(2) *Who did taste to him?* alluding to the royal taster who partook of the dishes and wine before the king—John V 6 28. Cf. Keep. *My lord, will't please you to fall to?* K. Rich. *Taste of it first, as thou art wont to do*—R2 V 5 98.

TATTERING

App., falling into rags: [We] *wound our tattering colours clearly up*—John V 5 7.

TAWDRY-LACE

Orig. a lace from the fair of St. Audrey (Ethelreda), said to have been held at the saint's shrine in the Isle of Ely: *You promised me a tawdry-lace* —Wint IV 4 252.

TAWNY COAT

The coat of this colour worn by ecclesiastical apparitors; hence, an ecclesiastical apparitor: *Draw, men. . . Blue coats to tawny coats*—1 H6 I 3 46. *Out, tawny coats!*—56. [*A noise within,* 'Down with the tawny-coats!'—III 1 73 (Stage Dir).

TAX (sb.)

Censure, charge: *Tax of impudence, A strumpet's boldness, a divulged shame*—All's II 1 173.

TAX (vb.)

(1) To censure, charge: *You tax Signior Benedick too much*—Ado I 1 46. *This heavy-headed revel . . . Makes us traduced and tax'd of other nations*—Hml I 4 17. *She'll tax him home*—III 3 29. *To tax of,* to charge with: *My fore-past proofs . . . Shall tax my fears of little vanity*—All's V 3 121. *Taxing,* censure, satire: *My taxing like a wild-goose flies*—As II 7 86.

(2) To lay a charge upon: *Tax not so bad a voice To slander music*—Ado II 3 46.

TAXATION

(1) A claim, demand: *I bring . . . no taxation of homage*—Tw I 5 224.

(2) Censure, satire: *You'll be whipped for taxation one of these days*—As I 2 90.

TEAR-FALLING

Shedding tears: *Tear-falling pity*—R3 IV 2 66. See *Fall* (vb.) (4).

TEEN

Grief, sorrow: *My heart bleeds To think o' the teen that I have turn'd you to*—Tp I 2 63. *Each hour's joy wreck'd with a week of teen*—R3 IV 1 97. *To my teen be it spoken*—Rom I 3 13. *My face is full of shame, my heart of teen*—Ven 808.

TELL

(1) To count: *Faster than you'll tell money*— Wint IV 4 184. *While one would tell twenty*— R3 I 4 122. *While one . . . might tell a hundred* —Hml I 2 238.

(2) In 2 H4 I 2 189 (*In some respects, I grant, I cannot go: I cannot tell*), perh., I cannot be counted in a reckoning, pass current; but the ordinary meaning suits also.

TEMPER (sb.)

(1) Temperament, frame of mind: *Never could the strumpet . . . Once stir my temper*—Meas II 2 183. *He holds your temper in a high respect*—1 H4 III 1 170. *A man of such a feeble temper*—Cæs I 2 129. *That dauntless temper of his mind*—Mcb III 1 52.

(2) Calmness, equanimity: *Keep me in temper: I would not be mad!*—Lr I 5 51.

(3) In Ant I 1 6 (*His captain's heart . . . reneges all temper*) the reference seems to be to loss of temper in the sense in which steel is said to lose its temper.

TEMPER (vb.)

(1) To mix, compound: *It is a poison temper'd by himself*—Hml V 2 339. *[She] oft importuned me To temper poisons for her*—Cymb V 5 249. Referring to the 'humours' (see *Humour* (3)): *I thought thy disposition better temper'd*—Rom III 3 115. See also *Ill-tempered*.

(2) To moisten: *The uncivil kerns of Ireland . . . temper clay with blood of Englishmen*—2 H6 III 1 310. *I'll pluck ye (i.e. his eyes) out, And cast you . . . To temper clay*—Lr I 4 324. To work into a desired consistency: *What wax so frozen but dissolves with tempering*—Ven 565. Generally, to bring into a proper state: *Lack of temper'd judgement*—Meas V 478. *Never durst poet touch a pen to write Until his ink were temper'd with Love's sighs*—LLL IV 3 346.

(3) To dispose (a person in a particular direction): *You may temper her . . . To hate young Valentine*—Gent III 2 64. *He that temper'd thee bade thee stand up*—H5 II 2 118. *'Tis she That tempers him to this extremity*—R3 I 1 64. *Now will I . . . temper him . . . To . . .*—Tit IV 4 108.

(4) *Tempered*, brought into a certain state, having a certain quality: *If the truth of thy love to me were so righteously tempered as mine is to thee*—As I 2 13. *The best-temper'd courage in his troops*—2 H4 I 1 115. *Were your days As green as Ajax' and your brain so temper'd*—Troil II 3 264. Disposed: *I'll talk to you When you are better temper'd to attend*—1 H4 I 3 234. *When was my lord so much ungently temper'd, To stop his ears against admonishment?*—Troil V 3 1.

(5) *To temper with*, to adapt oneself to, accord with: *Few men rightly temper with the stars*—3 H6 IV 6 29.

(6) To assume a desired state or quality: *I have him already tempering between my finger and my thumb*—2 H4 IV 3 140.

TEMPERANCE

Temperature, climate: *It (i.e. the island) must needs be of . . . delicate temperance*—Tp II 1 41.

TEMPLE

Used of a church: *He would meet her . . . at the temple, and there, before the whole congregation, shame her*—Ado III 3 171. *Here we have no temple (i.e. no church to be married in) but the wood*—As III 3 49.

TEMPORARY

A temporary meddler, perh., (an ecclesiastic) who meddles in temporal affairs: *A man divine and holy; Not . . . a temporary meddler*—Meas V 144.

TEMPORIZE

To come to terms, agree: *The Dauphin . . . will not temporize with my entreaties*—John V 2 124. *You will temporize with the hours*, will suit yourself to what your fortune may be—Ado I 1 276.

TENABLE

App., regarded as a thing to be kept: *Let it be tenable in your silence still*—Hml I 2 248.

TEND

(1) To be waiting or ready: *Your servants tend*—Hml I 3 83. *The associates tend*—IV 3 47.

(2) To attend, wait upon: *Had I not Four or five women once that tended me?*—Tp I 2 46. *Worthier than himself Here tend the savage strangeness he puts on*—Troil II 3 134. *Her gentlewomen . . . tended her i' the eyes*—Ant II 2 211. *So to tend on* or *upon*: *Three months this youth hath tended upon me*—Tw V 102. *Hitherto doth love on fortune tend*—Hml III 2 216. *The riotous knights That tend upon my father*—Lr II 1 96.

(3) *To tend to*, to attend to, give heed to: *Tend to the master's whistle*—Tp I 1 8.

TENDANCE

Persons in attendance: *His lobbies fill with tendance*—Tim I 1 80.

TENDER (adj.)

(1) Dear: *Whose life's as tender to me as my soul*—Gent V 4 37.

(2) Quick, keen: *Unapt for tender smell*—Lucr 695.

TENDER (sb.)

Regard, care: *Thou makest some tender of my life*—1 H4 V 4 49. *In the tender of a wholesome weal*—Lr I 4 230.

TENDER (vb.)

To regard, look upon: *How does your content Tender your own good fortune?*—Tp II 1 269. To care for, esteem, hold dear: *He shall not die; so much we tender him*—Err V 132. *We our kingdom's safety must so tender . . . that . . .*—H5 II 2 175. *Good Capulet,—which name I tender As dearly as my own*—Rom III 1 74. *For thine especial safety,—Which we do tender*—Hml IV 3 42. To regard (a suit) favourably: *Then, for thy husband and thy children's sake, Tender my suit*—Lucr 533. *Tendering my ruin*, protecting me in my extremity: *When my angry guardant stood alone, Tendering my ruin*—1 H6 IV 7 9.

TENDER-HEFTED

Having a tender or finely sensitive haft (heft) or handle, swayable by tender feelings: *Thy tender-hefted nature shall not give Thee o'er to harshness*—Lr II 4 174.

TENT (sb.)[1]

App., some part of the furniture of a bed: *My arras counterpoints, Costly apparel, tents, and canopies*—Shr II 353.

TENT (sb.)[2]

A roll of linen for searching or cleansing a wound, a probe: *The tent that searches To the bottom of the worst*—Troil II 2 16. With a play: Patr. *Who keeps the tent now?* Ther. *The surgeon's box, or the patient's wound*—V I 11.

TENT (vb).

To apply a tent to, probe (see *Tent* (sb.)[2]): *I'll tent him to the quick*—Hml II 2 626. *Well might they fester 'gainst ingratitude, And tent themselves with death*—Cor I 9 30. *'Tis a sore upon us, You cannot tent yourself* — III 1 235. *Mine ear . . . can take no greater wound, Nor tent to bottom that*—Cymb III 4 116.

TERCEL

The male of the goshawk: *The falcon as the tercel, for all the ducks i' the river*—Troil III 2 55. *Falcon* is, of course, feminine.

TERMAGANT

A supposed Moslem deity who appeared in the Miracle Plays as a ranting character like Herod: *That hot termagant Scot*—1 H4 V 4 114. *O'erdoing Termagant*—Hml III 2 15.

TERMINATION

A term, word: *If her breath were as terrible as her terminations*—Ado II 1 256.

TERMLESS

Indescribable; or perh., youthful: *His phœnix down began but to appear . . . on that termless skin*—Compl 93.

TERMS

The technical language of the courts of law: *Our city's institutions, and the terms For common justice*—Meas I 1 11.

TEST

Testimony, proof: *To vouch this, is no proof, Without more wider and more overt test*—Oth I 3 106.

TESTER

A sixpence: *Tester I'll have in pouch when thou shalt lack*—Wiv I 3 96. *There's a tester for thee*—2 H4 III 2 296.

TESTERN

To present (a person) with a testern (= *Tester* (q.v.)): *You have testerned me*—Gent I 1 152.

TESTIMONY

To bear witness to, display: *Let him be but testimonied in his own bringings-forth*—Meas III 2 152.

TESTRIL

Equivalent to *Tester* (q.v.): *There's a testril of me too*—Tw II 3 34.

THAN

Then: *Their ranks began To break upon the galled shore, and than Retire again*—Lucr 1439.

THANE

In Scotland, a hereditary tenant holding of the crown at a fixed rent: *The worthy thane of Ross*—Mcb I 2 45. *Hail to thee, thane of Glamis!*—I 3 48. And *passim* in the play.

THANKFUL

Deserving thanks: *That he can hither come so soon, Is by your fancy's thankful doom*—Per V 2 19.

THARBOROUGH

Equivalent to *Third-borough* (q.v.): *I am his grace's tharborough*—LLL I 1 185.

THAW

She told me . . . that I was duller than a great thaw — Ado II 1 249, app. in allusion to the depression of spirits felt on the setting in of a thaw.

THEFT

That which is stolen: *If he steal aught . . . I will pay the theft*—Hml III 2 93. Cf. *Offence* (5) and *Thievery*.

THEORIC

Theory: *That had the whole theoric of war in the knot of his scarf*—All's IV 3 162. *The art and practic part of life Must be the mistress to this theoric*—H5 I 1 51. *The bookish theoric*—Oth I 1 24.

THERE

Are you there with me?—Lr IV 6 148; *Are you thereabouts?*—Ant III 10 29, is that what you are thinking of?

THEREAFTER

According: *Thereafter as they be*—2 H4 III 2 56.

THERETO

Also, besides: *You are certainly a gentleman, thereto Clerk-like experienced*—Wint I 2 391. *If she be black, and thereto have a wit*—Oth II 1 133. *Yourself So out of thought, and thereto so o'ergrown*—Cymb IV 4 32.

THEREUNTO

In the same sense as the preceding word: *There's none so foul and foolish thereunto, But . . .*—Oth II 1 142.

THICK (vb.)

To make thick: *Thoughts that would thick my blood*—Wint I 2 171.

THICK (adv.)

Speak thick, speak fast: *Say, and speak thick*—Cymb III 2 58.

THICK-PLEACHED

See *Pleached.*

THIEVERY

That which is stolen: *Injurious time . . . Crams his rich thievery up*—Troil IV 4 44. Cf. *Theft.*

THINK

(1) To give way to melancholy: Cleo. *What shall we do, Enobarbus?* Eno. *Think, and die*—Ant III 13 1. Cf. *Thought.*

(2) *Thinks't thee?* seems it to thee? *Does it not, thinks't thee, stand me now upon?*—Hml V 2 63.

THIRD-BOROUGH

A constable: *I must go fetch the third-borough*—Shr Ind 1 11.

THIS

Thus: *What am I, that thou shouldst contemn me this?*—Ven 205.

THOROUGH (adv.)

Through: *It pierced me thorough*—Per IV 3 35.

THOROUGH (prep.)

Through: *Thorough bush, thorough brier*—Mids II 1 3. *Whose eyes do never give But thorough lust and laughter*—Tim IV 3 491. *Thorough the hazards of this untrod state*—Cæs III 1 136. *To show her bleeding body thorough Rome*—Lucr 1851.

THOUGHT

Care, melancholy, apprehension: *All that he can do Is to himself, take thought and die for Cæsar*—Cæs II 1 186. *Sicklied o'er with the pale cast of thought*—Hml III 1 85. *Thought and affliction . . . She turns to favour and to prettiness*—IV 5 188. *This blows my heart: If swift thought break it not, a swifter mean Shall out-strike thought*—Ant IV 6 34.

THOUGHTEN

Be you thoughten, have the thought, think: *Be you thoughten That I came with no ill intent*—Per IV 6 115.

THOUGHT-EXECUTING

Carrying out thought, doing execution with the rapidity of thought: *You sulphurous and thought-executing fires*—Lr III 2 4.

THOUGHT-SICK

Sick with apprehension: [The earth] *as against the doom, Is thought-sick at the act*—Hml III 4 50. See *Thought.*

THRASONICAL

After the style of Thraso, the braggart in Terence's Eunuchus, boastful: *His general behaviour vain, ridiculous, and thrasonical*—LLL V 1 13. *Cæsar's thrasonical brag*—As V 2 34.

THREAD AND THRUM

O Fates, come, come, Cut thread and thrum—Mids V 290. The thread is the substance of the weaver's warp, the thrum the small tuft where the thread is tied.

THREADEN

Woven of threads: *The threaden sails*—H5 III Chor 10. *Her threaden fillet*—Compl 33.

THREE-FARTHINGS

My face so thin That in mine ear I durst not stick a rose Lest men should say 'Look, where three-farthings goes!'—John I 141, alluding to the silver three-farthing pieces of Elizabeth, which were very thin, and the Queen's head on which was decorated with a rose.

THREE-HOOPED POT

The three-hooped pot shall have ten hoops—2 H6 IV 2 72, the old wooden drinking-pots being bound together with hoops.

THREE-MAN-SONG-MEN

Singers of songs in three parts: *The shearers, three-man-song-men all*—Wint IV 3 44.

THREE-NOOKED

Perh., having three corners, alluding to the three continents: *The three-nook'd world Shall bear the olive freely*—Ant IV 6 6. Cf. *Come the three corners of the world in arms*—John V 7 116.

THREE-PILE

Three-piled velvet (see the next word): *I have . . . in my time wore three-pile*—Wint IV 3 13. Cf. *Master Three-pile the mercer*—Meas IV 3 11.

THREE-PILED

Of velvet, having a treble pile or nap: *Thou art good velvet; thou'rt a three-piled piece*—Meas I 2 32. Fig., high-flown: *Three-piled hyperboles, spruce affectation*—LLL V 2 407. In Meas I 2

20

34 (*I had as lief be a list of an English kersey as be piled, as thou art piled, for a French velvet*) there seems to be a play on peeled, bald (from the ' French disease ').

THRENE

A threnody, dirge: *Whereupon it made this threne*—Phœn 49.

THRID

Thread: *I Have given you here a thrid of mine own life*—Tp IV 2.

THRIFT

Success: *I have a mind presages me such thrift, That I should questioniess be forturate*—Merch I 1 175. Profit: *My bargains and my well-won thrift*—Merch I 3 51. *Their profits, Their own particular thrifts*—Wint I 2 310. *Where thrift may follow fawning*—Hml III 2 67. *Base respects of thrift*—193.

THRIFTLESS

Unprofitable, useless: *What thriftless sighs shall poor Olivia breathe!*—Tw II 2 40. *An all-eating shame and thriftless praise*—Sonn 2 8.

THRIFTY

Dealt with after the manner of a thrifty man: *The thrifty hire I saved under your father*—As II 3 39.

THRONGED

Filled, oppressed: *The earth is throng'd By man's oppression*—Per I 1 101. So *thronged up*: *A man throng'd up with cold*—Per II 1 77.

THROUGH

(1) Thoroughly: *He's not yet through warm*—Troil II 3 232. Home: *I would revenges . . . would seek us through*—Cymb IV 2 159.
(2) *To be through with one*, to be under obligation to him, in his debt: *If a man is through with them in honest taking up*—2 H4 I 2 45. *To go through*, to come under obligation, make a bargain: *I have gone through for this piece*—Per IV 2 47.

THROUGHFARE

A thoroughfare: *The vasty wilds Of wide Arabia are as throughfares now*—Merch II 7 41. [*His body*] *is a throughfare for steel, if it be not hurt*—Cymb I 2 11.

THROUGHLY

Thoroughly: *I am informed throughly of the cause*—Merch IV 1 173. *I'll be revenged Most throughly for my father*—Hml IV 5 135. *My point and period will be throughly wrought*—Lr IV 7 97. *Caius Lucius Will do's commission throughly*—Cymb II 4 11.

THROW

To tumble past the throw, to overshoot the mark, go too far: *Like to a bowl upon a subtle ground, I have tumbled past the throw*—Cor V 2 20. *Ai this throw*, at this cast (as of dice): *You can fool no more money out of me at this throw*—Tw V 44.

THRUM

See *Thread and Thrum*.

THRUMMED

Made of thrums, *i.e.* tufts of wool: *Her thrummed hat*—Wiv IV 2 80. See *Thread and Thrum*.

THUNDER-STONE

A thunderbolt, the (supposed) solid body accompanying thunder: [I] *Have bared my bosom to the thunder-stone*—Cæs I 3 49. *The all-dreaded thunder-stone*—Cymb IV 2 271. Cf. *Are there no stones in heaven But what serve for the thunder?*—Oth V 2 234. *The gods throw stones of sulphur on me, if . . .*—Cymb V 5 240.

THWART (adj.)

Perverse: [*That her child may*] *be a thwart disnatured torment to her*—Lr I 4 305.

THWART (vb.)

To pass over, cross: *Pericles Is now again thwarting the wayward seas*—Per IV 4 9.

THWART (adv.)

Obliquely: *Every action . . . trial did draw Bias and thwart, not answering the aim*—Troil I 3 13.

TIB

A cant depreciative name for a woman: [*As fit*] *as Tib's rush for Tom's forefinger*—All's II 2 24. *Every Coistrel that comes inquiring for his Tib*—Per IV 6 175.

TICKLE

Unstable, critical: *Thy head stands so tickle on thy shoulders that . . .*—Meas I 2 176. *The state of Normandy Stands on a tickle point*—2 H6 I 1 215. Easily moved: *The clown shall make those laugh whose lungs are tickle o' the sere*—Hml II 2 336 (the first issue of the Globe has the inferior reading *tickled*).

TICKLE-BRAIN

The nickname of some strong liquor; applied to a person; or perh., a person of tickle or unsteady brain (see the foregoing word): *Peace, good pint-pot; peace, good tickle-brain*—1 H4 II 4 438.

TICK-TACK

A kind of backgammon; app. used in a wanton sense: *Who I would be sorry should be thus foolishly lost at a game of tick-tack*—Meas I 2 195.

TIDE

(1) A time, season: *It . . . should be set Among the high tides in the calendar*—John III 1 85. With a play: *Flow this way! A brave fellow! he keeps his tides well*—Tim I 2 56.

(2) *The tide of times*, the course of time: *The noblest man That ever lived in the tide of times*—Cæs III 1 256.

TIDY

As an epithet of vague commendation; capital, fine: *Thou whoreson little tidy Bartholomew boar-pig*—2 H4 II 4 250.

TIGHT

Smart, skilful: *My queen's a squire More tight at this than thou*—Ant IV 4 14.

TIGHTLY[1]

Smartly, skilfully: *He will clapper-claw thee tightly*—Wiv II 3 67.

TIGHTLY[2]

Quickly: *Bear you these letters tightly*—Wiv I 3 88.

TILLYVALLY

An interjection of contempt of uncertain origin: Tw II 3 83. So *Tilly-fally*: *Tilly-fally, Sir John, ne'er tell me*—2 H4 II 4 90.

TIME

(1) *In good time, in happy time*, happily, upon a wish: *In good time here comes the noble duke*—R3 II 1 45. Lord. *The king and queen and all are coming down*. Ham. *In happy time*—Hml V 2 212. *In good time*, used to express acquiescence: Duke . . . *Leave me awhile with the maid* . . . Prov. *In good time*—Meas III 1 180. To express indignation; forsooth: *He, in good time, must his lieutenant be, And I . . . his Moorship's ancient*—Oth I 1 32. *In happy time*, used to express content: La. Cap. . . . [Thy father] *Hath sorted out a sudden day of joy.* . . . Jul. *Madam, in happy time*—Rom III 5 110.

(2) *At more time*, at more leisure: *At more time . . . let us speak Our free hearts each to other*—Mcb I 3 153.

(3) The present state of things, the times: *The time is out of joint*—Hml I 5 189. *Beyond him in the advantage of the time*—Cymb IV 1 12. Sim. *the state of time*: *I would the state of time had first been whole*—1 H4 IV 1 25. *The time of scorn*, perh., the scornful age: *To make me A fixed figure for the time of scorn To point his slow unmoving finger at!*—Oth IV 2 53.

(4) *One's time*, his life: *Though his right arm might purchase his own time*—Tim III 5 77. His time of life: [The king] *Puts to him all the learnings that his time Could make him the receiver of*—Cymb I 1 43.

(5) All time to come, the future: *Mine, That brought you forth this boy, to keep your name Living to time*—Cor V 3 125. *When in eternal lines to time thou growest*—Sonn 18 12.

TIMELESS

Untimely: *Sorrows which would press you down . . . to your timeless grave*—Gent III 1 20. *The bloody office of his timeless end*—R2 IV 5. *Thy timeless cruel death*—1 H6 V 4 5. *Poison, I see, hath been his timeless end*—Rom V 3 162.

TIMELY

Early, soon: *He did command me to call timely on him*—Mcb II 3 51. *Thanks to you, That call'd me timelier than my purpose hither*—Ant II 6 51. *Bright orient pearl, alack, too timely shaded!*—Pilgr 133.

TIMELY-PARTED

Not having died untimely, having died a natural death: *Oft have I seen a timely-parted ghost*—2 H6 III 2 161.

TINCT

(1) A tincture, tint, hue: *Such black and grained spots As will not leave their tinct*—Hml III 4 90. *White and azure laced With blue of heaven's own tinct*—Cymb II 2 22.

(2) A tincture, solution, liquid extract: *Coming from him (i.e. Antony), that great medicine hath With his tinct gilded thee*—Ant I 5 36 (by *medicine* being no doubt meant the grand elixir of the alchemists, of which gold was an essential ingredient —whence *gilded*). The grand elixir: *Plutus himself, That knows the tinct and multiplying medicine*—All's V 3 101.

TINCTURE

Great men shall press For tinctures, stains, relics and cognizance—Cæs II 2 88, alluding to the practice of staining handkerchiefs with the blood of an honoured person.

TIRE (sb.)[1]

Furniture; here perh., bed-clothes: *I much marvel that your lordship, having Rich tire about you, should at these early hours Shake off . . . repose*—Per III 2 21.

TIRE (sb.)[2]

A head-dress: *The ship-tire, the tire-valiant, or any tire of Venetian admittance*—Wiv III 3 60 (see *Ship-tire* and *Tire-valiant*). *I like the new tire within excellently*—Ado III 4 13. [I] *put my tires and mantles on him*—Ant II 5 22. *You in Grecian tires are painted new*—Sonn 53 8.

TIRE (vb.)[1]

To dress; of hair: *To save the money that he spends in tiring*—Err II 2 98.

TIRE (vb.)²

Tiring, app. in a reflexive sense, riding hard to exhaustion: *The posts come tiring on*—2 H4 Ind 37. In LLL IV 2 131 ([So doth] *the tired horse* [imitate] *his rider) tired* no doubt expresses the sympathy of the horse with a wearied rider. Cf. *The beast that bears me, tired with my woe, Plods dully on*—Sonn 50 5.

TIRE (vb.)³

(1) *To tire on* or *upon*, of a bird of prey, to tear or devour (the prey); of an eagle: *Whose haughty spirit . . . Will . . . like an empty eagle Tire on the flesh of me and of my son*—3 H6 I 1 267. *As an empty eagle . . . Tires with her beak on feathers, flesh and bone*—Ven 55. Fig.: *Upon that were my thoughts tiring*—Tim III 6 4. *When thou shalt be disedged by her That now thou tirest on*—Cymb III 4 96.

(2) To glut: *In his will his wilful eye he tired*—Lucr 417.

TIRE-VALIANT

A kind of head-dress of unknown make: Wiv III 3 60 (quoted under *Tire* (sb.)²).

TIRING-HOUSE

A dressing-room: *This hawthorn-brake* [shall be] *our tiring-house*—Mids III 1 4.

TISICK

Phthisic; a consumption, a cough: *A whoreson tisick . . . so troubles me*—Troil V 3 101.

TISSUE

A fine, rich stuff: *Cloth-of-gold of tissue*—Ant II 2 204.

TITHE (adj.)

Tenth: *Every tithe soul*—Troil II 2 19. Cf. *One good woman in ten . . . we'ld find no fault with the tithe-woman*—All's I 3 86.

TITHE (sb.)

Our corn's to reap, for yet our tithe's to sow—Meas IV 1 76. Of this no satisfactory explanation has been given. Perh. *tilth* should be read.

TITHE (vb.)

To inflict (death) by the mode of decimation: *By decimation, and a tithed death*—Tim V 4 31.

TITHING

A subdivision of a county, containing about ten householders and forming a tenth of a Hundred: *Who is whipped from tithing to tithing*—Lr III 4 139.

TITLE

(1) An inscription: *Tell me once more what title thou dost bear*—Merch II 9 35 (to the silver casket).

(2) That to which one has or claims a title: *To know nothing, and to have nothing, is to be a great part of your title*—All's II 4 25. *The sword Which sways usurpingly these several titles*—John I 12. This seems to be the meaning in Mcb IV 2 6 (*To leave . . . His mansion and his titles (i.e.* his property and possessions in general) *in a place From whence himself does fly*).

TO

In addition to: *The Greeks are strong and skilful to their strength*—Troil I 1 7. *To that dauntless temper of his mind He hath a wisdom*—Mcb III 1 52. *New storms to those already spent*—Lucr 1589.

TO

An intensive prefix (see *All-to*): *Let them . . . fairy-like to-pinch the unclean knight*—Wiv IV 4 56.

TOAST

A piece of toast put into liquor: *Fetch me a quart of sack; put a toast in't*—Wiv III 5 3. *Made a toast for Neptune*—Troil I 3 45.

TOAZE

App. the same as *Touse (q.v.)*: *Thinkest thou, for that I insinuate, or toaze from thee thy business, I am therefore no courtier?*—Wint IV 4 758.

TOD (sb.)

An old weight, used chiefly for wool, commonly = 28 pounds: *Every tod yields pound and odd shilling*—Wint IV 3 34.

TOD (vb.)

To produce a tod (see above): *Every 'leven wether tods*—Wint IV 3 33.

TOFORE

Before, formerly: *Some obscure precedence that hath tofore been sain*—LLL III 83. *Would thou wert as thou tofore hast been!*—Tit III 1 294.

TOGE

Toga: *Why in this woolvish toge should I stand here?*—Cor II 3 122.

TOGED

Gowned, robed: *The toged consuls*—Oth I 1 25.

TOIL

To cause to toil: [Who] *now have toil'd their unbreathed memories With this same play*—Mids V 74. *Did my brother Bedford toil his wits, To . . .?*—2 H6 I 1 83. *Why this same . . . watch So nightly toils the subject of the land*—Hml I 71. *Toiled*, wearied: *Toil'd with works of war*—R2 IV 96.

TOKEN

To betoken: *That what in time proceeds May token to the future our past deeds*—All's IV 2 62.

TOKENED

Whose presence is indicated by 'tokens' (see the next word): *The token'd pestilence*—Ant III 10 9.

TOKENS

The Lord's tokens, spots indicating the infection of the plague: *These lords are visited; you (i.e. the ladies) are not free, For The Lord's tokens on you do I see*—LLL V 2 422 (with a play on *the lords' tokens*). Cf. *He is so plaguy proud that the death-tokens of it Cry 'No recovery'*—Troil II 3 187. *Corrupted blood some watery token shows*—Lucr 1748.

TOLL

(1) To levy taxes: *No Italian priest Shall tithe or toll in our dominions*—John III 1 153.

(2) *To toll for*, to pay toll as in a market for the liberty of selling: *I will buy me a son-in-law in a fair, and toll for this*—All's V 3 148.

TOMBOY

A loose woman: *To be partner'd With tomboys . . . with diseased ventures*—Cymb I 6 121.

TONGS

Prob. an instrument like a triangle, played with a key: *Let's have the tongs and the bones*—Mids IV 1 31.

TONGUE

To utter: *Such stuff as madmen Tongue and brain not*—Cymb V 4 146. To speak of: *How might she tongue me!*—Meas IV 4 28.

TOO MUCH

As a substantival expression, something present in excess: *The fellow has a deal of that too much (i.e. vanity), Which holds him (i.e. himself) much to have (i.e. to have many good qualities)*—All's III 2 92. *Goodness, growing to a plurisy, Dies in his own too much*—Hml IV 7 118.

TOPLESS

Without a superior, supreme: *Thy topless deputation he puts on*—Troil I 3 152.

TOP-PROUD

Proud in the highest degree: *This top-proud fellow*—H8 I 1 151.

TORCHER

A torch-bearer: *Ere twice the horses of the sun shall bring Their fiery torcher his diurnal ring*—All's II 1 164.

TOUCH (sb.)

(1) Natural sensibility, feeling: *He loves us not; He wants the natural touch*—Mcb IV 2 8. A sensibility or feeling: *Hast thou . . . a touch, a feeling Of their afflictions?*—Tp V 21. *The inly touch of love*—Gent II 7 18. *Have you no modesty . . . No touch of bashfulness?*—Mids III 2 285. *So excellent a touch of modesty*—Tw II 1 12. An acute feeling, a pang: *The most bitter touch of sorrow that e'er I heard virgin exclaim in*—All's I 3 122. *Not alone The death of Fulvia, with more urgent touches, Do strongly speak to us*—Ant I 2 186. *I am senseless of your wrath; a touch more rare Subdues all pangs*—Cymb I 1 135.

(2) A hint: *Give your friend Some touch of your late business*—H8 V 1 12.

(3) A trait: *Of many faces, eyes and hearts, To have the touches dearest prized*—As III 2 159. *I do remember in this shepherd boy Some lively touches of my daughter's favour*—V 4 26.

(4) The touchstone: *Now do I play the touch, To try if thou be current gold indeed*—R3 IV 2 8. *Thou touch of hearts!*—Tim IV 3 390. *To bide the touch*, to undergo trial: *A day Wherein the fortune of ten thousand men Must bide the touch*—1 H4 IV 4 8. *Of noble touch*, of tried nobleness: *My friends of noble touch*—Cor IV 1 49.

(5) A feat: *Hast thou kill'd him sleeping? O brave touch!*—Mids III 2 70.

(6) By confusion with Tache (a spot, stain), taint: *Your substitute, Who is as free from touch or soil with her As she from one ungot*—Meas V 140. *[Whether ever I have] spake one the least word that might Be to the . . . touch of her good person?*—H8 II 4 153. An evil trait: *One touch of nature makes the whole world kin*—Troil III 3 175.

TOUCH (vb.)

(1) To reach, touch at: *By his command Have I here touch'd Sicilia*—Wint V 1 138. *[They] shortly mean to touch our northern shore*—R2 II 1 288. *He touch'd the ports desired*—Troil II 2 76.

(2) To test, try (as with the touchstone): *A counterfeit . . . which, being touch'd and tried, Proves valueless*—John III 1 99. *Thus to have said . . . had touch'd his spirit And tried his inclination*—Cor II 3 198. *They have all been touch'd and found base metal*—Tim III 3 6. *A suit Wherein I mean to touch your love indeed*—Oth III 3 80.

(3) To taint, infect (cf. *Touch* (sb.) (6)): *I thank God I am not a woman, to be touched with so many giddy offences*—As III 2 366. *Hearing your high majesty is touch'd With that malignant cause*—All's II 1 113. *The life of all his blood Is touch'd corruptibly*—John V 7 1. *I'll touch my point With this contagion*—Hml IV 7 147.

TOUSE

To rend, pluck: *We'll touse you Joint by joint*—Meas V 313.

TOWARD

(1) In preparation, at hand: *What, a play toward!*—Mids III 1 81. *There is, sure, another flood toward*—As V 4 35. *O proud death, What feast is toward in thine eternal cell?*—Hml V 2 375. *Four feasts are toward*—Ant II 6 75.

(2) Promising, likely: *That is spoken like a toward prince*—3 H6 II 2 66.

TOWARDS

Like *Toward* (1): *We have a trifling foolish banquet towards*—Rom I 5 124.

TOWER

In falconry, of a hawk, to soar aloft in order to swoop down on her prey: *No marvel . . . My lord protector's hawks do tower so well*—2 H6 II 1 9. *A falcon, towering in her pride of place*—Mcb II 4 12. *Like a falcon towering in the skies*—Lucr 506. Of an eagle: *The gallant monarch is in arms And like an eagle o'er his aery towers*—John V 2 148.

TOY

(1) An idle fancy or impulse: *Such like toys as these Have moved his highness to commit me now*—R3 I 1 60. *For Hamlet and the trifling of his favour, Hold it a fashion and a toy in blood*—Hml I 3 5. *The very place puts toys of desperation . . . into every brain*—I 4 75. *No jealous toy Concerning you*—Oth III 4.156. *An inconstant toy*, a fickle freak: *If no inconstant toy, nor womanish fear, Abate thy valour*—Rom IV 1 119.

(2) A story, tale; *fairy toys*, idle tales: *I never may believe . . . these fairy toys*—Mids V 2.

(3) *There's toys abroad*, there's a little something afoot—John I 232.

TRACE

(1) To pace, traverse: *As we do trace this alley up and down*—Ado III 1 16. *To trace the forests wild*—Mids II 1 25.

(2) To follow: *All my joy Trace the conjunction!*—H8 III 2 44. To vie with: *Who else would trace him* [is] *his umbrage*—Hml V 2 124. To succeed: *All unfortunate souls That trace him in his line*—Mcb IV 1 152

TRACT¹

A trace: [It] *flies an eagle flight . . . Leaving no tract behind*—Tim I 1 49.

TRACT²

A track: *The eyes . . . now converted are From his* (*i.e.* the sun's) *low tract*—Sonn 7 11. The course (of an event): *The tract of every thing Would by a good discourser lose some life*—H8 I 1 40.

TRADE

(1) Traffic, coming and going: *In the king's highway, Some way of common trade*—R2 III 3

155. *Where most trade of danger ranged*—2 H4 I 1 174. A beaten track, general course: [He] *Stands in the gap and trade of moe preferments*—H8 V 1 36.

(2) Business or affairs in general: *My niece is desirous you should enter, if your trade be to her*—Tw III 1 82. *Have you any further trade with us?*—Hml III 2 346.

(3) A custom, practice: *Thy sin's not accidental, but a trade*—Meas III 1 149.

TRADED

Versed, practised: *Long traded in it*—John IV 3 109. *Two traded pilots*—Troil II 2 64.

TRADE-FALLEN

Out of service: *Revolted tapsters and ostlers trade-fallen*—1 H4 IV 2 31.

TRAIN (sb.)

An allurement, bait: *Macbeth By many of these trains hath sought to win me Into his power*—Mcb IV 3 117. See *Lure*.

TRAIN (vb.)

To allure, entice: *Train me not, sweet mermaid, with thy note*—Err III 2 45. *A call To train ten thousand English to their side*—John III 4 174. *We did train him on*—1 H4 V 2 21. *For that cause I train'd thee to my house*—1 H6 II 3 35.

TRAITORLY

Treacherous, perfidious: *These traitorly rascals*—Wint IV 4 820.

TRAMMEL

A net; hence as vb. *to trammel up*, to net, tie up: *If the assassination Could trammel up the consequence*—Mcb I 7 2. *Trammel* was also the name of a shackle used in teaching a horse to amble. (See *Amble*.) The allusion may be to this.

TRANECT

App., a ferry or a ferry-boat; perh. a misprint for *Traject*, to represent the Italian Traghetto, a ferry: *Bring them . . . Unto the tranect, to the common ferry Which trades to Venice*—Merch III 4 52.

TRANSFORMATION

App., mutilation: *Upon whose dead corpse there was such misuse, Such beastly shameless transformation*—1 H4 I 1 43.

TRANSLATE

To transfer: *If he see aught in you that makes him like, That any thing . . . I can with ease translate it to my will* (*i.e.* bring it into my liking)—John II 511. To describe, explain: *One that knows the youth . . . Did in great Ilion thus translate him to me*—Troil IV 5 110.   *There's matter in these sighs . . . You must translate: 'tis fit we understand them*—Hml IV 1 1.

TRANSLATION

A description, explanation: *Some thousand verses of a faithful lover, A huge translation of hypocrisy*—LLL V 2 50, app. meaning that the poem constitutes in effect an (unconscious) exemplification of the nature of hypocrisy.

TRANSPARENT

Bright: *The glorious sun's transparent beams*—2 H6 III 1 353.

TRANSPORT

(1) To bear, carry: *Her ashes . . . Transported shall be at high festivals*—1 H6 I 6 24.   *He cannot temperately transport his honours From where he should begin and end*—Cor II 1 240.

(2) To remove from this world: *To transport him in the mind he is Were damnable*—Meas IV 3 72.   Perh. also in Mids IV 2 3 (*He cannot be heard of.   Out of doubt he is transportea*).

TRANSPORTANCE

Conveyance, carriage: *Be thou my Charon, And give me swift transportance to those fields*—Troil III 2 11.

TRANSPOSE

To transform, change: *Things base and vile . . . Love can transpose to form and dignity*—Mids I 1 232.   *That which you are my thoughts cannot transpose*—Mcb IV 3 21.

TRASH (sb.)

Applied to persons in depreciation: Oth II 1 312 (quoted under *Trash* (vb.)).   *I do suspect this trash To be a party in this injury*—V 1 85.

TRASH (vb.)

To restrain by means of a trash, a strap attached to a hound, and allowed to drag along the ground or held by the huntsman: *This poor trash of Venice, whom I trash For his quick hunting*—Oth II 1 312.   *To trash for over-topping*, for outrunning the rest of the pack; fig.: *Being once perfected . . . who to advance and who To trash for over-topping*—Tp I 2 79.

TRAVAIL (sb.)

Labour, toil: *Is all our travail turn'd to this effect?*—1 H6 V 4 102.   *I have had my labour for my travail*—Troil I 1 70.   *Thy lovely argument Deserves the travail of a worthier pen*—Sonn 79 5.

TRAVAIL (vb.)

To labour, toil: *Obey our will, which travails in thy good*—All's II 3 165.   [It] *is very likely to load our purposes with what they travail for*—Tim V 1 16.

TRAVELLER

A labourer: *As fast lock'd up in sleep as guiltless labour When it lies starkly in the traveller's bones*—Meas IV 2 69.   *As motion and long-during action tires The sinewy vigour of the traveller*—LLL IV 3 307.

TRAVERSE (vb.)

(1) To march to and fro; as a word of command: *Hold, Wart, traverse*—2 H4 III 2 291.   *Traverse! go, provide thy money*—Oth I 3 378.

(2) In fencing, to parry: *To see thee fight . . . to see thee traverse*—Wiv II 3 24.

TRAVERSE (adv.)

Across; *to break traverse*, see *Break* (3).

TRAVERSED

Crossed, folded: [We] *Have wander'd with our traversed arms and breathed Our sufferance vainly*—Tim V 4 7.

TRAY-TRIP

A game played with dice in which success depended on throwing trays or treys (see *Trey*): *Shall I play my freedom at tray-trip?*—Tw II 5 208.

TREACHER

A traitor: *Knaves, thieves, and treachers*—Lr I 2 133.

TREASURE (sb.)

A treasury: *'Will' will fulfil the treasure of thy love*—Sonn 136 5.

TREASURE (vb.)

To enrich: *Treasure thou some place With beauty's treasure*—Sonn 6 3.

TREASURY

Treasure: *I would have ransack'd The pedlar's silken treasury*—Wint IV 4 359.   *Sunken wreck and sumless treasuries*—H5 I 2 165.   [They] *Have cost a mass of public treasury*—2 H6 I 3 134.

TREATISE

A discourse, tale: *I would have salved it with a longer treatise*—Ado I 1 317.   *My fell of hair Would at a dismal treatise rouse and stir*—Mcb V 5 11.   *Your treatise makes me like you worse and worse*—Ven 774.

TREATY

(1) A thing to be treated, an affair: *We are convented Upon a pleasing treaty*—Cor II 2 58.

(2) A proposal tending to an agreement: *Why answer not the double majesties This friendly treaty?*—John II 480.   *I must To the young man send humble treaties*—Ant III 11 61.

TREBLE-DATED

Living thrice as long as man: *Thou treble-dated crow*—Phœn 17.

TRENCH

To form by cutting: *A figure Trenched in ice*—Gent III 2 6. To incise: *With twenty trenched gashes on his head*—Mcb III 4 27. To cut a new channel for: *A little charge will trench him* (*i.e.* the Trent) *here And on this north side win this cape of land*—1 H4 III 1 112.

TRENCHANT

In a physical sense, cutting, keen: *Thy trenchant sword*—Tim IV 3 115.

TRENCHER-KNIGHT

A parasite: *Some mumble-news, some trencher-knight*—LLL V 2 464.

TREY

A throw of three at dice: Prin. . . . *There is three.* Biron. *Nay then, two treys*—LLL V 2 231.

TRIAL

Wantest thou eyes at trial? app., do you wish to be gazed at (and admired) during the trial? or perh., do you wish a trial of eyes, *i.e.* a bout of outstaring?—Lr III 6 26.

TRIBULATION OF TOWER-HILL

The tribulation of Tower-hill, The limbs of Limehouse, explained (not very satisfactorily) as allusions to some puritanical congregations: *That no audience, but the tribulation of Tower-hill, or the limbs of Limehouse, their dear brothers, are able to endure*—H8 V 4 64.

TRIBUNAL

A tribune, platform: *On a tribunal silver'd, Cleopatra and himself . . . Were publicly enthroned*—Ant III 6 3.

TRICK (sb.)

(1) Manner, habit; *by the trick*, according to the practice of the times: *I spoke it but according to the trick*—Meas V 509.

(2) A trait or peculiarity of visage, &c.: *Every line and trick of his sweet favour*—All's I 1 107. *[The] copy of the father . . . The trick of 's frown*—Wint II 3 99. *The trick of that voice I do well remember*—Lr IV 6 108. A trait of character: *A man that had this trick of melancholy*—All's III 2 8. *The fox . . . Will have a wild trick of his ancestors*—1 H4 V 2 9. A suggestion, reminder: *He hath a trick of Cœur-de-lion's face*—John I 85.

(3) A trifle, toy: ['Tis] *A knack, a toy, a trick*—Shr IV 3 67. *By some chance, Some trick not worth an egg*—Cor IV 4 20. *For a fantasy and trick of fame*—Hml IV 4 61. A puppet: *I Remain . . . a very trick For them to play at will*—Wint II 1 50.

TRICK (vb.)

In heraldry, to draw as a bearing: [Pyrrhus] *Hath now this dread and black complexion smear'd With heraldry more dismal; head to foot Now is he total gules; horridly trick'd With blood*—Hml II 2 477, *i.e.* the bearing figured to be displayed gules is 'tricked' in blood. The word, which strictly means to delineate without colour, the colours being indicated only, is here used with some latitude.

TRICKING

Dresses or ornaments for tricking out: *Go get us properties And tricking for our fairies*—Wiv IV 4 78.

TRIFLE

To reduce to insignificance: *This sore night Hath trifled former knowings*—Mcb II 4 3.

TRIGON

The fiery Trigon, his man—2 H4 II 4 288, an allusion, of course, to Bardolph's fiery complexion. In the language of astrology a trigon or triangle was the junction of three signs, the zodiac being divided into four trigons, the watery, the earthly, the airy and the fiery. The last included Aries, Leo and Sagittarius.

TRILL

To trickle: *An ample tear trill'd down Her delicate cheek*—Lr IV 3 14.

TRIPLE

Third: [Which] *He bade me store up, as a triple eye*—All's II 1 111. One of three: *The triple pillar of the world*—Ant I 1 12.

TRIPLE-TURNED

Three times faithless: *Triple-turn'd whore!*—Ant IV 12 13.

TRIPLEX

Triple time: *The triplex, sir, is a good tripping measure*—Tw V 40.

TRISTFUL

Sorrowful: *Convey my tristful queen*—1 H4 II 4 434. *With tristful visage*—Hml III 4 50.

TRIUMPH

(1) A public festivity or display: *Hold those justs and triumphs?*—R2 V 2 52. *Those triumphs held at Oxford*—V 3 14. *Thou art a perpetual triumph, an everlasting bonfire-light!*—1 H4 III 3 46. *With stately triumphs, mirthful comic shows*—3 H6 V 7 43.

(2) A trump-card: *She, Eros, has Pack'd cards with Cæsar, and false-play'd my glory Unto an enemy's triumph*—Ant IV 14 18.

TRIUMPHANTLY

As in a triumph (see *Triumph* (1)), festively: [We will] *Dance in Duke Theseus' house triumphantly*—Mids IV 1 93.

TRIUMVIRY

Triumvirate: *Thou makest the triumviry*—LLL IV 3 53.

TROJAN, TROYAN

A cant name for a dissolute fellow or a boon companion: *Hector was but a Troyan in respect of this*—LLL V 2 639. *Unless you play the honest Troyan, the poor wench is cast away*—681. *There are other Trojans that thou dreamest not of*—1 H4 II 1 76. *Base Trojan*—H5 V 1 20.

TROLL-MY-DAMES

Fr. *Trou-madame*, a game resembling bagatelle: *A fellow, sir, that I have known to go about with troll-my-dames*—Wint IV 3 91.

TROPICALLY

Metaphorically, figuratively: *The Mouse-trap. Marry, how? Tropically*—Hml III 2 247.

TROT (sb.)

An old woman: *An old trot with ne'er a tooth*—Shr I 2 79. Applied to a man: *What sayest thou, Trot?*—Meas III 2 52 (said to Pompey).

TROT (vb.)

I'll tell you . . . who Time trots withal—As III 2 327. [Time] *trots hard with a young maid between the contract of her marriage and the day it is solemnized*—331. The trot of the thick-set, straight-pasterned native Elizabethan horse was an uneasy, wearisome movement. For easy and swift travelling an ambling horse was used. See *Amble* and *Hard*.

TROTH-PLIGHT (adj.)

Betrothed: *Who . . . Is troth-plight to your daughter*—Wint V 3 150. *You were troth-plight to her*—H5 II 1 21.

TROTH-PLIGHT (sb.)

Betrothal, or here rather, marriage: *As rank as any flax-wench that puts to Before her troth-plight*—Wint I 2 277.

TROW

(1) To believe: *As I trow,—Which I do well; for I am sure . . .*—H8 I 1 184. *Learn more than hou trowest*—Lr I 4 135.

(2) To know; *trow you? can you tell? Trow you what he call'd me?*—LLL V 2 279. *Trow you who hath done this?*—As III 2 189. *Trow you whither I am going?*—Shr I 2 165. *I trow* or *trow* added to questions; expressing surprise; I wonder: *Who's there, I trow?*—Wiv I 4 140. *What is the matter, trow?*—Cymb I 6 47. With

some measure of contempt: *What tempest, I trow, threw this whale . . . ashore at Windsor?*—Wiv II 1 64. *What means the fool, trow?*—Ado III 4 59.

TROYAN

See *Trojan.*

TRUCE

Peace: *Keep then fair league and truce with thy true bed*—Err II 2 147. *Deep-sworn faith, peace, amity . . . And even before this truce . . .*—John III 1 231. *Since . . . it is thus agreed That peaceful truce shall be proclaim'd in France, We come to be informed . . . What the conditions of that league must be*—1 H6 V 4 116. See also *Take* (6).

TRUCKLE-BED

A bed on castors which could be pushed under the standing-bed: *There's his chamber . . . his standing-bed and truckle-bed*—Wiv IV 5 6. *I'll to my truckle-bed*—Rom II 1 39. See *Standing-bed.*

TRUE

A true man, an honest man, as opposed to a thief: *If you meet a thief, you may suspect him . . . to be no true man*—Ado III 3 53. *The most omnipotent villain that ever cried 'Stand' to a true man*—1 H4 I 2 121. *'Tis gold Which makes the true man kill'd and saves the thief*—Cymb II 3 75.

TRUEPENNY

A trusty fellow: *Say'st thou so? art thou there, truepenny?*—Hml I 5 150.

TRUMPET

A trumpeter: *Bid them bring the trumpets to the gate*—Meas IV 5 9. *Go, trumpet, to the walls, and sound a parle*—3 H6 V 1 16. *Thou, trumpet, there's my purse*—Troil IV 5 6. *Let the bird of loudest lay . . . Herald sad and trumpet be*—Phœn 1.

TRUNK SLEEVE

A wide, full sleeve: [A gown] *with a trunk sleeve*—Shr IV 3 142.

TRUST

Of my trust, on my credit: *I no question make To have it (i.e.* the money) *of my trust or for my sake*—Merch I 1 184.

TRY (sb.)

A trial, test: *A try for his friends*—Tim V 1 11.

TRY (vb.)

Bring her to try with main-course, bring her to the wind with the mainsail—Tp I 1 38. The orders for the manœuvre (adopted with a view to keeping the ship off the lee shore) seem to be resumed, after the altercation with the passengers, in the directions to the steersman given in 52.

TUB

Sweating or parboiling in a heated tub was the common mode of treatment of venereal disease: *She is herself in the tub*—Meas III 2 59. *Season the slaves For tubs and baths*—Tim IV 3 85. See also *Powdering-tub*.

TUB-FAST

Abstinence enjoined during the treatment of the tub (see above): *Bring down rose-cheeked youth To the tub-fast and the diet*—Tim IV 3 86.

TUCK

A rapier: *Dismount thy tuck*—Tw III 4 244. *A standing-tuck*, a rapier standing on end as a symbol of thinness: *You tailor's yard . . . you vile standing-tuck*—1 H4 II 4 272.

TUCKET

A trumpet signal: [*A tucket sounds*—Merch V 121 (Stage Dir). *Tucket. Enter* Montjoy—H5 III 6 120 (Stage Dir). Attrib.: *Let the trumpets sound The tucket sonance and the note to mount*—H5 IV 2 34.

TUITION

Protection, keeping: *To the tuition of God*—Ado I 1 283.

TUN-DISH

A funnel: *Filling a bottle with a tun-dish*—Meas III 2 182.

TUNEABLE

Harmonious, musical: *More tuneable than lark to shepherd's ear*—Mids I 1 184. *A cry more tuneable*—IV 1 128.

TURK

The Turk, the Sultan of Turkey: *A boy . . . that shall go to Constantinople and take the Turk by the beard*—H5 V 2 221. *The Turk, that two and fifty kingdoms hath*—1 H6 IV 7 73. *The importancy of Cyprus to the Turk*—Oth I 3 20. *To turn Turk*, lit., to be a renegade; hence, to be completely changed, to go to the bad: *An you be not turned Turk, there's no more sailing by the star*—Ado III 4 57 (meaning that Beatrice is in love). *If the rest of my fortunes turn Turk with me*—Hml III 2 286. *Turk Gregory*, supposed to refer to the warlike Hildebrand, Pope Gregory VII: *Turk Gregory never did such deeds in arms*—1 H4 V 3 46.

TURLYGOD

App. a name for a bedlam beggar, doubtfully said to be connected with Turlupins, the name borne by a French begging fraternity of about the fourteenth century: *Poor Turlygod! poor Tom!* —Lr II 3 20.

TURN

(1) To return, send back: *I will turn thy falsehood to thy heart*—R2 IV 39. *I'll turn my part thereof into thy throat*—1 H6 II 4 79.

(2) To modulate, adapt: [To] *turn his merry note Unto he sweet bird's throat*—As II 5 3.

(3) To return, come back: *Bring him . . . or turn thou no more*—As III 1 6. *Your own reasons turn into your bosoms*—H5 II 2 82. *Ere from this war thou turn a conqueror*—R3 IV 4 184. *Tarry with him till I turn again*—Tit V 2 141.

TURNBULL STREET

Properly (and now) Turnmill Street, Clerkenwell, long a noted haunt of harlots and disorderly people: *The feats he hath done about Turnbull Street*—2 H4 III 2 328.

TWELVE SCORE

I.e. twelve score yards: *As easy as a cannon will shoot point-blank twelve score*—Wiv III 2 33. *A march of twelve-score*—1 H4 II 4 598. *A would have clapped i' the clout at twelve score*—2 H4 III 2 51.

TWIGGEN

Covered with wicker-work: *I'll beat the knave into a twiggen bottle*—Oth II 3 152.

TWILLED

See *Pioned*.

TWIN

To bring forth as twins: *We were as twinn'd lambs*—Wint I 2 67. *Twinn'd brothers of one womb*—Tim IV 3 3. To be born as one of twins: *Though he had twinn'd with me*—Oth II 3 212. To be like twins or a twin: *Who twin, as 'twere, in love*—Cor IV 4 15. *Her inkle, silk, twin with the rubied cherry*—Per V Prol 8. *Twinned*, exactly resembling each other: *The twinn'd stones Upon the number'd beach*—Cymb I 6 35.

TWINK

A twinkling, instant: Ari. *Presently?* Pros. *Ay, with a twink*—Tp IV 42. *In a twink she won me to her love*—Shr II 312.

TWIRE

To twinkle: *When sparkling stars twire not*—Sonn 28 12.

TWO AND THIRTY

Two and thirty, a pip out (an expression derived from a card-game bone-ace or one-and-thirty), said to be a cant phrase meaning intoxicated: *Was it fit for a servant to use his master so, being perhaps, for aught I see, two and thirty, a pip out?*—Shr I 2 31.

TYBALT

A name given to a cat in Reynard the Fox, &c.; alluded to: Ben. *Why, what is Tybalt?* Mer. *More than prince of cats, I can tell you*—Rom II 4 18. *Tybalt, you rat-catcher*—iII 1 78.

TYBURN

The place of execution in London; hence a gallows, sometimes triangular: *The triumviry . . . The shape of Love's Tyburn that hangs up simplicity*—LLL IV 3 53.

TYPE

(1) A mark, badge: *The high imperial type of this earth's glory*—R3 IV 4 244 (the crown). *Renouncing clean . . . Short blister'd breeches, and those types of travel*—H8 I 3 29.

(2) A style, title: *Thy father bears the type of King of Naples*—3 H6 I 4 121. *I was a loyal wife . . . Of that true type hath Tarquin rifled me*—Lucr 1048.

TYRANNICALLY

Violently, noisily, referring to the noisy tyrants of the old plays: [That] *are most tyrannically clapped for't*—Hml II 2 356. Cf. *My chief humour is for a tyrant: I could play Ercles rarely, or a part to tear a cat in, to make all split*—Mids I 2 30.

U

UMBERED

Showing duskily in the gleam of the fires: *Fire answers fire, and through their paly flames Each battle sees the other's umber'd face*—H5 IV Chor 8.

UMBRAGE

A shadow: *His semblable is his mirror; and who else would trace him, his umbrage*—Hml V 2 124.

UNABLE

Weak, powerless: *Why does my blood thus muster to my heart, Making . . . it unable?*—Meas II 4 20. *You froward and unable worms!*—Shr V 2 169. *Sapless age and weak unable limbs*—1 H6 IV 5 4. *A love that makes breath poor, and speech unable*—Lr I 1 61.

UNACCOMMODATED

Not supplied or equipped: *Unaccommodated man is no more but such a poor . . . animal as thou art*—Lr III 4 111. Cf. *Accommodate* (2).

UNACCUSTOMED

Unseemly: *Set this unaccustom'd fight aside*—1 H6 III 1 93.

UNACTIVE

Inactive: *Idle and unactive*—Cor I 1 102.

UNADVISED

Of a wound, unintentionally inflicted: *Friend to friend gives unadvised wounds*—Lucr 1488. Cf. *Advise* (1).

UNAGREEABLE

Unsuitable: *The time is unagreeable to this business*—Tim II 2 41.

UNANELED

Not having received extreme unction: *Unhousel'd, disappointed, unaneled*—Hml I 5 77.

UNAPPROVED

Not made good, not justified by proof: *What unapproved witness dost thou bear!*—Compl 53. Cf. *Approve* (2).

UNAPTNESS

Disinclination: *That unaptness (i.e. his 'indisposition') [you] made your minister, Thus to excuse yourself*—Tim II 2 140.

UNATTAINTED

Unaffected, impartial: *With unattainted eye Compare her face with some that I shall show*—Rom I 2 90.

UNAVOIDED

Unavoidable, inevitable: *Unavoided is the danger now*—R2 II 1 268. *A terrible and unavoided danger*—1 H6 IV 5 8. *All unavoided is the doom of destiny*—R3 IV 4 217.

UNBARBED

Unarmoured; and hence, bare *Must I go show them my unbarbed sconce?*—Cor III 2 99. Barbs (properly bards) signified armour for men as well as that for horses mentioned under *Barbed.*

UNBATED

(1) Of a foil, unblunted, without a button: *You may choose A sword unbated*—Hml IV 7 138. *The treacherous instrument is in thy hand, Unbated and envenom'd*—V 2 327. Cf. *Bate* (vb.)[1] (1).

(2) Undiminished: *Unbated fire*—Merch II 6 11 (of a horse). Cf. *Bate* (vb.)[1] (2).

UNBID

Unbidden; and hence, unwelcome: *O unbid spite! is sportful Edward come?*—3 H6 V 1 18.

UNBOLTED

Unsifted; and hence, coarse, gross: *This un-bolted villain*—Lr II 2 71. Cf. *Bolt* (vb.).

UNBONNETED

Without bonneting, on equal terms: *My de-merits May speak unbonneted to as proud a fortune As this that I have reach'd*—Oth I 2 22. Cf. *Bonnet.*

UNBOOKISH

Unbookish jealousy, prob., such as may be expected from one unlearned in the books of love: *His unbookish jealousy must construe Poor Cassio's smiles . . . Quite in the wrong*—Oth IV 1 102.

UNBRACED

With the clothing loose: *Thus unbraced . . . [I] Have bared my bosom to the thunder-stone*—Cæs I 3 48. *Is it physical To walk unbraced?*—II 1 261. Unbuttoned: *Lord Hamlet, with his doublet all unbraced*—Hml II 1 78.

UNBRAIDED

Perh., not tarnished, fresh (braided = tarnished, faded): *Has he any unbraided wares?*—Wint IV 4 204.

UNBREATHED

Not exercised, unpractised: *Their unbreathed memories*—Mids V 74.

UNCAPABLE

Uncapable of, not open to, not susceptible of: *An inhuman wretch Uncapable of pity*—Merch IV 1 4. (Cf. *Capable* (2)). Incapable of holding (an office): *By making him uncapable of Othello's place*—Oth IV 2 235.

UNCAPE

Prob., to uncouple, to let loose the cape or collar: *I'll warrant we'll unkennel the fox . . . So, now uncape*—Wiv III 3 173. Cf. *Cape.*

UNCASE

To undress: *Do you not see Pompey is uncasing for the combat?*—LLL V 2 707. *Tranio, at once Uncase thee*—Shr I 1 211. Cf. *Case* (sb.)[1] (2).

UNCHARGE

To leave free of blame: *Even his mother shall uncharge the practice And call it accident*—Hml IV 7 68.

UNCHECKED

Uncontradicted: *It lives there unchecked that Antonio hath a ship . . . wrecked*—Merch III 1 2.

UNCIVIL

Uncivilized: *The uncivil kerns of Ireland are in arms*—2 H6 III 1 310. Barbarous, violent:

I have much to do To keep them from uncivil out-rages—Gent V 4 16. *Civil and uncivil arms*—R2 III 3 102. Unmannerly: *You would not give means for this uncivil rule*—Tw II 3 131. Cf. *Civil* (1) and (2).

UNCLASP

To disclose, reveal: *To my kingly guest* [he] *Unclasp'd my practice*—Wint III 2 167.

UNCLEW

To unwind; and hence, to undo, ruin: *If I should pay you for't as 'tis extoll'd, It would unclew me quite*—Tim I 1 167. Cf. *Clew.*

UNCOINED

Not stamped; and hence, not conventional, genuine, unfeigned: *A fellow of plain and un-coined constancy*—H5 V 2 160.

UNCOMELINESS

Unbecoming conduct: *Orderly and well-behaved reproof to all uncomeliness*—Wiv II 1 59.

UNCOMPREHENSIVE

Incomprehensible, unsounded: *The uncompre-hensive deeps*—Troil III 3 198.

UNCONFIRMED

Inexperienced, raw: *That shows thou art un-confirmed*—Ado III 3 124. *After his undressed, unpolished . . . unconfirmed fashion*—LLL IV 2 17.

UNCONSTANT

(1) Inconstant: *Unconstant womankind!*—Shr IV 2 14. *Unconstant children*—John III 1 243. *I will henceforth be no more unconstant*—3 H6 V 1 102.

(2) Uncertain, abrupt: *Such unconstant starts are we like to have from him as this*—Lr I 1 304.

UNCONTROLLED

(1) Unconquered: *Over my altars hath he hung his lance . . . his uncontrolled crest*—Ven 103. Cf. *Control* (vb.) (3).

(2) Not to be restrained: *My uncontrolled tide Turns not*—Lucr 645.

UNCOUTH

Unfamiliar, daunting, fearsome: *This uncouth forest*—As II 6 6. *I am surprised with an un-couth fear*—Tit II 3 211. *What uncouth ill event Hath thee befall'n?*—Lucr 1598.

UNCROSSED

Without cancellation, *i.e.* with the account still standing: *Such gain the cap of him that makes 'em fine, Yet keeps his book uncross'd*—Cymb III 3 25.

UNCTION

An ointment, salve: *I bought an unction of a mountebank*—Hml IV 7 142. Fig.: *Lay not that flattering unction to your soul*—Hml III 4 145.

UNCURABLE

Incurable: *Before the wound do grow uncurable* —2 H6 III 1 286. *Uncurable discomfit*—V 2 86.

UNCURRENT

Unwarranted: *I appeal To your own conscience . . . With what encounter so uncurrent I Have strain'd to appear thus*—Wint III 2 46.

UNDEAF

To free from deafness: *My death's sad tale may yet undeaf his ear*—R2 II 1 16.

UNDEEDED

Not put in action: *My sword . . . I sheathe again undeeded*—Mcb V 7 19.

UNDERBEAR

(1) To bear, endure: *Leave those woes alone which I alone Am bound to under-bear*—John III 1 64. *Patient underbearing of his fortune*—R2 I 4 29.

(2) To line (a dress): *round underborne*, lined round the base: *Round underborne with a bluish tinsel*—Ado III 4 21.

UNDERCREST

To live up to as one's crest: *I mean . . . at all times To undercrest your good addition To the fairness of my power*—Cor I 9 71.

UNDERGO

(1) To partake of, enjoy: *To undergo such ample grace and honour*—Meas I 1 24. *Their virtues else—be they . . . As infinite as man may undergo*—Hml I 4 33.

(2) To lie under, be subject or liable to: *I had rather crack my sinews . . . Than you should such dishonour undergo*—Tp III 1 26. *Claudio undergoes my challenge*—Ado V 2 57. *Much danger do I undergo for thee*—John IV 1 134. *You a world of curses undergo*—1 H4 I 3 164.

(3) To undertake, take upon oneself: *To undergo any difficulty imposed*—Troil III 2 86. *To undergo with me an enterprise*—Cæs I 3 123. *[I] would undergo what's spoken*—Cymb I 4 153. *If thou wouldst . . . undergo those employments wherein I should have cause to use thee*—III 5 109.

UNDERPRIZE

To underestimate: *The substance of my praise doth wrong this shadow In underprizing it*—Merch III 2 128. Cf. *Prize* (vb.) (1).

UNDER-SKINKER

An under-drawer, under-tapster: *This pennyworth of sugar, clapped even now into my hand by an under-skinker*—1 H4 II 4 24.

UNDERTAKE

(1) To assume (a name, &c.): *His name and credit shall you undertake*—Shr IV 2 106.

(2) To make an attempt upon, engage with: *You'll undertake her no more?*—Wiv III 5 127. *I would not undertake her in this company*—Tw I 3 61. *It is not fit your lordship should undertake every companion that you give offence to*—Cymb II 1 28.

(3) To take charge of (a person): *Sir Nicholas Vaux, Who undertakes you to your end*—H8 II 1 96.

(4) To take a risk, venture: *It is the cowish terror of his spirit, That dares not undertake*—Lr IV 2 12.

UNDERTAKER

One who undertakes

(1) Responsibility for something: *For Cassio, let me be his undertaker*—Oth IV 1 224.

(2) Another's responsibilities: *Nay, if you be an undertaker, I am for you*—Tw III 4 349.

UNDERVALUED

Inferior in worth: *Her name is Portia, nothing undervalued To Cato's daughter*—Merch I 1 165. *Ten times undervalued to tried gold*—II 7 53.

UNDERWRITE

To submit to: *Worthier than himself . . . underwrite . . . his humorous predominance*—Troil II 3 134.

UNDESERVING

Undeserved, or perh. sb., want of merit: *My lady . . . In courtesy gives undeserving praise*— LLL V 2 365.

UNDETERMINED

Indeterminable, endless: *In undetermined differences of kings*—John II 355.

UNDISPOSED

Not inclined to merriment: *That merry sconce of yours That stands on tricks when I am undisposed*—Err I 2 79. Cf. *Disposed.*

UNDISTINGUISHED

Undistinguishable; hence, illimitable: *O undistinguish'd space of woman's will!*—Lr IV 6 278. Inarticulate: *Shrieking undistinguish'd woe*— Compl 20.

UNDO

To solve: *If by which time our secret (i.e. the riddle) be undone*—Per I 1 117.

UNDOUBTED

Confident, fearless: *Hardy and undoubted champions*—3 H6 V 7 6.

UNEARED

Unploughed, untilled: *Where is she so fair whose unear'd womb Disdains the tillage of thy husbandry?*—Sonn 3 5. Cf. *Ear*.

UNEATH

Hardly, with difficulty: *Uneath may she endure the flinty streets*—2 H6 II 4 8.

UNEFFECTUAL

Ineffectual: *The glow-worm . . . gins to pale his uneffectual fire*—Hml I 5 89.

UNEQUAL

Unjust, unfair: *To lay a heavy and unequal hand Upon our honours*—2 H4 IV 1 102. *To punish me for what you make me do Seems much unequal*—Ant II 5 100. Cf. *Equal* (adj.) (1).

UNEVEN

Indirect, crooked: *Uneven is the course, I like it not*—Rom IV 1 5. Contradictory, incongruous: Escal. *Every letter he hath writ hath disvouched other.* Ang. *In most uneven . . . manner*—Meas IV 4 1. In confusion: *All is uneven, And every thing is left at six and seven*—R2 II 2 121. Perplexing, embarrassing: *Uneven and unwelcome news*—1 H4 I 1 50.

UNEXECUTED

Not put in practice: [You] *leave unexecuted Your own renowned knowledge*—Ant III 7 45.

UNEXPERIENCED

Inexperienced: *And thou return unexperienced to thy grave*—Shr IV 1 85.

UNEXPERIENT

Inexperienced: *Th' unexperient gave the tempter place*—Compl 318.

UNEXPRESSIVE

Inexpressible: *The fair, the chaste and unexpressive she*—As III 2 10.

UNFAIR

To take the beauty from: *Those hours . . . Will . . . that unfair which fairly doth excel*—Sonn 5 1.

UNFALLIBLE

Infallible: *Believe my words, For they are certain and unfallible*—1 H6 I 2 58.

UNFASHIONABLE

As adv., without bestowing proper form: *Scarce half made up, And that so lamely and unfashionable That dogs bark at me*—R3 I 1 21.

UNFATHERED

Without apparent progenitor: *The people fear me; for they do observe Unfather'd heirs*—2 H4 IV 4 121.

UNFELT

I.e. by the recipient, impalpable: *All my treasury Is yet but unfelt thanks*—R2 II 3 60.

UNFIRM

Unsteady: *All the sway of earth Shakes like a thing unfirm*—Cæs I 3 3. Inconstant: *Our fancies are more giddy and unfirm . . . Than women's are*—Tw II 4 34. In a weakened state: *So is the unfirm king In three divided*—2 H4 I 3 73. Crumbling: *The churchyard . . . Being loose, unfirm, with digging up of graves*—Rom V 3 5.

UNFOLD

To release from the fold; *the unfolding star,* the star which shows by its rising that it is time to unfold: *The unfolding star calls up the shepherd*—Meas IV 2 218.

UNFURNISH

To deprive, divest: *That which may Unfurnish me of reason*—Wint V 1 122. *Rome's royal empress, Unfurnish'd of her well-beseeming troop?*—Tit II 3 55. *Unfurnished,* lacking its fellow: *Having (i.e.* the painter having) *made one* [eye], *Methinks it should have power to steal both his And leave itself unfurnish'd*—Merch III 2 125.

UNGENITURED

Impotent: *This ungenitured agent*—Meas III 2 184.

UNGOT, UNGOTTEN

Unbegotten: *Your substitute, Who is as free from touch or soil with her As she from one ungot*—Meas V 140. *Ungotten and unborn*—H5 I 2 287. Cf. *Get.*

UNGRACIOUS

Graceless, wicked: *That word 'grace' In an ungracious mouth is but profane*—R2 II 3 88. *Swearest thou, ungracious boy?*—1 H4 II 4 490. *Do not, as some ungracious pastors do*—Hml I 3 47. Cf. *Gracious* (3).

UNHAPPILY

Wickedly: *Purest faith unhappily forsworn*—Sonn 66 4. Waggishly, censoriously: *You are a churchman, or, I'll tell you, cardinal, I should judge now unhappily*—H8 I 4 88. Sim.: *Would make one think there might be thought, Though nothing sure, yet much unhappily (i.e.* suggesting an evil interpretation)—Hml IV 5 12.

UNHAPPINESS

Capacity for mischief, wickedness: *If ever he have child, abortive be it . . . And that be heir to his unhappiness!*—R3 I 2 21. In Ado II 1 360 (*She hath often dreamed of unhappiness and waked herself with laughing*) perh., sportive mischief; but the usual modern sense suits equally well.

UNHAPPY (adj.)

(1) Of persons, wicked, pernicious: *O most unhappy strumpet!*—Err IV 4 127. *Thou old unhappy traitor*—Lr IV 6 232. *That unhappy guest Whose deed hath made herself herself detest*—Lucr 1565. Roguish, waggish: *A shrewd unhappy gallows*—LLL V 2 12. *A shrewd knave and an unhappy*—All's IV 5 66.

(2) Of things, mischievous, harmful, ill-omened: *Be thou arm'd for some unhappy words*—Shr II 140. *Upon a time,—unhappy was the clock That struck the hour!*—Cymb V 5 153. Ill fitted: *I have very poor and unhappy brains for drinking* —Oth II 3 34.

UNHAPPY (vb.)

To deprave: *A happy gentleman . . . By you unhappied and disfigured clean*—R2 III 1 9.

UNHATCHED

Unhacked: *He is knight, dubbed with unhatched rapier*—Tw III 4 257.

UNHEART

To dishearten: *To bite his lip And hum at good Cominius, much unhearts me*—Cor V 1 48.

UNHEEDY

Heedless, precipitate: *Wings and no eyes figure unheedy haste*—Mids I 1 237.

UNHOUSED

Free from domestic cares: *I would not my unhoused free condition Put into circumscription and confine For the sea's worth*—Oth I 2 26.

UNHOUSELED

Not having received the Eucharist: *Unhousel'd, disappointed, unaneled*—Hml I 5 77.

UNIMPROVED

Perh., unchastened (by experience), untrained: *Young Fortinbras, Of unimproved mettle hot and full*—Hml I 1 95.

UNINTELLIGENT

Without perception: *Your senses, unintelligent of our insufficience*—Wint I 1 15.

UNION

A fine pearl: *In the cup an union shall he throw*—Hml V 2 283. *Drink off this potion. Is thy union here?*—337.

UNJOINTED

Disjointed, disconnected: *This bald unjointed chat of his*—1 H4 I 3 65.

UNJUST

Dishonest: *This is the time that the unjust man* (*i.e.* the thief) *doth thrive*—Wint IV 4 687. *Discarded unjust serving-men*—1 H4 IV 2 30. False, faithless: *Theseus' perjury and unjust flight* — Gent IV 4 173. *O passing traitor, perjured and unjust!*—3 H6 V 1 106. *That same Diomed's a false-hearted rogue, a most unjust knave*—Troil V 1 95. *Unless thy lady prove unjust*—Pilgr 331.

UNJUSTLY

Dishonestly, wrongfully: *To cozen him that would unjustly win*—All's IV 2 76. *By this chaste blood so unjustly stain'd*—Lucr 1836.

UNKIND

(1) Childless: *Had thy mother borne so hard a mind, She had not brought forth thee, but died unkind*—Ven 203.

(2) Unnatural, not showing natural feelings: *Blow, blow, thou winter wind, Thou art not so unkind As man's ingratitude*—As II 7 174. *When envy breeds unkind division*—1 H6 IV 1 193. *Titus, unkind and careless of thine own*— Tit I 86. *What hast thou done, unnatural and unkind?*—V 3 48. Cf. *Kind* (adj.) (1).

UNKISS

To annul with a kiss: *Let me unkiss the oath 'twixt thee and me; And yet not so, for with a kiss 'twas made* (and for annulment inversion, not repetition of ritual would be required)—R2 V 1 74.

UNKNOWN

Perh., such as must not be indicated: *For divers unknown reasons, I beseech you, Grant me this boon*—R3 I 2 218. *I have frequent been with unknown minds*—Sonn 117 5.

UNLACE

To loosen the covering of; and so, fig., to expose to injury: *What's the matter, That you unlace your reputation thus?*—Oth II 3 193.

UNLIKE (adj.)

Unlikely, improbable: *Make not impossible That which but seems unlike*—Meas V 51. *The service that you three have done is more Unlike than this thou tell'st* — Cymb V 5 353. Of persons, not likely (to do a thing): Com. *You are like to do such business.* Bru. *Not unlike, Each way, to better yours*—Cor III 1 48. Cf. *Like* (adj.)

UNLIKE (adv.)

Improbably: Long. . . . *She is a most sweet lady.* Boyet. *Not unlike, sir, that may be*—LLL II 207.

UNLIMITED

Perh., disregarding the unity of place: *Scene individable, or poem unlimited*—Hml II 2 418.

UNLIVE
To deprive of life: *Where shall I live now Lucrece is unlived?*—Lucr 1754.

UNLOOKED
Unlooked for, unexpected: *By some unlook'd accident cut off*—R3 I 3 214.

UNMANNED
Of a hawk, not made subject to man, untrained; fig.: *Hood my unmann'd blood, bating in my cheeks*—Rom III 2 14. Cf. *Man* (2).

UNMERITABLE
Undeserving, having no merit: *My desert Unmeritable shuns your high request*—R3 III 7 154. *This is a slight unmeritable man*—Cæs IV 1 12.

UNNOBLE
Ignoble: *A most unnoble swerving*—Ant III 11 50.

UNNOTED
Undemonstrative: *With such sober and unnoted passion He did behave his anger*—Tim III 5 21.

UNOWED
Lacking an owner: *To part by the teeth The unowed interest of proud-swelling state*—John IV 3 146. Cf. *Owe* (1).

UNPARTIAL
Impartial: *The unpartial judging of this business*—H8 II 2 107.

UNPAVED
Without stones, emasculated: *The voice of unpaved eunuch*—Cymb II 3 34.

UNPAY
To annul the effect of (a payment); and hence, of an injury inflicted, to undo (it): *Pay her the debt you owe her, and unpay the villany you have done her*—2 H4 II 1 129.

UNPERFECT
Imperfect: *As an unperfect actor on the stage*—Sonn 23 1.

UNPERFECTNESS
Imperfection: *One unperfectness shows me another*—Oth II 3 298.

UNPINKED
App., lacking ornamental perforations: *Gabriel's pumps were all unpink'd i' the heel*—Shr IV 1 136. Cf. *Pinked*.

UNPLAUSIVE
Not applausive; and hence, neglectful: *He'll question me Why such unplausive eyes are bent on him*—Troil III 3 42. Cf. *Plausibly*.

UNPOSSESSING
Incapable of inheriting: *Thou unpossessing bastard!*—Lr II 1 69.

UNPOSSIBLE
Impossible: *For us to levy power Proportionable to the enemy Is all unpossible*—R2 II 2 124.

UNPREGNANT
(1) Unapt, unready: *This deed unshapes me quite, makes me unpregnant And dull to all proceedings*—Meas IV 4 23. Cf. *Pregnant*[2] (1).

(2) *Unpregnant of*, not receptive of the claims of, indifferent to: *[I] peak, Like John-a-dreams, unpregnant of my cause, And can say nothing*—Hml II 2 594. Cf. *Pregnant*[2] (2).

UNPREVAILING
Unavailing, vain: *We pray you, throw to earth This unprevailing woe*—Hml I 2 106. Cf. *Prevail*.

UNPRIZABLE
Not to be prized or valued (cf. *Prize* (vb.) (1)), as being
(1) Too great: *Your brace of unprizable estimations*—Cymb I 4 98.
(2) Too small; hence, insignificant: *A bawbling vessel . . . For shallow draught and bulk unprizable*—Tw V 57.

UNPRIZED
Either, not estimated at the due rate; or, inestimable, priceless: *This unprized precious maid*—Lr I 1 262. Cf. *Prize* (vb.) (1).

UNPROPER
Not appropriated to an individual: *There's millions now alive That nightly lie in those unproper beds Which they dare swear peculiar*—Oth IV 1 68.

UNPROPERLY
Improperly; *I kneel before thee; and unproperly Show duty*—Cor V 3 54.

UNPROPORTIONED
Not fitted to the occasion, unsuitable: *Give thy thoughts no tongue, Nor any unproportion'd thought his act*—Hml I 3 59.

UNPROVIDE
To unfurnish; and so, to deprive (of resolution): *I'll not expostulate with her, lest her body and beauty unprovide my mind again*—Oth IV 1 217. *Unprovided*, unprepared (for death): *If they die unprovided*—H5 IV 1 183.

UNPROVIDENT
Improvident: *Who for thyself art so unprovident*—Sonn 10 2.

UNQUALITIED

Deprived of one's proper qualities, unmanned: *He is unqualitied with very shame*—Ant III 11 44.

UNQUESTIONABLE

Not brooking question (see *Question* (sb.) (2)), disinclined to conversation: *An unquestionable spirit*—As III 2 393.

UNQUESTIONED

Not discussed: *Our haste . . . leaves unquestion'd Matters of needful value*—Meas I 1 54. Cf. *Question* (sb.) (1).

UNRAISED

Not rising to the due height, dull: *The flat unraised spirits*—H5 Prol 9.

UNREADY

Not dressed, not having finished one's toilet: 1 H6 II 1 38 (Stage Dir) (quoted under *Ready*). *How now, my lords! what, all unready so?*—39.

UNREASONABLE

Irrational: *Unreasonable creatures feed their young*—3 H6 II 2 26. *The unreasonable fury of a beast*—Rom III 3 111.

UNRECALLING

That cannot be recalled: *His unrecalling crime*—Lucr 993.

UNRECLAIMED

Untamed, undisciplined: *A savageness in unreclaimed blood, Of general assault*—Hml II 1 34. Cf. *Reclaim* (2).

UNRECONCILIABLE

Irreconcilable, incompatible: *That our stars, Unreconciliable, should divide Our equalness to this*—Ant V 1 46.

UNRECURING

That cannot be cured: *The deer That hath received some unrecuring wound*—Tit III 1 89. Cf. *Recure*.

UNRELENTING

Not dissolving: *Be your heart to them As unrelenting flint to drops of rain*—Tit II 3 140. Cf. *Relent* (1).

UNRESISTED

Irresistible: *Heedful fear Is almost choked by unresisted lust*—Lucr 281.

UNRESPECTED

Unregarded, unnoticed: *All the day they (i.e. his eyes) view things unrespected*— Sonn 43 2. *They live unwoo'd and unrespected fade*—54 10. Cf. *Respect* (vb.) (4).

UNRESPECTIVE

(1) Thoughtless, heedless: *I will converse with iron-witted fools And unrespective boys* — R3 IV 2 28. Cf. *Respective* (1).

(2) Undiscriminating; *unrespective sieve*, into which things are thrown without discrimination: *The remainder viands We do not throw in unrespective sieve, Because we now are full* — Troil II 2 70. Cf. *Respective* (2).

UNREVEREND

Irreverent, disrespectful: *Fie, fie, unreverend tongue!*—Gent II 6 14. *Thou unreverend boy*—John I 227.

UNREVERENT

The same as the foregoing: *See not your bride in these unreverent robes*—Shr III 2 114. *Unreverent Gloster!*—1 H6 III 1 49.

UNROLL

To strike off the roll (of thieves): *Let me be unrolled and my name put in the book of virtue!*—Wint IV 3 130.

UNROUGH

Smooth, beardless: *Many unrough youths*—Mcb V 2 10.

UNSATIATE

Insatiate: *That unsatiate Edward*—R3 III 5 87.

UNSEAM

To rip up, to cleave: *He unseam'd him from the nave to the chaps*—Mcb I 2 22.

UNSEASONED

Unseasonable: *This unseasoned intrusion*—Wiv II 2 174. Of late hours: *These unseason'd hours perforce must add Unto your sickness*—2 H4 III 1 105.

UNSEEM

To make as though one would not (do a thing): *[You] wrong the reputation of your name, In so unseeming to confess receipt Of that which hath so faithfully been paid*—LLL II 155.

UNSEMINARED

Deprived of virility, emasculated: *'Tis well for thee, That, being unseminar'd . . .*—Ant I 5 10.

UNSEPARABLE

Inseparable: *Who twin, as 'twere, in love Unseparable*—Cor IV 4 15.

UNSEVERED

Inseparable: *Honour and policy, like unsever'd friends, I' the war do grow together*—Cor III 2 42.

21

UNSHAPE

To derange, confound: *This deed unshapes me quite*—Meas IV 4 23.

UNSHUNNED

Unavoidable, inevitable: *An unshunned consequence*—Meas III 2 62.

UNSISTING

No doubt a corrupt word; explained as unfeeling, never at rest, &c.: *That spirit's possess'd with haste That wounds the unsisting postern with these strokes*—Meas IV 2 91.

UNSORTED

Not (wisely) chosen, ill-chosen: *The time itself [is] unsorted*—1 H4 II 3 13. Cf. *Sort* (vb.) (2).

UNSQUARED

Not fitted to the subject: *With terms unsquared*—Troil I 3 159.

UNSTANCHED

(1) Unquenchable, insatiate: *The villain whose unstanched thirst York and young Rutland could not satisfy*—3 H6 II 6 83. Cf. *Stanch.*

(2) *Urinae incontinens*: *As leaky as an unstanched wench*—Tp I 1 50.

UNSTATE

To unstate oneself, to divest oneself of one's dignities: *I would unstate myself, to be in a due resolution*—Lr I 2 108. *To unstate one's happiness*, to lay aside one's advantages: *Yes, like enough, high-battled Cæsar will Unstate his happiness!*—Ant III 13 29.

UNSURE

Unsafe, liable to danger (cf. *Sure* (1)): *An habitation giddy and unsure*—2 H4 I 3 89. *What is mortal and unsure*—Hml IV 4 51. Uncertain, liable to disappointment: *What's to come is still unsure*—Tw II 3 50. *Their unsure hopes*—Mcb V 4 19. Uncertain, liable to error: *His scattering and unsure observance*—Oth III 3 151.

UNSURED

Insecure: *Thy now unsured assurance to the crown*—John II 471.

UNTAINTED

Not attainted (see *Attaint* (vb.) (1)); and hence, app., loosely, not accused: *Within these five hours lived Lord Hastings, Untainted, unexamined, free, at liberty*—R3 III 6 8.

UNTEMPERING

Not tempering (in sense (3) given under *Temper* (vb.)), not winning: *Notwithstanding the poor and untempering effect of my visage*—H5 V 2 240.

UNTENTED

Not to be tented, incurable: *The untented woundings of a father's curse*—Lr I 4 322. See *Tent* (vb.).

UNTHRIFT

Prodigal, good for nothing: *With an unthrift love [she] did run from Venice*—Merch V 16. *What man didst thou ever know unthrift that was beloved after his means?*—Tim IV 3 311.

UNTIMELY

Unfitting, improper: *Your untimely claspings with your child*—Per I 1 128. As adv., amiss: *What's untimely done*—Hml IV 1 40.

UNTRADED

Unhackneyed: *Mock not, that I affect the untraded oath*—Troil IV 5 178.

UNTRIED

Unexamined, unnoticed: *I slide O'er sixteen years and leave the growth untried Of that wide gap*—Wint IV 1 5.

UNTRIMMED

Divested (of her wedding-gown): *The devil tempts thee here In likeness of a new untrimmed bride*—John III 1 208. *Untrimmed* is explained also as, with the hair dishevelled, as brides appear to have worn it.

UNTRUSSING

Undoing the points of the hose: *This Claudio is condemned for untrussing*—Meas III 2 189. See *Point* (sb.) (3) and *Hose.*

UNVALUED

(1) Inestimable, priceless: *Inestimable stones, unvalued jewels*—R3 I 4 27.

(2) Of small estimation, common: *He may not, as unvalued persons do, Carve for himself*—Hml I 3 19.

UNVIOLABLE

Inviolable: *This interchange of love . . . Upon my part shall be unviolable*—R3 II 1 26.

UNWARES

Unawares, unintentionally: *It is my father's face, Whom in this conflict I unwares have kill'd*—3 H6 II 5 61.

UNWARILY

Being taken at unawares, unexpectedly: *The best part of my power . . . Were in the Washes all unwarily Devoured by the unexpected flood*—John V 7 61.

UNWILLING

Unintentional, undesigned: *'Twas a fault unwilling*—Shr IV 1 159. *[Her eyes], being open'd, threw unwilling light Upon the wide wound*—Ven 1051.

UNWIT

To deprive of understanding: *As if some planet had unwitted men*—Oth II 3 182.

UNWORTHILY

In unmerited fashion, without cause: *Fearing lest my jealous aim might err And so unworthily disgrace the man*—Gent III 1 28.

UNWORTHY

Unmerited: *Which didst unworthy slaughter upon others*—R3 I 2 88.

UNYOKE

To disjoin, part: *Shall these hands . . . Unyoke this seizure?*—John III 1 239.

UNYOKED

Licentious, unrestrained: *The unyoked humour of your idleness*—1 H4 I 2 219.

UP

(1) *To be up*, to be in confinement: *So the poor third is up, till death enlarge his confine*—Ant III 5 12.

(2) *Up and down*, all over, precisely: *Here's his dry hand up and down*—Ado II 1 123 (with a play on the literal sense; cf. *Here's my mother's breath up and down*—Gent II 3 31). *Up and down she doth resemble thee*—Tit V 2 107.

UP-FILL

To fill up: *I must up-fill this osier cage of ours With . . .*—Rom II 3 7.

UPRIGHTEOUSLY

Righteously: *That you may most uprighteously do a poor wronged lady a merited benefit*—Meas III 1 205.

UPRISE

Of the sun, rising: *A lark, That gives sweet tidings of the sun's uprise*—Tit III 1 158. *O sun, thy uprise shall I see no more*—Ant IV 12 18.

UPRISING

Ascent, acclivity: *Was that the king, that spurr'd his horse so hard Against the steep uprising of the hill?*—LLL IV 1 1.

UPROAR

To throw into confusion: *Had I power, I should . . . Uproar the universal peace*—Mcb IV 3 97.

UPSHOOT

The decisive shot: *Then will she get the upshoot by cleaving the pin*—LLL IV 1 138.

UP-SPRING

The king . . . Keeps wassail, and the staggering up-spring reels—Hml I 4 8. Explained (1) as an upstart (referring to the King); (2) as a wild German dance; (3) as in apposition (in sense (2)) to, or, with a meaning such as light-footed, as an epithet of, *reels* (taking *reels* as sb. = revels, revelry, and as accusative after *keeps*) (see *Reels*).

UP-STARING

Standing on end: *With hair up-staring*—Tp I 2 213.

UP-SWARM

To bring (to the field) in swarms: *You have ta'en up . . . The subjects of . . . my father, And . . . Have here up-swarm'd them*—2 H4 IV 2 26.

UP-TILL

On, against: *She, poor bird, as all forlorn, Lean'd her breast up-till a thorn*—Pilgr 381.

UPWARDS

She shall be buried with her face upwards, i.e. in her lover's arms—Ado III 2 70. Cf. *Not like a corse; or if, not to be buried, But quick and in mine arms*—Wint IV 4 131.

URCHIN

(1) A hedgehog: *Ten thousand swelling toads, as many urchins*—Tit II 3 101.

(2) A hobgoblin: *Urchins Shall, for that vast of night that they may work, All exercise on thee*—Tp I 2 326. *We'll dress* [them] *Like urchins, ouphes and fairies*—Wiv IV 4 48. *Urchin-shows*, apparitions of hobgoblins: [They'll not] *Fright me with urchin-shows . . . unless he bid 'em*—Tp II 2 5.

URCHIN-SNOUTED

With a snout like a hedgehog's: *This foul, grim, and urchin-snouted boar*—Ven 1105. See *Urchin* (1).

URINAL

A vessel in which the water was kept for diagnosis: *These follies . . . shine through you like the water in an urinal*—Gent II 1 39. *I will knog his* (*i.e.* Doctor Caius's) *urinals about his knave's costard*—Wiv III 1 14. See *Cast* (vb.) (5).

USANCE

Interest on a loan: *He lends out money gratis and brings down The rate of usance*—Merch I 3 45. *My moneys and my usances*—109. [I would] *take no doit Of usance for my moneys*—141.

USE (sb.)

(1) A need, necessity: *My uses cry to me*—Tim II 1 20. *Requesting your lordship to supply his instant use with so many talents*—III 2 40. *I have a tree . . . That mine own use invites me to cut down*—V 1 208.

(2) Common occurrence, habitual experience: *These things are beyond all use*—Cæs II 2 25. *Against the use of nature*—Mcb I 3 137.

(3) *Uses*, usages, ways: *All the uses of this world*—Hml I 2 134. *Heaven me such uses send*—Oth IV 3 105.

(4) *In use*, in trust: *My full heart Remains in use with you*—Ant I 3 43. In Merch IV 1 382 (*So he will let me have The other half in use, to render it, Upon his death, unto* [Lorenzo]) the meaning is that Antonio was to hold the property in trust for Shylock for life with remainder for Lorenzo, *i.e.* on Shylock's death making the capital over to Lorenzo.

(5) Interest on a loan: [Nature] *determines Herself the glory of a creditor, Both thanks and use*—Meas I 1 39. *He lent it (i.e.* his heart) *me awhile; and I gave him use for it, a double heart for his single one*—Ado II 1 287. A putting out at interest: *That use is not forbidden usury Which happies those that pay the willing loan*—Sonn 6 5. So *to put to use: Being . . . put to use*—Tw III 1 56. *Gold that's put to use more gold begets*—Ven 768.

USE (vb.)

(1) *To use of*, to dispose of, deal with: [I] *brought him hither, To use as you think needful of the man*—Tit V 1 38.

(2) Refl., to behave: *If I have used myself unmannerly*—H8 III 1 176.

(3) To put out at interest: *Profitless usurer, why dost thou use So great a sum of sums?*—Sonn 4 7.

(4) *To use honour with*, app., to count oneself more honourable than: *We here below Recall not what we give, and therein may Use honour with you*—Per III 1 24.

USURING

Usurious: *The usuring senate*—Tim III 5 110. *A usuring kindness*—IV 3 516.

UTIS

The octave of a festival; festivity during the octave; and hence, stir, fun: *Here will be old Utis*—2 H4 II 4 21.

UTTER

To bring into the market, vend: *Beauty is bought by judgement of the eye, Not utter'd by base sale of chapmen's tongues*—LLL II 15. *Money's a medler, That doth utter all men's ware-a*—Wint IV 4 329. *Such mortal drugs I have; but Mantua's law Is death to any he that utters them*—Rom V 1 66.

UTTERANCE

To the utterance, at utterance, to extremity, to the death (*à outrance*): *Come fate into the list, And champion me to the utterance!*—Mcb III 1 71. *Which he to seek of me again, perforce, Behoves me keep at utterance*—Cymb III 1 72.

V

VADE

Fade: *Fair flower, untimely pluck'd, soon vaded*—Pilgr 131. *A shining gloss that vadeth suddenly*—170.

VAIL (sb.)

A sinking, declining: *The vail and darking of the sun*—Troil V 8 7.

VAIL (vb.)

(1) To lower, let fall: *Vail your regard Upon a wrong'd . . . maid*—Meas V 20. *Vailing her high-top lower than her ribs*—Merch I 1 28. *Thy vailed lids*—Hml I 2 70. *He vails his tail*—Ven 314. *Angels vailing clouds*, letting fall the clouds which hid them: *Fair ladies . . . Dismask'd . . . Are angels vailing clouds*—LLL V 2 295. Fig.: *The bloody Douglas . . . Gan vail his stomach*—2 H4 I 1 127. To cause to bow in token of submission: *If he have power, Then vail your ignorance*—Cor III 1 97.

(2) To do reverence: *She would with rich and constant pen Vail to her mistress Dian*—Per IV Prol 28.

VAIN

(1) Foolish, silly: *There's no man is so vain That would refuse so fair an offer'd chain*—Err III 2 185. *Every beardless vain comparative*—1 H4 III 2 67. *O vain fool!*—Lr IV 2 61.

(2) Light of tongue, not veracious: *'Tis holy sport to be a little vain, When the sweet breath of flattery conquers strife*—Err III 2 27.

(3) *For vain*, in vain: *An idle plume, Which the air beats for vain*—Meas II 4 11.

VAINLY

Idly, unreasonably: *Vainly thinking that she thinks me young*—Sonn 138 5. *At random from the truth vainly express'd*—Sonn 147 12. Erroneously, mistakenly: *My fore-past proofs . . . Shall tax my fears of little vanity, Having vainly fear'd too little*—All's V 3 121. *Which vainly I supposed the Holy Land*—2 H4 IV 5 239.

VALANCED

Fringed (with a beard): *Thy face is valanced since I saw thee last*—Hml II 2 442.

VALIDITY

(1) Worth, value: *This ring, Whose . . . rich validity Did lack a parallel*—All's V 3 191. *Of what validity and pitch soe'er*—Tw I 1 12. *More validity . . . lives In carrion-flies than Romeo*—Rom III 3 33. *No less in space, validity, and pleasure*—Lr I 1 83.

(2) Strength, force: *Purpose is . . . Of violent birth, but poor validity*—Hml III 2 198.

VALUE (sb.)

Estimation: *How much more is his life in value with him?*—H8 V 3 108.

VALUE (vb.)

(1) To be worth, be an equivalent of: *The peace . . . not values The cost that did conclude it*—H8 I 1 88. *It values not your asking*—II 3 52.

(2) Our business valued, taking into account what we have to do: *By which account, Our business valued, some twelve days hence Our general forces . . . shall meet*—1 H4 III 2 176. *Valued, of military power, rated (at a certain strength): The queen is valued thirty thousand strong*—3 H6 V 3 14.

VANITY

(1) In the mouth of a divine, the worldly life (not implying censure): *A lover may bestride the gossamer . . . And yet not fall; so light is vanity*—Rom II 6 18.

(2) An illusion: *I must Bestow upon the eyes of this young couple Some vanity of mine art*—Tp IV 39.

(3) *Vanity the puppet*, alluding to the Moralities, in which the vices were personified: [You] *take vanity the puppet's part against the royalty of her father*—Lr II 2 39.

VANTAGE

(1) Profit, gain: *Little vantage shall I reap thereby*—R2 I 3 218. *You have all the vantage of her wrong*—R3 I 3 310. [I have] *a brain that leads my use of anger To better vantage*—Cor III 2 30. *For my vantage, excellent*—Cymb V 5 198.

(2) Surplus, excess: *My fortunes every way as fairly rank'd, If not with vantage*—Mids I 1 101. *To the vantage*, over and above: *And as many to the vantage as would store the world*—Oth IV 3 85.

(3) Advantage, favourable condition, opportunity: *He that might the vantage best have took*—Meas II 2 74. *Which now to claim my vantage doth invite me*—Hml V 2 401. Imo. . . . *When shall we hear from him? Pis. . . . With his next vantage*—Cymb I 3 23. *Who lets go by no vantages that may Prefer you to his daughter*—II 3 50. *At your vantage*, taking your opportunity: *At your vantage . . . let him feel your sword*—Cor V 6 54.

(4) *Of vantage*, from the vantage-ground (of concealment): *'Tis meet that some more audience . . . should o'erhear The speech, of vantage*—Hml III 3 31.

VANTBRACE

A piece of armour for the forearm: *In my vantbrace* [I'll] *put this wither'd brawn*—Troil I 3 297.

VARIABLE

Various, different: *Variable complexions*—Cor II 1 228. *The seas and countries different With variable objects*—Hml III 1 179. *Your fat king and your lean beggar is but variable service*—IV 3 24. *Whiles he is vaulting variable ramps*—Cymb I 6 134.

VARLET

A servant to a knight or warrior: *My horse! varlet!*—H5 IV 2 2. *Call here my varlet; I'll unarm again*—Troil I 1 1.

VARY

Variation, change: [Such rogues] *turn their halcyon beaks With every gale and vary of their masters*—Lr II 2 84.

VASSALAGE

Vassalry, subjects: *Like vassalage at unawares encountering The eye of majesty*—Troil III 2 40.

VAST (adj.)

(1) Waste, desolate. More or less of this (obsolete) sense may be seen in many passages, *e.g.*: *The empty, vast and wandering air*—R3 I 4 39. *The ruthless, vast, and gloomy woods*—Tit IV 1 53. *No vast obscurity or misty vale*—V 2 36. *Vast sin-concealing chaos (i.e. Night)!*—Lucr 767.

(2) Very great and undefined: *Vast confusion waits . . . The imminent decay of wrested pomp*—John IV 3 152.

VAST (sb.)

Vast of night, the desolate and deserted period of night: *Urchins Shall, for that vast of night that they may work, All exercise on thee*—Tp I 2 326. *In the dead vast and middle of the night*—Hml I 2 198.

VASTIDITY

Vastness, immensity: *Though all the world's vastidity you had*—Meas III 1 69.

VASTLY

In a waste or desolate condition: *Her body . . . Who, like a late-sack'd island, vastly stood Bare and unpeopled*—Lucr 1739.

VASTY

Immense, boundless: *The vasty wilds Of wide Arabia*—Merch II 7 41. *The vasty deep*—1 H4 III 1 53. *Vasty Tartar*—H5 II 2 123.

VAULTAGE

A vaulted room or cellar: *Caves and womby vaultages of France*—H5 II 4 124.

VAULTY

Arched, concave: *Thy vaulty brows*—John III 4 30. *The vaulty top of heaven*—V 2 52. *The vaulty heaven*—Rom III 5 22. *Till sable Night . . . in her vaulty prison stows the Day*—Lucr 117.

VAUNT

The first part, beginning: *Our play Leaps o'er the vaunt and firstlings of those broils*—Troil Prol 26.

VAUNT-COURIER

A forerunner: *You sulphurous . . . fires, Vaunt-couriers to oak-cleaving thunderbolts*—Lr III 2 4.

VAWARD

(1) Vanguard; the advanced-guard of an army: *I beg The leading of the vaward*—H5 IV 3 129. *Their bands i' the vaward are the Antiates*—Cor I 6 53. There seems to be [some confusion in 1 H6 I 1 132 (*He, being in the vaward, placed behind With purpose to relieve and follow them*). Possibly the front of his own division is meant.

(2) In general, the early part: *We that are in the vaward of our youth*—2 H4 I 2 199. *To have the vaward of*, to be beforehand with: *Since we have the vaward of the day*—Mids IV 1 109.

VEGETIVE

A vegetable, plant: *The blest infusions That dwell in vegetives, in metals, stones*—Per III 2 35.

VELURE

Velvet: *A woman's crupper of velure*—Shr III 2 61.

VELVET-GUARDS

See *Guard* (sb.) (2)

VENERABLE

Deserving honour (without connotation of age): *This youth . . . I snatch'd one half out of the jaws of death . . . And to his image, which methought did promise Most venerable worth, did I devotion*—Tw III 4 393.

VENEY, VENUE

A bout in fencing: *Three veneys for a dish of stewed prunes*—Wiv I 1 295. *A quick venue of wit!*—LLL V 1 62.

VENGE

(1) To revenge (a person); refl.: *I am coming on, To venge me as I may*—H5 I 2 291.

(2) To revenge, take vengeance for: *To venge my Gloucester's death*—R2 I 2 36. *Would none but I might venge my cousin's death!*—Rom III 5

87. *It is an office of the gods to venge it*—Cymb I 6 92.

VENGEANCE

(1) Harm, mischief: *Whiles the eye of man did woo me, That could do no vengeance to me*—As IV 3 47. *Had you not . . . come, This vengeance on me had they executed*—Tit II 3 112. In imprecations: *A plague of all cowards, I say, and a vengeance too!*—1 H4 II 4 127. *The vengeance on the whole camp!*—Troil II 3 19. *Vengeance rot you all!*—Tit V 1 58.

(2) As adv., exceedingly, insufferably: *He's vengeance proud*—Cor II 2 5.

VENOM

Poisonous, pernicious: *Venom toads*—3 H6 II 2 138. *His venom tooth*—R3 I 3 291. [Why should] *toads infect fair founts with venom mud?*—Lucr 850. Fig.: *The venom clamours of a jealous woman*—Err V 69. *Lascivious metres, to whose venom sound . . .*—R2 II 1 19.

VENOMOUS

Venomous wights, perh., evil-minded, meditating evil, in antithesis to *love*: *With venomous wights she* (i.e. Night) *stays As tediously as hell, but flies the grasps of love*—Troil IV 2 12.

VENT[1]

A discharge, emission: *Here, on her breast, There is a vent of blood*—Ant V 2 351.

VENT[2]

Scent; *full of vent*, of a hound, excited by the scent, full of life; fig. of war: *Let me have war . . . it's spritely, waking, audible, and full of vent*—Cor IV 5 236.

VENTAGE

A finger-hole (of a wind instrument): *Govern these ventages with your fingers and thumb*—Hml III 2 372.

VENTRICLE

A cavity of the body; a division of the brain: *These are begot in the ventricle of memory*—LLL IV 2 70. The old anatomists divided the brain into three ventricles, one of which was supposed to be the seat of memory.

VENTURES

App., creatures who make a venture of their persons: *Diseased ventures That play with all infirmities for gold*—Cymb I 6 123.

VENUE

See *Veney.*

VERBAL

Verbose, full of talk or protestation: *You put me to forget a lady's manners, By being so verbal*—Cymb II 3 110.

VERBATIM

Orally: [That I] *am not able Verbatim to re-hearse the method of my pen*—1 H6 III 1 12.

VERGE

A circle or ring; of a crown: *The inclusive verge Of golden metal that must round my brow*—R3 IV 1 59.

VERIFY

(1) To affirm, maintain: *I will verify as much in his beard*—H5 III 2 75. *More truly now may this be verified*—1 H6 I 2 32.

(2) To back up, speak up for: *I have ever verified my friends*—Cor V 2 17.

VERITY

Faith, trustworthiness: *For his verity in love, I do think him as concave as a covered goblet*—As III 4 25. *The king-becoming graces, As justice, verity, temperance, stableness*—Mcb IV 3 91.

VERONESA

A ship furnished by Verona: *The ship is here put in, A Veronesa*—Oth II 1 25.

VERSE

To express in verse: *Versing love To amorous Phillida*—Mids II 1 67.

VERY

A very friend, a particular friend, one in the full sense of the word: *Against his very friend*—Gent III 2 41. *I bid my very friends . . . welcome*—Merch III 2 226.

VIA

An interjection of exultation or encouragement: *Have I encompassed you? go to; via!*—Wiv II 2 159. *Via! we will do't, come what will come*—LLL V 2 112. *'Via!' says the fiend; 'away!' says the fiend*—Merch II 2 11. *Why, Via! to London will we march amain*—3 H6 II 1 182.

VIAND

Food: *Still cupboarding the viand*—Cor I 1 103.

VICE (sb.)[1]

A stock character in the Moralities, often a buffoon, representing sometimes vice in general, sometimes a particular vice: *I'll be with you again . . . Like to the old Vice . . . with dagger of lath*—Tw IV 2 132. *Now is this Vice's dagger become a squire*—2 H4 III 2 343. *Like the formal vice, Iniquity*—R3 III 1 82. *A vice of kings*—Hml III 4 98.

VICE (sb.)[2]

A screw: *You must put in the pikes with a vice*—Ado V 2 20.

VICE (vb.)

To screw, to force as by a screw: *An instrument To vice you to't*—Wint I 2 415.

VICIOUS

Marking defect or imperfection: *Some vicious mole of nature*—Hml I 4 24. Censorious, suspicious: *Though I perchance am vicious in my guess*—Oth III 3 145. Blameworthy: *It had been vicious To have mistrusted her*—Cymb V 5 65.

VIE

At cards, to wager on (one's hand); hence, generally, to bring into competition, contend with respect to: *Nature wants stuff To vie strange forms with fancy*—Ant V 2 97. *So With the dove of Paphos might the crow Vie feathers white*—Per IV Prol 31. To shower (kisses) as if for a wager: *Kiss on kiss She vied so fast*—Shr II 310.

VIEW

(1) Appearance, aspect: *You that choose not by the view*—Merch III 2 132. *Alas, that love, so gentle in his view, Should be so tyrannous and rough in proof!*—Rom I 1 175.

(2) *Before this royal view*, in eye of this royal assembly—H5 V 2 32.

VILLAGERY

Village people, peasantry: *Are not you he That frights the maidens of the villagery?*—Mids II 1 34.

VILLAIN

A bondsman, servant: *Who should find them but the empress' villain?*—Tit IV 3 73. *My villain!*—Lr III 7 78. *The homely villain court'sies to her low*—Lucr 1338.

VILLANY

In softened sense, mischief roguery: *I will consent to act any villany against him, that may not sully . . . our honesty*—Wiv II 1 101.

VILLIAGO

The Italian *vigliacco*, a rascal: *Lording it in London streets, Crying 'Villiago!' unto all they meet*—2 H6 IV 8 47.

VINDICATIVE

Vindictive: *He in heat of action Is more vindicative than jealous love*—Troil IV 5 106.

VINEWED

Mouldy: *Speak then, thou vinewedst leaven*—Troil II 1 15.

VIOL-DE-GAMBOYS

A bass viol, represented by the modern violoncello: *He plays o' the viol-de-gamboys*—Tw I 3 26.

VIOLENT

To be violent, rage: [My grief] *violenteth in a sense as strong As that which causeth it*—Troil IV 4 4.

VIRGINAL (adj.)

Maidenly: *Tears virginal Shall be to me even as the dew to fire*—2 H6 V 2 52. *The virginal palms of your daughters*—Cor V 2 45. *Without any more virginal fencing*—Per IV 6 62.

VIRGINAL (vb.)

To finger as on a virginal, one of the predecessors of the pianoforte, in use in the 16th and 17th centuries: *Still virginalling Upon his palm!*—Wint I 2 125.

VIRTUE

(1) Valour: *Proud; which he is, even to the altitude of his virtue*—Cor I 1 40. *Trust to thy single virtue*—Lr V 3 103.

(2) Essence, essential quality: *The very virtue of compassion*—Tp I 2 27. *'' is the virtue of the law*—Tim III 5 8.

VIRTUOUS

Efficacious by inherent qualities, potent: *Whose liquor hath this virtuous property* — Mids III 2 367. *Like the bee, culling from every flower The virtuous sweets*—2 H4 IV 5 75. *By your virtuous means* — Oth III 4 111. *Virtuous season*, which in its nature tends to prevent corruption: [I] *Corrupt with virtuous season*—Meas II 2 168.

VISARD-LIKE

See under *Vizard*.

VISITATION

A visit, visiting: *Poor worm, thou art infected! This visitation shows it*—Tp III 1 31. *Nothing but peace and gentle visitation*—LLL V 2 179. *In loving visitation was with me a young doctor of Rome*—Merch IV 1 152. *The King of Sicilia means to pay Bohemia the visitation which he justly owes him*—Wint I 1 6.

VISITED

Attacked (by the plague): *These lords are visited; you are not free*—LLL V 2 422. *Strangely-visited*, attacked by a strange disease: *Strangely-visited people . . . he cures*—Mcb IV 3 150.

VIZARD, VISARD

Visor; a mask: *Was your vizard made without a tongue?*—LLL V 2 242. *I have vizards for you all*—1 H4 I 2 142. [We must] *make our faces vizards to our hearts*—Mcb III 2 34. *Visard-like*, like a mask: *Thy face is, visard-like, unchanging*—3 H6 I 4 116.

VIZARDED

Masked: *They must all be mask'd and vizarded*—Wiv IV 6 40. *Degree being vizarded*—Troil I 3 83.

VOICE (sb.)

(1) Talk, report: *The voice is now Only about her coronation*—H8 III 2 405. *The common voice, I see, is verified*—V 3 176. Similarly in pl.: *In voices well divulged*—Tw I 5 279.

(2) Expressed favourable opinion: [He] *Hath got the voice in hell for excellence*—H5 II 2 113. *Who . . . opinion crowns With an imperial voice*—Troil I 3 186. *Opinion . . . throws a more safer voice on you*—Oth I 3 225. A decision on a point submitted: *Till by some elder masters . . . I have a voice and precedent of peace*—Hml V 2 259.

(3) *In my voice*, in my name: *Implore her, in my voice, that she make friends To the strict deputy*—Meas I 2 185. So far as I have a say in the matter: *In my voice most welcome shall you be*—As II 4 87.

VOICE (vb.)

(1) To speak of (in such and such a way): *The Athenian minion, whom the world Voiced so regardfully*—Tim IV 3 80.

(2) To nominate by vote: *To voice him consul*—Cor II 3 242.

VOIDING LOBBY

An anteroom into which the inner rooms emptied themselves: *How in our voiding lobby hast thou stood And duly waited for my coming forth?*—2 H6 IV 1 61.

VOLABLE

Quick-witted: *A most acute juvenal; volable and free of grace!*—LLL III 67.

VOLQUESSEN

Afterwards Vexin, divided into Vexin français (cap. Pontoise) and Vexin normand (cap. Gisors): *Then do I give Volquessen, Touraine, Maine . . . With her to thee*—John II 527.

VOLUNTARY

A volunteer: *Rash, inconsiderate, fiery voluntaries*—John II 67. *Ajax was here the voluntary, and you as under an impress*—Troil II 1 105.

VOTARIST

A votary; *no idle votarist*, no insincere suppliant: *No, gods, I am no idle votarist*—Tim IV 3 26. A votaress: *The sisterhood, the votarists of Saint Clare*—Meas I 4 5. *The jewels . . . would half have corrupted a votarist*—Oth IV 2 188.

VOUCH

Testimony, attestation: *My vouch against you*—Meas II 4 156. *To the king I'll say't; and*

make my vouch as strong As shore of rock—H8 I
1 157. *To beg of Hob and Dick . . . Their needless
vouches*—Cor II 3 123. *A deserving woman indeed, one that . . . did justly put on the vouch of
very malice itself*—Oth II 1 146.

VOUCHSAFE

(1) To warrant, guarantee: *If Brutus will
vouchsafe that Antony May safely come to him*—
Cæs III 1 130.

(2) To deign to accept: *Our prayers come in,
If thou vouchsafe them*—John III 1 293. *If your
back Cannot vouchsafe this burthen*—H8 II 3 42.
Vouchsafe my labour—Tim I 1 152. *Vouchsafe
good morrow from a feeble tongue*—Cæs II 1 313.

(3) To permit: *Vouchsafe me speak a word*—
Err V 282. *I'll bring you thither, my lord, if
you'll vouchsafe me*—Ado III 2 3. *Sweet majesty,
vouchsafe me*—LLL V 2 888.

VULGAR (adj.)

(1) Of or pertaining to the common people: *He
that buildeth on the vulgar heart*—2 H4 I 3 90.
Apparent To the vulgar eye—Cor IV 7 20. *A
vulgar station*, a place in the throng: *Seld-shown
flamens . . . puff To win a vulgar station*—Cor II
1 229.

(2) Everyday, commonplace: *'Tis a vulgar
proof, That very oft we pity enemies*—Tw III 1
135. *Any the most vulgar thing to sense*—Hml
I 2 99. Making oneself common or cheap: *Be
thou familiar, but by no means vulgar*—Hml I 3 61.

(3) Commonly known, public: *Edg. Do you
hear aught, sir, of a battle toward? Gent. Most
sure and vulgar*—Lr IV 6 213. Passing from
mouth to mouth: *A vulgar comment will be made
of it*—Err III 1 100. *Unregister'd in vulgar fame*
—Ant III 13 119. *Vulgar scandal*—Sonn 112 2.
Common to all: *The vulgar air*—John II 387.

VULGAR (sb.)

(1) A common person: *As bad as those That
vulgars give bold'st titles*—Wint II 1 93.

(2) The common tongue: *Which to annothanize
in the vulgar*—LLL IV 1 68. *Abandon,—which
is in the vulgar leave*—As V 1 52.

VULGARLY

Publicly: *This worthy nobleman, So vulgarly
. . . accused*—Meas V 159.

W

WAFT

(1) To convey by water: *A braver choice of
dauntless spirits Than now the English bottoms
have waft o'er*—John II 72. *I charge thee waft
me safely cross the Channel*—2 H6 IV 1 114.
*Thou . . . our high admiral, Shalt waft them over
with our royal fleet*—3 H6 III 3 252. *Waft her
hence to France*—V 7 41.

(2) To beckon: *Who wafts us yonder?*—Err II
2 111. *Stood Dido . . . and waft her love To come
again to Carthage*—Merch V 10. *Whom Fortune
with her ivory hand wafts to her*—Tim I 1 70.

(3) To turn, direct: *Wafting his eyes to the
contrary*—Wint I 2 372.

WAFTAGE

Conveyance by water: *A ship you sent me to,
to hire waftage*—Err IV 1 95. *Like a strange
soul upon the Stygian banks Staying for waftage*—
Troil III 2 10.

WAFTURE

A waving, motion: *With an angry wafture of
your hand*—Cæs II 1 246.

WAG

To stir abroad: *The empress never wags But
in her company there is a Moor*—Tit V 2 87. To
go one's way, be off: *Let them wag; trot, trot*—

Wiv I 3 6. *Shall we wag?*—II 1 238. *If such a
one will . . . Bid sorrow wag*—Ado V 1 15.

WAGE

(1) To hazard, stake: *My life I never held but
as a pawn To wage against thy* (the first issue of
the Globe reads *thine*) *enemies*—Lr I 1 157. *I
will wage against your gold, gold to it*—Cymb I
4 144.

(2) To venture on, take the risk of: *Too weak
To wage an instant trial*—1 H4 IV 4 19. *To
wake and wage a danger profitless*—Oth I 3 30.

(3) To pay wages to, remunerate: *He waged
me with his countenance, as if I had been mercen-
ary*—Cor V 6 40.

(4) To contend, do battle: *[I] choose To wage
against the enmity o' the air*—Lr II 4 211.

(5) To be opposed as stakes; hence, to be
opposed in general: *His taints and honours Waged
equal with him*—Ant V 1 30. To be opposed as
(equal) stakes; hence, to be equal: *The commodity
wages not with the danger*—Per IV 2 34.

WAGGON

A chariot: *Dis's waggon*—Wint IV 4 118.
*Tear them on thy chariot-wheels; And then I'll
come and be thy waggoner . . . Provide thee two
proper palfreys . . . To hale thy vengeful waggon*
—Tit V 2 47. *Waggon-wheel*, chariot-wheel: *By*

the waggon-wheel [I will] *Trot*—Tit V 2 54.
Waggon-spoke, a spoke of a chariot-wheel: *Her
(i.e.* Queen Mab's) *waggon-spokes made of long
spinners' legs*—Rom I 4 59.

WAGGONER

A chariteer: Tit V 2 48 (quoted under *Waggon*).
Her (i.e. Queen Mab's) *waggoner a small grey-coated
gnat*—Rom I 4 64. *Such a waggoner As Phaethon*
—III 2 2.

WAGGON-SPOKE

See under *Waggon*.

WAGGON-WHEEL

See under *Waggon*.

WAKE (sb.)

(1) The state of being awake: *Such difference
'twixt wake and sleep*—1 H4 III 1 219. [Shall]
turn his sleep to wake—Lr III 2 34. App. as
adj., awake: *A whole tribe of fops, Got 'tween asleep
and wake*—Lr I 2 14.

(2) An annual festival in commemoration of the
dedication of a church: *He is wit's pedler, and
retails his wares At wakes and wassails*—LLL V
2 317. *He haunts wakes, fairs and bear-baitings*—
Wint IV 3 109. *Come, march to wakes and fairs*
—Lr III 6 77.

WAKE (vb.)

To hold a night-revel: *The king doth wake to-
night and takes his rouse*—Hml I 4 8. *For thee
watch I whilst thou dost wake elsewhere*—Sonn 61
13.

WALL-NEWT

A wall-lizard: *The tadpole, the wall-newt and
the water*—Lr III 4 135.

WAN

To turn pale: *That from her working all his
visage wann'd*—Hml II 2 580.

WANION

With a wanion, with a vengeance, and ill luck
to you: *Come away, or I'll fetch thee with a wanion*
—Per II 1 16.

WANTON (adj.)

Luxuriant: *The wanton green*—Mids II 1 99.
Four lagging winters and four wanton springs—
R2 I 3 214. *The wanton rushes*—1 H4 III 1 214.
My plenteous joys, Wanton in fulness—Mcb I 4 33.
Luxurious: *A guard too wanton for the head Which
princes . . . aim to hit*—2 H4 I 1 148. Mant-
ling: *Now comes the wanton blood up in your
cheeks*—Rom II 5 72.

WANTON (sb.)

(1) A spoilt or pampered person: *A cocker'd
silken wanton*—John V 1 70. *He, young wanton
and effeminate boy*—R2 V 3 10. *I am afeard you*

make a wanton of me—Hml V 2 310. [I am] *not
so citizen a wanton as To seem to die ere sick*—
Cymb IV 2 8.

(2) In slight depreciation, a skittish person, a
trifler: *Nay then, the wanton lies*—Gent V 2 10
(of Silvia). *Tarry, rash wanton*—Mids II 1 63
(to Titania). *Shall we play the wantons with our
woes?*—R2 III 3 164. *Let wantons light of heart
Tickle the senseless rushes with their heels*—Rom
I 4 35.

WANTONNESS

[You] *make your wantonness your ignorance,*
you make your wanton or dubious speech appear
(innocent) ignorance—Hml III 1 152.

WAPPENED

Over-worn, worn out: *This is it That makes
the wappen'd widow wed again*—Tim IV 3 37.

WARD (sb.)

(1) Confinement: *Ere they will have me go to
ward, They'll pawn their swords*—2 H6 V 1 112.

(2) A division of a prison, a cell: *If you have
any thing to say to me, come to my ward*—Meas
IV 3 65. [A prison] *in which there are many
confines, wards and dungeons*—Hml II 2 251.
Prison my heart in thy steel bosom's ward—Sonn
133 9. Fig. in pl., confinement: *To lock it in the
wards of covert bosom*—Meas V 10. Safe-keeping:
*That to my use it might unused stay . . . in sure
wards of trust*—Sonn 48 3.

(3) A bolt: *Doors, that were ne'er acquainted
with their wards*—Tim III 3 38. *Each [lock] by
him enforced retires his ward*—Lucr 303.

WARD (vb.)

To defend, protect: *God will in justice ward
you as his soldiers*—R3 V 3 254. *If I cannot
ward what I would not have hit*—Troil I 2 292.
A hand that warded him From thousand dangers
—Tit III 1 195.

WARDEN

A baking-pear; attrib.: *I must have saffron to
colour the warden pies*—Wint IV 3 48.

WARDER

A staff of authority: *Stay, the king hath thrown
his warder down*—R2 I 3 118. *When the king
did throw his warder down*—2 H4 IV 1 125.

WARE

The bed of Ware, a renowned bed of great size
in an inn at Ware: *As many lies as will lie in thy
sheet of paper, although the sheet were big enough
for the bed of Ware in England*—Tw III 2 49.

WARM

App., loving warmth, ease-loving: *Such a commodity of warm slaves, as had as lieve hear the
devil as a drum*—1 H4 IV 2 18.

WARN

(1) To summon: *Who is it that hath warn'd us to the walls?*—John II 201. [He] *sent to warn them to his royal presence*—R3 I 3 39. *A bell, That warns my old age to a sepulchre*—Rom V 3 206. To challenge to combat: *They mean to warn us at Philippi here*—Cæs V 1 5.

(2) *God warn us,* God protect us: *For lovers lacking—God warn us!—matter*—As IV 1 76.

WARP

To distort; and so, of frost, to wrinkle the surface of: *Though thou (i.e.* the 'bitter sky') *the waters warp*—As II 7 187.

WAR-PROOF

Of war-proof, proved in war: *Whose blood is set from fathers of war-proof*—H5 III 1 18.

WARRANT (sb.)

(1) A written authority for doing an act: *Who writes himself 'Armigero', in any bill, warrant, quittance*—Wiv I 1 9.

(2) *With modest warrant,* allowing yourselves only a reasonable or moderate scope (cf. *Modest*): *Do not cry havoc, where you should but hunt With modest warrant*—Cor III 1 275.

WARRANT (vb.)

(1) *God warrant us, Lord warrant us,* like *God warn us* (see *Warn* (2)): *Which . . . is the better; he for a man, God warrant us; she for a woman, God bless us*—Mids V 324. *Lord warrant us! what features?*—As III 3 5.

(2) *Upon a warranted need,* of absolute necessity: *The very stream of his life . . . must upon a warranted need give him a better proclamation*—Meas III 2 15c.

WARRANTIZE, WARRANTISE

A guarantee: *Break up the gates, I'll be your warrantize*—1 H6 I 3 13. *Such strength and warrantise of skill*—Sonn 150 7.

WARRANTY

Authorisation, permission: *From your love I have a warranty To unburden all my plots*—Merch I 1 132. *Her obsequies have been as far enlarged As we have warranty*—Hml V 1 249. *With such general warranty of heaven As I might love*—Oth V 2 60.

WARREN

A place to which a right of warren attached: *As melancholy as a lodge in a warren*—Ado II 1 221. Warren was a right, by grant from the Crown or prescription, to game found within a defined area.

WARRENER

The keeper of a warren (see above): *He hath fought with a warrener*—Wiv I 4 28.

WASH

I.e. with cosmetics: *When was he wont to wash his face?*—Ado III 2 56.

WASHFORD

Wexford: *Great Earl of Washford*—1 H6 IV 7 63.

WASSAIL

A festivity: *He is wit's pedler, and retails his wares At wakes and wassails*—LLL V 2 317. A drinking-bout: *Antony, Leave thy lascivious wassails*—Ant I 4 55. Revelry: *His two chamberlains Will I with wine and wassail so convince That . . .*—Mcb I 7 63. *The king . . . Keeps wassail*—Hml I 4 8. *Wassail candle,* a large candle lighted up at a revel: Ch. Just. *What! you are as a candle . . .* Fal. *A wassail candle, my lord*—2 H4 I 2 177.

WASTE (adj.)

Vacant, unoccupied: *What thy memory can not contain Commit to these waste blanks*—Sonn 77 9.

WASTE (sb.)

That which is wasted or destroyed: *The waste is no whit lesser than thy land*—R2 II 1 103 (referring to the legal sense, *i.e.* destruction done by the tenant to the prejudice of the freehold). *A naked subject to the weeping clouds And waste for churlish winter's tyranny*—2 H4 I 3 61. *In the way of waste,* prob. also with a reference to the legal sense, the honour of the wife being figured as the husband's freehold: *He will never, I think, in the way of waste, attempt us again*—Wiv IV 2 225.

WAT

A familiar name for a hare: *Poor Wat, far off upon a hill, Stands on his hinder legs*—Ven 697.

WATCH (sb.)

(1) Sleeplessness, wakefulness: [He] *Fell into a sadness . . . Thence to a watch*—Hml II 2 147. *To lie in watch there (i.e.* in his bed) *and to think on him*—Cymb III 4 43.

(2) A sentinel's cry: *Murder, Alarum'd by his sentinel, the wolf, Whose howl's his watch*—Mcb II 1 52.

(3) A candle marked out in sections each of which required a certain time to burn: *Give me a watch*—R3 V 3 63. Or perh. a sentinel is meant, as seems to be the meaning in Lucr 925 (*Mis-shapen Time . . . Base watch of woes*), the watch being perh. there figured as set over woes to see that the mourners grieve to the full.

(4) A clock: *Like a German clock, Still a-repairing . . . being a watch*—LLL III 192. *Mine eyes, the outward watch (i.e.* Time's 'numbering clock')—R2 V 5 52.

WATCH (vb.)

(1) Of a hawk, to keep her sleepless in order to tame her: *To watch her, as we watch these kites That bate and beat and will not be obedient*—Shr IV 1 198. *You must be watched ere you be made tame*—Troil III 2 45. *I'll watch him tame*—Oth III 3 23.

(2) To take by lying in wait: *Nay, do not fly; I think we have watch'd you now*—Wiv V 5 107.

WATCH-CASE

A sentry-box: *O thou dull god, why liest thou with the vile . . . and leavest the kingly couch A watch-case or a common 'larum-bell?*—2 H4 III 1 15.

WATCHFUL

Wakeful, sleepless: *Twenty watchful, weary, tedious nights*—Gent I 1 31. *Many a watchful night*—2 H4 IV 5 25. *What watchful cares do interpose themselves Betwixt your eyes and night?*—Cæs II 1 98.

WATER

Aquafortis: *Like water that doth eat in steel*—Lucr 755.

WATER-FLOWING

Flowing like a stream, copious: *Their water-flowing tears*—3 H6 IV 8 43.

WATER-GALL

A rainbow; properly a secondary rainbow: *Round about her tear-distained eye Blue circles stream'd, like rainbows in the sky: These water-galls in her dim element Foretell new storms*—Lucr 1586.

WATERING

Drinking: *When you breathe in your watering*—1 H4 II 4 17.

WATERISH

Well-watered; app. used in contempt: *Not all the dukes of waterish Burgundy*—Lr I 1 261.

WATER-RUG

Some kind of rough-haired water-dog: Mcb III 1 94.

WATERS

For all waters, app., up to anything: *Nay, I am for all waters*—Tw IV 2 68 (possibly with a play on topaz and his assumed name Sir Topas).

WATER-STANDING

Always filled with tears: *An orphan's water-standing eye*—3 H6 V 6 40.

WATER-WORK

Painting in water colours; *in water-work*, in water colours: *The German hunting in water-work*—2 H4 II 1 157.

WATERY

Watering (with desire): *When that the watery palate tastes indeed Love's thrice repured nectar*—Troil III 2 22.

WAVE

To vacillate, waver: *He waved indifferently 'twixt doing them neither good nor harm*—Cor II 2 19.

WAX

A wide sea of wax, app. referring to the practice of writing with a style on tablets coated with wax: *My free drift . . . moves itself In a wide sea of wax*—Tim I 1 45.

WAXEN (adj.)

A waxen epitaph, explained as a eulogy affixed to a tomb with wax: *Our grave . . . shall have a tongueless mouth, Not worshipp'd with a waxen epitaph*—H5 I 2 231. The practice of affixing papers in this way to tombs is said to have been formerly common.

WAXEN (vb.)

3rd pers. pl. pres. of To wax: *The whole quire . . . waxen in their mirth*—Mids II 1 55.

WEAL

The commonwealth, state: *The special watchmen of our English weal*—1 H6 III 1 66. *The charters that you bear I' the body of the weal*—Cor II 3 188. *Ere humane statute purged the gentle weal*—Mcb III 4 76. *The medicine of the sickly weal*—V 2 27.

WEALSMAN

A statesman, politician: *Two such wealsmen as you are*—Cor II 1 59.

WEALTH

Weal, welfare: *I once did lend my body for his wealth*—Merch V 249. *The imposthume of much wealth and peace*—Hml IV 4 27.

WEAR (sb.)

Fashion, vogue: *It (i.e. going bail) is not the wear*—Meas III 2 77. Fashion, style, make: *Motley's the only wear*—As II 7 34. *I like the wear well*—All's I 1 219. *Of the new'st and finest, finest wear-a*—Wint IV 4 327.

WEAR (vb.)

(1) To be in fashion: *Like the brooch and the tooth-pick, which wear not now*—All's I 1 171.

(2) To become adapted as a garment does by use: *So wears she to him*—Tw II 4 31.

WEATHER

To keep the weather of, in nautical phrase, to keep to the windward of, and so maintain a position of advantage in regard to: hence, to have the better of, keep in hand: *Mine honour keeps the weather of my fate*—Troil V 3 26.

WEATHER-FEND

To defend from the weather: *The line-grove which weather-fends your cell*—Tp V 10.

WEB

See *Pin* (2).

WEE

Little, tiny: *He hath but a little wee face*—Wiv I 4 22.

WEED

A garment: *Weed wide enough to wrap a fairy in*—Mids II 1 256. *With what contempt he wore the humble weed*—Cor II 3 229. *These weeds are memories of those worser hours*—Lr IV 7 7. *Thy youth's proud livery . . . Will be a tatter'd weed*—Sonn 2 3.

WEEDING

Weeds: *He weeds the corn and still lets grow the weeding*—LLL I 1 96.

WEEK

In by the week, caught, in captivity; and so perh., captivated, deeply in love: *That same Biron I'll torture ere I go: O that I knew he were but in by the week!*—LLL V 2 60.

WEEPING PHILOSOPHER

A name given to Heracleitus of Ephesus: *I fear he will prove the weeping philosopher when he grows old*—Merch I 2 52.

WEEPING-RIPE

See *Ripe.*

WEET

Wit; to know: *In which I bind . . . the world to weet We stand up peerless*—Ant I 1 38.

WEIGH

(1) To care for, regard: *You weigh me not? O, that's you care not for me*—LLL V 2 27. *For life, I prize it As I weigh grief*—Wint III 2 43. *My person; which I weigh not, Being of those virtues vacant*—H8 V 1 124. *Eternal love . . . Weighs not the dust and injury of age*—Sonn 108 9.

(2) *To weigh out,* to outweigh, make up for: *My friends, They that must weigh out my afflictions*—H8 III 1 87.

(3) To balance, hesitate: *The fair soul herself Weigh'd between loathness and obedience*—Tp II 1 129. *Weighed,* evenly balanced: *Equalities are so weighed, that . . .*—Lr I 1 5.

WEIRD

Connected with fate or destiny: *The weird sisters*—Mcb I 3 32. *By which title, before, these weird sisters saluted me*—I 5 8. *As the weird women promised*—III 1 2.

WELL-ADVISED

See *Advise* (1).

WELL-A-NEAR

Like well-a-day, alas! *The lady shrieks, and well-a-near Does fall in travail with her fear*—Per III Prol 51.

WELL-APPOINTED

Well equipped: *With well-appointed powers*—2 H4 I 1 190. *What well-appointed leader fronts us here?*—IV 1 25. *The well-appointed king*—H5 III Chor 4. Cf. *Appoint* (3).

WELL-BREATHED

Having long breath: *On thy well-breath'd horse*—Ven 678.

WELL FITTED

Well qualified: *Well fitted in arts, glorious in arms*—LLL II 45.

WELL-FOUND

Happily encountered, fortunate: *[The] last general In our well-found successes*—Cor II 2 47. *Well found,* well equipped, skilled: *In what he did profess, well found*—All's II 1 105.

WELL-LIKING

In good bodily condition; fig.: *Well-liking wits they have; gross, gross; fat, fat*—LLL V 2 268. Cf. *Like* (vb.)² (2).

WELL-RESPECTED

Duly weighed: *If well-respected honour bid me on*—1 H4 IV 3 10. Cf. *Respect* (vb.) (1).

WELL SAID

See *Said.*

WELL SEEN

Skilled: *A schoolmaster Well seen in music*—Shr I 2 133.

WELL TO LIVE

Well off, well to do: *His father . . . is an honest exceeding poor man and, God be thanked, well to live*—Merch II 2 54 (used app. with some confusion). *You're a made old man . . . you're well to live. Gold! all gold!*—Wint III 3 124.

WELSH HOOK

App. some sort of weapon; but nothing is really known about it: *[He that] swore the devil his true liegeman upon the cross of a Welsh hook*—1 H4 II 4 371.

WESTWARD-HO

Properly a cry of the Thames watermen inviting passengers to go westwards: Oli. . . . *There lies your way, due west.* Vio. *Then westward-ho!*—Tw III 1 145.

WEZAND

Weasand; the windpipe: [Thou mayst] *cut his wezand with thy knife*—Tp III 2 99.

WHARF

A river-bank: *The fat weed That roots itself in ease on Lethe wharf*—Hml I 5 32. *From the barge A . . . perfume hits the sense Of the adjacent wharfs*—Ant II 2 216.

WHAT

(1) Whatever: *I love thee not a jar o' the clock behind What lady-she her lord*—Wint I 2 43. *What will hap more to-night, safe 'scape the king!*—Lr III 6 121. Whoever: *That . . . my accusers, Be what they will, may stand forth face to face*—H8 V 3 46. *What in the world he is That names me traitor, villain-like he lies*—Lr V 3 97.

(2) Why: *What talk we of fathers, when there is such a man as Orlando?*—As III 4 41. *What should I don this robe?*—Tit I 189. Cleo. . . . *What should I stay*—[Dies. Char. *In this vile world?*—Ant V 2 316.

(3) How: *What dares the slave Come hither?*—Rom I 5 57.

(4) *What is he for a fool?* what manner of fool is he? *What is he for a fool that betroths himself to unquietness?*—Ado I 3 49.

WHEEL

(1) *O, how the wheel becomes it!*—Hml IV 5 172. Possibly the spinning-wheel of the girl supposed to sing the song; but the word is really unexplained.

(2) *To turn in the wheel*, to act the part of a turn-spit dog: *She had transform'd me to a curtal dog and made me turn i' the wheel*—Err III 2 151.

WHEELING

Hardly to be distinguished from *Extravagant* (q.v.): *An extravagant and wheeling stranger Of here and every where*—Oth I 1 137.

WHELK

A pustule, pimple: *His face is all bubukles, and whelks, and knobs*—H5 III 6 108.

WHELKED

With spiral ridges like those on a whelk's shell: *Horns whelk'd and waved like the enridged sea*—Lr IV 6 71.

WHEN

As an exclamation of impatience: *Come, thou tortoise! when?*—Tp I 2 316. *When, Harry,* when?—R2 I 1 162. *Kneel down; Nay, when? strike now, or else the iron cools*—3 H6 V 1 48. *When, Lucius, when? awake, I say!*—Cæs II 1 5.

WHEN AS, WHENAS

When: *When as your husband . . . Came to my house*—Err IV 4 140. *When as the enemy hath been ten to one*—3 H6 I 2 75. *When as thy love hath cast his utmost sum*—Sonn 49 3. *Whenas himself to singing he betakes*—Pilgr 1 14.

WHERE

Whereas: *Were my lord so, his ignorance were wise, Where now his knowledge must prove ignorance*—LLL II 102. *So we should; Where now remains a sweet reversion*—1 H4 IV 1 52. *You shall run a certain course; where, if you violently proceed . . .*—Lr I 2 88. *Fellowship in woe doth woe assuage . . . Where now I have no one to blush with me*—Lucr 790.

WHEREABOUT

On what errand: *I must not have you henceforth question me Whither I go, nor reason whereabout*—1 H4 II 3 106. As sb. = purpose: *For fear The very stones prate of my whereabout*—Mcb II 1 57.

WHERE AS, WHEREAS

Where: *Saint Alban's, Where as the king and queen do mean to hawk*—2 H6 I 2 57. *And make a conquest of unhappy me, Whereas no glory's got to overcome*—Per I 4 69. *He, spying her, bounced in, whereas he stood*—Pilgr 83.

WHIFFLER

An usher heading a procession to clear the way: *The deep-mouth'd sea, Which like a mighty whiffler 'fore the king Seems to prepare his way*—H5 V Chor 11.

WHILE (sb.)

The time, the age: *Alas the while!*—Merch II I 31. *God help the while!*—1 H4 II 4 144. *A bad, good, world the while*, a bad, good, age this of ours: *Bad world the while!*—John IV 2 100. *Here's a good world the while!*—R3 III 6 10.

WHILE (conj.)

Until: *Let the trumpets sound While we return these dukes what we decree*—R2 I 3 121.

WHILE (prep.)

Until: *While then, God be with you!*—Mcb III I 44.

WHILE AS

While: *While as the silly owner of the goods Weeps over them*—2 H6 I 1 225.

WHILE-ERE

Erewhile, a little while ago: *The catch You taught me but while-ere*—Tp III 2 126.

WHILES

(1) While: *I have drunk poison whiles he utter'd it*—Ado V 1 253. *Whiles I am a beggar*—John II 593. *Whiles thy consuming canker eats his falsehood*—1 H6 II 4 71. *The whiles*, meanwhile: *Take you your instrument, play you the whiles*—Shr III 1 22.

(2) Until: *He shall conceal it Whiles you are willing it shall come to note*—Tw IV 3 28.

WHILST

(1) *The whilst*, while: *The whilst his iron did on the anvil cool*—John IV 2 194. *The whilst this play is playing*—Hml III 2 93. Meanwhile: *I'll call Sir Toby the whilst*—Tw IV 2 3. *Where rode he the whilst?*—R2 V 2 22.

(2) Until: *We'll browse on that, Whilst what we have kill'd be cook'd*—Cymb III 6 38.

WHILST AS

Whilst: *Whilst as fickle Fortune smiled*—Pilgr 401.

WHIPPING-CHEER

A banquet consisting in whipping: *She shall have whipping-cheer enough, I warrant her*—2 H4 V 4 5.

WHIST

Still, hushed: *Courtsied when you have and kiss'd The wild waves whist, i.e.* kissed them into stillness—Tp I 2 378.

WHITE (adj.)

A white herring, a fresh herring as opposed to a red one: *Hopdance cries in Tom's belly for two white herring*—Lr III 6 32.

WHITE (sb.)

Equivalent to *Blank* (sb.) (1): *'Twas I won the wager, though you hit the white*—Shr V 2 186. An allusion to Bianca = white.

WHITE-LIVERED

Cowardly: *For Bardolph, he is white-livered and red-faced*—H5 III 2 33. *White-liver'd runagate*—R3 IV 4 465. See *Liver* (3).

WHITELY

White, pale-faced: *A whitely wanton with a velvet brow*—LLL III 198. This (in form *whitly*), the original reading, is by some changed to *wightly* (q.v.).

WHITHER

Whithersoever: *A fool go with thy soul, whither it goes!*—1 H4 V 3 22. *These three lead on this preparation Whither 'tis bent: most likely 'tis for you*—Cor I 2 15.

WHITING-TIME

Bleaching-time: *It is whiting-time*—Wiv III 3 140.

WHITSTER

A bleacher: *Carry it among the whitsters in Datchet-mead*—Wiv III 3 14.

WHITTLE

A small clasp-knife: *There's not a whittle in the unruly camp But I do prize it . . . before . . .*—Tim V 1 183.

WHOLESOME

(1) Healthy, sound: *The thin and wholesome blood*—Hml I 5 70. *On wholesome life usurp immediately*—III 2 271. *A mildew'd ear, Blasting his wholesome brother*—III 4 64.

(2) Sound, well ordered: *An honest method, as wholesome as sweet*—Hml II 2 465. *If it shall please you to make me a wholesome answer*—III 2 327. *In wholesome wisdom*—Oth III 1 49.

(3) Prosperous, well ordered: *In state as wholesome as in state 'tis fit*—Wiv V 5 63. *When shalt thou see thy wholesome days again?*—Mcb IV 3 105. *In the tender of a wholesome weal*—Lr I 4 230.

WHOO-BUB

Hubbub: *Had not the old man come in with a whoo-bub against his daughter*—Wint IV 4 627.

WHORESON

Properly a bastard: *The whoreson must be acknowledged*—Lr I 1 24. But applied merely jocularly: *The sly whoresons Have got a speeding trick to lay down ladies*—H8 I 3 39. *A merry whoreson, ha!*—Rom IV 4 19. As adj., expressing reproach, ludicrous dislike, even endearment, or as a mere expletive: *Hang, you whoreson, insolent noisemaker!*—Tp I 1 46. *A whoreson mad fellow's it was*—Hml V 1 193. *Come on, you whoreson chops: ah, rogue! i' faith, I love thee*—2 H4 II 4 235. *Your water is a sore decayer of your whoreson dead body*—Hml V 1 188.

WICKED

Baneful, pernicious: *As wicked dew as e'er my mother brush'd . . . from unwholesome fen*—Tp I 2 321. *Mumbling of wicked charms*—Lr II 1 41.

WIDOW

(1) *To widow* (a person) *with*, to give (her) a widow's rights in: *His possessions . . . We do instate and widow you withal*—Meas V 427.

(2) To become the widow of: *Let me be married to three kings in a forenoon, and widow them all*—Ant I 2 25.

WIDOWHOOD

Rights as a widow: *I'll assure her of Her widowhood*—Shr II 124.

WIGHTLY

Nimble: *A wightly wanton with a velvet brow* —LLL III 198.

WILD

Weald: *A franklin in the wild of Kent*—1 H4 II 1 60.

WILDERNESS

Wildness, wild growth: *Such a warped slip of wilderness Ne'er issued from his blood*—Meas III 1 142.

WILD-GOOSE CHASE

A kind of cross-country steeplechase in which the leader for the time being chose the line: *Nay, if thy wits run the wild-goose chase, I have done*— Rom II 4 75.

WILDLY

Like a wild, unpruned plant, shaggily: *Prisoners wildly overgrown with hair*—H5 V 2 43.

WILD-MARE

To ride the wild-mare, to play at see-saw: [Because he] *rides the wild-mare with the boys*—2 H4 II 4 268.

WILDNESS

Distraction, madness: *The happy cause Of Hamlet's wildness*—Hml III 1 39. *Ere wildn'ss Vanquish my staider senses*—Cymb III 4 9.

WILFUL-BLAME

Wilfully to blame: *You are too wilful-blame*— 1 H4 III 1 177.

WILFUL-OPPOSITE

Obstinately antagonistic: *The Dauphin is too wilful-opposite, And will not temporize with my entreaties*—John V 2 124.

WILL

To bid, desire: *He wills you . . . That you divest yourself*—H5 II 4 77. *God's mother . . . Will'd me to leave my base vocation*—1 H6 I 2 78. *They will'd me say so, madam*—H8 III 1 18. *Willing you to demand your hostages*—Tit V 1 160.

WIMPLED

Covered as with a wimple, a covering worn by women (and still by nuns) folded over the head and round the neck; blindfolded: *This wimpled, whining, purblind, wayward boy . . . Dan Cupid* —LLL III 181.

WINCHESTER GOOSE

Winchester goose, I cry, a rope!—1 H6 I 3 53 (addressed to the Bishop of Winchester). *Goose of Winchester: My fear is this, Some galled goose of Winchester would hiss*—Troil V 10 54. The Stews, a disorderly district on the Bankside in Southwark, were under the jurisdiction of the Bishop of Winchester. Hence *Winchester goose*, a cant name for a swelling caused by a disease contracted in such a place; applied also, as above, to a person supposed to be so suffering.

WIND (sb.)

(1) *To have in the wind*, to have scent of: *This same coxcomb that we have i' the wind*—All's III 6 122. *To recover the wind of*, of huntsmen, to get to windward of the hart, so that he may have them in the wind and break in the opposite direction into the toils (cf. *Recover* (2)): *Why do you go about to recover the wind of me, as if you would drive me into a toil?*—Hml III 2 361. So *to keep the wind*: *He knows the game: how true he keeps the wind!*—3 H6 III 2 14 (in order to drive Lady Grey into the toils).

(2) *To have the wind of*, to keep the weather of (see *Weather*): *My son and I will have the wind of you*—Tit IV 2 133. So *to sit in the wind*, to have (what ought to be) a dominating position: *Though my reason Sits in the wind against me*—Ant III 10 36.

WIND (vb.)

(1) As a term of horsemanship, to cause to turn or wheel: *To turn and wind a fiery Pegasus*— 1 H4 IV 1 109. Intrans. for refl.: *A creature that I teach to fight, To wind, to stop*—Cæs IV 1 31.

(2) To turn and go: *Wind away, Begone, I say* —As III 3 105.

(3) *To wind about*, to approach circuitously: [You] *spend but time To wind about my love with circumstance*—Merch I 1 153. *To wind into* (a person), to insinuate oneself into (his confidence): *Seek him out: wind me into him*—Lr I 2 106. *To wind oneself into*, to get surreptitiously: *To wind Yourself into a power tyrannical*—Cor III 3 64.

WINDGALLS

Enlargements near a horse's fetlock: *Full of windgalls*—Shr III 2 53.

WINDLASS

A circuitous or artful course: *Thus do we . . . With windlasses . . . By indirections find directions out*—Hml II 1 64.

WINDOW-BARS

Lattice-work on a woman's bodice: *Those milk-paps, That through the window-bars bore at men's eyes*—Tim IV 3 115.

WINDRING

Explained as winding: *The windring brooks*— Tp IV 128.

WINDY SIDE

To keep on the windy side of, to keep the weather of (see *Weather*): *It (i.e.* her 'merry heart') *keeps on the windy side of care*—Ado II 1 326. *Still you keep o' the windy side of the law*—Tw III 4 181.

WINK (sb.)

A closing of the eyes, a having them closed: [You] *To the perpetual wink for aye might put This ancient morsel*—Tp II 1 285. *To give mine enemy a lasting wink*—Wint I 2 317.

WINK (vb.)

(1) To close the eyes, to have them closed: [Thou] *wink'st Whiles thou art waking*—Tp II 1 216. *I'll wink and couch: no man their works must eye*—Wiv V 5 52. *I will wink and hold out mine iron*—H5 II 1 8. *When most I wink, then do mine eyes best see*—Sonn 43 1. Of the eyes, to close: *His eyes begun To wink, being blinded with a greater light*—Lucr 374. *Although to-day thou fill Thy hungry eyes even till they wink with fullness*—Sonn 56 5.

(2) *Winking,* having the eyes closed: *Two winking Cupids*—Cymb II 4 89. Of flowers, shut up, closed: *Winking Mary-buds*—Cymb II 3 26. So of gates: *Your city's eyes, your winking gates*—John II 215. As sb.: *What might you . . . think, If I had . . . given my heart a winking? (i.e.* shut his eyes to what was going on)—Hml II 2 134.

(3) Wince; to start aside: *He winks, and turns his lips another way*—Ven 90.

WINTER-GROUND

To cover so as to protect from frost: *Furr'd moss . . . To winter-ground thy corse*—Cymb IV 2 228.

WIPE

A scar, brand: *Worse than a slavish wipe or birth-hour's blot*—Lucr 537.

WIS

See *I wis.*

WISH

(1) To bid, desire: *I persuaded them . . . To wish him wrestle with affection*—Ado III 1 41. *The rest I wish thee gather*—1 H6 II 5 96. *When man was wish'd to love his enemies*—Tim IV 3 473.

(2) To recommend or introduce (a person *to* another): *I will wish him to her father*—Shr I 1 113. [Shall I] *wish thee to a shrewd ill-favour'd wife?*—I 2 60. *I'll not wish thee to her*—64.

WISP

A wisp of straw, the badge of a scold: *A wisp of straw were worth a thousand crowns, To make this shameless callet know herself*—3 H6 II 2 144.

WIST

See *Wit* (vb.).

WISTLY

Fixedly, attentively: *What a sight it was, wistly to view How she came stealing to the wayward boy!*—Ven 343. [She] *wistly on him gazed*—Lucr 1355. With notion of longing, wistfully: *Speaking it, he wistly look'd on me; As who should say, 'I would thou wert the man'*—R2 V 4 7. *The sun look'd on the world . . . Yet not so wistly as this queen on him (i.e.* Venus on Adonis)—Pilgr 81.

WIT (sb.)

The five wits, the intellectual faculties figured as five: *In our last conflict four of his five wits went halting off*—Ado I 1 65. *How fell you besides your five wits?*—Tw IV 2 92. *Bless thy five wits!*—Lr III 4 59. *My five wits nor my five senses*—Sonn 141 9.

WIT (vb.)

To know: *Now please you wit The epitaph is for Marina writ*—Per IV 4 31. 1st sing. and 2d pl. pres. ind. *wot: I wot well where he is*—Rom III 2 139. *Wot you what I found?*—H8 III 2 122. 3d sing. *wots: In gross brain [he] little wots What watch the king keeps*—H5 IV 1 299. Pres. pple. *witting: As witting I no other comfort have*—1 H6 II 5 16. Erroneously *wotting: The gods themselves, Wotting no more than I, are ignorant*—Wint III 2 76. 1st sing. past ind. *wist: An if I wist he did*—1 H6 IV 1 180.

WITCH

A wizard: *I (i.e.* Dromio) *could find in my heart to . . . turn witch*—Err IV 4 159. *Out, fool! I forgive thee (i.e.* the Soothsayer) *for a witch*—Ant I 2 40. *Such a holy witch That he enchants societies*—Cymb I 6 166.

WITH

(1) Used where modern usage would require (a) By: *We had like to have had our two noses snapped off with two old men*—Ado V 1 115. *He was torn to pieces with a bear*—Wint V 2 68. *Here is himself, marr'd, as you see, with traitors*—Cæs III 2 201. *Must I be unfolded With one that I have bred?*—Ant V 2 170. (b) Of: *To be possess'd with double pomp*—John IV 2 9. [Wishing me] *like him with friends possess'd*—Sonn 29 6. (c) On: *I am fain to dine and sup with water and bran*—Meas IV 3 159. *I live with bread like you*—R2 III 2 175. *How will you live? . . . With worms and flies?*—Mcb IV 2 31.

(2) *Not with himself,* beside himself: *He is not with himself: let us withdraw*—Tit I 368.

WITHAL (adv.)

(1) With it, with this, therewith: *He will scarce be pleased withal*—Gent II 7 67. *I was moved withal*—Cor V 3 194. *Mark Antony . . . ac-*

quainted My grieved ear withal—Ant III 6 57.
*His hand . . . May feel her heart . . . Beating her
bulk, that his hand shakes withal*—Lucr 463.

(2) *I could not do withal*, I could not help it—
Merch III 4 72.

WITHAL (prep.)

With: *Her cause and yours I'll perfect him
withal*—Meas IV 3 145. *What tedious homily
of love have you wearied your parishioners withal!*
—As III 2 163. *The strong conception That I do
groan withal*—Oth V 2 55. *Who hath she to
spend the night withal?*—Ven 847.

WITHOLD, ST.

St. Vitalis, said to have been invoked against
nightmare: *S. Withold footed thrice the old; He
met the night-mare, and her nine-fold*—Lr III 4
125.

WITHOUT (conj.)

Unless: *Without you were so simple, none else
would*—Gent II 1 38. *Such a one as a man may
not speak of without he say 'Sir-reverence'*—Err
III 2 91. *Not without the prince be willing*—Ado
III 3 86.

WITHOUT (prep.)

Beyond: [That could] *deal in her command
without her power*—Tp V 271. *Our intent Was
to be gone from Athens . . . Without the peril of
the Athenian law*—Mids IV 1 155.

WITNESS

With a witness, so as to leave a mark behind
as a testimony; and so, with a vengeance: *Here's
packing, with a witness, to deceive us all!*—Shr V
1 121.

WIT-OLD

A nonce-word, used for the sake of a play on
Wittol (*q.v.*): Arm. . . . *True wit!* Moth. *Offered
by a child to an old man; which is wit-old.* Hol.
What is the figure? . . . Moth. *Horns*—LLL V
1 64.

WIT-SNAPPER

One who affects repartee: *What a wit-snapper
are you!*—Merch III 5 55.

WITTILY

Cunningly, ingeniously: *Which cunning love
did wittily prevent*—Ven 471.

WITTOL

A cuckold: *Cuckold! Wittol!—Cuckold!*—Wiv
II 2 313.

WITTOLLY

Cuckoldly: *The jealous wittolly knave*—Wiv II
2 283.

WITTY

(1) Wise, intelligent, discreet: [The Kentish-
men] *are soldiers, Witty, courteous, liberal, full
of spirit*—3 H6 I 2 42. *She'll come straight:
you must be witty now*—Troil III 2 31.

(2) Cunning, artful: *A marvellous witty fellow,
I assure you*—Ado IV 2 27. *The deep-revolving
witty Buckingham*—R3 IV 2 42. *Our witty
empress . . . would applaud Andronicus' conceit*—
Tit IV 2 29. In Oth II 1 132 (Des. . . . *How if
she be black and witty?* Iago. *If she be black, and
thereto have a wit, She'll find a white that shall
her blackness fit*) the word seems to be meant by
Desdemona in sense (1) and to be taken by Iago
in sense (2).

WODE

See *Wood*.

WOE

Grieved, sorry: *I am woe for't*—Tp V 139.
Be woe for me—2 H6 III 2 73. *Woe are we*—
Ant IV 14 133.

WOMAN

Can woman me unto't, can subdue me to it and
make me show a woman's weakness—All's III 2
53.

WOMAN-QUELLER

A slayer of women: *Thou art . . . a man-queller,
and a woman-queller*—2 H4 II 1 57.

WOMAN-TIRED

Henpecked: *Thou art woman-tired, unroosted
By thy dame Partlet here*—Wint II 3 74. See
Tire (vb.)[3] (1).

WOMB

To enclose: *For all . . . The close earth wombs*
—Wint IV 4 499.

WOMBY

Hollow, capacious: *Caves and womby vaultages
of France*—H5 II 4 124.

WONDER

To wonder at: *You will wonder what hath
fortuned*—Gent V 4 169. To speculate in regard
to: *Both stood . . . wondering each other's chance*
—Lucr 1595. *To wonder of*, to wonder at: *I
wonder of their being here together*—Mids IV 1
135. So *I wonder on't*—Tim III 4 10.

WONDERED

Endowed with wonder, wonder-working: *So
rare a wonder'd father and a wife Makes this place
Paradise*—Tp IV 123 (*So rare a wondered* = so
rare-wondered a).

WONT

To be accustomed; Pres.: *I bear it on my shoulders, as a beggar wont her brat*—Err IV 4 39. *Have informed me How the English . . . Wont through a secret grate . . . to overpeer the city*—1 H6 I 4 8. Past: *Talbot is taken, whom we wont to fear*—1 H6 I 2 14. *My curtail dog, that wont to have play'd*—Pilgr 273.

WOOD, WODE

Mad, frantic: *O, that she could speak now like a wood woman!*—Gent II 3 30. *Here am I, and wode within this wood*—Mids II 1 192. *Life-poisoning pestilence and frenzies wood*—Ven 740. Cf. *Raging-wood.*

WOODBINE

Commonly = honeysuckle; but in Mids IV 1 45 (*So doth the woodbine the sweet honeysuckle Gently entwist*) perh. some species of convolvulus is meant.

WOODMAN

A huntsman: *You, Polydore, have proved best woodman*—Cymb III 6 28. *He is no woodman that . . .*—Lucr 580. Fig., a hunter (of women): *Am I a woodman, ha?*—Wiv V 5 30. [The duke is] *a better woodman than thou takest him for*—Meas IV 3 170.

WOOLLEN

In the woollen, in blankets without sheets: *I had rather lie in the woollen*—Ado II 1 32. Cf. *Woolward.*

WOOLVISH

Possibly, hirsute, shaggy: *Why in this woolvish toge should I stand here?*—Cor II 3 122.

WOOLWARD

With wool next the skin: *I have no shirt; I go woolward for penance*—LLL V 2 716.

WOO'T

Wilt: *Show me what thou'lt do: Woo't weep? woo't fight?*—Hml V 1 297. *Woo't thou fight well?*—Ant IV 2 7. *Noblest of men, woo't die?*—IV 15 59.

WORD (sb.)

(1) A motto borne on a shield: *The device he bears upon his shield Is a black Ethiope . . . The word, 'Lux tua vita mihi'*—Per II 2 19.

(2) *At a word,* in brief, indeed: *He hath wronged me . . . at a word, he hath*—Wiv I 1 108. *At a word, I am not*—Ado II 1 118. *No, at a word, madam; indeed, I must not*—Cor I 3 122. *I am at a word, I have spoke at a word,* you may take me at my word: *I am at a word; follow*—Wiv I 3 15. *Go to; I have spoke at a word*—2 H4 III 2 319.

WORD (vb.)

To ply with words, cajole: *He words me . . . that I should not Be noble to myself*—Ant V 2 191.

WORKING

Full of pathos: [Things] *Sad, high, and working, full of state and woe*—H8 Prol 3.

WORKINGS

Strivings of thought: [The] *intelligencer Between the grace, the sanctities of heaven And our dull workings*—2 H4 IV 2 20.

WORKY-DAY

Working-day; ordinary: *Tell her but a worky-day fortune*—Ant I 2 55.

WORLD

(1) *It is a world to see,* it is a wonderful sight: *God help us! it is a world to see*—Ado III 5 38. *'Tis a world to see, How tame . . . A meacock wretch can make the curstest shrew*—Shr II 313.

(2) *To go to the world,* to be married, commence housekeeper: *Thus goes every one to the world but I*—Ado II 1 330. *If I may have your ladyship's good will to go to the world, Isbel the woman and I will do as we may*—All's I 3 19. *A woman of the world,* a married woman: *I hope it is no dishonest desire to desire to be a woman of the world*—As V 3 3.

(3) *This world,* the present age: *Tongues to be your being shall rehearse When all the breathers of this world are dead*—Sonn 81 11.

WORM

A serpent, especially a small one: *Thou dost fear the soft and tender fork Of a poor worm*—Meas III 1 16. *Could not a worm, an adder, do so much?*—Mids III 2 71. *There the grown serpent lies; the worm that's fled Hath . . . No teeth for the present*—Mcb III 4 29. *Hast thou the pretty worm of Nilus there, That kills and pains not?*—Ant V 2 243.

WORSHIP (sb.)

Honour, dignity, authority: *Whom I . . . Have bench'd and rear'd to worship*—Wint I 2 313. *Till I have lent a glory to this hand, By giving it the worship of revenge*—John IV 3 71. *This double worship*—Cor III 1 142. *The worships of their name*—Lr I 4 288. *As I belong to worship,* by my nobility—H8 I 1 39.

WORSHIP (vb.)

To honour, dignify: *Not worshipp'd with a waxen epitaph*—H5 I 2 233.

WORSHIPFUL

Full of reverence: *Your very worshipful and loving friends*—R3 III 7 138. As adv.: *His master's son, as worshipful he terms it*—R3 III 4 41.

WORT

A plant, herb, vegetable: Evans. *Pauca verba, Sir John; goot worts.* Fal. *Good worts! good cabbage*—Wiv I 1 123 (with a play).

WORTH (adj.)

Valuable: *His health was never better worth* (*i.e.* more valuable) *than now*—1 H4 IV 1 27. *Better worth than all my father's lands*—2 H6 I 3 89. *A thing not ours nor worth to us*—Troil II 2 22.

WORTH (sb.)

(1) Substance, wealth: *The rich worth of your virginity*—Mids II 1 219. *Were my worth as is my conscience firm, You should find better dealing*—Tw III 3 17. *They are but beggars that can count their worth*—Rom II 6 32. *For the sea's worth*—Oth I 2 28.

(2) Dignity, nobility: *'Tis an office of great worth*—Gent I 2 44. *By the glorious worth of my descent*—R2 I 1 107.

(3) *To have his worth of contradiction*, to get good value out of disputes, come off best: *He hath been used . . . to have his worth Of contradiction*—Cor III 3 25.

WORTHY (adj.)

Merited, deserved: *He has much worthy blame laid upon him*—All's IV 3 7. *Worthy danger and deserved death*—R2 V 1 68. *Her worthy praise*—1 H6 V 5 11. *Doing worthy vengeance on thyself*—R3 I 2 87.

WORTHY (vb.)

To make a hero or worthy of: [He] *put upon him such a deal of man, That worthied him*—Lr II 2 127.

WOT

See *Wit* (vb.).

WRANGLER

A stubborn adversary: *He hath made a match with such a wrangler That . . .*—H5 I 2 264. *The seas and winds, old wranglers, took a truce*—Troil II 2 75.

WRATH (adj.)

Wroth; wrathful: *Oberon is passing fell and wrath*—Mids II 1 20.

WRATH (sb.)

Impetuosity in combat: *Harry Monmouth; whose swift wrath beat down The never-daunted Percy*—2 H4 I 1 109. *Hector in his blaze of wrath subscribes To tender objects*—Troil IV 5 105. *Aufidius was within my view, And wrath o'erwhelm'd my pity*—Cor I 9 85. So of impetuosity in love: *They are in the very wrath of love*—As V 2 43.

WREAK (sb.)

Vengeance: *If thou hast A heart of wreak in thee*—Cor IV 5 90. *With revengeful war Take wreak on Rome*—Tit IV 3 32. *Shall we be thus afflicted in his wreaks?*—IV 4 11.

WREAK (vb.)

To revenge: *Be wreak'd on him*—Ven 1004. To take vengeance for (a wrong): *To send down Justice for to wreak our wrongs*—Tit IV 3 51. To take vengeance on behalf of: *To wreak the love I bore my cousin Upon his body*—Rom III 5 102.

WREAKFUL

Revengeful, angry: *By working wreakful vengeance on thy foes*—Tit V 2 32. *All the spite Of wreakful heaven*—Tim IV 3 228.

WREST

A tuning-key; fig.: *This Antenor . . . is such a wrest in their affairs*—Troil III 3 22.

WRETCHED

Vile, hateful: *The wretched, bloody, and usurping boar*—R3 V 2 7. *O wretched villain!*—Oth V 1 41. *Such wretched hands such wretched blood should spill*—Lucr 999.

WRING

To writhe with anguish: *Those that wring under the load of sorrow*—Ado V 1 28. *Every fool, whose sense no more can feel But his own wringing*—H5 IV 1 252. *He wrings at some distress*—Cymb III 6 79.

WRIT

(1) Holy Writ: *Each man Thinks all is writ he speken can*—Per II Prol 11. Jestingly: *Let's see the devil's writ*—2 H6 I 4 60.

(2) A writing, document: *All too late I bring this fatal writ*—Tit II 3 264. [I] *Folded the writ up in form of the other*—Hml V 2 51. *For the law of writ and the liberty*, perh., for keeping to the book and for improvising: *For the law of writ and the liberty, these are the only men*—Hml II 2 420. Cf. *Let those that play your clowns speak no more than is set down for them*—III 2 42.

WRITE

To put oneself down as, reckon oneself to be: *I must tell thee, sirrah, I write man*—All's II 3 208. *As if he had writ man ever since his father was a bachelor*—2 H4 I 2 30. *About it; and write happy when thou hast done*—Lr V 3 35. *I'll write against them* (*i.e.* women)—Cymb II 5 32. *Writ as little beard*, could lay claim to as little: *I'd give bay Curtal . . . My mouth . . . writ as little beard*—All's II 3 65.

WRITHLED

Wrinkled: *This weak and writhled shrimp*—1 H6 II 3 23.

WROTH

Misfortune: *I'll keep my oath, Patiently to bear my wroth*—Merch II 9 77.

WRY

To swerve, go crooked: *How many Must murder wives . . . For wrying but a little!*—Cymb V 1 3.

Y

Y

A prefix common in Middle English; in Shakespeare's time an archaism, adding nothing appreciable to the sense: *y-clad*: *Her words y-clad with wisdom's majesty*—2 H6 I 1 33. *Ycleped, ycliped,* clept; named (see *Clepe*): *It is ycleped thy park*—LLL I 1 242. *Judas I am, ycliped Maccabæus*—V 2 602. *Y-ravish*: *The sum of this . . . Y-ravished the regions round*— Per III Prol 33. *Yslake*, to quiet, put to rest: *Now sleep yslaked hath the rout*—Per III Prol 1.

YARE

Nimble, dexterous: *You shall find me yare*—Meas IV 2 61. *Be yare in thy preparation*—Tw III 4 244. *Which does the hangman thank For being yare about him*—Ant III 13 130. Of ships, in good trim, readily handled: *Our ship . . . Is tight and yare and bravely rigg'd*—Tp V 222. *Their ships are yare; yours, heavy*—Ant III 7 39. As adv., nimbly, dexterously: *Cheerly, my hearts! yare, yare!*—Tp I 1 6. *Yare, yare, good Iras; quick*—Ant V 2 286.

YARELY

Nimbly, dexterously: *Fall to't, yarely*—Tp I 1 3. *Those flower-soft hands, That yarely frame the office*—Ant II 2 215.

Y-CLAD

See *Y.*

YCLEPED, YCLIPED

See *Y.*

YEAD

See *Yedward.*

YEA-FORSOOTH

Of one who says this in asseveration instead of swearing like a gentleman: *A rascally yea-forsooth knave!*—2 H4 I 2 41. Cf. *Forsooth.*

YEARN

(1) To vex, grieve: *It would yearn your heart to see it*—Wiv III 5 44. *How it yearn'd my heart!*—R2 V 5 76. *It yearns me not if men my garments wear*—H5 IV 3 26.

(2) To be grieved, sorrow: *My manly heart doth yearn*—H5 II 3 3. *Falstaff he is dead, And we must yearn therefore*—5. *That every like is not the same, O Cæsar, The heart of Brutus yearns to think upon!*—Cæs II 2 128.

YEARS

That smiles his cheek in years—LLL V 2 465, that smiles it into wrinkles (cf. *He does smile his face into more lines than is in the new map*—Tw III 2 84); or perh., that smiles though he is in years, is old.

YEDWARD, YEAD

Edward, Ned: *Hear ye, Yedward*—1 H4 I 2 149. *Yead [the] Miller*—Wiv I 1 160.

YELLOWNESS

Jealousy: *I will possess him with yellowness*—Wiv I 3 110. Cf.: *If thou (i.e. Nature) hast The ordering of the mind too, 'mongst all colours No yellow in't, lest she suspect . . .*—Wint II 3 105.

YELLOWS

Jaundice in horses: *Rayed with the yellows*—Shr III 2 54.

YEOMAN

(1) *Yeoman's service*, such as a sturdy yeoman did for his leader: *It did me yeoman's service*—Hml V 2 36.

(2) A gentleman attendant: *The lady of the Strachy married the yeoman of the wardrobe*—Tw II 5 44.

(3) A bailiff's follower: *Where's your (i.e.* Fang's) *yeoman?*—2 H4 II 1 4.

YERK

(1) To strike smartly: *I had thought to have yerk'd him here under the ribs*—Oth I 2 5.

(2) *To yerk out*, to kick out, lash out: *Their wounded steeds . . . Yerk out their armed heels at their dead masters*—H5 IV 7 81.

YEST

Yeast; foam, froth: *Swallowed with yest and froth*—Wint III 3 94.

YESTY

Yeasty; foamy, frothy: *The yesty waves*—Mcb IV 1 53. *A kind of yesty collection*—Hml V 2 199.

YIELD

To reward, requite: *The gods yield you for't!*—Ant IV 2 33. In contracted form *'ild*: *God 'ild you for your last company*—As III 3 76. *I teach you How you shall bid God 'ild us for your pains*—Mcb I 6 12.   *Well, God 'ild you!*—Hml IV 5 41.

YOKE

To be joined together as a couple, to pair: *'Twere pity To sunder them that yoke so well together*—3 H6 IV 1 22.   *We'll yoke together*—IV 6 49.   *Nor yoke with him for tribune*—Cor III 1 57.

YOKES

Do not these fair yokes Become the forest better than the town?—Wiv V 5 111, app. referring to Falstaff's horns.

YOND (adj.)

Yon: *Yond same black cloud* — Tp II 2 20. *Yond same star that's westward from the pole*— Hml I 1 36.   *Yond tall anchoring bark*—Lr IV 6 18.   *Up to yond hill*—Cymb III 3 10.

YOND (adv.)

Yonder, there: *Say what thou seest yond*—Tp I 2 409.   *Yond methinks he stands*—R2 III 3 91. *But, look! what lights come yond?*—Oth I 2 28.

YOUNG BONES

An unborn child: *Strike her young bones, You taking airs, with lameness!*—Lr II 4 165.

YOUNKER

A novice, greenhorn: *Will you make a younker of me?*—1 H4 III 3 92.

Y-RAVISH

See *Y.*

YSLAKE

See *Y.*

Z

ZANY

A buffoon who mimicked awkwardly the tricks of the real fool: *I take these wise men, that crow so at these set kind of fools, no better than the fools' zanies*—Tw I 5 94.   A fool or buffoon in general: *Some carry-tale, some please-man, some slight zany* —LLL V 2 463.

ZOUNDS, 'ZOUNDS

[By] God's wounds: *Zounds! I was never so bethump'd with words* — John II 466.   *'Zounds, where thou wilt, lad*—1 H4 I 2 112.   *'Zounds, he dies*—R3 I 4 128.   *'Zounds, sir, you're robb'd* —Oth I 1 86.

ADDENDA

ADAM

Add: Cf. *Young Adam Cupid, he that shot so trim*—Rom II 1 13.

AFTER-SUPPER

Add: *Come to me, Tyrrel, soon at after-supper* —R3 IV 3 31 (the hyphen seems to be required).

BELIE

Under sense (1) add: *I think my love as rare As any she belied with false compare*—Sonn 130 13.

CENSURE (sb.)

Under sense (2) add: A stating or forming of an opinion: *No discerner Durst wag his tongue*

in censure—H8 I 1 32.   *We will both our judgements join In censure of his seeming*—Hml III 2 91.

GENERAL (adj.)

Under sense (2) insert at the beginning: Whole: *His general behaviour [is] vain* — LLL V 1 13. *The general course of the action*—1 H4 II 3 23.

REVEREND

Reverent: *All is done in reverend care of her*— Shr IV 1 207.

REVERENT

Reverend, worthy of respect: *A very reverent body*—Err III 2 91.   *Thou art reverent Touching thy spiritual function, not thy life*—1 H6 III 1 49.